Real-World Algorithms
A Beginner's Guide

Panos Louridas

Real-World Algorithms
A Beginner's Guide

The MIT Press
Cambridge, Massachusetts   London, England

This book was set in LATEX by the author using the Linux Libertine and Inconsolata fonts. The figures were drawn with TikZ, except for a few that were made with Python. Printed and bound in the United States of America.

Library of Congress Cataloging-in-Publication Data

Names: Louridas, Panos, author.
Title: Real-world algorithms : a beginner's guide / Panos Louridas.
Description: Cambridge, MA : The MIT Press, [2017] | Includes bibliographical references and index.
Identifiers: LCCN 2016025660 | ISBN 9780262035705 (hardcover : alk. paper)
Subjects: LCSH: Computer algorithms—Popular works. | Computer programming—Popular works.
Classification: LCC QA76.9.A43 L67 2017 | DDC 005.1–dc23
LC record available at https://lccn.loc.gov/2016025660.

10 9 8 7 6 5 4 3 2 1

Contents

Preface

> Like most of my generation, I was brought up on the saying: "Satan finds some mischief for idle hands to do". Being a highly virtuous child, I believed all that I was told, and acquired a conscience which has kept me working hard down to the present moment. But although my conscience has controlled my actions, my opinions have undergone a revolution. I think that there is far too much work done in the world, that immense harm is caused by the belief that work is virtuous, and that what needs to be preached in modern industrial countries is quite different from what always has been preached.
>
> Bertrand Russell, *In Praise of Idleness* (1932)

This book is about *algorithms*; and algorithms are what we do in order *not to have to do something*. It is the work we do to avoid work. By virtue of our inventions we have always been good at using brain for brawn. With algorithms we are using brain for brain.

Reducing human effort is a noble task. It is well ingrained in our minds that we should use machines to reduce our toil whenever possible and this has allowed us to reduce back-breaking work that was the norm for centuries. That is a wonderful thing, and there is no reason to stop at avoiding physical effort when we can also avoid mental labor. Drudgery, dull, repetitive work are the bane of human creativity, and we should do our best to avoid it; and algorithms allow us to do that.

Besides, digital technology today can accomplish feats that do not seem to be mind-numbing, but the essence of human nature. Machines recognize and produce speech, translate texts, categorize and summarize documents, predict the weather, find patterns in mounts of stuff with uncanny accuracy, run other machines, do mathematics, beat us at games, and help us to invent yet other machines. All these they do with algorithms, and by doing them they allow us to do less, they give us time to pursue our interests, and they even give us time and opportunity to discover yet better algorithms that will reduce our daily grind even more.

Algorithms did not start with computers; they have been with us from ancient times; nor are they limited to computer science. It is difficult to come up with a discipline that has not be transformed in some way by algorithms. In this way, many people encounter algorithms through the back door, as it were: they discover that they have become an important part of their discipline, no matter how distant from computers it might appear to be. It behooves them then to learn about algorithms, to be able to reason with and use them.

Even with simple things and everyday tasks, it is amazing how much effort is squandered every day because some modicum of right thinking is not applied. Every time you find yourself doing something repetitive, chances are you should not be doing it. The author has encountered, time and again, that in the course of their daily office jobs, people perform sequences of operations that could be done in a blink of time, if only they knew how to apply themselves on how to avoid doing their work; not by shirking (some people are very adept at that), but getting a computer to do the job for them (more people should be more adept at that).

Intended Audience

This book was written to serve as a first encounter with algorithms. If you study computer science, you can benefit from it for an initial approach and then you can delve into more advanced texts; algorithms are the core of computing and an introduction such as this one can only skim the surface.

There are many others, though, that while pursuing other careers, or studying for them, become aware that algorithms have also become an essential part of their tool-chest. In many disciplines, it is pretty much impossible not to work with algorithms. This book intends to bring algorithms to this audience: those, and there are many, that need to use and understand algorithms as part, even though not as the center, of their job or studies.

And then there are all those who could use some algorithms, no matter how small or trivial, to simplify their work and avoid wasting time on chores. A task that would take hours for a diligent worker can be performed in virtually no time by using just a few lines of computer code in a modern scripting language. Sometimes this can come as an epiphany to the uninitiated, which is a pity because algorithmic thinking is not the prerogative of some illuminated elite.

In the same way that nobody could seriously argue today that a basic knowledge of mathematics and science is not essential to engage meaningfully with the modern world, it is no longer possible to be a productive member of contemporary society without a grasp of algorithms. They underlie your daily human experience.

What You Need to Know

It is wrong to believe that only computer scientists can understand algorithms. Algorithms consist of instructions to carry out tasks, and all humans can understand that. To work fruitfully with algorithms, however, and to benefit the most from a book such as this one, the reader should have a basic knowledge of some skills.

It is not necessary to be an experienced mathematician, but it is necessary to be comfortable with some fundamental mathematical ideas and notation. The mathematics we will encounter here are not beyond those taught normally in high school. It is not required to know higher mathematics, but it is necessary to know what a proof is like, because the way we prove that an algorithm works is by following logical steps, which is not different from mathematical proofs. That does not mean that we will be using full-blown mathematical proofs in this book, but the reader should understand how we work with proofs.

It is not necessary to be an accomplished programmer, but the reader should have a *basic* understanding of how computers work, how programs are written, and how computer languages are structured. The reader is not required to have a deep understanding of any of these; indeed, a good way to read this book is while you are also learning about them. The interplay between computer systems and algorithms is an intimate one and each of them elucidates the other.

It is necessary to have an inquisitive attitude. Algorithms are about solving problems that we face and ensuring that the solutions are *efficient*. Every time you think, "Is there a better way to do that?" you are really looking for an algorithm.

Matters of Style

The theme of this book is to make algorithms as simple as possible without humbling or insulting the reader's intelligence. If you read a book and realize that it goes over your head; if you start thinking that perhaps it is intended for people of higher mental powers than your own; if you feel in awe of what you read without understanding what it says, you are humbled by the book. We try to avoid getting into such a rut here. This requires some simplifications in what we present. It also means that some things may be given to you, without going the full length on how they can proved.

Simplifying some things and omitting some complex stuff does not mean that the result does not require active effort from the reader: this is where we get to not insulting the reader's intelligence. We assume that the reader really wants to learn about algorithms, that this does require effort and time, and that the more time you invest, the more you will benefit.

Taking a turn into literature for a moment, there are books that engage you and take you along a ride; you read them, you get absorbed by them, you finish them, and you have not realized how the time has passed. We are not talking about potboilers here. *The Plague*, by Albert Camus, is not a difficult book to read, but nobody will contend that it is not a serious and deep work of literature.

Other books require a full mental workout. That makes them more difficult to approach, but those that do so get a great sense of accomplishment, even a sense of exclusivity, from having managed to go through them: not everybody likes James Joyce's *Ulysses*, Thomas Pynchon, or David Foster Wallace. Yet you will not find many people regretting having strived to read them.

And then there are other books that sit somewhere in between. Perhaps *Gravity's Rainbow* is too much of a writer's book for you, but can you say the same for *The Brothers Karamazov* or *Anna Karenina*?

The book you are reading now tries to be in that place between; not as an intellectual achievement, of course, but in terms of the effort, you have to dedicate to it. The author will take your hand through algorithms but will not carry you on his arms; the book will help you to walk through algorithms, but it is *you* that will do the walking. So it will not insult your intelligence. It will assume that you are a bright person who wants to learn new things and who understands that learning does not come without vigorous effort; that you are somebody who knows that achievement does not come for free, while work is rewarded.

Pseudocode

In years past, a young person could expect to embark on a computer-related career with a good knowledge of a single programming language. That is no longer true. There are many fine programming languages currently in use; computers are doing many more things than they were doing just twenty years ago, and different languages are more appropriate for certain things than others. Language wars are silly and counterproductive. Also, a happy outcome of all the wonderful things that computers can do for us now is that people seek actively new ways to work with computers, and this effort leads to new programming languages being invented and older ones evolving.

The author does prefer some computer languages over others, but it is perhaps unfair to impose on the reader his own preferences. Moreover, computer languages go in and out of fashion, and yesterday's darling is frumpy today. Hoping to make the book as widely usable as possible and with an eye to longevity, there are no examples in an actual programming language in these pages. Algorithms are described using pseudocode. The pseudocode can be understood more easily than actual computer code, as it can glide over the foibles that real programming languages invariably have. It is often also easier to reason with pseudocode; when you try to develop a deep understanding of an algorithm, you must write down parts of it, and this is easier in pseudocode than in real code, where you need to attend carefully to syntax.

That said, it is difficult to work with an algorithm unless you do write computer code that implements it. The adoption of pseudocode in this book does not mean that the reader should also adopt a cavalier attitude towards computer code in general. Whenever possible, the algorithms presented should be implemented in a language of choice. Do not underestimate the sense of accomplishment you will get when you manage to create a computer program that implements an algorithm *correctly*.

How to Read this Book

The best way to read the book is sequentially, as earlier chapters provide instruction on concepts that are used later on. In the beginning, you will encounter basic data structures that all kinds of algorithms use, and that are indeed taken up in later chapters. However, once the foundation has been laid down, you may choose later chapters as you wish, if you find some more interesting than others.

You should therefore start with chapter 1 where you will see the way the rest of the chapters are structured: they begin with a description of a problem and then present algorithms that can solve it. Chapter 1 also introduces the pseudocode conventions used in the book and basic terminology and the first data structures you will encounter: arrays and stacks.

Chapter 2 gives a first glimpse of graphs and ways to explore them. It also covers recursion, so even if you have seen graphs before but you are not entirely sure about your grasp of recursion, you should not skip it. Chapter 2 presents additional data structures that we will see time and again in algorithms in other chapters. Then, in chapter 3, we turn to the problem of compression and how two different compressing schemes work: this allows us to introduce some further important data structures.

Chapters 4 and 5 treat cryptography. This is different from graphs and compression, but it is an important application of algorithms, especially in recent years where personal data can be found in all sort of places and devices, and all sort of entities are willing to peek into them. These two chapters can be read more or less independently from the rest, although some important pieces, such as how to pick large prime numbers, are left for chapter 16.

Chapters 6–10 describe problems related to graphs: ordering tasks, finding your way in a maze, how to decide the importance of things linked to other things (such as pages in the web), how graphs can be used in elections. Finding your way in a maze has more applications than you might initially think, from typesetting paragraphs, to Internet routing and financial arbitrage; a variant of it appears in the context of elections, so chapters 7, 8, and 10 can be treated as a unit.

Chapters 11 and 12 deal with two of the most fundamental problems in computing: searching and sorting. These two topics can fill entire volumes, and they have. We present some important algorithms that are in common use. When dealing with searching, we take the opportunity to deal with some additional material, such as online searching (searching for something among items that come streaming to you, without being able to revise your decision afterwards) and scale-free distributions, which researchers have found pretty much everywhere they have cared to look. Chapter 13 gives another way of storing and retrieving data, that of hashing, which is extremely useful, common, and elegant.

Chapter 14 covers a classification algorithm: the algorithm learns how to classify data, based on a set of examples, and then we can use it to classify new, unseen instances. This is an example of Machine Learning, a field whose importance has increased immensely as computers have become more and more powerful. The chapter also covers basic ideas on Information Theory, another beautiful field related to algorithms. Chapter 14 is different from the other chapters in the book because it also presents how an algorithm works by calling on smaller algorithms to do part of its work, in the same way that computer programs are composed of small building parts, each one of which does a particular job. It also shows how data structures that have been introduced elsewhere into the book play an essential role in implementing the classification algorithm. The chapter should appeal particularly to readers who would like to see how the details of a high-level algorithm are worked out—an important step in the process of turning algorithms into programs.

Chapter 15 goes into sequences of symbols, called strings, and how we can find things inside them. It is an operation we call our computers to do every time we look for something inside a text, yet it is not obvious how to do it efficiently. Fortunately, there are ways to do it fast and gracefully. Moreover, sequences of symbols can represent many other kinds of things, so that string matching has applications in many areas, for example, in biology.

Finally, chapter 16 treats algorithms that work with chance. It is surprising how many applications of such randomized algorithms exist, so it is only possible to include a smattering of them here. Among other things, they provide answers to problems we have encountered previously in the book, such as how to find large prime numbers, required in cryptography. Or, again related to voting, how you count the impact of your vote.

Course Use

The material in the book can be used for a full semester course that covers algorithms and focuses on understanding the main ideas without going deep into a technical treatment of the subject. Students in diverse disciplines such as business and economics; life, social, and applied sciences; or formal sciences like mathematics and statistics, can use it as the main text in an introductory course, supplemented with programming assignments in which they are called to implement working instances of real, practical algorithms. Those studying computer science per se could use it as an informal introduction that would spur them to appreciate the full depth and beauty of algorithms as presented in a more technical book on the subject.

Acknowledgments

When I first broached the idea about this book to MIT Press, little did I know what it would take to realize it, and it would not exist without the support of the wonderful people there. Marie Lufkin Lee guided me through the whole process, ever gently, even when I was treading over deadlines. Virginia Crossman, Jim Mitchell, Kate Hensley, Nancy Wolfe Kotary, Susan Clark, Janice Miller, Marc Lowenthal, and Justin Kehoe all helped at various stages, as did the anonymous reviewers. Amy Hendrickson assisted when I was having fun with LaTeX arcana.

Marios Fragkoulis provided detailed feedback on parts of the manuscript and Diomidis Spinellis found the time to give me great suggestions on how to improve it. Stephanos Androutsellis-Theotokis, George Theodorou, Stephanos Chaliasos, Christina Chaniotaki, and George Pantelis were kind enough to point out errors. The embarassment of any remaining slips and oversights is entirely my own.

And of course my respect to Eleni, Adrian, and Hector, *who really bore the brunt of this book.*

Last First Words

If you write *algorhythm* instead of algorithm, you get a portmanteau word that means "the rhythm of pain," as *algos* is Greek for pain. In reality, the word algorithm comes from al-Khwārizmī, the name of a Persian mathematician, astronomer, and geographer (c. 780–c. 850 CE). Hoping that this book will engage you and not pain you, let's get on with algorithms.

1 Stock Spans

Imagine that you are given daily price quotes for a stock. That is, you have a series of numbers, each one representing the closing price of a given stock at a given day. The days are in chronological order. No quote is given for the days on which the stock market is closed.

The *span* of a stock's price on a given day is the number of consecutive days, from the given day going backwards, on which its price was less than or equal to its price on the day we are considering. The Stock Span Problem then is, given a series of daily price quotes for a stock, to find the span of the stock on each day of the series. So, for instance, consider figure 1.1. The first day is day zero. On day six of our data the span is five days, on day five it is four days, and on day four it is one day.

In reality the series can contain thousands of days, and we may want to compute the span for many different series, each one describing the evolution of a different stock price. We therefore want to use a computer to give us the solution.

In many problems that we use computers to solve, there is usually more than one way to arrive at a solution, more than one way to solve it. Usually some of them are better than others. Now, "better" by itself does not really mean anything; when we say better, we actually mean better in terms of something. This can be in terms of speed, memory, or something else that impacts on a resource such as time or space. We will have more to say on this in a bit, but it is important to keep that in mind from the outset because a solution to a problem may be simple but may not be optimal according to some constraint or criterion we have placed.

Suppose you are on day m of the series. One way you could find the span of the stock on day m is to go back one day, so you will be on day $m - 1$. If the price on day $m - 1$ is greater than the price on day m, then you know that the span of the stock on day m is just one. But if the price on day $m - 1$ is less

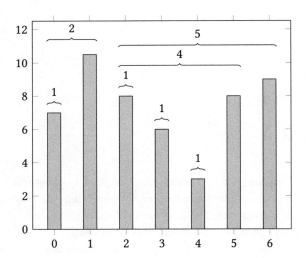

Figure 1.1
A stock span example.

than or equal to the price on day m, then the span of the stock on day m is at least two, and may be more, depending on what price the stock had earlier on. So we go on and check the price on day $m - 2$. If the price is not greater than the price on day m, then we check one day still earlier, and so on. Then two things may happen. We may run out of days (i.e., we got to the start of our series). Then the stock price is less than or equal for all days preceding day m, and so the span is exactly m. Or we find that on day k, where $k < m$, the stock had a higher price than on day m; then the span is exactly $m - k$.

If the series has n days, then to answer the problem you will have to repeat the procedure we just described n times, one for the span of each day. You can verify that the procedure works by going through it with the example of figure 1.1.

Now, this is not a very good way to describe the procedure. Prose is superb at communicating pretty much everything in this world apart from procedures to be fed to computers because we need to be precise in how we describe things to computers.

If we are precise enough so that a computer will be able to understand our procedure, then we will have created a *program*. But describing a procedure in a computer program may not be the best way for humans to understand it, because you have to tell a computer all sorts of details that have to do with the

---

Algorithm 1.1: A simple Stock Span algorithm.

SimpleStockSpan(*quotes*) → *spans*
    Input: *quotes*, an array with n stock price quotes
    Output: *spans*, an array with n stock price spans

1   *spans* ← CreateArray(n)
2   **for** i ← 0 **to** n **do**
3   k ← 1
4   *span_end* ← FALSE
5   **while** $i - k \geq 0$ **and not** *span_end* **do**
6   **if** $quotes[i - k] \leq quotes[i]$ **then**
7   k ← $k + 1$
8   **else**
9   *span_end* ← TRUE
10   *spans*[i] ← k
11 **return** *spans*

---

way computers work, but are not really related to the solution of the problem. A description that is detailed enough to be understood by computers may be so detailed that it becomes more difficult to understand by humans.

So we can go somewhere in the middle, and describe the procedure via some sort of structured language that is more precise than simple text, yet humans have little trouble understanding it. That structured language may not be directly executable by a computer, but turning it into an actual computer program should be a straightforward job.

1.1   Algorithms

Before we do that for our solution to the stock span problem, it is good if you get familiar with an important term. An *algorithm* is a procedure, but a special kind of procedure. It must be described by a finite sequence of steps, and it must finish at some finite time. Each step must be well defined, to the point that it can be executed by a human equipped with a pen and paper. An algorithm does something based on some input that we provide to it, and it produces some output that reflects the work it performed. Algorithm 1.1 implements the procedure we just described.

Algorithm 1.1 shows how we will be describing algorithms. Instead of using a computer language, which would force us to deal with implementation details that are not relevant to the logic of the algorithm, we will be using a form of *pseudocode*. Pseudocode is something between real programming code and an informal description. It employs a structured format and adopts a set of words that it endows with specific meaning. However, pseudocode is not real computer code. It is not meant to be executed by computers, but to be understood by humans. By the way, programs should also be understood by humans, but not all programs are—there are a lot of running, badly written, incomprehensible computer programs out there.

Each algorithm has a name, takes some input, and produces some output. We will write the name of the algorithm in `CamelCase` and its input in parentheses. Then we will indicate the output with a →. In the lines that follow, we will be describing the algorithm's inputs and outputs. The name of the algorithm followed by its input in parentheses can be used to *call* the algorithm. Once an algorithm has been written, we can treat it as a black box that we can use by feeding it with some input; the black box will return the algorithm's output. When implemented in a programming language, an algorithm is a named piece of computer code, a *function*. In a computer program, we call the function that implements the algorithm.

Some algorithms do not produce an output that they explicitly return. Instead, their actions impact some part of their context. For example, we may provide the algorithm with some space where to write its results. In this case, the algorithm does not return its output in the conventional sense, but there is an output anyway, the changes it effects on its context. Some programming languages make the distinction between pieces of named program code that explicitly return something, calling them *functions*, and pieces of named program code that do not return something but have nevertheless other side effects, calling them *procedures*. The distinction comes from mathematics, where a function is something that must return a value. For us an algorithm, when coded as an actual program, may turn out to be either a function or a procedure.

Our pseudocode will use a set of keywords in **bold** whose meaning should be self-explanatory if you have some acquaintance with how computers and programming languages work. We will be using the character ← for assignment, and the equals sign (=) for equality. The usual five symbols are adopted for the four mathematical operations (+, −, /, ×, ·); hence we have two signs for multiplication; we will be using both, basing our choice on aesthetics.

We will not be using any keywords or symbols to demarcate blocks of pseudocode; we will rely on indentation.

In this algorithm, we use *arrays*. An array is a structure holding data that allows us to manipulate its data in specific ways. A structure holding data that allows specific operations on the data it contains is called a *data structure*. An array is therefore a data structure.

Arrays are to computers what series of objects are to people. They are ordered sequences of elements. These elements are stored in the computer's memory. To obtain the space required for holding the elements and create an array that can hold n elements, we call an algorithm CreateArray in line 1 of algorithm 1.1. If you are familiar with arrays, then you may think it strange that the creation of an array requires an algorithm. And yet it does. To get a block of memory to hold data, you must at least search for the available memory inside the computer and mark it for use by the array. The CreateArray(n) call does all that is required. It returns an array with space for n elements; initially there are no elements in there, just the space that can hold them. It is the responsibility of the algorithm that calls CreateArray(n) to fill the array with the actual data.

For the array A, we denote and access its ith element by $A[i]$. The position of an element in the array, such as i in $A[i]$, is called its *index*. An array of n elements contains elements $A[0], A[1], \ldots, A[n-1]$. This may strike you as strange because its first element is the zeroth, and its last element is the $(n-1)$th. You may have expected them to be first and nth instead. However, this is how arrays work in most computer languages, so you had better get used to it now. Because it is so common, when we iterate over an array of size n, we iterate from place 0 to place $n-1$. In our algorithms, when we say that something will take the values from a number x to a number y (assuming that x is less than y), we mean all the values from x up to but not including y; check out line 2 of the algorithm.

We assume that accessing the ith element takes the same time, no matter what i actually is. So accessing $A[0]$ requires the same time as $A[n-1]$. That is an important feature of arrays: elements are uniformly accessible at a constant time; the array does not have to search for an element when we want to access it by its index.

Concerning notation, when describing algorithms we will be using lowercase letters for the variables that appear in them; but when a variable refers to a data structure we may be using uppercase characters, such as the array A, to help them stand out; but this will not always be necessary. When we want to give to a variable a name consisting of many words, we will be using an underscore (_) as a_connector; that is necessary because computers do not understand that a set of words separated by spaces constitute a single variable name.

Algorithm 1.1 uses arrays that store numbers. Arrays can hold any type of item, although each array can hold items of a single type in our pseudocode. This is also the case in most programming languages. For example you may have an array of decimal numbers, an array of fractions, an array of items that represent people, and another array of items that represent addresses. You may not have an array that contains both decimal numbers and items representing people. As to what the "items that represent people" may be, that is down to the specific programming language used in a program. All programming languages provides the means to represent meaningful stuff.

A particularly useful kind of array is an array that contains characters. An array of characters represents a *string*, which is a sequence of letters, numbers, words, sentences, or whatever. As in all arrays, the individual characters that the array contains can be referenced individually by the index. If we have the string s = "Hello, World", then $s[0]$ is the letter "H" and $s[11]$ is the letter "d".

Summing up, an array is a data structure that holds a sequence of items of the same type. There are two operations on arrays:

- CreateArray(n) creates an array that can hold n elements. The array is not initialized, that is, it does not hold any actual elements, but the required space for them has been reserved and can be used to store them.

- As we have seen, for an array A and its ith element, $A[i]$ accesses the element, and accessing any element in the array takes the same time. It is an error to try to access $A[i]$ when $i < 0$.

Back to algorithm 1.1. Following the above, the algorithm contains a loop, a block of code that executes repeatedly, in lines 2–10. The loop is executed n times, once for the calculation of a span, if we have prices for n days. The current day whose span we are considering is given by variable i. Initially, we are at day zero, the earliest point in time; each time we go through line 2 of the loop, we will be moving to day $1, 2, \ldots, n - 1$.

We use a *variable k* to indicate the length of the current span; a variable is a name that refers to some piece of data in our pseudocode. The contents of those data, to be precise, the *value* of the variable may change during the execution of the algorithm; hence its name. The value of k when we start to calculate a span is always 1, which we set in line 3. We also use an *indicator variable, span_end*. Indicator variables take the values TRUE and FALSE and indicate that something holds or does not hold. The variable *span_end* will be true when we reach the end of a span.

At the start of each span's calculation *span_end* will be false, as in line 4. The length of the span is calculated in the inner loop of lines 5–9. Line 5 tells us to go backwards in time as far as we can, and as long as the span has not ended. As far as we can is determined by the condition $i - k \geq 0$: $i - k$ is the index of the day to which we go back to check if the span ends, and the index cannot be zero, as this corresponds to the first day. The check for the end of a span is at line 6. If the span does not end, then we increase it in line 7. Otherwise we note the fact that the span ends in line 9 so that the loop will stop when execution goes back to line 5. At the end of each iteration of the outer loop of lines 2–10, we store the value of k in the appropriate place in the array *span* in line 10. We return *spans*, which contains the results of the algorithm, in line 11 after exiting the loop.

Note that when we start we have $i = 0$ and $k = 1$. That means that the condition in line 5 will certainly fail for the earliest point in time. That is as it should, as its span can only be equal to 1.

At this point, remember what we just said about algorithms, pen, and paper. The proper way to understand an algorithm is to execute it yourself, manually. If at any time an algorithm seems complicated, or you are not sure you have grasped it entirely, then write down what it does on some example. It will save you a lot of time, old-fashioned though it may seem. If you are unsure about algorithm 1.1 go and do it now, then return here when the algorithm is clear.

1.2   Running Times and Complexity

Algorithm 1.1 is a solution to the Stock Span Problem, but we can do better. Here better means that we can do faster. When we talk about speed in algorithms, we are really talking about the number of steps the algorithm will execute. No matter how fast computers get, although they will execute computational steps faster and faster, the number of steps will remain the same, so evaluating the performance of an algorithm in terms of the steps it requires makes sense. We call the number of steps the *running time* of the algorithm, although this is a pure number, not measured in any time units. Using time units would make any running time estimate relative to a specific computer model, which is not useful.

Consider how long it takes to calculate the spans of n stock quotes. The algorithm consists of a loop, starting at line 2, that will execute n times, one for each quote. Then there is an inner loop, starting in line 5, that for each iteration of the outer loop will try to find the quote's span. For each quote it will compare the price of the quote with all previous quotes. In the worst case, if the quote is the highest price yet, then it will examine all previous quotes. If quote k is the highest of all previous quotes, then the inner loop will execute k times. Therefore, in the worst case, which is if the quotes are in ascending order, line 7 will execute the following number of times:

$$1 + 2 + \cdots + n = \frac{n(n + 1)}{2}$$

If the equation is not clear, then you can easily see that this is indeed so if you add the numbers $1, 2, \ldots, n$ twice:

$$
\begin{array}{cccccc}
 & 1 & + & 2 & + \cdots + & n \\
+ & n & + & n - 1 & + \cdots + & 1 \\
\hline
 & n + 1 & + & n + 1 & + \cdots + n + 1 & = n(n + 1)
\end{array}
$$

Because line 6 is the step of the algorithm that will execute most times, $n(n + 1)/2$ is the worst case running time of the algorithm.

When we talk about algorithm running times, we are really interested in the running time when our input data is large (in our case, the number n). That is the *asymptotic* running time of an algorithm because it deals with the behavior of the algorithm when the input data increase without bounds. There is some special notation that we use for this purpose. For any function $f(n)$, if for all values of n greater than some initial positive value the function $f(n)$ is less than or equal to another function $g(n)$ scaled by some positive constant value c, that is, $cg(n)$, we say that $O(f(n)) = g(n)$. In a more precise way, we say that $O(f(n)) = g(n)$ if there exist positive constants c and n_0 such that $0 \leq f(n) \leq cg(n)$ for all $n \geq n_0$.

The notation $O(f(n))$ is called "big-Oh notation." Keep in mind that we are interested in *big values* of our input, because that is where we will have the biggest savings. Take a look at figure 1.2, where we plot two functions, $f_1(n) = 20n + 1000$ and $f_2(n) = n^2$. For small values of n it is $f_1(n)$ that takes biggest values, but the situation changes drastically quite early, after which n^2 grows much faster.

The big-Oh notation allows us to simplify functions. If we have a function like $f(n) = 3n^3 + 5n^2 + 2n + 1000$, then we have simply $O(f(n)) = n^3$. Why?

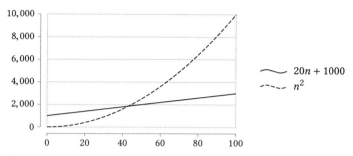

Figure 1.2
$O(f(n))$ comparison.

Because we can always find a value c so that $0 \le f(n) \le cn^3$. In general, when we have a function with many terms, it is the biggest term that quickly dominates the growth of the function, and we take out the smallest terms when we work with big-Ohs. So, $O(a_1 n^k + a_2 n^{k-1} + \cdots + a_n n + b) = O(n^k)$.

The running time of the algorithm in the way we have described it is usually called the *computational complexity* of an algorithm, or *complexity* for short. As we use simplified forms of functions when we study the running time of algorithms, it turns out that most algorithms have running times whose functions are among a small number of simplified functions. That means that the complexity of algorithms usually falls under one of a few common categories, or families.

First of all, we have the *constant function*, $f(n) = c$. This simply means that the function always has the same value, c, no matter what n is. Unless c is a preposterously high value, this is the best we can hope for in an algorithm. In terms of big-Oh notation, we have by definition that there exist positive constants c and n_0, such that $0 \le f(n) \le cg(n) = c \cdot 1$. Indeed, c is the function's constant value and $n_0 = 1$. Therefore, $O(c) = O(1)$. We call an algorithm that behaves in this way a *constant time algorithm*. This is actually a misnomer because it does not mean that the algorithm will always take the same amount of time irrespective of its input. It means that the upper bound in the running time of the algorithm is irrespective of its input. For example, a trivial algorithm that adds a value y to a value x if $x > 0$ does not always take the same amount of time to run: if $x > 0$ it performs an addition, otherwise it does nothing. The upper bound, though, is constant, the time it takes for the addition, and so it falls into the $O(1)$ family. Unfortunately, there are not many algorithms that run in constant time. The most common operation that runs in constant time is accessing an element in an array, which we take to be constant and not dependent on the index of the element we are accessing; as we saw, in an array A of n elements, accessing $A[0]$ takes the same time as accessing $A[n-1]$.

After constant time algorithms, we have algorithms that run in *logarithmic time*. The logarithmic function, or *logarithm*, is $\log_a(n)$, which is defined to be the power that we have to raise a to get n: if $y = \log_a(n)$ then $n = a^y$. The number a is the *base of the logarithm*. From the definition of the logarithm, it follows that $x = a^{\log_a x}$, which shows that the logarithm is the inverse of raising a number to an exponent. Indeed, $\log_3 27 = 3$ and $3^3 = 27$. If $a = 10$, that is, a logarithm to base ten, then we simply write $y = \log(n)$. In computers we frequenty encounter *base two logarithms*, called binary logarithms, so we use a special notation for them, $\lg(n) = \log_2(n)$. This is different from the so-called *natural logarithm*, which is the base e logarithm, where $e \approx 2.71828$. Natural logarithms also have a special notation, $\ln(n) = \log_e(n)$.

A short aside if you wonder where the number e comes from. The number e is sometimes called Euler's number, after the 18th-century Swiss mathematician Leonhard Euler, and arises in many different areas. It is the limit of the expression $(1 + 1/n)^n$ as n approaches infinity. Although named after Euler, it was actually discovered by another Swiss mathematician, this time living in the 17th century, Jacob Bernoulli. Bernoulli was trying to come up with a formula for calculating interest that is applied continuously.

Imagine you put d dollars in the bank, and the bank gives you an interest of $R\%$. If the interest is calculated once per year, then after a year your money will have grown to $d + d(R/100)$. Setting $r = R/100$, your money will be $d(1 + r)$. You can verify that if $R = 50$, $r = 1/2$, your money will have grown to $1.5 \times d$. If the interest is calculated twice per hear, then the interest rate at every six months interval will be $r/2$. After six months you will have $d(1 + r/2)$. Then after another six months, at the end of the year, you will have $d(1 + r/2)(1 + r/2) = d(1 + r/2)^2$. If interest is applied, or *compounded*, to use the technical term, n times per year, then you will have $d(1 + r/n)^n$ at the end of the year. For $R = 100\%$, a substantial rate, you get $r = 1$; if you compound continuously, that is, in ever smaller time intervals, n will get to infinity. Then if $d = 1$, your dollar at the end of the year will have grown to $(1 + 1/n)^n = e$. End of aside.

A basic property of logarithms is that logarithms to different bases differ by a constant multiplier because $\log_a(n) = \log_b(n)/\log_b(a)$. For example, $\lg(n) = \log_{10}(n)/\log_{10}(2)$. Therefore, we bundle all logarithmic functions under the same complexity family, which we usually denote by $O(\log(n))$, although the more specific $O(\lg(n))$ is also used a lot. Algorithms with $O(\lg(n))$ complexity arise when the algorithm repeatedly divides a problem in two because if you divide something repeatedly by two, you are essentially applying the logarithmic function to it. Important logarithmic time algorithms are algorithms related to searching: the fastest searching algorithms run on base two logarithmic time.

More time consuming than logarithmic time algorithms are *linear time algorithms* that run in time $f(n) = n$, that is, in time proportional to their input. For these algorithms, the complexity is $O(n)$. These algorithms may have to scan their whole input in order to find an answer. For example, if we search a random set of items that are not ordered in any way, then we may have to go through all of them to find the one we want. Therefore, such a search runs in linear time.

Slower than linear time are the *loglinear time algorithms*, where $f(n) = n \log(n)$, and we therefore write $O(n \log(n))$. As before, the logarithm can be to any base, although in practice algorithms to base two are common. These algorithms in some way are a combination of a linear time algorithm and a logarithmic time algorithm. That may involve repeatedly dividing a problem and applying a linear time algorithm to each of the divided parts. Good sorting algorithms have a loglinear time complexity.

When the function describing the running time of the algorithm is a polynomial $f(n) = (a_1 n^k + a_2 n^{k-1} + \cdots + a_n n + b)$ we have, as we saw, a complexity of $O(n^k)$ and the algorithm is a *polynomial time algorithm*. Many algorithms run in polynomial time; an important sub-family are algorithms that run in $O(n^2)$ time, which we call *quadratic time algorithms*. Some not efficient sorting methods run in quadratic time, as does the standard way to multiply two numbers with n digits each—note that there are actually more efficient ways to multiply numbers, and we use these more efficient ways in applications where we want high performance arithmetic calculations.

Slower than polynomial time algorithms are *exponential time algorithms*, where $f(n) = c^n$, with c a constant value, so $O(c^n)$. Be sure to notice the difference between n^c and c^n. Although we swapped the place of n and the exponent, it makes for a huge difference in the resulting function. As we said, exponentiation is the reverse of the logarithmic function and is simply raising a constant to a variable number. Careful: exponentiation is c^n; the *exponential function* is the special case where $c = e$, that is, $f(n) = e^x$, where e is the Euler number we met before. Exponentiation occurs when we have to handle

Table 1.1

Growth of functions.

Function	Input size				
	1	10	100	1000	1,000,000
$\lg(n)$	0	3.32	6.64	9.97	19.93
n	1	10	100	1000	1,000,000
$n\ln(n)$	0	33.22	664.39	9965.78	1.9×10^7
n^2	1	100	10,000	1,000,000	10^{12}
n^3	1	1000	1,000,000	10^9	10^{18}
2^n	2	1024	1.3×10^{30}	10^{301}	$10^{10^{5.5}}$
$n!$	1	3,628,800	9.33×10^{157}	4×10^{2567}	$10^{10^{6.7}}$

a problem of input n, where each of the n inputs can take a number of c different values and we must try all possible cases. We have c values for the first input, and for each of these we have c values for the second input; in total $c \times c = c^2$. For each of these c^2 cases, we have c possible values for the third input, which makes it $c^2 \times c = c^3$; and so on until the last input that gives c^n.

Still slower than exponential time algorithms are *factorial time algorithms* with $O(n!)$, where the factorial number is defined as $n! = 1 \times 2 \times \cdots \times n$ and the degenerate case $0! = 1$. The factorial comes into play when in order to solve a problem we need to try all possible *permutations* of input. A permutation is a different arrangement of a sequence of values. For example, if we have the values $[1, 2, 3]$, then we have the following permutations: $[1, 2, 3]$, $[1, 3, 2]$, $[2, 1, 3]$, $[2, 3, 1]$, $[3, 1, 2]$, and $[3, 2, 1]$. There are n possible values in the first position; then because we have used one value, there are $n - 1$ possible values in the second position; this makes $n \times (n - 1)$ different permutations for the first two positions. We go on like this for the remaining positions until the last position where there is only one possible value. In all, we have $n \times (n - 1) \cdots \times 1 = n!$. In this way the factorial number arises in shuffles: the number of possible shuffles of a deck of cards is 52!; that's an astronomical number.

A rule of thumb is that algorithms with up to polynomial time complexity are good, so our challenge is often to find algorithms with such performance. Unfortunately, for a whole class of important problems, we know of no polynomial time algorithms! Take a look at table 1.1; you should realize that if for a problem we have only an algorithm with a running time of $O(2^n)$, then the algorithm is pretty much worthless for anything apart from toy problems, with very small values of input. You can also check that with figure 1.3; in the bottom row, $O(2^n)$ and $O(n!)$ start skyrocketing for small values of n.

In figure 1.3, we show the plots of functions as lines, although in reality the number n when we study algorithms is a natural number, so we would expect to see scatter plots, showing points instead of lines. Logarithmic, linear, loglinear, and polynomial functions are of course directly defined for real numbers, so there is no problem in plotting them with lines by using the normal functional definitions. The usual interpretation of exponentiation is for integers, but powers with rational exponents are also possible because $x^{(a/b)} = (x^a)^{(1/b)} = \sqrt[b]{x^a}$. Then powers with exponents that are real numbers are defined as $b^x = (e^{\ln b})^x = e^{x \ln b}$. Concerning factorials, with some more advanced mathematics, it turns out that they can also be defined for all real numbers (negative factorials are taken to be infinite). So we are justified in drawing the complexity functions with lines.

Lest you think that complexity $O(2^n)$ or $O(n!)$ rarely occurs in practice, consider the famous (or infamous) Traveling Salesman Problem. In this problem, a traveling salesman must travel to a number of cities, visiting each one of them only once. Every city is directly connected to every other city (perhaps the salesman travels by plane). The twist is that the salesman must do that while traveling as few kilometers as possible. A direct solution is to try all possible permutations of the cities. For n cities, this is $O(n!)$. There is a better algorithm that solves the problem in $O(n^2 2^n)$—a bit better, but not much of a practical difference. Then how do we solve this (and other similar problems)? It turns out that, although we may not know a good algorithm that will give us a precise answer, we may know good algorithms that will give us approximate results.

The big-Oh provides an *upper bound* on the performance of an algorithm. The converse is a *lower bound*, when we know that its complexity will be always no better than a certain function, after some initial values. This is called "big-Omega," or $\Omega(n)$, and the precise definition is that $\Omega(f(n)) = g(n)$ if there exist positive constants c and n_0 such that $f(n) \geq cg(n) \geq 0$ for all $n \geq n_0$. Having defined big-Oh and big-Omega, we can also define the situation when we have both an upper and a lower bound. This is "big-Theta," and we say that $\Theta(f(n)) = g(n)$ if and only if $O(f(n)) = g(n)$ and $\Omega(f(n)) = g(n)$. Then we know that the algorithm has a running time that is bounded both from below and from above by the same function, scaled by a constant. You can think of it as the algorithm running time lying in a band around that function.

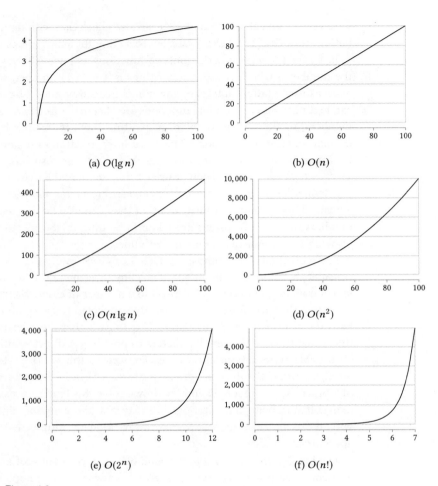

(a) $O(\lg n)$

(b) $O(n)$

(c) $O(n \lg n)$

(d) $O(n^2)$

(e) $O(2^n)$

(f) $O(n!)$

Figure 1.3
Different complexity families.

1.3   Stock Span Using a Stack

Let's return to the Stock Span Problem now. We have found an algorithm with a complexity of $O(n(n + 1/2))$. According to what we have been saying, this is equivalent to $O(n^2)$. Can we do better? Go back to figure 1.1. Notice that when we are at day six, we do not need to compare with all the previous days until day one. Because we have gone through all days up to day six, we already "know" that days two, three, four, and five all have quotes less than or equal to that of day six. If we somehow keep that knowledge, then instead of doing all these comparisons, we only need to compare with the quote on day one.

This is a general pattern. Imagine you are on day k. If the stock price quote on day $k - 1$ is less than or equal to the stock price on day k, so that we have $quotes[k - 1] \leq quotes[k]$ or equivalently $quotes[k] \geq quotes[k - 1]$, then there is no reason to even compare with $k - 1$ again. Why? Take a future day $k + j$. If the quote on $k + j$ is less than the quote on day k, $quotes[k + j] < quotes[k]$, then we do not have to compare with $k - 1$ because the span starting from $k + j$ ends at k. If the quote on $k + j$ is greater than the quote on k, then we know already that it must be $quotes[k + j] \geq quotes[k - 1]$ because $quotes[k + j] \geq quotes[k]$ and $quotes[k] \geq quotes[k - 1]$. So each time that we are searching backwards for the end of the span, we may throw away all days with values less than or equal to the day whose span we are examining and we may exclude the thrown away days from consideration in any future span.

The following metaphor may help: Imagine you are sitting on top of the column for day six in figure 1.4. You look straight back, not below. You see the column for day one only. That is the only column with which you need to compare the stock value of day six. In general, at each day you only need to compare what is directly in your line-of-sight.

That means that we waste our time in algorithm 1.1 when in the inner loop starting in line 5 we start comparing with each and every previous day. We can save the waste by using some mechanism by which we have at hand the limits of the highest established spans.

We can do that by using a special data structure for holding data called a *stack*. A stack is a simple data structure. It is something on which we can put data, one after the other, and retrieve them. Each time we can retrieve the last one we have put. The stack works like a stack of trays in a restaurant, piled on top of each other. We can only take the top tray, and we can only add trays on top of the pile. Because the last tray to be added to the stack is the first one to be removed, we call a stack a Last In First Out (LIFO) structure. You

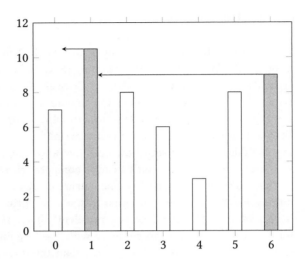

Figure 1.4
Stock spans optimized.

Figure 1.5
Insertion and removal from a stack.

can see the tray-like operations of adding and removing an item in a stack in figure 1.5.

When we talk about data structures we need to describe the operations that we can perform on them. For arrays, we saw that the two operations are array creation and element access. For stacks, based on what we have just said, the five stack operations are:

- CreateStack() creates an empty stack.
- Push(S, i) pushes item i on the top of the stack S.

- Pop(S) pops the item that is on the top of the stack S. The operation returns the item. If the stack is empty, then the operation is not allowed (we get an error).

- Top(S) we get the value of the item on the top of the stack S without removing it. The stack remains the same. If the stack is empty, then the operation again is not allowed and we get an error.

- IsStackEmpty(S) returns TRUE if stack S is empty, or FALSE otherwise.

In reality a stack is finite: we can only push a certain amount of elements on it before reaching a limit—after all there is only finite memory in a computer. In actual stack implementations there are additional operations for checking the number of elements in the stack (its size) and whether it is full or not. These are not relevant to our algorithms using pseudocode, so we are not going to include them further in our discussion; similarly for related operations in the other data structures we will be using.

Using a stack we can solve the Stock Span Problem with the idea we just developed in algorithm 1.2. We start with creating an array of size n, in line 1, as we did before. The span of the first day is by definition one, so we initialize $spans[0]$ accordingly in line 2. This time we use a stack to store the days we need to compare. For that purpose, we create a new empty stack in line 3. In the beginning we have the trivial fact that the price of the stock in the first day is not lower than the price in the first day, so in line 4 we push zero, the index of the first day, in the stack.

The loop in lines 5–12 handles all subsequent days. The inner loop of lines 6–7 looks backwards in time to find the latest day with a stock price higher than the day we are handling. It does that by popping an item from the stack (line 7) , as long as the day at the top of the stack has a stock price less than or equal to the price of the day we are handling (line 6). If we exit the inner loop by exhausting the stack (line 8) and we are at day i, then all days before that have lower stock prices, so the span is $i + 1$. We set $spans[i]$ to that value in line 9. Otherwise (line 10), the span extends from day i to the day at the top of the stack, so we use the difference between the two to set $spans[i]$ in line 11. Before returning to the start of the loop, we push day i at the top of the stack. In this way at the end of the outer loop, the stack will contain the days where the stock price is not lower than the stock price in the day we are checking. In the next iteration of the loop, this will allow us to compare only with the days that matter, the days that are above our line-of-sight, which is what we want.

Algorithm 1.2: Stack Stock Span algorithm.

StackStockSpan(*quotes*) → *spans*
>   **Input:** *quotes*, an array with n stock price quotes
>   **Output:** *spans*, an array with n stock price spans

1   *spans* ← CreateArray(n)
2   *spans*[0] ← 1
3   S ← CreateStack()
4   Push($S, 0$)
5   **for** i ← 1 **to** n **do**
6   **while not** IsStackEmpty(S) **and** *quotes*[Top(S)] ≤ *quotes*[i] **do**
7   Pop(S)
8   **if** IsStackEmpty(S) **then**
9   *spans*[i] ← $i + 1$
10   **else**
11   *spans*[i] ← $i -$ Top(S)
12   Push(S, i)
13 **return** *spans*

Table 1.2

Boolean short circuit evaluation.

operator	a	b	result
	T	T	T
and	T	F	F
	F	T/F	F
	T	T/F	T
or	F	T	T
	F	F	F

There is a detail in line 6 of the algorithm that merits our attention. It is an error to evaluate Top(S) if S is empty. This will not happen, thanks to an important property about how conditions are evaluated, called *short circuit evaluation*. The property means that when we evaluate an expression involving logical boolean operators, the evaluation of the expression stops as soon as we know its final result, without bothering to evaluate any remaining parts of the expression. Take for example the expression **if** $x > 0$ **and** $y > 0$. If we know that $x \leq 0$, then the whole expression is false, regardless of the value of

y; we do not need to evaluate the second part of the expression at all. Similarly, in the expression **if** $x > 0$ **or** $y > 0$, if we know that $x > 0$, then we do not need to evaluate the second part of expression, the one involving y, because we already know that the whole expression is true having established that the first part is true. Table 1.2 shows the general situation for any two-part boolean expression with an **and** or an **or** operator. The shaded rows indicate that the result of the expression does not depend on the second part and therefore the evaluation can stop as soon as we know the value of the first part. With short circuit evaluation, when IsStackEmpty(S) returns TRUE, which means that **not** IsStackEmpty(S) is FALSE, we will not try to evaluate the right hand of **and** containing Top(S), thereby avoiding an error.

You can see how the algorithm works and the line-of-sight metaphor in figure 1.6. At each panel of the figure we show, on the right, the stack at the start of each loop iteration; we also indicate the days in the stack with filled bars, whereas the days we have not handled yet are in dashed bars. The current day we are handling is in the black circle below the panel.

In the first panel we have $i = 1$, and we have to check the value of the current day with the values of the other days in the stack, which is just day zero. Day one has a higher price than day zero. That means that from now on there is no need to compare with the days before day one; our line-of-sight will stop there; so in the next iteration, with $i = 2$, the stack contains the number 1. Day two has a lower price than day one. That means that any span starting from day three may end on day two, if the value on day three is lower than the value on day two, or it may end on day one, if the value on day three is no less than the value on day two. There is no way it can end on day zero, though, as the price on day zero is less than on day one. A similar situation occurs with $i = 3$ and $i = 4$. But when we arrive at $i = 5$, we realize that we no longer need to compare with days two, three, and four in the future. These days lie in the shadow, as it where, of day five. Or, with the line-of-sight metaphor, our view is unobstructed way back until day one. Everything in-between can be popped from the stack and the stack will contain 5 and 1, so that at $i = 6$ we only need to compare at most with these two days. If a day has a value greater than or equal to that of day five, it will certainly surpass the values of days four, three, and two; what we cannot be certain about is whether it reaches the value of day one. When we are done with day six, the stack will contain the numbers 6 and 1.

Is this better than before? In algorithm 1.2 the loop starting in line 5 is executed $n - 1$ times. For each one of these times, say at the ith iteration,

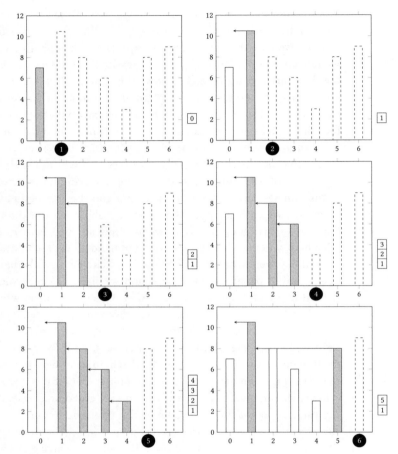

Figure 1.6
Lines-of-sight of stock spans.

the Pop operation in the inner loop that starts in line 6 is executed p_i times. That means that in total the Pop operation will be executed $p_1 + p_2 + \cdots + p_{n-1}$ times, p_i times for each iteration of the outer loop. We do not know what the number p_i is. But if you pay close attention to the algorithm, you will see that each day is pushed on the stack only once, the first day at line 3 and the subsequent days at line 11. Therefore each day can be popped from the stack in line 7 at most once. So, throughout the whole execution of the algorithm, in all iterations of the outer loop, we cannot execute line 6 more than n times. In other words, $p_1 + p_2 + \cdots + p_{n-1} = n$, which means that the whole algorithm is $O(n)$; line 7 is the operation that will be executed most times because it is in an inner loop, whereas the rest of the code in lines 5–12 is not.

We can also proceed in our analysis and see that, in contrast to algorithm 1.1, where we could only arrive at a worst-case estimate, here our estimate is also a lower bound on the algorithm's performance—there is no way the algorithm can complete with less than n steps because we need to go through n days. So the computational complexity of the algorithm is also $\Omega(n)$, and so it follows that it is $\Theta(n)$.

Stacks, like all the other data structures we will encounter, have many uses. A LIFO behavior is common in computers, so you will find stacks from low-level programs written in machine language, to the biggest problems running in supercomputers. That is why data structures in general exist in the first place. They are nothing but the essence of years of experience with problem solving with computers. It turns out, time and again, that algorithms use similar ways to organize the data they process. People have codified these ways so that, when looking our way around a problem, we reach to them, availing ourselves of their functionality to develop algorithms.

Notes

The definitive text on algorithms is the multi-volume work by Donald Knuth [112, 113, 114, 115]. The work is 50 years in the making and some volumes are yet to be written, which the existing books do not cover all areas of algorithms, but what they cover they treat with rigor and unsurpassed style. These books are not for the faint-hearted, yet they reward their reader many times over.

A thorough, classic introduction to algorithms is the book by Cormen, Leiserson, Rivest, and Stein [42]. Thomas Cormen has also written another popular book [41] that gives a shorter and gentler introduction to important algorithms. A lay person's introduction to algorithms is MacCormick's book [130]. Other popular introductions to algorithms include the books by Kleinberg and Tardos [107], Dasgupta, Papadimitriou, and Vazirani [47], Harel and Feldman [86], and Levitin [129].

There are also many fine books that deal with algorithms and their implementation in a particular programming language [180, 176, 178, 177, 179, 188, 82].

Stacks are about as old as computers. According to Knuth [112, pp. 229 and 459], Alan M. Turing proposed it in a design for an Automatic Computing Engine (ACE) written in 1945 and presented in 1946; the stack operations were called BURY and UNBURY instead of "push" and "pop" [205, pp. 11–12 and 30].

Algorithms are much older than computers, hailing at least since ancient Babylonian times [110].

Exercises

1. A stack is a simple data structure to implement. A straightforward implementation is using an array; go ahead and write an array-based stack implementation. In the text we mentioned that in practice a stack has more operations than the five we mentioned: operations returning its size and checking whether it is full. Make sure you also implement them.

2. We showed two solutions for the Stock Span Problem, one using a stack and one without a stack. We argued that the solution with the stack is faster. Check that it is indeed so by implementing the two algorithms in your programming language of choice and timing how long it takes for each approach to solve the problem. Note that to time a program's execution, you must feed it with enough data so that it does take a reasonable amount of time to finish; then, because lots of things happen to a computer at once and each run may be affected by different factors, you need to to run it repeatedly to get a stable measurement. So this is a good opportunity to look around and read on how programs are benchmarked.

3. Stacks are used for implementing arithmetic calculations written in *Reverse Polish Notation* (RPN), also known as *postfix notation*. In RPN every operator follows all its operands, in contrast to the usual infix notation where the operator is placed between its operands. So, instead of writing 1 + 2, we write 1 2+. "Polish" refers to the nationality of Jan Łukasiewicz who invented the *Polish* or *prefix notation* in 1924 and in which we write +1 2. The advantage of RPN is that there is no need for parentheses: $1 + (2 \times 3)$ in infix notation becomes 1 2 3 * + in postfix notation. To evaluate it, we read it from left to right. We push numbers on a stack. When we encounter an operator, we pop from the stack as many items as it needs as operands, we perform the operation, and we push the result in the stack. At the end we get the result at the top (and only element of the stack). For example, when evaluating 1 2 3 * + 2 − the stack, written horizontally in brackets, becomes [ ], [1], [1 2], [1 2 3], [1 6], [7] [7 2], [5]. Write a calculator that evaluates arithmetic expressions given by the user in RPN.

4.   In many programming languages, we have expressions set off by a matching set
      of delimiters, such as parentheses or round brackets ( ), brackets [ ], and curly
      brackets { }. Write a program that reads a sequence of delimiters, such as ( ) { [
      ] ( ) { } }, and reports whether the delimiters are balanced, or whether there are
      unmatched delimiters, for instance (( ), or delimiters that match with the wrong
      kind, such as (}. Use a stack to remember the currently opened delimiters.

2 Exploring the Labyrinth

Finding your way in a labyrinth is an ancient problem. The story goes that king Minos of Crete had forced Athens to send to him seven youths and seven maidens every seven years. They would be thrown into the dungeons of Minos's palace, where the Minotaur lived, a monster with the body of a man and the head of a bull. The dungeons formed a maze, and the hapless sacrificial offerings would be devoured by the Minotaur. The third time that this tribute was due, Theseus volunteered to be among the youths to be sacrificed. When he got to Crete, he charmed the daughter of Minos, Ariadne, who gave him a ball of thread. He unwound the thread as he went along in the maze, found the Minotaur, slaughtered him, and then used the thread to find his way to the exit, instead of getting lost and perishing.

Maze exploration is not of interest just because it appears in an ancient myth or because it gives us amusement in beautifully landscaped parks. A maze is not different from any situation where we have to explore a set of spaces connected with specific paths. A road network is an obvious example; but the problem becomes more interesting if we realize that there are cases when we want to explore more abstract things. We may have a network of computers, connected to each other, and want to find out whether one computer is connected to some other computer. We may have a network of acquaintances, that is, people somehow connected to each other, and want to find out whether we can get from one person to another.

The myth suggests that to find our way in a maze, we must somehow know where we have already been. Otherwise a maze exploration strategy will fail. Let's take an example maze and think of a strategy. Figure 2.1 shows a maze, where we depict rooms as circles and the corridors between them as lines connecting the circles.

In figure 2.2 you can see what happens when we explore the maze systematically, following a specific strategy called "hand on the wall." We indicate

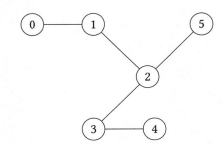

Figure 2.1
The maze.

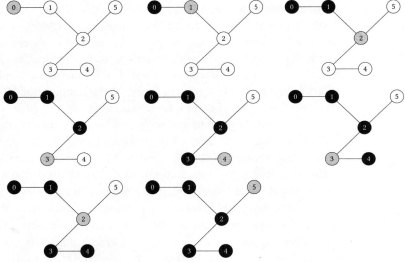

Figure 2.2
Keep the hand on the wall strategy: it works!

the current room as gray and the visited rooms as black. It is a simple strategy. You place your hand on a wall and you never lift your hand from the wall. As you proceed from one room to another, you take care to keep the hand touching the wall as you go. Apparently, the strategy works. But then see the maze in figure 2.3. By following the strategy, you will visit the rooms on the periphery of the maze, and you will miss the room on the interior, as you can verify in figure 2.4.

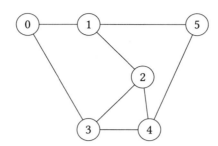

Figure 2.3
Another maze.

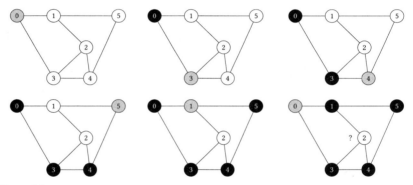

Figure 2.4
Keep the hand on the wall strategy: it fails…

2.1 Graphs

Before we proceed on how we can solve the problem, we have to deal with how we are going to represent mazes in general. The way we have described them, mazes consist of rooms and corridors among them. We hinted that they become more interesting when we realize that they are similar to other structures; in fact they are similar to anything consisting of objects and connections among these objects. This is a fundamental data structure, perhaps the most fundamental of all, because many things in the real world can be represented as objects and connections among objects. Such structures are called *graphs*. A succinct definition is that a graph is a set of *nodes* and *links* among them. Alternatively, we may speak of *vertices*, in singular *vertex*, and *edges*. An edge connects exactly two vertices. A series of edges, in which every two

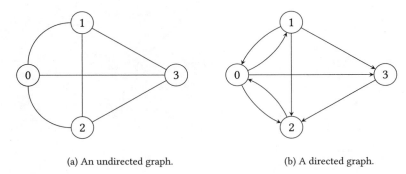

(a) An undirected graph.   (b) A directed graph.

Figure 2.5
Directed and undirected graphs.

edges share a node in common, is called a *path*. So, in figure 2.2 there is a
path connecting nodes 0 and 2 passing through node 1. The number of edges
in a path is called its *length*. An edge is a path with length 1. If a path exists
between two nodes, then we say that the two nodes are *connected*. In certain
graphs we may want the edges to be directed; these graphs are *directed graphs*,
or *digraphs* for short. Otherwise, we deal with *undirected graphs*. Figure 2.5
shows an undirected graph on the left and a directed graph on the right. As
you can see, there may be a number of different edges starting or ending on
a single node. The number of edges adjacent to a node is called its *degree*. In
directed graphs we have the *in-degree*, for incoming edges, and the *out-degree*,
for outgoing edges. In figure 2.5a it so happens that all edges have degree 3.
In figure 2.5b the rightmost node has in-degree 2 and out-degree 1.

The applications of graphs can fill whole volumes: it is amazing how many
things can be represented as graphs, how many problems can be rendered in
graph terms, and how many algorithms exist for solving graph-related problems. This is because many things consist of objects and connections among
them, as we just observed; this deserves some further attention.

Perhaps the most obvious graph application, at which we already hinted,
is in representing *networks*. Points in a network are nodes in the graph, and
links are edges between them. There are many different kinds of networks; we
have *computer networks*, of course, with computers connected to each other,
but there are *transport networks* as well, with cities linked by roads, airplane
routes, or railway lines. In computer networks, the *Internet* is the biggest
example of all, and the *web* is also a network with pages as nodes connected

by hyperlinks between them. The *Wikipedia* is an especially large network, a subset of the web network. In the domain of electronics, *circuit boards* consist of electrical components, such as transistors, connected via circuits. In biology we encounter *metabolic networks* that contain, among other things, metabolic pathways: chemicals are connected through chemical reactions. *Social networks* are modeled as graphs, with people as nodes and the relationships among them as edges. *Scheduling* of jobs and tasks among people or machines can also be modeled via graphs, with the tasks as nodes and the dependencies among them, such as which task should precede which other tasks, represented by the edges.

For all the above applications, and more, there exist different kinds of graphs that are suitable for representing varied situations. If there is a path from any node to any other node in a graph, the graph is called *connected*. Otherwise it is called *disconnected*. Figure 2.6 shows a connected and a disconnected graph, both undirected. Note that in a directed graph we have to take into account the direction of the edges to determine whether it is connected. A directed graph in which there is a *directed path* between any two nodes is called *strongly connected*. If we somehow forget about directions and we are interested in whether it is an *undirected path* between any two nodes, then the graph is called *weakly connected*. If a directed graph is not strongly connected nor weakly connected, then it is simply disconnected. Figure 2.7 shows the possibilities. The question of graph connectivity arises whenever we want to determine whether something, which is modeled as a graph, represents a whole entity, or is composed from separate sub-entities. Connected sub-entities in undirected graphs and strongly connected sub-entities in directed graphs are called *connected components*. Therefore, a graph is connected, or strongly connected if it is a directed graph, when it consists of a single connected component. A related question is that of *reachability*, which is whether it is possible to reach some node from some other node.

In a directed graph, or digraph, it may be possible to start from a node, jump from edge to edge, and come back to the node we started from. When this happens, we have traveled in a circle, and the path we have made is a *cycle*. In an undirected graph, we may always return to where we started from by going backward, so we say that we travel in a circle if we can get back to the node we started without going backward on an edge. Graphs with cycles are called *cyclic*; graphs without cycles are called *acyclic*. Figure 2.8 shows two directed graphs with several cycles. Note that the graph on the right has some edges that start and end on the same node. These are cycles of length one, and

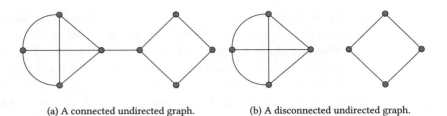

(a) A connected undirected graph.   (b) A disconnected undirected graph.

Figure 2.6
Undirected connected and disconnected graphs.

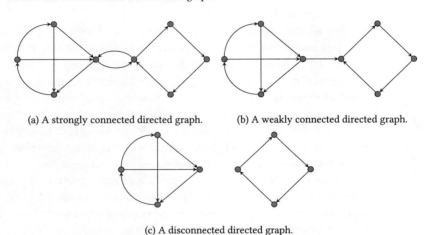

(a) A strongly connected directed graph.   (b) A weakly connected directed graph.

(c) A disconnected directed graph.

Figure 2.7
Connected and disconnected directed graphs.

we call them *loops*. Loops are possible in undirected graphs as well, but they are not common. Directed acyclic graphs arise in many applications, to the point that they have been given a name: a directed acyclic graph is called *dag* for short. To complete the picture, figure 2.9 shows two acyclic graphs, one undirected and one dag.

If it is possible to separate the nodes of a graph in two sets so that all the edges connect a node from one set to a node to the other set, then we have a *bipartite graph*. A classic application involving bipartite graphs is *matching*, where we want to match two sets of entities to each other (e.g., they may be people or tasks to be assigned to persons). The entities are represented as nodes, and the compatible connections between them are represented as

(a) A directed cyclic graph.

(b) A directed cyclic graph with loops.

Figure 2.8
Cyclic directed graphs.

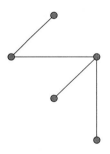

(a) An acyclic undirected graph.

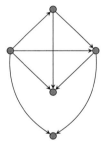

(b) A directed acyclic graph.

Figure 2.9
Acyclic graphs.

edges. To avoid running into trouble, it is important to match exactly one entity to another entity. It is not always clear from inspection, unless we rearrange the position of the nodes, that a graph is bipartite, as in figure 2.10.

An important distinction is made between graphs that have a large number of edges and those that do not. A graph with a large number of edges is called *dense*, otherwise we have a *sparse graph*. At one extreme, a graph may be such that any node is connected to any other node. A graph like that is a *complete graph*, and you can see one in figure 2.11. Obviously it has a large number of

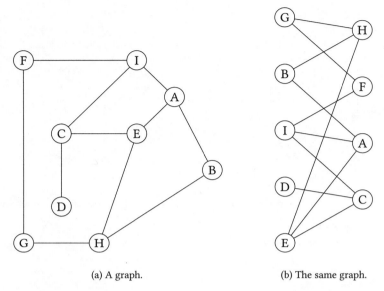

(a) A graph.   (b) The same graph.

Figure 2.10
A bipartite graph.

edges. For n nodes, because every node is connected to all other $n - 1$ nodes, we have $n(n - 1)/2$ edges. In general we may say that a graph with n nodes is dense if it has close to n^2 number of edges, and sparse if it has about n edges. This leaves a fuzzy area between n and n^2, but usually we know from the context of an application if we are dealing with a sparse or dense graph; most of the applications use sparse graphs in fact. For example, imagine that we have a graph representing friendship relationships between people. We take the graph to contain 7 billion nodes, or $n = 7 \times 10^9$, assuming that pretty much everybody on this planet is in it. We also assume that everybody is connected to 1,000 friends, which is probably impossible. Then the number of edges is 7×10^{12}, or 7 trillion. The number $n(n - 1)/2$ for $n = 7 \times 10^9$ is about 2.5×10^{25}, or 7 septillion. That is much bigger than 7 trillion. The graph would have a very large number of edges, but would still be sparse.

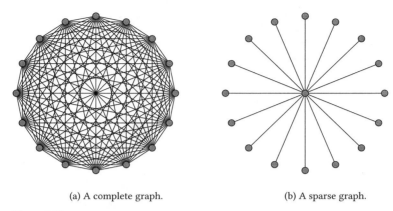

(a) A complete graph.   (b) A sparse graph.

Figure 2.11
Complete and sparse graphs.

2.2   Graph Representation

Before we can do any work with graphs in computers, we need to see how graphs are represented in computer programs. But before that, a brief excursion into how graphs are actually defined in mathematics is necessary. Usually we call the set of vertices V and the set of edges E. A graph G is then $G = (V, E)$. In undirected graphs, the set E is a set consisting of two element sets $\{x, y\}$ for each edge between two nodes x and y of the graph. We usually write (x, y) instead of $\{x, y\}$. In both cases, the order of x and y does not matter. The graph in figure 2.5a is then defined as:

$$V = \{0, 1, 2, 3\}$$
$$E = \{\{0, 1\}, \{0, 2\}, \{0, 3\}, \{1, 2\}, \{1, 3\}, \{2, 3\}\}$$
$$ = \{(0, 1), (0, 2), (0, 3), (1, 2), (1, 3), (2, 3)\}$$

In directed graphs the set E is a set consisting of two element tuples (x, y) for each edge between two nodes x and y of the graph. This time the order of x and y is important and corresponds to the order of the edge it represents. The graph in figure 2.5b is then defined as:

$$V = \{0, 1, 2, 3\}$$
$$E = \{(0, 1), (0, 2), (0, 3), (1, 0), (1, 2), (1, 3), (2, 0), (3, 2)\}$$

Table 2.1

Adjacency matrix for the graph in figure 2.3.

	0	1	2	3	4	5
0	0	1	0	1	0	0
1	1	0	1	0	0	1
2	0	1	0	1	1	0
3	1	0	1	0	1	0
4	0	0	1	1	0	1
5	0	1	0	0	1	0

The mathematical definition of a graph shows that to represent it we need somehow to represent the vertices and the edges. A straightforward way to represent G is with a matrix. This matrix, called an *adjacency matrix*, is a square matrix with a row and a column for each vertex. The contents of the matrix are 0 or 1. If the vertex represented by the ith row is connected to the vertex connected by the jth row, then the (i, j) element of the matrix will be 1, otherwise it will be 0. In an adjacency matrix, vertices are represented by row and column indices, and vertices are represented by the contents of the matrix.

Following these rules, the adjacency matrix for the graph in figure 2.2 is shown in table 2.1. You can check that the adjacency matrix is symmetric. Also, the diagonal will be all zero, except if there are loops in the graph. If we call the matrix A, then $A_{ij} = A_{ji}$ for any two nodes i and j. This is true for all undirected graphs, but it is not true for all directed graphs (unless for every edge from node i to node j there exists an edge from node j to node i). You can also see that many of the values in the matrix are zero. This is typical of sparse graphs.

Even if a graph is not sparse, we may be wary of the space wasted for all those 0 entries in the adjacency matrix. To get over it, there is an alternative representation for graphs that uses less space. Because real-world graphs can have millions of edges, most of the times we use the alternative representation to save what we can. In this representation, we use an array to represent the vertices of the graph. Each element of the array stands for one vertex and is the start of a *list* that contains the vertices that are neighbors of a given vertex. This list is called the *adjacency list* of the vertex in the graph.

Now what exactly is a list? A list is a data structure that contains elements. Each element in the list, called a *node,* has two parts. The first part contains

Figure 2.12
A linked list.

some data that describe the element. The second part contains a link to the next element in the list. The second part is usually a *pointer*, as it points to the next element. A pointer in computers is something that points to a location in the computer's memory; it is also called a *reference*, as it refers to that location. So the second part of a list element is usually a pointer holding an address where the next node in the list is located. A list has a *head*, its first element. We follow the elements in the list as if following the links in a chain. When an element has no next element, we say that it points to nowhere, or *null*; we use the term null to refer to nothingness in computers; because it is a special value, we'll denote it by NULL in text and pseudocode. A list constructed this way is more accurately called a *linked list*, and you can see one in figure 2.12. We use a crossed square to show NULL in the figure.

The basic operations that we need to be able to perform with lists are:

- CreateList(), creates and returns a new, empty list.

- InsertListNode(L, p, n), adds node n after node p in list L. If p is NULL, then we insert n as the new head of the list. The function returns a pointer to n. We assume that the node n has already been created with some data that we want to add in the list. We will not get into the details on how nodes are actually created. Briefly, some memory must be allocated and initialized, so that the node contains the data we want and a pointer. InsertListNode then needs only change pointers. It must make the pointer of n point to the next node, or to NULL, if p was the last node of the list. It must also change the pointer of p to point to n, if p is not NULL.

- InsertInList(L, p, d), adds a node containing d after node p in list L. If p is NULL, then we insert the new node as the new head of the list. The function returns a pointer to the newly inserted node. The difference with InsertListNode is that InsertInList creates the node that will contain d, whereas InsertListNode takes an already created node and inserts it in the list. InsertListNode inserts *nodes*, whereas InsertInList inserts *data* contained in nodes it creates. That means that InsertInList can use InsertListNode to insert in the list the node it creates.

- RemoveListNode(L, p, r), removes node r from the list and returns that node; p points to the node preceding r in the list, or NULL if r is the head. We will see that we need to know p in order to remove the item pointed by r efficiently. If r is not in the list, it returns NULL.

- RemoveFromList(L, d), removes the first node containing d from the list and returns the node. The difference with RemoveListNode is that it will search the list for the node containing d, find it, and remove it; d does not point to the node itself; it is the data contained inside the node. If there is no node containing d in the list, RemoveFromList returns NULL.

- GetNextListNode(L, p), returns the node following p in list L. If p is the last node in the list, then it returns NULL. If p is NULL, then it returns the first node of L, the head. The returned node is not removed from the list.

- SearchInList(L, d), searches the list L for the first node containing d. It returns the node, or NULL if no such node exists; the node is not removed from the list.

To create a representation of graph using adjacency lists, only CreateList and InsertInList are essential. To go through the elements of a list L, we need to call $n \leftarrow$ GetNextListNode(L, NULL) to get the first element; then, as long as $n \neq$ NULL, we call repeatedly $n \leftarrow$ GetNextListNode(L, n). Note that we need a way to access the data inside a node, for example, a function GetData(n) that returns the data d stored inside the node n.

To see how insertion works, suppose we have an empty list and we insert into it three nodes, each one of which contains a number. When we write a list in the text, we will enumerate its elements inside brackets, like this [3, 1, 4, 1, 5, 9]. An empty list will be simply [ ]. If the numbers are 3, 1, and 0 and we insert them in this order in the beginning of the list, then the list will grow as in figure 2.13 from [ ] to [0, 1, 3]. Insertion at the front of the list works by passing NULL repeatedly as the second argument to InsertInList.

Alternatively, if we want to append a series of nodes at the end of the list, we make a series of calls to InsertInList passing as second argument the return value of the previous call; you can see the pattern in figure 2.14.

Removal of a node from the list entails taking the node out and making the previous node, if it exists, point to the node following the node to be removed. If we remove the head of the list, then there is no previous node, and the next node becomes the new head of the list. Figure 2.15 shows what happens when we remove the nodes with data 3, 0, 1 from the list we created in figure 2.13. If we do not know the previous node, we have to start from the head of the

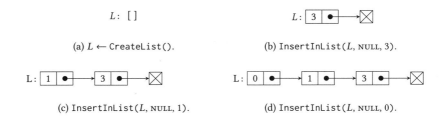

Figure 2.13
Inserting nodes in the beginning of a list.

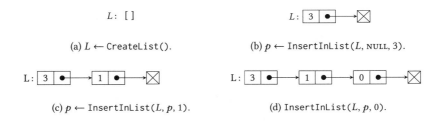

Figure 2.14
Appending nodes to a list.

list and go through the nodes until we find the one pointing to the node we want to remove. That is why we include it in the calls of RemoveListNode.

Although in our examples the nodes in a list carry only a number, a list is a much more general data structure, and we could have any kind of information carried in it. It is convenient to keep it simple right now, but you must be aware that we can have lists of anything, as long as they consist of elements containing data and each element points to the next element in the list, or NULL.

Our lists are the simplest possible, with just one link from one element to the next. There are other kinds of lists. We may have two links in an element, one pointing to the previous element and one pointing to the next element in the list; this is a *doubly linked list*. By contrast, when we want to be specific, we use the term *singly linked list* to make clear that we are really talking about lists with only one link. You can see an example of a doubly linked list in figure 2.16. In a doubly linked list, both the head and the final element of the list point to NULL. Doubly linked lists allow us to traverse them both forward

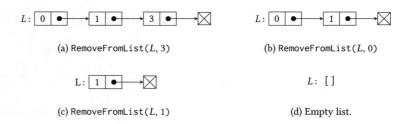

(a) RemoveFromList(L, 3)   (b) RemoveFromList(L, 0)

(c) RemoveFromList(L, 1)   (d) Empty list.

Figure 2.15
Removing nodes from a list.

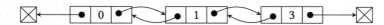

Figure 2.16
A doubly linked list.

and backward, whereas singly linked lists allow only forward traversal. At the same time, they require some more space, as each node in the list needs two links, one to the next element and one to the previous element. Moreover, addition and removal are a bit more complicated as we must make sure that both forward and backward links are set and updated in the proper way. That said, to remove a node, we no longer need to know the node that points to it, as we can find it immediately by following the backward link.

Another kind of list is when the final element in the list does not point to NULL but back to the first element of the list. This is called a *circular list*, and you can see one in figure 2.17.

All this is good to know, and the different kinds of lists are widely used, but we'll stick to singly linked lists here for now.

Using lists, we create the adjacency list representation of a graph. In this representation, we have one adjacency list for each vertex. All these are brought together with an array that points to the heads of the adjacency lists.

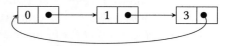

Figure 2.17
A circular list.

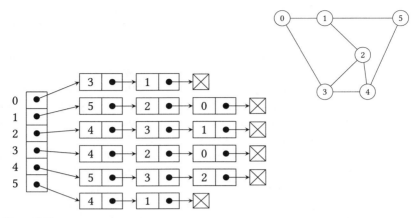

Figure 2.18

The adjacency list representation of a graph.

If the array is A, then item $A[i]$ of the array points to the head of the adjacency list of node i of the graph. If node i has no neighbors, $A[i]$ will point to NULL.

The adjacency list representation of the graph of figure 2.4 is in figure 2.18. For convenience a minimized version of the graph is on the upper right corner of figure 2.18. The figure shows on the left the array that contains the heads of the adjacency lists of the graph; each item of the array corresponds to one vertex. The adjacency lists contain the edges of the vertex in their head. So the third element of the array contains the head of the adjacency list for node 2 of the graph. Each adjacency list was constructed by taking the neighbors of each node in their numerical order. For example, to create the adjacency list of node 1, we called Insert three times, for nodes 0, 2, and 5, in this order. This explains why the nodes appear in reverse order in this and in every other adjacency list in the figure: nodes are inserted in the head of each list, so inserting them in the order 0, 2, 5 will result in the list [5, 2, 0].

It is straightforward to compare the space requirements of the adjacency matrix and the adjacency list representation of a graph $G = (V, E)$. If $|V|$ is the number of vertices in a graph, the adjacency matrix will have $|V|^2$ elements. Similarly, if $|E|$ is the number of edges in the graph, then the adjacency list representation of it will contain an array of size $|V|$ and then $|V|$ lists that all of them will contain $|E|$ edges. So the adjacency list representation will require $|V| + |E|$ items, much less than $|V|^2$, except if the graph is dense and many vertices are connected to each other.

You may think then that there is no reason to bother with adjacency matrices at all. There are two reasons. First, adjacency matrices are simpler. You only need to know about matrices and nothing else; no bother with lists. Second, adjacency matrices are faster. We take for granted that accessing an element in a matrix is an operation that takes constant time, that is, we can retrieve every edge, or element, as fast as any other—it does not matter whether it is near, say, the upper left corner of the matrix or the bottom right one. When we use adjacency lists, we have to access the right element on the array of vertices on the left side of figure 2.18 *and* find the required edge by traversing the list headed by the vertex. So, to see whether nodes 4 and 5 are connected, we need to go first at node 4 on the vertices matrix and then jump to 2, 3, and finally 5. To see whether nodes 4 and 0 are connected, we need to go through all the list headed by 4 until its end and then report that we have not found 0, so they are not connected by link. You may counter that it would be faster if we had searched the list headed by 0 because it is shorter, but we had no way of knowing that.

Using big-Oh notation, determining whether a vertex is connected to another vertex takes constant time, so the complexity is $\Theta(1)$ if we use an adjacency matrix. The same operation using adjacency lists takes $O(|V|)$ time because it is possible that in a graph a vertex is connected to all other vertices, and we may have to search the whole of its adjacency list for a neighbor. As you know, there is no such thing as a free lunch. In computers this translates to trade-offs: we exchange space for speed. This is something we do often, and it even has a name: *space-time tradeoff*.

2.3   Depth-first Graph Traversal

Now back to maze exploration. To explore a maze fully we need two things: some way to keep track of where we have been, and some systematic way to visit all unvisited rooms. Suppose that the rooms are somehow ordered. In the graphs we have seen, we can assume that the order is numeric. Then to visit all rooms we can go to the first room and mark it as visited. We then go to the *first* of the rooms connected to it. We mark it as visited. We go again to the first unvisited room connected to it, and we repeat the procedure: we mark it as visited, and we go to the first unvisited room connected to the room we are. If there are no unvisited rooms connected to a room, then we go back to where we came from, and we try to see whether any unvisited rooms remain there. If yes, we visit the first unvisited room there, and so on. If no, then we

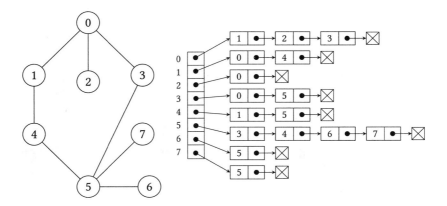

Figure 2.19
Maze to be explored depth-first.

go retrace our steps back another room. We do that until we come back to the room we started in and find that we have visited all rooms connected to it.

It is easier to see that in practice. The procedure is called *depth-first search*, or DFS for short, because we are exploring the maze in depth rather than in breadth. An example maze is in figure 2.19, along with its adjacency list representation on the right. Note that again we inserted nodes in the list in reverse order. For example, in the adjacency list for node 0, we inserted the neighboring nodes in order 3, 2, 1, so the list is [0, 1, 2, 3].

Tracing depth-first search in figure 2.20, we start at node, or room, 0. We indicate with gray the current node and with black the nodes we have already visited. A double indicate shows a virtual thread that we are holding in our hand during our exploration. Much like Theseus, we use the thread to go back and retrace our steps when we cannot or should not go any farther.

The first unvisited room there is room 1, so we go to room 1. The first unvisited room from room 1 is 4. Then the first unvisited room from 4 is 5. In the same way we get from 5 to 3. At that point we find no unvisited room, so we go back by picking up the thread. We go back to 5. There we find room 6 that is still unvisited. We visit it, and we return to 5. Room 6 still has one unvisited room, 7. We visit that room, and we go back to 5 again. Now 5 has no unvisited rooms next to it, so we go back to room 4. In turn, 4 has no unvisited rooms next to it, so we trace our steps back once more to 1, and

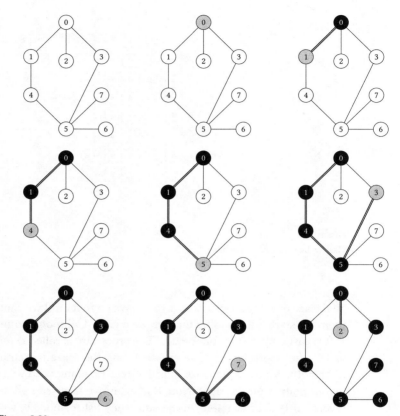

Figure 2.20
Depth-first maze exploration.

then for the same reason we return to 0. There we see that 2 is unvisited; we visit it, and we go back to 0. Now that 1, 2, and 3 are visited, we are done. If you have followed the path we described, you may have verified that we are going deep rather than wide. When in room 0, we went to 1 and then 4, instead of going to 2 and 3. Room 2, although it was next to us when we started, was the last room we visited. So indeed we go as deep as we can before we have to consider any alternatives.

Algorithm 2.1 implements depth-first search. The algorithm takes as input a graph G and a node from where it will start exploring the graph. It also uses an array *visited* that indicates for each node whether it has been visited.

Algorithm 2.1: Recursive graph depth-first search.

DFS(*G, node*)

    Input: $G = (V, E)$, a graph

          node, a node in G

    Data: *visited*, an array of size $|V|$

    Result: *visited*[*i*] is TRUE if we have visited node *i*, FALSE otherwise

1   *visited*[*node*] ← TRUE

2   **foreach** v in AdjacencyList(*G, node*) **do**

3   **if not** *visited*[*v*] **then**

4   DFS(*G, v*)

In the beginning we have visited no node, so *visited* is all FALSE. Although *visited* is required by the algorithm, we do not include it in its inputs, as it is not something that we pass to the algorithm when we call it; it is an array, created and initialized outside the algorithm, which the algorithm can access, read, and modify. Because *visited* is modified by the algorithm it is really its output, even if we do not really say so. We do not specify any output for the algorithm, because it does not return any; yet, it communicates its results to its environment through the *visited* array, so the changes in *visited* are the algorithm's results. You can think of *visited* as a newly cleaned blackboard to which the algorithm writes its progress.

Algorithm DFS(*G, node*) is *recursive*. Recursive algorithms are algorithms that call themselves. DFS(*G, node*) marks the current vertex as visited, in line 1, and then calls itself for every unvisited vertex linked to it by walking down the adjacency list; we assume we have a function AdjacencyList(*G, node*) that given a graph and a node returns its adjacency list. In line 2 we go through the nodes in the adjacency list; that is easy to do because from any node we can go directly to the next one, by the definition of a list, because each node in a list is linked to the next. If we have not visited that neighboring node (line 3), then we call DFS(*G, v*) for *the neighboring node v*.

The tricky part in understanding the algorithm is understanding the recursion it performs. Let's take a trivial graph, consisting of four nodes, shown in figure 2.21a. We start with node 0. If the graph is called G, then we call DFS(*G*, 0). The function gets the adjacency list of node 0, which is [1, 3]. The loop in lines 2–4 will be executed twice: the first time for node 1 and the second time for node 3. In the first execution of the loop, as node 1 is not visited,

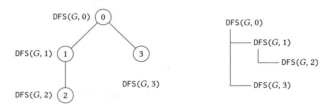

(a) Graph and visiting order.   (b) Call trace of depth-first search.

Figure 2.21
Depth-first search in depth.

we will reach line 4. Now this is the important part. In line 4 we call DFS(G, 1), but the current call *is not finished yet*. We start executing DFS(G, 1) while putting DFS(G, 0) on the shelf, as it were; we will take it from the shelf when DFS(G, 1) finishes and we will resume its execution then at the point right after the call to DFS(G, 1). When we execute DFS(G, 1), we take its adjacency list, which is [2]. The loop in lines 2–4 will be executed once, for node 2. As node 2 is not visited yet, we reach line 4. As we did before, we call DFS(G, 2), but DFS(G, 1) is again not finished, but rather put on the shelf, waiting for DFS(G, 2) to finish. DFS(G, 2) has an empty adjacency list, so the loop in lines 2–4 is not executed at all, and the function returns immediately.

Where? We take DFS(G, 1) off the shelf and go to the place in DFS(G, 1) where we had left it waiting for us; that is, at line 4 but right after the call to DFS(G, 2). Because there is no other node apart from node 2 in the adjacency list of node 1, the loop in DFS(G, 1) terminates, and the function finishes. We return to DFS(G, 0), taking it from the shelf and going where we left it. That was at line 4 right after the call to DFS(G, 1). That is the end of the execution of the first iteration of the loop. We therefore start the second iteration of the loop. That leads us to call DFS(G, 3), while putting DFS(G, 0) on the shelf again. Node 3 has an empty adjacency list, and so, like in node 2, DFS(G, 3) will finish and return to DFS(G, 0). That will let DFS(G, 0) finish the second iteration of the loop, complete its whole execution, and return.

We call a trace of a series of function calls, unsurprisingly, *call trace*. Figure 2.21b shows the call trace that starts with DFS(G, 0). The trace is read from top to bottom, left to right. It is a tree, where calls initiated from another

---

Algorithm 2.2: Factorial function.

Factorial(n) → !n
    Input: n, a natural number
    Output: $n!$, the factorial of n

1   **if** $n = 0$ **then**
2   **return** 1
3   **else**
4   **return** $n \cdot$ Factorial($n-1$)

---

call are children of that call. Control flows from a parent to child, from child to grandchild, and so on, until there are no more offspring, where we take the opposite route, from offsprings to ancestors. It's like going: down DFS(G, 0) → DFS(G, 1) → DFS(G, 2); up DFS(G, 2) → DFS(G, 1) → DFS(G, 0); down again DFS(G, 0) → DFS(G, 3); up again DFS(G, 3) → DFS(G, 0); and finish. Observe that when we visit a node, we go recursively to its children if any; we visit its siblings only after we have visited the children. For example, we went from node 1 to node 2, and not to node 3. By using recursion in this way, we do indeed go deep first, performing a depth-first traversal.

In case recursion still appears a bit obscure, it's worth making a small diversion to explain it a bit more. The archetypical recursive function is the factorial, $n! = n \times (n-1) \times \ldots \times 1$ with the corner case $0! = 1$. We can render the factorial function as algorithm 2.2; figure 2.22 shows the call trace for calculating 5!.

In this call trace, we include the statement in each call that causes the recursive call; in this way we can show, via arrows, where exactly the called function returns. For example, when we are in Factorial(1), we reach line 4 of algorithm 2.2. At this point you can think of Factorial(0) in figure 2.22 as a placeholder that is filled in when Factorial(0) returns. The returning path in the call trace, filling in the placeholders, is indicated by the bottom up arrows that wind up the recursive series of calls. We go down the call trace following the steps on the left, and we return following the arrows on the right.

A crucial part of all recursive functions is a condition that will stop the recursion. In the factorial function, when we reach $n = 0$, we stop the recursive calls, and it's time to go back. In algorithm 2.1 the stopping condition is in line 3. If we have visited all neighbors of a node, then there are no more

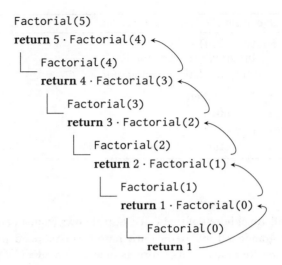

```
Factorial(5)
  return 5 · Factorial(4)
      │  Factorial(4)
          return 4 · Factorial(3)
              │  Factorial(3)
                  return 3 · Factorial(2)
                      │  Factorial(2)
                          return 2 · Factorial(1)
                              │  Factorial(1)
                                  return 1 · Factorial(0)
                                      │  Factorial(0)
                                          return 1
```

Figure 2.22
Factorial call trace.

recursive calls for that node; it's time to go back. *This is very important.* Forgetting to specify when to end a recursion is a recipe for disaster. A recursive function without a stopping condition will go on calling itself, and do so ad infinitum. Programmers who forget that are in for nasty bugs. The computer will keep calling and calling the function, until it runs out of memory and the program crashes. You are left with a message that talks about a "stack overflow" or something similar, for reasons we'll explain in a little bit.

Hoping that recursion is clear now (if it is not, give it another go), note that the depth-first search algorithm works from whatever node we start. We used node 0 in our example simply because it is on the top. We can start the algorithm from node 7, or node 3, as you can see in figure 2.23, where we put the order we visit a node next to it. The order that we visit the nodes is different, but we still explore the graph fully.

This would not happen if the graph were undirected and disconnected, or if it were directed and not strongly connected. In such graphs, we must call algorithm 2.1 for each node in turn if it has not been visited. In this way, even nodes that are unreachable from one node will have their turn as start nodes.

How does recursion work in a computer? How is all this housekeeping done, putting functions on hold, calling other functions, and then knowing

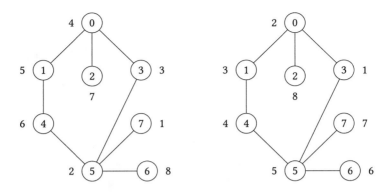

(a) Depth-first search starting from node 7.   (b) Depth-first search starting from node 3.

Figure 2.23
Depth-first exploration from different starting nodes.

where to return? The way a computer knows where to return from a function is by using an internal stack, called *call stack*. The stack holds the current function on top. Below it there is the function which called it with all the information to resume execution where we left it. Below that, the function that called that function, if any, and so on. That's why a recursion gone awry will cause a crash: we cannot have an infinite stack. You can see snapshots of the stack when running algorithm 2.1 in figure 2.24. We show the contents of a stack when the algorithm visits a node, painted gray below the stack. When it hits a dead end, which is a node with no unvisited neighbors to visit, the function returns, or *backtracks* to its caller; the process of retracing our steps is called *backtracking*. We call popping the top of the call stack *unwinding* (although in the case of maze exploration, this corresponds to winding our thread). So from node 3 we go to node 5, painted black to show that we have already visited it. A series of unwinding actions happens in the second row of the figure, when we go from node 7 all the way to node 0 to visit node 2.

All this stack activity happens automatically. However, there is no reason that you cannot do the same magic yourself. Instead of using recursion to perform depth-first search, which uses a stack implicitly, you can use a stack explicitly, in which case you do away with recursion altogether. The idea is that at every node we add the unvisited nodes in the stack, and when we search for nodes to visit, we simply pop elements from the stack. Algorithm 2.3 shows the stack-based implementation of depth-first search. You

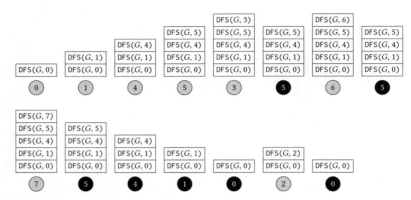

Figure 2.24

Stack evolution in depth-first search for figure 2.20.

can see the contents of the stack in figure 2.25b; we only show snapshots of the stack upon visiting a node, not when backtracking on it, in the interests of space and ink.

The algorithm works in the same way as algorithm 2.1 but uses an explicit stack instead of relying on recursion. We create the stack in line 1. This time we do not rely on an externally provided array to record our progress, creating the array *visited* ourselves in line 2; we then initialize it to all FALSE values in lines 3–4.

To emulate recursion, we push on the stack the nodes that we have yet to visit, and when we are looking for a node to visit, we go to the one at the top of the stack. To get things in motion, we push on the stack the starting node, in line 5. Then as long as there is something on the stack (line 6), we pop it (line 7), mark it as visited (line 8), and push on the stack every node in its adjacency list that we have not already visited (lines 9–11). When we are done, we return the array *visited* so that we report which nodes we were able to reach.

Because of the order nodes are put on the stack, graph traversal is depth-first but goes from higher-numbered nodes to lower-numbered ones. Whereas the recursive algorithm goes counterclockwise in our maze, this one goes clockwise.

You may notice from figure 2.25b, in the third column from the right, that node 1 is added to the stack twice. This does not make the algorithm incorrect, but we can fix it anyway. We need a *no-duplicates stack*, in which an item is

---

Algorithm 2.3: Graph depth-first search with a stack.

StackDFS(G, *node*) $\rightarrow$ *visited*
    Input: $G = (V, E)$, a graph
            node, the starting vertex in G
    Output: *visited*, an array of size $|V|$ such that *visited*[i] is TRUE if we
             have visited node i, FALSE otherwise

1    $S \leftarrow$ CreateStack()
2   *visited* $\leftarrow$ CreateArray($|V|$)
3   **for** $i \leftarrow 0$ **to** $|V|$ **do**
4   *visited*[i] $\leftarrow$ FALSE
5   Push(S, *node*)
6   **while not** IsStackEmpty(S) **do**
7        $c \leftarrow$ Pop(s)
8   *visited*[c] $\leftarrow$ TRUE
9   **foreach** v **in** AdjacencyList(G, c) **do**
10   **if not** *visited*[v] **then**
11   Push(S, v)
12   **return** *visited*

---

added only if it is not already in the stack. To do this we use an additional array. An element of that array will be true if that element is currently in the stack and false otherwise. Algorithm 2.4 is the result. The algorithm is pretty much the same as algorithm 2.4 but uses the additional array *instack*, where we record those nodes that are in the stack. You can see what is happening in the stack in figure 2.25c.

You may wonder why, given that we already had algorithm 2.1, we went on to develop algorithm 2.4. Apart from it being instructive, to show how recursion really works, implicit recursion requires that the computer puts all the necessary memory state of the function on the stack at each recursive call. So it will transfer more things on the stack in figure 2.24 (where we only show the function calls) instead of simple numbers as in figure 2.25. An algorithm implemented with an explicit stack may be more economical than an equivalent recursive one.

To finish depth-first exploration, let's go back to algorithm 2.1 and examine its complexity. The complexity of algorithms 2.3 and 2.4 will be the same

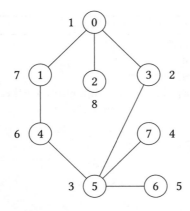

(a) The order of visiting the rooms.

(b) The evolution of the stack.

(c) The evolution of the no-duplicates stack.

Figure 2.25
Walkthrough and stack contents of algorithms 2.3 and 2.4.

as that of algorithm 2.1 because only the implementation of the recursive mechanism changes, not the overall exploration strategy. Line 2 is executed $|V|$ times, once per each vertex. Then DFS(G, *node*) is called exactly once per edge, in line 4, that is, $|E|$ times. All in all, the complexity of depth-first search is $\Theta(|V| + |E|)$. We can explore the graph in time proportional to its size, which makes sense.

2.4 Breadth-first Search

As we saw, the graph exploration in depth-first search goes deep rather than wide. Suppose we would like to explore the maze in a different way, so that when we start at node 0 we visit nodes 1, 2, and 3 before we go on to visit node 4. That means that we would be casting our net wide, instead of deep. Such a search strategy is called, not surprisingly, *breadth-first search*, or BFS for short.

In breadth-first search, we can no longer rely on a thread (implicit or real) to carry us through. There is no physical means by which we can get directly from node 3 to node 4 because they are not directly connected, so the analogy

---

Algorithm 2.4: Graph depth-first search with a no-duplicates stack.

NoDuplicatesStackDFS(G, *node*) → *visited*
    Input: $G = (V, E)$, a graph
           node, the starting vertex in G
    Output: *visited*, an array of size $|V|$ such that *visited*[i] is TRUE if we
           have visited node i, FALSE otherwise

1   $S \leftarrow$ CreateStack()
2   *visited* $\leftarrow$ CreateArray($|V|$)
3   *instack* $\leftarrow$ CreateArray($|V|$)
4   **for** $i \leftarrow 0$ **to** $|V|$ **do**
5   *visited*[i] $\leftarrow$ FALSE
6   *instack*[i] $\leftarrow$ FALSE

7   Push(S, *node*)
8   *instack*[*node*] $\leftarrow$ TRUE
9   **while not** IsStackEmpty(S) **do**
10      $c \leftarrow$ Pop(S)
11   *instack*[c] $\leftarrow$ FALSE
12   *visited*[c] $\leftarrow$ TRUE
13   **foreach** v **in** AdjacencyList(G, c) **do**
14   **if not** *visited*[v] **and not** *instack*[v] **then**
15   Push(S, v)
16   *instack*[v] $\leftarrow$ TRUE
17   **return** *visited*

---

with real-world mazes breaks down. For a breadth-first traversal to work, we need to assume that we can get from the node we are currently visiting to a node we know it exists but we have not visited yet. We cannot disappear from node 3 and move to node 4 if it were an actual labyrinth, but there is no problem doing such a move in an algorithm, provided we know that node 4 does exist. The allowed moves in this version of the maze exploration game are all moves from a node to another known, yet unvisited, node.

You can follow breadth-first search in figure 2.26. Below each snapshot of the exploration we show the nodes that we know we have to visit, read from the right to the left—we will see why in a moment. When we start our breadth-first exploration from node 0, the only node we know exists is node 0. At that

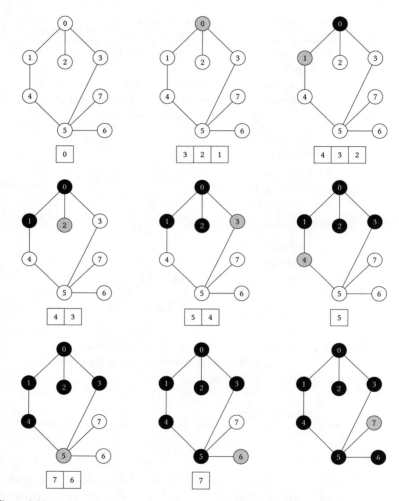

Figure 2.26
Breadth-first maze exploration.

Figure 2.27
Addition and removal in a queue.

node we record its three neighbors, nodes 1, 2, and 3. We visit them in that order. When we visit node 1, we record its unvisited neighbor, node 4; that means we know we have to visit nodes 2, 3, and 4. We visit node 2, which has no unvisited neighbors, and then we go to node 3, where we record that we will have to visit node 5. The known unvisited nodes now are 4 and 5. We visit 4, then 5. When we are at node 5, we record that we need to visit nodes 6 and 7. We then visit them in that order and we are done.

To implement breadth-first search we need to use a new data structure called a *queue*, which gives us the functionality we need to keep track of the unvisited nodes below each snapshot of the graph exploration in 2.26. A queue is a sequence of things. We add things on the back of the sequence, and we remove things from its front; it works like a queue in real life, where the first one in is the first one out (unless somebody is jumping the queue). To make this clear we talk about First In First Out (FIFO) queues. We call the back of the queue its *tail* and the front of the queue its *head* (so both lists and queues have heads). You can see how addition and removal works in a queue in figure 2.27. It follows that the basic operations on a queue are:

- CreateQueue(), creates an empty queue.
- Enqueue(Q, i) adds item i to the tail of the queue Q.
- Dequeue(Q) removes an item from the front of the queue. In essence, it removes the head and makes the element following it the new head. If the queue is empty, then the operation is not allowed (we get an error).
- IsQueueEmpty(Q) returns TRUE if the queue Q is empty, FALSE otherwise.

With these operations at hand, we can write algorithm 2.5, which implements breadth-first search in a graph. Because the queue is filled at the tail and emptied from the head, we visit the nodes it contains by reading its contents from the right to the left, as in figure 2.26.

The algorithm is similar to algorithm 2.4. It returns an array *visited*, which indicates the nodes that we were able to reach. It uses an array *inqueue* that

---

Algorithm 2.5: Graph breadth-first search.

BFS(G, *node*) $\rightarrow$ *visited*
      Input: $G = (V, E)$, a graph
              node, the starting vertex in G
      Output: *visited*, an array of size $|V|$ such that *visited*[i] is TRUE if we
              have visited node i, FALSE otherwise

1    $Q \leftarrow$ CreateQueue()
2   *visited* $\leftarrow$ CreateArray($|V|$)
3   *inqueue* $\leftarrow$ CreateArray($|V|$)
4   **for** $i \leftarrow 0$ **to** $|V|$ **do**
5   *visited*[i] $\leftarrow$ FALSE
6   *inqueue*[i] $\leftarrow$ FALSE

7   Enqueue(Q, *node*)
8   *inqueue*[*node*] $\leftarrow$ TRUE
9   **while not** IsQueueEmpty(Q) **do**
10        $c \leftarrow$ Dequeue(Q)
11   *inqueue*[c] $\leftarrow$ FALSE
12   *visited*[c] $\leftarrow$ TRUE
13   **foreach** v **in** AdjacencyList(G, c) **do**
14   **if not** *visited*[v] **and not** *inqueue*[v] **then**
15   Enqueue(Q, v)
16   *inqueue*[v] $\leftarrow$ TRUE
17   **return** *visited*

---

keeps track of which nodes are currently in the queue. In the beginning of the algorithm, we initialize the queue we will be using (line 1), then we create and initialize *visited* and *inqueue* (lines 2–6).

The queue will always contain the nodes we know exist but we have not visited yet. In the beginning we only node the starting node, so we add it to the queue (line 7) and we keep track of that in *inqueue*. Then as long as the queue is not empty (lines 9–16), we take off the element at the head of the queue (line 10), record the fact (line 11), and mark it as visited (line 12). Then for every node in its adjacency list (lines 13–16) that is neither visited nor in the queue (line 14), we put it in the queue (line 15) and record that the node entered the queue (line 16). In this way it will come off the queue in some

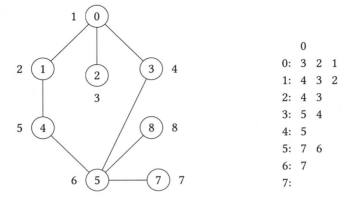

(a) The order of visiting the rooms.   (b) The evolution of the queue.

Figure 2.28
Walkthrough and queue contents of algorithm 2.5.

future iteration of the main loop of the algorithm. Figure 2.28 is a condensed version of figure 2.26.

Examining the algorithm's complexity, line 9 will be executed $|V|$ times. Then the loop starting at line 13 will be executed once for every edge of the graph, or $|E|$ times. So the complexity of breadth-first search is $\Theta(|V| + |E|)$, the same with depth-first search. That is quite pleasant; it means that we have two algorithms for graph search at our disposal, with the same complexity, but each one of them will explore the graph with a different, yet correct strategy. We can choose and pick which one fits better a particular problem we have to solve.

Notes

The foundations of graph theory were laid down by Leonhard Euler in 1736, when he presented a paper examining whether it would be possible to cross the seven bridges of Königsberg once and only once (back then Königsberg was in Prussia, today it is called Kaliningrad and it is in Russia, and only five bridges remain). The answer was negative [56]; because the original paper is in Latin, which may not be your forte, you can check the book by Biggs,

Lloyd, and Wilson [19], which contains a translation, along with lots of other interesting historical material on graph theory.

For an easy approach to graph theory, you can read the introductory book by Benjamin, Chartrand, and Zhang [15]. If you want to go deeper, you can check the book by Bondy and Murty [25]. In recent years, offshoots of graph theory treat many different aspects of all kinds of networks; see for example the books by Barabási [10], Newman [150], David and Kleinberg [48], and Watts [214]. The study of graphs in networks (of different kinds), the web, and the Internet can be seen as three different disciplines [203], where graphs are applied to explain different phenomena arising from large interconnected structures.

Depth-first search has a long provenance; a 19th-century French mathematician, Charles Pierre Trémaux, published a version of it; for a comprehensive account of this and other aspects of graph theory, see the book by Even [57]. Hopcroft and Tarjan presented depth-first search in computers and argued for representing graphs using adjacency lists [197, 96]; see also the short, classic text by Tarjan on data structures and graphs [199].

Maze exploration lay behind breadth-first search, published in the 1950s by E. F. Moore [145]. It was also discovered independently as an algorithm for routing wires on circuit boards by C. Y. Lee [126].

Exercises

1. There are good quality implementations of lists in all popular programming languages, but it is instructive, and not difficult, to implement your own. The basic ideas are in figures 2.13 and 2.15. An empty list is a pointer to NULL. When you insert an element in the list's head, you need to adjust the list to point to the new head and make the newly inserted head point to where the list was pointing before its insertion—that is, the previous head or NULL. To insert an element after an existing element, you need to adjust the previous element's link to point to the newly inserted element and make the newly inserted element point to where the previous element was pointing before the insertion. To search for an item in the list, you need to start from the head and check each item, following the links, until you find the one you are looking for or NULL. To remove an item, you have to look for it first; once you find it, you need to make the pointer pointing to it point to the next item, or NULL if you are removing the last item.

2.   A queue can be implemented using an array, in which you keep track of the index of the head, h, and the tail, t, of the queue. Initially both the head and the tail are equal to 0:

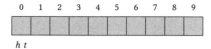

When you insert an item in the queue, you increase the index of the head; similarly, when you remove an item from the queue, you increase the index of the tail. After inserting 5, 6, 2, and 9 and removing 5, the array will be:

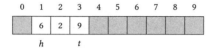

If the array can hold n items, when the head or the tail reach the $(n-1)$th item they wrap around to position 0. So, after several more insertions and removals the queue may look like this:

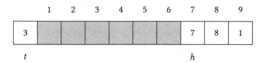

Implement a queue with this idea. The queue will be empty when the head reaches the tail and full when the tail is about to trample the head.

3.   Implement depth-first search (either recursively or not) and breadth-first search using the adjacency matrix representation instead of the adjacency list one that we have used.

4.   Depth-first search can be used to create mazes, not just to explore them. We start with a graph with $n \times n$ nodes that are arranged in a grid; for example, if $n = 10$ and we name the nodes by their (x, y) position we have:

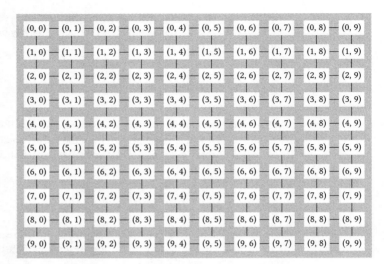

We start from a node in the graph. We mark the node as visited, and we take its neighbors in some random order. For each one of them, if we have not visited the node we record the link that we traverse and we go to that node, where we continue the procedure recursively. That means that we perform a depth-first traversal in which we visit the neighbors in random order, keeping a record of the links we follow. When we have finished the depth-first search, we have in our hands a new graph: it consists of the same $n \times n$ nodes and the subset of the original links that we followed. That is our maze. Write a program that creates such mazes. It is worth learning a drawing library so that you can visualize the results.

5.   As you can see in figure 2.10, it is not easy to determine whether a graph is bipartite simply by visual inspection. Instead we can perform the following procedure. We traverse the graph, coloring the nodes in two different, alternate colors. When we color a node we do not really paint it, of course; we just mark it as having that color. If the colors as "red" and "green," we will color the first node as red, the next one as green, and so on. If at any time during the traversal we encounter a neighbor that is already painted the same color as the color we have used for the current node, then the graph is not bipartite. If we finish the traversal without this occurring, then the graph is bipartite. Implement the procedure as an algorithm for detecting bipartite graphs.

3 Compressing

We store digital data using series of 0s and 1s, or bits. Any text you are reading, including this one, is represented as such a sequence of bits. Consider the phrase "I am seated in an office". What is this to a computer?

The computer needs to encode each letter of the sentence to a pattern of bits. There are various ways to do that, but in English the most straightforward is to use the ASCII encoding. ASCII stands for American Standard Code for Information Interchange, and it is an encoding that uses 128 characters to represent the English alphabet, plus punctuation and some control characters. It is not a recent standard; it has been around since the 1960s, with various revisions. It works well for languages that use the Latin character set but cannot accommodate other languages that do not, so in those languages we must use other encodings, such as Unicode that can represent more than 110,000 characters from different language scripts. ASCII can represent only 128 characters because it uses seven bits per character, and the number of possible characters that can be represented with seven bits is $2^7 = 128$. This follows from the fact that with seven bits we can represent 2^7 different numbers, and we will use each one of these numbers to stand for a character.

The number of different characters we can represent with seven bits is equal to the number of different bit patterns that are possible with seven bits, which you can see in figure 3.1. Each bit, shown as a box in the figure, can take the value 0 or 1, so there are two distinct patterns, 0 and 1 for every single bit. Starting from the end of a series of bits, if we take the last two bits, there are two possible patterns for each one of them, so 2×2 possible patterns for the two of them together (these are 00, 01, 10, 11). With three bits we have two possible patterns for every possible pattern of two bits, so $2 \times 2 \times 2$ altogether, and so on until we cover all seven bits. In general, if we have n bits, we can represent 2^n different numbers.

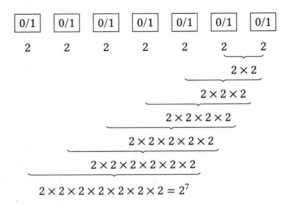

Figure 3.1
Number of possible characters represented by 7 bits.

You can see the ASCII encoding in table 3.1. Each character corresponds to a unique bit pattern, which in turn corresponds to a unique number, the value of the pattern in the binary system. The table runs in 8 rows of 16 elements each; for convenience we use the hexadecimal number system for the columns. There is nothing special about hexadecimal numbers. Instead of using the nine digits $0, 1, \ldots, 9$, we use the sixteen digits $0, 1, \ldots, 9$, A, B, C, D, E, F. The number A in hexadecimal is 10, the number B is 11, until the number F, which is 15. Remember that in decimal numbers, the value of a number such as 53 is $5 \times 10 + 3$, and in general a number made up of digits $D_n D_{n-1} \ldots D_1 D_0$ has value $D_n \times 10^n + D_{n-1} \times 10^{n-1} + \cdots + D_1 \times 10^1 + D_0 \times 10^0$. In hexadecimal the logic is exactly the same, but instead of 10 we use 16 as the base of our calculations. The number $H_n H_{n-1} \ldots H_1 H_0$ in hexadecimal has value $H_n \times 16^n + H_{n-1} \times 16^{n-1} + \cdots + H_1 \times 16^1 + H_0 \times 16^0$. For example, the number 20 in hexadecimal has value $2 \times 16 + 0 = 32$ and the number 1B in hexadecimal has value $1 \times 16 + 11 = 27$. Usually we prefix hexadecimal numbers by 0x to make clear we are using the hexadecimal number system and avoid any confusions. So we write 0x20 to make clear that this is written in hexadecimal and not in decimal. We also write 0x1B, although it is clear that this cannot be a number in decimal, just to keep things consistent.

By the way, the logic we described above works with other bases apart from 10 and 16; the *binary number system* directly follows when we adopt the number 2 as the *base* of our calculations. The value of a binary number made up of bits $B_n B_{n-1} \ldots B_1 B_0$ is $B_n \times 2^n + B_{n-1} \times 2^{n-1} + \cdots + B_1 \times 2^1 + B_0 \times 2^0$.

All these are examples of *positional number systems*, that is, number systems where the value of a number is derived by the position of the digits in it and the base of the number system. The general rule for finding the value is in a base b system is:

$$X_n X_{n-1} \ldots X_1 X_0 = X_n \times b^n + X_{n-1} \times b^{n-1} + \cdots + X_1 \times b^1 + X_0 \times b^0$$

If you substitute 2, 10, or 16 for b, then you get the formulas we used above. A generic notation to work with number in different number systems is $(X)_b$. For example, $(27)_{10} = (1B)_{16}$.

You may wonder at this point why we go into all this trouble with hexadecimal numbers. Computers store data in memory in multiples of bytes, where a byte contains 8 bits. If you go back to figure 3.1, you will see that four bits make up $2 \times 2 \times 2 \times 2 = 2^4 = 16$ patterns. With a single hexadecimal digit, we can represent all patterns made from four bits. Then by splitting a byte in two components of four bits each, we can represent all possible bytes by splitting them down in half and using just two hexadecimal characters, from 0x0 to 0xFF. Take, for instance, the byte 11100110. If we split it in half, we get 1110 and 0110. We treat each one of them as a binary number. The binary number 1010 has value 14, as it is $2^3 + 2^2 + 2^1$. The binary number 0110 has value 6, as it is $2^2 + 2^1$. The hexadecimal number with value 14 is 0xE and the hexadecimal number with value 6 is 0x6. Therefore, we can write byte 11100110 as 0xE6. That is more elegant than 230, which is the decimal representation of the number; also, there is no easy way to derive 230 apart from doing the full calculations $2^7 + 2^6 + 2^5 + 2^2 + 2^1$, while from the hexadecimal equivalent we have immediately $E \times 16 + 6 = 14 \times 16 + 6$.

If you are still not convinced of the usefulness of hexadecimal, note that you can write down cool numbers such as 0xCAFEBABE. As it happens, 0xCAFEBABE is used to identify compiled files of programs written in the Java programming language. Spelling English words using hexadecimal characters is called *Hexspeak*, and if you search around you will find some resourceful examples.

Back to ASCII, the first 33 characters and the 128th character are control characters. These were originally intended to control devices, for instance, printers, that use ASCII. Most of them are not used anymore, apart from some exceptions that are still relevant. So the character 32 (0x20, the 33rd character since we start from 0) is the space character; character 127 (0x7F) stands for delete; character 27 (0x1B) is the escape character, and characters 10 (0xA) and 13 (0xD) stand for carriage return and line feed, respectively: these are

Table 3.1

The ASCII encoding.

	0	1	2	3	4	5	6	7	8	9	A	B	C	D	E	F
0	NUL	SOH	STX	ETX	EOT	ENQ	ACK	BEL	BS	HT	LF	VT	FF	CR	SO	SI
1	DLE	DC1	DC2	DC3	DC4	NAK	SYN	ETB	CAN	EM	SUB	ESC	FS	GS	RS	US
2	SP	!	"	#	$	%	&	'	(	)	*	+	,	-	.	/
3	0	1	2	3	4	5	6	7	8	9	:	;	<	=	>	?
4	@	A	B	C	D	E	F	G	H	I	J	K	L	M	N	O
5	P	Q	R	S	T	U	V	W	X	Y	Z	[	\	]	^	_
6	`	a	b	c	d	e	f	g	h	i	j	k	l	m	n	o
7	p	q	r	s	t	u	v	w	x	y	z	{			}	~	DEL

Table 3.2

ASCII encoding example.

I		a	m		s	e	a
0x49	0x20	0x61	0x6D	0x20	0x73	0x65	0x61
1001001	100000	1100001	1101101	100000	1110011	1100101	1100001

t	e	d		i	n		a
0x74	0x65	0x64	0x20	0x69	0x6E	0x20	0x61
1110100	1100101	1100100	100000	1101001	1101110	100000	1100001

n		o	f	f	i	c	e
0x6E	0x20	0x6F	0x66	0x66	0x69	0x63	0x65
1101110	100000	1101111	1100110	1100110	1101001	1100011	1100101

used to start a new line (depending on the operating system of the computer, only carriage return or both of them are required). Other characters are more exotic. For instance, character 7 was intended to ring a bell on teletypes.

By using table 3.1 you can find that the sentence "I am seated in an office" corresponds to the ASCII sequences in hexadecimal and binary of table 3.2. Because each character corresponds to a binary number with seven bits and the sentence contains 24 characters, we need $24 \times 7 = 168$ bits.

3.1   Compression

Can we do better than that? If we can somehow find a way to represent text in a more compact way, we could save many storage bits; and taking into account the amount of textual digital information that we store every day, the savings could turn out to be huge. Indeed, a lot of the information we store is compressed in one way or another and decompressed when we want to read it.

To be more precise, *compression* is the process by which we encode some amount of information, representing it using fewer bits than its original representation. There are two kinds of compression, depending on how we reduce the amount of bits required.

If the reduction comes as a result of detecting and eliminating redundant information, then we talk about *lossless compression*. A simple form of lossless compression is *run-length encoding*. For example, consider a black and white image. Each line of the image is a series of black and white pixels, like for example:

□□□□■□□□□□□□□□□■■□□□□□□□□□□□□□□□□□□■■□□□□□□□□□□□□□

Run-length encoding uses *runs of data*, that is, sequences of the same value that are represented as the value and its count. The above line would be represented as the following sequence:

□4■1□9■2□15■2□13

That is much less than before and no information is lost: we can reconstruct the initial line from it exactly as it was.

In *lossy compression* reduction comes from detecting information that we deem is not really necessary so that it can be removed without discernible loss. For example, JPEG images are lossy versions of their originals, as is MPEG-4 video, and MP3 music files: an MP3 audio file can be much less than the original sound file it came from, yet it may be indistinguishable to the human ear (or at least to most human ears).

To see how we can proceed let us go on a trip down memory lane and consider an older encoding for representing information. In table 3.3 we see the Morse code, originally developed by Samuel F. B. Morse, Joseph Henry, and Alfred Vail in 1836 for transmitting messages with the telegraph (actually this is the modern version of the Morse code; the original Morse code had some differences). The Morse code encodes characters and numbers using dots and dashes. If you look at it you will see that it does not use the same number of dots and dashes for all characters. Vail, when trying to figure out how to represent the various letters, had the idea to use smaller encodings for more frequent characters, longer encodings for less frequent ones. In this way, the overall number of dots and dashes would decrease. To find the frequencies of letters in English, Vail went to the office of the local newspaper of his town, Morristown, New Jersey. There he counted the characters in the type-cases used by the compositors. There would be more characters in the type-cases of the more frequent characters because they appeared more times in the text.

Table 3.3

The Morse code.

A	.-	8.04%	J	.---	0.16%	S	...	6.51%	2	..---
B	-...	1.48%	K	-.-	0.54%	T	-	9.28%	3	...--
C	-.-.	3.34%	L	.-..	4.07%	U	..-	2.73%	4	....-
D	-..	3.82%	M	--	2.51%	V	...-	1.05%	5	.....
E	.	12.49%	N	-.	7.23%	W	.--	1.68%	6	-....
F	..-.	2.4%	O	---	7.64%	X	-..-	0.23%	7	--...
G	--.	1.87%	P	.--.	2.14%	Y	-.--	1.66%	8	---..
H	....	5.05%	Q	--.-	0.12%	Z	--..	0.09%	9	----.
I	..	7.57%	R	.-.	6.28%	1	.----		0	-----

Table 3.4

Character frequencies for the word "effervescence".

E: 5	F: 2	R: 1	V: 1	S: 1	C: 2	N: 1

Table 3.3 also includes the frequencies of letters in English as we know them today. You can verify that Vail and the typesetters did a good job.

We can use the same idea today to represent text more frugally: we can use fewer bits for letters that appear more frequently in a test, and more bits for letters that appear less frequently.

Suppose then that we want to encode "effervescence" so that we use shorter bit patterns for more frequent letters. You can see the letter frequencies for this word in table 3.4. We would like the letter E to have the shortest bit pattern, followed by letters F and C, and then the other letters.

Before we go on to find the code, think how much space you should need to encode effervescence in plain ASCII. Because the word is 13 characters long, you will need $13 \times 7 = 91$ bits. But now notice that this word contains only seven different characters, so you do not need the whole ASCII code to represent it. You have only seven different characters, which you can represent all in an encoding using just three bits: $2^3 = 8 > 7$. You could therefore enumerate the different bit patterns with three bits, creating an encoding like table 3.5, a *fixed-length encoding* because all characters require the same, fixed length. In this encoding we need only $13 \times 3 = 39$ bits to represent the word. That is an improvement from 91 bits with ASCII.

The encoding in table 3.5 still uses the same number of bits for all characters. What about our goal to use different number of bits for the characters depending on their frequencies, that is, a *variable-length encoding*? You could

Table 3.5

Fixed-length encoding for the word "effervescence".

E: 000	F: 001	R: 010	V: 011	S: 100	C: 101	N: 110

Table 3.6

Variable-length encoding for the word "effervescence": wrong!

E: 0	F: 1	R: 11	V: 100	S: 101	C: 10	N: 110

Table 3.7

Correct prefix-free variable-length encoding for the word "effervescence".

E: 0	F: 100	R: 1100	V: 1110	S: 1111	C: 101	N: 1101

start with an encoding like in table 3.6, only this is wrong. The encoded word would start with 011110, and there is no way to know whether, when we want to decode it, it starts with an E (0) followed by two Fs (1 and 1) or an R (11). To ensure that we can decode the encoded word unambiguously, we must have a variable-length encoding in which no character starts with the same sequence of bits as another character, in other words, in which no character's code is a prefix of another character's code. We call such encodings *prefix-free encodings*.

Table 3.7 shows a prefix-free variable-length encoding for effervescence. The word is encoded as 01001000110011100111101011011010, in 32 bits, even better than before. It is true that we had to use four bits for some characters for which we used three bits with fixed-length encoding, but this overhead is offset by the fact that we used just one bit for the most common letter and two bits for the next most frequent ones, so it sums up nicely. How did we come up with table 3.7? Surely there must be an algorithm to create prefix-free variable-length encodings?

Indeed there is, but before we describe it, you need to become familiar with a couple of data structures.

3.2   Trees and Priority Queues

A *tree* is an undirected connected graph in which there are no cycles, in other words, an acyclic undirected connected graph. In figure 3.2 you can see two graphs. The graph on the left is not a tree, the graph on the right is.

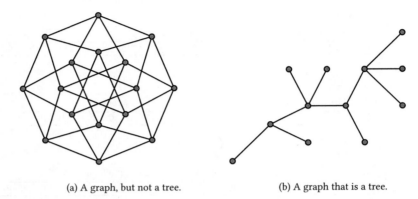

(a) A graph, but not a tree.   (b) A graph that is a tree.

Figure 3.2
Graphs and trees.

Usually we draw trees in such a way that remind us of real-world trees. We designate one of the nodes the *root* of the tree, and we draw the nodes connected to it, which are called its *children*, below or above it. Nodes without children are called *leaves*. For each child of the root we follow the same rule. This gives us an alternative, recursive definition of what is a tree: a tree is a structure with a root node that may have a set of nodes connected to it. Each one of these nodes is the root of another tree. You can see a tree in figure 3.3. On the left-hand side, the tree grows upwards, like a normal tree. On the right-hand side, the same tree grows downward. Most of the trees you will encounter in relation to computers grow downward.

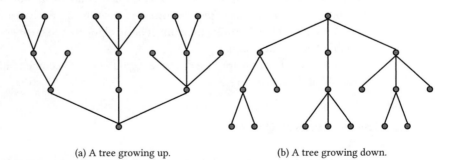

(a) A tree growing up.   (b) A tree growing down.

Figure 3.3
Trees, growing up and down.

The number of children of a node is called the *degree* of the node. Right now we will be dealing with *binary trees*. A binary tree is a tree in which each node has at most two children, that is, its degree will be at most two. A precise definition is that a binary tree is a structure with a root node that may have up to two nodes connected to it. Each one of these nodes is the root of another binary tree.

A tree is useful not just because of its structure, but because each node carries some data with it. The data are the payload of the node, and it bears some relationship to the data carried by the children of the node. The relationship is hierarchical, reflecting the hierarchical structure of the tree.

Trees are a common data structure and arise in many different contexts. There are many operations on them, like inserting nodes, deleting nodes, and looking for a node, but for the time being we only need an operation to create a tree with a root and two children:

- CreateTree(d,x,y) takes d, a piece of data, and two nodes, x and y to create a new node with payload d and x, y as its children, left and right; it then returns the new node. Either or both of x and y may be NULL, so that we can create a tree with zero, one, or two children.

Trees being graphs, they can be traversed breadth-first, visiting all the nodes in one level before going to the next one, or depth-first, going to the leaves and then back upwards. They can be represented as graphs, but usually we use other representations. A common one is a linked representation, where each node contains two links to its two children or to NULL: nodes with one child only or leaves have such links to NULL. The CreateTree operation is then simply a matter of creating a node and initializing its links to x and y.

Figure 3.4 shows how we can represent a binary tree using linked nodes. To create such a tree, we work bottom-up, from children to parents. The left sub-tree of this particular tree would be the result of the following operations:
$n_1 \leftarrow$ CreateTree(7, NULL, NULL)
$n_2 \leftarrow$ CreateTree(1, NULL, NULL)
$n_3 \leftarrow$ CreateTree(5, n_1, n_2)
and continuing in this way, we could construct the whole tree.

The next data structure we will need to create our encoding is a *priority queue*. A priority queue is a data structure in which when we remove items we remove the item with the largest value, or the smallest value, depending on whether we have a maximum priority queue (max-priority) or a minimum priority queue (min-priority). In a maximum priority queue, if you remove an

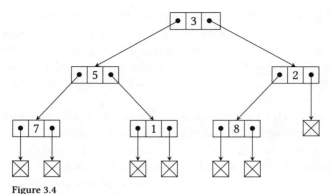

Figure 3.4
A binary tree represented with linked nodes.

item, you remove the item with the largest value, or highest priority. Then if you remove an item again, you will remove the item with the largest value among the remaining items, so it will be the item with the second highest priority, and so on. Conversely, in a minimum priority queue, you remove the item with the lowest priority, then the item with the second lowest priority, and so on. So a priority queue has the following operations:

- `CreatePQ()` creates a new, empty priority queue.
- `InsertInPQ(`*pq*`, `*i*`)` inserts item *i* to the priority queue *pq*.
- `FindMinInPQ(`*pq*`)` or `FindMaxInPQ(`*pq*`)` returns the minimum, for a min-priority queue, or the maximum, for a max-priority queue, of the items in the queue. `FindMinInPQ(`*pq*`)` and `FindMaxInPQ(`*pq*`)` just return the minimum or maximum value, but they do not alter the queue—the value remains there.
- `ExtractMinFromPQ(`*pq*`)` or `ExtractMaxFromPQ(`*pq*`)` removes and returns the minimum, for a min-priority queue, or the maximum, for a max-priority queue, of the items in the queue.
- `SizePQ(`*pq*`)` returns the number of elements in the priority queue *pq*.

3.3   Huffman Coding

If we have a min-priority queue at our disposal, then we can build a prefix-free code as a binary tree. This code is called *Huffman code*, after David A. Huffman, who devised the scheme in 1951 while he was a 25-year-old graduate student. Huffman coding is, as we will see, an efficient lossless compression scheme that exploits the frequencies of the symbols in the information we want to compress.

We start with a priority queue whose elements are binary trees. The leaves of these binary trees will contain a letter and its frequency in the text. Initially each binary tree will contain a single node, which will therefore be both leaf and root. For the word "effervescence" that we met before, we start with a priority queue as in the first row of figure 3.5, where the minimum value is on the left.

We take twice the minimum element of the queue. These are two single node trees with minimum frequencies, for the letters R and N. We then create a new binary tree with a new root whose children are the two trees we took out of the priority queue. The root of the new tree has as frequency the sum of the frequencies of the letters R and N and stands for the combined frequencies of both letters. We put the newly created tree in the queue, as you can see in the second row of figure 3.5. We do the same for the next two nodes, V and S, in the third row. Then we combine the two trees we created in the previous two steps, creating a tree with all four nodes R, N, S, V. We proceed until in the end all nodes are put into a single tree.

The procedure is described in algorithm 3.1. We pass to the algorithm a priority queue. Each element of the priority tree is a single-element tree containing a letter and its frequency. In the algorithm we assume we have a function GetData(*node*) that returns the data stored in the node; here it is the frequency stored in each node. As long as the priority queue contains more than one element (line 1), the algorithm extracts two elements from the priority queue (lines 2 and 3), adds their frequencies (line 4), creates a new binary tree with the sum as root and the two items as children (line 4), and inserts the tree back in the queue (line 6). At the end of the algorithm, the priority queue contains a single binary tree that specifies our code, which we extract from the queue and return (line 7). To find the encoding of a letter, we traverse the tree from the root to the leaf corresponding to the letter. Each time we go left we put 0 in the encoding, and each time we go right we put 1 in the encoding. The resulting series is the Huffman encoding for the letter. So in our example,

E is 0, F is 100, C is 101, and so on for the other letters until we fill out table 3.7; you can see the paths in figure 3.6.

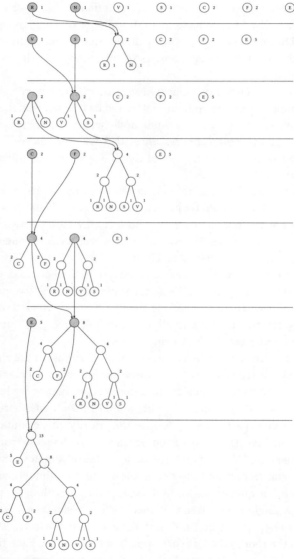

Figure 3.5
Construction of Huffman code for effervescence.

Algorithm 3.1: Huffman code creation.

CreateHuffmanCode(pq) $\rightarrow$ hc
    Input: pq, a priority queue
    Output: hc, a binary tree representing a Huffman code

1 **while** Size(pq) > 1 **do**
2      $x \leftarrow$ ExtractMinFromPQ(pq)
3      $y \leftarrow$ ExtractMinFromPQ(pq)
4      $sum \leftarrow$ GetData(x) + GetData(y)
5      $z \leftarrow$ CreateTree(sum, x, y)
6   InsertInPQ(pq, z)
7 **return** ExtractMinFromPQ(pq)

Note that to encode a string using Huffman encoding we need to pass twice over it, so it is a *two-pass* method. First we need to go over it, measure the letter frequencies, and construct its Huffman code. Then we need to go over it again and encode each letter with its Huffman code. The resulting encodings are the compressed text.

To decompress something that has been compressed with a Huffman code, we need the Huffman code tree that has been used during compression. This should be stored as part of the compressed file. We first extract the Huffman code tree from the file (it should be stored in some agreed, known format), and then we start reading the rest of the file as a series of bits. We descend the Huffman code tree, following the paths indicated by the bits we read from the file. Each time we arrive at a leaf node, we output a letter and move back to the root of the Huffman code tree before we read another bit from the file.

For example, if we are given to decompress the binary sequence of bits 01001000110011100111110101101010 and the tree in figure 3.6, we start at the root of the tree. We read bit 0, which takes us to the letter E, the first letter of our output. We go back to the root of the tree. We read bit 1, which takes us to the right, then bit 0, and again bit 0, which take us to letter F, the second letter of the output. We go back to the root of the tree and so on, until we exhaust all the remaining bits.

Algorithm 3.1 uses a priority queue whose contents are binary trees. You are now entitled to ask how the priority queue does its magic; how can we have ExtractMinFromPQ(pq) and InsertInPQ(pq, i) work?

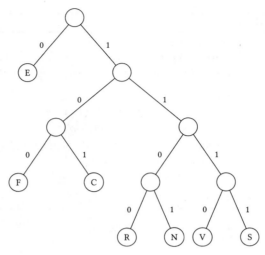

Figure 3.6
The Huffman code for effervescence.

Priority queues can be implemented as trees. To see that, first consider the two trees in figure 3.7. Both are binary trees, and both have the same number of nodes, 11. But the left one goes deeper than the right one. The tree on the right has the minimum number of levels for its number of nodes. A tree with the minimum number of levels is called a *complete tree*. In a binary tree, we call the rightmost node at its lowest level its *last node*.

Priority queues are implemented in terms of *heaps*. Heaps are complete binary trees, in which each node is greater than or equal to or less than or equal to its children. A *maximum heap* (max-heap) is a binary tree in which the value of each node is greater than or equal to the values of its children. That means that the root of the heap has the greatest value of all nodes in the tree. Conversely, a binary tree in which the value of each node is less than or equal to the values of its children is a *minimum heap* (min-heap). In a min-heap, the root has the smallest value in the tree. So a minimum priority queue is implemented in terms of a minimum heap.

It helps to view a minimum heap as a set of weights, its nodes, floating in a liquid. Nodes with greater weights go below lighter nodes. To add a node to a minimum heap, we add it to its lowest level, making it the last node. Then if it is larger than its parent, it floats up and exchanges places with its parent. This is repeated, if necessary, until the node floats up to its proper place. The

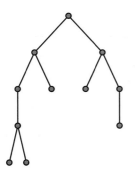
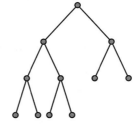

(a) A binary tree.   (b) A complete binary tree.

Figure 3.7
A binary tree and a complete binary tree.

proper place may be the root, or somewhere below it if we find a node that
is lighter, which then becomes its parent. This is described in algorithm 3.2
and illustrated in figure 3.8. In this algorithm we assume we have function
AddLast(pq, c) that adds a node c as last node to the priority queue pq, function Root(pq) that returns the root of a priority queue, Parent(c) that returns
the parent of a node c in the priority queue, GetData(x) that returns the data
stored in node x, and Exchange(pq, x, y) that swaps the *values* of nodes x and
y in the tree. Note the emphasis: we want to swap the values of the nodes, not
the nodes themselves. Swapping the nodes themselves would entail taking all
the subtree rooted in a node with the node we are moving to its new position.
In line 1 of the algorithm, we add the item to the end of the queue; then the
loop in lines 2–5 raises it to the appropriate place. The item goes up as long
as it has not reached the root of the three and its value is less than that of
its parent (line 2); if these conditions hold, we exchange it with the parent
(lines 3–5). To do that we use p to point to the parent of node c in line 3, we
call Exchange(pq, c, p) in line 4, and we make c point to p (c's parent) in line 5.
With the last operation we ascend one level up the tree.

   To extract the minimum from a priority queue, we work in a similar way.
We take out the root of the queue, which by definition is the node with the
minimum value. Then we take the last node and put it at the root. If it is less
than its children, then we are done. If not, then it sinks down one level: we
exchange it with the smallest of its children. We repeat this until we either
find that it is larger than its children, or we arrive at the bottom of the tree.

Algorithm 3.2: Priority queue, minimum heap insert.

InsertInPQ(*pq*, *c*)
    Input: *pq*, a priority queue
             c, an item to insert to the queue
    Result: item *c* is added to *pq*

1   AddLast(*pq*, *c*)
2   **while** $c \neq$ Root(*pq*) **and** GetData(c) < GetData(Parent(c)) **do**
3       $p \leftarrow$ Parent(c)
4   Exchange(*pq*, *c*, *p*)
5       $c \leftarrow p$

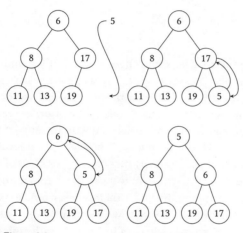

Figure 3.8
Walkthrough of insertion in a priority queue.

Algorithm 3.3 shows how this is done, and figure 3.9 shows the algorithm in action. We introduce a few new functions, namely, ExtractLastFromPQ(*pq*) that extracts the last item of the priority queue *pq*, Children(*i*) that returns the children of a node, HasChildren(*i*) that returns TRUE if the node has children and FALSE otherwise, and Min(*values*) that returns the minimum of the values passed to it.

ExtractMinFromPQ starts by putting the root of the priority queue in a variable *c* (line 1); this is the minimum that we want to extract from the queue. The whole job of the algorithm is to restructure the queue after the minimum has

---

Algorithm 3.3: Priority queue, minimum heap extract minimum.

ExtractMinFromPQ(*pq*) → *c*
    Input: *pq*, a priority queue
    Output: *c*, the minimum element of the queue

1   *c* ← Root(*pq*)
2   Root(*pq*) ← ExtractLastFromPQ(*pq*)
3   *i* ← Root(*pq*)
4   **while** HasChildren(*i*) **do**
5   *j* ← Min(Children(*i*))
6   **if** GetData(*i*) < GetData(*j*) **then**
7   **return** *c*
8   Exchange(*pq*, *i*, *j*)
9   *i* ← *j*
10 **return** *c*

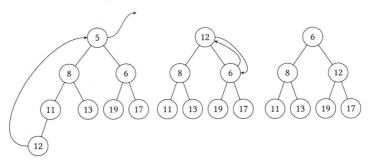

Figure 3.9
Walkthrough of extract minimum from a priority queue.

been removed, so that it remains a minimum heap. We put the last element to the root position in line 2 and store the new, provisional root in variable *i* in line 3. Then the loop of lines 4–9 takes *i* to its appropriate position. While *i* has children (line 4), it gets the child with the minimum value of them, say *j* (line 5). If the value of *j* is not less than the value of *i*, then we are done, the restructuring is complete, and we can return *c* from line 7. If not, then the value of *i* has to change place with the value of *j*, in line 8, and *i* must point to *j*, in line 9. If we exit the loop because we got to the bottom of the tree, then we return *c* (line 10).

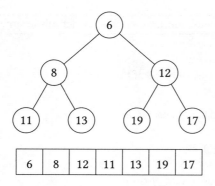

Figure 3.10
Array representation for a priority queue.

One last thing on these algorithms. We have mentioned a number of helper functions in algorithms 3.2 and 3.3. It turns out that these are trivial to write if we implement the priority queue as an array with the root of the heap at position 0. Then for each node, i, its left child is at position $2i + 1$ and its right child is at position $2i + 2$; see figure 3.10. Conversely, if we are at node i, its parent is at position $\lfloor (i - 1)/2 \rfloor$, where $\lfloor x \rfloor$ is the integer part of a number x (or, equivalently, its floor). If the priority queue has n elements, then to check that a node at position i has children we only need to check that $2i + 1 < n$. Finally, to extract the last item of a priority queue with n elements, we only need to take the nth element and decrease the size of the queue by one. Remember that we said that a common way to represent trees is using a linked structure; common does not mean always, and here indeed we see that it is convenient to represent a heap, which is a tree, in terms of an array.

In this way, to create a Huffman encoding, we use two different representations for trees. We use a matrix to represent the tree underlying the priority queue; we use linked trees to represent the tree containing the Huffman code. The top of the rows of figure 3.5 can be implemented as an array whose elements are linked trees.

Is the algorithm for constructing Huffman codes efficient? If you go back to algorithm 3.1, you can see that the loop is executed exactly $n - 1$ times, where n is the number of characters we want to encode. The reasoning is as follows. In each iteration, we do two extractions and one insertion, so the size of the priority queue is reduced by one. The iterations stop when the priority queue has only one element. Initially it has n elements, one for each character we want to encode, so after $n - 1$ iterations the size of the queue will be equal to one and we can return the sole element.

Now we must account for the insertions and extractions. In algorithm 3.2 an insertion can require at most as many iterations as the depth of the heap. Because the heap is a complete binary tree, this is the binary logarithm of its size, $\lg n$, since to go from a node to its parent we have to divide by two, and to reach the root we need to do that for each level up to the top. Similarly, in algorithm 3.3 an extraction can require as many iterations as the depth of the heap. Overall, the construction of a Huffman code may take up to $n - 1$ times two extractions and one insertion, or $O((n - 1)3 \lg n)$, which is equal to $O(n \lg n)$.

3.4   Lempel-Ziv-Welch Compression

The idea behind the Huffman code is to use shorter encodings for common items and longer encodings for items that occur less frequently. What if, instead of varying the length of the encodings for our items, we vary the length of the *items we want to encode*? This is the idea behind the Lembel-Ziv-Welch (LZW) compression scheme, an efficient and notably simple to implement algorithm invented by Abraham Lempel, Jacob Ziv, and Terry Welch.

Suppose we have a text encoded in ASCII. That requires, as we have seen, seven bits per character. At this point we go a bit out of our way and decide to use more bits for our encoding: say, we will encode each item with eight bits, instead of the minimum of seven that is required. That seems crazy, yet there is method in the madness. With eight bits we can represent $2^8 = 256$ different items. We use the numbers from 0x00 (0) to 0x7F (127) to represent the ASCII characters (recall table 3.1); then we have the numbers from 0x80 (128) to 0xFF (255) available to represent whatever else we want. We will use these 128 numbers to represent sequences of two, three, or more characters, instead of just one. Sequences of two letters are called *bigrams*, sequences of three letters are called *trigrams*, larger sequences are called by their value plus the "gram" suffix, like "four-gram," and in general we have *n-grams*. An n-gram with a single item is called a *unigram*. Therefore, the numbers from 0 to 127 will be used to represent unigrams while the numbers from 128 to 255 will be used to represent n-grams of size greater than one, n-grams that are not unigrams.

Which n-grams? We don't know in advance which n-grams appear in our text. For an alphabet of 26 letters, there are $26 \times 26 = 26^2 = 676$ possible

$t = \{\ldots, \_ : 32, \ldots,$

A: 65, B: 66, C: 67, D: 68, E: 69, F: 70, G: 71, H: 72, I: 73

J: 74, K: 75, L: 76, M:77, N: 78, O: 79, P: 80, Q: 81, R: 82

S: 83, T: 84, U: 85, V: 86, W: 87, X: 88, Y: 89, Z: 90, ... $\}$

	M	E	L	L	O	W	_	Y	E	L	L	O	W	_	F	E	L	L	O	W	
M ◁ 77	M	E	L	L	O	W	_	Y	E	L	L	O	W	_	F	E	L	L	O	W	{ ME: 128 } → t
E ◁ 69	M	E	L	L	O	W	_	Y	E	L	L	O	W	_	F	E	L	L	O	W	{ EL: 129 } → t
L ◁ 76	M	E	L	L	O	W	_	Y	E	L	L	O	W	_	F	E	L	L	O	W	{ LL: 130 } → t
L ◁ 76	M	E	L	L	O	W	_	Y	E	L	L	O	W	_	F	E	L	L	O	W	{ LO: 131 } → t
O ◁ 79	M	E	L	L	O	W	_	Y	E	L	L	O	W	_	F	E	L	L	O	W	{ OW: 132 } → t
W ◁ 87	M	E	L	L	O	W	_	Y	E	L	L	O	W	_	F	E	L	L	O	W	{ W_ 133 } → t
_ ◁ 32	M	E	L	L	O	W	_	Y	E	L	L	O	W	_	F	E	L	L	O	W	{ _Y: 134 } → t
Y ◁ 89	M	E	L	L	O	W	_	Y	E	L	L	O	W	_	F	E	L	L	O	W	{ YE : 135 } → t
	M	E	L	L	O	W	_	Y	E	L	L	O	W	_	F	E	L	L	O	W	
EL ◁ 129	M	E	L	L	O	W	_	Y	E	L	L	O	W	_	F	E	L	L	O	W	{ ELL: 136 } → t
	M	E	L	L	O	W	_	Y	E	L	L	O	W	_	F	E	L	L	O	W	
LO ◁ 131	M	E	L	L	O	W	_	Y	E	L	L	O	W	_	F	E	L	L	O	W	{ LOW: 137 } → t
	M	E	L	L	O	W	_	Y	E	L	L	O	W	_	F	E	L	L	O	W	
W_ ◁ 133	M	E	L	L	O	W	_	Y	E	L	L	O	W	_	F	E	L	L	O	W	{ W_F: 138 } → t
F ◁ 70	M	E	L	L	O	W	_	Y	E	L	L	O	W	_	F	E	L	L	O	W	{ FE: 139 } → t
	M	E	L	L	O	W	_	Y	E	L	L	O	W	_	F	E	L	L	O	W	
	M	E	L	L	O	W	_	Y	E	L	L	O	W	_	F	E	L	L	O	W	
ELL ◁ 136	M	E	L	L	O	W	_	Y	E	L	L	O	W	_	F	E	L	L	O	W	{ ELLO: 140 } → t
	M	E	L	L	O	W	_	Y	E	L	L	O	W	_	F	E	L	L	O	W	
OW ◁ 132	M	E	L	L	O	W	_	Y	E	L	L	O	W	_	F	E	L	L	O	W	

Figure 3.11
LZW compression.

bigrams, $26^3 = 17{,}576$ trigrams, and 26^n n-grams, for any n. We will be able to select only a small subset of them. In particular, we will find the n-grams as we go through the text we want to compress. That means that we will build our encoding step by step as we proceed: we will be creating the compressing codes and doing the compressing in one go, which is neat.

Let's see how we can do this with an example. Assume we want to compress the phrase "MELLOW YELLOW FELLOW". As we said, we start by deciding that for every unigram, every single letter that we will encounter, we will use an 8-bit number. The lower seven bits will correspond to the ASCII encoding of that character; the leftmost bit will be left to zero. We are going to use a table that will contain the mappings from items to numerical values.

In figure 3.11 you can see on the top the table t that contains the mappings. For brevity we show the mappings for the uppercase ASCII characters and space (␣). Below that, in each line of the figure we show how we read the phrase character by character; the current character has a border around it.

In the first line of the figure, we read the character, unigram, "M". We check to see whether "M" is in the table. It is. Instead of outputting its numerical value, we prefer to wait and see whether it starts a longer n-gram stored in the table. Right now there are no longer n-grams in the table, but this is the overall logic, so we will apply for consistency.

In the second line of the figure, we read the character "E". We now have the bigram "ME"; throughout the figure, we indicate with grayed characters the part of the n-gram that we know it is in the table. We check whether "ME" it is in the table—it is not. We then output the value for the n-gram that exists in the table, "M", 77, and we insert into the table the new bigram "ME", assigning to it the next available numerical value, which is 128. We use the symbol ◁ to stand for output; you can think of it as an idealized loudspeaker. We show the compressed output on the left side of the figure: M ◁ 77 means that we output 77, standing for "M". We show the insertions in the table in the right side of the figure: { ME : 128 } → t means that we insert 128 as the encoding of "ME" in the table t. From now on, if we meet "ME" somewhere later in our text, we will output 128, standing for both characters. As we have just output the encoding of "M", we do not need that n-gram anymore. We keep only the character we read last, "E", as the start of the next n-gram to use. As before, "E" is a unigram that exists in the table, but we want to try to find a longer n-gram starting with "E".

In the third line of figure we read the character "L". This extends "E" to produce the bigram "EL". It is not in the table, so we output the value of "E" 69, insert "EL" in the table with value 129, and keep the character "L" as the start of the next n-gram.

We continue in exactly the same way even when we encounter a space at the end of "MELLOW". The bigram "W␣" does not exist in the table, so we output the encoding for "W" and insert the mapping for "W␣" in the table. We discard "W" and read "Y" from "YELLOW", forming the bigram "␣Y", which does not exist in the table, so we output the encoding for the space, we discard the space, and we form a new bigram "YE" by reading "E".

Now notice what is happening when we read the first "L" in "YELLOW". The current n-gram is "EL". When we check whether it exists in the table, we find that it does, as we have inserted it into the table before. So we can try to extend the n-gram by one more character and we read the second "L". We get the trigram "ELL" that does not exist in the table, so we insert it with the value 136. Then we output the value of the bigram "EL" (129), discard it, and start a new n-gram with "L", the last character we read.

The overall logic is: read a character. Use it to extend the current n-gram. If the resulting n-gram is in the table, repeat by reading the next character. Otherwise insert the new n-gram into the table, output the code for the previous n-gram, start a new n-gram with the character just read, and repeat by reading the next character. In short, we try to encode the longest n-grams possible. Each time we encounter an n-gram we have not seen before, we assign it a code so that we will be able to use it the next time we see it. After a while, we will have encoded a set of n-grams that we hope will appear many times later in the text and so we will save on the space needed for representing our message. The idea works in practice: the n-grams we find do repeat in the text and we do save space.

In our example, the phrase is 20 characters long and so it requires $20 \times 7 = 140$ bits to represent in ASCII. Using LZW with 8 bits per code, the phrase is encoded as [77, 69, 76, 76, 79, 87, 32, 89, 129, 131, 133, 70, 136, 132], which contains 14 numbers each 8 bits long, totaling $14 \times 8 = 112$ bits. We compressed the phrase to 80% of its original size.

You may counter that this 80% is not that impressive, considering that the phrase "YELLOW MELLOW FELLOW" is an artificial phrase that contains more repeated n-grams than you would expect in three words. That is true, but the phrase was selected so that it could exemplify the workings of the algorithm even in such a short text. We used seven bits for the initial alphabet and eight bits for each encoding. In a real application, these numbers can be larger, so that we can accommodate bigger alphabets and more n-grams: say 8-bit alphabets and 12 bits for encoding. Then the codes from 0 up to and including 255 represent the individual characters, and the values from 256 to 4095 are used to represent n-grams. In longer texts there are more opportunities for repeating n-grams, and they will get longer and longer. If we run LZW with these parameters on James Joyces's *Ulysses*, we reduce the text to about 41% of its original size. In figure 3.12 you can see the distribution of n-grams that were derived during that compression. Most n-grams are three or four characters long, but there is even an n-gram of size ten ("Stephen's⌴") and two of size nine ("Stephen⌴b" and "Stephen's"). Stephen Dedalus is one of the main characters in the book.

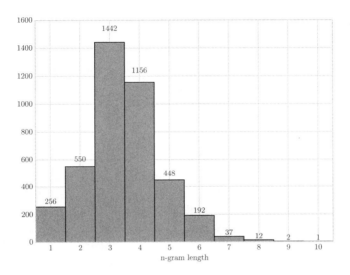

Figure 3.12
The distribution of LZW n-grams in James Joyce's *Ulysses*.

Algorithm 3.4 shows the LZW algorithm. The algorithm assumes that we have a table that works as described, allowing us to look up numerical values corresponding to strings and insert new mappings from strings to values. Such a table is implemented by a data structure called a *map, dictionary,* or *associative array*. It is called a map because it maps items, called *keys,* to corresponding values. This is similar to when we look up something in a dictionary, where the key is a word, and its value is its definition, although dictionaries in computers need not have just word for keys, nor definitions as values. It is an associative array in that it works as an array, but instead of associating a numerical index with a value, it can associate anything, such as a string, with a value. Because the need to store values associated with items arises often, maps are common in programs. We will have much more to say about maps and how they work in chapter 13. In particular, it is important that with maps we can perform our lookup and insertion operations in constant time, $O(1)$, so that they work as fast as normal arrays. For the time being, though, it suffices to know their basic operations. A map provides the following functions that we use in LZWCompress:

- CreateMap() creates a new empty map.
- InsertInMap(t, k, v) inserts item k into the map t with value v. The notation $\{\,ME: 128\,\} \rightarrow t$ in figure 3.11 means that we call InsertInMap(t, "ME", 128).
- Lookup(t, k) performs a lookup for item k in the map t; it returns the value associated with v, if it exists, or NULL if the map t does not contain k. The notation OW $\lhd$ 132 in figure 3.11 means that the call Lookup(t, "OW") returns the value 132.

LZWCompress works on strings, so we need some functionality on strings as well. The function CreateString creates a new, empty string. If we have two strings a and b, we can concatenate them with the addition symbol: $a + b$. If we have a string, then we can go through all the characters in the string with a **foreach** statement. Finally, the length of a string a is given by $|a|$.

The algorithm takes as input the string s to be compressed, the number of bits, nb, that we will use to encode each item, and the number of items, n, in the alphabet of the string that we want to compress. We start in lines 1–6 by setting the ground for the main part of the algorithm. We create an empty list, *compressed*, that will contain the compression results (line 1). The possible encoding values are from 0 to $2^{nb} - 1$, which we store in *max_code* in line 2. In our example, the encoding values range from 0 up to and including 255, as we have 8 bits for each one of them, so *max_code* will be set to 255. Then, in line 3, we create an empty map t. In the loop of lines 4–6, we insert into t associations of the form $k: v$, where k is a single letter string and i is the corresponding numerical code. To this purpose we use the function Char(i), which returns the ASCII character that has ASCII value i; Char("A") returns the value 65. In line 6 we store in the variable *code* the encoding for the next item that will be inserted in the table; when we start it will be equal to the size of the alphabet. In our example, *code* will be set to 128. At the end of line 6, we have filled the table, as in the top of figure 3.11, and we are ready to insert new mappings into it.

We will use w to hold the n-gram we have read and have determined that it is contained in our table. This n-gram is indicated by the grayed characters in figure 3.11. Initially we have no n-gram at all, so we set it to an empty string in line 7. We will also use a pointer p to point to the last item of the list *compressed*; initially it is an empty list, so this is NULL (line 8). Then the real works starts, in the loop of lines 9–20. For each character c in the string s that we want to compress (line 9), we form a new n-gram, wc, by appending it to

---

Algorithm 3.4: LZW compression.

LZWCompress(s, nb, n) $\rightarrow$ *compressed*
     Input: s, a string to compress
               nb, the number of bits used to represent an item
               n, the number of items in the alphabet
     Output: *compressed*, a list containing the numbers representing s
                   according to LZW compression

1   *compressed* $\leftarrow$ CreateList()
2   *max_code* $\leftarrow 2^{nb} - 1$
3    $t \leftarrow$ CreateMap()
4   **for** $i \leftarrow 0$ **to** n **do**
5   InsertInMap(t, Char(i), i)
6    $code \leftarrow n$

7    $w \leftarrow$ CreateString()
8    $p \leftarrow$ NULL
9   **foreach** c **in** s **do**
10        $wc \leftarrow w + c$
11        $v \leftarrow$ Lookup(t, wc)
12   **if** $v \neq$ NULL **then**
13            $w \leftarrow wc$
14   **else**
15            $v \leftarrow$ Lookup(t, w)
16            $p \leftarrow$ InsertInList(*compressed*, p, v)
17            $w \leftarrow c$
18   **if** $code \leq max\_code$ **then**
19   InsertInMap(t, wc, $code$)
20                $code \leftarrow code + 1$

21   **if** $|w| > 0$ **then**
22   InsertInList(*compressed*, p, v)
23   **return** *compressed*

---

our current n-gram (line 10). We try to find it in the map (line 11). If the new n-gram is in the map (line 12), we will try to find a larger one, so we set *w* to *wc* (line 13) and we repeat the loop.

If the new n-gram is not in the map (line 14), then we look up the current n-gram *w* (line 15), which we know exists in the map. How do we know that? The only way that *w* gets longer is by assigning it to *wc* in line 13 during a previous iteration of the loop *after* we have established that *wc* is included in the table *t*.

We insert the encoding value for *w* at the end of the *compressed* list (line 16). Note that InsertInList returns a pointer to the newly inserted item, so *p* will point to the new end of the list, allowing us in the next call to append the next encoding value at the end of the list, after the newly inserted item.

Having done that, we have dealt with *w* so we discard its contents and reset it to the last character we have read (line 17) in preparation for the next iteration of the loop. But before that, we will store the extended n-gram *wc* in the table, if possible. That will happen if we have not exhausted all the possible encodings (line 18). If so, we insert it into *t* (line 19), and we increase the value that we will use for the next encoded n-gram (line 20).

Lines 21–22 take care of the situation when we are in the midst of looking for a greater n-gram and then realize we have reached the end of the text to be compressed. This is what happens in the last line of figure 3.11. When this occurs we just output the encoding of the current n-gram and we are done.

To decompress a message compressed with LZW, we follow the reverse process. We are given a sequence of encodings, and we want to derive the text behind the encodings. We do not know, at the beginning, which n-grams have been encoded by which encodings *except for* the encodings for unigrams, which is just the reverse of the original table that we used at the start of the compression process.

If we go back to figure 3.11, then we see that every time we output something, we create an n-gram with the output and the next character we read. To reconstitute the encoding table in reverse form, we therefore have to record the output, read the next encoding, find the corresponding encoded value, and insert into the table the n-gram constituted by our previous output and the first character of the decoded value we have just found.

In figure 3.13 you can see the decompression process. At the top we have the initial state of the decoding table, *dt*. In each line we read an encoding, and then we look it up in the decoding table. We must take care so that, as we proceed, we fill the decoding table with the encodings of the n-grams

$dt = \{\ldots, 32: \_, \ldots,$

65: A, 66: B, 67: C, 68: D, 69: E, 70: F, 71: G, 72: H, 73: I

74: J, 75: K, 76: L, 77: M, 78: N, 79: O, 80: P, 81: Q, 82: R

83: S, 84: T, 85: U, 86: V, 87: W, 88: X, 89: Y, 90: Z, $\ldots \}$

77 ◁ M	77	69	76	76	79	87	32	89	129	131	133	70	136	132	
69 ◁ E	77	69	76	76	79	87	32	89	129	131	133	70	136	132	{ 128: ME } → dt
76 ◁ L	77	69	76	76	79	87	32	89	129	131	133	70	136	132	{ 129: EL } → dt
76 ◁ L	77	69	76	76	79	87	32	89	129	131	133	70	136	132	{ 130: LL } → dt
79 ◁ O	77	69	76	76	79	87	32	89	129	131	133	70	136	132	{ 131: LO } → dt
87 ◁ W	77	69	76	76	79	87	32	89	129	131	133	70	136	132	{ 132: OW } → dt
32 ◁ _	77	69	76	76	79	87	32	89	129	131	133	70	136	132	{ 133: W_ } → dt
89 ◁ Y	77	69	76	76	79	87	32	89	129	131	133	70	136	132	{ 134: _Y } → dt
129 ◁ EL	77	69	76	76	79	87	32	89	129	131	133	70	136	132	{ 135: YE } → dt
131 ◁ LO	77	69	76	76	79	87	32	89	129	131	133	70	136	132	{ 136: ELL } → dt
133 ◁ W_	77	69	76	76	79	87	32	89	129	131	133	70	136	132	{ 137: LOW } → dt
70 ◁ F	77	69	76	76	79	87	32	89	129	131	133	70	136	132	{ 138: W_F } → dt
136 ◁ ELL	77	69	76	76	79	87	32	89	129	131	133	70	136	132	{ 139: LOW } → dt
132 ◁ OW	77	69	76	76	79	87	32	89	129	131	133	70	136	132	{ 140: ELLO } → dt

Figure 3.13
LZW decompression.

that we encounter. In the first line there is nothing to do, as we only have a unigram. From the second line onward, however, we must enter into the decompression table the n-gram that is made up from our previous output and the first character of the current output. In this way the decoding table keeps up with our input, and when we read, for instance, 129, we can look it up successfully as we have already entered it into the decompression table before.

But does the decoding table always keep up with the current encoding we read, so that we can find it there? In our example, every n-gram that we look up has been entered into the decoding table several steps (rows) back. That happens because in the mirror situation, the encoding for the corresponding n-gram was also created several steps behind. What happens when, during compression, we create an encoding for an n-gram and output it immediately in exactly the next step?

This is an example of a *corner case*. A corner case is an extreme situation handled by an algorithm or a computer program. It is always a good idea to test our algorithms on corner cases because they may not be typical. It follows that we must be extra vigilant on corner cases when we are checking our work for bugs. For example, our program may work for a set of values, but not for the smallest or the largest. That's a bug lurking in a corner case.

As we said, in LZW decompression the corner case is when, during compression, we create an n-gram and output its encoding immediately. Such a situation occurs in figure 3.14a. We are compressing the string "ABABABA". We encode "AB", then "BA", and then "ABA", whose encoding is the very next thing we output. The compressed result is the list [65, 66, 128, 130].

If we are given the list [65, 66, 128, 130] to decompress, then we start with the number 65, which according to the table *dt* is equal to "A"; see figure 3.14b. Then we take the number 66, which is encoded to "B". We add to the decoding table the bigram "AB", keyed by the value 128. Next we take 128 from the list, which decompressed is "AB". So far, so good, even though we just managed to enter "AB" in the decoding table. We get the value 130 last; and here things are not so good because 130 has not been entered into the decoding table yet.

To see how we can handle this, we need to step back a bit and remember that this can happen only when during the encoding process we encoded something and we immediately output that encoding. Suppose we have read the string $x[0], x[1], \ldots, x[k]$, which we have found in the encoding table. Then we read $x[k+1]$ and cannot find $x[0], x[1], \ldots, x[k], x[k+1]$ in the encoding table. We compress $x[0], x[1], \ldots, x[k]$ by using its encoding and then create a new encoding for $x[0], x[1], \ldots, x[k], x[k+1]$. If the next thing we compress is exactly $x[0], x[1], \ldots, x[k], x[k+1]$, then this can only happen if the input string is of the form:

$$\ldots \quad x[0] \quad x[1] \quad \ldots \quad x[k] \quad x[k+1]$$
$$x[0] \quad \quad x[1] \quad \ldots \quad x[k] \quad x[k+1] \quad \ldots$$

That is, $x[0] = x[k+1]$ and the newly created n-gram is equal to the previous n-gram with its first character appended to the end. This is indeed what happens in figure 3.14.

Going back to decompression, when we encounter an encoded value that we have not entered into the decoding table yet, we can enter into the decoding table a new entry whose key will be the last n-gram we entered with its first character appended to it. Then we can output that newly created n-gram.

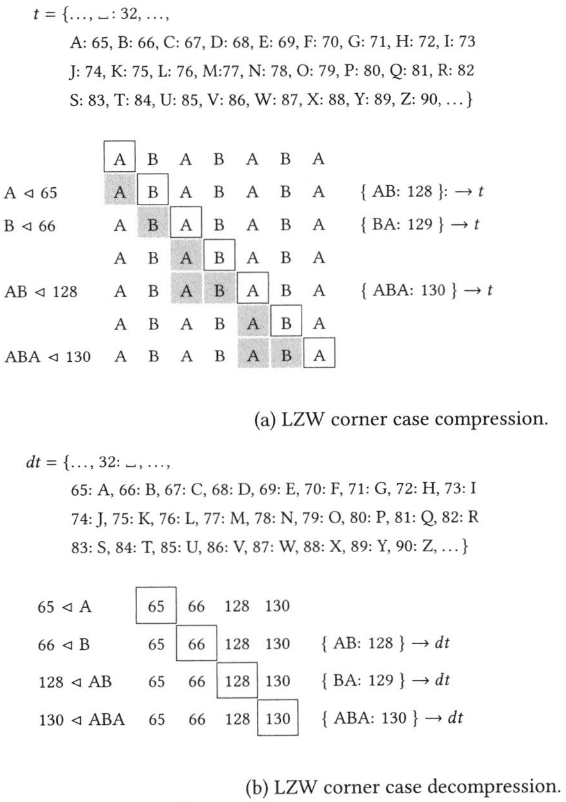
t = {..., ␣: 32, ...,
A: 65, B: 66, C: 67, D: 68, E: 69, F: 70, G: 71, H: 72, I: 73
J: 74, K: 75, L: 76, M:77, N: 78, O: 79, P: 80, Q: 81, R: 82
S: 83, T: 84, U: 85, V: 86, W: 87, X: 88, Y: 89, Z: 90, ...}
A B A B A B A
A ◁ 65 A B A B A B A { AB: 128 }: → t
B ◁ 66 A B A B A B A { BA: 129 } → t
A B A B A B A
AB ◁ 128 A B A B A B A { ABA: 130 } → t
A B A B A B A
ABA ◁ 130 A B A B A B A
(a) LZW corner case compression.
dt = {..., 32: ␣, ...,
65: A, 66: B, 67: C, 68: D, 69: E, 70: F, 71: G, 72: H, 73: I
74: J, 75: K, 76: L, 77: M, 78: N, 79: O, 80: P, 81: Q, 82: R
83: S, 84: T, 85: U, 86: V, 87: W, 88: X, 89: Y, 90: Z, ...}
65 ◁ A 65 66 128 130
66 ◁ B 65 66 128 130 { AB: 128 } → dt
128 ◁ AB 65 66 128 130 { BA: 129 } → dt
130 ◁ ABA 65 66 128 130 { ABA: 130 } → dt
(b) LZW corner case decompression.

Figure 3.14
LZW corner case compression and decompression.

In our example, when we read 130, we note that it does not exist in the decoding table. We have just entered "AB" in the decoding table. We append "A" to "AB" creating "ABA", which we enter into the decoding table and also output immediately.

To do this we use algorithm 3.5, the counterpart of algorithm 3.4. The algorithm takes as input a list containing encoded values for the compressed string, the number of bits that we use represent an item and the total number of items in the alphabet. We calculate the maximum encoding value, in line 1. In lines 2–4 we create the initial version of the decoding table. It is similar to

---

Algorithm 3.5: LZW decompression.

LZWDecompress(*compressed, nb, n*) $\rightarrow$ *decompressed*

    Input: *compressed*, a list representing a compressed string

              nb, the number of bits used to represent an item

              n, the number of items in the alphabet

    Output: *decompressed*, the original string

1    $max\_code \leftarrow 2^{nb} - 1$

2    $dt \leftarrow$ CreateMap()

3   **for** $i \leftarrow 0$ **to** n **do**

4   InsertInMap($dt, i,$ Char(i))

5    $code \leftarrow n$

6    $decompressed \leftarrow$ CreateString()

7    $c \leftarrow$ GetNextListNode(*compressed*, NULL)

8   RemoveListNode(*compressed*, NULL, c)

9    $v \leftarrow$ Lookup(dt, GetData(c))

10   $decompressed \leftarrow decompressed + v$

11   $pv \leftarrow v$

12   **foreach** c **in** *compressed* **do**

13       $v \leftarrow$ Lookup(dt, c)

14   **if** $v =$ NULL **then**

15          $v \leftarrow pv + pv[0]$

16       $decompressed \leftarrow decompressed + v$

17   **if** $code \leq max\_code$ **then**

18   InsertInMap($dt, code, pv + v[0]$)

19          $code \leftarrow code + 1$

20       $pv \leftarrow v$

21   **return** *decompressed*

---

the encoding table, only it maps the other way round, from integer encodings to strings. In line 5 we note that we have used up to n encodings to this point.

In line 6 we create an empty string that will grow to contain the results of the decompression. To kick-start the decompression process per se, we get the first encoding (line 7), we remove it from the list (line 8), and we look it up in the decoding table (line 9). We are sure to find it because the first encoding is always for a single alphabet character. We add the decoded value to the decompression results (line 10). In the rest of the algorithm, we will use a variable pv that will hold the last decompressed value; we initialize it in line 11.

The loop in lines 12–20 decompresses the remaining list, that is, all the list but the first item that we have already taken care of. For each list item we look it up in the decoding table (line 13). If we find it there, then we again add the decoded value to the decompression results (line 16). If we do not find it (line 14), then we have run against the corner case we explained above, so the decoded value is really the previously decoded value with its first character appended to its end (line 15); then we add that value to the decompression results in line 16.

In lines 17–19, if there is room in the decoding table (line 17), we add the new mapping into the table (line 18) and note that we have one more entry in the table (line 19). Before the next loop iteration, we store in pv the new decompressed value (line 20). Finally we return the string we have built (line 21).

The LZW algorithm can be implemented efficiently, as it needs only a single pass through its input: it is a *single-pass* method. It encodes as it reads the input and it decodes as it goes through the compressed values. The operations that both compression and decompression perform are simple; in essence the speed of the algorithm depends on the speed with which we can manipulate the encoding and decoding tables. A map can be implemented so that insertion and lookup can be performed in constant, $O(1)$ time; therefore, compression as well as decompression need linear time, $O(n)$, where n is the length of the input.

Notes

For the history and development of ASCII and related codes up to 1980, see the account written by Mackenzie [132]. Data compression is woven in our every-day lives, and there are plenty of sources should you wish to delve deeper into it; see the book by Salomon [170], Salomon and Motta [171], and Sayood [172]. An earlier survey was written by Lelewer and Hirschberg [128].

The story of the development of the Morse code is told in Russel W. Burn's history [32, p. 68]. The English letter frequencies in table 3.3 are those counted by Peter Norvig and are available at `http://norvig.com/mayzner.html`. Tabulating letter frequencies is an interesting task in itself; we will have more to say in chapter 4.

In 1951, David A. Huffman was an electrical engineering graduate student at MIT attending a course in information theory. The students were left to choose a term paper or a final exam; the term paper required them to find the most efficient representation method for numbers, text, and other symbols, using binary code. Huffman encoding is the solution he invented. The story is told nicely in a *Scientific American* profile [192]. Huffman coding is widely used thanks to its simplicity and to the fact that he never tried to patent his invention. Huffman's original article was published in 1952 [99].

Abraham Lempel and Jacob Ziv published the LZ77 algorithm, also known as LZ1, in 1977 [228], and the LZ78 compression algorithm, also known as LZ2, in 1978 [229]. LZ78 was improved by Terry Welch in 1984 [215], giving us LZW. In the original LZW paper, data comes in 8-bit characters (instead of the 7-bit ASCII we described) and is encoded in 12-bit codes. The LZW algorithm was patented, but the patents have since expired. Before that, the Unisys corporation, which held the patent for LZW, tried to enforce licensing fees for GIF images, which use LZW compression, thereby receiving general opprobrium.

Exercises

1. In the film "The Martian," astronaut Mark Watney (played by Matt Damon) is left stranded on Mars. The only way to communicate with mission control back on Earth is by using a rotating camera. Watney devises the following plan. Because every ASCII character can be encoded with two hexadecimal symbols, he places boards with hexadecimal symbols in the circumference of a circle. In this way, for every word he wants to send to Earth, he breaks it into ASCII

characters and then for each character he sends two pictures with the camera, one for each hexadecimal symbol. Watney is a botanist by profession, so he could use some help. Write a program that takes as input an ASCII message and outputs the series of rotation angles of the camera.

2. Implement a minimum and a maximum priority queue using an array with the convention described in the text: the element at position 0 will be the minimum, or maximum, and for each node i its left child will be at position $2i + 1$ and its right child at position $2i + 2$. Try to design your code so that you reuse as much as possible so that both the minimum and maximum priority queue implementations share as much code as possible.

3. An alternative convention for implementing priority queues using an array is to leave empty the element at position 0 so that for each node its left child will be at position $2i$ and its right child at position $2i + 1$. Do the previous exercise using this convention.

4. We have described how Huffman codes are built, but we have not gone into the details of how they can be programmed in a computer. Before we can call algorithm 3.1, we need to go through the text to be encoded and do the frequency counts for the characters in the text. After algorithm 3.1 has completed, we can create a table like the one in table 3.7, which we use to encode each character in the text with its Huffman encoding. The compressed output, usually a file, must contain two things: the table we have created and the actual encoded text. We need the table, otherwise we will not know how to decode the text in the future. The encoded text consists of a series of bits *not characters*. Taking table 3.7 again, you should not output the string "1110" for V, but the four digits 1, 1, 1, 0. This may not be straightforward, as many programming languages output bytes by default, so you need to pack the bits into the bytes that will be output. With all these, you can write your own Huffman encoder and decoder.

5. Using a Huffman encoder, encode a substantial amount of English text and check how close the length of the encodings for each letter are to the encodings used by the Morse code.

6. Write a program that will generate random sequences of characters so that each character appears with equal probability in the output. The program would take as input the size of the output. Run a Huffman encoder through the program's output and verify that with such an input, the Huffman encoder will not perform better than a fixed-length encoding.

7. We have described LZW decompression using a decoding table. However, this table maps from numerical values to strings, so we could use an array of strings instead. Rewrite and implement algorithm 3.5 using an array for the decoding table *dt*.

4 Secrets

How do you keep a secret? Say you want to write something that only its intended recipient will be able to read, and nobody else. More plausibly in everyday life, you want to buy something from an online vendor. You need to give the vendor the details of your credit card. You want the credit card details to remain a secret between you and your vendor and to be sure that nobody that might intercept your communication will be able to get your credit card details.

To keep some information secret, we use *cryptography*. In cryptography we use some *encryption* mechanism, with which we take an initial message, called *plaintext*, and we *encrypt* it; that is, we turn it to something that by itself cannot be read, called a *ciphertext*. To read the ciphertext, it is necessary to *decrypt* it; this process is called *decryption*. This should only be done by somebody we approve. Otherwise we say that the encryption is broken. Encryption and decryption work, as you will see, by using some *encryption key* that is instrumental in hiding and unveiling the information we want to protect.

We use encryption to safeguard our privacy. In the words of Philip Zimmermann, a cryptography pioneer:

It's personal. It's private. And it's no one's business but yours. You may be planning a political campaign, discussing your taxes, or having a secret romance. Or you may be communicating with a political dissident in a repressive country. Whatever it is, you don't want your private electronic mail (email) or confidential documents read by anyone else. There's nothing wrong with asserting your privacy. Privacy is as apple-pie as the Constitution.

Every time you enter a password, you use cryptography. Every time you perform a financial transaction on the Internet, you use cryptography. If you want to have a secure voice or video call, where secure means that nobody but the participants in the call can attend it, then you have to use cryptography.

Zimmermann, again, has put it pithily: you should be able to "whisper in somebody's ear a thousand miles away."

A good place to start a journey in cryptography is with an obvious way to encrypt messages, onto which pretty much every child has stumbled; it has also been used in some guise since ancient times. The way is to invent some fictitious alphabet, and substitute every letter in our message with a letter from the fictitious alphabet. Alternatively, we can substitute every letter in our message with another letter from our own alphabet. This encryption is a *substitution cipher*. A famous substitution cipher is the so-called *Caesar cipher*, reportedly used by Julius Caesar. In this cipher each letter is substituted by the letter on which we land when we move along the alphabet by a specific number of letters, wrapping around if necessary. The number of letters that we use to find the substitute is the key of the cipher. If the key is 5, then A becomes F, B becomes G, ..., and so on until Z becomes E. You can check that the plaintext "I am seated in an office" is encoded as the plaintext N FR XJFYJI NS FS TKKNHJ. To decrypt the message you only need to shift back by 5 characters. Such ciphers are also called *shift ciphers*.

4.1   A Decryption Challenge

Imagine now you are given the cipher text in figure 4.1. Can you make sense out of it? Initially it may seem a bunch of gibberish. But you may suspect that it represents some English text. Because up to now we have only spoken of substitution ciphers, you may suspect that this is a text encrypted using one such cipher, substituting letters from the English alphabet by letters from another one.

The thing about language and texts is that they obey rules. Words are made of characters, following the rule of the grammar; sentences are made of words, following the rule of syntax. Some words are more frequent than others. Also, some letters are more frequent than others, and some sequences of letters (say, two or three of them in a row) are more frequent than others. If we have a large corpus of text, we can determine the letter frequencies in a language. Mark Mayzner published tables with letter frequencies in 1965. Using the technology of the time, he was able to cull a corpus of 20,000 words. On December 17, 2012, he contacted Peter Norvig, Director of Research at Google, inquiring whether Google could use its resources to update the letter frequency tables. Norvig did so and published the results. From them we find table 4.1, compiled

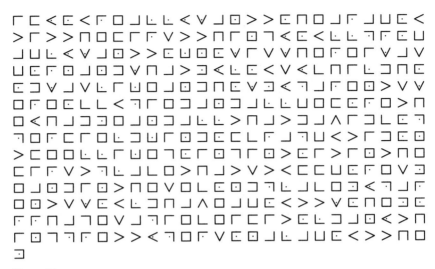

Figure 4.1
An encryption challenge.

after counting 3,563,505,777,820 letters in Google's corpus. The numbers next to each letter are the count in billions and its corresponding percentage.

Now go back to figure 4.1. If you count the various symbols in the encrypted text, you will see that the most common one is $\square$ with 35 occurrences. Then comes $>$ with 33 occurrences and $\lrcorner$ with 32 occurrences. If you go make the substitutions $\square \to$ E, $> \to$ T, and $\lrcorner \to$ A to the encrypted text then you will get the three texts in figure 4.2.

This does not seem to make sense yet, so you go on and make more substitutions. Next in the ciphertext frequencies comes $\sqsubset$ with 28 occurrences, $\ulcorner$ with 24 occurrences, and $\boxdot$ with 22 occurrences. By doing the substitutions $\sqsubset \to$ O, $\ulcorner \to$ I, and $\boxdot \to$ N you have several characters filled it, as you can see in figure 4.3a.

Now note that it is not just individual characters that appear with different frequencies, but two-letter sequences, *bigrams*, that appear with different frequencies, shown in table 4.2, as given by Norvig—the numbers are again billions. The most frequent bigram in English texts is TH; in the ciphertext the most frequent bigram, with 9 occurrences, is T$\sqcap$, so it makes sense to try H for $\sqcap$.

Table 4.1

English letter frequencies.

E	445.2	12.49%	M	89.5	2.51%
T	330.5	9.28%	F	85.6	2.40%
A	286.5	8.04%	P	76.1	2.14%
O	272.3	7.64%	G	66.6	1.87%
I	269.7	7.57%	W	59.7	1.68%
N	257.8	7.23%	Y	59.3	1.66%
S	232.1	6.51%	B	52.9	1.48%
R	223.8	6.28%	V	37.5	1.05%
H	180.1	5.05%	K	19.3	0.54%
L	145.0	4.07%	X	8.4	0.23%
D	136.0	3.82%	J	5.7	0.16%
C	119.2	3.34%	Q	4.3	0.12%
U	97.3	2.73%	Z	3.2	0.09%

Table 4.2

Top ten of bigrams.

TH	100.3	3.56%
HE	86.7	3.07%
IN	68.6	2.43%
ER	57.8	2.05%
AN	56.0	1.99%
RE	52.3	1.85%
ON	49.6	1.76%
AT	41.9	1.49%
EN	41.0	1.45%
ND	38.1	1.35%

Things look better; you can see some words, like THE and THAT appearing in the ciphertext in figure 4.3b. The second most frequent bigram in the ciphertext is ⌐E with 8 occurrences. In English texts, RE is a frequent bigram, so you can try R for ⌐.

We have arrived at figure 4.4a where you can see in the first line the sequence REA∟∟<. Could this be REALLY? By performing the substitution we are at figure 4.4b, and it seems it was a good choice because now we can guess more letters. In the first two lines there are two YO<, which is probably YOU. In the last line there is the word ANYTHIN⌐, which is probably ANYTHING. Then ⌐RETTY is probably PRETTY. Proceeding with such educated guesses it is not difficult to reach figure 4.4.

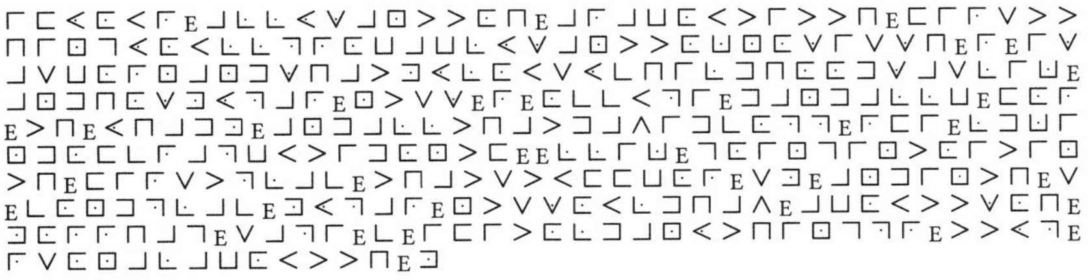

```
⌐⊏<⊏<⌐ᴇ⌐⊔⊔<∨⌐o>>⊏⊓ᴇ⌐⌐⌐⊔⊏<>⌐>>⊓ᴇ⊏⌐⌐∨>>
⊓⌐o⌐<⊏<⊔⊔⌐⌐⊏⊔⌐⊔⊔⊔<∨⌐o>>⊏⊔o⊏∨⌐∨∨∨⊓ᴇ⌐ᴇ⌐∨
⌐∨⊔⊏⌐o⌐o⌐∨⊓⌐⌐>⌐<⊔⊏<∨<⊔⊓⌐⊔⌐⊐⊏⊏⌐∨⌐∨⊔∨⌐⌐⊔ᴇ
⌐o⌐⊓⊏∨⌐<⌐⌐⌐⌐ᴇo>∨∨ᴇ⌐ᴇ⊏⊔⊔<⌐⌐ᴇ⌐⌐o⌐⌐⊔⊔⊔ᴇ⊏ᴇ⌐
ᴇ>⊓ᴇ<⊓⌐⌐⌐ᴇ⌐o⌐⊔⊔⊔>⊓⌐⌐>⌐⌐⌐⌐⌐⌐⊏⌐⌐ᴇ⌐⊏⌐ᴇ⊔⌐⌐
o⌐⊏⊏⊔⌐⌐⌐⊔⌐<>⌐⌐⊏o>⊏ᴇᴇ⊔⊔⌐⌐⊔ᴇ⌐⊏⌐o⌐⌐o>⊏⌐>⌐o
>⊓ᴇ⊏⌐⌐∨>⌐⊔⌐⊔ᴇ>⊓⌐>∨><⊏⊏⊔⊏⌐ᴇ∨⌐ᴇ⌐o⌐⌐o>⊓ᴇ∨
ᴇ⊔⊏o⌐⌐⊔⊔⊔ᴇ⌐<⌐⌐⌐⌐ᴇo>∨∨ᴇ<⊔⌐⊓⌐∧ᴇ⌐⊔⊏<>>∨⊏⊓ᴇ
⌐⊏⌐⌐⊓⌐⌐ᴇ∨⌐⌐⌐ᴇ⊔ᴇ⌐⊏⌐>⊏⊔⌐⊔o<>⊓⌐o⌐⌐⌐ᴇ>><⌐ᴇ
⌐∨⊏o⊔⊔⌐⊔⊏<>>⊓ᴇ⌐
```

(a) Decryption: □ → E.

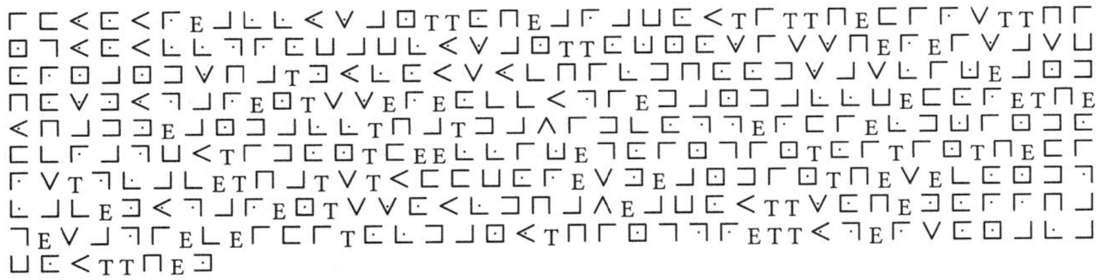

```
⌐⊏<⊏<⌐ᴇ⊔⊔⊔<∨⌐oᴛᴛ⊓ᴇ⌐⌐⌐⊔⊏<ᴛ⌐ᴛᴛ⊓ᴇ⊏⌐⌐∨ᴛᴛ⊓⌐
o⌐<⊏<⊔⊔⌐⌐⊏⊔⌐⊔⊔<∨⌐o⊔ᴛᴛ⊏⊔o⊏∨⌐∨∨⊓ᴇ⌐ᴇ⌐∨
⊏⌐o⌐o⌐∨⊓⌐⊔ᴛ⌐<⊔⊏<∨<⊔⊓⌐⊔⌐⊐⊏⊏⌐∨⌐∨⊔∨⌐⌐⊔ᴇ⌐o⌐
⊓ᴇ∨⌐<⌐⌐⌐ᴇoᴛ∨∨ᴇ⌐ᴇ⊏⊔⊔<⌐⌐ᴇ⌐⌐o⌐⌐⊔⊔⊔ᴇ⊏ᴇ⌐ᴇᴛ⊓ᴇ
<⊓⌐⌐⌐ᴇ⌐o⌐⌐⊔⊔⊔ᴛ⊓⌐⊔ᴛ⌐⌐∧⌐⊏⊔ᴇ⌐⌐ᴇ⌐⊏⌐ᴇ⊔⌐o⌐o
⊏⊔⌐⌐⌐⊔<ᴛ⌐⊏ᴇoᴛ⊏ᴇᴇ⊔⊔⌐⌐⊔ᴇ⌐⊏⌐o⌐⌐oᴛᴇ⌐⌐o⌐⊓ᴇ⊏⌐
⌐∨ᴛ⌐⊔⊔ᴇᴛ⊓⌐⊔ᴛ∨ᴛ<⊏⊏⊔⊏⌐ᴇ∨⌐ᴇ⌐o⌐⌐o⌐oᴛ⊓ᴇ∨ᴇ⊏o⌐ᴛ
⊔⊔⊔ᴇ⌐<⌐⌐⌐ᴇoᴛ∨∨ᴇ<⊔⌐⊓⌐∧ᴇ⌐⊔⊏<ᴛᴛ∨⊏⊓ᴇ⌐⊏⌐⌐⊓⌐
ᴛᴇ∨⌐⌐⌐ᴇ⊔ᴇ⌐⊏⌐⌐ᴛ⊏⊔⌐⌐o<ᴛ⊓⌐oᴛᴛ⌐ᴇᴛᴛ<ᴛᴇ⌐∨⊏o⊔⊔
⊔⊏<ᴛᴛ⊓ᴇ⌐
```

(b) Decryption: > → T.

```
⌐⊏<⊏<⌐ᴇᴀ⊔⊔<∨ᴀoᴛᴛ⊏⊓ᴇᴀ⌐ᴀ⊔⊏<ᴛ⌐ᴛᴛ⊓ᴇ⊏⌐⌐∨ᴛᴛ⊓⌐o
⌐<⊏<⊔⊔⌐⌐⊏⊔ᴀ⊔⊏<∨ᴀoᴛᴛ⊏⊔o⊏∨⌐∨∨⊓ᴇ⌐ᴇ⌐∨ᴀ∨⊔⊏⌐
oᴀo⌐∨⊓ᴀᴛ⌐<⊔⊏<∨<⊔⊓⌐⊔⌐⊐⊏⊏⌐∨ᴀ∨⊔⌐⌐⊔ᴇᴀo⌐⊓⊏∨
⌐<ᴛᴀ⌐ᴇoᴛ∨∨ᴇ⌐ᴇ⊏⊔⊔<ᴛ⌐ᴇ⌐ᴀo⌐ᴀ⊔⊔⊔ᴇ⊏ᴇ⌐ᴇᴛ⊓ᴇ<⊓ᴀ⌐
⊐ᴇᴀo⌐ᴀ⊔⊔ᴛ⊓ᴀᴛ⌐ᴀᴀ⌐⊏⊔ᴇᴛᴛᴇ⌐⊏⌐ᴇ⊔⌐o⌐ᴇ⊏⊏⊔⌐ᴀᴛ⊔
<ᴛ⌐⌐⊏ᴇoᴛ⊏ᴇᴇ⊔⊔⌐⌐⊔ᴇ⌐⊏⌐o⌐⌐oᴛᴇ⌐⌐oᴛ⊓ᴇ⊏⌐⌐∨ᴛ⌐⊔ᴀ
⊔ᴇᴛ⊓ᴀᴛ∨ᴛ<⊏⊏⊔⊏⌐ᴇ∨⌐ᴇᴀo⌐⌐oᴛ⊓ᴇ∨ᴇ⊏o⌐ᴛ⊔ᴀ⊔ᴇ⌐<ᴛ
ᴀ⌐ᴇoᴛ∨∨ᴇ<⊔⌐⊓ᴀ∧ᴇᴀ⊔ᴇ<ᴛᴛ∨⊏⊓ᴇ⌐⊏⌐⌐⊓ᴀᴛᴇ∨ᴀᴛ⌐ᴇ⊔ᴇ
⌐⊏⌐ᴛ⊏⊔⌐ᴀo<ᴛ⊓⌐oᴛᴛ⌐ᴇᴛᴛ<ᴛᴇ⌐∨⊏o⊔ᴀ⊔ᴀ⊔⊏<ᴛᴛ⊓ᴇ⌐
```

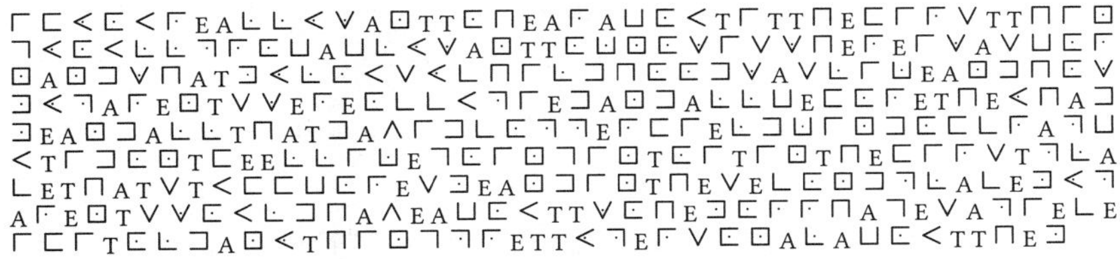

(c) Decryption: ⌐ → A.

Figure 4.2
Decrypting the challenge.

From there with further guesses, which become easier as more words make sense, we can arrive at figure 4.5, where we have derived the original plaintext. If it looks peculiar it is because it lacks punctuation and capitalization, which we left out for simplicity. If we do add punctuation, the text reads:

If you really want to hear about it, the first thing you'll probably want to know is where I was born, and what my lousy childhood was like, and how my parents were occupied and all before they had me, and all that David Copperfield kind of crap, but I don't feel like going into it. In the first place, that stuff bores me, and in the second

```
I⊏<O<ΓEA⊔⊔<∨ANTTO⊓EAΓA⊔O<TITT⊓E⊏IΓ∨TT⊓IN˥<O<
⊔⊔˥ΓO⊔A⊔⊔<∨ANTTO⊔NO∨I∨∨⊓EΓEI∨A∨⊔OΓNAN⊐∨⊓AT
⊐<⊔O<∨<⊔⊓I⊔⊐⊓OO⊐∨A∨⊔I⊔EAN⊐⊓O∨⊐<˥AΓENT∨∨E
ΓEO⊔⊔<˥IE⊐AN⊐A⊔⊔⊔EΓETΓ⊓E<⊓A⊐⊐EAN⊐A⊔⊔T⊓AT⊐
A∧I⊐⊔O˥˥EΓ⊏IE⊔⊐⊔IN⊐O⊏⊔ΓA˥⊔<TI⊐ONT⊏EE⊔⊔I⊔E˥OI
N˥INTOITINT⊓E⊏IΓ∨T˥⊔A⊔ET⊓AT∨T<⊏⊏⊔OΓE∨⊐EAN⊐INT
⊓E∨E⊔ON⊐˥⊔A⊔E⊐<˥AΓENT∨∨O<⊔⊐⊓A∧EA⊔O<TT∨O⊓E
⊐OΓΓ⊓A˥E∨A˥IE⊔EI⊏ITO⊔⊐AN<T⊓IN˥˥ΓETT<˥EΓ∨ONA⊔
A⊔O<TT⊓E⊐
```

(a) Decryption: ⊏ → O, Γ → I, □ → N.

```
I⊏<O<ΓEA⊔⊔<∨ANTTOHEAΓA⊔O<TITTHE⊏IΓ∨TTHIN˥<O<
⊔⊔˥ΓO⊔A⊔⊔<∨ANTTO⊔NO∨I∨∨HEΓEI∨A∨⊔OΓNAN⊐∨HAT
⊐<⊔O<∨<⊔HI⊔⊐HOO⊐∨A∨⊔I⊔EAN⊐HO∨⊐<˥AΓENT∨∨EΓE
O⊔⊔<˥IE⊐AN⊐A⊔⊔⊔EΓETΓETHE<HA⊐⊐EAN⊐A⊔⊔THAT⊐A∧I
⊐⊔O˥˥EΓ⊏IE⊔⊐⊔IN⊐O⊏⊔ΓA˥⊔<TI⊐ONT⊏EE⊔⊔I⊔E˥OIN˥I
NTOITINTHE⊏IΓ∨T˥⊔A⊔ETHAT∨T<⊏⊏⊔OΓE∨⊐EAN⊐INTHE∨E
⊔ON⊐˥⊔A⊔E⊐<˥AΓENT∨∨O<⊔⊐HA∧EA⊔O<TT∨OHE⊐OΓΓH
A˥E∨A˥IE⊔EI⊏ITO⊔⊐AN<THIN˥˥ΓETT<˥EΓ∨ONA⊔A⊔O<TT
HE⊐
```

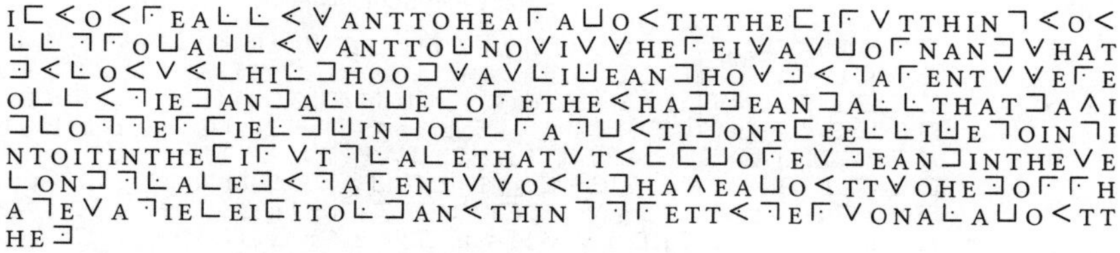

(b) Decryption: ⊓ → H.

Figure 4.3
Continuing to decrypt the challenge.

place, my parents would have about two hemorrhages apiece if I told anything pretty personal about them.

That is, the beginning of J. D. Salinger's "The Catcher in the Rye."

This was a fun exercise, but it has a moral. If it is possible for a human to break them with some guesswork and a bit of effort, then it is a completely worthless encryption scheme and definitely not a match for a computer that would do guessing much faster, combined with dictionary lookups. If we want to keep a secret, then we have to try harder than that.

As an aside, the symbols used in the substitution cipher form the so-called "pigpen cipher," which dates at least to the 18th century. We still find it in popular culture and children puzzles. If you wonder where the symbols come from, they are derived from the placement of the letters of the alphabet on a grid, drawing lines around them, and adding some dots. See figure 4.6: each letter is substituted by the lines and dots around it.

We were able to break the code because we took advantage of the regularities in the encrypted text; these regularities mirrored the regularities of language. That is the way all code breaking works: by detecting and taking advantage of regularities in the encrypted text. It follows that if we want a code to be unbreakable, we must make sure that all regularities are wiped out

I⌐ < O < R E A L ∟ ∟ < ∨ A N T T O H E A R A ⊔ O < T I T T H E ⌐ I R ∨ T T H I N ⌐ < O < ∟
∟ ⌐ R O ⊔ A ⊔ ∟ < ∨ A N T T O ⊔ N O ∨ I ∨ ∨ H E R E I ∨ A ∨ ⊔ O R N A N ⌐ ∨ H A T ⌐ <
∟ O < ∨ < ∟ H I ∟ ⌐ H O O ⌐ ∨ A ∨ ∟ I ⊔ E A N ⌐ H O ∨ ⌐ < ⌐ A R E N T ∨ ∨ E R E O ∟
∟ < ⌐ I E ⌐ A N ⌐ A ∟ ∟ ⊔ E ⌐ O R E T H E < H A ⌐ ⌐ E A N ⌐ A ∟ ∟ T H A T ⌐ A ∧ I ⌐ ∟
O ⌐ ⌐ E R ⌐ I E ∟ ⌐ ⊔ I N ⌐ O ⌐ ∟ R A ⌐ ⊔ < T I ⌐ O N T ⌐ E E ∟ ∟ I ⊔ E ⌐ O I N ⌐ I N T O I
T I N T H E ⌐ I R ∨ T ⌐ ∟ A ∟ E T H A T ∨ T < ⌐ ⌐ ⊔ O R E ∨ ⌐ E A N ⌐ I N T H E ∨ E ∟ O N
⌐ ⌐ ∟ A ∟ E ⌐ < ⌐ A R E N T ∨ ∨ O < ∟ ⌐ H A ∧ E A ⊔ O < T T ∨ O H E ⌐ O R R H A ⌐ E ∨
A ⌐ I E ∟ E I ⌐ I T O ∟ ⌐ A N < T H I N ⌐ ⌐ R E T T < ⌐ E R ∨ O N A ∟ A ⊔ O < T T H E ⌐

(a) Decryption: ⌐ → R.

I ⌐ Y O < R E A L L Y ∨ A N T T O H E A R A ⊔ O < T I T T H E ⌐ I R ∨ T T H I N ⌐ Y O < L L ⌐ R O
⊔ A ⊔ L Y ∨ A N T T O ⊔ N O ∨ I ∨ ∨ H E R E I ∨ A ∨ ⊔ O R N A N ⌐ ∨ H A T ⌐ Y L O < ∨ Y ∟
H I L ⌐ H O O ⌐ ∨ A ∨ L I ⊔ E A N ⌐ H O ∨ ⌐ Y ⌐ A R E N T ∨ ∨ E R E O L ∟ < ⌐ I E ⌐ A N ⌐
A L L ⊔ E ⌐ O R E T H E Y H A ⌐ ⌐ E A N ⌐ A L L T H A T ⌐ A ∧ I ⌐ L O ⌐ ⌐ E R ⌐ I E L ⌐ ⊔ I N
⌐ O ⌐ L R A ⌐ ⊔ < T I ⌐ O N T ⌐ E E L L I ⊔ E ⌐ O I N ⌐ I N T O I T I N T H E ⌐ I R ∨ T ⌐ ∟ A L
E T H A T ∨ T < ⌐ ⌐ ⊔ O R E ∨ ⌐ E A N ⌐ I N T H E ∨ E ∟ O N ⌐ ⌐ L A L E ⌐ Y ⌐ A R E N T ∨
∨ O < ∟ ⌐ H A ∧ E A ⊔ O < T T ∨ O H E ⌐ O R R H A ⌐ E ∨ A ⌐ I E ∟ E I ⌐ I T O L ⌐ A N Y T H
I N ⌐ ⌐ R E T T Y ⌐ E R ∨ O N A L A ⊔ O < T T H E ⌐

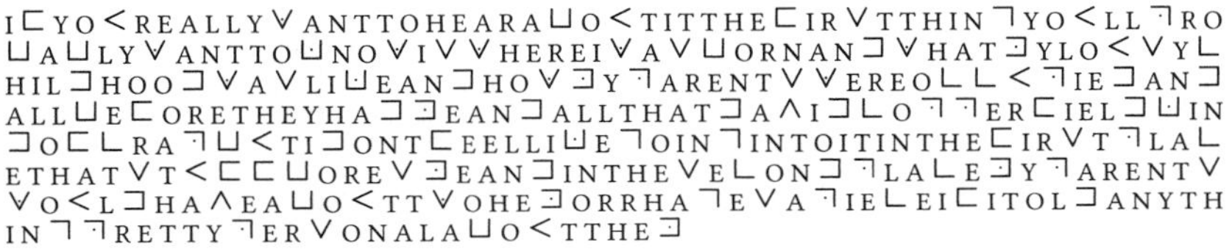

(b) Decryption: ∟ → L, < → Y.

Figure 4.4

More on decrypting the challenge.

I F Y O U R E A L L Y W A N T T O H E A R A B O U T I T T H E F I R S T T H I N G Y O U L L P R O B A B L
Y W A N T T O K N O W I S W H E R E I W A S B O R N A N D W H A T M Y L O U S Y C H I L D H O O D
W A S L I K E A N D H O W M Y P A R E N T S W E R E O C C U P I E D A N D A L L B E F O R E T H E Y H
A D M E A N D A L L T H A T D A V I D C O P P E R F I E L D K I N D O F C R A P B U T I D O N T F E E L L
I K E G O I N G I N T O I T I N T H E F I R S T P L A C E T H A T S T U F F B O R E S M E A N D I N T H E
C O N D P L A C E M Y P A R E N T S W O U L D H A V E A B O U T T W O H E M O R R H A G E S A P I E
C E I F I T O L D A N Y T H I N G P R E T T Y P E R S O N A L A B O U T T H E M

Figure 4.5

The challenge deciphered.

during the encryption. In other words, we must make the encrypted text be as random as possible. Ideally, it should be completely random. A complete random sequence of symbols cannot be decrypted back to the plaintext message by detecting regularities because there are none to be found.

4.2   One-time Pad

There is an encryption method that makes the ciphertext random, and it is the only encryption method that is guaranteed to be unbreakable. We assign a number to each letter in the alphabet, starting with A and zero, then B and one, until Z and 25. We take the original message one letter at a time. We also use a completely random sequence of letters as the encryption key. We walk through the random sequence one letter at a time, in tandem with the

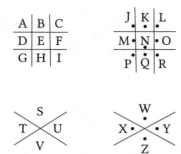

Figure 4.6
The pigpen cipher.

plaintext. At each step we have one letter from the plaintext and one letter from the encryption key. For example, we may have the plaintext letter W and the ciphertext letter G; that is, the numbers 22 and 6. We add them together: 22 + 6 = 28. Because Z is 25, we wrap around to the beginning of the alphabet and count three characters, arriving at C. This is the character that goes out to the ciphertext.

This kind of wrap around addition is common in cryptography and is called *modular addition* because it boils down to adding two numbers and finding the *remainder* of a division with a given number. We call this the *modulo* operation. It is what we do when we add minutes in the hour: if we reach 60, we take the remainder of the division of minutes by 60, which we call the minutes modulo 60; see for example figure 4.7. The symbol for the modulo is mod, so 23 mod 5 = 3. In our example we have (22 + 6) mod 26 = 28 mod 26 = 2 and 2 corresponds to the character C.

The mathematical definition of the modulo, x mod y, is the number $r \geq 0$, the remainder, such that $x = qy + r$, where q is the floor of the division of x/y, $\lfloor x/y \rfloor$. Therefore, we get $r = x - y\lfloor x/y \rfloor$. This definition covers the modulo of a negative dividend. Indeed, -6 mod $10 = 4$ because $\lfloor -6/10 \rfloor = -1$ and $r = -6 - 10(-1) = -6 + 10 = 4$.

Decryption is similar, using subtraction instead of addition. We take the ciphertext and the same encryption key we used for encryption and we walk through them character by character. If we have C in the ciphertext and G in the encryption key, then we get $(2 - 6)$ mod $26 = -4$ mod $26 = 22$, which is the letter W.

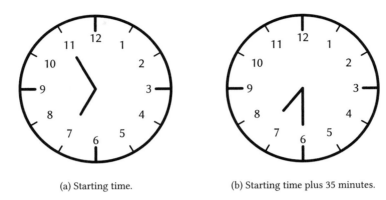

(a) Starting time.   (b) Starting time plus 35 minutes.

Figure 4.7
Adding minutes is modulo 60.

This encryption method is called a *one-time pad*, as in figure 4.8. As we said, it is completely secure because we get a completely random ciphertext. Each letter of the plaintext, $m[i]$, is added modulo 26, if our message contains only letters from the English alphabet, with the corresponding random letter of the one-time pad $t[i]$, to produce the ciphertext $c[i]$, so we have $c[i] = (m[i] + t[i])$ mod 26. If $t[i]$ is random, then so is $c[i]$. As you can see, there are no detectable patterns in the ciphertext. The same letter is encrypted to different letters on the ciphertext, so we cannot take advantage of any regularities to carry out frequency analysis. Decryption is easy, if we have the one-time pad. If encryption is given by $c[i] = (m[i] + t[i])$ mod 26, then decryption is $m[i] = (c[i] - t[i])$ mod 26. But if we are not given the one-time pad, then there is no way to guess it. Worse, we may guess a wrong one-time pad that decrypts to some other message: because every character in the one-time pad is random, each one-time pad is as likely as any other. We may start guessing and stumble at a wrong guess, as in figure 4.9. In figure 4.9a we take the encrypted text and the correct one-time pad, so we produce the original plaintext. In figure 4.9b we see that some other, equally likely one-time pad, on which we might have chanced while trying to break the code, produces perfectly legible results.

We can simplify the operations in one-time pads by using the binary exclusive-or (XOR) operation instead of modular addition. The XOR operation, whose symbol is usually ⊕, takes as input two binary digits. If they are the same digit, that is, if both of them are 1 or both of them are 0, then it outputs 0. If they are different, then it outputs 1. In other words, we have $1 \oplus 1 = 0$,

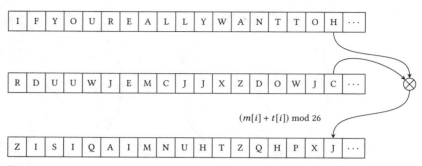

Figure 4.8
One-time pad.

Table 4.3
The exclusive-or (XOR)
operation.

		x	
		0	1
y	0	0	1
	1	1	0

$0 \oplus 0 = 0$, $1 \oplus 0 = 1$, $0 \oplus 1 = 1$. So it is an "either-or," or exclusive-or, illustrated in table 4.3. To use XOR we take the plaintext to be a sequence of binary digits. This is always possible, because each character is represented by a binary number; for instance, A is usually represented as 1100001 when using the ASCII encoding. Then the one-time pad is a random binary sequence, such as 1101011...We take the XOR of the plaintext with the one-time pad, bit by bit. The result is the ciphertext, in our case 0001010. The interesting thing about XOR is that, apart from being straightforward, it is immediately reversible. If $c = a \oplus b$, then $c \oplus b = a$. So to decrypt we just XOR again the ciphertext with the one-time pad. You can check that $0001010 \oplus 1101011 = 1100001$. Working with XOR is more general than working with the modulo operator, as it will work with binary string and not just some particular letter encoding. Moreover, the XOR operator is very fast.

Unfortunately, one-time pads are not practical. The random sequence of letters must be exactly that: completely random. It is not easy to produce truly random letters in large quantities. Computer methods do exist for producing seemingly random sequences, but they are only pseudo-random. If you think

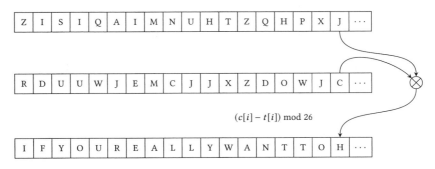

(a) Correct decryption.

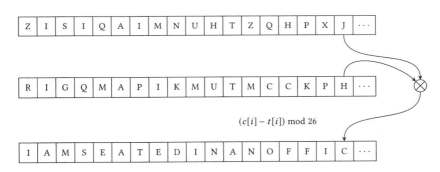

(b) Wrong decryption.

Figure 4.9
One-time pad, correct and wrong decryptions.

about it, it is not possible to produce something random by following a well-defined procedure, which is what a computer can do. You need some measure of chaos, something unpredictable. This is the subject of 16.1.

Apart from that, the one-time pad can be used only once. If we start repeating the sequence, then the same substitutions will occur after the length of the sequence: it will degenerate to a kind of shift cipher. Also, the one-time pad must be as long as the message, or again we will start repeating the substitutions.

These drawbacks mean that, except for exceptional circumstances, one-time pads are not used in practice. Typically large random sequences are saved on some portable medium and sent over to the recipient. The sender and recipient start using the random sequences until they get to the end of the saved sequence. Then they must use a newly issued one. So the logistics are complicated, with big bulks of random sequences being transferred every now and then, in addition to the burden of actually generating them in the first place.

4.3   The AES Cipher

Modern cryptography works by producing ciphertexts using specific mathematical methods. These methods take a relatively small key: hundreds or thousands of bits long. They take the plaintext and the key and transform the plaintext in complex ways that cannot be reversed unless you have the encryption key. We will describe a method, the Advanced Encryption Standard (AES), that is almost ubiquitous in use. Chances are that every time you transmit encrypted information using your browser, you are using AES behind the scenes. AES is a standard, adopted by the U.S. National Institute of Standards and Technology (NIST) in 2001, as a result of an open process to substitute an older standard, the Data Encryption Standard (DES). The process lasted from 1997 to 2000. NIST asked for submissions of proposals from the cryptographic community; after serious analyses, on October 2, 2000, NIST announced that a submission by two Belgian cryptographers, Joan Daemen and Vincent Rijmen, called Rijndael, was selected.

AES is a complicated algorithm. It is normal for the newcomer to despair when first encountering it. The reader is not expected to memorize each and every step of AES. The reader is expected, however, to appreciate the effort that goes into designing a solid cipher and what must go into a cipher in the computer age to resist decryption by computers. The reader will then be wary of any magic privacy preserving technologies or tools that may be peddled around without having survived intense, public scrutiny by cryptographers and computer scientists. So, dear reader, prepare for a bumpy ride.

AES performs a series of operations on the plaintext. First, we break the plaintext in blocks of 128 bits, or 16 bytes. AES works on blocks of bits, and so it is a *block cipher*. By contrast, a *stream cipher* works on individual bytes or bits. It uses keys that may be 128, 192, or 256 bits long. The bytes are put in a matrix in column-order, that is, we proceed by filling the matrix column by column. This matrix is called the *state*. If the block is composed of bytes $p_0, p_1, \ldots, p_{15}$, then byte p_i is put in the state matrix as byte $b_{j,k}$, where $j = i \bmod 4$ and $k = i/4$. The transformation is shown in figure 4.10; we assume it is implemented in an operation called `CreateState` that takes as input a block b and returns the state matrix s.

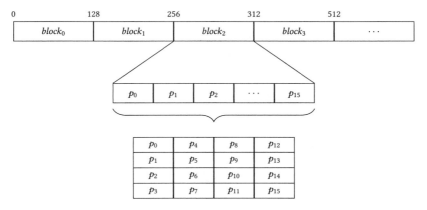

Figure 4.10
AES `CreateState` operation.

Then we take the encryption key and use it to derive a series of additional keys of bytes arranged in column-order, similarly to the state. These keys are called *round keys* because we will see that we use one key for each *round*, or iteration, of the core AES algorithm. In fact, the number of keys we will use is actually one more than the number of rounds because we need one key before the rounds start. The generation of the additional keys is called `KeyExpansion`. The idea of altering the key so that the encryption is more resistant to certain kinds of attacks is called *key whitening*. We will not delve further into `KeyExpansion`; this is a small and subtle algorithm in itself.

Assuming we have extended the key, we take the first round key. We XOR each byte of the round key with the corresponding byte of the state. This operation is called `AddRoundKey`. We get a new state with elements $x_{i,j} = p_{i,j} \oplus k_{i,j}$, as shown in figure 4.11.

Now we perform a series of rounds to the results of the `AddRoundKey` operation. The number of rounds depends on the length of the key. We do 10 rounds for 128-bit keys, 12 rounds for 192-bit keys, and 14 rounds for 256-bit keys.

p_0	p_4	p_8	p_{12}
p_1	p_5	p_9	p_{13}
p_2	p_6	p_{10}	p_{14}
p_3	p_7	p_{11}	p_{15}

k_0	k_4	k_8	k_{12}
k_1	k_5	k_9	k_{13}
k_2	k_6	k_{10}	k_{14}
k_3	k_7	k_{11}	k_{15}

$\oplus$

x_0	x_4	x_8	x_{12}
x_1	x_5	x_9	x_{13}
x_2	x_6	x_{10}	x_{14}
x_3	x_7	x_{11}	x_{15}

Figure 4.11

AES AddRoundKey operation.

Table 4.4

The AES S-box.

	0	1	2	3	4	5	6	7	8	9	A	B	C	D	E	F
0	63	7C	77	7B	F2	6B	6F	C5	30	01	67	2B	FE	D7	AB	76
1	CA	82	C9	7D	FA	59	47	F0	AD	D4	A2	AF	9C	A4	72	C0
2	B7	FD	93	26	36	3F	F7	CC	34	A5	E5	F1	71	D8	31	15
3	04	C7	23	C3	18	96	05	9A	07	12	80	E2	EB	27	B2	75
4	09	83	2C	1A	1B	6E	5A	A0	52	3B	D6	B3	29	E3	2F	84
5	53	D1	00	ED	20	FC	B1	5B	6A	CB	BE	39	4A	4C	58	CF
6	D0	EF	AA	FB	43	4D	33	85	45	F9	02	7F	50	3C	9F	A8
7	51	A3	40	8F	92	9D	38	F5	BC	B6	DA	21	10	FF	F3	D2
8	CD	0C	13	EC	5F	97	44	17	C4	A7	7E	3D	64	5D	19	73
9	60	81	4F	DC	22	2A	90	88	46	EE	B8	14	DE	5E	0B	DB
A	E0	32	3A	0A	49	06	24	5C	C2	D3	AC	62	91	95	E4	79
B	E7	C8	37	6D	8D	D5	4E	A9	6C	56	F4	EA	65	7A	AE	08
C	BA	78	25	2E	1C	A6	B4	C6	E8	DD	74	1F	4B	BD	8B	8A
D	70	3E	B5	66	48	03	F6	0E	61	35	57	B9	86	C1	1D	9E
E	E1	F8	98	11	69	D9	8E	94	9B	1E	87	E9	CE	55	28	DF
F	8C	A1	89	0D	BF	E6	42	68	41	99	2D	0F	B0	54	BB	16

The first operation in each round is called SubBytes and it consists of taking the current state and substituting each byte in it by another byte from another matrix, called *S-box*. The S-box is a 16×16 matrix, whose contents are calculated using functions with specific cryptographic properties. You can see the matrix in table 4.4. If the entry $x_{i,j}$ of the state is equal to the number X, then because X is a byte it can be represented by two hexadecimal digits, $h_1 h_2$. The result of the SubBytes operation for $x_{i,j}$ is the (h_1, h_2) element of the S-box, or s_{h_1, h_2}. Figure 4.12 illustrates the procedure.

It may seem more complicated than it really is. Suppose that in figure 4.12 we have $x_4 = 168$; 168 in decimal is A8 in hexadecimal. We go to row A and column 8 of table 4.4, where we find the number C2 in hexadecimal, or 194 in decimal. That means that $sb_4 = 194$. We do the same for all numbers in the state.

x_0	x_4	x_8	x_{12}
x_1	x_5	x_9	x_{13}
x_2	x_6	x_{10}	x_{14}
x_3	x_7	x_{11}	x_{15}

$s_{0,0}$	$s_{0,1}$	$\cdots$	$s_{0,F}$
$s_{1,0}$	$s_{1,1}$	$\cdots$	$s_{1,F}$
$\cdots$	$\cdots$	$\cdots$	$\cdots$
$s_{F,0}$	$s_{F,1}$	$\cdots$	$s_{F,F}$

$$x_i = h_1 h_2 \rightarrow sb_i = s_{h_1, h_2}$$

sb_0	sb_4	sb_8	sb_{12}
sb_1	sb_5	sb_9	sb_{13}
sb_2	sb_6	sb_{10}	sb_{14}
sb_3	sb_7	sb_{11}	sb_{15}

Figure 4.12
AES SubBytes operation.

The second operation in each round, following the SubBytes operation, is to shift the rows of the resulting state. This is called, not surprisingly, the ShiftRows operation. It shifts left each row of the state apart from the first by an increasing number of positions. Row 2 is shifted left 1 position, row 3 is shifted left 2 positions, and row 4 is shifted left 3 positions, wrapping around if necessary as shown in figure 4.13.

The third operation on each round is called MixColumns, and it is where we work on the columns, taking each column of the current state and transforming it into a new column. The transformation is performed by multiplying each column by a fixed matrix, as in figure 4.14, which shows the operation for the second column; the matrix is the same for all columns. You may notice that instead of the usual notation for addition and multiplication we use $\oplus$ and $\bullet$, respectively. This is because we do not perform the usual arithmetic operations. Addition and multiplication are performed on polynomials modulo an irreducible polynomial of degree 8 in the finite field $GF(2^8)$. That is a mouthful of a phrase. Fortunately, you do not need to know exactly what it

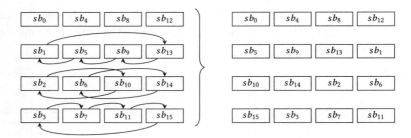

Figure 4.13
AES ShiftRows operation.

means to understand what AES does. Addition is simply xor of the underlying bit patterns. Multiplication is a bit more involved but essentially simple, nonetheless.

Indeed, it turns out that, although the underlying theory is complex for the uninitiated, the actual multiplication operation is straightforward. If a stands for one of the sb_i values, then from figure 4.14 we only need to define the multiplication by 1, 2, or 3. We observe that:

$$1 \bullet a = a$$
$$3 \bullet a = 2 \bullet a \oplus a$$

That means we only need to know how to calculate $2 \bullet a$. We consider the binary representation of a, which is $a = (a_7, a_6, \ldots, a_0)$ where each of the a_i is an individual bit. Then we have:

$$2 \bullet a = \begin{cases} (a_6, \ldots, a_0, 0) & \text{if } a_7 = 0 \\ (a_6, \ldots, a_0, 0) \oplus (0, 0, 0, 1, 1, 0, 1, 1) & \text{if } a_7 = 1 \end{cases}$$

For those who implement AES, the whole MixColumns operation can be written in a few lines of optimized computer code. The complexity in the MixColumns description does not translate to an unwieldy implementation.

The final operation in a round is to add the round key on the state again, that is, to perform operation AddRoundKey on the state as it is right now.

We do the same series of operations for all rounds except for the last one, in which we do not perform the MixColumns operation. In summary, AES works as in algorithm 4.1. We create the state in line 1, then we expand the keys in

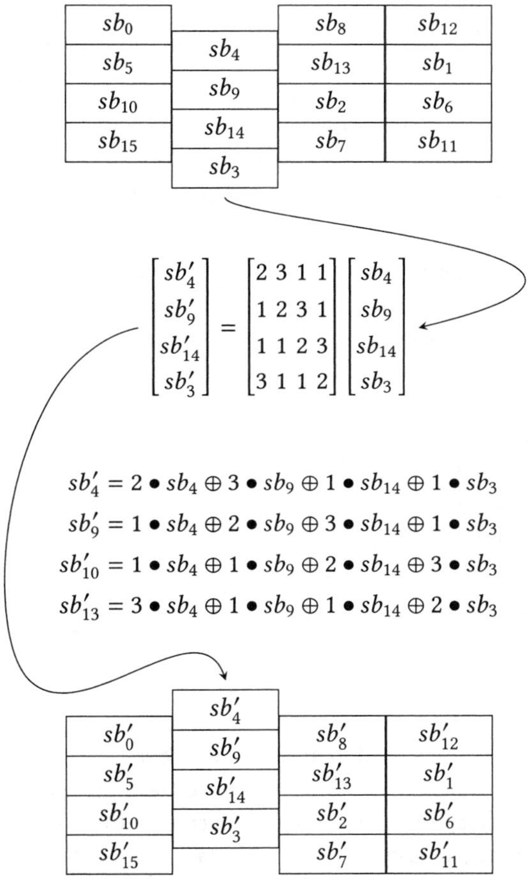

sb0 sb4 sb8 sb12
sb5 sb9 sb13 sb1
sb10 sb14 sb2 sb6
sb15 sb3 sb7 sb11
$\begin{bmatrix} sb'_4 \\ sb'_9 \\ sb'_{14} \\ sb'_3 \end{bmatrix} = \begin{bmatrix} 2 & 3 & 1 & 1 \\ 1 & 2 & 3 & 1 \\ 1 & 1 & 2 & 3 \\ 3 & 1 & 1 & 2 \end{bmatrix} \begin{bmatrix} sb_4 \\ sb_9 \\ sb_{14} \\ sb_3 \end{bmatrix}$
$sb'_4 = 2 \bullet sb_4 \oplus 3 \bullet sb_9 \oplus 1 \bullet sb_{14} \oplus 1 \bullet sb_3$
$sb'_9 = 1 \bullet sb_4 \oplus 2 \bullet sb_9 \oplus 3 \bullet sb_{14} \oplus 1 \bullet sb_3$
$sb'_{10} = 1 \bullet sb_4 \oplus 1 \bullet sb_9 \oplus 2 \bullet sb_{14} \oplus 3 \bullet sb_3$
$sb'_{13} = 3 \bullet sb_4 \oplus 1 \bullet sb_9 \oplus 1 \bullet sb_{14} \oplus 2 \bullet sb_3$
sb'0 sb'4 sb'8 sb'12
sb'5 sb'9 sb'13 sb'1
sb'10 sb'14 sb'2 sb'6
sb'15 sb'3 sb'7 sb'11

Figure 4.14
AES `MixColumns` operation.

Algorithm 4.1: AES cipher algorithm.

AESCipher(b, k, n) $\rightarrow$ s

    Input: b, a block of 16 bytes
           k, the encryption key
           n, the number of rounds
    Output: s, the ciphertext corresponding to b

1   $s \leftarrow$ CreateState(b)
2   $rk \leftarrow$ ExpandKey(k)
3   $s \leftarrow$ AddRoundKey(s, $rk[0]$)
4   **for** $i \leftarrow$ 1 **to** n **do**
5      $s \leftarrow$ SubBytes(s)
6      $s \leftarrow$ ShiftRows(s)
7      $s \leftarrow$ MixColumns(s)
8      $s \leftarrow$ AddRoundKey(s, $rk[i]$)
9   $s \leftarrow$ SubBytes(s)
10 $s \leftarrow$ ShiftRows(s)
11 $s \leftarrow$ AddRoundKey(s, $rk[n]$)
12 **return** s

---

line 2. The keys are stored in array rk of size $n + 1$, where n is the number of rounds. Line 3 adds the first round key to the state. Lines 4–8 carry out the first $n - 1$ rounds, whereas lines 9–11 carry out the last round.

Of course, any encryption algorithm is worthless without a corresponding decryption algorithm. It turns out that decryption in AES is straightforward. All the steps in algorithm 4.1 are reversible, provided that in the SubBytes operation we use a special inverse S-box, which you can see in table 4.5. The inverse AES cipher is algorithm 4.2. The operations are prefixed with Inv to show that they are simple variants of the operations in the original cipher. Beyond some changes in the order of the operations, the logic is pretty much the same; note that the round keys are used in the reverse order than the one used for encryption.

In summary, if you want to encrypt a message securely, you can use AES. You pick an encryption key, feed it into an implementation of the algorithm, and send the resulting ciphertext to the recipient. The recipient uses the same key and runs the inverse of the AES cipher to recover your message.

Algorithm 4.2: AES decipher algorithm.

AESDecipher(b, k, n) $\longrightarrow$ s
  Input: b, a block of 16 bytes
     k, the encryption key
     n, the number of rounds
  Output: s, the plaintext corresponding to b

1 $s \leftarrow$ CreateState(b)
2 $rk \leftarrow$ ExpandKey(k)
3 $s \leftarrow$ AddRoundKey(s, $rk[n]$)
4 **for** $i \leftarrow 1$ **to** n **do**
5 $s \leftarrow$ InvShiftRows(s)
6 $s \leftarrow$ InvSubBytes(s)
7 $s \leftarrow$ AddRoundKey(s, $rk[n - i]$)
8 $s \leftarrow$ InvMixColumns(s)
9 $s \leftarrow$ InvShiftRows(s)
10 $s \leftarrow$ InvSubBytes(s)
11 $s \leftarrow$ AddRoundKey(s, $rk[0]$)
12 **return** s

AES has been in use for many years, and no practical weaknesses have been found against it. That means that there is no known practical way to recover the plaintext from a ciphertext unless one has the encryption key. AES is an example of a *symmetric cipher*. The same encryption key is used for encryption and decryption. When one key is used for encryption and a different key is used for decryption we have an *asymmetric cipher*.

All security hinges on the security key. That means that your secrets are as secure as your key is. If it is leaked, then AES is compromised. That is not a defect of AES. All ciphers use some sort of key. What's more, it is a feature, not a bug, that the security of AES and any other good cipher rests on the confidentiality of the key and only on the confidentiality of the key. Back in 1883, August Kerckhoffs, a Dutch linguist and cryptographer who was professor of languages at the École des Hautes Études Commerciales in Paris in the late 19th century, argued that the working of the cipher should not be required to be a secret, and it should not be a problem if it falls into the hands of the enemy. In today's terms, all secrecy of a cipher should rest on the key itself and not on the cipher.

Table 4.5

The inverse AES S-box.

	0	1	2	3	4	5	6	7	8	9	A	B	C	D	E	F
0	52	09	6A	D5	30	36	A5	38	BF	40	A3	9E	81	F3	D7	FB
1	7C	E3	39	82	9B	2F	FF	87	34	8E	43	44	C4	DE	E9	CB
2	54	7B	94	32	A6	C2	23	3D	EE	4C	95	0B	42	FA	C3	4E
3	08	2E	A1	66	28	D9	24	B2	76	5B	A2	49	6D	8B	D1	25
4	72	F8	F6	64	86	68	98	16	D4	A4	5C	CC	5D	65	B6	92
5	6C	70	48	50	FD	ED	B9	DA	5E	15	46	57	A7	8D	9D	84
6	90	D8	AB	00	8C	BC	D3	0A	F7	E4	58	05	B8	B3	45	06
7	D0	2C	1E	8F	CA	3F	0F	02	C1	AF	BD	03	01	13	8A	6B
8	3A	91	11	41	4F	67	DC	EA	97	F2	CF	CE	F0	B4	E6	73
9	96	AC	74	22	E7	AD	35	85	E2	F9	37	E8	1C	75	DF	6E
A	47	F1	1A	71	1D	29	C5	89	6F	B7	62	0E	AA	18	BE	1B
B	FC	56	3E	4B	C6	D2	79	20	9A	DB	C0	FE	78	CD	5A	F4
C	1F	DD	A8	33	88	07	C7	31	B1	12	10	59	27	80	EC	5F
D	60	51	7F	A9	19	B5	4A	0D	2D	E5	7A	9F	93	C9	9C	EF
E	A0	E0	3B	4D	AE	2A	F5	B0	C8	EB	BB	3C	83	53	99	61
F	17	2B	04	7E	BA	77	D6	26	E1	69	14	63	55	21	0C	7D

That is a sound engineering principle and a precaution against the notion of *security by obscurity*, which is the idea that if the adversaries do not know how it works, they will not be able to break it. That is wrong; if that is your best defense, you must keep in mind that the adversaries have the best minds at their disposal and will find out how your system works. Or they can probably just bribe somebody. Be that as it may, constraining the security on the key makes it possible to guarantee secrecy as long as the key remains secret, a far easier proposition than trying to keep the whole design secret.

There are other symmetric encryption ciphers apart from AES, and in all of them security rests on keeping the key hidden. They also require that both parties of the communication have agreed on the same key. And here is the rub. If you want to encrypt something to send to somebody, then you must somehow agree on the key to use. If you happen to be in physical proximity, that may be easy: you just meet and exchange keys. But if you are not, you cannot simply go forth and send the recipient the key. Because the key is not encrypted, it can be intercepted in transit, and all security is lost.

4.4   Diffie-Hellman Key Exchange

The solution to the problem of key exchange is what really enabled secure digital communications. At first glance it appears as if it works by magic. Two parties, say Alice and Bob (typically names of parties in cryptography follow the alphabet), want to exchange a key to use in encrypting and decrypting a message. Before they do that, they exchange a series of other messages. These messages are in plaintext, and they do not contain the key they want to share. Yet, when they finish with these messages, both Alice and Bob have at their hands the same key. Because the key was never sent from one another, nobody could have intercepted it.

Let's see how this is possible. Alice and Bob perform the following sequence of steps. First, Alice and Bob agree on two numbers. A prime number, p, and another number, not necessarily prime, g, such that $2 \leq g \leq p - 2$ (if the limits do not seem to make sense, please be patient, they will). Because all calculations they will perform are done modulo p, p is the *modulus* of the scheme; g is called the *base*. Suppose that Alice and Bob pick $p = 23$ and $g = 14$. They do not need to keep these two numbers secret; they can agree on these numbers in public and publish them anywhere.

Alice then chooses a secret number a, $1 \leq a \leq p - 1$. Suppose she chooses $a = 3$. She calculates the number

$$A = g^a \bmod p = 14^3 \bmod 23 = 2744 \bmod 23 = 7$$

Because the calculations are modulo p, it would not have made sense for Alice to select $a \geq p$. Alice sends the number A, that is, 7, to Bob. Now Bob chooses a secret number b, again $1 \leq b \leq p - 1$. Suppose he chooses $b = 4$. He performs the same operations on it that Alice did on her secret number. That is, he calculates the number

$$B = g^b \bmod p = 14^4 \bmod 23 = 38\,416 \bmod 23 = 6$$

Bob sends the number B, that is, 6, to Alice. Alice calculates the number

$$B^a \bmod p = 6^3 \bmod 23 = 216 \bmod 23 = 9$$

Bob calculates the number

$$A^b \bmod p = 7^4 \bmod 23 = 2401 \bmod 23 = 9$$

That's it: 9 is Alice's and Bob's secret. Notice that they never exchanged this number, yet they ended up with the same result after their calculations. Moreover, there is no known practical way to derive their secret by anybody who intercepts their communication. In other words, there is no way to derive the secret by knowing p, g, A, and B. You can verify in figure 4.15 that the actual secret is not sent to each other.

This method for exchanging keys is called *Diffie-Hellman key exchange*, after Whitfield Diffie and Martin Hellman, who published it in 1976. The

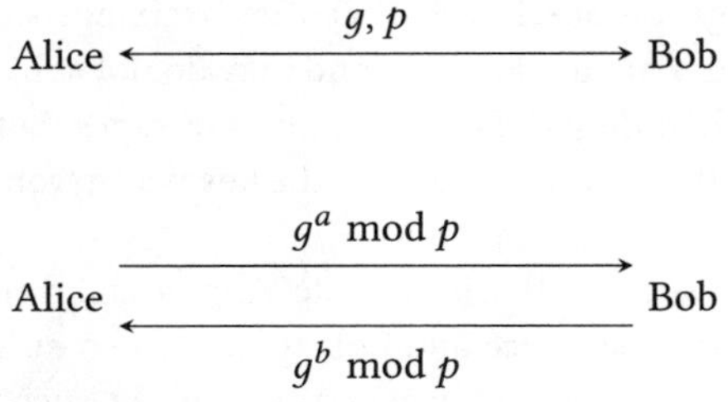

$$\text{Alice} \xleftarrow{\quad\quad g, p \quad\quad} \text{Bob}$$

$$\text{Alice} \xrightarrow{\quad g^a \bmod p \quad} \text{Bob}$$
$$\text{Alice} \xleftarrow{\quad g^b \bmod p \quad} \text{Bob}$$

Figure 4.15
Diffie-Hellman communication.

method had been invented some years earlier by Malcolm Williamson working at the Government Communications Headquarters (GCHQ), the UK government agency responsible for communications intelligence, but was kept classified, so Diffie, Hellman, and pretty much everybody else were unawares. Table 4.6 shows the Diffie-Hellman key exchange method. You can see why it works: both Alice and Bob calculate the same number because $g^{ba} \bmod p = g^{ab} \bmod p$. To arrive at that, we need to know that from the basic laws of modulo arithmetic we have:

$$(u \bmod n)(v \bmod n) \bmod n = uv \bmod n$$

from which it follows:

$$(u \bmod n)^k \bmod n = u^k \bmod n$$

so that:

$$(g^b \bmod p)^a \bmod p = g^{ba} \bmod p$$

and

$$(g^a \bmod p)^b \bmod p = g^{ab} \bmod p$$

The Diffie-Hellman key exchange method is secure, as long as Alice and Bob keep a and b secret, which they have no reason not to. In fact, they can throw them away after the exchange because they are no longer needed.

The security rests on the difficulty of the following problem. If we have a prime number p, a number g, and $y = g^x \bmod p$, the *discrete logarithm problem* is finding the integer x in this equation, where $1 \le x \le p - 1$. The integer x is called the *discrete logarithm of y to the base g*, and we can write $x = \log_g y \bmod p$. The problem is difficult because $y = g^x \bmod p$ is an example of a *one-way function*. It is easy to calculate y given g, x, and p (shortly we

Table 4.6

Diffie-Hellman key exchange.

Alice	Bob
Alice and Bob agree on p and g	
Choose a Calculate $A = g^a \bmod p$ Send A to Bob	Choose b Calculate $B = g^b \bmod p$ Send B to Alice
Calculate $s = B^a \bmod p$ $ = (g^b \bmod p)^a \bmod p$ $ = g^{ba} \bmod p$	Calculate $s = A^b \bmod p$ $ = (g^a \bmod p)^b \bmod p$ $ = g^{ab} \bmod p$

Table 4.7

Raising to a power and taking the remainder for $g = 2$, $p = 13$.

x	1	2	3	4	5	6	7	8	9	10	11	12
g^x	2	4	8	16	32	64	128	256	512	1024	2048	4096
$g^x \bmod p$	2	4	8	3	6	12	11	9	5	10	7	1

will see efficient computational methods for that), but we know of no effective method to calculate x given y, g, and p. What we can do is try different values for x until we find the correct one.

Indeed, while the behavior of the exponentiation function is predictable, producing increasing values for increasing powers of a number, the behavior of raising to a power modulo a prime appears to be erratic; see table 4.7. You can easily get x from g^x to x by taking the logarithm. You *cannot* get x from $g^x \bmod p$ by taking the logarithm, or by using any other known formula.

In table 4.7, while the normal powers of 2 are produced by successive doubling, the powers of 2 modulo 13 go through all the numbers in the range from 1 to 12 inclusive, with no apparent pattern. From then on they will start going around the same cycle. Indeed, from the equality $2^{12} \bmod 13 = 1$ we get $2^{13} \bmod 13 = (2^{12} \times 2) \bmod 13 = ((2^{12} \bmod 13) \times (2 \bmod 13)) \bmod 13 = (1 \times 2) \bmod 13 = 2$; we use again the property of modulo arithmetic that allows us to move the modulo operation in and out of multiplication. In general, you can see that the function $2^x \bmod 13$ is periodic with period 12 since $2^{12+k} \bmod 13 = ((2^{12} \bmod 13) \times (2^k \bmod 13)) \bmod 13 =$

Table 4.8

Raising to a power and taking the remainder for $g = 3$, $p = 13$.

x	1	2	3	4	5	6	7	8	9	10	11
g^x	3	9	27	81	243	729	2187	6561	19683	59049	177147
$g^x \bmod p$	3	9	1	3	9	1	3	9	1	3	9

$(1 \times 2^k) \bmod 13 = 2^k \bmod 13$. Moreover, 12 is the fundamental period; there is no other period smaller than that.

Note that this does not happen always. Table 4.8 shows the situation with successive powers of 3 modulo 13. This time the modular powers do not go through all the values from 1 to 12 but only through a subset of them; the fundamental period of $3^x \bmod 13$ is 3. If we had such a choice of g and p we would have to try only 3 different values to find the solution to the discrete algorithm problem instead of possibly all 12 values.

If the successive values of $g^x \bmod p$ cover all the numbers from 1 up to and including $p - 1$, then we say that g is a *generator* or a *primitive element*. To be more precise, it is called a *group generator* or a *group primitive element* because the numbers $1, 2, \ldots, p - 1$ when p is a prime form a *multiplicative group* when we multiply them modulo p, an important concept in algebra and number theory. We therefore need to pick as g a generator. In fact, we can make do without a generator, if the successive values of $g^x \bmod p$ are a large enough subset of the numbers $1, 2, \ldots, p - 1$ so that trying to find the solution to the discrete logarithm problem is impractical.

The values will start repeating once a power $g^x \bmod p$ becomes 1. If we have $g = p - 1$, then $g^1 \bmod p = (p - 1) \bmod p = p - 1$; $g^2 \bmod p = (p - 1)^2 \bmod p = 1$, because $(p - 1)^2 = p(p - 2) + 1$, so that all the powers will be alternating between $p - 1$ and 1. If we have $g = 1$, then all powers will be equal to 1. That is why we demanded that Alice and Bob should pick g such that $2 \leq g \leq p - 2$.

To return to Diffie-Hellman, to ensure that the key exchange cannot be broken, we need to ensure that from $g^x \bmod p$ one cannot guess x. That means that p should be quite large. We can choose p to be a prime whose binary representation is 4096 bits long, which is a number with at least 1233 decimal digits. There are good methods for finding such primes, we do not search blindly for them. We examine a popular method for finding primes in section 16.4 We should also choose an appropriate g. In contrast to p, it is not necessary to choose a large value for g to get a generator (or something close to a generator); it can even be as low as 2. Then we can start exchanging keys.

Taking everything together, if Alice wants to communicate securely with Bob, they will first use Diffie-Hellman to establish some secret key that only the two of them know. They will use the key to encrypt their messages using AES. When they are finished, they will throw away the secret key, as the whole sequence can be performed again any time they want in the future.

There is a small caveat. What we have said holds true for computers as we know them. An algorithm devised for *quantum computers* solves the discrete logarithm problem in polynomial time. If quantum computers become practical, then the implications for Diffie-Hellman, as well as other cryptographic methods, will be severe. With this in mind, researchers are already working for cryptographic algorithms that are resistant to quantum computation.

4.5   Fast and Modular Exponentiation

The Diffie-Hellman key-exchange method requires raising to powers modulo a prime number; this is called *modular exponentiation*. We can of course calculate $g^x \bmod p$ by raising g to the xth power and then calculating the modulo of the division by p. However, with a little thought we can see that this is wasteful. A number like g^x can get very large; yet the final result will always be less than p. It would be nice if we could find a way to calculate the expression without having to calculate potentially very big powers only to reduce them modulo p in the end. Using the properties of modulo arithmetic we have:

$$g^2 \bmod p = g \cdot g \bmod p = ((g \bmod p)(g \bmod p)) \bmod p$$
$$g^3 \bmod p = g^2 \cdot g \bmod p = ((g^2 \bmod p)(g \bmod p)) \bmod p$$
$$\vdots$$
$$g^x \bmod p = g^{x-1} \cdot g \bmod p = ((g^{x-1} \bmod p)(g \bmod p)) \bmod p$$

We can therefore avoid the calculation of big powers modulo p by starting with the square modulo p, then using that result to calculate the cube modulo p, and so on until the xth power.

There is an even more efficient way, which is the standard way to do modular exponentiation. To arrive at it we need to derive a fast way to do exponentiation (not modular) in general. This will give us a general tool for calculating large powers, which we will adapt to calculate large modular powers.

To see how it works, we start by writing the exponent in binary notation:

$$x = b_{n-1}2^{n-1} + b_{n-2}2^{n-2} + \cdots + b_0 2^0$$

where each b_i is a single bit in the binary representation of x. Having that, we can calculate g^x as follows:

$$g^x = g^{b_{n-1}2^{n-1} + b_{n-2}2^{n-2} + \cdots + b_0 2^0}$$

The last equation is equivalent to:

$$g^x = (g^{2^{n-1}})^{b_{n-1}} \times (g^{2^{n-2}})^{b_{n-2}} \times \cdots \times (g^{2^0})^{b_0}$$

Taking the expression from the right to the left, we start by calculating $(g^{2^0})^{b_0}$. Then we calculate $(g^{2^1})^{b_1}$, $(g^{2^2})^{b_2}$, $(g^{2^3})^{b_3}$, and so on. But $g^{2^0} = g^1 = g$, g^{2^1} is the square of g, g^{2^2} is the square of g^{2^1}, g^{2^3} is the square of g^{2^2}, and in general $g^{2^k} = (g^{2^{k-1}})^2$, because $(g^{2^{k-1}})^2 = g^{2 \cdot 2^{k-1}}$. That means we can calculate the exponentiation base, g^{2^i} for $i = 1, 2, \ldots, n-1$, of each factor from the right to the left by squaring the base of the previous factor. This leads to algorithm 4.3, exponentiation by repeated squaring.

The algorithm takes as input g and x and returns g^x. It works by performing the calculations we described in a right to left order. In line 1 we set the base, c, equal to g, which is equal to g^{2^0}. We use the variable d, initially set to x in line 2, to get the binary representation of x. The result is calculated in the variable r, initially set to 1 in line 3. The loop in lines 4–8 executes as many times as the number of bits in the binary representation of x. If the rightmost bit of d is 1, which we check in line 5, then we multiply our current result by the factor, c, that we have calculated. Then we need to move one bit to the left in the binary representation of x. We do that by taking the integer division of d by 2; this chops off one bit from the right, in line 7. At the end of each loop iteration, we square the current c, in line 8. In this way we start the kth iteration with c equal to $g^{2^{k-1}}$ and that covers the first iteration where we saw that we have $g^{2^0} = g^1 = g$.

The modulo 2 operation in line 5 does not really require a division. A number is divisible by 2 if its last bit is 0; otherwise it does not. So we only need to check whether the last digit of d is 0. That is easy to do, with an operation

---

Algorithm 4.3: Exponentiation by repeated squaring.

ExpRepeatedSquaring(g, x) $\rightarrow r$
    Input: g, the integer base
              x, the integer exponent
    Output: r, equal to g^x

1   $c \leftarrow g$
2   $d \leftarrow x$
3   $r \leftarrow 1$
4   **while** $d > 0$ **do**
5   **if** $d \bmod 2 = 1$ **then**
6         $r \leftarrow r \times c$
7      $d \leftarrow \lfloor d/2 \rfloor$
8      $c \leftarrow c \times c$
9   **return** r

---

called *bitwise* AND, which takes two numbers bit by bit and returns a number whose ith bit is 1 if both ith bits of the two numbers are 1; otherwise it is 0. In our case we just perform the bitwise AND of d and a number with equal number of bits, with all bits set to 0 apart from the last one, which is 1. We will meet again the bitwise AND operation in section 13.7. You can peek ahead at table 13.4 to see how it works.

Similarly, the integer division by 2 in line 7 does not really require a division. We just need to drop off the rightmost bit. This is equivalent to shifting all bits to the right by one position (so that the rightmost falls off). This is implemented in an operation called *shift right*. We will see the bitwise shift right operation in detail in section 16.1; in the meantime you can check figure 16.1.

An example of the operation of the algorithm is in table 4.9, where we use it to calculate 13^{13}. Each row, apart from the last, corresponds to the values of c, r, and d at line 5 of the algorithm's loop. The last row shows the end result at the exit of the loop. You can verify that when the last digit of d is 1, the value of r in the next row is the product of c and r in the current row; otherwise it remains unchanged. The full calculation took four iterations; that is much less than doing 13 multiplications to calculate 13^{13} in the conventional way.

We can deduce the performance of the algorithm from the number of loop iterations. As we said, these are equal to the number of bits in the binary

Table 4.9
Exponentiation by repeated squaring: 13^{13}.

$c = g^{2^i} = 13^{2^i}$	r	d
13	1	1101
169	13	110
28561	13	11
815730721	371293	1
	302875106592253	

representation of the exponent x, which is $\lg x$. Therefore, exponentiation by repeated squaring takes $O(\lg x)$ iterations.

The question then is how much time each iteration requires. The modulo and the division by 2 do not take much time, as they are performed with simple binary operations. The multiplication in line 6 and the squaring in line 8 may take some time. In general, computers use a fixed number of bits to represent an integer, say 32 or 64 bits. Operations involving such numbers are carried out very fast and are called *single-precision* operations; arithmetic with these operations is called *single-precision arithmetic*. If our numbers cannot fit in the number of bits offered by the computer, then the computer has to use *multiple-precision arithmetic*, also called *arbitrary-precision arithmetic*, or *bignum arithmetic*. Multiple precision arithmetic is more computationally demanding than single-precision arithmetic. For an analogy, consider multiplication carried out by humans. Early in our school years we learn by heart the multiplication table. As a result, we can multiply single-digit numbers in an instant. To multiply multiple-digit numbers, however, we have to employ long multiplication, which takes considerable more time (if you think of it, for two n-digit numbers it involves n^2 multiplications, plus additions). It is the same with machines. Multiple-precision multiplication of two numbers a and b of n and m bits respectively using the appropriate algorithm (an adaptation of the traditional long multiplication taught in school) requires nm single-precision multiplications, so it is $O(nm) = O(\lg a \lg b)$. Squaring can be twice as fast as multiplication, with a complexity of $O((n^2 + n)/2)$ for a number of n bits. Although halving the time may be significant in applications, the complexity remains at $O(n^2)$, and does not change the overall complexity of algorithm 4.3.

We assume that in each iteration we get numbers with double the number of bits they had in the previous iteration. Line 6 is executed fewer times than

---

Algorithm 4.4: Modular exponentiation by repeated squaring.

ModExpRepeatedSquaring(g, x, p) $\rightarrow r$
    Input: g, the integer base
             x, the integer exponent
             p, the divisor
    Output: r, equal to $g^x \bmod p$

1    $c \leftarrow g \bmod p$
2    $d \leftarrow x$
3    $r \leftarrow 1$
4   **while** $d > 0$ **do**
5   **if** $d \bmod 2 = 1$ **then**
6            $r \leftarrow (r \times c) \bmod p$
7        $d \leftarrow \lfloor d/2 \rfloor$
8        $c \leftarrow (c \times c) \bmod p$
9   **return** r

---

line 8 and r is less than c, so we only need to deal with line 8. The first iteration involves the multiplication of numbers up to g, requiring $O((\lg g)^2)$ time. The second iteration involves the multiplication of numbers of size g^2, requiring $O((\lg g^2)^2) = O((2 \lg g)^2)$ time. The last iteration involves the multiplication of numbers of size $g^{x/2}$, requiring $O((\lg g^{x/2})^2) = O((x/2 \lg g)^2)$. Summing it up, we have $O((\lg g)^2) + O((2 \lg g)^2) + \cdots + O((x/2 \lg g)^2)$. Each term in the sum has the form $O((2^{i-1} \lg g)^2)$, for $i = 1, 2, \ldots, \lg x$ (we have $\lg x$ iterations). We have many terms contributing to the overall complexity of the calculation, but it is the biggest term that dominates the growth of the complexity function, so the overall complexity is $O((x/2 \lg g)^2) = O((x \lg g)^2)$.

Here we are in a kind of conundrum because we have arrived at two different complexity measures. Which of the two then holds? Is the complexity $O(\lg x)$, or $O((x \lg g)^2)$? The answer depends on what we want to include in our estimates. $O(\lg x)$ is the number of iterations. If we care about the complexity of multiplications that need to be carried out by multiple-precision arithmetic, then we use $O((x \lg g)^2)$.

Recall now that we want an efficient way to carry out modular exponentiation; this is just a short step from algorithm 4.3. Thanks to the arithmetic properties of the modulo operator, we can take the modulo each time we calculate c and r. This leads to algorithm 4.4, modular exponentiation by repeated

Table 4.10

Modular exponentiation by repeated squaring: 155^{235} mod 391.

$c = g^{2^i} = 155^{2^i}$ mod 391	r	d
155	1	11101011
174	155	1110101
169	382	111010
18	382	11101
324	292	1110
188	229	111
154	42	11
256	232	1
	314	

squaring. This is the same algorithm as before, but we perform all our multiplications modulo the divisor p. An example of the algorithm in action is in table 4.10; it is rather impressive that we can calculate a number such as 155^{235} mod 391 with only a few multiplications and without having to deal with any large numbers anywhere. The loop of lines 4–8 is executed $\lg x$ times; if we do not care about the time taken up by the multiplication in line 6 and the squaring in line 8, the complexity of the algorithm is $O(\lg x)$. But we may care about the time taken by them because they may involve multiple-precision arithmetic. Again, because line 6 is executed fewer times than line 8 and r is less than c, we only need to examine line 8. Also, because of the modulo operator, we have $c < p$. The squaring of a number with $\lg p$ digits can be performed, as we saw, in $O((\lg p)^2)$ time. This gives us an overall complexity of $O(\lg x(\lg p)^2)$. If we assume that $x \leq p$, then we get $O((\lg p)^3)$.

Notes

Cryptography has a long and fascinating history. An excellent account has been given by David Kahn [104]. Another popular history of codes and codebreaking has been written by Simon Singh [187]. Philip Zimmermann's first quote comes from a piece he wrote as part of the original PGP User's Guide [224]; PGP (Pretty Good Privacy) was the first strong cryptographic application available to the public at large. His second quote is from an audio interview with *The Guardian* [225].

Peter Norvig's results containing letter frequencies are published at http://norvig.com/mayzner.html.

For more information on the design of AES, you can check the design of Rijndael as documented by it creators [46]. Details on how to implement AES on a specific architecture can be found in [74]. AES has been published by the National Institute of Standards and Technology [206]. Public key cryptography first became publicly known with the groundbreaking paper by Whitfield Diffie and Martin Hellman [50].

Bruce Schneier has written many books on cryptography and privacy. His *Applied Cryptography* is a classic in the field [174]; see also [63] for a higher-level treatment. The textbook by Katz and Lindell covers many aspects of cryptography, combining theoretical and practical considerations [105]. A trusty companion to cryptographers and computer scientists has been the *Handbook of Applied Cryptography* [137], which is freely available online.

If you are interested in understanding the mathematical concepts behind cryptography, see [153]. A comprehensive description of the theoretical foundations is the two-volume work by Oded Goldreich [79, 80]. A deep understanding of cryptography requires a good knowledge of number theory; Silverman's introduction is a good place to start [186].

According to Knuth [113, pp. 461–462], the idea evaluating powers by repeated squaring is ancient, having appeared before 200 BCE in India. The modular exponentiation algorithm we use was published in 1427 CE in Persia.

In 1994, Peter Shor presented an algorithm that solves the discrete logarithm problem in polynomial time (the algorithm was published in journal form in 1997) [185]. For an introduction to quantum computing, see [151].

Exercises

1. Implement a program for decrypting ciphertexts produced by substitution ciphers. Use the frequency tables available on the Internet. For guessing words, you can use word lists. These are available as spelling dictionaries in operating systems, or you can also find them online.

2. Implement a one-time pad encryption and decryption program. Make it work on two different modes: one that encrypts and decrypts using arithmetic modulo operations, and one that encrypts and decrypts using XOR. Measure the performance of each mode of operation.

3. To appreciate how AES works, it is a good idea to work out how it alters a message in just a single round. Follow the evolution of the AES state for a

single round where all the input bits are zero. Do the same with all the input bits apart from the last set to zero.

4.   Write a program that, given a prime p, finds primitive elements for its multiplicative group. To do that you can pick a random number from $2, 3, \ldots, p - 1$ and check whether it is a generator. Generators are not very rare, so you should be able to come across them.

5.   Implement the exponentiation by repeated squaring in two ways. First, use standard division and modulo operators, as provided by the language of your choice. Then, use the bitwise AND and the right shift operators. Measure the performance of each implementation.

5   Split Secrets

Imagine that you run a company called Super Trustworthy Boxes (STB). Your company has developed a novel kind of safe box. Normal safe boxes come with a lock and a key. STB boxes come with a lock and two keys. The two keys are made in such a way that if you lock the box with one of the two, you can only unlock it with the other.

What is the advantage your product has compared to traditional safe boxes? If somebody, let's call her Alice, wants to send something to somebody else, let's call him Bob, she may put it in a traditional safe box, and send it over to Bob. Nobody can break the box on the way, and only Bob can open it, provided that he has a copy of the key. That is a problem because you cannot send the key along with the box; somebody along the way, let's call her Eve (for eavesdropper), would just open the box with the key. You must find a way to give the key to Bob so that nobody else gets it.

Enter STB safe boxes. Alice can send the box to Bob, along with the second key. She keeps the first key secret. Bob puts his message in the box, locks it, and sends it back to Alice. Only Alice has the first key, and she has neither shared it with anybody nor sent it to Bob. So only Alice can unlock the box and recover Bob's message.

Moreover, STB safe boxes allow your clients some extra functionality. Alice can put a message in the box and lock it using the first key. She sends the box to Bob along with the second key. Bob can open it knowing that only somebody who has the first key could have locked it. If he knows that the first key belongs to Alice, he can be sure that Alice, and not anybody else, was the sender of the box.

5.1   Public Key Cryptography

From the analog to the digital world, and specifically to cryptography. When you want to keep a message, you encrypt your message using a key, and the recipient of the message uses a key to decrypt the message. Note that we used the expression "a key" and not "the key." If the two keys, for encryption and decryption, are identical, then the encryption is symmetric. But that is not necessary. You can imagine a scheme, like the one we described for STB, where different keys are used. This is *asymmetric cryptography*. It works by having two keys, one used for encryption and one used for decryption. For the scheme to work, one of the keys is *public* and the other is *private*. Alice will always keep her private key secret, but she can give away the public key. Anyone can use Alice's public key to encrypt a message. Only Alice, however, can decrypt the message because only she has the corresponding private key. Because one key is public, the whole approach is called *public key cryptography*.

Public key cryptography solves the key distribution problem, that is, the problem of how Alice and Bob can exchange a key to encrypt their messages. Simply, they need not do that at all. Bob can use Alice's public key to encrypt messages to Alice, which she can decrypt using her private key. Alice can use Bob's public key to encrypt messages to Bob, which he can decrypt using his private key. Keys come in pairs, so we can call $P(A)$ the public key of pair A and $S(A)$ the secret key of pair A. Only one private key corresponds to a public key, so each key pair is unique. If M is the original plaintext message, then the operation of encrypting the message using the public key $P(A)$ is

$$C = E_{P(A)}(M)$$

The reverse operation of decrypting the message encrypted with the public key $P(A)$ using its secret counterpart $S(A)$ is

$$M = D_{S(A)}(C)$$

The encryption process follows directly from the above.

1. Bob generates a key pair $B = (P(B), S(B))$.

2. Alice gets Bob's public key $P(B)$. This may happen in a number of ways. For example, Bob may publish it in some public server, or send it to Alice directly via e-mail.

3. Alice encrypts her message M using $P(B)$:
   $C = E_{P(B)}(M)$.

4. Alice sends C to Bob.

5. Bob decrypts C using his secret key:
   $M = D_{S(B)}(C)$.

The fact that only one secret key corresponds to a public key means that, like Alice locking the safe box, we can also use the secret, private key to encrypt a message:

$$C = E_{S(A)}(M)$$

The resulting encrypted message can only be decrypted with the corresponding public key:

$$M = D_{P(A)}(C)$$

Why should anybody want to do that? Because the public key corresponds to only a single private key, Bob can be sure that the message he received has been encrypted by the owner of the private key. So if he knows that the owner is Alice, then he knows that the message he received comes from Alice. Thus, encrypting with the private key and decrypting with the public key is a way to prove where the message comes from. It is equivalent to what we do when we sign a sheet of paper. Because our signature is unique, anybody who knows our signature can verify that we have signed the sheet of paper. Encrypting with the private key is therefore called *signing the message,* and a message encrypted with a private key is a *digital signature.* Overall the signing process proceeds in a way analogous to encryption.

1. Alice generates a key pair $A = (P(A), S(A))$. She distributes $P(A)$ to Bob in any convenient way.

2. Alice signs her message M with her secret key $S(A)$:
   $C = E_{S(A)}(M)$.

3. Alice sends (M, C) to Bob.

4. Bob verifies C using Alice's public key $P(A)$:
   $M \stackrel{?}{=} D_{P(A)}(C)$.

To recap, in public key cryptography, each participant has a set of two keys instead of a single one. One key can be shared with anybody or put in a public repository. The other key must be kept secret. Anybody can use the public key to encrypt a message, which can be decrypted only using the private key. If an eavesdropper, say Eve, listens to the communications between Alice and Bob, she can get only the public keys and encrypted messages, so she cannot decrypt the underlying plaintext, as you can check in figure 5.1. In addition, we can use the private key to encrypt a message, that is, to sign a message. Anybody can get the public key and confirm that the message has been signed using the private key. If they know the owner of the private key, they know the owner has signed it.

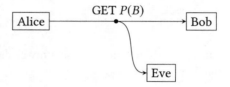

(a) Alice asks Bob for his public key.

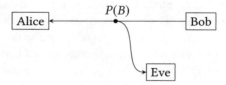

(b) Bob sends his public key to Alice.

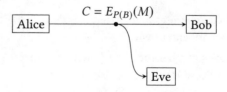

(c) Alice sends Bob her encrypted message.

Figure 5.1
Public key encryption between Alice and Bob.

Having the two operations, encryption and signing, you can combine them so that you can both encrypt a message and sign it. First, you sign the message using your private key. Then you encrypt the message and the signature with your recipient's public key. The recipient first decrypts the encrypted message using the corresponding private key, getting the plaintext message and the signature. Then the recipient decrypts the signature message with your public key and verifies it matches the decrypted plaintext message. Alice and Bob would perform the following steps:

1. Alice generates a key pair $A = (P(A), S(A))$. She distributes $P(A)$ to Bob in any convenient way.

2. Bob generates a key pair $B = (P(B), S(B))$. He distributes $P(B)$ to Alice in any convenient way.

3. Alice signs her message M with her secret key $S(A)$:
   $C_1 = E_{S(A)}(M)$.

4. Alice encrypts her message and the signature she calculated, that is, (M, C_1), using Bob's public key $P(B)$:
   $C_2 = E_{P(B)}(M, C_1)$.

5. Alice sends C_2 to Bob.

6. Bob decrypts C_2 using his secret key:
   $(M, C_1) = D_{S(B)}(C_2)$.

7. Bob verifies C_1 using Alice's public key $P(A)$:
   $M \stackrel{?}{=} D_{P(A)}(C_1)$.

To complete the picture, we now need to see how these encryptions, decryptions, and signings really take place. They follow straightforward processes based on results obtained from number theory.

5.2   The RSA Cryptosystem

One of the first public key cryptosystems to be used in practice, and in wide use today, is the RSA cryptosystem. The name comes from its inventors, Ron Rivest, Adi Shamir, and Leonard Adleman, who first published the system in 1977, although it had been independently discovered earlier, in 1973 by Clifford Cocks working for the UK Government General Communications Headquarters (GCHQ); Cock's work was classified, however, until 1997. We saw in section 4.4 that the same thing happened with the Diffie-Hellman key exchange mechanism, which had been discovered by Malcolm Williamson at GCHQ before Diffie and Hellman. In fact, Cocks's discovery came first.

Williamson was his friend and learned his discovery, which prompted him to go on and develop the Diffie-Hellman key exchange.

RSA provides a method to generate a public-private key pair. Before we go into the steps of the method, a definition is required. If two numbers are prime between them, that is, if they have no divisors in common apart from 1, then they are called *relatively prime*, or *coprime*. With that definition in place, RSA comprises the following series of steps.

1. Choose two large prime numbers, say p and q for which $p \neq q$.

2. Calculate their product, $n = pq$.

3. Choose an integer e that is relatively prime to $(p - 1)(q - 1)$.

4. Find a number d, $1 \leq d < (p - 1)(q - 1)$ such that:

$$(e \cdot d) \bmod [(p - 1)(q - 1)] = 1$$

5. The public-private key pair is $A = (P(A), S(A)) = ((e, n), (d, n))$.

6. The tuple $P(A) = (e, n)$ is your RSA public key.

7. The tuple $S(A) = (d, n)$ is your RSA private key.

We have to explain how we select d in step 4. We will see how, but first let's see how RSA works in practice.

We said that the two numbers p and q should be large. The larger, the better, but the larger, the more computational effort is required for encryption and decryption. There is no reason, however, why they should not be 2048 bits each, and 4096 is better.

There is no such size requirement for e; it can even be equal to 3. A popular choice is $e = 2^{16} + 1 = 65537$; this number has some good properties that make it more unlikely to break messages encrypted with RSA using it.

Both encryption and decryption use the same function:

$$f(m, k, n) = m^k \bmod n$$

The arguments passed to the function are different in encryption and decryption, however. So when encrypting, m is the plaintext message and k is equal to e from the public key of the participant. In decryption, m is the ciphertext and k is equal to d from the private key of the participant.

In other words, with this scheme, encryption of a message M is done by computing the ciphertext C of M using:

$$C = E_{P(A)}(M) = M^e \bmod n$$

Decryption of a ciphertext C is done by computing:

$$M = D_{S(A)}(C) = C^d \bmod n$$

Signing a message is

$$C = E_{S(A)}(M) = M^d \bmod n$$

and the verification of the signature is

$$D_{P(A)}(C) = C^e \bmod n$$

Because for any integers u, v, it holds:

$$(u \bmod n)(v \bmod n) \bmod n = uv \bmod n$$

decryption is:

$$M = D_{S(A)}(C) = C^d \bmod n = (M^e \bmod n)^d \bmod n = M^{ed} \bmod n$$

and similarly signature verification is:

$$D_{P(A)}(C) = C^e \bmod n = (M^d \bmod n)^e \bmod n = M^{de} \bmod n$$

You can see that in fact they calculate the same thing, as they should. When you decrypt an encrypted message, you get the plaintext back. When you verify a signature, you get again the original message back. The only thing that changes is the sequence of applying the keys. In encryption and decryption, first the public key is applied and then the private key. In signing and verifying, first the private key is applied and then the public key.

Now suppose Alice wants to encrypt a message M. If p and q are 2048 bits each, then $p - 1$ and $q - 1$ must be 2047 bits each, and n must be $2047 + 2047 = 4094$. Therefore, M must be less than 4094 bits long. If it is not, then Alice must break M to chunks less than 4094 bits each. Alice knows Bob's public key $P = (e, n)$. To send M to Bob, Alice will compute C as above, and Bob will receive C and decrypt it.

For the calculations to work, the plaintext message M must be an integer number. That does not limit the usefulness of RSA. A text message in a computer is actually a series of bits, encoding the text via a suitable encoding, such as ASCII. We then break the text in chunks of bits of the required length. The decimal value of a chunk is the number M.

You can verify that RSA actually works with an example. Bob wants to encrypt the message $M = 314$ and send it to Alice.

1. Alice takes $p = 17$ and $q = 23$.

2. Alice calculates $n = pq = 17 \times 23 = 391$.

3. She chooses $e = 3$. You can check that e is relatively prime to

$$(p - 1)(q - 1) = (17 - 1)(23 - 1) = 16 \times 22 = 352$$

4. Alice finds $d = 235$, which satisfies $1 \leq d < 352$ and
    $(e \cdot d) \bmod [(p - 1)(q - 1)] = 1$,
    or equivalently $(3 \times 235) \bmod 352 = 1$.

5. The public-private key pair is $A = ((3, 391), (235, 391))$.
    The tuple $P(A) = (3, 391)$ is the RSA public key.
    The tuple $S(A) = (235, 391)$ is the RSA private key.

6. Bob gets $P(A)$ from Alice and encrypts M with the operation:

$$C = M^e \bmod n = 314^3 \bmod 391 = 155$$

7. Bob sends C to Alice.

8. Alice decrypts C with the operation:

$$C^d \bmod n = 155^{235} \bmod 391 = 314$$

which is the original plaintext message.

If an expression like $155^{235} \bmod 391 = 314$ seems forbidding, you can see exactly how it can be computed efficiently in table 4.10 of section 4.5.

That is fine, but step 4 remains a mystery. To arrive at how d is found, we need some background material from number theory. We know that the *multiplicative inverse*, or *reciprocal*, of a number x, is the number $1/x$ or x^{-1} such that $xx^{-1} = 1$. In modular arithmetic, the *modular multiplicative inverse* of an integer x modulo n $(n > 0)$ is the integer x^{-1}, $1 \leq x^{-1} \leq n - 1$, such that $xx^{-1} \bmod n = 1$. That is equivalent to $xx^{-1} = kn + 1$, or $1 = xx^{-1} - kn$, for some integer k. So when in step 4 we find the number d, $1 \leq d < (p - 1)(q - 1)$, so that $(e \cdot d) \bmod [(p - 1)(q - 1)] = 1$, we are really finding the modular multiplicative inverse of e modulo $(p - 1)(q - 1)$, for which it holds:

$$1 = ed + k(p - 1)(q - 1)$$

for some integer k. That follows directly from $1 = xx^{-1} - kn$, with a different sign before k, which does not matter because k is just an integer, so that we can take its negative. In the realm of real numbers, we can always find the inverse of any number $x \neq 0$. But how do we find the modular inverse? Moreover, does a modular inverse always exist?

The modular multiplicative inverse of x modulo n exists if and only if x and n are coprime. That is why when we picked e we insisted that it should be coprime with $(p - 1)(q - 1)$. With such an e, we know there is a d with the properties we want. We need to see how we can find it.

The *greatest common divisor* (gcd) of two integers is the greatest integer that divides them both. To find the gcd of two positive integers, we use a venerable algorithm, found in Euclid's *Elements*, shown in algorithm 5.1. Euclid's algorithm follows from the fact the gcd of two integers $a > 0$ and $b > 0$ is the gcd of b and the remainder of the division of a by b, unless b divides a, in which case, by definition, the gcd is b itself. Algorithm 5.1 works by making recursive calls, substituting b and $a \bmod b$ for a and b in each call (line 4). The recursion stops when $b = 0$ (lines 1–2), where b is the result of $a \bmod b$ of the previous recursion call.

The proof that a and $a \bmod b$ have the same gcd relies on the basic properties of division. If d is a common divisor of a and b, then $a = k_1 d$ and $b = k_2 d$, for some positive integers k_1, k_2. Also, if $r = a \bmod b$, we have $r = a - k_3 b$ for some positive integer k_3. Substituting the values for a and b, we get $r = k_1 d - k_3 k_2 d = (k_1 - k_3 k_2)d$, so d divides r, which means that all the divisors of a and b are also divisors of b and $a \bmod b$.

Conversely, if d is a common divisor of both b and $r = a \bmod b$, then $b = z_1 d$ and $r = z_2 d$, for some positive integers z_1, z_2. At the same time, we have $a = z_3 b + r$ for some positive integer z_3. Substituting the values for r and b, we get $a = z_3 z_1 d + z_2 d = (z_3 z_1 + z_2)d$, so d divides a, which means that all the divisors of b and $a \bmod b$ are also divisors of a and b. Hence, a and b have exactly the same divisors with b and $a \bmod b$, and then they must have the same greatest common divisor.

Table 5.1 shows an example of the operation of Euclid's algorithm to determine the gcd of 160 and 144, which you can see is 16. Each row of the table shows what happens in each recursive call. It can be shown that, if $a > b$, the number of recursive calls required by the algorithm is $O(\lg b)$. If $b > a$, then it is $O(\lg a)$. That is because the first call just reverses a and b: trace the operation of the algorithm to determine the gdc of 144 and 160 to see that.

A generalization of Euclid's algorithm, the extended Euclid's algorithm, can be used to find, apart from the gcd of two positive integers, the way we can get

---

Algorithm 5.1: Euclid's algorithm.

Euclid(a, b) → d
  Input: a, b, positive integers
  Output: d, the greatest common divisor of a and b

1   **if** $b = 0$ **then**
2   **return** a
3   **else**
4   **return** Euclid(b, a mod b)

Table 5.1

Example run of Euclid's algorithm.

a	b	a mod b
160	144	16
144	16	0
16	0	

the gcd of these numbers by combining them with multiplication and addition. Specifically, if $r = \gcd(a, b)$, then we can find integers x and y such that:

$$r = \gcd(a, b) = xa + yb$$

The extended Euclid's algorithm is algorithm 5.2, and it is the key in finding modular multiplicative inverses. The number of recursive calls is again $O(\lg b)$, if $a > b$, or $O(\lg a)$, if $a < b$. It can be proven that:

$$|x| \leq \frac{b}{\gcd(a, b)} \quad \text{and} \quad |y| \leq \frac{a}{\gcd(a, b)}$$

where the equality holds when a is a multiple of b, or b is a multiple of a. If a and b are relatively prime, then we have $\gcd(a, b) = 1$. That means we can use the extended Euclid's algorithm to find two integers x and y such that:

$$1 = xa + yb \quad \text{with } |x| < b \text{ and } |y| < a$$

This in turn means that if $0 < x < b$, then x is the multiplicative inverse of a modulo b. If $x < 0$, then by adding and deleting ab to the above formula we get $1 = xa + ab + yb - ab = (x + b)a + (y - a)b$, with $0 < x + b < b$. So if $x < 0$, then the multiplicative inverse of a modulo b is $x + b$.

Algorithm 5.2: Extended Euclid's algorithm.

ExtendedEuclid(a, b) $\rightarrow$ (r, x, y)
    Input: a, b, positive integers
    Output: r, x, y, such that $r = \gcd(a, b) = xa + yb$

1   **if** $b = 0$ **then**
2   **return** $(a, 1, 0)$
3   **else**
4       $(r, x, y) =$ ExtendedEuclid(b, $a \bmod b$)
5   **return** $(r, y, x - \lfloor a/b \rfloor \cdot y)$

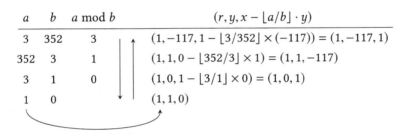

a	b	$a \bmod b$	$(r, y, x - \lfloor a/b \rfloor \cdot y)$
3	352	3	$(1, -117, 1 - \lfloor 3/352 \rfloor \times (-117)) = (1, -117, 1)$
352	3	1	$(1, 1, 0 - \lfloor 352/3 \rfloor \times 1) = (1, 1, -117)$
3	1	0	$(1, 0, 1 - \lfloor 3/1 \rfloor \times 0) = (1, 0, 1)$
1	0		$(1, 1, 0)$

Figure 5.2
Example run of the extended Euclid's algorithm.

Algorithm 5.3 shows the procedure of finding the modular multiplicative inverse in algorithmic form. You may notice that if the extended Euclid's algorithm returns a gcd different from 1, then the modular multiplicative inverse does not exist, so we return zero, which is an invalid value.

An example run of the extended Euclid's algorithm for the numbers 3 and 352, which are relatively prime, is in figure 5.2. To read this table you must read columns a, b, and $a \bmod b$ from the top to the bottom, and then the last column from the bottom to the top, as this is the way the triplet (r, x, y) is constructed at the return of each recursive call. At the end of the algorithm we have:

$$1 = 3 \times (-117) + 352 \times 1$$

which you can verify is true. Therefore, the multiplicative inverse of 3 modulo 352 is $-117 + 352 = 235$. That is the value of d that we used in the RSA example above.

Algorithm 5.3: Modular inverse algorithm.

ModularInverse(a, n) $\rightarrow r$
    Input: a, n, positive integers; n is the modulus
    Output: r, such that $r = a^{-1}$ mod n, if it exists, or 0 otherwise

1   $(r, x, y) = $ ExtendedEuclid(a, n)
2   **if** $r \neq 1$ **then**
3   **return** 0
4   **else if** $x < 0$ **then**
5   **return** $x + n$
6   **else**
7   **return** x

In summary, to find the number d of the secret RSA key, we need to find the multiplicative inverse modulo $(p-1)(q-1)$ of e. To do that, we use the extended Euclid's algorithm with input e and $(p-1)(q-1)$. The output is a triplet $(1, x, y)$. If $x > 0$, x is the number we are looking for. If $x < 0$, $x + (p-1)(q-1)$ is the number we are looking for.

We have now explained how the different steps of RSA are implemented; the question that remains is why RSA works in the first place. We need some more number theory for that. For any positive integer n, the number of integers k with $1 \leq k \leq n$ such that k and n are coprime is the value of a function, called *Euler's totient function* or *Euler's phi function* and symbolized as $\varphi(n)$. If n is a prime, then it is relatively prime with all smaller positive natural numbers, so for n prime we have $\varphi(n) = n - 1$.

In RSA, we use $p - 1 = \varphi(p)$ and $q - 1 = \varphi(q)$. When two numbers p and q are coprime, $\varphi(pq) = \varphi(p)\varphi(q) = (p-1)(q-1)$. Both p and q are prime and therefore coprime, which means that in step 3 we choose an integer e that is relatively prime to $\varphi(pq) = \varphi(n)$. In fact, we could have substituted $\varphi(n)$ for the more cumbersome $(p-1)(q-1)$ in our presentation.

Euler's phi function appears in Euler's theorem, which states that for any n that is a positive integer, and any $0 < a < n$, $a^{\varphi(n)}$ mod $n = 1$. A special case of Euler's theorem arises when n is prime. If we use p to stand for such n, we have a^{p-1} mod $p = 1$. This is called Fermat's Little Theorem, to distinguish it from the other Fermat's Theorem, known as Fermat's Last Theorem, which baffled mathematicians for centuries.

Back to RSA, where to show that it works we must verify that indeed the result of the decryption is the original message. Because signing and verifying is the same with encryption and decryption, we only need to prove encryption and decryption. Because we have:

$$D_{S(A)}(C) = C^d \bmod n = (M^e \bmod n)^d \bmod n = M^{ed} \bmod n$$

we must show that:

$$M^{ed} \bmod n = M \bmod n = M$$

First, consider the case that $M = 0$. Then we have:

$$M^{ed} \bmod n = 0^{ed} \bmod n = 0 \bmod p = 0 = M$$

so we are done; we still have to show that it holds if $M \neq 0$. If $M \neq 0$ and p is prime, then from Fermat's Little Theorem $M^{p-1} \bmod p = 1$. Recall that:

$$1 \doteq ed + k(p-1)(q-1)$$

for some integer k, or equivalently :

$$ed = 1 + k'(p-1)(q-1)$$

by using $k' = -k$. So we get:

$$
\begin{aligned}
M^{ed} \bmod p &= M^{1+k'(p-1)(q-1)} \bmod p \\
&= MM^{k'(n-1)(p-1)} \bmod p \\
&= [(M \bmod p)((M^{p-1})^{k'(q-1)} \bmod p)] \bmod p \\
&= [(M \bmod p)((M^{p-1} \bmod p)^{k'(q-1)} \bmod p)] \bmod p \\
&= [(M \bmod p)((1 \bmod p)^{k'(q-1)} \bmod p)] \bmod p \\
&= [(M \bmod p)(1^{k'(q-1)} \bmod p)] \bmod p \\
&= M \bmod p
\end{aligned}
$$

In exactly the same way, using the fact that from Fermat's Little Theorem $M^{q-1} \bmod q = 1$ we have:

$$M^{ed} \bmod q = M \bmod q$$

That is why we worked with the product $(p-1)(q-1)$: we use Fermat's Little Theorem with $p-1$ and $q-1$. Now from another theorem of number theory, the Chinese Remainder Theorem, published by the Chinese mathematician Sun Tzu somewhere in the 3rd to 5th century CE, given that we have found:

$$M^{ed} \bmod p = M \bmod p$$

and:

$$M^{ed} \bmod q = M \bmod q$$

we get:

$$M^{ed} \bmod pq = M \bmod pq$$

But $pq = n$, so:

$$M^{ed} \bmod n = M \bmod n = M$$

which is what we wanted to show.

RSA solves the key distribution problem and has been analyzed for years. Its security rests on the difficulty of *prime factorization*. A *factor* of a number is an integer that divides the number without leaving a remainder. A *prime factor* is a factor that is also a prime. Prime factorization is finding the prime factors of a number and expressing it as a product of them. The current known algorithms to solve the problem are computationally very intensive, so it takes an awful amount of time to factor a large integer. In our case, given n it is very difficult to find the numbers p and q. If you had an efficient prime factorization method at your disposal, then you would just use it to find the numbers p and q; since e is public you would calculate yourself d as in step 4 of RSA, and you would have the private key.

Of course somebody could just start checking all positive integers less then n hoping to find its factors; it is for this reason that it is important that p and q should be large. As in Diffie-Hellman, we do not search blindly for primes; we can use algorithms to find the primes we need. section 16.4 shows an efficient prime finding method.

RSA is potentially vulnerable to advances in quantum computation, as it is possible to carry out factorization in polynomial time on a quantum computer. For the time being, though, RSA is secure.

As long as RSA remains secure and solves the key distribution problem, you may ask why we still use symmetric cryptography at all. You could encrypt any message using RSA anyway. The answer is that RSA is much slower than symmetric cryptography like AES. So usually RSA is used in a hybrid way. In such a system, participants use RSA to negotiate a key that they use then with AES, instead of doing so with the Diffie-Hellman key exchange:

1. Alice, who wants to send a long message M to Bob, in which case RSA would be slow, selects a random key K that she will use with a symmetric cipher such as AES.

2. Alice encrypts K with Bob's public key:
    $C_K = E_{P(B)}(K)$.

3. Alice encrypts M using K with AES:
    $C_M = E_{AES(K)}(M)$.

4. Alice sends (C_K, C_M) to Bob.

5. Bob decrypts the message C_K, which contains the AES key, using his private key:
    $K = D_{S(B)}(C_K)$.

6. Bob uses the key K to decrypt the message M:
    $M = D_{AES(K)}(C_M)$.

In this way we combine the best of both worlds: we leverage RSA to obtain a secure secret key for our communication and then AES to encrypt the bulk of our data. Instead of RSA we could use the Diffie-Hellman key exchange for the same purpose. Both methods are popular. If we want to both sign and encrypt with the same method, however, then we go for RSA.

5.3   Message Hashing

The same concern about speed applies to digital signing as well. It may be slow to sign the entire message M if the message is long. Alice can then sign a *digital fingerprint*, or simply *fingerprint*, of the message. A fingerprint of a message is a short piece of identifying data that we get by applying a special fast function $h(M)$ to the message. It is also called a *message digest*. The function is such that from any message it produces a sequence of bits, of a small fixed size, say 256 bits. The function is called a *hash function*; for this reason the fingerprint may also be called *message hash*. We also require that it is very difficult to find two messages with the same fingerprint, that is, M and M' such that $h(M) = h(M')$. We call hash functions with this property *collision-resistant hash functions*. In this way the fingerprint identifies the message because it is difficult to forge another message with the same fingerprint. Alice will sign M by going through the sequence of steps below.

1. Alice calculates the fingerprint of M:
    $H = h(M)$.

2. Alice signs the fingerprint of M:
   $C = E_{S(A)}(H)$.

3. Alice sends $(M, C = E_{S(A)}(H))$ to Bob.

4. Bob computes $H = h(M)$ himself.

5. Bob verifies that the signature he received comes from Alice:
   $H \stackrel{?}{=} D_{P(A)}(C)$.

6. Bob verifies that the fingerprint he calculated in step 4 is the same with the signature he verified in step 5.

Of course it is impossible not to have collisions, that is, different messages having the same fingerprint. For example, if messages are 10 Kbytes long, then there are 2^{80000} possible messages because 10 Kbytes have 10,000 bytes or 80,000 bits. The hash function maps these 2^{80000} messages to a much lower number of possible fingerprints. If it produces digests that are 256 bits long, then the number of possible fingerprints is 2^{256}. Thus, theoretically there is an extremely high number of collisions: $2^{80000}/2^{256} = 2^{79744}$. However, in practice we will only encounter a small minority of the theoretically possible 2^{80000} messages; we will want to sign the messages in this minority only. We want $h(M)$ to be highly unlikely to map two of them to the same fingerprint, and it turns out there are such functions, but we must be careful to choose one that the research community has judged resistant enough against collisions.

We should note that the term *hash* is overloaded and means many related, yet distinct, things; *hashing* is an important technique for storing and retrieving data. We will explore this hashing in chapter 13. In general, a hash function is a function that maps data of arbitrary size to data of a fixed, much smaller size. Good hash functions are collision-resistant. The hash functions we use for digital signatures and fingerprinting have the added property that they are one-way functions: given the output of the hash function, it is not possible to derive the input data that was given to the hash function. Such a hash function is called a *cryptographic hash function*. A cryptographic hash function with a good security record in widespread use is SHA-2 (Secure Hash Standard-2).

5.4   Internet Traffic Anonymization

The combination of symmetric and public key cryptography can solve other problems as well. One example, which combines RSA, AES, and the Diffie-Hellman key exchange, involves the anonymization of Internet traffic. This is an instance of a more general problem involving the encryption not just of data but also of *metadata*. Metadata refers not to the data itself but to data related to the data. In a telephone communication, metadata comprises the identities of the persons making the call and the date and time of the call. In the Internet, metadata on the traffic may refer not to the actual information that is transferred but to the details of the parties involved in the communication. If Alice sends an e-mail to Bob, the contents of the e-mail message are the data; the date and time of the e-mail as well as the fact that Alice sends an e-mail to Bob are metadata. If Alice visits a web site, the contents of the web site are the data. The facts that Alice visited the particular web site on a particular date are metadata.

Using Diffie-Hellman or RSA, we can obtain secure private keys with which to encrypt the content of our communications. No eavesdropper will be able to know what Alice tells Bob. But an eavesdropper will know that Alice is talking to Bob, and that in itself may be important. Even if it is not, it may be nobody's business but Alice's and Bob's.

When Alice visits Bob's web site, the information between Alice and Bob travels in packets, hopping from computer to computer, from Alice's computer to Bob's computer and back. Each computer on the way that directs Internet traffic, called *router*, knows that it carries data from Alice to Bob. Even if the communication between them is encrypted, the encryption applies to the contents of the communication, that is, the data. The addresses of Alice and Bob in the packets that transmit the encrypted data are still in plaintext and can be captured by anybody snooping in the computers in between; see figure 5.3 for an example of a message traveling from Alice to Bob routed through three routers.

It is possible to anonymize communication on the Internet by using cryptography with an idea called *onion routing*. It works by encapsulating the packet in a series of layered packets, like an onion, as in figure 5.4. The first router that gets the packet from Alice can only read the outer layer, which gives the address of the next router to which it will forward the packet. The second router will get the packet without the outer layer, and will only be able to read the new outer layer (that is, the second layer of the initial layered

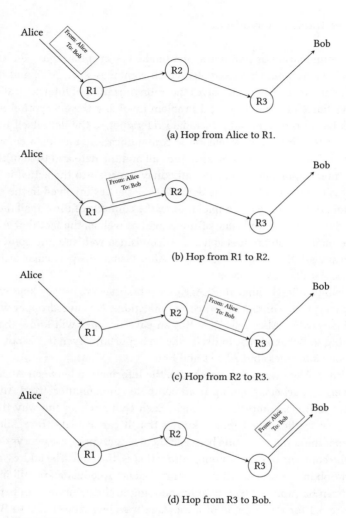

(a) Hop from Alice to R1.

(b) Hop from R1 to R2.

(c) Hop from R2 to R3.

(d) Hop from R3 to Bob.

Figure 5.3
Message traveling from Alice to Bob.

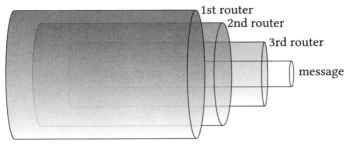

Figure 5.4
A layered packet for onion routing.

packet). This will give the second router the address of the third router to
which it will forward the packet. The same process, stripping another layer,
will take place in the third router, and so on until the packet reaches Bob.

Notice now that the first router only knows that it got a packet from Alice to
the second router. The second router only knows that it got a packet from the
first router to the third router. Bob will only know that it got a packet from
some router. Nobody knows, apart from Alice, that the packet was initially
sent from Alice to Bob.

How does Alice create the onion layered packet, and how does she create
the route to Bob without the intermediate routers knowing about it? A well-
known onion router is Tor (short for The onion router), which works roughly
as follows.

Tor consists of a number of intermediate routers that are available to Alice.
First, Alice picks the set of intermediate routers that she will use. These are
called Onion Routers (ORs). Suppose she picks three ORs: OR_1, OR_2, OR_3.
Alice wants her message to travel through the route Alice $\rightarrow OR_1 \rightarrow OR_2 \rightarrow$
$OR_3 \rightarrow$ Bob. Only Alice will know that route. The message will travel from
router to router, with layers of encryption getting peeled off at each router.
You can see an illustration in figure 5.5, where we assume that Tor comprises
OR_{n3} onion routers arranged nicely as a matrix; the true Tor topology of
course is not like that and changes as onion routers are added or removed
through time. She may choose different routers next time she wants to communicate with Bob, so that it will not be possible to track her communications
over time.

Alice starts by communicating with OR_1 using RSA and sending instructions on how to set up the communications routing. As this is a packet with

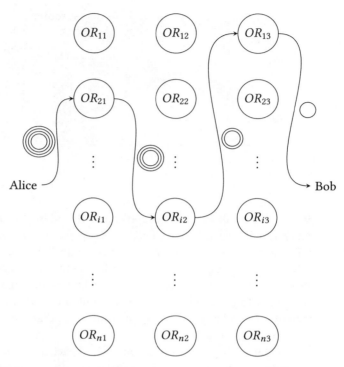

Figure 5.5
Alice sending a message to Bob through onion routers.

which Alice commands OR_1 to do certain things, we can think of it as a command packet. It contains her part of a Diffie-Hellman key exchange with OR_1. In addition, it contains a command that tells OR_1 that she will be tagging her packets with a special ID she picks, called a *circuit id*, say C_1. Let us call this command packet a CreateHop(C_1, g^{x1}) packet, abbreviating the Diffie-Hellman part in our notation. OR_1 replies with its part of the Diffie-Hellman key exchange. All messages that Alice will be sending to OR_1 will be encrypted with the key they established, say DH_1.

Next Alice communicates again with OR_1 and tells it that from now on she wants OR_1 to forward all messages from her to OR_2. To do that she sends a command packet to OR_1 with the command to extend the route and her part of a new Diffie-Hellman key exchange. The Diffie-Hellman part is encrypted with the RSA public key of OR_2. The whole packet is encrypted with DH_1. Let us call that command packet an ExtendRoute(OR_2, g^{x2}) packet. When OR_1 gets the packet it decrypts it. It then creates a new CreateHop(C_2, g^{x2}) packet that it sends to OR_2. The command packet contains the Diffie-Hellman part from Alice to OR_2, and tells OR_2 that it will be tagging packets with another circuit ID, say C_2. It tells that to OR_2, without telling it that the messages will be coming from Alice. OR_1 records the fact that packets tagged with C_1 will be sent to OR_2, and packets received from OR_2 tagged with C_2 will be passed back to Alice. OR_1 passes back the Diffie-Hellman response it receives from OR_2 to Alice, so Alice and OR_2 share a Diffie-Hellman key, DH_2.

To create the route to OR_3, Alice creates an ExtendRoute(OR_3, g^{x3}) command packet to extend the route from OR_2 to OR_3. The packet contains her part of a Diffie-Hellman key she wants to establish with OR_3. The Diffie-Hellman part is encrypted with the RSA public key of OR_3. The whole packet is encrypted with DH_2 and then encrypted on top with DH_1. Alice sends the packet to OR_1. When OR_1 gets the packet, it is able to decrypt the first layer only. OR_1 knows that cells tagged with C_1 must be forwarded to the destination associated with C_2, OR_2, but it does not know its contents. It tags the packet with C_2 and forwards the packet with one layer peeled off to OR_2.

OR_2 gets the packet from OR_1 and decrypts it using DH_2, retrieving ExtendRoute(OR_3, g^{x3}). It follows the same sequence of steps that OR_1 did before, as OR_2 has received a command packet to extend the route and which contains Alice's part of the Diffie-Hellman key exchange with OR_3. It creates and sends a new command packet CreateHop(C_3, g^{x3}) to OR_3. The command packet contains the Diffie-Hellman part from Alice to OR_3 and tells it that it will be tagging packets with another circuit ID, say C_3. OR_3 records the fact that packets tagged with C_2 will be sent to OR_3, and packets received from OR_3 tagged with C_3 will be passed back to Alice. OR_2 passes back the Diffie-Hellman response from OR_3 to Alice via OR_1, so Alice and OR_3 share a Diffie-Hellman key, DH_3.

Now Alice can send her message to Bob knowing that not just the contents, but also the route will be kept secret. To send a message to Bob, Alice creates a packet with her message addressed to Bob encrypted with DH_3, in turn encrypted with DH_2, in turn encrypted with DH_1 and tagged with C_1. The packet goes first to OR_1. Because the packet is tagged with C_1, OR_1 knows it must forward it to OR_2. OR_1 peels off the first layer using DH_1 and forwards it to OR_2, tagged with C_2. OR_2 peels off the second layer using DH_2. It knows that packets tagged with C_2 must be forwarded to OR_3, so it tags it with C_3 and sends it to OR_3.

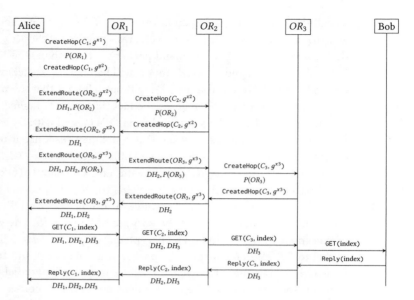

Figure 5.6

A Tor exchange.

OR_3 gets the packet from OR_2 and decrypts it using DH_3. It sees that it is a message addressed to Bob, so it just forwards it there. The response from Bob will follow exactly the reverse route, Bob $\rightarrow OR_3 \rightarrow OR_2 \rightarrow OR_1 \rightarrow$ Alice, encrypted again with DH_1, then DH_2, then DH_3, routed in the same way using C_3, C_2, C_1. You can see the whole interaction in figure 5.6, reading from top to bottom and left to right. Each arrow corresponds to a message. The label above the arrow corresponds to the message contents and the label below corresponds to the encryption that is applied, either Diffie-Hellman or RSA with the public key of the recipient. Alice asks Bob's web server to send her its home page, and Bob replies with that page. To ask for the home page, she must issue a GET request to Bob's server using the Hypertext Transfer Protocol (HTTP), but the details do not concern us here.

Tor also allows the creation of the Diffie-Hellman keys using a newer protocol that does not use RSA; the newer protocol is faster and better but more difficult to describe. Also, all communication between two points in Tor (Alice, Onion Routers, and Bob) uses authentication and encryption protocols. Overall, Tor is robust and a staple for maintaining Internet anonymity.

Notes

For material in cryptography see the notes of the previous chapter. The RSA algorithm was described publicly by Ron Rivest, Adi Shamir, and Leonard Adleman in 1977 and was filed as U.S. Patent 4,405,829. Martin Gardner announced their algorithm in his "Mathematical Games" column in the August 1977 issue of *Scientific American* [75]. RSA was published as a paper one year later [165]. RSA is vulnerable to quantum computers running Shor's algorithm [185], if they are built.

The notion of digital signatures was described by Whitfield Diffie and Martin Hellman in the paper in which they introduced their key-exchange scheme [50], but they did not give an actual signature method. This came with the RSA algorithm. Other signature schemes have been introduced since then. Merkle signatures [138], named after Ralph Merkle, are resistant to quantum computing attacks and are used in file systems to guarantee integrity and in peer to peer protocols, for example, BitTorrent.

SHA-2 (Secure Hash Algorithm 2) is a family of hash functions designed by the National Security Agency (NSA) and released as a standard by the National Institute of Standards and Technology (NIST) [207]. The SHA-2 family comprises hash functions that produce digests, that is, hash values, of 224, 256, 384, or 512 bits and are named SHA-224. SHA-256, SHA-384, and SHA-512, respectively; among them SHA-256 is most popular. In August 2015, NIST published a new cryptographic hash function, SHA-3 [208], not as a replacement of SHA-2 (as it has not been compromised), but as an alternative. The selected algorithm was the winner of a hash function competition organized by NIST. For a rigorous introduction to cryptographic hash functions, see [167].

For a technical description of Tor, see [52]. An earlier discussion of the underlying principles is [81]. Onion routing was initially developed by the U.S. Naval Research Laboratory in the mid-1990s and then by the Defense Advanced Research Projects Agency (DARPA). The Naval Research Laboratory released the Tor code under a free license; the Tor project was then established as a non-profit organization in 2006 to further support and develop Tor.

Exercises

1. Public key encryption has not eclipsed symmetric encryption because it is slower. Find a software library implementing RSA and one implementing AES and compare their performance on messages of different sizes. Make sure that the software libraries are implemented in the same underlying programming language. In particular, scripting languages have pure implementations, written in the scripting language, and implementations that interface to libraries written in a faster, compiled language. It is not fair to compare among them.

2. An application of cryptographic hash functions like SHA-2 is to check that parts data are already stored somewhere. For example, instead of storing a file as a monolithic piece, it is broken into blocks of fixed size. The blocks are stored, retrievable by their SHA-2 hash value. If another file is to be stored that is identical, or similar to the first, then all or many of the blocks will have the same SHA-2 hash values, so only those blocks with hash values that do not match any of those already seen need to be stored. This is the basis of a storage technique called *deduplication* because it removes duplicate blocks. Write a program that takes a file and a block size, breaks the file into blocks, and calculates its SHA-2 hashes.

6   Tasks in Order

A set of tasks that you have to accomplish seldom comes without limitations. The tasks may be related to each other, so that one task cannot be started unless some other task, or tasks, are completed first. Limiting ourselves to personal tasks, we learn at an early age that in order for the kettle to boil, we first have to put water in it and connect its plug to the electricity socket. We may do this task (or rather the kettle will do it for us) in parallel with the task that the toaster will do for us when it is toasting a couple of slices of bread. The production of a cup of coffee, however, needs to wait for the kettle to do its job.

The tasks may not be personal; they may be parts of a project that require completion in a specific order, with specific dependencies among them. Or they may be academic tasks. To earn a degree, you have to accomplish a certain number of courses, some of which usually have other courses as prerequisites. In general, you can think of tasks as jobs that have ordering constraints among them, so that some jobs must precede other jobs and must be completed before more jobs can start.

The archetypal example of such tasks is the problem of getting dressed. Most human beings master this capability in their toddler years (although getting dressed does not mean that one is dressed *well*), so we take it for granted. Still, it involves a remarkable number of steps, if you come to think of it. In a winter day, there are underwear, socks, several layers of garments, jacket, hat, gloves, and boots. There are specific constraints, so that a boot cannot be put on before a sock on the same leg. There is also some leeway, so that you can put the left boot on before the right one, and then your jacket; or you may put the right boot on, then your jacket, and then your left boot. When we learn to get dressed, we also learn how to order these tasks.

For another example, consider a campaign. We want to contact a number of people with an offer, or we want to ask them for something: we may be offering a coupon or a free trial for a service, or we may be soliciting donations for a cause. A well-established fact is that the best way to influence people's decisions is to show them what other people are doing, especially people they know or respect. So if we know in general that if Alice responds to our campaign then Bob is also likely to respond, it makes sense to approach first Alice, then Bob. Imagine that in our campaign we have a cast of characters for which we have identified and plotted these relationships. You can see the resulting graph in figure 6.1.

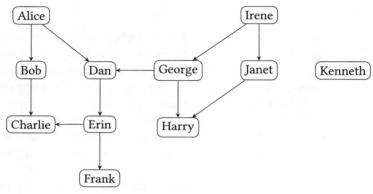

Figure 6.1
A graph with our cast of characters.

The problem then is, in which order do we contact these people? We do not want to contact Charlie before we have contacted Bob and Erin. Similarly, we do not want to contact Bob before we have contacted Alice. Kenneth is a hermit; we can contact him whenever we want. There is no single solution to the problem. In figure 6.2 you can see two different, valid orderings, shown by rearranging the cast of characters graph. In both of them the order of the relationships between people are not violated because there are no arrows going backward.

6.1   Topological Sort

We want to find a general way to obtain such orderings. In graph terms, we are interested in a specific way of sorting directed acyclic graphs or dags. A *topological ordering* or *topological sort* of a directed acyclic graph $G = (V, E)$ is an ordering of the vertices V of the graph such that for every edge (u, v) that appears in E, the vertex u appears in the ordering before vertex v.

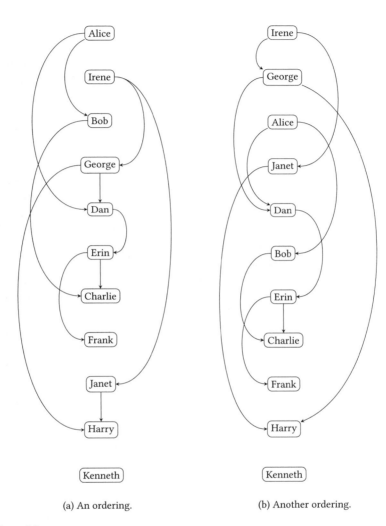

(a) An ordering.   (b) Another ordering.

Figure 6.2
Contacts orderings; order is top to bottom.

As figure 6.2 shows, a graph may have more than one topological order. The contrary is also true: a graph may have no topological order. Specifically, consider what happens with a directed cyclic graph. In our example, we want to have Alice before Bob, and Bob before Charlie, so Alice before Charlie. If there were an edge from Charlie to Alice, then we would also want to contact Charlie before Alice, so we would arrive at a deadlock. In directed cyclic graphs, topological sorts do not exist because they simply do not make sense. So the first thing you have to do to derive a topological sort of a graph is to ensure it is acyclic, in other words, that it is a dag.

Go back to our example, which is a dag, so you can work on it. You want a topological sort of that graph, which will be an ordering of the persons who you can use to contact somebody only when you have already contacted the persons preceding them. It is easier to solve the problem by thinking in the opposite way: which person would you contact *last*? Clearly, you would contact last the person who would give you no leads; that is, the person who has no outgoing edges, who does not link *to* any other person. In our example, Frank, Harry, Kenneth, or Charlie would be such candidates for the last person to contact. Now that you have found the last person to contact, who would you contact before that person? Again, you would apply the same rule. You would contact a person who would give you no leads. If you had picked Frank as the last person before, then now you would be left to choose among Charlie, Harry, and Kenneth. Say that you now pick Charlie. You would contact Frank last, and Charlie before Frank. Who would you contact before Charlie? You could choose among Harry and Kenneth, but also Bob because he only leads to Charlie, who you have already put in the topological sort as next to last.

This way of choosing persons to contact, going from the last person backward, is equivalent to exploring the graph as deep as you can: go to the deepest node you can, from where you start, and then move backward to where you started. Exploring a graph by going deep as much as we can is what depth-first search does; and indeed, applying depth-first search in a dag will produce a topological sort of it.

Along these lines, algorithm 6.1 shows a modification of depth-first search; it works like normal depth-first search, but it uses some additional data: *sorted* is a list in whose head we add each element when we reach a dead-end in depth-first search and we need to backtrack. In particular, the idea behind algorithm 6.1 is that when we encounter a dead-end in depth-first search and we start backtracking, we are in line 5. By adding the current *node*, the dead-end in the corresponding recursive call, at the head of the list, we fill the list from the back to the front. That means that we fill the list from back to front with each dead-end that we encounter.

With algorithm 6.1 at hand, we can now arrive at algorithm 6.2 that implements topological sort. Essentially the algorithm sets the scene for

---

Algorithm 6.1: DFS for topological sort.

DFSTopologicalSort(*G, node*)

    Input: $G = (V, E)$, a dag

              node, a node in G

    Data: *visited*, an array of size $|V|$

             sorted, a list

    Result: *visited*[*i*] is TRUE if node *i* is reachable from *node*

               sorted contains in its start, in reverse order, the dead-ends we

               reached using depth-first search starting from *node*

1   *visited*[*node*] ← TRUE

2   **foreach** v in AdjacencyList(*G, node*) **do**

3   **if not** *visited*[v] **then**

4   DFSTopologicalSort(*G*, v)

5   InsertInList(*sorted*, NULL, *node*)

DFSTopologicalSort. It initializes *visited* and *sorted*. Then it only needs to call DFSTopologicalSort until all nodes are visited, in the loop of lines 5–7. If we can visit all nodes from node 0, then the loop will be executed only once. If not, the loop will be re-run for the first unvisited node, and so on.

Performance-wise, as the algorithm is really a depth-first traversal of the graph, and because a depth-first traversal requires $\Theta(|V| + |E|)$ time, topological sort also requires $\Theta(|V| + |E|)$.

Let's see the algorithm in action. As we said, before running the algorithm we assign unique indices to the nodes. If we assign the indices alphabetically, then Alice becomes 0, Bob becomes 1, and so on. The graph of figure 6.1 becomes then the equivalent graph in figure 6.3a. You can see the depth-first traversal of the graph in figure 6.3b. The numbers next to the nodes indicate the order in which we visited them. The dashed rectangles overlayed on the graph show how the graph is visited in each call of DFSTopoloticalSort.

Because the graph is not strongly connected, the traversal proceeds by first visiting the nodes that are reachable from node 0. Then it visits the nodes that are reachable from node 6, except node 3, because we have already visited it, so it visits only node 7. Then it goes to node 8 and visits the only unvisited neighbor, node 9. Last, it visits node 10. So the loop of algorithm 6.2 is executed four times. We examined the unvisited nodes and the neighbors of each node in increasing numerical order in line 5 of the algorithm, but this is

---

Algorithm 6.2: Topological sort on a dag.

TopologicalSort(G) → *sorted*
    Input: $G = (V, E)$, a dag
    Output: *sorted*, a list of size $|V|$ with the nodes of the graph in
            topological order

1   *visited* ← CreateArray($|V|$)
2   *sorted* ← CreateList()
3   **for** $i ← 0$ **to** $|V|$ **do**
4   *visited*[i] ← FALSE
5   **for** $i ← 0$ **to** $|V|$ **do**
6   **if not** *visited*[i] **then**
7   DFSTopologicalSort(G, i)
8   **return** *sorted*

---

not necessary. The algorithm will run correctly with any order we choose to examine the nodes.

Let's zoom in and see what is going on in each iteration of the loop of algorithm 6.2. In the first iteration we call DFSTopologicalSort for node 0. Remember that after visiting every neighbor of a node, we know that the current node is the last of the remaining nodes that we need to contact. So when we start at node 0, and then via node 1 we arrive at node 2, we see that there are no leads from node 2, and therefore we insert 2 in the beginning of the (empty) list *sorted*. Then we go back to node 1, we see that there are no leads we have not visited, so we insert node 1 in the beginning of *sorted*. Node 0 still has node 3 unvisited, so we go and visit 3, and from there 4 and 5. Node 5 has no leads, so we insert it at the front of *sorted*. Then we insert node 4, node 3, and finally node 0 at the front of *sorted*. At the end of the first iteration we have *sorted* = $[0, 3, 4, 5, 1, 2]$. From there, we call DFSTopologicalSort for node 6 and we get *sorted* = $[6, 7, 0, 3, 4, 5, 1, 2]$. Then, we call DFSTopologicalSort for node 8 and we get *sorted* = $[8, 9, 6, 7, 0, 3, 4, 5, 1, 2]$. Finally, we call DFSTopologicalSort for node 10 and we get *sorted* = $[10, 8, 9, 6, 7, 0, 3, 4, 5, 1, 2]$.

In figure 6.4 you can see for each node the order it is visited and its topological order. The topological sort of the graph is $10 → 8 → 9 → 6 → 7 → 0 →$

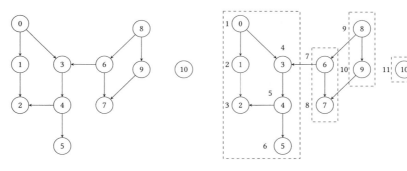

(a) The cast of characters graph with numerical indices.

(b) Depth-first traversal of the cast of characters graph.

Figure 6.3
Numerical cast of characters graph and its depth-first traversal.

$3 \rightarrow 4 \rightarrow 5 \rightarrow 1 \rightarrow 2$. Going back to names instead of indices, we have Kenneth → Irene → Janet → George → Harry → Alice → Dan → Erin → Frank → Bob → Charlie. You can check in figure 6.5 that there are no arrows going up, so this is a correct solution. Also, this solution is different than either of the solutions in figure 6.2.

In algorithm 6.2 we assumed that the graph G is a dag. What if it isn't? Then a topological sort does not make sense. A cycle in a graph means that we have a sequence of precedence relations $u_k \rightarrow \cdots \rightarrow u_k$; in other words, a node must somehow precede itself. In our cast of characters example, if we had a link from Charlie to Alice, then there is no way to say which one we should contact first, Alice or Charlie.

We can use topological sort anywhere we need to find an order in which to do some tasks. In our example, we wanted to contact people, but tasks can be anything. For instance, they can be processes that must be performed subject to constraints, so that certain processes must precede others. Some books have navigation maps in their introductory material specifying the order in which the reader should approach the chapters. A glossary of terms may be ordered alphabetically, or it may be ordered in such a way that no term appears after a term whose definition depends on it.

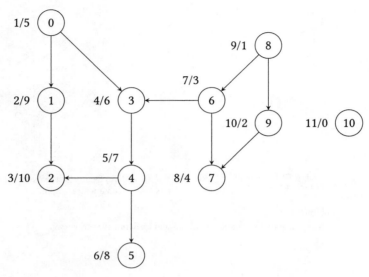

Figure 6.4
Depth-first traversal of the cast of characters graph with topological sort; the label i/j next to a node means that the node was the ith node to visit during depth-first traversal and the jth node in topological order.

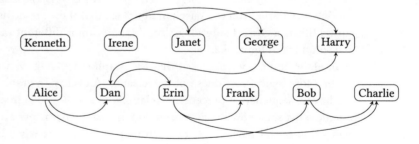

Figure 6.5
Topological sort of the cast of characters graph; order is left to right, top to bottom.

6.2 Weighted Graphs

Up to this point we have used graphs that show entities as nodes and their connections as edges. We can extend graphs so that we assign a number, called

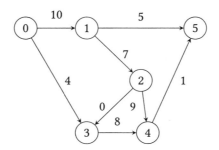

Figure 6.6
A weigthed graph.

weight, to each edge. Such graphs are called *weighted graphs*. They are a generalization of unweighted graphs, because an unweighted graph can be seen as a weighted graph where all edges have the same weight, say one, which we ommit. We will denote the weight of an edge (u, v) by $w(u, v)$. Weighted graphs are useful because the allow us to represent more information. If a graph is a road network, the weights may represent distances, or the time required to travel between two points.

In figure 6.6 you can see a weighted, directed graph. It may seem familiar, you have seen an unweighted, undirected version of it before in chapter 2, in figure 2.3. Although all weights in the figure are nonnegative integers, that is not necessary. We may have positive and negative weights: the nodes may correspond to achievements and weights may be rewards or penalties. The weights can also be real numbers; it depends on the requirements of our application. In a weighted graph, when we talk about the length of a path between two nodes, we take it to mean not the number of edges between the nodes, but the sum of the weights of those edges. Hence, in figure 6.6, the length of the path from 0 to 2 is not 2 but 17.

We can represent a weighted graph similarly to an unweighted graph. The adjacency matrix for a weighted graph has as entries the weights of its edges or a special value for the entries that are not connected. Table 6.1 shows the adjacency matrix for the graph in figure 6.6. When there is no connection we used ∞ as a special value, but we could have used any other value that does not make sense as a weight. If our weights are nonnegative, we can use -1; or we can use NULL, or something else. Again, it depends on the requirements of our application.

Table 6.1

Adjacency matrix for the graph in figure 6.6.

	0	1	2	3	4	5
0	∞	10	∞	4	∞	∞
1	∞	∞	7	∞	∞	5
2	∞	∞	∞	0	9	∞
3	∞	∞	∞	∞	8	∞
4	∞	∞	∞	∞	∞	1
5	∞	∞	∞	∞	∞	∞

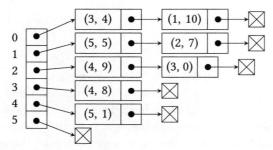

Figure 6.7

The adjacency list representation for the weighted graph in figure 6.6.

Alternatively, we can use an adjacency list representation. In each node of the list we store not only the name of the vertex, but also the weight of the corresponding edge. The adjacency list representation for the weighted graph of figure 6.6 is in figure 6.7.

6.3   Critical Paths

Focusing on scheduling tasks, a problem that is close to topological sort is that of finding a *critical path* in a dag that represents the steps to be performed in a process. In that problem, the process to be completed is represented as a graph where nodes are the tasks and the links represent the ordering constraints between the process tasks. To each edge (u, v) we assign a weight $w(u, v)$, which is the time it takes for task u to complete so that task v can start. Figure 6.8 shows such a *scheduling graph*. The nodes correspond to discrete tasks (number coded from zero onward) and the weights correspond to time units, for example weeks, required to get from one task to another.

In figure 6.8, we need 17 weeks to get from task 0 to task 1. The problem arising here is, what is the least amount of time that will be required to complete the process?

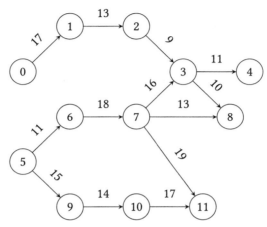

Figure 6.8
A task scheduling graph.

Some of the tasks can be performed in parallel, for example, we can start executing tasks 0 and 5. Similarly, tasks 1, 6, and 9 can also be executed without waiting for each other, when tasks 0 and 5 complete. However, not all tasks can be performed in parallel: task 3 can start only after tasks 2 and 7 complete. Taking then into account the possibility of running tasks in parallel, what is the minimum time that will be required to complete all of them?

To find the answer, we work as follows. First, we add two additional nodes to the graph. A start node, *s*, which we assume is the starting point of the whole process. We call node *s* the *source node*. We connect *s* to each of the nodes without predecessors in the graph to show the tasks that we can begin executing at the start of the process. The edges we add have weight zero. We also add another node, *t*, which we assume is the end of the whole process. We call node *t* the *sink node*. We connect each of the nodes without successors to *t*. The edges have again weight zero. We then arrive at figure 6.9.

When we have the source and sink nodes added, our problem becomes the following: what is the *longest path* from node *s* to node *t*? Because we need to visit all nodes of the graph, we need to go through every path from *s* to *t*. We may be able to work on some paths in parallel. There is no way, however,

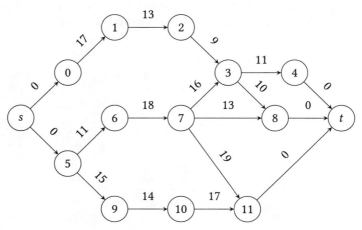

Figure 6.9
A task scheduling graph with source and sink nodes.

to complete the process until we complete the path that requires the longest amount of time. The longest path in a process is called its critical path. As a minimal example, consider figure 6.10.

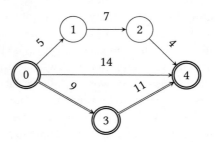

Figure 6.10
A critical path example.

The path $0 \rightarrow 1 \rightarrow 2 \rightarrow 4$ has length 16; the path $0 \rightarrow 4$ has length 14, and the path $0 \rightarrow 3 \rightarrow 4$ has length 20. If length is in weeks, there is no way we can start task 4 before 20 weeks, so the critical path is $0 \rightarrow 3 \rightarrow 4$; we indicate the nodes in the path with double edges and borders. In the same way, in the graph in figure 6.9, there is no way we can start task t, which is just a placeholder for the end of the process, before the time required for the longest path from s to t.

How do we find the longest path? We need to traverse the graph in an ordered way. In particular we want to start from s, visit every node in the graph, and at each node calculate the length of the path from s to that node. Initially the only length we know is the length to s, which is zero. We will be visiting the nodes and updating the length to them as we go. Suppose we are visiting node u, we have found the longest path from s to u, and u is connected to node v. If the longest path we have found from s to v is longer than the path from s to u plus the weight of the edge (u, v), then we need not do anything. But if the longest path we have found from s to v is less than or equal to the path from s to u plus the weight of the edge (u, v), then we need to record the information that the longest path we have found to v passes from u, and update the calculated length accordingly. Beceause we want to update the length each time we find a longest path, when we start, we set all lengths we do not know, that is, all lengths apart from the length to s, to the lowest possible estimate, which is $-\infty$. To see what we mean, check figure 6.11a, where we show a graph with two paths from s to v; we use $l(u)$ for the length of the path from s to a node u.

We are traversing the graph and we visit node u_1. This is the first node during our traversal that is connected to v, so we record the fact that the longest path we have found until now to v passes from u_1, and has a length $l(v) = l(u_1) + w(u_1, v)$; see figure 6.11b. Then afterward, sometime during our traversal, we visit node u_2. We check the length of the path from s to v passing through u_2, $l'(v) = l(u_2) + w(u_2, v)$, compared to the length of the path we had previously established. If it is longer, then we record that actually the longest path is the one passing from u_2, as we do in figure 6.11c. If there is another node u_3 that links to v, then we will do the same comparison and update if necessary when we visit node u_3. The process of checking and updating if necessary an estimate on a graph metric by a more accurate measurement is typical in many graph algorithms, to the point that it has a name: *relaxation*. Here our initial estimate on the path length is extreme on the low side, $-\infty$, and it is relaxed to a less extreme, and more accurate value, each time we update the path length.

It is necessary that the first time we check the path to v we find it has the smallest possible value, $-\infty$, so that we can update it correctly to the length of the path passing from u_1. That explains why initially we set the length of all paths to $-\infty$, apart from the path to s, which is set to 0, to make sure

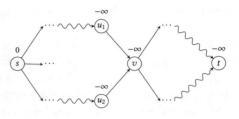

(a) Graph with two paths to v.

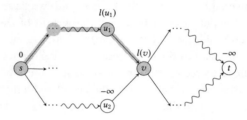

(b) First visit to v.

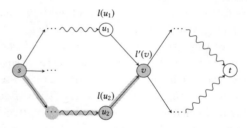

(c) Second visit to v.

Figure 6.11
Longest path update.

everything will work, as in figure 6.11a. In addition, it is necessary that we do not visit node v before we have visited all nodes that point to v. This is easy to achieve, by traversing the graph in topological order. Algorithm 6.3 brings all the strands together. We assume that, as before, we assign unique indices to the nodes, so when you see s, you should think of it as an integer different from other node indices.

We use two data structures: an array *pred* and an array *dist*. Element i in *prev*, that is, *prev*[i], indicates the node that comes before i in the critical

---

Algorithm 6.3: Critical path.

CriticalPath(G) $\rightarrow$ ($pred$, $dist$)

    Input: $G = (V, E, s)$, a weighted dag with a source s

    Output: $pred$, an array of size $|V|$ such that $pred[i]$ is the predecessor
             of node i along the critical path from s to i
             $dist$, an array of size $|V|$ such that $dist[i]$ contains the length
             of the critical path from s to i

1   $pred \leftarrow$ CreateArray($|V|$)
2   $dist \leftarrow$ CreateArray($|V|$)
3   **for** $i \leftarrow 0$ **to** $|V|$ **do**
4       $pred[i] \leftarrow -1$
5       $dist[i] \leftarrow -\infty$
6   $dist[s] \leftarrow 0$
7   $sorted \leftarrow$ TopologicalSort(V, E)
8   **foreach** u **in** $sorted$ **do**
9   **foreach** v **in** AdjacencyList(G, u) **do**
10   **if** $dist[v] < dist[u] +$ Weight(G, u, v) **then**
11             $dist[v] \leftarrow dist[u] +$ Weight(G, u, v)
12             $pred[v] \leftarrow u$
13   **return** ($pred$, $dist$)

---

path we have found to the node corresponding to i. Element i in $dist$, that is, $dist[i]$, contains the length of the critical path we have found to the node corresponding to i. We also use a function Weight(G, u, v) that returns the weight between the nodes u and v in the graph G. Note that algorithm 6.3 does not need t as an input. It suffices to know which node it is; then the length of the critical path is given by $dist[t]$, and to find the path we trace $pred$ starting from $pred[t]$.

In lines 1–6 we create and initialize the data structures $pred$ and $dist$. We set each element of $pred$ to an invalid, non-existent node called -1, and the length to each node, that is, each element of $dist$, to $-\infty$, apart from the source node s, which we set to 0. Then we perform a topological sort on the graph. In lines 8–12 we deal with every node in topological order. For each node in turn, we iterate over its neighbors, by going through its adjacency list. In lines 10–12 we check whether the length of the path to each neighbor going

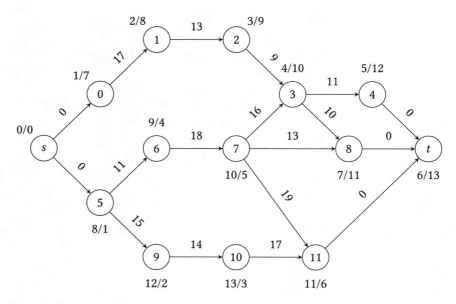

Figure 6.12
The task scheduling graph with topological order. As in figure 6.4, the label i/j next to a node means that the node was the ith node to visit during depth-first traversal and the jth node in topological order.

through the current node is greater than the parent we have calculated to this point. If it is, then we update the length and the predecessor of the neighbor in the longest path to be the current node. This is relaxation in practice. In algorithm 6.3 we first relax from $-\infty$ to a length the first time we visit a node, and then we relax to a longer length each time we find one.

The algorithm is efficient. The topological sort takes $\Theta(|V| + |E|)$ time. The loop in lines 3–5 takes $\Theta(|V|)$ time. Then the loop in lines 8–12 goes through lines 11–12 once per edge: each edge is relaxed one time. This means that overall the loop takes $\Theta(|E|)$ time. In summary, the whole algorithm requires $\Theta(|V| + |E| + |V| + |E|) = \Theta(|V| + |E|)$ time.

An example run of the algorithm for the graph in figure 6.9 is in figures 6.13 and 6.14. We indicate with gray the node we are currently visiting in topological order. Look at what happens when we visit node 7, when we update the length to node 11 that we had calculated previously. The same thing happens again when we visit nodes 3, 8, and 4, when relaxation results in changing the previously calculated path length. The matrix below each graph in the two figures displays the contents of the *pred* array. As we have explained, s and t are in fact node indices, so we could have $s = 12$ and $t = 13$, but it is nicer to draw the matrix with s on the left and t on the right. At the end of the execution of the algorithm, we retrieve the critical path by going to *pred*[t], which is 4; then we go to *pred*[4], which is 3, and so on. The critical path then is

$$s \rightarrow 5 \rightarrow 6 \rightarrow 7 \rightarrow 3 \rightarrow 4 \rightarrow t$$

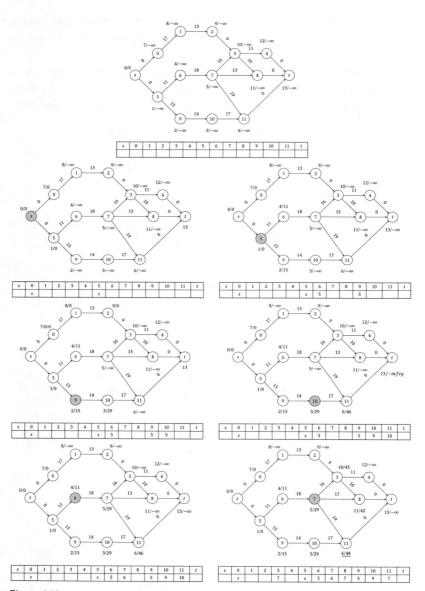

Figure 6.13

Finding the critical path. The label i/j next to a node means that the node has topological order i and distance j. The matrix below each panel shows *pred*, with empty entries instead of -1 to reduce clutter.

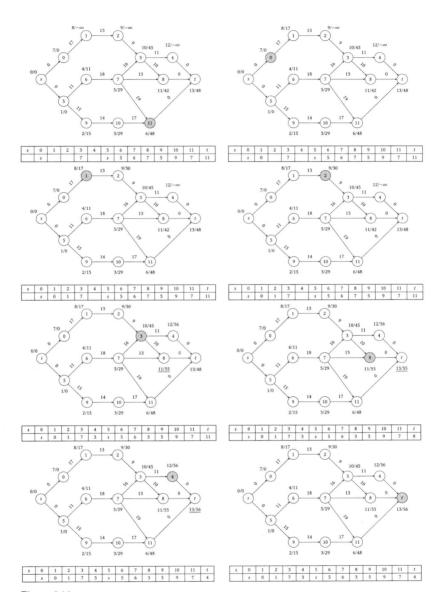

Figure 6.14
Finding the critical path (continued).

Notes

Donald Knuth [112] gives an algorithm for topological sorting—not the one we present here. The algorithm we describe here is given by Cormen, Leiserson, Rivest, and Stein [42]; a precursor was described by Robert Tarjan [198].

As a project modeling technique, the use of critical paths is known as the Critical Path Method (CPM) and also lies behind the Program Evaluation and Review Technique (PERT). In graph terms, finding the critical path is equivalent to finding the longest path.

Exercises

1.   Depth-first search and topological sort do not require that we examine the nodes of the graph in a particular order. Implement the topological sort algorithm so that the nodes are examined in increasing, or decreasing order, and check the results. Verify that they are correct, although not necessarily the same.

2.   Topological sort does not work on graphs with cycles because it does not after all make sense to have a topological ordering in such graphs. When we are not sure that our graph is acyclic, it is convenient to be able to detect cycles during the execution of the topological sort algorithm and report the problem. It turns out that it is not difficult to do that. In depth-first search, we follow edges as far as we can go. If we keep the nodes that are in our recursive sequence of calls, the recursive call stack, then if the node we are about to visit is in the nodes in the current recursive sequence of calls, we know there is a cycle. For example, in figure 6.4, when we are at node 2, the recursive call stack contains nodes 0, 1, and 2, in this order. If there were an edge from 2 to 0 or from 2 to 1, then we would have a cycle. We could detect it immediately by checking that 0, or 1, is present in our recursive call stack. Modify DFSTopologicalSort so that it detects cycles and reports the situation when it arises.

3.   To find the critical path in a graph G we need to add a source node s and a sink node t. We have not described the exact way to do that, but it is not difficult. If we have $|V|$ nodes initially in the graph, numbered from 0 to $|V| - 1$, we add another two nodes in the graph: s will be numbered $|V|$ and t will be numbered $|V| + 1$. We then find the nodes that have no node pointing to them: these will be connected with s. Following that, we find the nodes that point to no other node: these will be connected to t. Implement this scheme so that you have a program that carries out the whole procedure for detecting critical paths.

7   Lines, Paragraphs, Paths

The text that you are reading is composed of letters, grouped in words, arranged in lines, split into paragraphs. When you write in longhand, you start writing a line, and as you approach the end of the line on your notepad, you arrange the last word so that it either ends the line, or you hyphenate it if possible.

Similarly, when you write a text in a word processor, the program will append words in the line until you approach the end of the line. Then when you type a word that does not fit into the line, the word processor has to decide what to do with it. It may be possible to leave it in the line by squeezing the spaces between the preceding words, so that the line will be compressed a bit to accommodate the last word. It may be possible to put the whole word in the next line and expand the spaces between the preceding words. If neither of these solutions works well, because the line gets too compressed or too loose, then the word processor will try to hyphenate the word and leave a part of it in the current line and start the next line with the remaining part.

Separating text into lines is called *line breaking*; we do that pretty much effortlessly when we write longhand, and the word processor takes a decision for each line as we type it. In figure 7.1a you can see the results of applying this line breaking method to the opening paragraph of brothers Grimm's *The Frog Prince*. The method broke lines when their length approached thirty characters (including spaces and punctuation). The paragraph does not look very bad, but then look at figure 7.1b. That's the same paragraph, but instead of using the above approach for line breaking, we went for a different line breaking method. The paragraph is two lines shorter, and overall uses white space more judiciously, thus having a more polished look.

If you think of it, the method we described considers each line in isolation. However, it has been shown that you can get better results if you consider together all the lines that make up a paragraph when you decide where to

In olden times when wishing
still helped one, there lived
a king whose daughters were
all beautiful, but the youngest was so beautiful that
the sun itself, which has seen
so much, was astonished
whenever it shone in her face.
Close by the king's castle lay
a great dark forest, and under
an old lime-tree in the forest
was a well, and when the day
was very warm, the king's
child went out into the forest
and sat down by the side of
the cool fountain, and when
she was bored she took a
golden ball, and threw it up
on high and caught it, and
this ball was her favorite
plaything.

In olden times when wishing still
helped one, there lived a king
whose daughters were all beautiful, but the youngest was so beautiful that the sun itself, which
has seen so much, was astonished
whenever it shone in her face.
Close by the king's castle lay a
great dark forest, and under an old
lime-tree in the forest was a well,
and when the day was very warm,
the king's child went out into the
forest and sat down by the side of
the cool fountain, and when she
was bored she took a golden ball,
and threw it up on high and caught
it, and this ball was her favorite
plaything.

(a) A paragraph broken into lines.   (b) A paragraph broken into lines, better.

Figure 7.1
Breaking lines into paragraphs.

split them. In this way it is possible to arrive at better-looking paragraphs
that take into account the whole of their material, instead of rushing to break
lines as soon as possible.

The way we can do that is by considering different ways to break up a
paragraph into lines, and assign a numerical value to each possible line. The
numerical value should correspond to how desirable the line break is. The
lower the value, the more we would like to use that line break in our paragraph; the higher the value, the more we would want to penalize that line and
try for alternative line breaks.

You can see this other process at work in figure 7.3, which corresponds to
figure 7.2. On the left you can see line numbers. For each line we considered

In olden times when wishing still helped one, there lived a
king whose daughters were all beautiful, but the youngest
was so beautiful that the sun itself, which has seen so much,
was astonished whenever it shone in her face. Close by the
king's castle lay a great dark forest, and under an old lime-
tree in the forest was a well, and when the day was very
warm, the king's child went out into the forest and sat
down by the side of the cool fountain, and when she was
bored she took a golden ball, and threw it up on high and
caught it, and this ball was her favorite plaything.

Figure 7.2
A paragraph broken into lines, traced in figure 7.3.

possible break points, so that the paragraph would not exceed a certain width.
The first line could be broken at two places, "lived", and "a". The numbers on
the edges of the figure correspond to how bad each break point is. The second
break point is better than the first. In line three there is only one feasible
breakpoint. In the eighth and ninth lines there are four possible breakpoints,
before we arrive at the last line, where there is of course just one.

Figure 7.3 is really a graph, with the nodes representing the possible breakpoints. The edges have weights that are measures of how bad a breakpoint is;
they are calculated with a specific algorithm that does not concern us here.
We only need to know that for each line the algorithm produces a number
that shows how bad it is; worse lines get higher marks. We want the paragraph with the lowest possible "badness." Then the problem of laying out the
paragraph in an aesthetically pleasing way reduces to the problem of finding
the shortest path from the top of the graph to the bottom, where the path is
defined as the sum of the weights of the edges along the way. For an example
of what badness really means here, look at figure 7.4. The first line corresponds to taking the left branch at node "much" of the third line of figure 7.3,
whereas the second line corresponds to the right, selected, branch.

You may be tempted to think that the difference is small, but it is important if you are concerned about quality in a publication. The method we
have just described was invented by Donald Knuth and Michael Plass and
has been implemented in a typesetting program popular in scientific publishing, called TEX. The name comes from the Greek stem τεχ, which means art
as well as technology; therefore, TEX is not pronounced with an x sound but

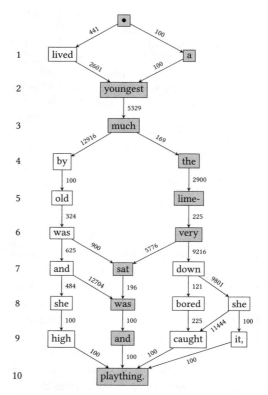

Figure 7.3
Optimizing line-breaking.

with a Greek chi sound. A document composition system called LᴬTᴇX, an off-shoot of TᴇX, is used to write this text. Again, the pronunciation follows the Greek sound of chi. Search engines seem to have come around to the fact that searches for LᴬTᴇX issues are not related to rubber.

7.1   Shortest Paths

Word wrapping, or breaking a paragraph into lines, is just one of the applications of the *shortest path* problem, in which we try to find the shortest possible path from a start node to a destination node in a graph. The shortest path problem is one of the most common in algorithms; plenty of real-world

was   astonished   whenever   it   shone   in   her   face.   Close   by
was astonished whenever it shone in her face. Close by the

Figure 7.4
Badness examples.

problems are in fact shortest path problems, and different algorithms exist
for different settings of the problem. Navigating through a road network is of
course a shortest path problem, where you want to go from your departure
point to your destination by using the shortest route possible through a series
of cities. The shortest route may be defined in terms of the total distance you
have to cover, or in terms of the time, if instead of distances you have time
estimates for getting through the intermediate cities in your route.

To examine the problem in more detail, imagine you have to navigate
through a grid, where intersection points are crossroads and estimates are
given for the time required to go from one intersection point to another. The
grid may be a regular one, if it happens to represent a city laid out geometri-
cally; this is not necessary, but it will make the presentation easier. Figure 7.5
shows such a grid. We have not put names on the grid nodes, to avoid clut-
tering the figure; the numbers correspond to the weights between the nodes,
which may stand for the minutes required to get from one node to the other. If
we want to refer to a particular node, we will be referring to node (i, j) for the
node in row i, column j, where both rows and columns have indices starting
from zero.

To solve the problem of navigating from a starting point to a destination,
we will consider the more general problem of finding all shortest paths from
a starting point to any other point in our grid. That is the *single source shortest
paths problem*. To solve it we need to apply a relaxation technique. Initially,
the only distance we do know is the distance to our starting point, which is
zero. We initialize our estimate of all other distances to the largest possible
value, which is ∞. Then we pick the node with the lowest estimate. At the
beginning, this is the starting node with estimate zero, as we just established.
We examine all its adjacent nodes. We find the weight of the link from the
current node to each adjacent node, and if it is less than the current estimate
we have, then we adjust that estimate and note that the predecessor of the
adjacent node in the shortest path is the current node we are visiting. When
we are done, we pick again the node with the lowest estimate and relax its
adjacent nodes. We finish when there are no more nodes to examine. You can

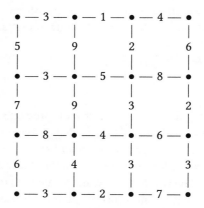

Figure 7.5
A traffic grid.

trace the process in figures 7.6 and 7.7, where we find the shortest paths from the upper left corner to every other node in the graph.

We start by estimating the cost of the path to the node at the upper left corner, which is zero. Then we pick the node with the lowest path estimate; that is the node in the upper left corner, node $(0, 0)$. We visit that node, marking it black, and estimate the costs to get to its neighbors. That's three for the node $(0, 1)$, and five for the node below it, node $(1, 0)$. We indicate the shortest path to these nodes by painting it with a thicker line. Node $(0, 1)$ has the lowest path estimate right now, so this will be the next node we will visit; we mark it gray. We go and visit node $(0, 1)$ and calculate the estimates for its neighbors. We continue this procedure until there are no more nodes to consider for updating the estimates to their neighbors.

Pay attention to what is going on when we visit node $(1, 1)$, in the fifth panel of figure 7.6. We already had an estimate for the node $(1, 1)$, which was 12, arriving from the node $(0, 1)$. But now if we go to node $(1, 1)$ from node $(1, 0)$ we get a shorter path, with length eight; we underline node $(1, 2)$ to indicate that, and we update our path lines. The same thing happens in figure 7.7 when we update the paths for nodes $(3, 0)$ and $(3, 3)$. At the end of the algorithm, the path from $(0, 0)$ to $(3, 3)$ has length 18, and it goes $(0, 0) \rightarrow (1, 0) \rightarrow (2, 0) \rightarrow (2, 1) \rightarrow (2, 2) \rightarrow (3, 2) \rightarrow (3, 3)$.

The shortest paths from our starting node to every other node in the graph form a tree, which you can see in figure 7.8. A tree whose nodes are the nodes

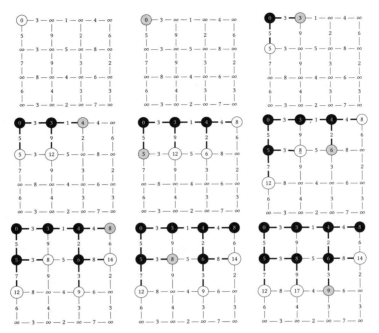

Figure 7.6
Shortest paths from upper left corner.

of a graph and whose edges are a subset of the edges of the graph is called a *spanning tree*. Spanning trees are important for a number of applications, especially spanning trees that have minimum weight, that is, the sum of the weights of their edges is minimum with respect to other ways of selecting the edges that form the spanning tree. Such spanning trees are called *minimum spanning trees*. Note that the shortest path method we have described derives a spanning tree, but not necessarily a minimum spanning tree.

7.2   Dijkstra's Algorithm

The way we calculated the shortest paths corresponds to *Dijkstra's algorithm*, named after the Dutch computer scientist Edsger Dijkstra who found it in 1956 and published it in 1959. Algorithm 7.1 describes the method in algorithmic form. It takes as input a graph and a starting node in the graph and it returns two arrays.

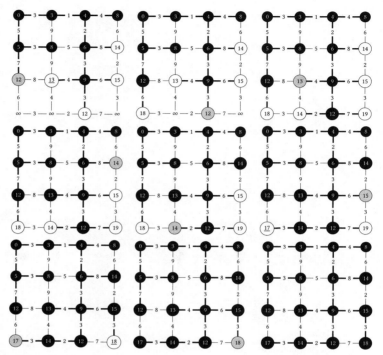

Figure 7.7
Shortest paths from upper left corner (continued).

The algorithm uses a minimum priority queue to keep track of which node we must visit next. The priority queue must support the operations we described in section 3.2, but with some modifications to cater for the needs of Dijkstra's algorithm. In the priority queue we will be inserting nodes and distances. We will also need to update in-place the distance of a node that is stored in the priority queue. That means that the required operations are:

- CreatePQ() creates a new, empty priority queue.
- InsertInPQ(*pq*, *n*, *d*) inserts the node *n* with distance *d* to the priority queue.
- ExtractMinFromPQ(*pq*) removes from the queue and returns the node with the minimum distance.
- SizePQ(*pq*) returns the number of elements in the priority queue *pq*.

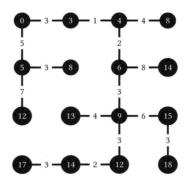

Figure 7.8
Spanning tree of the traffic grid.

- UpdatePQ(*pq*, *n*, *d*) updates the priority queue by changing the stored distance associated with *n* to the distance *d*.

The algorithm uses two additional data structures: an array *pred* and an array *dist*. Element *i* in *pred*, that is, *pred*[*i*], indicates the node that comes before *i* in the shortest path we have found from node *s* to the node corresponding to *i*. Element *i* in *dist*, that is, *dist*[*i*], contains the length of the shortest path we have found to the node corresponding to *i*. Lines 1–10 of the algorithm initialize the data structures, so there is no predecessor node for any node (there is no node −1). Also, the only shortest path we know is to the start node, equal to zero; so the distances to all other nodes are set initially to ∞ in line 7, except for the starting node whose distance is set to 0 in line 9. Then we add the current node *v* of the loop to the priority queue in line 10. The loop in lines 11–17 repeats as long as the priority queue is not empty (line 11). It extracts the minimum element from it (line 12), and relaxes the path estimate for any adjacent node that gets a better path estimate in the inner loop of lines 13–17. Specifically, it checks whether the distance to the neighbor *v* of the current node *u* is greater than the distance we would get if we followed the path that ends with the link (*u*, *v*), in line 14. If yes, it updates the distance to *v* to the distance of that path (line 15) and then updates the predecessor node of *v* in the path to be *u* (line 16). If it does relax the path estimate for a neighbor, it must ensure that the priority queue is updated, in line 17. Finally, the algorithm returns the two arrays *pred* and *dist* (line 18).

Algorithm 7.1: Dijkstra's algorithm.

Dijkstra(G, s) $\rightarrow$ ($pred, dist$)

    Input: $G = (V, E)$, a graph

          s, the starting node

    Output: $pred$, an array of size $|V|$ such that $pred[i]$ is the predecessor of node i in the shortest path from s

          $dist$, an array of size $|V|$ such that $dist[i]$ is the length of the shortest path calculated from node s to i

1   $pred \leftarrow$ CreateArray($|V|$)

2   $dist \leftarrow$ CreateArray($|V|$)

3   $pq \leftarrow$ CreatePQ()

4   **foreach** v in V **do**

5      $pred[v] \leftarrow -1$

6   **if** $v \neq s$ **then**

7         $dist[v] \leftarrow \infty$

8   **else**

9         $dist[v] \leftarrow 0$

10   InsertInPQ($pq, v, dist[v]$)

11 **while** SizePQ(pq) $\neq 0$ **do**

12     $u \leftarrow$ ExtractMinFromPQ(pq)

13   **foreach** v in AdjacencyList(G, u) **do**

14   **if** $dist[v] > dist[u] +$ Weight(G, u, v) **then**

15           $dist[v] \leftarrow dist[u] +$ Weight(G, u, v)

16           $pred[v] \leftarrow u$

17   UpdatePQ($pq, v, dist[v]$)

18 **return** ($pred, dist$)

Note that each node is removed from the priority queue exactly once. That is because when we extract it from the priority queue, all nodes adjacent to it will get shortest path estimates that are at least as long as the path to the node we extracted. In fact, from that point to the end of the algorithm run, all nodes will get shortest paths that are at least as long as the path we extracted. So there is no way for the node to re-enter the priority queue, as the condition in line 14 will fail.

There is a fine little detail in algorithm 7.1. In line 14, we add the weight of an edge to a path estimate. What happens if the path estimate is ∞? This will occur when a node is not reachable from the source, so that when we extract it from the priority queue, its path estimate has not changed from its initial value. We will add something to infinity. In mathematics, that is not a problem; adding something to infinity produces infinity. But in many computer languages there is no infinity. A common workaround is to use the largest possible number as a replacement for infinity. If we add to that number, we do not get infinity; in most cases we wrap around and get something added to the smallest negative number. The test in line 11 will test $dist[v]$ with something negative, will succeed, and the algorithm will go on producing gibberish. So translating line 11 from the algorithmic ideal to an actual implementation may require checking that $dist[u]$ is not ∞, before adding to it. We will have more to say about such facets of computer arithmetic in section 11.7.

Is it possible that we miss the shortest path to a node? Suppose that we extract from the priority queue node v with shortest path estimate $dist[v]$. If that estimate is not correct, there is some other path that we have not found that is shorter than the one we have found. As we explained above, all path calculations using nodes not yet extracted from the priority queue will not have shorter paths. So there must be some path to node v using nodes we have already extracted that is shorter than the one we have already found. This path would end at node v. If u were the node just before v in that path, then when we extracted u we would have found that shortest path because we would have $dist[u] + \text{Weight}(G, u, v) < dist[v]$. So we cannot miss the shortest path; therefore, each time we extract a node from the priority queue we have already found the shortest path to it. During the execution of the algorithm, the set of nodes extracted from the priority queue is the set of nodes for which we have found the correct shortest paths.

That means that Dijkstra's algorithm can be used to find the shortest path to a single node. As long as a node is extracted from the priority queue, we have found the shortest path to it, so if that's all we are interested in, we may just stop the algorithm and return the result.

Let's assume that we implement the priority queue as a simple array. Then InsertInPQ(pq, n, d) is equal to setting $pq[n] \leftarrow d$, which takes constant time, that is, $O(1)$. Because an array has a fixed number of items from the time of its creation, we need to keep track of the number of elements we insert into the priority queue by incrementing a counter each time we call InsertInPQ.

UpdatePQ(pq, n, d) is also equal to $pq[n] \leftarrow d$ and therefore takes time $O(1)$. ExtractMinFromPQ(pq) requires searching through the entire array, as this is not sorted in any way, and we have to look through to its end to find the smallest element. For n elements in the priority queue this requires time $O(n)$. Because we cannot really extract an item from an array, it suffices to set its value to ∞ and then decrement the counter holding the number of items in the queue. Even if this is no real extraction, it does behave as such and does not alter the correctness of the algorithm. In section 3.3 we saw that priority queues can be implemented as heaps. That is not necessary; if we are not interested in getting the best performance from a priority queue, then we can always implement it as a simple array, with the disadvantage that finding the minimum item takes longer than in a heap.

The whole initialization part of the algorithm, lines 1–7, is executed $|V|$ times; as all operations in it take constant time, it requires time $O(|V|)$. The algorithm extracts each node as the minimum element exactly once, in line 12, so we have $|V|$ ExtractMinFromPQ(pq) operations, each taking time $O(|V|)$, in overall taking time $O(|V|^2)$. The relaxation sequence in lines 14–17 is performed at most $|E|$ times, once per edge in the graph, so we have at most $|E|$ UpdatePQ(pq, n, d) operations, requiring time $O(|E|)$. In total, Dijkstra's algorithm runs in $O(|V| + |V|^2 + |E|) = O(|V|^2)$. It is possible to use more efficient priority queues reducing the time to $O((|V| + |E|) \lg |V|)$. If all graph nodes are reachable from the source, then the number of nodes cannot be more than the number of edges, so in such graphs Dijkstra's algorithm runs in $O(|E| \lg |V|)$ time.

Dijkstra's algorithm works for both directed and undirected graphs. Cycles do not matter because a cycle will only add to the length of a path, so the path will not be the shortest. However, negative weights do matter; you may have negative weights when weights do not represent actual distances but some other metric that can take both positive and negative values. The correct execution of the algorithm depends on finding paths of increasing length. If there are negative weights present, then we cannot be sure that all paths calculated in the future will not be shorter than the path we have already calculated when we extract a node from the priority queue. In short, if your graph may have negative weights, then you cannot use Dijkstra's algorithm.

Consider the graph in figure 7.9. The shortest path from node 0 to node 3 is the path $0 \rightarrow 1 \rightarrow 2 \rightarrow 3$, with total length $5 - 4 + 1 = 2$. However, look at a trace of Dijkstra's algorithm in figure 7.10. The trace shows that because we have extracted node 2 from the priority queue before, it cannot be re-extracted when we update the shortest path coming from node 1. Hence, the shortest path to node 3 will never be updated or found.

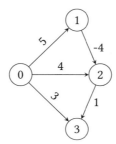

Figure 7.9
A graph with negative weights.

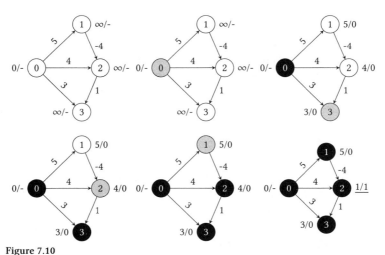

Figure 7.10
Dijkstra's algorithm on graph with negative edges. The label d/p next to a node means that that the path estimate is d and the predecessor node is p.

You may be tempted to think that a simple solution exists, by adding a constant to the weight of each edge, so that all edges have positive weights. It does not work. Figure 7.11 shows the results of re-weighting the graph. Now the shortest path from node 0 to node 3 has changed and is the path $0 \rightarrow 3$, so we cannot use the transformation to get the same results. The reason is that we added four not only to one edge in the path from node 0 to node 3, but to three edges in the path from node 0 to node 3 through nodes 1 and 2, which messed up the relationships between paths and lengths.

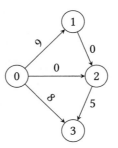

Figure 7.11
The graph re-weighted.

Apart from that restriction, you can use Dijkstra's algorithm to get other sorts of additional information on a graph. It is straightforward to calculate all shortest paths from any node to any other node in a graph; that is called the *all pairs shortest paths problem*. You only need to execute Dijkstra's algorithm $|V|$ times, starting each time at a different node, as in algorithm 7.2. To store the results we use two $|V|$ element arrays, *preds* and *dists*, whose elements point to arrays of results produced by Dijkstra; so each time we call Dijkstra for a node u, we set *preds*[u] and *dists*[u] to the *pred* and *dist* arrays returned by Dijkstra.

Having calculated the shortest paths between all pairs of nodes in a graph, you can calculate a metric on the topology of the whole graph. The *diameter of a graph* is the length of the longest shortest path between two nodes. If in a graph there are two nodes v and u with a shortest path between them of length d, such that the shortest path connecting any other pair of nodes is less than d, then the longest shortest path we can travel across the graph is along the path from v to u. As the diameter of a shape is understood as the longest distance between two points in the shape, if we take the graph as a shape and the nodes as points, then the path from v to u corresponds to the diameter of the shape, hence its name. To calculate the diameter of a graph you first run the all pairs shortest paths algorithm; then you search among the results to find the longest path returned; that's the graph diameter.

The diameter of a graph gives us the largest number of links we need to cross across a graph to get between any two nodes in the graph. In this way, it is related to the so-called "six degrees of separation" theory, by which every

---

Algorithm 7.2: All pairs shortest paths.

AllPairsShortestPaths(G) $\rightarrow$ ($preds$, $dists$)
    Input: $G = (V, E)$, a graph
    Output: $preds$, an array of size $|V|$ such that $pred[u]$ is the array of
           predecessors resulting from calling Dijkstra for node u
           $dists$, an array of size $|V|$ such that $dist[u]$ is the array of
           distances resulting from calling Dijkstra for node u

1   $preds \leftarrow$ CreateArray($|V|$)
2   $dists \leftarrow$ CreateArray($|V|$)

3   **foreach** u **in** V **do**
4   ($preds[u]$, $dists[u]$) $\leftarrow$ Dijkstra(G, u)
5   **return** ($preds$, $dists$)

---

person is six or fewer persons away from any other person in the world. This is also called "the small world problem". Perhaps counterintuitively, it has been found that nodes in large networks are on average much closer to each other than we might think.

Notes

The line breaking algorithm described here and used in TEX and LATEX is due to Knuth and Plass [117]. TEX is presented in inimitable style in the TEXbook [111]. LATEX was created by Leslie Lamport and described in [120].

Edsger Dijksra found the shortest path algorithm that bears his name in 1956 and published it in 1959 [51]. In an interview Dijkstra related the circumstances surrounding his inventions: "What's the shortest way to travel from Rotterdam to Groningen? It is the algorithm for the shortest path, which I designed in about 20 minutes. One morning I was shopping in Amsterdam with my young fiancée, and tired, we sat down on the café terrace to drink a cup of coffee and I was just thinking about whether I could do this, and I then designed the algorithm for the shortest path. As I said, it was a 20-minute invention" [141].

The performance of Dijkstra's algorithm is improved if we use appropriate priority queue implementations [71]. There are further improvements in Dijkstra's algorithm that are based on using other data structures instead of priority queues implemented as heaps: see the algorithms proposed by Ahuja, Melhorn, and Tarjan [1], Thorup [201], and Raman [163].

Dijkstra's algorithm can be seen as a specialization of a more general algorithm called *best-first search* that can in fact be more efficient [60]. Another generalization of Dijkstra's algorithm is the A* algorithm invented by Hart, Nilsson, and Raphael in 1968 [87] (with the proofs strengthened in 1972 [88]); A* is in widespread use and is a common choice for path finding in computer games.

Because Dijkstra's algorithm can be used to find the shortest route between a city and other cities in a road network, it has been adopted in *networking routing protocols* where the goal is to move data packets among nodes in the network. Such protocols are the Open Shortest Path First (OSPF) protocol [147] and the Intermediate System to Intermediate System (IS-IS) protocol [34].

The most famous investigation of the small world problem was by Stanley Milgram in the 1960s [139, 204]; John Guare's play *Six Degrees of Separation* [84] and a movie based on the play helped popularize the idea.

Exercises

1. In algorithm 7.1 we insert all the nodes of the graph in the priority queue during the initialization steps of the algorithm. If the priority queue provides an operation to check whether it contains an item, then that is not necessary. When we treat a neighbor v of a node u and find, in the relaxation step, that a better path goes through u, we can check whether u is already inside the priority queue. If it is, we can update it as in algorithm 7.1; otherwise we can insert it in the priority queue right then. Modify `Dijkstra` so that it works with this change.

2. Write two implementations of Dijkstra's algorithm, one using an array for a priority queue in the way we described in the text and the other using a priority queue implemented as a heap. Benchmark the performance of the two implementations.

3. Today it is easy to check the diameters of real-world graphs, as there are publicly available dumps of various kinds of networks; get one and check how big the diameter is and how it fares with respect to the six degrees of separation theory. If the graph is big you will need to make sure that your implementations are efficient.

8 Routing, Arbitrage

When you visit a web page, a lot of things happen behind the scenes. Your browser sends a command to the server you are visiting. The command instructs the server to send to your browser the contents of the page you want to see. This is what is happening couched in human language, but it is not what computers understand. Computers do not just send commands, or talk to each other. They communicate in a carefully prescribed way, in which each party in a communication can only say specific things in a precisely choreographed way.

The way communication is organized is through *protocols*. You can think of a communication protocol as a set of instructions, like a role play, laying down who says what and when. Communication protocols are not limited to computers. Take as an example an everyday telephone conversation. When Alice calls Bob and Bob replies, Alice expects Bob to indicate that by saying "Hello," or "Bob speaking," or something similar. If nothing comes from Bob's end of the line, Alice may try to elicit a response by asking "Hello? Who am I speaking to?", although this is not the normal way of starting a phone conversation. Then, as both parties talk, they, perhaps unconsciously, acknowledge each other's talk snippets. If Bob embarks on some long speech, Alice will occasionally emit something like "Uh-uh," or "Right," or "I see." She does not really "see" anything, of course, but if a long time passes with Bob talking and not getting some feedback like that, he will on his part try to elicit some response by asking, "Are you following me?" or "Are you with me?"

We take all this for granted because it occurs countless times every day, but it is not trivial, as you can verify any time the line is bad or a connection is lost, especially on cell phones.

When your browser communicates with a web server and gets a web page it also follows a well-defined protocol, called HTTP, for *Hypertext Transfer Protocol*. The protocol is remarkably simple, with just a number of commands that the browser can send to the server and a set of responses that the server can send back to the browser. Only these commands and responses can be sent between the browser and the server during an HTTP communication.

The simplest such command is called GET. The browser sends a GET command to the server, passing along with it the address of the web page that it wants. An example command is:

GET http://www.w3.org/pub/WWW/TheProject.html HTTP/1.1

The command asks the server named www.w3.org to send to the browser the web page identified as /pub/WWW/TheProject.html using version 1.1 of the HTTP protocol. The server will retrieve this page and send it back to the browser.

When we say that the browser asks the server to do something, we are glossing over a lot of details. The browser sends this command to the server via a connection to the server. The browser is *not* concerned with how the connection is set up or with how it works. It assumes that there is a reliable connection between itself and the server and that it can send stuff through this connection to the server. Similarly, the server can send stuff back through the same connection to the browser, and it also is not concerned with how the connection is set up or how it works. You can think of the connection as a pipe set up between the browser and the server, in which data flow in both directions.

Because neither the browser nor even the server is concerned with how the connection is established and how data flow through it, something else must take care of these things. This is the responsibility of a different protocol, called Transmission Control Protocol (TCP). The TCP protocol is responsible for giving to its users, here the HTTP protocol, a connection through which data are moved in both ways. The TCP protocol knows nothing about the commands it may transfer along the connection. It has no idea what HTTP is, and what GET is. It only knows to take some data, which may be a GET command, make sure it makes its way to the end of the connection, wait for the response from that end, and make sure that the response makes it back to the original sender of the GET command. It puts the HTTP commands and responses in chunks called *segments*, which it sends over the connection. If the data are too large, then it may break them to chunks of up to a certain size. The HTTP protocol is oblivious to all this; TCP will combine all chunks to create a complete request or a response that it will present to HTTP.

TCP is responsible for setting up the connection and the flow of data between the two computers that are connected through it, but it is not responsible for actually moving the data between the two computers. It is responsible for creating the illusion that a reliable connection exists, although no such physical circuit, as a pipe, or more probably a cable, is in place. Moreover, it does not even know how the data should travel to its destination. It is as if it were running a connection, but it actually has no idea how the connection is built up. Imagine a pipe consisting of many parts. TCP knows how to put things on the pipe, push them to it, get them from it, and notice whether some things that were put into the pipe never got out at the other end, but it does not know how the pipe itself is constructed, out of which parts, or even how many parts. Throughout its operation the pipe may even change, with parts added or removed, if things get clogged on the way. The pipe may even be leaking and data get lost. TCP will notice that and require the re-transmission of the data that are missing, but it has no idea what happens to the data once they get into the pipe. This is the job of a different protocol, the Internet Protocol (IP).

IP takes data, in the form of segments, from TCP and encapsulates them in *packets*, each one of which contains the address of the source and the destination. The packets may be up to a certain size, depending on the physical network on which they will be sent, so each segment may be fragmented to a number of packets. The sender takes each IP packet and forwards it to its destination via a network interface that will put the data on the underlying physical network, and then it forgets about it. Occasionally the destination may be a computer directly connected to the source, but more often than not it will not be so. Computers are connected to each other, and the route from the source to the destination may span many connections across different computers, in the same way that a road network may connect two cities directly, but usually we go from our source to the destination traveling city by city. The IP protocol does not guarantee delivery, and it does not track packets. It does not guarantee that packets will be delivered in order. It does not guarantee that all packets will travel to their destination using the same way. It just forwards packets to their destination. It only knows where to forward a packet it receives, or to deliver it directly if it has reached its destination. When packets arrive at the destination, it presents them to TCP as segments, re-assembling fragmented packets if necessary. It is up to TCP to take these segments and put them back in order, detect missing segments, and ask its counterpart on the other side of the communication to resend them. Overall,

TCP will make everything required to create that illusion of a reliable connection over an unreliable transport layer that simply forwards packets and forgets about them.

A metaphor that may help you understand the interplay between TCP and IP is a city with some fictitious water mains. Imagine that in that city water faucets work the way they are supposed to work: water pours down from them in a stream. Yet if you cared to look in how water travels down to your faucet, you would discover that no pipe exists from the reservoir to your house. There are water carriers at the reservoir, filling their buckets with water. When you turn on your tap, these water carriers take their buckets and carry them to a water tank outside your house. They fill the water tank that feeds the faucet, so you have the impression that water flows uninterruptedly from the reservoir to the faucet, even though this is the result of many buckets traveling around the city. Moreover, each water carrier is free to choose the best way to get to your house; it is not necessary that all of them follow the same route. Yet, if they travel fast enough you will have the illusion that you live in a city with full water plumbing. The water carriers are the IP protocol; what you see as a flow of water is the TCP protocol, which takes care to shield you from the underlying reality.

The whole process is shown in figure 8.1. At each level the protocols operate with the impression that they communicate with their peer on the other side of the communication. In reality, everything goes first down from the upper protocols to the physical network, being broken up if necessary, and then goes up from the physical network on the other side towards the upper protocol layers, re-assembled if necessary.

Another way to think about what is going on is going from the bottom to the top. At the bottom layer of figure 8.1 there is the physical network that moves bits around using, for example, light waves, if the physical network is built with light fibers. A computer communicates with the physical network via its network interface. The network interface pushes data on the network and also receives data from it. Data must know where to go. This is the responsibility of the IP protocol, which handles the routing of the data along the computers that make up the Internet. The IP protocol does not guarantee the delivery of data, it is just a fire and forget protocol. The guarantee of delivery and the establishment of a reliable connection over an unreliable data movement mechanism is the purview of the TCP protocol. The TCP protocol will notice that some data that it asked IP to send have not actually been delivered and will ask its TCP counterpart to resend them. In this way

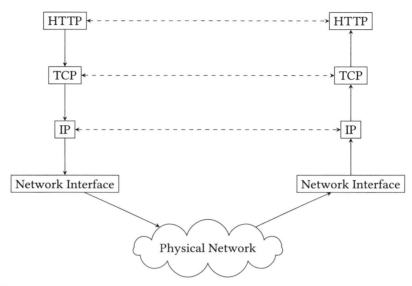

Figure 8.1
The TCP/IP protocol stack with HTTP.

it allows HTTP or any other application-level protocol to issue its commands
and get their responses without thinking about it.

It is pretty amazing that the whole Internet is built on top of an unreliable
transport mechanism, but the combination of the TCP and IP protocols makes
it possible. They are usually bundled together and called the TCP/IP protocol suite. A definition of Internet is the set of computers in the world that is
connected via the TCP/IP protocol suite.

8.1   Internet Routing

As we said above, unless two computers are directly connected to each other,
by which we mean they are on the same physical network, IP cannot forward
the packet from the source to the destination directly, but it has to send it
to intermediaries. We call the intermediaries *routers* because they are routing the data along the network. The way it works is that IP knows, for each
address it sees on a packet, to which router to send the packet, hoping that
this router will know better what to do with it and that it will be closer to the
destination. To understand this it helps to think of a series of messengers in

different towns. If a messenger receives a message from another messenger, it checks to see whether the destination is a local one in town. If it is, it delivers it directly. If it is not and it is to a town directly connected to it, it knows that it must go there. Otherwise, it checks its records and reasons like this: "All packets with addresses of these form should be forwarded to this town, which to the best of my knowledge will know what to do with them." For example, it may know that everything that has a destination in the "north" should go to its northern neighbor, who will know what to do about the packets.

How does IP know where to forward the packets? There is no centralized authority in the Internet, and no central network map. The Internet is composed of big sub-networks, called *autonomous systems*. Each autonomous system may correspond to a campus-wide network, or the network of a big Internet Service Provider (ISP). A complex protocol, called Border Gateway Protocol (BGP) is responsible for arranging the routes between the routers of different autonomous systems. A different protocol, called Routing Information Protocol (RIP), is responsible for arranging the routes between the routers in each autonomous system.

To understand how RIP works, go back to the messengers metaphor. Imagine that each messenger is a bona fide bureaucrat. When the messengers take their places, they know nothing, apart from the fact that their town is directly connected to some other town or towns. The only other thing they can do is send packets to the neighboring towns and receive packets from them. They also have a ledger laying down the forwarding instructions. Initially the ledgers are pretty much empty, containing only the instructions for delivering packets to the neighboring towns.

The messengers send between themselves some special messages that describe to which towns they are connected and the distance to these towns. These messages are crucial. When a messenger receives a message from a town connected to it, it will see that *that* town is connected to towns further afield. From now on the messenger knows that messages that have as their destination the neighboring town *or any of the neighbors' neighboring towns* will be delivered to that neighboring town because the messenger over there will know what to do about them.

Now, the neighboring town will be also receiving these kind of messages, so it will know how to deliver messages farther away. And it will periodically update the first messenger on its knowledge. In this way, after some time all messengers will have a good picture of where to forward the messages they receive. Moreover, sometimes a messenger may receive a message specifying

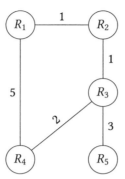

Figure 8.2
An autonomous system with five routers.

that a route through a neighbor is shorter than a previous route it knew about, in which case it will update the ledger accordingly.

If all this looks a bit like a sleight of hand, it can be explained with an example. In figure 8.2 there is an autonomous system with five routers. The operation of RIP is shown in figure 8.3.

Although figure 8.3 shows a single table with all the routes from router to router, no such table really exists. Each router has its own table, which is like a row of the table in the figure, only there are no empty cells in it. As each router does not know how many routers there are, the router's table is only as big as the routers it knows about at each point in time. So in the beginning the table for R_1 has three entries, then it has four, and later on it has five. At each cell (R_i, R_j) in the figure we show the distance from R_i to R_j and the next router to which the packet should be forwarded. So if cell (R_5, R_2) contains the value $4/R_3$, this means that the distance from R_5 to R_2 is 4 and packets to R_2 should be forwarded to R_3. We put D to indicate that there is a direct connection.

In figure 8.3a the only entries in the table are of the form x/D, as we only know of direct connections. Then in figure 8.3b we show what happens after R_1 has received a message from R_2. R_1 now knows that it can forward messages to R_3 via R_2; because R_2 can forward messages to R_3 traveling a distance of one, the total distance from R_1 to R_3 is two, via R_2; we underline the updated entry. Then in figure 8.3c, R_2 receives a message from R_3. R_2 now knows to forward messages to R_4 and R_5 via R_3, so the relevant entries are updates.

	R_1	R_2	R_3	R_4	R_5
R_1	0	1/D	-	5/D	-
R_2	1/D	0	1/D	-	-
R_3	-	1/D	0	2/D	3/D
R_4	5/D	-	2/D	0	-
R_5	-	-	3/D	-	0

(a) Initial state.

	R_1	R_2	R_3	R_4	R_5
R_1	0	1/D	2/R_2	5/D	-
R_2	1/D	0	1/D	-	-
R_3	-	1/D	0	2/D	3/D
R_4	5/D	-	2/D	0	-
R_5	-	-	3/D	-	0

(b) $R_2 \rightarrow R_1$

	R_1	R_2	R_3	R_4	R_5
R_1	0	1/D	2/R_2	5/D	-
R_2	1/R_1	0	1/D	3/R_3	4/R_3
R_3	-	1/D	0	2/D	3/D
R_4	5/D	-	2/D	0	-
R_5	-	-	3/D	-	0

(c) $R_3 \rightarrow R_2$

	R_1	R_2	R_3	R_4	R_5
R_1	0	1/D	2/R_2	4/R_2	5/R_2
R_2	1/R_1	0	1/D	3/R_3	4/R_3
R_3	-	1/D	0	2/D	3/D
R_4	5/D	-	2/D	0	-
R_5	-	-	3/D	-	0

(d) $R_2 \rightarrow R_1$

	R_1	R_2	R_3	R_4	R_5
R_1	0	1/D	2/R_2	4/R_2	5/R_2
R_2	1/R_1	0	1/D	3/R_3	4/R_3
R_3	-	1/D	0	2/D	3/D
R_4	5/D	3/R_3	2/D	0	5/R_3
R_5	-	-	3/D	-	0

(e) $R_3 \rightarrow R_4$

	R_1	R_2	R_3	R_4	R_5
R_1	0	1/D	2/R_2	4/R_2	5/R_2
R_2	1/R_1	0	1/D	3/R_3	4/R_3
R_3	-	1/D	0	2/D	3/D
R_4	5/D	3/R_3	2/D	0	5/R_3
R_5	-	4/R_3	3/D	5/R_3	0

(f) $R_3 \rightarrow R_5$

	R_1	R_2	R_3	R_4	R_5
R_1	0	1/D	2/R_2	4/R_2	5/R_2
R_2	1/R_1	0	1/D	3/R_3	4/R_3
R_3	2/R_2	1/D	0	2/D	3/D
R_4	5/D	3/R_3	2/D	0	5/R_3
R_5	-	4/R_3	3/D	5/R_3	0

(g) $R_2 \rightarrow R_3$

	R_1	R_2	R_3	R_4	R_5
R_1	0	1/D	2/R_2	4/R_2	5/R_2
R_2	1/R_1	0	1/D	3/R_3	4/R_3
R_3	2/R_2	1/D	0	2/D	3/D
R_4	5/D	3/R_3	2/D	0	5/R_3
R_5	5/R_2	4/R_3	3/D	5/R_3	0

(h) $R_3 \rightarrow R_5$

Figure 8.3
Trace of the RIP protocol for figure 8.2.

When we leave off the trace of RIP in figure 8.3, R_4 is aware of the direct route to R_1 and not of the better alternative through R_3. That's because it has not received a message from R_3 after R_3 received a message from R_2. Once it does, R_4 will be aware of the best route to R_1 and will update its table entry. At some point all necessary messages between the routers will have been exchanged so that all routers will know the best, shortest paths to all other routers.

To understand fully why RIP works, it is easier to consider what happens at a single router. When it starts, it only knows the paths to the routers one link away from it. Then it receives a packet from one such router. Suppose that second router has not received any packet itself from any other router. Then the packet it has sent to the first router tells the first router of only the second router's direct connections. The first router then knows of paths up to two links away from it, going from the second router. If the second router receives a packet from a third router, which has not received any packets from any other router, it will know of paths up to two links from it. When it sends a new packet to the first router, the first router will know of paths up to three links away from it, passing through the second router.

This looks like a relaxation procedure, where each time we get a packet we may relax paths of an increasing number of links. That is indeed what happens: a repeated application of relaxation across paths of an increasing number of links. To convince yourself that RIP works, you need to see how such an application of relaxation finds shortest paths in a graph.

Instead of having all routers talking to each other, take a graph in which we want to find shortest paths from a starting node. We start with the graph initialized with every shortest path estimate set to ∞ apart from the estimate to our starting node, which we set to zero.

Next we take each edge in the graph and relax the path estimate to its destination. In other words, we take each edge in the graph and check whether it is possible to use it to get to its destination from our starting node with a shorter path than the one we have already found. The first time we do that, we will find shortest path estimates for the nodes that are directly connected to our starting node, so these will be the shortest paths containing only one edge. That's the starting point for RIP at a single node.

We repeat the procedure, and we relax again along all edges of the graph. This time, the second one, we will find shortest path estimates for the nodes that are directly connected to our starting node or directly connected to nodes that are directly connected to our starting node. That means we will find shortest path estimates for the nodes that are up to two edges away from our starting node. Then if we repeat the procedure $|V| - 1$ times, we will find shortest path estimates for the nodes that are up to $|V| - 1$ edges away from our starting node. There is no way there can be a path from a node to another node in the graph with more than $|V| - 1$ nodes in it, unless there are cycles in it. If the cycles have paths with positive length, then they cannot be in any shortest path. If the cycles have paths with negative length, then anyway there is no notion of shortest path in the graph because we can go around them for ever reducing our path length to $-\infty$. Either way, after $|V| - 1$ iterations of the relaxation process for all edges we will have found the shortest paths from our starting node to every other node in the graph.

8.2   The Bellman-Ford(-Moore) Algorithm

The procedure is a high-level description of the Bellman-Ford algorithm, shown in algorithm 8.1. It is named after Richard Bellman and Lester Ford, Jr., who published the algorithm. The algorithm is also called Bellman-Ford-Moore because Edward F. Moore also published the algorithm at the same time. The RIP protocol then is a distributed version of the Bellman-Ford algorithm for finding not just the shortest paths from a starting node, but all shortest paths between any two pairs of nodes. In other words, it solves the all-pairs shortest paths problem in a distributed fashion.

Back to the basic, meaning not the distributed, version of the Bellman-Ford algorithm. It uses an array *pred* to hold the predecessor of each node in the shortest path to it and *dist* to hold the value of the shortest path.

The Bellman-Ford algorithm starts with initializing the data structures, in lines 1–8, so that they reflect the situation where we know of no shortest path apart from the path to our starting node. Hence, no node has a predecessor and the lengths of all shortest paths are set to ∞, apart from the trivial path from our starting node to our starting node, which is equal to zero. After the initialization it checks for shortest paths of an ever-increasing number of edges. Initially paths may have one edge, then two, until we reach the maximum number of edges in path. A path with the maximum number of edges will contain all nodes in the graph exactly one, and therefore will have $|V| - 1$ edges. All this happens in lines 9–13. The loop works as follows:

• After the first iteration, we have found shortest paths containing no more than one link.

Algorithm 8.1: Bellman-Ford.

BellmanFord(G, s) $\longrightarrow$ ($pred, dist$)
    Input: $G = (V, E)$, a graph
           s, the starting node
    Output: $pred$, an array of size $|V|$ such that $pred[i]$ is the predecessor
           of node i in the shortest path from s
           $dist$, an array of size $|V|$ such that $dist[i]$ is the length of the
           shortest path calculated from node s to i

1   $pred \leftarrow$ CreateArray($|V|$)
2   $dist \leftarrow$ CreateArray($|V|$)
3   **foreach** v **in** V **do**
4        $pred[v] \leftarrow -1$
5   **if** $v \neq s$ **then**
6            $dist[v] \leftarrow \infty$
7   **else**
8            $dist[v] \leftarrow 0$
9   **for** $i \leftarrow 0$ **to** $|V|$ **do**
10   **foreach** (u, v) **in** E **do**
11   **if** $dist[v] > dist[u] +$ Weight(G, u, v) **then**
12               $dist[v] \leftarrow dist[u] +$ Weight(G, u, v)
13               $pred[v] \leftarrow u$
14 **return** ($pred, dist$)

- After the second iteration, we have found shortest paths containing no more than two links.

- After the kth iteration, we have found shortest paths containing no more than k links.

- After $|V| - 1$ iterations, we have found shortest paths containing no more than $|V| - 1$ links.

Because there can be no shortest path with more than $|V| - 1$ links, or we would go into circles, we are done.

As with Dijkstra's algorithm, if you are to implement algorithm 8.1, be careful with line 11. If the programming language you are using does not know

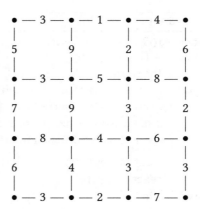

Figure 8.4
A traffic grid.

infinity and you use a big number instead, make sure you are not adding to a big number and getting a small number due to overflows.

A trace of the Bellman-Ford algorithm for the traffic grid graph in figure 8.4, is in figure 8.5. To refer to nodes on the grid we will use their coordinates, indexed from zero, so that $(0, 0)$ is the node at the upper left corner, $(3, 3)$ is the node at the bottom right corner, and so on.

Each sub-figure in the figure corresponds to an iteration of the relaxation process for all edges. The first sub-figure contains paths with zero edges, the second sub-figure contains paths with one edge, until the last sub-figure, which contains paths with up to seven edges. We underline edges in which the relaxation process involves a choice between paths, that is, a choice between two edges leading to that particular node in that iteration. So, in the second iteration there are two paths with two edges to the node at position $(1, 1)$ and we select the best one. In the fifth iteration, the node at position $(2, 1)$ gets an improved path by choosing to go through the node at position $(3, 2)$ instead of going from the node at position $(1, 1)$. In general, we do not have a set of nodes for which we know that their estimate is not going to change; the shortest path of a node may be subject to change in the future, until the end of the algorithm. Moreover, even after we have seemingly examined all nodes, as in the sixth iteration, there may still be better paths with more edges in them. This is what happens in the eighth iteration,

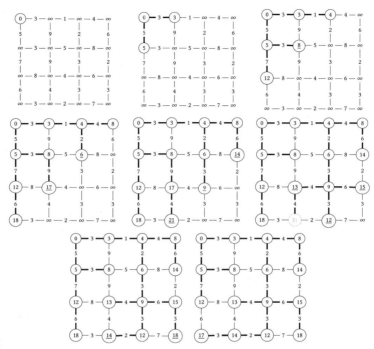

Figure 8.5
Shortest paths with the Bellman-Ford algorithm.

when node (3, 0) gets a better path via node (3, 1), where the new path contains seven edges, going through $(0, 0) \rightarrow (0, 1) \rightarrow (0, 2) \rightarrow (1, 2) \rightarrow (2, 2) \rightarrow (3, 2) \rightarrow (3, 1) \rightarrow (3, 0)$ instead of the old path that contained only three edges going through $(0, 0) \rightarrow (1, 0) \rightarrow (2, 0) \rightarrow (3, 0)$.

We have put (3, 1) with gray text in a dotted line in the fifth iteration to highlight that it is right now in a limbo state. The path to node (2, 1) has been updated, and from a path with three edges, in the fourth iteration, now has a shorter path with five edges. At iteration i the algorithm finds shortest paths with up to i edges, but not longer. So the path to node (3, 1) from the updated path to node (2, 1) is not really found at the fifth iteration because this has six edges. It just happened to be there. It *may* be found, by accident, if we relax edge $(2, 1) \rightarrow (3, 1)$ after we relax $(2, 2) \rightarrow (2, 1)$, but there is nothing in the algorithm that specifies the order in which we consider edges to relax. This is not to worry, however, because node (3, 1) will get the correct path at the next iteration, and that path is not even the one coming from (2, 1).

In terms of running time, the Bellman-Ford algorithm performs $|V|$ iterations in the initialization part. The initialization involves setting values in arrays, which takes constant, $O(1)$, time, so it takes $O(|V|)$ time. The loop in lines 9–13 is repeated $|V| - 1$ times, and each time it examines all the edges of the graph, so it takes $O((|V| - 1)|E|) = O(|V||E|)$ time. The whole algorithm takes $O(|V| + |V||E|)$ time, that is, $O(|V||E|)$ time.

Note that the algorithm as we have described it does not stop at the seventh iteration. It will continue trying to find shortest paths with more edges, until it reaches fifteen iterations. However, in this particular graph no shorter paths will be found for the remaining iterations, so we have cut they story short and left the trace there. In general, though, this shows an opportunity for optimization with respect to algorithm 8.1. Suppose we are at the ith iteration of the algorithm, and we relax, and therefore update, the shortest paths to, say, m nodes. Let's call these nodes $i_1, i_2, \ldots, i_m$. The shortest paths to these nodes will have no more than i edges. At the $(i + 1)$th iteration of the algorithm the only edges we really need to check are the edges adjacent to the nodes $i_1, i_2, \ldots, i_m$. Why? Because at the $(i + 1)$th iteration of the algorithm we will be looking for shortest paths with no more than $i + 1$ edges because we have already found paths with no more than i edges. But these paths with i edges are the paths whose last edge ends at one of the nodes $i_1, i_2, \ldots, i_m$. Therefore, at each iteration of the algorithm, instead of checking all edges, we need to check only the edges of the nodes whose estimates we updated at the previous iteration.

Before we go on to take advantage of this optimization, you may wonder why the algorithm works in the first place. The argument is somewhat similar to the one above on optimization and works by induction. When we start, before the first iteration, the *dist* array contains for every node the length of the shortest path from the starting node s, to that node, with no more than zero edges. Indeed, it is so, as $dist[s] = 0$ and $dist[u] = \infty$ for all $u \neq s$. Suppose the same holds at iteration i. Then for every node u, $dist[u]$ contains the length of the shortest path from s to u with no more than i edges. Consider then what happens at the $(i + 1)$th iteration. The paths from s to any node u at this iteration may have no more than $i + 1$ edges. If all such paths contain no more than i edges, we have already found them in the previous iterations, and so $dist[u]$ does not change in the current iteration. If there are paths with $i + 1$ edges, then for each such path we reason as follows. The path will consist of two parts. It will start from node s and arrive at some node w after i edges; after that there will be an edge from node w to node u: $s \overset{i}{\rightsquigarrow} w \rightarrow v$. The first part, $s \overset{i}{\rightsquigarrow} w$, contains i edges, and so we must have found it in the ith iteration. That means that it cannot be longer than the shortest path from s to w. In the $(i + 1)$th iteration we found the edge $w \rightarrow v$ that has the least possible weight to add to the weight of the path $s \overset{i}{\rightsquigarrow} w$, so the path $s \overset{i}{\rightsquigarrow} w \rightarrow v$ is the shortest path with up to $i + 1$ links.

Returning to how to optimize the algorithm, we can keep the nodes whose estimates we update at each iteration by putting them in a First-In First-Out (FIFO) queue. We also need a way to know whether an item is in the queue. An easy way to do that is to use a boolean array *inqueue* in which *inqueue*[i] will be true if i is in q and false otherwise. We can then recast Bellman-Ford as in algorithm 8.2. Let's return to the graph in figure 8.5 and trace the execution of algorithm 8.2. The trace is in figure 8.6. Beneath each grid you can see the contents of the queue. You can also see them on the grid: the nodes that are currently in the queue are filled with grey.

This time the algorithm does stop at the ninth iteration, so you see the advantage over the previous implementation. Pay attention to what happens in the sixth, seventh, and eighth iterations: nodes that had been in the queue before re-enter the queue, as we find shorter paths with more edges in them. In the fourth iteration we found a path to node $(2, 1)$, then in the sixth iteration we found a better path to it. In the fourth iteration we also found a path to node $(3, 0)$, then we found a better one at the eighth iteration. And in the fifth iteration we found a path to node $(3, 1)$, which we changed for a better path in the seventh iteration.

The running time of the Bellman-Ford algorithm, at $O(|V||E|)$, is in general worse than the running time of the Dijkstra algorithm, which can be as low as $O(|E| \lg |V|)$. Figures 8.5 and 8.6 are a bit deceptive because they show a snapshot of each iteration, while lots of things happen in each one of them. In the queue-based version, all edges adjacent to nodes on the queue are checked between two snapshots. In the simpler version, all edges of the graph are checked anew at each transition between two snapshots. The queue-based algorithm improves the running time from algorithm 8.1 in many cases but not always. It may happen that in each iteration of the graph we update the path estimates of all nodes, so that at each iteration we have to check all edges again. In practice, though, Bellman-Ford is efficient.

Algorithm 8.2: Queue-based Bellman-Ford.

BellmanFordQueue(G, s) $\rightarrow$ (*pred*, *dist*)

    Input: $G = (V, E)$, a graph

          s, the starting node

    Output: *pred*, an array of size $|V|$ such that *pred*[i] is the predecessor

          of node i in the shortest path from s

          dist, an array of size $|V|$ such that *dist*[i] is the length of the

          shortest path calculated from node s to i

1   *inqueue* $\leftarrow$ CreateArray($|V|$)

2    $Q \leftarrow$ CreateQueue()

3   **foreach** v **in** V **do**

4   *pred*[v] $\leftarrow -1$

5   **if** $v \neq s$ **then**

6   *dist*[v] $\leftarrow \infty$

7   *inqueue*[v] $\leftarrow$ FALSE

8   **else**

9   *dist*[v] $\leftarrow 0$

10   Enqueue(Q, s)

11   *inqueue*[s] $\leftarrow$ TRUE

12   **while** Size(Q) $\neq 0$ **do**

13       $u \leftarrow$ Dequeue(Q)

14   *inqueue*[u] $\leftarrow$ FALSE

15   **foreach** v **in** AdjacencyList(G, u) **do**

16   **if** *dist*[v] $>$ *dist*[u] $+$ Weight(G, u, v) **then**

17   *dist*[v] $\leftarrow$ *dist*[u] $+$ Weight(G, u, v)

18   *pred*[v] $\leftarrow u$

19   **if not** *inqueue*[v] **then**

20   Enqueue(Q, v)

21   *inqueue*[v] $\leftarrow$ TRUE

22   **return** (*pred*, *dist*)

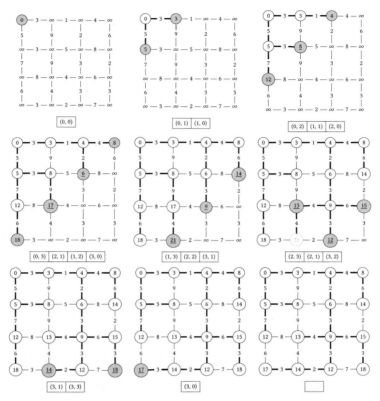

Figure 8.6
Shortest paths with the queue-based Bellman-Ford algorithm.

8.3   Negative Weights and Cycles

We may not always have the luxury of choice between Dijkstra and Bellman-Ford. The Bellman-Ford algorithm does handle negative weights properly, in contrast to Dijkstra's algorithm, which produces wrong results. Indeed, if you take the graph in figure 8.7 and apply the Bellman-Ford algorithm, as you see in figure 8.8, you will get the right results.

Now, let's give another turn to the screw and ask what will happen if the graph contains negative weights as well as negative cycles, such as the graph in figure 8.9?

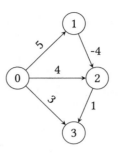

Figure 8.7
A graph with negative weights.

Algorithm 8.1 will stop after $|V|$ iterations and will output its results, which will not make sense because as we said the shortest path along a cycle with negative weights is the path going around it forever, with weight $-\infty$. Algorithm 8.2 will do even worse, as it will never stop. When it encounters a cycle it will get stuck forever in a loop inserting and extracting the nodes of the cycle in the queue it uses, as you can see in figure 8.10.

All this means that in order for the queue-based algorithm to terminate in the presence of negative cycles, we have to do some extra work. We can detect a cycle if we find a path with more than $|V| - 1$ edges because the longest path in a graph with $|V|$ nodes includes all of them and has $|V| - 1$ edges. Paths with more edges retrace their steps over nodes they have already visited.

Recall that the basic idea behind Bellman-Ford is that we investigate paths of increasing number of edges. Initially, when we start at the source node s, we have paths of zero edges. When we add the neighbors of s in the queue, we have paths with one edge. When we add the neighbors *of the neighbors* of s, we have paths with two edges, and so on. The problem is how to know when we stop processing one set of neighbors and proceed to another set of neighbors. When this happens $|V| - 1$ times we know that the algorithm must terminate.

We can solve the problem by using a special *sentinel* value in the queue. In general, sentinel values are invalid values that signal some specific event. In our case we will use the number $|V|$ as a sentinel value, as there is no such node; nodes go from 0 to $|V| - 1$. In particular, we will use the number $|V|$ to demarcate in the queue a set of neighbors at the same number of links away from s. You can see how this works in figure 8.11.

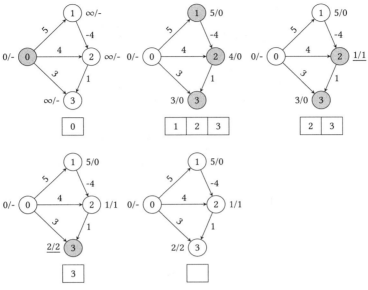

Figure 8.8
Bellman-Ford algorithm on graph with negative edges.

When we start, we put the source node, 0, and the sentinel, 5, in the queue. We keep a counter, i, to indicate the number of edges in paths. Initially this is zero. Each time 5 reaches the head of the queue, we increment i and put 5 back in the end of the queue. Take a look at what happens when node 3 is in the head of the queue. We remove 3 from the head and add the two neighbors of 3, nodes 1 and 4, at the back of the queue. Now 5 comes to the head of the queue, so we increment i. We put 5 back again at the end of the queue to indicate that nodes 1 and 4 are at the same number of links away from node 0. When the sentinel makes it again to the head of the queue and i becomes 5, we know that we have started going in circles and we can stop. The amended Bellman-Ford that takes care of all this is algorithm 8.3. Algorithm 8.3 returns, apart from the arrays *pred* and *dist*, a boolean value that will be true when no negative cycle was detected and false when a negative cycle was found. It initializes the sentinel in line 10 and handles the counter i in lines 16–17. We check the value of i in line 14; notice that now we do not expect the queue ever to be empty as the sentinel will always be in there.

Algorithm 8.3: Queue-based Bellman-Ford with negative cycles.

BellmanFordQueueNC(G, s) $\rightarrow$ ($pred, dist, ncc$)

    Input: $G = (V, E)$, a graph

             s, the starting node

    Output: $pred$, an array of size $|V|$ such that $pred[i]$ is the predecessor

               of node i in the shortest path from s

               $dist$, an array of size $|V|$ such that $dist[i]$ is the length of the

               shortest path calculated from node s to i

               nnc, TRUE if there is no negative cycle, FALSE otherwise.

1    $inqueue \leftarrow$ CreateArray($|V|$)
2    $Q \leftarrow$ CreateQueue()
3   **foreach** v **in** V **do**
4        $pred[v] \leftarrow |V|$
5   **if** $v \neq s$ **then**
6            $dist[v] \leftarrow \infty$
7            $inqueue[v] \leftarrow$ FALSE
8   **else**
9            $dist[v] \leftarrow 0$
10   Enqueue(Q, s)
11   $inqueue[s] \leftarrow$ TRUE
12   Enqueue($Q, |V|$)

13   $i \leftarrow 0$
14   **while** Size(Q) $\neq 1$ **and** $i < |V|$ **do**
15       $u \leftarrow$ Dequeue(Q)
16   **if** $u = |V|$ **then**
17           $i \leftarrow i + 1$
18   Enqueue($Q, |V|$)
19   **else**
20           $inqueue[u] \leftarrow$ FALSE
21   **foreach** v **in** AdjacencyList(G, u) **do**
22   **if** $dist[v] > dist[u] +$ Weight(G, u, v) **then**
23                   $dist[v] \leftarrow dist[u] +$ Weight(G, u, v)
24                   $pred[v] \leftarrow u$
25   **if not** $inqueue[v]$ **then**
26   Enqueue(Q, v)
27                      $inqueue[v] \leftarrow$ TRUE
28   **return** ($pred, dist, i < |V|$)

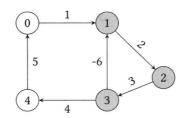

Figure 8.9
A graph with a negative cycle.

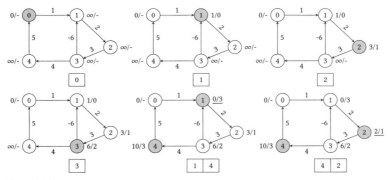

Figure 8.10
Trace of the Bellman-Ford algorithm with a negative cycle.

8.4   Arbitrage

You should not think that getting across negative cycles is some obscure phenomenon. Negative weight cycles do arise in real-world problems. A real-world application involving the detection of negative weight cycles is the detection of *arbitrage opportunities*. An arbitrage is like a free lunch. It involves a set of commodities that can be exchanged, bought, and sold for each other. Such commodities may involve industrial metals, for example, copper, lead, and zinc, currencies, such as euros and U.S. dollars, or anything that is traded on a market. Arbitrage is taking advantage of the price difference between different markets to make a profit. As a simple example, suppose that in London the exchange rate between euros and U.S. dollars is €1 = $1.37, while in New York the exchange rate between U.S. dollars and euros is $1 = €0.74. Then a trader can buy in London with €1,000,000 a total of

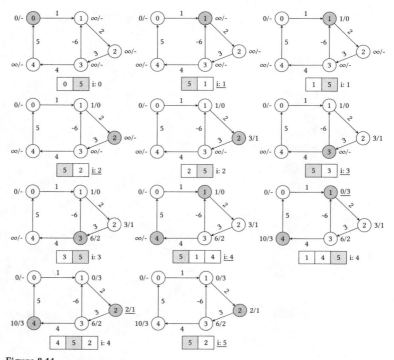

Figure 8.11
Trace of the amended Bellman-Ford algorithm with a negative cycle.

$1,370,000, wire them over to New York, and buy back Euros there. The trader will end up with $1,370,000 × 0.74 = €1,013,800, making a risk-free tidy profit of €13,800 out of thin air.

The reason this does not happen often is that once an arbitrage opportunity appears, traders will sniff it out and the markets will adjust to make it disappear. So, to continue with our example, after a number of arbitrage trades, the exchange rate in New York will go down, or in London will go up so that one should be the exact inverse of the other: for rate x in London we will very quickly end up with rate $1/x$ in New York.

For the short time window that an arbitrage opportunity appears, however, there is serious money to be made, and an arbitrage opportunity may not be so obvious to spot as a simple back and forth conversion between two currencies. Table 8.1 contains the top ten traded currencies by value in April

2013. As currency trading involves pairs, the percentages sum up to 200% for all currencies (including those not in the top ten).

Table 8.1
Top ten most traded currencies by value, April 2013.

Rank	Currency	Code	% Daily Share
1	U.S. dollar	USD	87.0%
2	European Union euro	EUR	33.4%
3	Japanese yen	JPY	23.0%
4	United Kingdom pound sterling	GBP	11.8%
5	Australian dollar	AUD	8.6%
6	Swiss franc	CHF	5.2%
7	Canadian dollar	CAD	4.6%
8	Mexican peso	MXN	2.5%
9	Chinese yuan	CNY	2.2%
10	New Zealand dollar	NZD	2.0%

If we can convert between any two currencies in that table, then an arbitrage opportunity may appear involving any path in the graph of figure 8.12. The table beneath the graph shows the cross-currency exchange rates for the currencies in the graph. They are the weights of the edges, but they would not fit in the graph very easily.

Suppose you have a U.S. dollar and an arbitrage opportunity exists by exchanging them to Australian dollars, these to Canadian dollars and these back to U.S. dollars. The whole conversion sequence would be:

$$1 \times (\text{USD} \rightarrow \text{AUD}) \times (\text{AUD} \rightarrow \text{CAD}) \times (\text{CAD} \rightarrow \text{USD})$$

You would end up better off if the result of the above product is greater than one. In general, if $c_1, c_2, \ldots, c_n$ are currencies, then an arbitrage a exists if we have:

$$a = 1 \times (c_1 \rightarrow c_2) \times (c_2 \rightarrow c_3) \times \cdots \times (c_n \rightarrow c_1)$$

so that:

$$a > 1$$

Going to the graph in figure 8.12, such a sequence of conversions corresponds to the cycle in the graph going through those currency nodes. Any arbitrage opportunity will be a cycle in the graph, in which cycle the product of the weights should be greater than one.

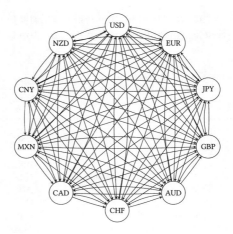

(a) Cross-currency rates graph.

	USD	EUR	JPY	GBP	AUD	CHF	CAD	MXN	CNY	NZD
USD	1	1.3744	0.009766	1.6625	0.9262	1.1275	0.9066	0.07652	0.1623	0.8676
EUR	0.7276	1	0.007106	1.2097	0.6739	0.8204	0.6596	0.05568	0.1181	0.6313
JPY	102.405	140.743	1	170.248	94.8421	115.455	92.8369	7.836	16.6178	88.8463
GBP	0.6016	0.8268	0.005875	1	0.5572	0.6782	0.5454	0.04603	0.09762	0.5219
AUD	1.0799	1.4842	0.010546	1.7953	1	1.2176	0.979	0.08263	0.1752	0.9369
CHF	0.8871	1.2192	0.008663	1.4748	0.8216	1	0.8042	0.06788	0.144	0.7696
CAD	1.1033	1.5163	0.010775	1.8342	1.0218	1.2439	1	0.08442	0.179	0.9572
MXN	13.0763	17.9724	0.1277	21.7397	12.1111	14.7435	11.8545	1	2.122	11.345
CNY	6.167	8.4761	0.06023	10.2528	5.7118	6.9533	5.5908	0.4719	1	5.3505
NZD	1.153	1.5846	0.01126	1.9168	1.0678	1.2999	1.0452	0.08822	0.1871	1

(b) Cross-currency graph adjacency matrix.

Figure 8.12

Cross-currency rates graph and adjacency matrix.

We do not have at our disposal an algorithm to identify such cycles, but a mathematical trick will allow us to use the tools that we do already have. Instead of using the currency exchange rates as weights in the graph, we can use the negative logarithm of the exchange rates. That is, if the weight in the edge between nodes u and v is $w(u, v)$, then we substitute $w'(u, v) = -\log w(u, v)$. Some of these logarithms will be positive and some will be negative; in particular, $w'(u, v) \geq 0$ if $w(u, v) > 1$. We run the Bellman-Ford algorithm for negative weight cycles on the graph and watch to see whether it reports the existence of negative weight cycles. If it does, then we find the cycle. Suppose that the cycle contains n edges; then its sum one time around it will be $w'_1 + w'_2 + \ldots + w'_n < 0$, where $w'_1, w'_2, \ldots w'_n$ are the weights of the n edges constituting the cycle between the two nodes. We have:

$$w'_1 + w'_2 + \ldots + w'_n = -\log w_1 - \log w_2 - \cdots - \log w_n$$

so we get for the sum of the path along the negative weight cycle:

$$-\log w_1 - \log w_2 - \cdots - \log w_n < 0$$

A basic property of logarithms is that for any numbers x and y the product of their logarithm $\log(xy)$ corresponds to the sum of their logarithms $\log x + \log y$ and similarly $\log(1/x \; 1/y)$ corresponds to $\log(1/x) + \log(1/y) = -\log x - \log y$. It follows that the last inequality above corresponds to:

$$\log(\frac{1}{w_1} \times \frac{1}{w_2} \times \cdots \times \frac{1}{w_n}) < 0$$

Exponentiating to remove the logarithm, it becomes:

$$\frac{1}{w_1} \times \frac{1}{w_2} \times \cdots \times \frac{1}{w_n} < 10^0 = 1$$

But this is equivalent to:

$$w_1 w_2 \ldots w_n > 1$$

which is what we wanted to find in the first place; a cyclical path with weights whose product is greater than one. You detect an arbitrage opportunity whenever you find a negative weight cycle in the graph. Don't delay!

Notes

There are many books on TCP/IP and how the internet works; the book by
Stevens (revised by Fall) is the classic reference [58]; see also Comer's textbook [38]. To see how general concepts are translated to networking protocols, see the book by Perlman [157]. For general introductions to networking
see the textbook by Kurose and Ross [119] as well as the one by Tanenbaum
and Wetherall [196].

Lester Ford published the algorithm in 1956 [69]; then Richard Bellman
published it in 1958 [13], while Edward Moore presented it in 1957 [145]. If the
graph does not have cycles with negative weights, then it can be improved, as
shown by Yen [221]. Another improvement, again applicable when the graph
does not have cycles with negative cycles, was given more recently by Bannister and Eppstein [8].

9 What's Most Important

At each moment, incessantly, the web is trawled by *web crawlers*, programs that jump from page to page, taking each one of them and indexing it. They break each page to words, sentences, and phrases, and they get the links the page contains to other pages of the web. The crawlers take the derived contents of the page and store them in a big data structure called an *inverted index*. It is an index like the index you find at the end of a book, where you see terms associated with the set of pages in which they appear. It is called inverted because its purpose is to allow retrieving the original content, the web page, from one of its parts, a term that appears in the page. Usually we get the contents of a page from the page when we read the page; when we get the page from the contents we go the other way round, hence inverse.

Apart from the index, the crawlers use the links contained inside the web pages to find other web pages to visit and do the indexing process; they also use the links to create a big map of the web, showing which pages link to which other pages.

All this happens so that when you search for something in a search engine, the search engine will give you, hopefully, the results that you are looking for. The search engine uses the inverted index to find the pages that correspond to your search. But like an index in a book, more than one page may match your search. In a book that is not a big problem because the pages will not be that many, and usually you are interested in the first page that a term appears. But in the web there is no first page, while the number of pages that match your search may be in the billions. You are not going to look through all of them, of course. You want to find the most relevant of them.

For example, when you search for the White House on the web, there will definitely be umpteen web pages that feature the words "White House" in them. A simple list of all pages that match your search query will be pretty much useless. However, probably some web pages are more relevant to you than others; it is more likely that the web page of the White House itself is what you are looking for, rather than the web page of a little known blog offering idiosyncratic views on White House policy—unless you really asked for it.

One way to solve the problem of which page to give you as a search result is to order them in terms of significance, or importance. The problem then is how to define what is important in the realm of web pages.

9.1   The PageRank Idea

A solution that has proved to be hugely successful is the one invented by the founders of Google, Sergey Brin and Larry Page. The solution, published in 1998, is called PageRank, and it assigns to each web page a number, also called its PageRank. The highest the PageRank of a page, the more important it is. The essential idea behind PageRank is that the importance of a page, its PageRank, depends on the importance of the pages that link to it.

Each page may link to a number of other pages through outgoing links, and a number of other pages may link to that particular page through incoming links. We denote page i by P_i. If a page P_j has m outgoing links, then we use the notation $|P_j|$ for the number m; in other words, $|P_j|$ is the number of outgoing links of page P_j. We then assume that the importance of the page $|P_j|$ is contributed evenly to the pages it links to. For example, if P_j links to three pages, then it will contribute $1/3$ of its importance to each one of the three linked pages. We use the notation $r(P_j)$ for the PageRank of the page P_j. Following the above, if P_j links to P_i and has $|P_j|$ outgoing links, then it will contribute to P_i a part of its PageRank equal to $r(P_j)/|P_j|$. The PageRank of a page is the sum of the PageRank contributions it takes from all pages that link to it. If we call B_{P_i} the set of pages that link to P_i, that is the set of pages with *backlinks* to P_i, then we have:

$$r(P_i) = \sum_{P_j \in B_{P_i}} \frac{r(P_j)}{|P_j|}$$

If, for example, we have the graph at figure 9.1, then:

$$r(P_1) = \frac{r(P_2)}{3} + \frac{r(P_3)}{4} + \frac{r(P_4)}{2}$$

So, to find the PageRank of a page we need to know the PageRank of the pages that link to it; to find the PageRank of *those* pages, we need to find the

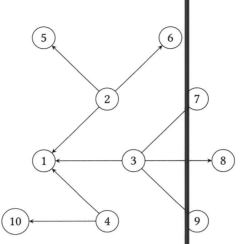

Figure 9.1
A minimal web graph.

PageRank of the pages that link to them, and so on. At the same time, pages may link between themselves in cycles. It appears we have a chicken-and-egg problem, where in order to find the PageRank of a page we need to calculate something that may require the PageRank of that page.

The solution to the chicken or the egg problem is to use an iterative procedure. At the beginning we assign a PageRank to each and every page. If we have n pages, then we may assign the number $1/n$ as the PageRank of every page. Then we use the following iteration:

$$r_{k+1}(P_i) = \sum_{P_j \in B_{P_i}} \frac{r_k(P_j)}{|P_j|}$$

The subscripts $k + 1$ and k denote the value of $r(P_i)$ and $r(P_j)$ at iteration $k + 1$ and k, respectively. The above formula means that the PageRank of the page is calculated using the PageRank of the pages linking to it in the previous iteration. We iterate a number of times, hoping that after a while the PageRank calculations will converge to some stable and sensible values.

Immediately there are two questions to consider:

- Does the iterative procedure for calculating PageRank converge after a reasonable number of iterations?
- Does the iterative procedure for calculating PageRank converge to a reasonable result?

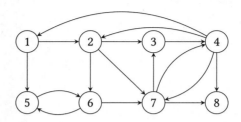

Figure 9.2
Another web graph.

9.2   The Hyperlink Matrix

The procedure we just described shows what happens at each individual page. We can cast it in a form that describes what is happening on all pages by using matrices. In particular, we start by defining a matrix, called *hyperlink matrix*. The hyperlink matrix is a square matrix with the number of rows, or columns, equal to the number of pages. Each row and each column corresponds to a page. Each element of the matrix is defined as:

$$H[i,j] = \begin{cases} 1/|P_i|, & P_i \in P_{B_j} \\ 0, & \text{otherwise} \end{cases}$$

In other words, element $H[i,j]$ is zero if there is no link from page P_i to page P_j, or the inverse of the number of outgoing links of page P_i if one of the links goes to page P_j.

Consider the graph in 9.2. The H matrix for the graph, with indices added for clarity, is:

$$H = \begin{array}{c} \\ P_1 \\ P_2 \\ P_3 \\ P_4 \\ P_5 \\ P_6 \\ P_7 \\ P_8 \end{array} \begin{array}{cccccccc} P_1 & P_2 & P_3 & P_4 & P_5 & P_6 & P_7 & P_8 \\ \left[\begin{array}{cccccccc} 0 & 1/2 & 0 & 0 & 1/2 & 0 & 0 & 0 \\ 0 & 0 & 1/3 & 0 & 0 & 1/3 & 1/3 & 0 \\ 0 & 0 & 0 & 1 & 0 & 0 & 0 & 0 \\ 1/4 & 1/4 & 0 & 0 & 0 & 0 & 1/4 & 1/4 \\ 0 & 0 & 0 & 0 & 0 & 1 & 0 & 0 \\ 0 & 0 & 0 & 0 & 1/2 & 0 & 1/2 & 0 \\ 0 & 0 & 1/3 & 1/3 & 0 & 0 & 0 & 1/3 \\ 0 & 0 & 0 & 0 & 0 & 0 & 0 & 0 \end{array}\right] \end{array}$$

You can check a couple of properties of this matrix. The sum of each row is one because the denominator of each element in a row is the number of non-zero elements in that row, except if a page has no outgoing links, in which case the whole row is zero. This is what happens in the eighth row of this hyperlink matrix.

We can put the PageRank values in a matrix, or more precisely a vector, as well. By convention vectors are considered to be one-column matrices. If the vector containing the PageRanks is π, we have for a set of n pages:

$$\pi = \begin{bmatrix} r(P_1) \\ r(P_2) \\ \vdots \\ r(P_n) \end{bmatrix}$$

When we want to transform a column vector to a row vector, we use the notation:

$$\pi^T = \begin{bmatrix} r(P_1) \ r(P_2) \ \cdots \ r(P_n) \end{bmatrix}$$

It may not look beautiful, but it is in widespread use so you must get accustomed to it; T stands for transpose. Also, remember that we use arrays to represent matrices in computers and arrays are in most computer languages zero based, so we have:

$$\pi^T = \begin{bmatrix} r(P_1) \ r(P_2) \ \cdots \ r(P_n) \end{bmatrix} = \begin{bmatrix} \pi[0] \ \pi[1] \ \cdots \ \pi[n-1] \end{bmatrix}$$

With these definitions in place, let's take the matrix product of π^T and H and use that as the basis for an iterative procedure

$$\pi_{k+1}^T = \pi_k^T H$$

A quick inspection shows that indeed, these matrix multiplications are completely equivalent to the iterative procedure we started with. Because the multiplication of two matrices C and D where C has n columns and D has n rows is defined as the matrix E such that:

$$E[i,j] = \sum_{t=0}^{n-1} C[i,t]D[t,j]$$

the ith element of $\pi_{k+1}^T = \pi_k^T H$ is really:

$$\pi_{k+1}[i] = \sum_{t=0}^{n-1} \pi_k[t]H[t,i]$$

$$= \pi_k[0]H[0,i] + \pi_k[1]H[1,i] + \cdots + \pi_k[n-1]H[n-1,i]$$

In our example each iteration calculates:

$$r_{k+1}(P_1) = \frac{r_k(P_4)}{4}$$

$$r_{k+1}(P_2) = \frac{r_k(P_1)}{2} + \frac{r_k(P_4)}{4}$$

$$r_{k+1}(P_3) = \frac{r_k(P_2)}{3} + \frac{r_k(P_7)}{3}$$

$$r_{k+1}(P_4) = r_k(P_3) + \frac{r_k(P_7)}{3}$$

$$r_{k+1}(P_5) = \frac{r_k(P_1)}{2} + \frac{r_k(P_6)}{2}$$

$$r_{k+1}(P_6) = \frac{r_k(P_2)}{3} + r_k(P_5)$$

$$r_{k+1}(P_7) = \frac{r_k(P_2)}{3} + \frac{r_k(P_4)}{4} + \frac{r_k(P_6)}{2}$$

$$r_{k+1}(P_8) = \frac{r_k(P_4)}{4} + \frac{r_k(P_7)}{3}$$

which is what it should indeed calculate.

9.3   The Power Method

The successive matrix multiplications form the *power method* because they involve raising a vector, in our instance the vector of PageRank values, to successive powers. The two questions we stated in the original iterative procedure are now transferred in the realm of the power method. In essence, we want to know whether the series of multiplications will converge to a stable, reasonable π^T after a number of iterations. If the power method converges, then we call the vector to which it converges a *stationary vector* because further iterations of the power method calculations will not change its values. Does the power method succeed in finding a stationary vector?

A simple counter-example suffices to show that it does not always succeed. See figure 9.3. There are only three nodes, and a single link from one to the other.

The way we described PageRank, in each iteration a page gives part of its importance to the pages it links to. At the same time, it takes importance from

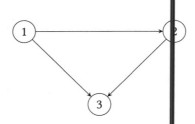

Figure 9.3
A PageRank sink.

the pages they link to it. In our counter-example, page P_1 will be contributing
importance to page P_2, but will not be getting any importance from anywhere.
This will result in all PageRanks getting drained in just three iterations:

$$\begin{bmatrix} 1/3 & 1/3 & 1/3 \end{bmatrix} \begin{bmatrix} 0 & 1/2 & 1/2 \\ 0 & 0 & 1 \\ 0 & 0 & 0 \end{bmatrix} = \begin{bmatrix} 0 & 1/6 & 1/2 \end{bmatrix}$$

then

$$\begin{bmatrix} 0 & 1/6 & 1/2 \end{bmatrix} \begin{bmatrix} 0 & 1/2 & 1/2 \\ 0 & 0 & 1 \\ 0 & 0 & 0 \end{bmatrix} = \begin{bmatrix} 0 & 0 & 1/6 \end{bmatrix}$$

and finally

$$\begin{bmatrix} 0 & 0 & 1/6 \end{bmatrix} \begin{bmatrix} 0 & 1/2 & 1/2 \\ 0 & 0 & 1 \\ 0 & 0 & 0 \end{bmatrix} = \begin{bmatrix} 0 & 0 & 0 \end{bmatrix}$$

Our counter-example involves just three nodes, but this is a general problem.
Pages with no outgoing links act in this way and take out importance from
pages in the web graph without giving anything in return. They are called
dangling nodes.

   To get around dangling nodes, we have to add some notions of probability
in our model. Imagine a random surfer who jumps from page to page. The
hyperlink matrix, H, gives the probability that if the surfer lands on page P_i
the next page to visit will be page P_j with probability equal to $H[i, j]$, where
j is any non zero entry in the row of the page P_i. Hence, for the H matrix
corresponding to figure 9.2, if the surfer lands on page 3, there is 1/2 probability that the next page to visit will be page 4 and 1/2 probability that it will
be page 7. The problem is what happens when the surfer lands on page 8.

Currently there is no way out of it. To get out of the dead end we decide that when the surfer arrives on a page with no outgoing links, it will be possible to go to any other page in the graph with probability $1/n$. It is like assuming that the random surfer has a teleportation device that can transport the bearer to any other point in the graph in random when stuck in a page with no exit. This teleportation device is equivalent to setting any row full of zeros to a row full of $1/n$.

To achieve that mathematically, we need to add to H a matrix whose rows are zeros, except from those rows corresponding to the zero rows of H; these we set to $1/n$. We call this matrix A and the resulting matrix S, and for figure 9.3 we have:

$$S = H + A = \begin{bmatrix} 0 & 1/2 & 1/2 \\ 0 & 0 & 1 \\ 0 & 0 & 0 \end{bmatrix} + \begin{bmatrix} 0 & 0 & 0 \\ 0 & 0 & 0 \\ 1/3 & 1/3 & 1/3 \end{bmatrix} = \begin{bmatrix} 0 & 1/2 & 1/2 \\ 0 & 0 & 1 \\ 1/3 & 1/3 & 1/3 \end{bmatrix}$$

Matrix A can be defined by using a column vector w with elements:

$$w[i] = \begin{cases} 1, & |P_i| = 0 \\ 0, & \text{otherwise} \end{cases}$$

that is, w is a column vector such that the ith element is zero if page P_i has outgoing links, or one if the page P_i has no outgoing links. Equivalently, the ith element of w is one if all the elements of the ith row of H are zero, or zero otherwise. With w, A becomes:

$$A = \frac{1}{n} w \mathbf{e}^T$$

where $\mathbf{e}$ is a column vector of ones and $\mathbf{e}^T$ is a row vector of ones, so

$$S = H + A = H + \frac{1}{n} w \mathbf{e}^T$$

The S matrix corresponds to a new graph, shown in figure 9.4. The edges of the original graph are drawn with thick links and the new, added edges are drawn with dashed lines.

The matrix S is a *stochastic matrix*; stochastic matrices are those matrices where all entries are non-negative and the sum in every row is equal to one. To be more precise, these are called *right stochastic* matrices; if the sum in every column is equal to one, they are called *left stochastic matrices*. They are called this way because they give the probability for moving from one cell to another using a probabilistic, or stochastic process. The sum of all probabilities in a

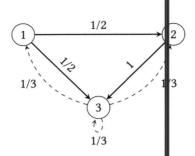

Figure 9.4
A PageRank sink plugged.

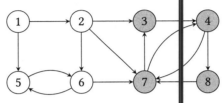

Figure 9.5
A web graph with a disconnected cycle.

given state, represented by the random surfer being in a node, that is, a row of the S matrix, is equal to one, and no probability is negative.

We can verify that the dead end at node 3 of the graph in figure 9.3 does not exist anymore in the graph of figure 9.4, as the power method converges to the values:

$$\pi^T = \begin{bmatrix} 0.18 & 0.27 & 0.55 \end{bmatrix}$$

The S matrix solves the problem of getting out of a dead end, so the power method converges, but a more devious problem may appear for the random surfer. The graph in figure 9.5 is similar to the graph in figure 9.2 with the links from node 4 to nodes 3 and 2 removed, and the link from node 7 to node 8 substituted by a link from node 8 to node 7. Now if the random surfer reaches one of the nodes 3, 4, 7, 8, it is not possible to ever get out of that cycle.

This is again an instance of a general issue: how to deal with dead ends that appear when a graph is not strongly connected. In such graphs, when the random surfer lands in part of the graph that does not link to the rest of the graph, it is impossible to escape from it.

Let's see how the power method will manage. The matrix H for the graph of figure 9.5 is:

$$H = \begin{array}{c} \\ P_1 \\ P_2 \\ P_3 \\ P_4 \\ P_5 \\ P_6 \\ P_7 \\ P_8 \end{array} \begin{array}{c} \begin{array}{cccccccc} P_1 & P_2 & P_3 & P_4 & P_5 & P_6 & P_7 & P_8 \end{array} \\ \left[\begin{array}{cccccccc} 0 & 1/2 & 0 & 0 & 1/2 & 0 & 0 & 0 \\ 0 & 0 & 1/3 & 0 & 0 & 1/3 & 1/3 & 0 \\ 0 & 0 & 0 & 1 & 0 & 0 & 0 & 0 \\ 0 & 0 & 0 & 0 & 0 & 0 & 1/2 & 1/2 \\ 0 & 0 & 0 & 0 & 0 & 1 & 0 & 0 \\ 0 & 0 & 0 & 0 & 1/2 & 0 & 1/2 & 0 \\ 0 & 0 & 1/2 & 1/2 & 0 & 0 & 0 & 0 \\ 0 & 0 & 0 & 0 & 0 & 0 & 1 & 0 \end{array} \right] \end{array}$$

There are no zero rows anyway, so $S = H$. Yet if we run the power method, we find that it converges to the following values:

$$\pi^T = \begin{bmatrix} 0 & 0 & 0.17 & 0.33 & 0 & 0 & 0.33 & 0.17 \end{bmatrix}$$

What happens is that the dead end cycle consisting of the nodes 3, 4, 7, and 8 drains the PageRanks of the other pages in the graph. The dead end cycle acts again as a sink.

We adopt a solution similar to the one for single node sinks. We extend the capabilities of the teleportation device so that the random surfer does not always jump from node to node using the matrix S; the surfer will use S with a probability a between zero and one, or not use S and just jump anywhere with probability $1 - a$. That is, the surfer picks a random number between zero and one. If the number is less than or equal to α, then the surfer will go to the destination indicated by the matrix S. Otherwise, the teleportation device will kick into action and transport the random surfer to some other, random, page in the graph.

This functionality of the teleportation device corresponds in some way to what an everyday human user does when surfing the web. For some time, the user follows links from one page to another. But at some point in time the user stops following links and goes to a completely different page by typing a new URL, using a bookmark, or checking out a link sent by a friend.

9.4 The Google Matrix

The way we can express this mathematically is by using a new matrix, G, instead of S. The matrix G will have the probabilities as we described them above, which means that it can be defined as:

$$G = \alpha S + (1 - \alpha)\frac{1}{n}J_n$$

where J_n is the $n \times n$ square matrix whose entries are all equal to 1. As $\mathbf{e}$ is the column vector with all ones and $\mathbf{e}^T$ is the row vector with ones we have:

$$J_n = \mathbf{e}\mathbf{e}^T$$

With this, we prefer to write:

$$G = \alpha S + (1 - \alpha)\frac{1}{n}\mathbf{e}\mathbf{e}^T$$

The reason is that J_n, being an $n \times n$ matrix, takes up space n^2, whereas $\mathbf{e}\mathbf{e}^T$ is the product of two vectors each taking space n, which may be of use if we do not actually need to store the whole $n \times n$ matrix during our calculations. This is indeed what happens, as you will see later.

Matrix G is stochastic. This follows from the definition of G. Take a row i of the S matrix. The row will have some entries, say k, that are positive, whereas the rest of them are zero. Row i of the S matrix has sum:

$$\sum_{S_{i,j}>0} S_{i,j} + \sum_{S_{i,j}=0} S_{i,j} = k\frac{1}{k} + (n-k)0 = 1$$

The same row i in matrix G has sum:

$$\sum_{S_{i,j}>0} G_{i,j} + \sum_{S_{i,j}=0} G_{i,j}$$

But the first term of the sum is:

$$\sum_{S_{i,j}>0} G_{i,j} = \alpha k\frac{1}{k} + (1-\alpha)k\frac{1}{n} = \alpha + (1-\alpha)k\frac{1}{n}$$

and the second term is:

$$\sum_{S_{i,j}=0} G_{i,j} = (1-a)(n-k)\frac{1}{n}$$

So the sum for the whole row is:

$$\sum_{S_{i,j}>0} S_{i,j} + \sum_{S_{i,j}=0} S_{i,j} = \alpha + (1-\alpha)k\frac{1}{n} + (1-a)(n-k)\frac{1}{n}$$

$$= \frac{\alpha n + (1-\alpha)k + (1-\alpha)(n-k)}{n}$$

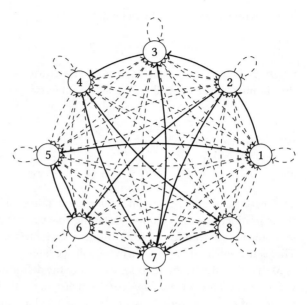

Figure 9.6
The graph corresponding to G for figure 9.5.

$$= \frac{\alpha n + k - \alpha k + n - k - \alpha n + \alpha k}{n}$$

$$= 1$$

G has another important property. It is a *primitive matrix*. A matrix M is primitive if for some power p, all the elements of the matrix M^p are positive numbers. That is easy to see. All zero entries of S were transformed to positive numbers with value $(1 - \alpha)1/n$, so G is primitive for $p = 1$.

The graph corresponding to G, shown in figure 9.6, differs from the original graph in figure 9.5: again we show the original edges with thick lines, and all the edges we added with dashed lines; we see that G is in fact a complete graph.

We have now arrived at a key juncture: linear algebra shows that when a matrix is stochastic and primitive, the power method converges to a unique vector of positive values; moreover that vector has components that sum up to one. It also does not matter which vector we started with. So, although we did start with an initial vector with $1/n$ for all PageRank values, we could have started with anything and we would still get the same result. Therefore, if the power method converges after k iterations for the matrix G, we have:

$$\pi^T G = 1\pi^T$$

with

$$\pi_1 > 0, \pi_2 > 0, \ldots, \pi_n > 0$$

and

$$\pi_1 + \pi_2 + \cdots + \pi_n = 1$$

These conditions correspond to a set of sensible values for our PageRanks, as all of them are positive.

Going back to our example, the G matrix of figure 9.6 for $\alpha = 0.85$ is:

$$G = \begin{bmatrix} \frac{3}{160} & \frac{71}{160} & \frac{3}{160} & \frac{3}{160} & \frac{71}{160} & \frac{3}{160} & \frac{3}{160} & \frac{3}{160} \\[2mm] \frac{3}{160} & \frac{3}{160} & \frac{29}{96} & \frac{3}{160} & \frac{3}{160} & \frac{29}{96} & \frac{29}{96} & \frac{3}{160} \\[2mm] \frac{3}{160} & \frac{3}{160} & \frac{3}{160} & \frac{139}{160} & \frac{3}{160} & \frac{3}{160} & \frac{3}{160} & \frac{3}{160} \\[2mm] \frac{3}{160} & \frac{3}{160} & \frac{3}{160} & \frac{3}{160} & \frac{3}{160} & \frac{3}{160} & \frac{71}{160} & \frac{71}{160} \\[2mm] \frac{3}{160} & \frac{3}{160} & \frac{3}{160} & \frac{3}{160} & \frac{3}{160} & \frac{139}{160} & \frac{3}{160} & \frac{3}{160} \\[2mm] \frac{3}{160} & \frac{3}{160} & \frac{3}{160} & \frac{3}{160} & \frac{71}{160} & \frac{3}{160} & \frac{71}{160} & \frac{3}{160} \\[2mm] \frac{3}{160} & \frac{3}{160} & \frac{71}{160} & \frac{71}{160} & \frac{3}{160} & \frac{3}{160} & \frac{3}{160} & \frac{3}{160} \\[2mm] \frac{3}{160} & \frac{3}{160} & \frac{3}{160} & \frac{3}{160} & \frac{3}{160} & \frac{3}{160} & \frac{139}{160} & \frac{3}{160} \end{bmatrix}$$

If we do some iterations, we find that the power method now converges to the PageRank vector:

$$\pi^T = \begin{bmatrix} 0.02^+ & 0.03^+ & 0.15^+ & 0.26^- & 0.06^+ & 0.04^+ & 0.28^- & 0.13^- \end{bmatrix}$$

The plus or minus suffixes next to the numbers denote whether in rounding the results to two decimals places we got a number greater than or less than the real value. Note that if we add up the numbers, due to this rounding, they sum up to 1.01 instead of 1; that is better than having to pile here digits upon digits.

The matrix G is called the *Google matrix*. The Google matrix is huge; for the whole World Wide Web it counts billions and billions of rows and columns. It is worth seeing if something can be saved in terms of memory. Recall that:

$$G = \alpha S + (1 - \alpha)\frac{1}{n}\mathbf{e}\mathbf{e}^T$$

so we have:

$$\pi_{k+1}^T = \pi_k^T \left(\alpha S + (1 - \alpha)\frac{1}{n}\mathbf{e}_{n \times n}\right)$$

Recall also that:

$$S = H + A = H + \frac{1}{n}\mathbf{w}\mathbf{e}^T$$

so we get:

$$\pi_{k+1}^T = \pi_k^T \left(\alpha H + \alpha\frac{1}{n}\mathbf{w}\mathbf{e}^T + (1 - \alpha)\frac{1}{n}\mathbf{e}\mathbf{e}^T\right)$$

$$= \alpha\pi_k^T H + \pi_k^T \left(\alpha\mathbf{w}\mathbf{e}^T\frac{1}{n} + (1 - \alpha)\mathbf{e}\mathbf{e}^T\frac{1}{n}\right)$$

$$= \alpha\pi_k^T H + \pi_k^T \left(\alpha\mathbf{w} + (1 - \alpha)\mathbf{e}\right)\mathbf{e}^T\frac{1}{n}$$

$$= \alpha\pi_k^T H + \left(\pi_k^T\alpha\mathbf{w} + (1 - \alpha)\pi_k^T\mathbf{e}\right)\mathbf{e}^T\frac{1}{n}$$

$$= \alpha\pi_k^T H + \left(\pi_k^T\alpha\mathbf{w} + (1 - \alpha)\right)\mathbf{e}^T\frac{1}{n}$$

$$= \alpha\pi_k^T H + \pi_k^T\alpha\mathbf{w}\mathbf{e}^T\frac{1}{n} + (1 - \alpha)\mathbf{e}^T\frac{1}{n}$$

In the last but one step we used the fact that $\pi_k^T\mathbf{e} = 1$ because this multiplication is equal to the sum of all the PageRanks, which is one. In the final line note that $\alpha\mathbf{w}\mathbf{e}^T(1/n)$ and $(1 - \alpha)\mathbf{e}^T(1/n)$ are actually constant values, and need to be calculated only once. Then at each iteration we only need to multiply π_k with a constant value and add another constant value to it. Moreover, the matrix H is extremely sparse because every web page has about ten links to other pages, instead of the matrix G, which is extremely dense (being complete). So we never need to actually store G, and the total number of operations is much less than if we just used the definition of G.

Notes

PageRank, invented by Larry Page and Sergey Brin, was published in 1998 and named after Larry Page [29]. It was the first algorithm used by the Google search engine; today Google employs more algorithms to produce its results, and the exact mechanisms it uses are not publicly known. Still, PageRank continues to be influential because it is conceptually simple and it formed part of the foundation of one of the largest corporations in history.

For the mathematics behind PageRank, look at the paper by Bryan and Leise [31]. An accessible introduction to PageRank and search engines in general is the book by Langville and Meyer [121]; see also the short book by Berry and Browne [18]. The book by Manning, Raghavan, and Hinrich Schütze is a more general introduction to information retrieval, covering indexing . Büttcher, Clarke, and Cormack cover information retrieval and also treat retrieval efficiency and effectiveness [33].

PageRank is not the only algorithm to use links for ranking. Another important algorithm in the field is HITS, developed by Jon Kleinberg [108, 109].

10 Voting Strengths

A company wishes to select a catering service that will provide daily meals to its employees. After some market research, the company has found there are three services that meet quality and price requirements. However, there is a catch. The first catering service, called "MeatLovers," or M for short, offers a selection of mostly meat menus, with a sprinkling of pasta dishes on the side. The second catering service, called "BitOfEverything," E for short, offers a more varied menu, ranging from meat to vegetarian dishes. The third catering service, called "VegForLife," or V, offers strictly vegetarian dishes.

The Human Resources department of the company decides to ask the employees about their preferred catering service. They put the matter to a vote. The results of the vote are as follows: 40% of the employees prefer M, 30% of the employees prefer E, and 30% of the employees prefer V. The contract is awarded to M, as all due process has been followed.

Can you spot a problem? It is unlikely that the vegetarians in the company would like to abide by such a decision, and yet they must; or rather they will have to bring their own food every day.

If you pay attention, you may notice that the way the election was framed created the problem. Although 30% of the employees chose V, a relative minority, it is probable that they prefer E to M. The employees who favor M, on their part, most likely prefer E to V. Finally, those who chose E may prefer V over M. Let's tabulate these preferences:

40%:	$[M, E, V]$
30%:	$[V, E, M]$
30%:	$[E, V, M]$

Now let's calculate the *pairwise preferences* among the choices, that is, for every pair of choices, how many of the voters prefer one to the other? We start by examining M and E for the three groups of voters above: 40% of the voters prefer M to E, having M as their first choice. At the same time, 30% of the voters prefer E to M, with their first choice being V, and another 30% of the voters prefer E to M, with E being their first choice. Thus, 60% of the voters prefer E to M. So E beats M by 60% to 40%.

We proceed with M and V. We reason in the same way: 40% of the voters prefer M to V, having M as their first choice. However, 30% of the voters prefer V to everything else, and the 30% of the voters who have E as their first choice also prefer V to M. So V beats M by 60% to 40%.

Finally, to compare E with V, 40% of the voters listed M as their first choice and prefer E to V and 30% of the voters listed V as their first choice and also prefer V to E. The 30% of the voters who listed E as their first choice prefer, obviously, E over V. Therefore, E beats V by 70% to 30%.

Taking it all together, E beats both the other two contestants in their pairwise comparisons, M by 60% to 40% and V by 70% to 30%, while V beats one contestant, and M beats none. We therefore declare E the winner of the election process.

10.1   Voting Systems

The example showed an issue that arises with well-known and popular election system, *plurality voting*. In plurality voting, voters record on their ballot their first preference. The candidate with the most ballots wins the election. The problem with plurality voting is that the voters do not record their full set of preferences. They only record their top one. So, it is possible that one candidate may be preferred to any other candidate, but that candidate will not win the election if it is not the top choice of the majority of the voters.

The requirement that in an election the winner should be the candidate that when compared with any other candidate is preferred by most voters is called the *Condorcet criterion*. The winner is called the *Condorcet candidate*, or *Condorcet winner*. The name comes from Marie Jean Antoine Nicolas Caritat, the Marquis de Condorcet, an 18th-century French mathematician and philosopher who described the situation in 1785.

Lest you think that the Condorcet criterion is an arcane concept embedded in culinary discussions or 18th-century France, consider two more recent examples.

In the 2000 U.S. presidential election the voters were called to select among George W. Bush, Al Gore, and Ralph Nader. In the United States, the president is elected by an Electoral College. The Electoral College is based on the election results of the particular U.S. states. After much drama, the 2000 election was decided by the results in the state of Florida. The final results gave to the candidates the following count:

- George W. Bush received 2,912,790 votes, equal to 48.847% of voters.
- Al Gore received 2,912,253 votes, equal to 48.838% of voters.
- Ralph Nader received 97,421 votes, or 1.634% percent of voters.

George W. Bush won with a wafer-thin 537-vote margin, or 0.009% of the votes in Florida. It is generally thought, however, that most of the Ralph Nader voters preferred Al Gore to George W. Bush. If that is true, and the U.S. elections used a voting method that allowed voters to express their second choices as well, then Al Gore would have been the winner.

Changing continents and moving to France, in the 2002 French presidential election on April 21, Jacques Chirac, Lionel Jospin, and fourteen other candidates were competing. To be elected president in France, a candidate has to secure more than 50% of the vote. If this does not happen, then the first two candidates are selected to participate in a second election round. It came as a shock to the world that instead of Lionel Jospin, Jacques Chirac would face the far-right Jean-Marie Le Pen in the second round.

That does not mean that most of French voters support the far-right. The count of the first round on April 21, 2002, was:

- Jacques Chirac received 5,666,440 votes, equal to 19.88% of the vote.
- Jean-Marie Le Pen received 4,805,307 votes, equal to 16.86% of the vote.
- Lionel Jospin received 4,610,749 votes, equal to 16.18% percent of the vote.

In the second round of the elections, which took place two weeks later on May 5, 2002, Jacques Chirac received more than 82% of the vote, while Jean-Marie Le Pen got less than 18% of the vote. It seems that while Chirac got pretty much the votes of all the other fourteen eliminated candidates, Le Pen barely moved from his performance on the first round.

The problem arose because initially there were sixteen candidates, from which two would be chosen to go to the second round. With sixteen candidates, it is not difficult to find a situation where support among them is spread so much that an extreme candidate, with no support beyond its own supporters, will manage to get enough votes from voters with hardcore views to prevail over a more moderate candidate. More generally, a candidate who is fairly liked by most people, but is not necessarily their first choice, will fail against a candidate who is hated by most people, but is the first choice of some sizable minority.

Plurality voting is not the only voting method that fails the Condorcet criterion, but due to its popularity, it is the one that can be easily picked upon by critics.

In *approval voting*, voters can select any number of candidates, not just one, on the ballot. The winner is the candidate with the most votes. Suppose in an election we have three candidates A, B, and C, and we obtained the following count (we do not use square brackets around the ballots to emphasize that the sequence does not matter):

60%: $[A, B]$
40%: $[C, B]$

Because B was selected by all 100% of the voters, B carries the day. Suppose that 60% of the voters favor A over B over C and 40% of the voters favor C over B over A, although they are not able to express that on the ballot. In other words, if they were, the ballots would be:

60%: $[A, B, C]$
40%: $[C, B, A]$

Then A beats B by 60% to 40%; so although most voters prefer A to B, A is not elected.

Another voting method is the *Borda count*, named after another 18th-century Frenchman, the mathematician and political scientist Jean-Charles de Borda, who described it in 1770. In Borda count, voters award points to the candidates. If there are n candidates, their first choice gets $n - 1$ points, their second choice $n - 2$ points, down to the last choice that will get zero points. The winner is the candidate who collects the most points. Consider an election in which three candidates, A, B, and C, compete and the ballots are as follows:

60%: $[A, B, C]$
40%: $[B, C, A]$

If there are n voters, then candidate A gets $(60 \times 2)n = 120n$ points, candidate B gets $(60 + 2 \times 40)n = 140n$ points, and candidate C gets $40n$ points. The winner is candidate B. Yet most candidates prefer candidate A to candidate B.

Returning to the Condorcet criterion, the problem is to find a method that will pick the Condorcet winner of an election, if such a winner exists. A Condorcet winner might not necessarily exist. For example, say we have three candidates, A, B, and C, for which we received the following ballots:

$$30: \quad [A, B, C]$$
$$30: \quad [B, C, A]$$
$$30: \quad [C, A, B]$$

If we do the pairwise comparisons, then we find that A beats B by 60 to 40, B beats C by 60 to 40, and C beats A by 60 to 40. Therefore each candidate beats some other candidate, and no candidate beats more candidates than others, so no overall winner emerges.

Now see another election involving three candidates, where the ballots were cast in a different way:

$$10 \times [A, B, C]$$
$$5 \times [B, C, A]$$
$$5 \times [C, A, B]$$

A is preferred over B by 15 to 5, B is preferred over C by 15 to 5, and C and A tie up with 10 each. Because both A and B have a pairwise win, we cannot declare a winner.

That's a bit strange because it is not a case where all ballots take an equal share of the voters, as the previous one. It is clear that more voters cast the first ballot, but somehow this does not make its way to the results. We would therefore like to have a method that respects the Condorcet criterion but is less prone to ties than the simple method we have been using until now.

10.2   The Shulze Method

A method that finds the Condorcet winner of an election, if such a winner exists, is the Schulze method, developed in 1997 by Markus Schulze. It is a method used among technological organizations, and is not prone to ties. The basic idea in the Schulze method is that we use the pairwise preferences of the voters to construct a graph. Then the preferences between candidates are found by tracing paths on that graph.

The first step in the Schulze method is exactly finding the pairwise preferences for the candidates. Suppose we have n ballots and m candidates. The ballots are $B = B_1, B_2, \ldots, B_n$ and the candidates are $C = c_1, c_2, \ldots, c_m$. We take each ballot B_i in turn, where $i = 1, 2, \ldots n$. Each ballot contains a series of candidates, in decreasing preference order, so a candidate who precedes other candidates in a ballot is preferred by the voter who cast that ballot to any of the candidates who follow in the ballot. In other words, for any two candidates c_j and c_k in ballot B_i, the voter prefers c_j to c_k if c_j appears before c_k. To tally the preferences, we use an array P of size $m \times m$. To calculate the contents of the array, we first initialize it to all zero values. Then as we read each ballot B_i, for every pair c_j and c_k of candidates in the ballot such that c_j precedes c_k, we add one to element $P[c_j, c_k]$ of array P. When we are done reading all ballots, each element of P, $P[c_j, c_k]$, will show how many voters in total prefer candidate c_j to candidate c_k.

For example, a ballot might be $[c_1, c_3, c_4, c_2, c_5]$, meaning that the voter prefers candidate c_1 over all other candidates, candidate c_3 over candidates c_4, c_2, c_5, candidate c_4 over candidates c_2, c_5, and candidate c_2 over candidate c_5. In that ballot candidate c_1 is before candidates c_3, c_4, c_2, and c_5, so we add one to elements $P[c_1, c_3]$, $P[c_1, c_4]$, $P[c_1, c_2]$, and $P[c_1, c_5]$. Candidate c_3 is before candidates c_4, c_2, and c_5, so we add one to elements $P[c_3, c_4]$, $P[c_3, c_2]$, and $P[c_3, c_5]$, and so on, up to candidate c_2, where we add one to element $P[c_2, c_5]$:

$$
\begin{array}{c c c c c c}
 & c_1 & c_2 & c_3 & c_4 & c_5 \\
c_1 & - & +1 & +1 & +1 & +1 \\
c_2 & - & - & - & - & +1 \\
c_3 & - & +1 & - & +1 & +1 \\
c_4 & - & +1 & - & - & +1 \\
c_5 & - & - & - & - & -
\end{array}
$$

Algorithm 10.1 does that. The algorithm creates the array P that will hold the pairwise preferences in line 1 and initializes the pairwise preferences for all candidates to 0 in lines 2–4. This requires $\Theta(|B|^2)$ time. Then it takes each of the $|B|$ ballots, in the loop in lines 5–11. In each ballot, it takes each candidate in turn in the nested loop in lines 7–11. Because the ballots contain the candidates in the preference of the voter, each time we enter the nested loop, the selected candidate is preferred by all the following candidates in the ballot. So, if the candidate is c_j, then for every other candidate c_k that follows c_j in the ballot, we add one to the element $P[c_j, c_k]$. It does the same thing starting with all the other candidates in the ballot in sequence. If the ballot contains all $|C|$ candidates, then it will update the preferences array $(|C| - 1) + (|C| - 2) + \ldots + 1 = |C|(|C| - 1)/2$ times. In the worst case all ballots contain all $|C|$ candidates, so the time required for each ballot is

---

Algorithm 10.1: Calculate pairwise preferences.

CalcPairwisePreferences(*ballots, m*) → *P*

    Input: *ballots*, an array of ballots, where each ballot is an array of
           candidates

           m, the number of candidates

    Output: *P*, an array of size $m \times m$ with the pairwise preferences for
           candidates; $P[i, j]$ is the number of voters that prefer
           candidate i to candidate j

1   $P \leftarrow$ CreateArray$(m \cdot m)$
2   **for** $i \leftarrow 0$ **to** m **do**
3   **for** $j \leftarrow 0$ **to** m **do**
4         $P[i][j] \leftarrow 0$
5   **for** $i \leftarrow 0$ **to** $|ballots|$ **do**
6      $ballot \leftarrow ballots[i]$
7   **for** $j \leftarrow 0$ **to** $|ballot|$ **do**
8         $c_j \leftarrow ballot[j]$
9   **for** $k \leftarrow j + 1$ **to** $|ballot|$ **do**
10            $c_k \leftarrow ballot[k]$
11            $P[c_j, c_k] \leftarrow P[c_j, c_k] + 1$
12 **return** P

$O(|C|(|C| - 1)/2) = O(|C|^2)$ and the time for all ballots is $O(|B||C|^2)$. In total, algorithm 10.1 runs in $O(|C|^2 + |B|^2)$ time.

As an example, take an election with four candidates, A, B, C, and D. In the election 21 voters took part. After counting the ballots we found that the following had been cast:

$$6 \times [A, C, D, B]$$
$$4 \times [B, A, D, C]$$
$$3 \times [C, D, B, A]$$
$$4 \times [D, B, A, C]$$
$$4 \times [D, C, B, A]$$

That is, six ballots $[A, C, D, B]$, four ballots $[B, A, D, C]$, and so on. In the first six ballots, the voters preferred candidate A to candidate C, candidate C to candidate D, and candidate D to candidate B.

To calculate the preference array, we find that candidate A is preferred to B in only the first set of ballots, so the entry in the array for the pairwise preferences between A and B will be 6. Similarly, we find that candidate A is preferred to C in the first, second, and fourth set of ballots, so the pairwise preferences between A and C will be 14. Continuing in this way, we find that the preference array for the candidates of our election is:

$$
\begin{array}{c}
 & A & B & C & D \\
\begin{array}{c} A \\ B \\ C \\ D \end{array}
\begin{bmatrix}
0 & 6 & (6+4+4) & (6+4) \\
(4+3+4+4) & 0 & (4+4) & 4 \\
(3+4) & (6+3+4) & 0 & (6+3) \\
(3+4+4) & (6+3+4+5) & (4+4+4) & 0
\end{bmatrix}
\end{array}
$$

that is:

$$
\begin{array}{c}
 & A & B & C & D \\
\begin{array}{c} A \\ B \\ C \\ D \end{array}
\begin{bmatrix}
0 & 6 & 14 & 10 \\
15 & 0 & 8 & 4 \\
7 & 13 & 0 & 9 \\
11 & 17 & 12 & 0
\end{bmatrix}
\end{array}
$$

The second step of the Schulze method starts by constructing a graph, where the candidates are the nodes and the margins of the preferences of one candidate over another are the weights of the links. If for two candidates c_i and c_j the number $P[i, j]$ of voters that prefer c_i over c_j is greater than the number of voters $P[j, i]$ that prefer c_j over c_i, we add the link $c_i \rightarrow c_j$ and we assign the number $P[i, j] - P[j, i]$ as the weight of the link $c_i \rightarrow c_j$. We use $-\infty$ for the other pairs to show that the corresponding link does not exist. To do that we start by doing the comparisons and operations as necessary:

$$
\begin{array}{c}
 & A & B & C & D \\
\begin{array}{c} A \\ B \\ C \\ D \end{array}
\begin{bmatrix}
0 & (6 < 15) & (14 - 7) & (10 < 11) \\
(15 - 6) = 9 & 0 & (8 < 13) & (4 < 17) \\
(7 < 14) & (13 - 8) & 0 & (9 < 12) \\
(11 - 10) = 1 & (17 - 4) & (12 - 9) & 0
\end{bmatrix}
\end{array}
$$

and then substituting $-\infty$ for negative and zero entries:

$$
\begin{array}{c}
 & A & B & C & D \\
\begin{array}{c} A \\ B \\ C \\ D \end{array}
\begin{bmatrix}
-\infty & -\infty & 7 & -\infty \\
9 & -\infty & -\infty & -\infty \\
-\infty & 5 & -\infty & -\infty \\
1 & 13 & 3 & -\infty
\end{bmatrix}
\end{array}
$$

You can see the corresponding graph in figure 10.1. As explained, the graph has the candidates as its nodes and the positive margins of the differences in preferences between each pair of candidates as its edges.

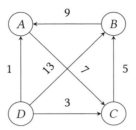

Figure 10.1
An election graph.

Having constructed the graph, we proceed to calculate the *strongest paths* between all nodes in the preference graph. We define the *strength of a path*, or equivalently the *width of a path*, as the minimum weight in the links that make up the path. If you imagine a path as a sequence of bridges between nodes, then the path is only as strong as its weakest link, or bridge. There may be multiple paths between two nodes in the preference graph, each with a different strength. The path with the greatest strength among them is the strongest path. Returning to the bridges metaphor, the strongest path is the path that allows us to transport the heaviest vehicle between the two nodes. Figure 10.2 shows a graph and two strongest paths. The strongest path between node 0 and node 4 passes through node 2 and has strength 5; similarly, the strongest path between node 4 and node 1 passes through node 3 and has strength 7.

Finding the strongest paths is a problem that arises in other areas as well. In computer networks, it is equivalent to finding the maximum bandwidth between two computers in the Internet when between any two computers or routers in the network the link has a limited bandwidth capacity. It is also called the *widest path problem* because strength is synonymous with width, and *maximum capacity path problem* because it boils down to finding the maximum capacity of a path in a graph. The maximum capacity of the path is constrained by its weakest link; the maximum capacity path between two nodes is the maximum capacity among the capacities of the paths between the two nodes.

To find the strongest path between all pairs of nodes in the graph, we reason as follows. We take all nodes of the graph in sequence, $c_1, c_2, \ldots, c_n$. We find

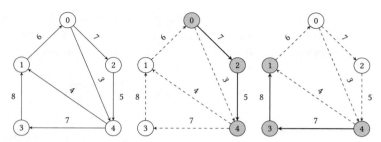

Figure 10.2
Strongest path examples.

the strongest path between all pairs of nodes, c_i and c_j in the graph using zero intermediate nodes from the sequence $c_1, c_2, \ldots, c_n$. The strongest path between the two nodes using no intermediate nodes exists if there is a direct link between c_i and c_j; otherwise it does not exist at all.

We proceed to find again the strongest path between all pairs of nodes c_i and c_j using the first of the nodes in the sequence, node c_1, as an intermediate node. If we have already found a strongest path between c_i and c_j in the previous step, then if there exist paths $c_i \rightarrow c_1$ and $c_1 \rightarrow c_j$, we compare the strength of the path $c_i \rightarrow c_j$ with the strength of the path $c_i \rightarrow c_1 \rightarrow c_j$, and we take the strongest of the two as our new estimate for the strongest path between c_i and c_j.

We continue the same procedure until we have used all n nodes in the sequence. Suppose we have found the strongest path between all pairs of nodes in the graph, c_i and c_j, using the first k nodes of the sequence as intermediate nodes. We now try to find the strongest path between the two nodes c_i and c_j using the first $k + 1$ nodes in the sequence. If we find a path from c_i to c_j using the $(k + 1)$th node, it will consist of two parts. The first part will be a path from c_i to c_{k+1} using the first k nodes of the sequence as intermediate nodes, and the second part will be from c_{k+1} to c_j using again the first k nodes of the sequence as intermediate nodes. We have already found the strengths of these two paths in the previous steps of the procedure. If we call $s_{i,j}(k)$ the strength of the path from c_i to c_j using the first k nodes, the two paths using node $(k + 1)$ are $s_{i,k+1}(k)$ and $s_{k+1,j}(k)$. The strength of the path going from c_i to c_j through c_{k+1} is by definition the minimum of the strength of the paths $s_{i,k+1}(k)$ and $s_{k+1,j}(k)$ and we have already found both of them previously. So:

$$s_{i,j}(k + 1) = max\Big(s_{i,j}(k), min\big(s_{i,k+1}(k), s_{k+1,j}(k)\big)\Big)$$

In the end, after using all n nodes in the sequence, we will have found all the strongest paths between any two pairs in the graph. Algorithm 10.2 shows the procedure in detail.

In lines 1–2 of the algorithm we create the two output arrays. In lines 2–10, we initialize the strength of the path between two nodes to their direct links between them, if they exist. They correspond to finding the strongest paths using zero intermediate nodes. Then in lines 11–18, we calculate strongest paths using more and more intermediate nodes. The outer loop, over variable k, corresponds to the intermediate node we are adding to our set of intermediate nodes. Each time we increase k we check all pairs of nodes, given by i and j, and adjust their strongest path estimates, if needed, in lines 14–16. We also keep track of the paths using an array *pred* that gives, at each position (i, j) in the array, the predecessor node along the strongest path from node i to node j.

The algorithm is efficient. The first loop in lines 2–10 executes n^2 times and the second loop in lines 11–18 executes n^3 times, where n is the number of vertices in the graph. Because the graph is represented as an adjacency matrix, all graph operations take constant time, so in total it takes $\Theta(n^3)$ time. If we take the discussion to elections, then n is the number of candidates. In the notation we have adopted, the time required is $\Theta(|C|^3)$.

You can see a trace of the execution of the algorithm in our example in figure 10.3. At each sub-figure we indicate with a gray fill the intermediate node that is used to form a new path at each step. Note that in the last step, when we add node D in our set of intermediate nodes, we find no path stronger from those already found. This may happen, but we cannot know it in advance. It is also possible to happen in one of the previous steps, even though it did not happen in this case. Be that as it may, we have to carry out the execution of the algorithm to the end, examining all nodes of the graph in sequence as intermediate nodes.

The paths are returned from algorithm 10.2 via array *pred*. If you want to see the paths on the graph, you can check them in figure 10.4. Verify that the strongest path from node D to node C is through nodes B and A and not the direct path from D to C; at the third sub-figure the earlier estimate gets overwritten by the better estimate when we use node B as an intermediate node. By contrast, when we add A as an intermediate node we can obtain the path $D \rightarrow A \rightarrow B$ with strength 1; but we already have path $D \rightarrow A$ with strength 1, so there is no need to update the strongest path between A and D. By the same token, we can obtain the path $D \rightarrow A \rightarrow C$ with strength 1; but

---

Algorithm 10.2: Calculate strongest paths.

CalcStrongestPaths(W, n) $\rightarrow$ (S, $pred$)

    Input: W, an array of size $n \times n$ representing the adjacency matrix of a graph; $W[i, j]$ is the weight of the edge between nodes i and j

        n, the size of each dimension of W

    Output: S, an array of size $n \times n$ such that $S[i, j]$ is the strongest path between nodes i and j

        $pred$, an array of size $n \times n$ such that $pred[i, j]$ is the predecessor of node i in the strongest path to node j

1   $S \leftarrow$ CreateArray($n \cdot n$)

2   $pred \leftarrow$ CreateArray($n \cdot n$)

3   **for** $i \leftarrow 0$ **to** n **do**

4   **for** $j \leftarrow 0$ **to** n **do**

5   **if** $W[i, j] > W[j, i]$ **then**

6              $S[i][j] \leftarrow W[i, j] - W[j, i]$

7              $pred[i, j] \leftarrow i$

8   **else**

9              $S[i][j] \leftarrow -\infty$

10             $pred[i, j] \leftarrow -1$

11   **for** $k \leftarrow 0$ **to** n **do**

12   **for** $i \leftarrow 0$ **to** n **do**

13   **if** $i \neq k$ **then**

14   **for** $j \leftarrow 0$ **to** n **do**

15   **if** $j \neq i$ **then**

16   **if** $S[i, j] < $ Min($S[i, k], S[k, j]$) **then**

17                          $S[i, j] \leftarrow$ Min($S[i, k], S[k, j]$)

18                          $pred[i, j] \leftarrow pred[k, j]$

19   **return** (S, $pred$)

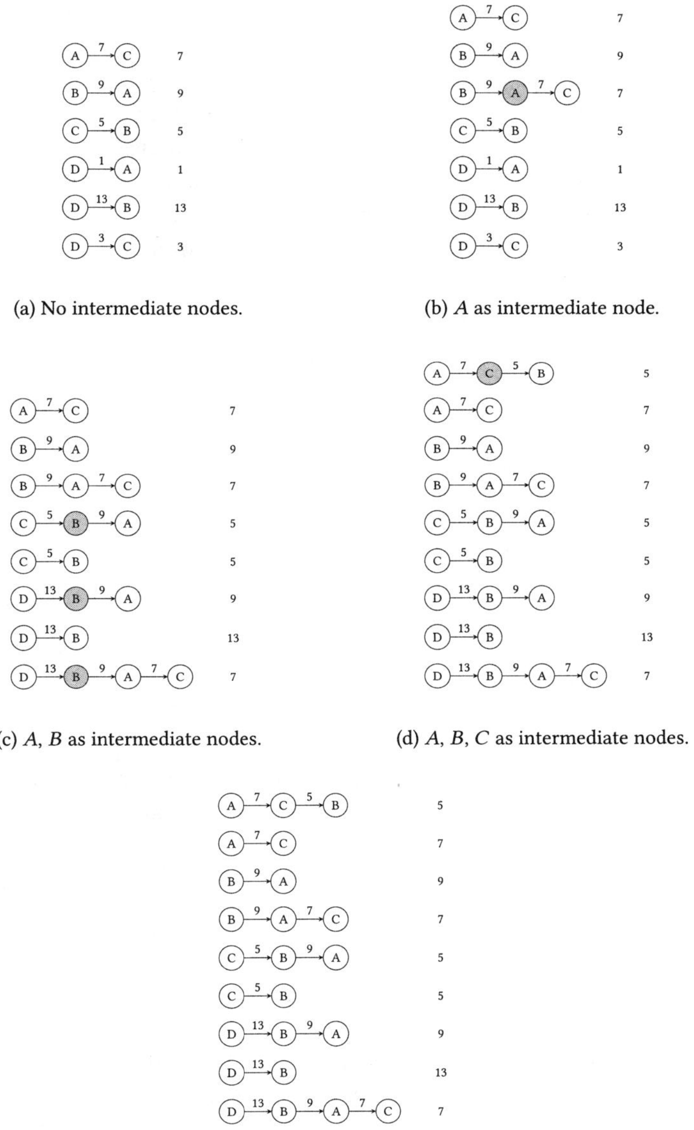

(a) No intermediate nodes.

(b) A as intermediate node.

(c) A, B as intermediate nodes.

(d) A, B, C as intermediate nodes.

(e) A, B, C, D as intermediate nodes.

Figure 10.3
Calculation of strongest paths.

we already have path $D \rightarrow C$ with strength 3, so the strongest path between D and C remains unchanged.

What the algorithm really does is calculate parts of the solution to our problem and combine them incrementally to arrive at the overall solution. It finds shorter strongest paths that it combines, if possible, producing longer strongest paths. This strategy, of solving part of the problem and combining the solved parts to produce the final solution, is called *dynamic programming* and lies behind many interesting algorithms.

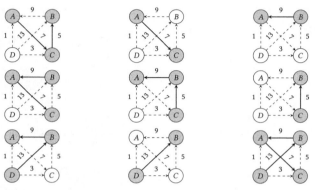

Figure 10.4
Strongest paths for the election graph.

In our example, algorithm 10.2 produces an array S with the strengths of the strongest paths between any pair of nodes:

$$
\begin{array}{c c c c c}
 & A & B & C & D \\
A & \begin{bmatrix} -\infty \\ 9 \\ 5 \\ 9 \end{bmatrix} & \begin{matrix} 5 \\ -\infty \\ 5 \\ 13 \end{matrix} & \begin{matrix} 7 \\ 7 \\ -\infty \\ 7 \end{matrix} & \begin{matrix} -\infty \\ -\infty \\ -\infty \\ -\infty \end{bmatrix} \\
\end{array}
$$

With these available, we can go on in the third step of the Schultze method. We have established, for any two candidates c_i and c_j how much support there is for candidate c_i to c_j as well as how much support there is for candidate c_j to c_i. They are the strengths of the paths from c_i to c_j and from c_j to c_i, respectively. If the strength of the path from c_i to c_j is greater than the strength of the path from c_j to c_i, then we say that candidate c_i wins over candidate c_j. We want then to find, for each candidate c_i, over how many other candidates

---

Algorithm 10.3: Calculate results.

CalcResults(S, n) → *wins*

    Input: S, an array of size $n \times n$ with the strongest paths between nodes; $s[i, j]$ is the strongest path between nodes i and j

           n, the size of each dimension of S

    Output: *wins*, a list of size n; item i of *wins* is a list containing m integer items $j_1, j_2, \ldots, j_m$ for which $s[i, j_k] > s[j_k, i]$

1   *wins* ← CreateList()
2   **for** $i \leftarrow 0$ **to** n **do**
3   *list* ← CreateList()
4   InsertInList(*wins*, NULL, *list*)
5   **for** $j \leftarrow 0$ **to** n **do**
6   **if** $i \neq j$ **then**
7   **if** $S[i, j] > S[j, i]$ **then**
8   InsertInList(*list*, NULL, j)
9   **return** *wins*

---

c_i wins. That is easy to do, by just going over the array with the path strengths that we calculated using algorithm 10.2 and adding up the times c_i is preferred over c_j. We do this in algorithm 10.3, which returns a list *wins* such that item i of the list *wins* contains a list with the candidates over which candidate i prevails.

In our example we find that A beats C, B beats A and C, C is beaten by all, and D beats A, B, and C. In particular, *wins* = $[[2], [2, 0], [], [2, 1, 0]]$. Because the number of times a candidate wins other candidates is $A = 1$, $B = 2$, $C = 0$, and $D = 3$, D is the preferred candidate. Algorithm 10.3 requires $O(n^2)$ time, where n is the number of candidates, or $|C|$ in the notation that we have been using, so the time required is $O(|C|^2)$. Because algorithm 10.1 runs in $O(|C|^2 + |B|^2)$ time, algorithm 10.2 runs in $\Theta(|C|^3)$ time, and algorithm 10.3 runs in $O(|C|^2)$ time, the whole Schulze method requires polynomial time and is efficient.

Note that we did not just get a winner for the election; we got an ordering of the candidates. Thus, the Schulze method can also be used when we want to pick the first k out of a total n candidates. We just select the first k in the ordering it produces.

In our example we did not have ties. Candidates were ordered in a clear way. That may not always happen. The Schulze method will produce a Condorcet winner, when there is one, but of course it cannot invent one if there is none. Also, there may be ties lower down in the order, with an overall winner and two candidates tied up in second place. For example, there could be an election scenario in which D would beat B, C, and D, while A would beat C, B would beat D, and C would beat nobody. D would be the winner, and A and B would both get second place.

Now let's return to the example that got us started on the Schulze method. Recall that we had the following ballots for three candidates, A, B, and C:

$$10 \times [A, B, C]$$
$$5 \times [B, C, A]$$
$$5 \times [C, A, B]$$

We found that with simple comparisons, without using the Schulze method, A is preferred over B by 15 to 5, B is preferred over C by 15 to 5, and C and A tie up with 10 each. Because both A and B have a pairwise win, we ended up with a tie. How does the Schulze method fare? The preference array for the candidates is:

$$
\begin{array}{c c c c}
 & A & B & C \\
A & 0 & 15 & 10 \\
B & 5 & 0 & 15 \\
C & 10 & 5 & 0
\end{array}
$$

From that we get the adjacency matrix for the election graph:

$$
\begin{array}{c c c c}
 & A & B & C \\
A & -\infty & 10 & -\infty \\
B & -\infty & -\infty & 10 \\
C & -\infty & -\infty & -\infty
\end{array}
$$

The graph itself is in figure 10.5. It's easy to see that there are two (strongest) paths starting from A, the path $A \rightarrow B$ and the path $A \rightarrow B \rightarrow C$, whereas there is only one strongest path from B, $B \rightarrow C$. As there are no reverse paths to compare, the Schulze method will give as a result that A wins over both B and C, B wins over C, and C beats nobody. It will therefore declare A as a winner, resolving the earlier tie. The Schulze method will in general produce fewer ties than a simple pairwise comparison. It can be proven that it meets the criterion of *resolvability*, which means that there is a low possibility of tied results.

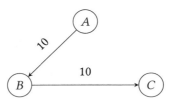

Figure 10.5
Another election graph.

Caveat emptor. We have presented the Condorcet criterion and showed that it is a reasonable requirement for an election. We have also presented the Schulze method, which is a reasonable voting method that meets the Condorcet criterion. This does not mean that the Schulze method is the one best voting method, or even that the Condorcet criterion is the one criterion that should guide a polity's decisions as it looks to decide how to run its elections. It can be proven, as it was by the Nobel prize winner Kenneth Joseph Arrow in his PhD thesis, that there exists no perfect voting system where voters express their preferences in the ballots. That is called Arrow's Impossibility Theorem. What is important is that the choice of a voting method should be an informed one, and not made unthinkingly, or perhaps guided by custom. Voters must decide how to vote wisely. That said, the Schulze method does provide a nice example to introduce a graph algorithm, and that is why we chose it here.

10.3 The Floyd-Warshall Algorithm

Algorithm 10.2 for calculating the strongest paths is a variant of a venerable algorithm for calculating the shortest paths between all pairs in a graph, the Floyd-Warshall algorithm. It was published by Robert Floyd, but similar algorithms have been published by Bernard Roy and Stephen Warshall. This is algorithm 10.4. Like algorithm 10.2, this also runs in time $\Theta(n^3)$. That makes it in general slower than the Dijkstra algorithm, but it performs well in dense graphs. It is also simple to implement, with no requirements for any special data structures, and it works in graphs with negative weights as well. Attention is needed in line 16 to watch for overflows in computer languages that have no notion of infinity and you use big numbers to stand in for them. In these settings you need to check whether $dist[i, k]$ and $dist[k, j]$ are not equal

---

Algorithm 10.4: Floyd-Warshall all pairs shortest paths.

FloydWarshall(W, n) $\rightarrow$ ($dist$, $pred$)

    Input: W, an array of size $n \times n$ representing the adjacency matrix of
        a graph; $W[i,j]$ is the weight of the edge between nodes i and j
        n, the size of each dimension of W

    Output: $dist$, an array of size $n \times n$ such that $dist[i,j]$ is the shortest
        path between nodes i and j
        $pred$, an array of size $n \times n$ such that $pred[i,j]$ is the
        predecessor of node i in the shortest path to node j

1    $dist \leftarrow$ CreateArray($n \cdot n$)
2    $pred \leftarrow$ CreateArray($n \cdot n$)
3   **for** $i \leftarrow 0$ **to** n **do**
4   **for** $j \leftarrow 0$ **to** n **do**
5   **if** $W[i,j] \neq 0$ **then**
6                $dist[i,j] \leftarrow W[i,j]$
7                $pred[i,j] \leftarrow i$
8   **else**
9                $dist[i,j] \leftarrow +\infty$
10               $pred[i,j] \leftarrow -1$

11   **for** $k \leftarrow 0$ **to** n **do**
12   **for** $i \leftarrow 0$ **to** n **do**
13   **if** $i \neq k$ **then**
14   **for** $j \leftarrow 0$ **to** n **do**
15   **if** $j \neq i$ **then**
16   **if** $dist[i,j] > dist[i,k] + dist[k,j]$ **then**
17                            $dist[i,j] \leftarrow dist[i,k] + dist[k,j]$
18                            $pred[i,j] \leftarrow pred[k,j]$
19   **return** ($dist$, $pred$)

---

to what you use to represent ∞. If they are, there is no point in adding them, and the shortest path from i to j will not go through them anyway.

Notes

Condorcet described his criterion in his book *Essay on the Application of Analysis to the Probability of Majority Decisions* [39]. The Schulze method is described in [175].

Voting theory is a fascinating topic, and there is no reason that informed citizens should not be aware of its main results. See the books by Saari [169], Brams [27], Szpiro [195], and Taylor and Pacelli [200].

Robert Floyd published his version of the Floyd-Warshall algorithm in [67]; Stephen Warshall published his also in 1962 [213], while Bernard Roy had published his earlier, in 1959 [168]. The version with three nested loops is due to Ingerman [101].

11 Brute Forces, Secretaries, and Dichotomies

Do you enjoy searching for your keys, your socks, your glasses? Rummaging around your things is probably among the most frustrating endeavors, and yet you are lucky. You only have to look for physical things that you may have misplaced. You do not have to look for the phone number of a friend, a song among your audio collection, a payment slip for a bank transaction in an overflowing folder. Computers now take care of these things. They keep track of things for us, they look them up when we ask them to, and they are so efficient in doing so that we hardly notice. Searching is ubiquitous in computers; it is hard to think of any useful computer program that does not involve some form of searching in order to work.

Computers are natural searchers. They are much better at doing repetitive things than humans are, they never tire, they never complain. Their attention will not stray away, even after checking whether the millionth item is the one they are looking for.

We are using computers to search for anything that we store in them. There are whole books on search algorithms and research on search still goes on actively. We store more and more data in computers. Data are useless unless you can locate in a timely manner what you are looking for—where timely may be a tiny fraction of a second. There is no single way to search: depending on the nature of data and the nature of your search, one algorithm may be suitable, whereas another one may be woefully inefficient. The nice thing with search, though, is that the basic ideas are easy to grasp and even familiar from everyday experience. The other nice thing is that search algorithms provide a wonderful window through which we can observe the relationship between algorithms in the abstract and the nitty-gritty of getting them to work. You will see that this can be a lot trickier than you may initially think.

11.1   Sequential Search

An fundamental distinction that we must make when we are talking about search is whether the data we are searching through are ordered or processed in any way. Searching in unordered data is like looking for a particular card in a well-shuffled deck. Searching in ordered data is like looking for a word in a dictionary.

Let's start with unordered data. What strategy would you follow to find a card in a deck? The simplest one is to get the first card on the deck and see whether it is the one you are looking for. If it is not, then try with the second. Then with the third, and so on until you find the card. Alternatively, you could start with the last card, then try the previous one, and so on. A third strategy would be to get a card at random. Then if it is not the correct card, get another one at random, then another... Or you could go through every other card or every five cards, discarding them from the deck until you come to the right card.

All these strategies are correct, and no strategy is better than any other. What they share is that we examine the cards, or, in general, our data, in some specific way, making sure that we try each card at most once. As the cards are not in any known order, meaning that there are no patterns in our data that we may exploit, the only thing we can really do is hunker down and go through the tedium of examining our data, piece by piece. There is no cleverness here in how we can solve the problem. We can only apply *brute force*, that is, an exhaustive search through our material, where our only resource is in effect how quickly we can go through it. No room for subtlety or ingenuity here.

The simplest brute force search is a straightforward application of sequential search described at the beginning. Go to square one and start examining each piece of data until you find the one that matches what you are looking for. There are two possible outcomes. Either you find it or you exhaust your data, being confident that what you are looking for is not there. Algorithm 11.1 is a description of sequential search. The algorithm assumes that we are looking for an element in an array. We go through each element of the array (line 1) and check to see whether it is the one we want (line 2) by using a function $Matches(x, y)$, for which we'll have more to say in a bit. If it is, we return from the algorithm the index of the element in the array. If we do not find it, we reach the end of the array without returning any index; we then return the value -1, which is not a valid index, to show that we did not

---

Algorithm 11.1: Sequential search.

SequentialSearch(A, s) $\rightarrow$ i
 Input: A, a array of items
   s, a element we are searching for
 Output: i, the position of s in A if A contains s, or -1 otherwise

1 **for** $i \leftarrow 0$ **to** $|A|$ **do**
2 **if** Matches($A[i], s$) **then**
3   **return** i
4 **return** -1

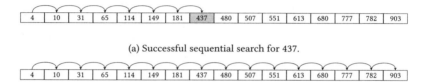

| 4 | 10 | 31 | 65 | 114 | 149 | 181 | 437 | 480 | 507 | 551 | 613 | 680 | 777 | 782 | 903 |

(a) Successful sequential search for 437.

| 4 | 10 | 31 | 65 | 114 | 149 | 181 | 437 | 480 | 507 | 551 | 613 | 680 | 777 | 782 | 903 |

(b) Unsuccessful sequential search for 583.

Figure 11.1
Sequential search.

find the item anywhere in the array. In figure 11.1 you can see an example of a successful and an unsuccessful sequential search.

If the array A has n elements, that is, $|A| = n$, then what is the expected performance of sequential search? If the elements in A are in completely random order, then s can be in any position of A with equal probability: s can be in the first position with probability $1/n$, in the second position with the same probability $1/n$, up to last position with probability always $1/n$. If s is the first item in A the loop of lines 1–3 will be executed once. If s is the second item in A the loop will be executed twice. If s is at the very end of A, or not found at all, the loop will be executed n times. Because the probability of each of these cases is $1/n$, the average number of times that the loop will be executed is:

$$\frac{1}{n} \times 1 + \frac{1}{n} \times 2 + \cdots + \frac{1}{n} \times n = \frac{1 + 2 + \cdots + n}{n} = \frac{n+1}{2}$$

The last part of the equation follows from the fact that:

$$1 + 2 + \cdots + n = \frac{n(n+1)}{2}$$

Hence, the performance of a successful sequential search is on average $O((n+1)/2) = O(n)$. Searching sequentially among n items will take you, on average, time proportional to n. If the item you are searching for is not present, then you will go through all the items in the array to discover that it is not here, so the time for an unsuccessful sequential search is $\Theta(n)$.

11.2 Matching, Comparing, Records, Keys

In the algorithm we use the function Matches(x, y). The function checks whether two elements are the same and returns TRUE if they are and FALSE if they are not. Later on we will also use another function, Compare(x, y), which compares two items and returns +1 if x is better than y, −1 if y is better than x, and 0 if they are considered equal. Such three-valued comparison functions are common in programming, as the result of a single call covers all three possible outcomes. How do these two functions work, and why instead of Matches don't we check simply whether $x = y$? That's because this is probably not what we really want. To see that, we must spend some time dissecting what we are really looking for.

A common term for the data among which we search is *records*. A record may contain several *fields*, or *attributes*, like a person's attributes. Each attribute in a record has a *value* associated with it. An attribute or a set of attributes that identifies a record is called a *key*. Usually, when we search for a record, we search for a record with a particular key. For example, to search for a person, we would search for a person with a particular passport number because passport numbers are unique. You can see an example record for a person in figure 11.2a.

We may of course search for a person with some other attribute, other than a key, for example, the surname. In that case a match does not mean that a single matching person exists. Sequential search will find the first person we come across with the given surname, but there may be others further on.

A key may be made by more than one attribute. When this happens, we call it a *composite* or a *compound key*. In figure 11.2b there is a record for a complex number. The key of the record would be the combination of both its real and complex parts.

A record may have more than one key. For instance, a passport number and a social security number. It may also have both simple and compound keys.

first name: John
surname: Doe
passport no: AI892495
age: 36
occupation: teacher

real: 3.14
imaginary: 1.62

(a) A person record.   (b) A complex number record.

Figure 11.2
Record examples.

For example, a student record may have a registration number as a key and the combination of name, surname, year of birth, department, and enrollment year as another, composite key. We assume that the combination of all these attributes is unique. When there are more than one keys, we usually designate one of them as the key we will be using most of the time. This we call *primary key*, and the other keys we call *secondary keys*.

To simplify the discussion we will simply say that we are searching for something, an item, or a record; we will not be insisting on saying precisely that we are searching for something with a particular key. And we will be using Matches(x, y) for that. With this in mind, in figure 11.1 we showed only the key of the record we are searching for, as this is what really matters. We will follow the same convention in the coming figures.

What about $x = y$? It means something different. All records, all items, are stored in the computer's memory at a particular location with a particular address. The comparison $x = y$ for two records means "tell me if x is stored in the same memory location, if it has the same address, as y." Similarly $x \neq y$ means "check whether x and y are stored in different memory locations, whether they have different addresses."

Figure 11.3 contrasts the two situations. In figure 11.3a we have two variables, x and y, that point to two different locations in memory where records are stored. The two locations have the same contents, but different memory addresses, shown on top of them. The records to which x and y point are equal, but not the same. In figure 11.3b we have two variables, x and y, that point to the same location in memory. The two variables are *aliases* of one another.

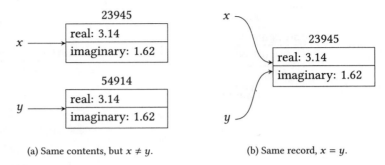

(a) Same contents, but $x \neq y$.   (b) Same record, $x = y$.

Figure 11.3
Two kinds of equality.

Checking $x = y$ or $x \neq y$ for two records is faster than comparing their keys, because we are just comparing their address, which is simply an integer number. The comparison $x = y$ is called *strict comparison*. So we are to gain in speed if a strict comparison is really appropriate to our situation. Hence, in algorithm 11.1 we could use $A[i] = s$ in line 2 if we are not looking for a record based on its contents, or keys, but we are instead trying to find out whether s is an alias to a particular record in $A[i]$. In most cases when we are searching we are not using strict comparisons.

11.3   The Matthew Effect and Power Laws

If you are lucky and the items you are looking for appear early in the array $|A|$ then the performance of sequential search will be much better. This hints at an opportunity for using sequential search when you have a set of items that are not ordered by one of their attributes (like name or surname) but by the frequency of their appearance. If you have the most common object first in the array, then the second most common object second in the array, continuing to less frequent objects, sequential searching will work in your favor.

This proposition becomes more interesting given that a great deal of things are distributed not only unequally but grossly unequally. Wealth is one such thing; a small percentage of people hold a large percentage of global wealth. The frequency of words in a language is another such thing: some words are much more common than others. We see the same pattern in the size of cities:

most human settlements do not count in the millions, but a few of them count up to multi-millions. In the digital realm, most web sites get a few visits, but a few get an enormous number. In literature, most books are hardly read at all, but a few of them become best-sellers. All these recall the phenomenon where "the rich get richer and the poor get poorer," also called The Matthew Effect, after verse 25:29 in the Gospel of Matthew, which goes: "For unto every one that hath shall be given, and he shall have abundance: but from him that hath not shall be taken even that which he hath."

In linguistics, the phenomenon is called Zipf's law, after Harvard linguist George Kingsley Zipf, who observed that the ith most common word in a language appears with a frequency proportional to $1/i$. Zipf's law states that the probability of coming across the ith most common word in a corpus of n words is:

$$P(i) = \frac{1}{i} \frac{1}{H_n}$$

where:

$$H_n = 1 + \frac{1}{2} + \frac{1}{3} + \cdots + \frac{1}{n}$$

The number H_n arises frequently enough in mathematics to be given a name: it is called the nth *harmonic number*. Whence the name? It comes from the overtones, or harmonics, in music. A string vibrates in a fundamental wavelength, and also in harmonics that are $1/2$, $1/3$, $1/4, \ldots$ of the fundamental wavelength: this corresponds to the infinite sum that we get when $n = \infty$, which is called *harmonic series*.

As Zipf's law gives probabilities for an event, Zipf's law is also a namesake probability distribution. In table 11.1 you can see the 20 most common words in an English language corpus (the Brown language corpus, containing 981,716 words of which 40,234 are distinct), their empirical probabilities as calculated by counting their occurrences in the corpus, and their theoretical probabilities, according to Zipf's law, or distribution. In short, we show rank, word, empirical, and theoretical distributions.

A plot of table 11.1, is in figure 11.4. Note that the distribution is defined only for integer values; we included an interpolated line to show the overall trend. Note also that there is not a complete overlap over the theoretical and empirical probabilities. That is a reality we have to face when applying a mathematical model to the real world.

When we see a trend going down rapidly, like in figure 11.4, it is worth checking what happens if instead of using our familiar x and y axes we use

Table 11.1

20 most common words in the Brown English corpus with their associated probabilities and those given by Zipf's law.

Rank	Word	Empirical Probability	Zipf Law
1	THE	0.0712741770532	0.0894478722533
2	OF	0.03709015642	0.0447239361267
3	AND	0.0293903735907	0.0298159574178
4	TO	0.0266451804799	0.0223619680633
5	A	0.0236269959948	0.0178895744507
6	IN	0.0217343916163	0.0149079787089
7	THAT	0.0107913082806	0.0127782674648
8	IS	0.0102972753831	0.0111809840317
9	WAS	0.00999779977101	0.00993865247259
10	HE	0.00972582702126	0.00894478722533
11	FOR	0.00966572817393	0.0081316247503
12	IT	0.00892315089089	0.00745398935445
13	WITH	0.0074247542059	0.00688060555795
14	AS	0.00738808372279	0.00638913373238
15	HIS	0.00712629721834	0.00596319148356
16	ON	0.00686654796295	0.00559049201583
17	BE	0.0064957686337	0.00526163954431
18	AT	0.00547205098012	0.0049693262363
19	BY	0.00540482176108	0.00470778275018
20	I	0.00526017707769	0.00447239361267

logarithmic axes. In logarithmic axes, we transform all values to their logarithms and plot the result. A logarithmic plot equivalent of figure 11.4 is in figure 11.5: for each y we use $\log y$ and for each x we use $\log x$. As you can see, the trend now for the theoretical distribution is a straight line; the empirical distribution seems to stay a bit upwards from what theory would predict. In most cases there will be a difference from a theoretical distribution to what we observe in practice. Also, the two figures show only a subset containing the first 20 most common words, so we cannot really judge the fit based on them. To really see what's going on, check figure 11.3 and 11.7 where the full distributions for all 40,234 different words of the Brown corpus are shown. Two things stand out. First, unless we work on logarithmic scales the plot is useless. That's a striking demonstration of how uneven the probability distribution is. We have to take the logarithm of the values for any trend to become

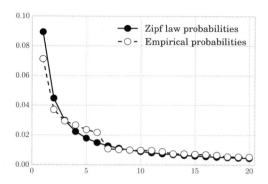

Figure 11.4
Zipf's distribution for the most common 20 words of the Brown corpus.

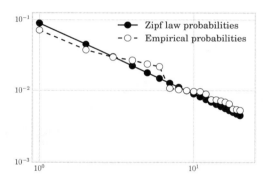

Figure 11.5
Zipf's distribution for the most common 20 words of the Brown corpus in logarithmic axes.

visible. Second, once we go logarithmic, the fit between the theoretical values and the empirical observations is much better.

We see everything clearer in logarithmic scales because Zipf's law is a specific instance of a *power law*. A power law occurs when the probability of a value is proportional to a negative power of that value, or in mathematical terms:

$$P(X = x) \propto cx^{-k} \quad \text{where } c > 0, k > 0$$

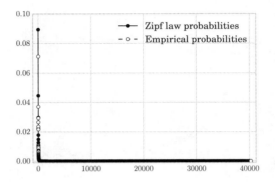

Figure 11.6
Empirical and Zipf distributions of the Brown corpus.

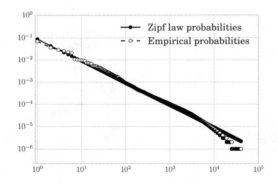

Figure 11.7
Empirical and Zipf distributions of the Brown corpus in logarithmic axes.

In the above formula, the symbol $\propto$ means "is proportional to." Now we can explain why the logarithmic plot is a straight line. If we have $y = cx^{-k}$, then we get $\log y = \log(cx^{-k}) = \log c - k \log x$. The last part is a line with y intercept equal to $\log c$ and slope equal to $-k$. So when we encounter data that plot as a straight line in a logarithmic plot, that is a tell-tale sign that their theoretical distributions could be a power law.

In economics an example of a power law is the Pareto principle, which states that about 20% of the causes are responsible for about 80% of the effects. In management and popular folklore this is usually taken to mean that 20%

of the people do about 80% of the work. In the case of the Pareto principle, it can be proven that $P(X = x) = c/x^{1-\theta}$, where $\theta = \log.80/\log.20$.

The pervasiveness of power laws has spawned a whole field of study of related phenomena over the last twenty years or so; it seems that wherever we look there is a power law lurking underneath. In addition to the example we mentioned when we introduced the Matthew Effect, we find power laws in such different areas as in the citations of scientific papers, the magnitude of earthquakes, and the diameter of moon craters. We also find it in the increase of biological species over time, in fractals, in the foraging patterns of predators, and in peak gamma-ray intensity of solar flares. And the list goes on: the number of long distance calls in a day, the number of people affected by blackouts, the occurrence of family names, and so on.

Such regularities sometimes appear to arise out of nowhere. For example, a related law is *Benford's law*, named after the physicist Frank Benford, or *First-Digit law*. This refers to the frequency distribution of digits in many kinds of data. Specifically, the law states that the first digit of a number is the digit 1 in about 30% of the time. Each digit, from 2 to 9 occurs in the first position with decreasing frequency. Mathematically, the law states that the probability that the leading digit of a number will be $d = 1, 2, \ldots, 9$ is:

$$P(d) = \log\left(1 + \frac{1}{d}\right)$$

If we calculate the probabilities for each digit, we find the results in table 11.2. The numbers in the table tell us that if we have a set of numbers in a dataset, the leading digit should be 1 about 30% of the time: about 30% of the numbers will start with 1, about 17% of the numbers will start with 2, about 12% of the numbers will start with 3, and so on.

You can see a plot of Benford's law in figure 11.8. This does not look very different from the Zipf distribution, so we may wonder what will happen if we draw it in logarithmic axes. The result is in figure 11.9. That is almost a straight line, suggesting that Benford law is related to power laws.

The breadth of Benford's law is stunning. It applies to such varying datasets as physical constants, the height of tallest buildings in the world, population numbers, stock prices, street addresses, and more. Indeed, it seems to be so pervasive that a test for detecting fraudulent data is to check whether the numbers they contain *do not* obey Benford's law. Fraudsters change true values or substitute random values for them, without paying attention to whether the numbers that result follow Benford's law. So if we come across a

Table 11.2

Benford's law, giving the probability that a value will have each digit as its leading number.

Leading Digit	Probability
1	0.301029995664
2	0.176091259056
3	0.124938736608
4	0.0969100130081
5	0.0791812460476
6	0.0669467896306
7	0.0579919469777
8	0.0511525224474
9	0.0457574905607

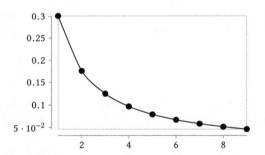

Figure 11.8
Benford's law.

dataset that seems suspect, a good starting point is to see whether the leading digit follows the Benford probabilities.

Benford's law may impact our search, if our search pattern mirrors the distribution pattern: that is, if the keys of the records follow Benford's law and the keys we are searching for also follow Benford's law. If this happens, there will be more records with keys starting with 1 and more searches for these records, fewer for keys starting with 2, and so on.

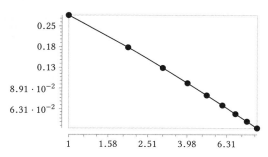

Figure 11.9
Benford's law in logarithmic axes.

11.4   Self-Organizing Search

Going back to searching, if we have evidence that our search records are searched in patterns such that some searches are more popular than others, then shouldn't we take advantage of the fact? That is, if we know that most of our searches will be for one particular item, fewer searches for another item, and still fewer searches for another, and we detect that the popularity of the searches follows a power law, it makes sense to make something out of it. In particular, if we can bring the data in the form where the most frequent items come up first, then we are certain to gain a lot in performance. This idea is called *self-organizing search* because we are using the search pattern to organize our data so as to get a better arrangement of the data.

In algorithm 11.2 we work out this idea when we have to search among a list of items by using a *move-to-front method*. We go through the elements in a list, in the loop of lines 1–9. As we go through the loop, we keep track of the previous item than the one we are currently visiting in the list. We use the variable p for the previous item. Initially we set p to NULL, in line 1, and we update it each time through the loop, in line 9. If we find a match, we check to see, in line 4, whether the match is in the head of the list. That will happen if $p \neq$ NULL, as $p =$ NULL only the first time through the loop. Note that comparisons with NULL are strict comparisons because we are simply checking whether a variable points to nothing. If we are not at the head of the list, then we take the current item and put it in front of the list; then we return it. If we have found a match but we are at the head of the list, then we just return the match. If we do not find a match, then we want to return nothing; therefore, we return NULL.

Algorithm 11.2: Self-organizing search with move-to-front.

MoveToFrontSearch(L, s) $\rightarrow s$ or NULL
    Input: L, a list of items
             s, a element we are searching for
    Output: the element we are looking for, or NULL if it does not exist

1   $p \leftarrow$ NULL
2   **foreach** r in L **do**
3   **if** Matches(r, s) **then**
4   **if** $p \neq$ NULL **then**
5              $m \leftarrow$ RemoveListNode(L, p, r)
6   InsertListNode(L, NULL, m)
7   **return** m
8   **return** r
9       $p \leftarrow r$
10 **return** NULL;

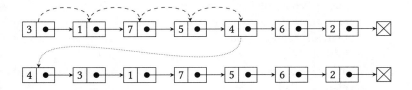

Figure 11.10
Self-organizing search: move-to-front method.

We show how this works in figure 11.10. We are searching for item 4. We find it and take it from its place it and move it on the head of the list. To move an item to the front of a list, we need to use the function RemoveListNode followed by the function InsertListNode. This means that removing an item from a list and adding an item in its front is something that can be done without moving other items around; we only need to manipulate the links among the items. That is not true when we are talking about arrays. Deleting an item from an array entails leaving a hole or moving all following elements one position forward. Inserting an item in the front of an array entails moving all array elements one position. That is not efficient, and that is why algorithm 11.2 is meant for lists.

Algorithm 11.3: Self-organizing search with transposition.

TranspositionSearch(A, s) $\rightarrow$ s or NULL
    Input: L, a list of items,
           s, a element we are searching for
    Output: the element we are looking for, or NULL if it does not exist

1   $p \leftarrow$ NULL
2   $q \leftarrow$ NULL
3   **foreach** r **in** L **do**
4   **if** Matches(r, s) **then**
5   **if** $p \neq$ NULL **then**
6            $m \leftarrow$ RemoveListNode(L, p, r)
7   InsertListNode(L, q, m)
8   **return** m
9   **return** r
10      $q \leftarrow p$
11      $p \leftarrow r$
12 **return** NULL;

Another, related, method for self-organizing search proposes not moving the matched item to the front but just interchanging it with its previous item. For example, if we search for an item and find it at the fifth position of our data, we interchange it with the item in front of it, the fourth element. In this way, popular items will still move-to-front, although not in one jump, but one position for each search for them. Algorithm 11.3 shows how this is done; this is called the *transposition method*.

Here we need to keep track of two list elements: the previous one p, and the one before p, which we call q. Initially both are set to NULL, in lines 1–2. As we go through the items in the list we make q point to p, in line 10, before updating p to point to the item we just visited, in line 11. In the transposition method, we use a slightly different version of Insert. We need to insert an item in some arbitrary location in the list, so we have Insert(L, p, i), which means that we insert item i just after item p. If $q =$ NULL, as would happen if r is the second item in the list and p the first item in the list, Insert will insert m to the head of the list. In figure 11.11 we illustrate what would happen in

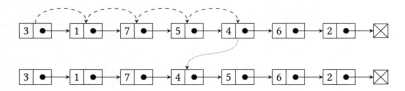

Figure 11.11
Self-organizing search: transposition method.

Algorithm 11.4: Self-organizing search with the transposition method in an array.

TranspositionArraySearch(A, s) $\rightarrow i$
    Input: A, a array of items
            s, a element we are searching for
    Output: i, the position of s in A if A contains s, or -1 otherwise

1   **for** $i \leftarrow 0$ **to** $|A|$ **do**
2   **if** Matches($A[i], s$) **then**
3   **if** $i > 0$ **then**
4   Swap($A[i-1], A[i]$)
5   **return** $i - 1$
6   **else**
7   **return** i
8   **return** -1

---

the same search as in figure 11.11 but when we transpose elements instead of moving to front.

Interchanging two elements is efficient for both lists and arrays, so the transposition method is suitable for both of them. In algorithm 11.4 we show how self-organizing search with transposition is done in an array. We only need a function Swap(x, y) that changes x to y and y to x. In an array, Swap would copy one element to the other. The logic of algorithm 11.4 is similar to that of algorithm 11.3, but we are returning the index of an item, instead of the item itself. As we are working with the index, it is easy to know where we are, at line 3: we simply compare the index with 0 to find out whether we are at the first item.

We can reap substantial savings with self-organizing search. If the probabilities of our keys follow Zipf's law, it can be shown that the average number of comparisons required in the move-to-front method is $O(n/\lg n)$, which is considerably better than $O(n)$, which we get with simple sequential search. The transposition method requires even fewer comparisons than the move-to-front method, but that happens in the long run. This means that move-to-front is better, unless we will be searching for a long time.

11.5   The Secretary Problem

Let us turn to a different formulation of our search problem: suppose that we are looking for the best among a set of elements. What "best" means will depend on the context, of course. We may be looking for the cheapest item, the one with the highest quality, or whatever. We only need to assume that we can evaluate one item with another and see whether it is better or not. That is quite straightforward. If we are looking, say, for the cheapest item, then we just go through the whole set of items, noting down their prices, and then select the one with the lowest price.

But now let us add a twist. Suppose that each time we examine an item we must decide *on the spot* if it is the one. If we reject it, then we cannot recall it later. If we choose it, then we will ignore any other items further on.

This is typical of situations when the data come to us from some external source; we have no control of their order, we have to select the best match among them, and we cannot go back to an item we have rejected. This is sometimes called the Secretary Problem. Imagine that you are about to hire a new secretary. You have a pile of CVs in front of you, and you must select the secretary from that list. The catch is that if you go over a CV and reject it, you cannot go back: your decision must be made on the spot, and it must be final. What is the best way to choose the new secretary?

It turns out that if you have n CVs, your best course of action is to go through and reject the first n/e of them, where $e \approx 2.7182$ is Euler's number. The ratio n/e is equal to about 37% of all. While rejecting the first 37% of the secretaries, note the best applicant in this set of CVs. Then, pick up the first candidate you find in the remaining CVs who is better than that best candidate of the first n/e candidates. If you do not find any, pick up the last one in the pile. Your probability of hiring the best candidate is at least $1/e$, about 37%, and it is the best you can do.

Algorithm 11.5: Secretary search.

SecretarySearch(A, s) $\rightarrow i$
> **Input**: A, a array of items
> **Output**: i, the position of the element in A that we should choose,
> or -1 if we failed to find the best element

1   $m \leftarrow \lceil |A|/e \rceil$
2   $c \leftarrow 0$
3   **for** $i \leftarrow 1$ **to** m **do**
4   **if** Compare($A[i], A[b]$) > 0 **then**
5         $c \leftarrow i$
6   **for** $i \leftarrow m + 1$ **to** $|A|$ **do**
7   **if** Compare($A[i], A[c]$) > 0 **then**
8   **return** i
9   **return** -1

Algorithm 11.5 describes this search mechanism, where decisions must be made on each item on the spot, with no capability to revisit past items. We either reject, or accept an item, and the decision for each item is irrevocable.

In line 1 we calculate the number of items that we will reject while looking for the best one among them. Because $|A|/e$ is not an integer, we take the nearest integer m greater than the ratio $|A|/e$. We use a variable c to hold the index of the best item among the first m. Initially we set it to zero, the first item. In lines 3–5 we search for the best item in the first m items. We use the Compare(x, y) function that compares two items and returns $+1$ if x is better than y, -1 if y is better than x, and 0 if they are considered equal. The comparison is carried out using the keys of the records; when we say we are comparing items or records we really mean that we are comparing their keys. Having found the best among the first m items, $A[c]$, we proceed to find the first one that is better than $A[c]$. If we find it we return it immediately; otherwise we return -1 to indicate that our strategy failed because the best candidate was among the initial m.

Keep in mind that algorithm 11.5 will not necessarily give you the best item in A. If the best item is among the first m, then unfortunately you will miss it and end up empty-handed. But no other strategy will do better. It may be a good idea to either make sure your CV does not appear among the top of the pile or not send your CV to companies that engage in such practices.

Algorithm 11.5 applies to any problem where we must decide to select or reject an item on the spot. A problem that fits this description is when we wait for a set of inputs or events and have to decide to act on only one of them. We know how many events we will get, but we have no prior indication which one would be the best one to select. Suppose we are given bids. Once we open each one in turn, we can either accept or reject it. We can accept only one bid. Once we reject a bit, it is no longer valid. All such situations belong to the theory of *optimal stopping*, which deals with choosing when to take an action to maximize a reward or minimize a cost. In a sense, what we are searching for is not simply an item: we are searching for a way to know when to stop searching. Other situations similar to the Secretary Problem are the so-called *online algorithms*, where input is presented and processed in a serial function, piece by piece, without having the entire input available to us from the start. *Streaming algorithms*, where the input comes as a sequence of items that can be examined in a single pass as they come, are examples of online algorithms.

Regarding the complexity of algorithm 11.5, in lines 1–5, we go through the first m items. Then lines 6–8 are similar in structure to lines 1–3 of algorithm 11.1, but instead of n items we have $n - m$ items. Therefore, the overall complexity is $O(m + (n - m + 1)/2) = O(m/2 + (n + 1)/2 = O(n/2e + (n - 1)/2) = O(n)$.

The Secretary Problem assumes that you want to find the absolutely best candidate and only that candidate is important to you. You have about 37% probability of getting *the one*, but you may end up with nobody at all. The ideal secretary is worth everything to you and all others are worth nothing. Suppose now that you lower your standards a bit. Instead of valuing only the single best candidate, or in general the single best item in your search, and judging the rest to be worthless, you may decide to value each one of the items according to their worth. Thus, you decide that all choices have a worth, which is the value you use to do your comparisons. For example, if you are to buy cars and your criterion is speed, then the uncompromising stance is to value only the fastest car and deem all the others as clunkers. A bit of compromise means that you value the fastest car the most, but you still value the rest of them. The value of the second fastest car to you will be less than the value of the fastest car, but it will not be nothing, and so on for the third car and the rest of them. You do not bag all cars but the fastest as worthless. If you do that, then it can be proven that you must not examine and disregard the first n/e of the candidates, but the first $\sqrt{n}$ of them. Moreover, as the number n increases, your probability of ending up with the best candidate

1	1.0079	2	4.0025	3	6.941	4	9.0122	5	10.811	6	12.011	7	14.007	8	15.999	9	18.998	10	20.180
H		He		Li		Be		B		C		N		O		F		Ne	
Hydrogen		Helium		Lithium		Beryllium		Boron		Carbon		Nitrogen		Oxygen		Fluorine		Neon	

(a) First ten chemical elements ordered by atomic number.

89	227	13	26.982	95	243	51	121.76	18	39.948	33	74.922	85	210	56	137.33	97	247	4	9.0122
Ac		Al		Am		Sb		Ar		As		At		Ba		Bk		Be	
Actinium		Aluminium		Americium		Antimony		Argon		Arsenic		Astatine		Barium		Berkelium		Beryllium	

(b) First ten chemical elements ordered alphabetically.

89	227	47	107.87	13	26.982	95	243	18	39.948	33	74.922	85	210	79	196.97	5	10.811	56	137.33
Ac		Ag		Al		Am		Ar		As		At		Au		B		Ba	
Actinium		Silver		Aluminium		Americium		Argon		Arsenic		Astatine		Gold		Boron		Barium	

(c) First ten chemical elements ordered by chemical symbol.

Figure 11.12
Different orderings of chemical elements. Each element is shown with its chemical symbol, atomic number, and atomic weight.

goes to 1, instead of being $1/e$. That seems strange. You make a slight change in the formulation of a problem and you end up with a different solution and different chances of arriving at the best solution. There are many such instances in computer science and mathematics, where a seemingly minor change alters the nature of a problem.

11.6   Binary Search

To this point we have assumed that we have no control over the order in which items appear to us. Let's turn our attention now to how we can benefit if the items are ordered in some way.

It is important that your items are ordered on the key by which you are searching for them. In figure 11.12 you see the first ten chemical elements ordered in three different ways: by their atomic number, alphabetically by their name, or alphabetically by their chemical symbol.

You can see that the orderings are different. Even the orderings by name and chemical symbol differ, as chemical symbols are based on Latin, not English, names. If you were to search for a chemical element by atomic number, you should have the elements sorted by that key, whereas if you were to search by its chemical symbol, the third ordering of figure 11.12 would be the one to use. Pretending to search ordered items when the wrong ordering is used makes no sense, and it may not make much difference in practice than using simple sequential searching.

When we do know that items are in the correct order, the opposite holds: it does not make sense to start searching sequentially. If you have a pile of CVs on your desk ordered by the candidate's surname, then when you want to look for a surname starting with "D", you expect the CV to appear closer to the top of the pile than to the bottom. Conversely, if you want to look for a surname starting with "T", you expect the CV to appear closer to the bottom of the pile than to the front.

This is a good educated guess, and we can take it further if we think about the simple number guessing game where one player says, "I have in mind a number between 0 and 100, can you guess which one with the fewest guesses? For each of your guesses I will tell you if you got the number right, or if the number is greater than or lower than your guess." Unless you are not psychic, the winning strategy is to start by taking the middle number, that is, 50, as your guess. If you got it right, you are done. If 50 is greater than the chosen number, then now you know the number is between 0 and 50. You split again the difference and put forward 25 as your guess. If you go on like this, you are guaranteed to find the chosen number in at most seven guesses; we'll see why when we wrap up our discussion of how to search in ordered items.

The method we described has a name, *binary search*. The word binary comes from the fact that at each decision point we cut our search space in two. Initially all we knew was that the number was between 0 and 100. Then we knew that it was between 0 and 50 or between 50 and 100; and then between 0 and 25 or between 25 and 50. Algorithm 11.6 renders binary search in algorithmic form.

The algorithm uses two variables, l and h, to refer to the low and the high end of our search space, respectively. Initially l is the index of the first element of the array in which we are searching and h is the index of the last element of the array. At line 4 we calculate the midpoint, m, of the array by taking the average of l and h and rounding down to the closest integer. If the midpoint is less than the item we are looking for, we know that we have to search from the midpoint upward and adjust l in line 7. If the midpoint is more than the item we are looking for, we know that we have to search from the midpoint

---

Algorithm 11.6: Binary search.

BinarySearch(A, s) → i
    Input: A, a sorted array of items
            s, a element we are searching for
    Output: i, the position of s in A if A contains s, or -1 otherwise

1   $l \leftarrow 0$
2   $h \leftarrow |A|$
3   **while** $l \leq h$ **do**
4       $m \leftarrow \lfloor (l + h)/2 \rfloor$
5       $c \leftarrow$ Compare$(A[m], s)$
6   **if** $c < 0$ **then**
7          $l \leftarrow m + 1$
8   **else if** $c > 0$ **then**
9          $h \leftarrow m - 1$
10   **else**
11   **return** m
12 **return** -1

---

downward and this time we adjust h in line 8. If the midpoint is what we are looking for we just return it.

This procedure is repeated as long as there is something in which to search. Every time we cut our search space in half. Or, rather, about half: if we have to search among seven elements, then half is not an integer number, so we take three as the midpoint and split our search space between the first two and the last four elements if the third element is not the one we are looking for. This does not change the picture. At some point there will be nowhere to search into. If this happens, then we return -1 to indicate that we did not find our item.

You can think of it in another way. Each time in the loop of lines 3–11 either l is increased or h is decreased. Therefore, at some point the condition $l \leq h$ in line 3 will definitely cease to hold. Then we know we can stop.

You can check the behavior of binary search in figures 11.13 and 11.14. Our sorted array of numbers is 4, 10, 31, 65, 114, 149, 181, 437, 480, 507, 551, 613, 680, 777, 782, 903. We carry out a successful search for 149 in figure 11.13a. In the figure we indicate the variables l, h, and m of algorithm 11.6. We gray

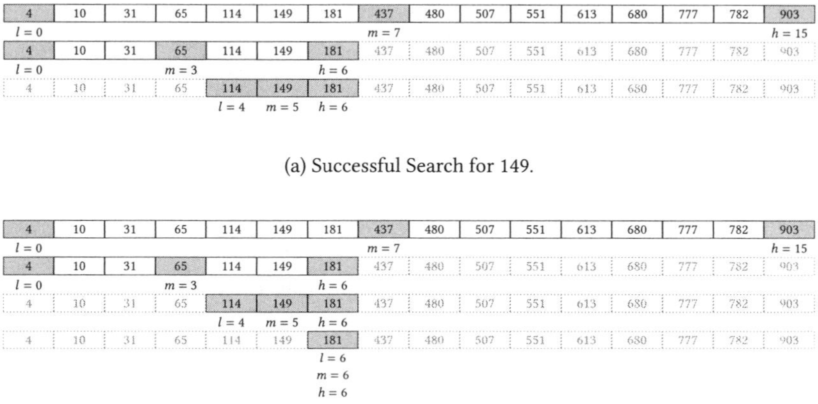

(a) Successful Search for 149.

(b) Successful search for 181.

Figure 11.13
Binary search, successful search examples.

out the discarded part of our search space, so you can see how this is reduced. When we search for 149, we reach our target in the third iteration, when the middle point of our search space falls on it. In figure 11.13b we search, successfully, for 181. This time we land on it when the search space has been reduced to a single item—the one we are looking for.

When we search unsuccessfully for an item, as in figure 11.14a and 11.14b, we keep reducing our search space until we run out of it completely, without having found what we are looking for. In figure 11.14a the left boundary of our search space moves to the right of its right boundary, which does not make sense. This violates the condition in line 3 of algorithm 11.6, so the algorithm returns −1. Similarly, in figure 11.14b the right boundary of our search space moves to the left of its left boundary, producing the same result.

Binary search is an algorithm developed in the dawn of the computer age. Still, the details of implementing binary search correctly continued to trip programmers for a long time. A prominent programmer and researcher, Jon Bentley, found in the 1980s that about 90% of professional programmers fail to get a correct working implementation of binary search, even after working several hours on it. Another researcher in 1988 found that only 5 out of 20 textbooks had accurate descriptions of the algorithm (hopefully the situation

4	10	31	65	114	149	181	437	480	507	551	613	680	777	782	903
l=0							m=7								h=15
4	10	31	65	114	149	181	437	480	507	551	613	680	777	782	903
								l=8			m=11				h=15
4	10	31	65	114	149	181	437	480	507	551	613	680	777	782	903
								l=8	m=9	h=10					
4	10	31	65	114	149	181	437	480	507	551	613	680	777	782	903
										l=10					
										m=10					
										h=10					
4	10	31	65	114	149	181	437	480	507	551	613	680	777	782	903
										m=10	l=11				
										h=10					

(a) Unsuccessful search for 583.

4	10	31	65	114	149	181	437	480	507	551	613	680	777	782	903
l=0							m=7								h=15
4	10	31	65	114	149	181	437	480	507	551	613	680	777	782	903
								l=8			m=11				h=15
4	10	31	65	114	149	181	437	480	507	551	613	680	777	782	903
								l=8	m=9	h=10					
4	10	31	65	114	149	181	437	480	507	551	613	680	777	782	903
								l=8							
								m=8							
								h=8							
4	10	31	65	114	149	181	437	480	507	551	613	680	777	782	903
							h=7	l=7							
							m=7								

(b) Unsuccessful search for 450.

Figure 11.14
Binary search, unsuccessful search examples.

has since improved). In a twist of fate, it was found that Jon Bentley's program was also broken, and the bug had gone undetected for about 20 years. It was discovered by Joshua Bloch, an acclaimed software engineer who implemented many features of the Java programming language. In fact, the bug that Bloch found had infected his own implementation of binary search in Java and had gone undetected for years.

What was that bug? Go back to algorithm 11.6 and examine line 4. That is a simple mathematical expression to calculate the average of two numbers and rounding down to the closest integer. We calculate the average by adding l and h and halving the result. There is nothing wrong with the mathematics, but when we turn from mathematics to implementations, things can get messy. The two numbers l and h are positive integers. Adding them will always produce an integer larger than either of them. Unless you are adding them on a computer.

11.7   Representing Integers in Computers

Computers have limited resources: no computer has infinite memory. That means it is impossible to add arbitrary large numbers. A large number will have more digits than we can put in the computer's memory. If l and h fit into the available memory but $l + h$ does not, then the addition will not be possible.

Often the limit is much smaller than the available memory. Many programming languages do not allow us to use arbitrary sized integers anyway. They will not allow us to exhaust the memory because for efficiency reasons they have limits on the size of numbers they can handle. They use a sequence of n bits to represent an integer as a binary number, where n is a predetermined number, a power of 2, such as 32 or 64.

Suppose we want to represent only unsigned numbers, that is, positive numbers. If a binary number is made up of n bits $B_{n-1} \ldots B_1 B_0$, then its value is $B_{n-1} \times 2^{n-1} + B_{n-2} \times 2^{n-2} + \cdots + B_1 \times 2^1 + B_0 \times 2^0$, where each of $B_{n-1}, B_{n-2}, \ldots, B_0$ is either 1 or 0. The first bit (B_{n-1}) has the highest value and is called the *most significant bit*. The last bit is the *least significant bit*.

Which numbers can we represent with n bits? Take four bits numbers as an example. With four bits, when all bits are zero, we get the binary number $0000 = 0$, whereas when all the bits are one, we get the binary number 1111, which is $2^3 + 2^2 + 2^1 + 2^0$. That is one less than the binary number 10000, which is $2^4 + 0 \times 2^3 + 0 \times 2^2 + 0 \times 2^1 + 0 \times 2^0 = 2^4$. Let us introduce a bit of notation now. To avoid any confusion of whether a number b is binary, we will write $(b)_2$. So to make clear that 10 is the number 2 in binary and not the number 10 in decimal, we will write $(10)_2$. Using this notation we have $(10000)_2 = (1111)_2 + 1$. That means that we have $(1111)_2 = (10000)_2 - 1 = 2^4 - 1$. With four bits we can represent all numbers from 0 to $2^4 - 1$, 2^4 numbers in total.

We can generalize that. Another helpful bit of notation is to use $d\{k\}$ to mean that the digit d is repeated k times. Using this notation we can write $1\{4\}$ instead of 1111. With n bits we can represent the numbers from zero to $(1\{n\})_2$, which is equal to $2^{n-1} + 2^{n-2} + \cdots + 2^1 + 2^0$. That is one less than $(10\{n\})_2$: $(10\{n\})_2 = (1\{n\})_2 + 1$. Therefore, $(1\{n\})_2 = (10\{n\})_2 - 1$, and because $(10\{n\})_2 = 2^n$, we get $(1\{n\})_2 = 2^n - 1$. Therefore, with n bits we can represent all numbers from 0 to $2^n - 1$, 2^n numbers in total.

To see how addition works with these numbers, you can think of them as placed on a wheel, like in figure 11.15, which shows the numbers wheel for numbers represented with four bits. Addition works by going clockwise

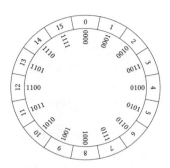

Figure 11.15
Numbers wheel.

around the wheel. To calculate $4 + 7$, start at 0, go around four steps to 4, and then go around another 7 steps. You get to 11, the result of the addition, as in figure 11.16.

So far so good, but if you try to calculate $14 + 4$, as in figure 11.17, you first go around from 0 to 14. Then the additional four steps take you to number 2, which is the result of the addition. This situation is called *overflow* because the calculation flows over the allowable upper limit of numbers. If we do the arithmetic, we get $14 + 4 = (1110)_2 + (0100)_2 = (10010)_2$. The last number has five bits instead of four. What computers do is simply drop the extra bit on the left, the most significant bit; that is the same as going around the wheel, as we get $(0010)_2 = 2$.

Going back to line 4 of algorithm 11.6, if the sum of the two numbers l and h is greater than the greater allowable integer, we will not get the correct result, as it will overflow: the number $l + h$ will be wrong, and from then on the algorithm will not work. If we have 32 bits to represent unsigned integers in a programming language, then the range of integers that can be represented is from 0 to $2^{32} - 1$, or from zero to 4,294,967,295. If you add numbers that will sum up to a value greater than about 4.29 billion, then you will get an overflow. Four billion might have seen astronomical some years back, but data sets of such sizes are pretty common now.

We have assumed so far that we represent only positive integers, but what happens when our programming language represents signed numbers, that is, negative as well as positive integers? A common way to represent negative integers is to use those sequences of bits that start with 1 to stand for negative numbers, keeping those sequences of bits that start with 0 for the positive

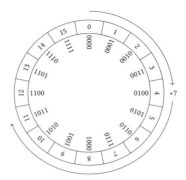

Figure 11.16
Calculating 4 + 7.

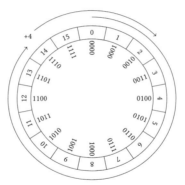

Figure 11.17
Calculating 14 + 4.

numbers. In this convention we call the most significant bit the *sign bit*, as it denotes the sign of the number. That means we are left with $n - 1$ digits to represent our numbers, so we can represent 2^{n-1} different positive numbers and 2^{n-1} negative numbers. We include zero among the positive numbers as its sign bit is zero. If, when we are adding, our numbers are too large, we may get a negative number as a result: half of our wheel of numbers (the right side) will be filled with positive numbers, and half with negative numbers (the left side). Overflow will happen every time we add to a positive number another positive number that takes us from the realm of the positives to the realm of the negatives.

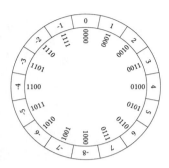

Figure 11.18
Two complement's numbers wheel.

Figure 11.19
Calculating 4 + 2 in two complement's representation.

For example, check figure 11.18 that shows signed four-bit integers. It shows the integers represented with a scheme called *two complement's representation*. Positive numbers have a sign bit of zero, and they range from 0 to 7 or $(0000)_2$ to $(0111)_2$. Negative numbers follow this rule: take a positive number of x with n bits. The representation of its negative in binary will be the number $c = 2^n - x$, that is, the number that added to x will produce 2^n. That explains the name, as we are complementing with a power of 2. So the negative of number $5 = (0101)_2$ is the binary number that results from $2^4 - 5 = 16 - 5 = 11 = (1011)_2$. You can verify that with this scheme we will get negative overflows: while 4 + 2 produces the right result, as in figure 11.19, 4 + 7 produces a negative number because of overflow, −5, as in figure 11.20.

In general, if we have n digits, because we have 2^{n-1} digits for positive numbers plus 0 and 2^{n-1} digits for negative numbers, then we can represent

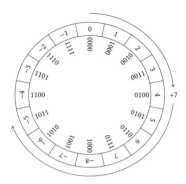

Figure 11.20
Calculating 4 + 7 with two complement's representation.

the numbers from 0 to $2^{n-1} - 1$ and from -1 to -2^{n-1}. For 32 bits, the largest positive number is 2,147,483,647. This is a large number but not outlandish for today's applications. If you venture beyond that, instead of getting to a larger number you will go to $-2^{32} = -2,147,483,648$. This is what humanity did in 2014 by watching the video of the popular song "Gangnam Style." On December 1, we learned that the number of views of that video on YouTube had exceeded 2,147,483,647. Apparently when YouTube was designed this was not thought possible. The service was updated so that the views counter uses a 64-bit integer. This will overflow after $2^{63} - 1 = 9,223,372,036,854,775,807$ views.

Two's complement representation may seem a strange contraption, as there appear to be simple solutions. One alternative is to form the opposite of a number by flipping all its bits. So, for example, the opposite of $(0010)_2 = 2$ would be $(1101)_2$. This is called *ones' complement representation*. Be careful where the apostrophe is. It's not "one's complement," it's "ones' complement," because we are complementing each individual digit with respect to 1: we are forming its opposite by adding the number required to get 1. Another alternative, called *signed magnitude representation*, is to form the opposite of a number by flipping its sign bit only. So the opposite of $(0010)_2 = 2$ would be $(1010)_2$.

Two's complement is the most popular way of representing signed integers for two reasons. First, in one's complement and signed magnitude representations, you end up with two zeros, $(0000)_2$ and $(1111)_2$, which is kind of messy.

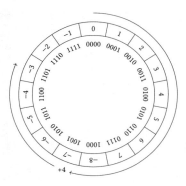

Figure 11.21
Calculating $4 - 7$ with two complement's representation.

Second, both addition and subtraction are easier to do with two's complement numbers. Subtraction works as the addition of numbers with opposite signs. To find $x - y$ you go to the number wheel, find $-y$, and proceed x steps clockwise, as you can see in figure 11.21.

11.8   Binary Search Revisited

Back to binary search. Fortunately, the situation is easy to fix. Instead of calculating $\lfloor (l + h)/2 \rfloor$ we may calculate the equivalent $l + \lfloor (h - l)/2 \rfloor$, which will give us a correct value for m, avoiding overflows. Instead of finding the midpoint between two numbers by first adding them and then halving their sum, we find it by calculating the difference of the two numbers, cutting it in half, and adding it to the lowest number. Indeed, because l is an integer, we have $l + \lfloor (h - l)/2 \rfloor = \lfloor l + (h - l)/2 \rfloor = \lfloor (l + h)/2 \rfloor$. Figure 11.22 shows the two equivalent midpoint calculations. There is no risk of overflow by calculating $(h - l)$, which is less than h anyway; adding $\lfloor (h - l)/2 \rfloor$ to l will not get beyond h, so again there is no risk of overflow. The fix is in algorithm 11.7, line 4.

You may think that all this is pretty obvious, and it is, in hindsight. We did not relate the story of the bug to point fingers at some extremely intelligent people. It is exactly the fact that even extremely intelligent people can fall into such subtle traps, which highlights one of the most important virtues computer programmers should have: humility. No matter how clever you are, no matter how good at programming, you will never be immune from bugs.

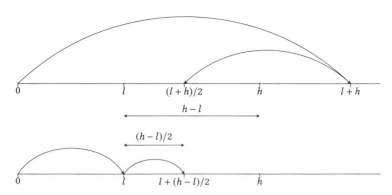

Figure 11.22
Avoiding overflow in calculation of midpoint.

People who brag that their code is ironclad and bug-free have usually not writ-ten any valuable production code. Maurice Wilkes, another computer pioneer, reminiscing about the early computing days of 1949, when he was program-ming the EDSAC computer in Cambridge, wrote:

It was on one of my journeys between the EDSAC room and the punching equipment that "hesitating at the angles of stairs" the realization came over me with full force that a good part of the remainder of my life was going to be spent in finding errors in my own programs.

That must rank among the most prescient thoughts in the history of com-puting. By the way, punching equipment refers to paper punching equipment that was used for computer input, not boxing. The phrase "hesitating at the angles of stairs" is from T. S. Eliot's "Murder in the Cathedral."

Binary search is an efficient algorithm. In fact, on average we cannot search faster than with binary search. Each time we carry out a comparison in line 5 of algorithm 11.7 we either find what we are looking for or we cut our search space in half, going on to search either in the upper or the lower half. There-fore, each time we are dividing by two the number of items in which we search. We cannot go on dividing by two forever: the number of times we can divide a number by two is the logarithm base two of that number: for n, it is $\lg n$.

Algorithm 11.7: Safe binary search without overflows.

SafeBinarySearch(A, s) $\rightarrow i$
 Input: A, a sorted array of items
    s, a element we are looking for
 Output: i, the position of s in A if A contains s, or -1 otherwise

1 $l \leftarrow 0$

2 $h \leftarrow |A|$

3 **while** $l \leq h$ **do**

4 $m \leftarrow l + \lfloor (h - l)/2 \rfloor$

5 $c \leftarrow$ Compare($A[m], s$)

6 **if** $c < 0$ **then**

7   $l \leftarrow m + 1$

8 **else if** $c > 0$ **then**

9   $h \leftarrow m - 1$

10 **else**

11   **return** m

12 **return** -1

11.9 Comparison Trees

One way to visualize what is going on is by using a *comparison tree* as in figure 11.23. The tree shows the different comparisons that can take place in an array of 16 elements, $A[0], A[1], \ldots A[15]$. When we start the algorithm we compare the element we are looking for, s, with element $A[\lfloor (0 + 15) \rfloor /2] = A[7]$. If $s = A[7]$ we stop, if $s < A[7]$ we go down on the left subtree, and if $s > A[7]$ we go down the right subtree. The left subtree contains items $A[0], A[1], \ldots, A[6]$ and the right subtree contains items $A[8], A[9], \ldots, A[15]$. In the left subtree we compare s with $A[\lfloor (0 + 6) \rfloor /2] = A[3]$. In the right subtree we compare s with $A[\lfloor (8 + 15) \rfloor /2] = A[11]$. The tree grows downwards by splitting the search space in half until we arrive at search spaces containing just one element. These are the leaves of the tree. Hanging from the leaves of the tree you can see rectangular nodes: these correspond to values of s that are not in array A. If we arrive at a point where we compare s with $A[8]$ and we find that $s > A[8]$, then we fail in our search because s is between $A[8]$

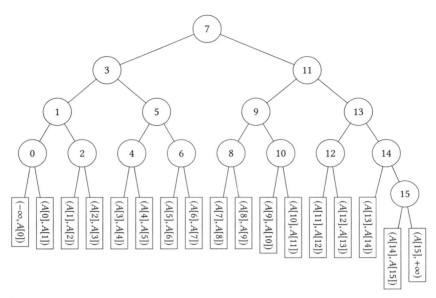

Figure 11.23
Comparison tree representing binary search for 16 items.

and $A[9]$, that is, $s \in (A[8], A[9])$. Similarly, if we arrive at a point where we compare s with $A[0]$ and we find $s < A[0]$, then we fail because $s \in (-\infty, A[0])$.

The general pattern for constructing the comparison tree is that if n is the number of elements of array A, then we take element $A[\lfloor n/2 \rfloor]$ as the root of the tree. We put the first $\lfloor n/2 \rfloor - 1$ elements in the left subtree and the remaining $n - \lfloor n/2 \rfloor$ in the right subtree. We proceed in the same way in each of the subtrees until we have subtrees of size one, in which case we only have a single, root node for them.

Comparison trees allow us to study the performance of binary search. The number of comparisons depends on the number of round nodes in the tree—we do not consider the rectangular nodes as proper nodes in the tree. The way we construct the tree, by creating subtrees in a recursive way, means that all levels apart from the last one are full. Indeed, at every node we split the search space of the tree hanging from that node. Figure 11.24 shows the trees corresponding to values of n from 1 to 7. If the search space contains more than one node, then we will get two subtrees, and the number of elements in the two subtrees cannot differ by more than one, which will happen if the elements cannot be divided evenly by two. It's impossible to start a new level unless the previous one is full. Lopsided trees, like the one in figure 11.25, cannot happen.

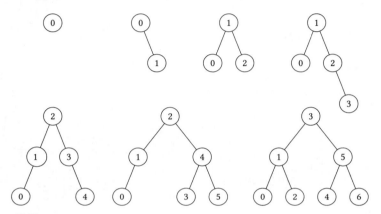

Figure 11.24

Comparison trees for searches in 1 to 7 items.

The root level, level zero, of a comparison tree has one node. Level one of the tree can have up to two nodes. It is not necessary that it has two nodes. A comparison tree can have two levels with just a single node at level one; a root with just one child, as the second tree of figure 11.24. Level two can have up to $2 \times 2 = 2^2$ nodes. Again, it may have less; this number is the maximum number when the level is completely full. Proceeding in this way we find that level k can have up to 2^k nodes. Therefore, a comparison tree whose last level is level k can have up to $1 + 2 + \cdots + 2^k$ nodes in total. Note that $1 = 2^0$ and $2 = 2^1$, so a comparison tree where the last level is level k can have up to, and including, $2^0 + 2^1 + \cdots + 2^k$ nodes. But we have already met this number: it is the number $(1\{k + 1\})_2$, which we know is equal to $2^{k+1} - 1$. Therefore, we have $n \le 2^{k+1} - 1$, or equivalently $n < 2^{k+1}$.

Because level k is the last level, all levels up to and including level $k - 1$ will be completely full. Using the same line of thought as above, the tree will have $2^k - 1$ nodes in the levels up to and including level $k - 1$. So we have $n > 2^k - 1$, or equivalently $n \ge 2^k$. Combining our results we get $2^k \le n < 2^{k+1}$.

A successful search may stop at any level of tree, including reaching level k, requiring anything from one to $k + 1$ comparisons, so if $2^k \le n < 2^{k+1}$ the minimum number of comparisons is one and the maximum is $k + 1$. Regarding unsuccessful searches now, if $n = 2^{k+1} - 1$, then the last level is full and we

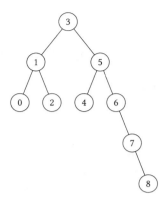

Figure 11.25
This comparison tree cannot happen.

need exactly $k + 1$ comparisons. If $2^k \leq n < 2^{k+1} - 1$, then the last level is not full, and we may need either k or $k + 1$ comparisons.

To cast the above in terms of complexity, a successful search is $O(\lfloor \lg n \rfloor) = O(\lg n)$. An unsuccessful search is $\Theta(\lg n)$. Remember that in the guessing game you could find the answer in at most seven guesses? Now we know why. With a binary search among 100 elements, you need $\lg 100 \approx 6.65 < 7$ guesses to find the secret.

Recall that $2^{32} - 1 = 4,294,967,295$. That means that any search in a sorted array of 4,294,967,295 will take no more than 32 comparisons. Compare that to the billions of comparisons required on average for a sequential search on the same array.

You can appreciate the power of repeated division, which is what the logarithm does, by taking a look at its reverse, repeated multiplication, or raising to a power. A nice illustration is the probably apocryphal myth on the invention of chess. It is said that when the game of chess was invented, the ruler of the country liked it so much that he asked the inventor to name his reward. The inventor asked his reward to be a quantity of rice (or wheat, depending on the version of the story), calculated as follows: one grain in the first square, two grains in the second square, four grains in the third square, and so on. The ruler granted the wish, until the treasurer informed him that all the provisions stored in the country would not suffice.

You can see why in figure 11.26. The exponent increases each time we proceed to the next square; therefore, the growth is exponential. In the last square we have 2^{63} grains. That is about equal to 9 followed by 18 zeroes. Ponder that for a minute: we can search among about 9×10^{18} sorted items with no more than 63 comparisons. A logarithm is as powerful as exponential growth in reverse.

The idea of solving a problem by dividing it in pieces is a powerful tool. A *divide and conquer* approach is applicable in many problems we have to solve using computers. It is also applicable to brain teasers. Suppose that you are asked to solve this problem: You have nine coins, one of which is counterfeit and lighter than the other. You also have one balance. How can you find the fake one with no more than two weighings?

The key to answer the problem is to observe that with a careful procedure we can use a weighing to split our search space in three (instead of two, as in binary search). Suppose we label the coins as $c_1, c_2, \ldots, c_9$. We take coins c_1, c_2, c_3 and we weigh them against coins c_7, c_8, c_9. If they balance, then we know the counterfeit is among coins c_4, c_5, c_6. Now we take coins c_4, c_5. If they balance, then the counterfeit is coin c_6. If they do not, then the fake one is the one that shows up as lighter on the balance. If c_1, c_2, c_3 and c_7, c_8, c_9 do not balance, then again we know immediately which triplet contains the

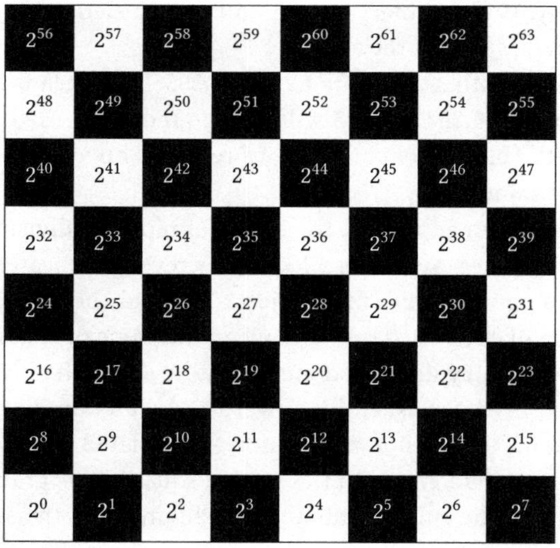

2^{56}	2^{57}	2^{58}	2^{59}	2^{60}	2^{61}	2^{62}	2^{63}
2^{48}	2^{49}	2^{50}	2^{51}	2^{52}	2^{53}	2^{54}	2^{55}
2^{40}	2^{41}	2^{42}	2^{43}	2^{44}	2^{45}	2^{46}	2^{47}
2^{32}	2^{33}	2^{34}	2^{35}	2^{36}	2^{37}	2^{38}	2^{39}
2^{24}	2^{25}	2^{26}	2^{27}	2^{28}	2^{29}	2^{30}	2^{31}
2^{16}	2^{17}	2^{18}	2^{19}	2^{20}	2^{21}	2^{22}	2^{23}
2^{8}	2^{9}	2^{10}	2^{11}	2^{12}	2^{13}	2^{14}	2^{15}
2^{0}	2^{1}	2^{2}	2^{3}	2^{4}	2^{5}	2^{6}	2^{7}

Figure 11.26
Exponential growth on a chessboard.

fake one, and we do with that triplet the same thing we described for coins c_4, c_5, c_6. You can see the full picture as a coin weighing tree in figure 11.27, where we denote by $w(c_i c_j c_k)$ the weight of coins c_i, c_j, c_k. Each internal node corresponds to a weighting and each leaf node to a fake coin.

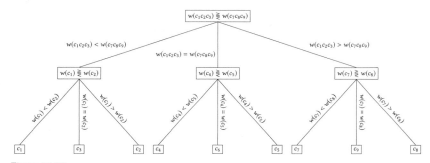

Figure 11.27
Coin weighing tree.

As at each level we split the search space in three, the total number of steps required for a complete search is calculated with a logarithm base 3, instead of base 2 as before. For nine coins, we have $\log_3(9) = 2$, which is indeed the height of the tree in figure 11.27.

Notes

George Kingsley Zipf popularized his observations in two books in 1935 [226] and in 1949 [227]. The Brown language corpus was compiled in the 1960s by Henry Kučera and W. Nelson Francis of Brown University from 500 English text samples. Vilfredo Pareto described a power law distribution, although nobody called them that way back then in the 19th century [154]. In the early 20th century, G. Udny Yule also discovered power laws in his study of the creation of biological species [223]. Power laws were brought into the limelight by Barabasi [10, 11]. For a history see the account by Mitzenmacher [143]. For a cautionary view on power laws see the commentary by Stumpf and Porter [194].

Frank Benford stated the law that bears his name in 1938 [14]; however, he was not the first to publish it. The astronomer and mathematician Simon

Newcomb had published it previously in 1881 [149]. For a derivation of Benford's law see the paper by Hill [92], and for an explanation see the paper by Fewster [65].

Apart from the transposition and the move-to-front methods, the *count method* also falls into that category. In this method we count the number of times an item is counted, and we keep the list arranged so that the items with the higher counts appear at the front of the list. Self-organizing search was proposed by John McCabe [135]. The proof that the transposition method uses fewer comparisons in the long run than the move-to-front method was given by Ronald Rivest [166]. Sleator and Tarjan showed that the move-to-front method has a total cost within a constant factor of four from the optimum; this does not hold for the transposition or the count method [189]. Their results supported the experiments by Bentley and McGeoch, which showed that the most-to-front rule is generally the best in practice [17]. For more recent analyses and approaches, see the papers by Bachrach and El-Yaniv [5] and Bachrach, El-Yaniv, and Reinstädtler [4].

The Secretary Problem has an interesting history; it first appeared in print in the February 1960 column of Martin Gardner in *Scientific American*, with a solution in the March 1960 issue; see the account by Ferguson [64], where he points out that similar problems go back to Keppler. The solution to the variant where all candidates are ranked according to their value was given by Bearden [12].

According to Knuth [114], binary search harks back to the beginning of the computer age. John Mauchly, one of the designers of the ENIAC, the first general purpose electronic digital computer, described it in 1946. However, it was not clear what should be done when the number of items in the array in which the search was carried out was not a power of two. The first description of binary search that could handle arrays without that restriction appeared in 1960, by Derrick Henry Lehmer, a pioneering mathematician who also contributed significantly to the advancement of computing. Jon Bentley's description of the problems professional programmers face in implementing binary search is in his book [16]. The study which found that three-quarters of textbooks had errors in their descriptions of binary search was by Richard Pattil [155]. Joshua Bloch reported his own mishap in the Google research blog [21]. Maurice Wilkes's quote is from his memoirs [217, p. 145].

12 A Menagerie of Sorts

What do organizing a list of names, a library of songs, putting things in chronological order have in common, arranging our e-mails in alphabetical order based on sender name, or subject, or received date? All of them require sorting items. That these applications involve putting items in order is no surprise, but sorting is not limited to such obvious uses. Consider computer graphics. An important problem when painting a picture on a computer is to paint the different parts in order. In particular, distant parts of a scene should be painted first and parts that are closer to the viewer should be painted last. In this way we ensure that only objects closer to the viewer may obscure or hide objects that are farther away. So we need to identify the different parts, sort them, and paint them in the right order, from back to front—this is called the *painter's algorithm*.

Moving from computer graphics to biology, sorting is an important ingredient of computational biology algorithms; moving from there to data compression, sorting lexicographical variants of data is used in an important compression method, the so-called *Burrows-Wheeler transform*, also called block-sorting compression.

In the hours we spend online, it is likely that we come across recommendations for items to buy, or things to look at. Recommendation systems must do two things: they must filter out things that they reckon are of no interest to us, and they must sort those things that we may find interesting so that the most interesting ones come up on top.

Indeed it is difficult to come across a computing application that does not involve sorting; also to the point, the need for sorting mechanically predates the advent of digital computers. A "sorting box" was developed to be used alongside Herman's Hollerith tabulating machine in the 1880s. Hollerith developed the tabulating machine to assist in the counting during the

1890 U.S. census, when population growth had ensured that manual counting would require 13 years to complete—well into the next scheduled census of 1900.

As sorting is pretty much everywhere, people have been devising sorting methods for quite a long time; the first sorting methods for use by computers were developed at the same time computers were developed, in the second half of the 20th century. Research on sorting methods is still active, either for improvements in known methods and implementations, or for new algorithms that correspond ideally in a specific application area. Fortunately, although it is not possible to cover the field of sorting, it is possible to see the main concepts and basic algorithms. It is rather gratifying that algorithms that we encounter, unbeknownst to us, in our every day lives, are not difficult to approach and examine. As we'll see, fundamental sorting algorithms take no more than a few lines of pseudocode to describe.

Sorting is related to searching, as searching is more efficient if we perform it on sorted data. The same terminology is used in sorting as in searching: data consist of records. The records may have several attributes, but we are sorting them using a subset of them, which we call a key. If a key is composed by more than one attribute, then it is a composite key.

12.1   Selection Sort

Perhaps the simplest sorting algorithm is the intuitive approach of finding the minimum element of our items, take it out, find the minimum element of the remaining items, and place it next to the one we took out, repeating until we have been through all the elements. If you have a heap of paper scraps with numbers of it, then you search for the minimum number in the heap and you take it out. Then you go back to the heap and search again for the minimum number. You place it next to the number you found previously. You continue until you empty the heap.

This simple procedure is called *selection sort* because each time we search for the smallest item among the remaining items. Algorithm 12.1 implements selection sort on an array A, which is its input; it sorts A itself, so it does not need to return anything because it performs the sorting procedure *in-place*; the same A now sorted is the result of the algorithm, as we indicate.

If we have n items to sort, then selection sort works by searching for the minimum of all n items, then the minimum of $n - 1$ items, then the minimum of $n - 2$ items, until we are left with a single item. Line 1 of algorithm 12.1

Algorithm 12.1: Selection sort.

```
SelectionSort(A)
     Input: A, a array of items to be sorted
     Result: A is sorted
1    for i ← 0 to |A| − 1 do
2         m ← i
3         for j ← i + 1 to |A| do
4              if Compare(A[j], A[m]) < 0 then
5                   m ← j
6         Swap(A[i], A[m])
```

---

defines a loop through all items in the array. Each time through the loop we search for the minimum from the item corresponding to the current value of i to the end of the array. As with the binary search algorithm, we use a function Compare(a, b) that compares two items using their keys and returns +1 if a is better than b, −1 if b is better than a, and 0 if they are considered equal.

We use variable m to search for the minimum of the remaining items. Initially m holds the index of our starting item in our search for each minimum. In lines 3–5 we search for the minimum, by going from the element in $A[i + 1]$ to the end of the array. That is, for every i of the outer loop, we search for the minimum in the remaining $n - i$ items. Once we find the minimum, we use a function Swap(a, b) to put the minimum in its correct place in the array.

Figure 12.1 shows selection sort in operation in an array of 14 elements. On the left column you can see the value of i; the other columns contain the array. In each iteration we find the minimum of the remaining unsorted items in the array, and we exchange it with the first of the unsorted remaining items. We indicate these two items in each iteration with a circle. The lower-left, grayed-out area corresponds to the elements that are already sorted and in place. In each iteration we search for the minimum on the right part of the figure, which you can see it is decreasing. Take a moment to examine what happens when $i = 8$. The minimum of the remaining unsorted items is the first of these items. Therefore, there is only one circled item in that row.

To study the performance of selection sort, note that if we have n items, the outer loop is executed $n - 1$ times, so we have $n - 1$ exchanges. For each pass through the outer loop we compare all items from $i + 1$ to the end of A. In the first pass, we compare all items from $A[1]$ to $A[n - 1]$, so we have

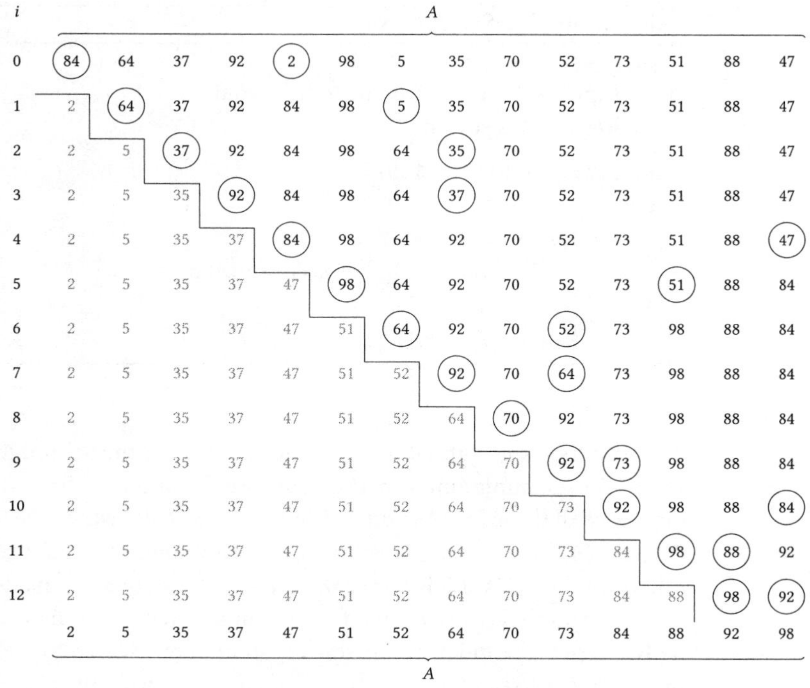

i							A							
0	84	64	37	92	2	98	5	35	70	52	73	51	88	47
1	2	64	37	92	84	98	5	35	70	52	73	51	88	47
2	2	5	37	92	84	98	64	35	70	52	73	51	88	47
3	2	5	35	92	84	98	64	37	70	52	73	51	88	47
4	2	5	35	37	84	98	64	92	70	52	73	51	88	47
5	2	5	35	37	47	98	64	92	70	52	73	51	88	84
6	2	5	35	37	47	51	64	92	70	52	73	98	88	84
7	2	5	35	37	47	51	52	92	70	64	73	98	88	84
8	2	5	35	37	47	51	52	64	70	92	73	98	88	84
9	2	5	35	37	47	51	52	64	70	92	73	98	88	84
10	2	5	35	37	47	51	52	64	70	73	92	98	88	84
11	2	5	35	37	47	51	52	64	70	73	84	98	88	92
12	2	5	35	37	47	51	52	64	70	73	84	88	98	92
	2	5	35	37	47	51	52	64	70	73	84	88	92	98

A

Figure 12.1
Selection sort example.

$n - 1$ comparisons. In the second pass, we compare all elements from $A[2]$ to $A[n-1]$, so we have $n - 2$ comparisons. In the last pass, we compare the last two elements, $A[n-2]$ and $A[n-1]$ and one comparison. It follows that the total number of comparisons is:

$$1 + 2 + \cdots + (n-1) = 1 + 2 + \cdots + (n-1) + n - n$$
$$= \frac{n(n+1)}{2} - n = \frac{n(n-1)}{2}$$

The complexity of selection sort is therefore $\Theta(n-1) = \Theta(n)$ exchanges and $\Theta(n(n-1)/2) = \Theta(n^2)$ comparisons. We treat exchanges and comparisons separately because one operation may have a different computational cost than the other. Typically, comparisons are faster than exchanges because

---

Algorithm 12.2: Selection sort with no unnecessary exchanges.

```
SelectionSortCheckExchanges(A)
```
       Input: A, a array of items to be sorted
       Result: A is sorted

1   **for** $i \leftarrow 0$ **to** $|A| - 1$ **do**
2      $m \leftarrow i$
3   **for** $j \leftarrow i + 1$ **to** $|A|$ **do**
4   **if** Compare$(A[j], A[m]) < 0$ **then**
5            $m \leftarrow j$
6   **if** $i \neq m$ **then**
7   Swap$(A[i], A[m])$

---

exchanges involve moving data around. The difference becomes greater as the data that are moved around are bigger.

Recall now what happened in row eight of figure 12.1: at that point, an item was exchanged with itself. That seems like a waste: there is no need to exchange anything with itself. When the first of the unsorted items is the minimum of the unsorted items we can just let it be. We can do that with a slight modification, which you can see in algorithm 12.2. Here in line 6 we check whether the minimum item is different from the first of the unsorted items, and we do the exchange only if it is. That means that the number n is an upper limit for the number of exchanges. The complexity of the modified algorithm is $O(n)$ exchanges and $\Theta(n^2)$ comparisons.

The difference in the behavior of the two algorithms is more pronounced whenever parts of the array A are already in the correct place. If A is already sorted, algorithm 12.1 will still exchange all n items (with themselves). Algorithm 12.2 will only check that the array is sorted.

That said, it is not certain that we will see an improvement in practice by using algorithm 12.2 over algorithm 12.1. It is true that we made the exchanges optional; elements will be swapped when they have to. At the same time, however, we added one extra comparison, in line 6. As line 6 is executed $n - 1$ times, we added $n - 1$ comparisons in the execution of the algorithm. These act to balance any performance benefits we get from the reduced number of exchanges. So, algorithm 12.2 is not a better, optimized version of selection sort that everybody should adopt, disregarding algorithm 12.1. If we implement and measure them, we may find their performance to be about the same,

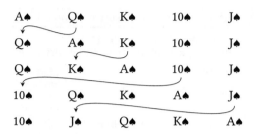

Figure 12.2
Sorting cards.

depending on the relative cost of copying versus comparing, and how sorted our data are in the first place. Is it good to have an understanding of why this happens. It is also good to take into account any performance hits that are not immediately obvious when trying to optimize things.

Selection sort has a couple of things going for it. It is a simple method and easy to implement. It needs a small number of exchanges; this may be important when moving data around is computationally expensive. It is suitable for small arrays, where it will perform fast enough, but it is not used for large arrays, where better sorting algorithms will deliver much better results.

12.2   Insertion Sort

Another intuitive method for sorting is the one used by card players to sort their hand. Imagine you are dealt a hand, card by card. You take the first card. Then you take the second card, and you place it in the correct place with respect to the first card. After that you take the third card, and you place it in the correct place with respect to the first two cards. You proceed like this for all the cards you are dealt. You can see how this works in figure 12.2 where five cards of the same suit are sorted in ascending order, with ace being the highest-ranking card. In reality card players may prefer to sort their hand with the highest-ranking cards on the left, but let us not delve into card playing niceties.

This sorting procedure is called insertion sort, because we insert each item in its correct place with respect to the items we have already sorted. To craft an algorithm from the procedure we have described, we need a way to

---

Algorithm 12.3: Insertion sort.

InsertionSort(*A*)
    Input: *A*, a array of items to be sorted
    Result: *A* is sorted

1   **for** $i \leftarrow 1$ **to** $|A|$ **do**
2        $j \leftarrow i$
3   **while** $j > 0$ **and** Compare$(A[j-1], A[j]) > 0$ **do**
4   Swap$(A[j], A[j-1])$
5            $j \leftarrow j - 1$

---

describe accurately the movement of cards, indicated by arrows, in figure 12.2. In the first card that we sort, Q♠, we just swap it with A♠. We do the same with K♠, swapping it with A♠. The movement of 10♠ is a bit more complicated because it does not involve a single swap. However, it can be described accurately as a series of swaps. First we swap 10♠ with A♠. Then we swap 10♠ with K♠. Finally we swap 10♠ with Q♠. It is as if we rearranged our hand as follows: Q♠K♠A♠10♠J♠ ⇝ Q♠K♠10♠A♠J♠ ⇝ Q♠10♠K♠A♠J♠ ⇝ 10♠Q♠K♠A♠J♠. Thus, for each card we want to put in the correct place, we swap it repeatedly with the card on its left, as long as its value is higher than the value of the card on its left. This is rendered in algorithmic terms in algorithm 12.3.

The algorithm starts with setting j in line 2 to the position of the second item in the array A of items to be sorted. Then in lines 3–5, it compares that item with its previous item and swaps it if necessary. Going back to line 2, we do the same thing for the third item of the array, setting j to the new value of i. Each time we go through line 2, the variable j holds the initial position of the item we move in each iteration of the outer loop. The value of j is reduced in line 5 of the inner loop as long as $A[j]$ is higher than the $A[j-1]$. The condition $j > 0$ in the inner loop is necessary to ensure that we do not fall off the start of the array as we go backwards comparing and swapping. It comes into play when we have moved the item in the beginning of the array: then $j = 0$ and there is no $A[j-1]$, so the second check would produce an error. Note that here we use short circuit evaluation; we will not evaluate $A[j-1] > A[j]$ when $j > 0$ is false.

Figure 12.3 shows insertion sort on the array of numbers we also used in 12.1. The overall behavior of insertion sort is somewhat similar to that of selection sort, with one part, the lower left, being sorted. The difference is

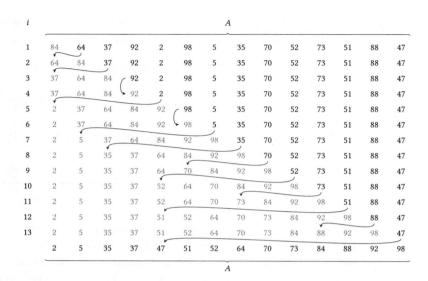

Figure 12.3
Insertion sort example.

that whereas in selection sort the grayed-out items are sorted and placed in the final positions, in insertion sort the grayed-out items are sorted among themselves but not necessarily in their final positions, as items from the right can be inserted between them.

Moving an item in each iteration of the outer loop may involve a series of exchanges. For instance, the transition from the row with $i = 6$ to the row with $i = 7$ is not atomic, but a number of operations take place: figure 12.4 shows what is really happening.

To study the performance of insertion sort, we have to find the number of comparisons and exchanges, like we did with selection sort. It is easier to start with the number of exchanges. In the first row of figure 12.3 we have one exchange because $64 < 84$. In the second row we have two exchanges because $37 < 84$ and $37 < 64$. In the third row we do not need to change anything, while on the fourth row we need four exchanges. You can see a pattern emerging: the number of exchanges in each row is equal to the number of items on the left of the item we are examining that are greater than that item. Indeed, in row eight, the items 98, 92, and 84 are greater than item 70, so there are three exchanges in that row. When we have a sequence of values and a value

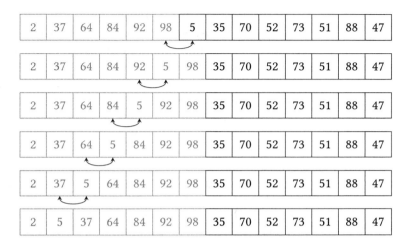

Figure 12.4
Swaps when $i = 6$ in figure 12.3.

is greater than a value on its left, we say in mathematics that we have an *inversion* because these two items are in inverse order to each other. In short, an inversion appears whenever two items are out of order. In every row then the number of exchanges is equal to the number of inversions involving the item we are moving. Taking all rows together, the total number of exchanges is equal to the total number of inversions for all items in the original array. For example, if we have an array with contents 5, 3, 4, 2, 1, then we have the following inversions: (5, 3), (5, 4), (5, 2), (5, 1), (3, 2), (3, 1), (4, 2), (4, 1), (2, 1). That means that to sort it using insertion sort we need nine exchanges—you may want to check that this is indeed so.

If an array is already sorted, then the number of inversions is zero. If an array with n elements is sorted in reverse order, then if we start with the last element of the array, that element has $n - 1$ inversions because it stands in reverse order to every other element before itself. If we go to the one but last element, that element has $n - 2$ inversions for the same reason. The same goes on until the second element of the array, which has exactly one inversion, as it is out of order with respect to the first element of the array. In total, therefore, an array that is in reverse order has: $1 + 2 + \cdots + (n - 1) = n(n - 1)/2$ inversions. It can be proven that an array that is in random order has fewer inversions, specifically $n(n-1)/4$ inversions. We saw that the number of inversions is equal to the number of exchanges, therefore insertion sort has at the best case zero exchanges, at the worst case $n(n-1)/2$ exchanges, and on average $n(n-1)/4$ exchanges.

Let's deal now with the number of comparisons between elements $A[j]$ and $A[j-1]$ in line 3 of the algorithm. If the array is sorted, then for each iteration of the outer loop, that is, for every value of i, we have exactly one comparison: therefore, we have $n-1$ comparisons. If the array is sorted in reverse order, then we saw that we need to do $n(n-1)/2$ exchanges. For this to happen we need to do $n(n-1)/2$ successful comparisons in line 3: each item will be compared with all previous items up to the first item, giving us yet again the familiar formula $1 + 2 + \cdots + (n-1) = n(n-1)/2$.

If the array is sorted in some random order, because we need to do $n(n-1)/4$ exchanges we need to perform $n(n-1)/4$ successful comparisons. However, we may need to perform unsuccessful comparisons as well. For example, consider the array 1, 2, 5, 4, 3. Suppose we are handling item 4. We will do the comparison $5 > 4$, which will be successful and then the comparison $2 > 4$, which will be unsuccessful. We will perform unsuccessful comparisons every time we go through line 3 having $j = 0$. Although we do not know how many times this can happen, we can be sure that this cannot happen more than $n-1$ times because this is the maximum number of times it can happen (if the array is sorted in reverse order it will happen exactly n times, but we have already handled this case). Adding the two comparison measures, we have at most $n(n-1)/4 + (n-1)$ comparisons. The factor $n-1$ does not change the overall complexity of $n(n-1)/4$ that we have already found.

To recap, the number of exchanges in insertion sort is 0 for a sorted array, $\Theta(n(n-1)/2) = \Theta(n^2)$ for an array in reverse order, and $\Theta(n(n-1)/4) = \Theta(n^2)$ for an array in random order. The number of comparisons is $\Theta(n-1) = \Theta(n)$ for a sorted array, $\Theta(n(n-1)/2) = \Theta(n^2)$ for an array in reverse order, and $\Theta(n(n-1)/4) + O(n) = \Theta(n(n-1)/4) = \Theta(n^2)$ for an array in random order.

Insertion sort, like selection sort, is simple to implement. In practice insertion sort implementations run typically faster than selection sort implementations. This makes insertion sort suitable for small datasets. It is also possible to use it as an online algorithm, that is, an algorithm that sorts a sequence of elements as it receives them: it is not necessary to have all elements available when the algorithm starts.

A complexity of order $\Theta(n^2)$ may be acceptable for small datasets, but is impractical for big datasets. If we have 1 million items, n^2 runs up to 1 trillion: a number with 12 zeroes. This is way too slow. If you think that 1 million items is too big a number, which is not, for 100,000 items n^2 runs up to 10 billion, which is again a big number. If we want to be able to handle sizable datasets, then we have to do better than either selection sort or insertion sort.

12.3 Heapsort

We can arrive at a better way to sort by going back to selection sort and think a bit more about the process we are following there. For each item we search for the smallest of the unsorted items. We do this search by going through all of the unsorted items. But perhaps we can find a more clever method. First, let's flip the logic and imagine a sorting procedure like selection sort where we start by finding the maximum item and putting it at the end. Then we find the maximum of the remaining items and put it just before the end. We continue until we exhaust our items. That's selection sort in reverse: instead of finding the minimum for position 1, we find the maximum for the last position, $|A| - 1$. Instead of finding the second smallest for the second position, we find the second largest for position $|A| - 2$. Clearly, this would work. Now, if we somehow process the items so that it is easier each time to find the maximum among the unsorted, we will end up with a better algorithm, provided that we do not spend much time doing this kind of processing.

Suppose that we manage to arrange the items in array A so that we have $A[0] \geq A[i]$ for all $i < |A|$. Then $A[0]$ is the maximum, which we must put in the end of A: we can exchange $A[0]$ and $A[n-1]$. Now $A[n-1]$ contains the maximum of our items and $A[0]$ the previous value of $A[n-1]$. If we manage to arrange the items from $A[0]$ to $A[n-2]$ so that again we have $A[0] \geq A[i]$, for all $i < |A| - 1$, then we can repeat the same procedure: exchange $A[0]$, which is the maximum of items $A[0], A[1], \ldots, A[n-2]$, with $A[n-2]$. Now $A[n-2]$ will contain the second biggest of our items. Again then we can continue with rearranging $A[0], A[1], \ldots, A[n-3]$ so that we have $A[0] \geq A[i]$, for all $i < |A| - 2$, and exchange $A[0]$ with $A[n-3]$. If we continue doing this, finding the maximum of our remaining items and putting it at the appropriate position at the end of A, at the end we will have all items in place.

At this point it helps to treat array A as a tree, where each item $A[i]$ corresponds to a node with children $A[2i + 1]$ and $A[2i + 2]$. Figure 12.5 shows the correspondence between the array we have been using as our example for

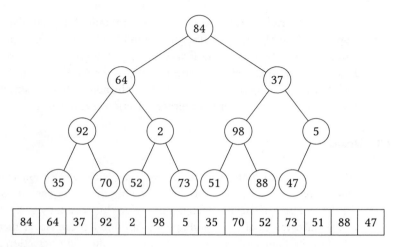

Figure 12.5
Correspondence between array and tree.

sorting and its tree representation. You must understand that the tree is only a fiction. Everything is stored in the underlying array; however, viewing the array as a tree with the above rule will illuminate what is going on.

If for every i we have $A[i] \geq A[2i + 1]$ and $A[i] \geq A[2i + 2]$, then every node of the tree is greater than or equal to its children. Then the root is greater than all other elements in the tree, which is our initial requirement that $A[0] \geq A[i]$, for all $i < |A|$. Moreover, this structure, where a node is at least equal to its children, is a *heap*, in particular a maximum heap (max-heap). The question is, how do we arrange A to be like that? In other words, how do we transform A to a max-heap? We have seen heaps before, in Huffman compression. Although the mechanism is somewhat different here, you may want to review section 3.3 for a different application and implementation. The same data structure can have many uses, the more the merrier, and many different implementation variants.

If the last level of the tree is level h, we start with the nodes at level $h - 1$, taking them from right to left. We compare each node with its children. If it is larger than the children, that's fine. If not, we exchange it with the maximum of the children. Once we are done with level $h - 1$, we know that for all nodes in that level we have $A[i] \geq A[2i + 1]$ and $A[i] \geq A[2i + 2]$. You can see that in figure 12.6a, where we have worked on level two of the tree. On the left there is the original tree, as in figure 12.5. We indicate with grey the nodes that are exchanged. For reasons that will become clear later on, we process the nodes of the level again from the right to the left; first node 5, then node 98, for which we don't need to do anything, then node 2, and finally node 92, which again does not need anything. The resulting tree is on the right. Below each tree there is the array A where the action really happens. You can verify that the array changes mirroring the changes in the tree (or rather, as only the array really exists, the tree illusion changes mirroring the array).

We do the same thing with level $h-2$, only this time if we effect an exchange, we have to check what is going on with the level below, the one we have just fixed. In the left of figure 12.6b we replicate the right of figure 12.6a, to pick up where we left the process. We have to exchange node 37 with node 98. If we do that, then we will find out that 37 has as children nodes 51 and 88, which violates our condition. We can fix it by doing the same thing as before: finding the maximum of 51 and 88 and exchanging it with the new position of 37. Similar exchanges happen with node 64 going down to node 70. After we are done with level two, the tree will look as in the right of figure 12.6b.

Finally, we arrive at the root level. There we need to exchange 84 with 98. Once this happens, we need to exchange 84 with 88, and then we are done. The series of exchanges is in figure 12.6c. Please trace now, if you have not done so already, what is going on when we start from figure 12.5 and work as in figure 12.6.

Because you have traced how the nodes move during the construction of the max-heap, we may say that nodes seem to *sink* from the level they happen to be at the right level for them. They go to the level below, while the node whose place they assume moves up and takes their place. Algorithm 12.4 is the algorithm for the sink procedure.

The algorithm takes as input an array A and the index i of the item that we want to sink in its correct place. It also takes as input the number of items, n, that we will consider during the algorithm. You may wonder why we need that because the number of items should be equal to the number of items in the array, $|A|$. That is because we want to treat only *part* of A as a heap. Recall that when we start we want to have $A[i] \geq A[i]$, for all $i < |A|$, so the whole array A is a heap. After we take the maximum, $A[0]$ and exchange it with $A[n-1]$, we want to find the maximum of $A[0], A[1], \ldots A[n-2]$, so we treat the first $n-1$ elements of A as a heap. Each time we put an item in its correct place, we start working with a smaller heap.

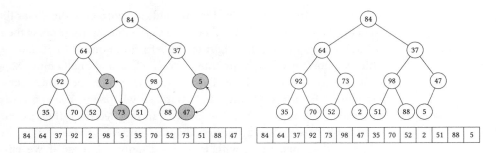

(a) Making a max-heap at level two.

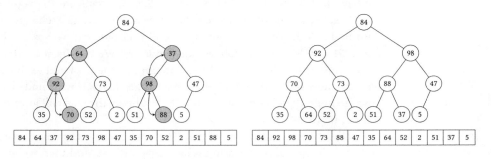

(b) Making a max-heap at level 1.

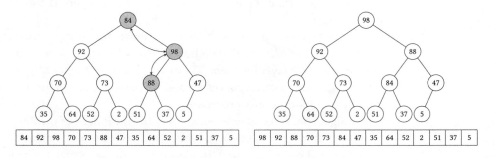

(c) Making a max-heap at the root level.

Figure 12.6
Making a max-heap.

Algorithm 12.4: Sink.

Sink(A, i, n)
    Input: A, a array of items
            i, the index of the item to sink into place
            n, the number of items we will consider
    Result: A with item $A[i]$ sunk into place

1   $k = i$
2   $placed \leftarrow$ FALSE
3   $j \leftarrow 2k + 1$
4   **while not** $placed$ **and** $j < n$ **do**
5   **if** $j < n - 1$ **and** Compare($A[j], A[j + 1]$) < 0 **then**
6           $j \leftarrow j + 1$
7   **if** Compare($A[k], A[j]$) ≥ 0 **then**
8           $placed =$ TRUE
9   **else**
10   Swap($A[k], A[j]$)
11      $k \leftarrow j$
12      $j \leftarrow 2k + 1$

In the algorithm, we use k for the index of the item. Initially this is set to i, but this will change as the item will move down the tree. The variable *placed* will indicate whether the item has been put into its correct position. The children of an item with index k are in positions $2k + 1$ and $2k + 2$, if they exist. We set j to point to the first, left, child. Then we enter a loop that will repeat for as long as the node is not in its correct position and there are children to the node ($j < n$). First, we want to find the maximum of the two children, if the node does have two children. This we do in lines 5–6. Then we check whether the node we are sinking is greater than the maximum of its children. If it is, we are done; this is the purpose of lines 7–8. If not, then we have to sink the node down and bring the maximum of the children up, in lines 9–10. Then we prepare to repeat the loop one level down by updating k to point to the new location of the item we are sinking and j to the location where we expect to find its first child, if it exists.

The neat thing about the sink algorithm is that it not only provides the means for constructing a max-heap; it is also the main vehicle by which we

---

Algorithm 12.5: Heapsort.

HeapSort(A)
    Input: A, a array of items
    Result: A is sorted

1    $n \leftarrow |A|$
2   **for** $i \leftarrow \lfloor (n-1)/2 \rfloor$ **to** -1 **do**
3   Sink(A, i, n)
4   **while** $n > 0$ **do**
5   Swap($A[0], A[n-1]$)
6        $n \leftarrow n - 1$
7   Sink($A, 0, n$)

---

can create the new sorting algorithm we are after. First we use it as in figure 12.6 to turn our data into a heap. Figure 12.6a shows what happens with Sink($A, i, |A|$), for $i = 6, 5, 4, 3$; figure 12.6b shows what happens with Sink($A, i, |A|$), for $i = 2, 1$; and finally, figure 12.6c shows the situation for Sink($A, 0, |A|$). After that, having a heap, we know that the maximum of all our items is at the root of the tree. This should be the last item when the items are put in order. So we take it from the root of the heap and exchange it with the item in the last item of the heap, $A[n-1]$: always remember that the tree is really an array in disguise. The first $n-1$ items of the array are not a heap any more because the root is not greater than its children. But that's easy to fix! We just need to run the sink algorithm for the first $n-1$ items in order to sink the newly exchanged $A[0]$ to its proper place: Sink($A, 0, |A|-1$). In effect, we are working with a heap that is smaller by one element. That's why we passed the number of items as input in the algorithm, because we need to indicate that we are working with a smaller heap. After the sink algorithm finishes, we will have a max-heap again, with the second largest of our items on top. We can then exchange $A[0]$ with the last item of our current heap, item $A[n-2]$. Items $A[n-2]$ and $A[n-1]$ will then be in their correct, ordered positions, allowing us to continue in the same way to remake the remaining $n-2$ items a max-heap with Sink($A, 0, |A|-2$). At the end, all items will be sorted, going from the back of A to the front. This is *heapsort*, algorithm 12.5.

Heapsort is remarkably terse, provided we have Sink. Initially we set a variable n equal to the size of A in line 1, and we start the first phase of heapsort, in which we turn the array to a max-heap in lines 2–3. To do that we need to call

Sink(A, i, $|A|$) for all i that correspond to internal nodes of the tree. The last internal node of the tree is the one that has node at position $n - 1$ as a child. That node is at position $\lfloor (n - 1)/2 \rfloor$. The values of i that correspond to positions of internal nodes are therefore $\lfloor (n - 1)/2 \rfloor, \lfloor (n - 1)/2 \rfloor - 1, \ldots, 0$. Recall that in **for** loops the **to** boundary is not included, so to get 0 the loop range must be **to** -1. The heap construction phase of heapsort is exactly what we did in figure 12.6. We take the values of i in decreasing order, which explains why in figure 12.6 we took the nodes from the right to the left.

Once we have constructed a heap, we start the second phase of heapsort, in which we enter the loop in lines 4–7. We will repeat the loop as many times as there are items in A. We take the first item, $A[0]$, which is the maximum of $A[0], A[1], \ldots, A[n - 1]$. We exchange it with $A[n - 1]$, we reduce n by one, and we re-create a heap out of the first $n - 1$ items in A.

In our example array A, the second phase of heapsort starts as in figure 12.7. Each item is taken from the top of the heap, that is, the first position of A, and put back to positions $n - 1, n - 2, \ldots, 1$. Each time this happens the item it replaced at the back is put provisionally on top of the heap and then sinks to its proper position in the tree. After that the maximum of the remaining unsorted elements is again at the first position of A, and we can repeat the same steps but with a smaller heap. In the figure we gray out the items that reach their final position and remove them from the tree to indicate the shortening of the heap each time around the loop.

Heapsort is an elegant procedure, but what about performance? We started out by noting that we would follow in the steps of selection sort by putting each item in its correct, final position. Instead of looking for the maximum unsorted item from start to finish, we resorted to a more intelligent procedure by which we always get the maximum unsorted item in the top of a max-heap. Is it worth it?

It is. Let us count exchanges first. To make a max-heap, when we reach the root we may need up to h exchanges, where h is the last level of the tree. For each node of level 1 we need $h - 1$ exchanges, until the last but one level, where we need one exchange per node. As the heap is a complete binary tree, there is one node at level zero (the root), $2 = 2^1$ nodes at level one, $2 \times 2 = 2^2$ nodes at level two, and so on; at the last but one level, which is the $(h - 1)$th, there are 2^{h-1} nodes. All these exchanges sum up as $2^0 \times h + 2^1 \times (h - 1) + 2^2 \times (h - 2) + \cdots + 2^{h-1}$. That is the sum of all terms $2^k(h - k)$, for $k = 0, 1, \ldots, h - 1$. The sum is equal to $2^{h+1} - h - 2$. Because h is the last level, if n is the number of items in the tree we have $n = 2^{h+1} - 1$, so the sum becomes $n - \lg n - 1$. The number of exchanges to create the max-heap is then $O(n - \lg n - 1) = O(n)$. The number of comparisons is double that: for each exchange, we need one comparison between the children and one comparison with the parent and the maximum of the children, so the number of comparisons to create the max-heap is $O(2n)$. In the second phase of heapsort, the worst case is remaking a heap with h levels, which requires h exchanges and $2h$ comparisons. We have $h = \lfloor \lg n \rfloor$. The second phase is repeated n times; we therefore conclude that we can have no more than $n\lfloor \lg n \rfloor$ exchanges and $2n\lfloor \lg n \rfloor$ comparisons. That is $O(n \lg n)$ and $(2n \lg n)$, respectively.

Summing up, if we have n elements we need less than $2n \lg n + 2n$ comparisons and $n \lg n + n$ exchanges to sort them using heapsort. In terms of complexity, we have $O(2n \lg n + 2n) = O(n \lg n)$ comparisons and $O(n \lg n + n) = O(n \lg n)$ exchanges.

An improvement from $\Theta(n^2)$ to $O(n \lg n)$ is nothing to sneeze at. If you have 1,000,000 objects to sort, insertion sort and selection sort will need $(10^6)^2 = 10^{12}$ comparisons; one trillion of them. Heapsort will need $10^6 \lg 10^6$, which is less than 20 million. We have made a transition from the realm of the astronomical to the realm of the eminently possible.

Heapsort is an algorithm that can, and is, used for sorting big datasets, especially because it does all the sorting without needing any auxiliary space to do its work: it just manipulates the existing data. Heapsort shows how much extra mileage we can get from an algorithm if we employ a better data structure.

12.4   Merge Sort

Imagine now that you have two sets of sorted items. How would you produce a single set of sorted items? A solution would be to concatenate them into a single sorted set and then sort it. If we do that using insertion sort or selection sort, then we are limited by the size of the dataset. Moreover, we fail to take advantage of the fact that the two sets with which we start are already sorted. Surely there must be a way to leverage this?

Indeed there is. Let's return to playing cards again, and suppose you have two piles of sorted cards. To produce one pile of sorted cards, you can proceed as follows. You examine the first card from each pile. You put the card with the smallest value on a third, initially empty, pile. You examine the first card from each pile again; one pile will be the same as before, whereas in the other pile its top card has been moved to the third pile. You put the card with the

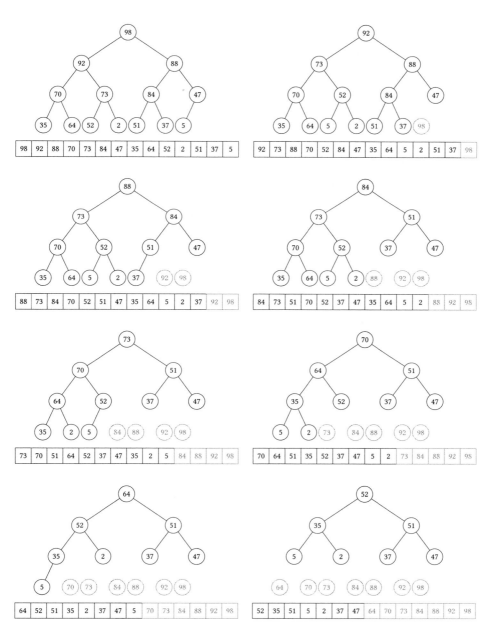

Figure 12.7
Heapsort second phase.

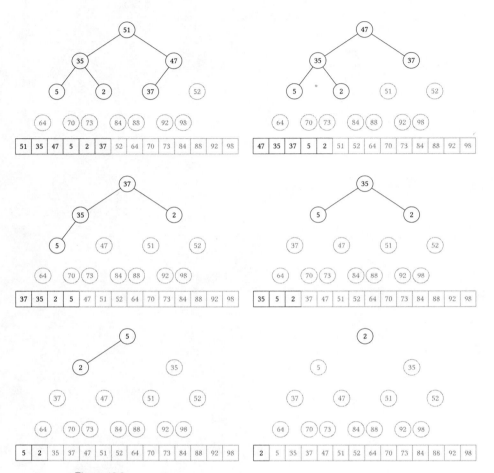

Figure 12.8
Heapsort second phase, continued.

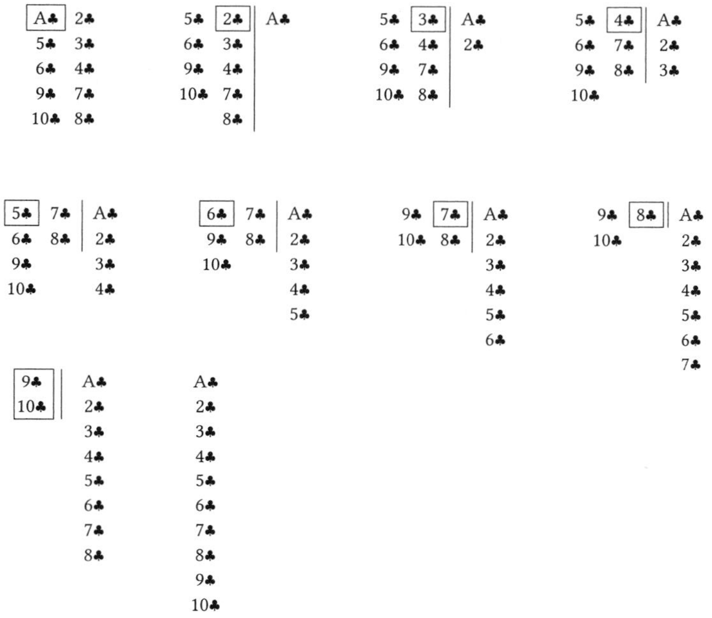

[A♣] 2♣	5♣ [2♣] A♣	5♣ [3♣] A♣	5♣ [4♣] A♣
5♣ 3♣	6♣ 3♣	6♣ 4♣ 2♣	6♣ 7♣ 2♣
6♣ 4♣	9♣ 4♣	9♣ 7♣	9♣ 8♣ 3♣
9♣ 7♣	10♣ 7♣	10♣ 8♣	10♣
10♣ 8♣	8♣		

[5♣] 7♣ │ A♣	[6♣] 7♣ │ A♣	9♣ [7♣] ‖ A♣	9♣ [8♣] │ A♣
6♣ 8♣ 2♣	9♣ 8♣ 2♣	10♣ 8♣ 2♣	10♣ 2♣
9♣ 3♣	10♣ 3♣	3♣	3♣
10♣ 4♣	4♣	4♣	4♣
	5♣	5♣	5♣
		6♣	6♣
			7♣

[9♣] ‖ A♣	A♣
[10♣] 2♣	2♣
3♣	3♣
4♣	4♣
5♣	5♣
6♣	6♣
7♣	7♣
8♣	8♣
	9♣
	10♣

Figure 12.9
Merging two piles of sorted cards.

smallest value on the third pile on top of the card already there. You go on like this until you run out of cards in the two piles. If one pile runs out before the other, it means that all the remaining cards in that pile have larger face values than the cards in the third pile, so you just add them all on top of the existing cards in the third pile. Figure 12.9 shows an example of combining in this way, or *merging*, two sorted piles of cards.

Going back to arrays of elements, take the array *A* we have been using in our examples and split it in two. Then sort the two parts with some method (don't worry about which method right now). You end up with two sorted arrays, like we want. Then to get a single sorted array you proceed as follows. You take the first element of the first sorted array and the first element of the second sorted array. The smallest of them will be the first element of the new sorted array. You remove the smallest from each array and put it in the new array. You then repeat the same procedure until you run out of elements in

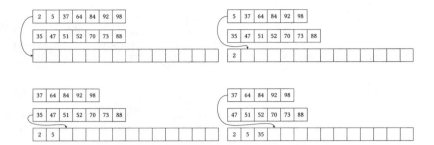

Figure 12.10
Merge of two arrays.

the sorted arrays. If one of the sorted arrays runs out of elements before the other, then you just add the remaining elements at the end of the new array. In figure 12.10 you can see how the process goes for the first four elements of two arrays. The merge process forms the basis of an efficient sorting method called *merge sort*.

Before we proceed to see merge sort itself, there are a few things to note about merging. Figure 12.10 shows what happens conceptually, but in practice we do not merge in this way. The reason is that we would like to avoid removing items from an array, which may be inefficient and complicated. It is better to leave the items in the two original arrays in place and just keep track of where we are in each array. We can do this by using two pointers that will show the beginning of the remaining part of each array as we process it. With this modification we get from figure 12.10 to figure 12.11.

We now turn what is happening in figure 12.11 into algorithm 12.6. We have two arrays, A and B, as input, and an array C as output, whose length $|C|$ is equal to the sum of the lenghts of A and B: $|C| = |A| + |B|$. We use a pointer i that runs through array A, a pointer j that runs through array B, and a pointer k that runs through array C.

In line 1 of the algorithm we create the output array C; in lines 2 and 3 we initialize the two points i and j to 0. Then we enter the loop of lines 4–16, which is executed once for each item of A and B. Lines 5–7 deal with what is happening when we have put all elements of A into C. In this case, all remaining elements of B are added at the end of C. Lines 8–10 deal with the mirror case when we have put all elements of B into C. Then we add all remaining elements of A at the end of C. If we still have elements in both A

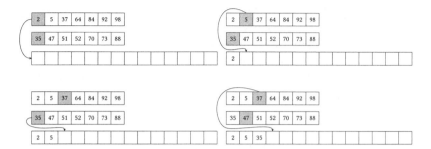

Figure 12.11
Merge of two arrays using pointers.

and B, then we examine which one of the two current elements, $A[i]$ and $B[j]$, is smaller than or equal to the other, and we put it at the end of C. If $A[i]$ is smaller it gets into C, in lines 11–14; otherwise $B[j]$ goes into C, in lines 14–16. Note that in each iteration, apart from k, we advance i or j, depending on whether we put an element from A or B into C.

We assumed to this point that we have two sorted arrays and we want to produce a single sorted array. Let us remove the requirement that we have two sorted arrays, and assume instead that we have one array that consists of two sorted parts. The items of the array from its beginning to some position $m - 1$ are sorted, and the items of the array from position m to its end are also sorted. Thus, instead of having the two arrays of figures 12.10 and 12.11 we have a single array consisting of the two arrays concatenated one after the other. Can we merge them in way similar to algorithm 12.6? We can, with a slight modification.

First, we need a temporary array, which we'll use as scratch space. We'll copy the items that belong to the two sorted parts to the temporary array. Then we'll proceed as in algorithm 12.6, only instead of copying from two different arrays to a new output array, we will be copying from the temporary array on the initial, existing array. Because we'll be modifying our initial array directly, we call this *in-place* array merge, and you can see it in algorithm 12.7.

Algorithm 12.7 is a bit more general, in that it does not require that the whole array consists of two sorted parts. It only requires that the array contains two sorted parts, one of which follows the other. There may be other elements before the first part and other elements after the second part. In a

---

Algorithm 12.6: Array merge.

ArrayMerge(A, B) $\rightarrow$ C
>**Input**: A, a sorted array of items
>
> B, a sorted array of items
>
>**Output**: C, a sorted array containing the items of A and B

1   $C \leftarrow$ CreateArray($|A| + |B|$)
2   $i \leftarrow 0$
3   $j \leftarrow 0$
4   **for** $k \leftarrow 0$ **to** $|A| + |B|$ **do**
5   **if** $i \geq |A|$ **then**
6           $C[k] \leftarrow B[j]$
7           $j \leftarrow j + 1$
8   **else if** $j \geq |B|$ **then**
9           $C[k] \leftarrow A[i]$
10          $i \leftarrow i + 1$
11   **else if** Compare($A[i], B[j]$) ≤ 0 **then**
12          $C[k] \leftarrow A[i]$
13          $i \leftarrow i + 1$
14   **else**
15          $C[k] \leftarrow B[j]$
16          $j \leftarrow j + 1$
17   **return** C

---

little while we'll see why this is useful. The algorithm takes as input the array A to be sorted, and three indices, l, m, and h. These indices indicate that the elements $A[l], \ldots, A[m]$ are sorted and that the elements $A[m + 1], \ldots, A[h]$ are sorted. If the two sorted parts cover the whole array, then we have $l = 0$ and $h = |A| - 1$.

The in-place merge uses again two pointers, only this time they do not point to two different arrays, but to two different locations of the same array. We need an auxiliary array C, which we create in line 1 and fill with the elements of the two sorted parts of A in lines 2–3. Because the two sorted parts are in locations $l, l + 1, \ldots, h$, to copy the items we need to loop $h - l$ times: $|C| = h - l$. We use again two pointers, i and j, that move through the two sorted parts, only this time they move on the copied items in array C. The first

---

Algorithm 12.7: In-place array merge.

ArrayMergeInPlace(A, l, m, h)
    Input: A, an array of items
           l, m, h, array indices such that items $A[l], \ldots, A[m]$ and
           $A[m + 1], \ldots, A[h]$ are sorted
    Result: A with items $A[l], \ldots, A[h]$ sorted

1   $C \leftarrow$ CreateArray$(h - l + 1)$
2   **for** $k \leftarrow l$ **to** $h + 1$ **do**
3      $C[k - l] = A[k]$

4   $i \leftarrow 0$
5   $cm \leftarrow m - l + 1$
6   $ch \leftarrow h - l + 1$
7   $j \leftarrow cm$

8   **for** $k \leftarrow l$ **to** $h + 1$ **do**
9   **if** $i \geq cm$ **then**
10        $A[k] \leftarrow C[j]$
11        $j \leftarrow j + 1$
12   **else if** $j \geq ch$ **then**
13        $A[k] \leftarrow C[i]$
14        $i \leftarrow i + 1$
15   **else if** Compare$(C[i], C[j]) \leq 0$ **then**
16        $A[k] \leftarrow C[i]$
17        $i \leftarrow i + 1$
18   **else**
19        $A[k] \leftarrow C[j]$
20        $j \leftarrow j + 1$

---

sorted part contains $m - l$ elements and the second sorted part contains $h - l$ elements. Therefore, the second sorted part starts at position $cm = m - l + 1$ of C and it ends in position $ch = h - l + 1$ of C. The pointer i will start at position 0 and the pointer j will start at position cm. We put these definitions in lines 4–7. Having done that, lines 8–20 of algorithm 12.7 are essentially the same as lines 4–16 of algorithm 12.6.

During the execution of the algorithm, after we have copied the items to be merged in array C, we proceed along the two sorted parts of array C and

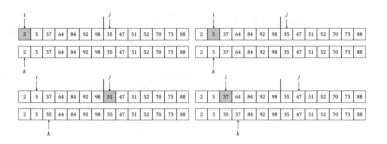

Figure 12.12
In-place merge.

merge them by taking each time the smallest element and writing it in array
A. This is exactly what we did before in algorithm 12.6. At the end of the
algorithm, array *A* will contain a merge of the two sorted parts.

Figure 12.12 shows what is going on in an array that is split in two equal
parts, that is, so $l = 0$ and $h = |A| - 1$. We indicate the start of the second sorted
part with a vertical bar. You can see four array pairs; the upper array in each
pair is array *C* and the lower array pair is array *A*. Initially *C* is a copy of
A—it would be a copy of part of *A* if $l > 0$ or $h < |A| - 1$. As the algorithm
progresses, items are copied from *C* to *A* and *A* gets sorted.

Now stand back a bit to take stock of what we have achieved so far: provided we have two sorted arrays, or two sorted parts of an array, we can merge
them in a single sorted sequence. In general, then, if we are given a sequence
of sort, we can break it in two. We sort the first part and the second part. Then
we have two sorted parts, which we combine with a merge, as we have seen.

This may seem like a sleight of hand, because we started with the requirement to sort a single sequence and somehow we waived the problem away
by assuming that we can sort its two halves. How do we sort each one of
them then? We do the same: we split it in half, and we sort each of its two
halves, and then we merge them. It seems again that we are just postponing
the real work because instead of doing the sorting right there and then we
assume that somehow even though we do not know how to sort all items,
half of them will be sorted and merged. This recalls the Siphonaptera nursery
rhyme:

Big fleas have little fleas,
Upon their backs to bite 'em,

And little fleas have lesser fleas,
and so, ad infinitum.

We are saved from an infinite regression, however, by the fact that we cannot divide a sequence in two indefinitely. At some point as we continue dividing a sequence we arrive at a sequence of one. This sequence, though, is already sorted: a single item is always sorted with respect to itself. This is the key to the solution. By dividing and dividing we arrive at sequences of one item. These are already sorted, and we can readily merge them: merging them means taking two items and putting them in order. Then we can take the larger sequences that are the result of the merging of the smaller ones and merge them, and so on, until eventually we have two sorted sequences that make up the whole sequence.

For example, how would we sort a poker hand like A♡ 10♡ K♡ J♡ Q♡? We start by breaking the hand in two: A♡ 10♡ K♡ and J♡ Q♡. The two parts are not sorted and so we cannot merge them. We take the first part and break it again: A♡ 10♡ and K♡. This time the second part, K♡, is already sorted, being a single card, but the first part is not, so we break it in two: A♡ and 10♡. These two cards are individually sorted so we can merge them and get 10♡ A♡. Now we merge them with K♡ and get 10♡ K♡ A♡. We return to J♡ Q♡. We break it in two and we get J♡ and Q♡. Each one of them is trivially sorted, so we merge them and we get J♡ and Q♡. We now have two sorted parts: 10♡ K♡ A♡ and J♡ and Q♡. These we merge to get the final sorted hand 10♡ J♡ Q♡ K♡ A♡. The whole process is depicted in figure 12.13.

You may have observed that when we are handling J♡ Q♡ we are really wasting our time because they are already sorted. That is true; however, we choose to live with it because checking that an array is sorted requires going through the whole array and checking that every element is greater than or equal to its previous element. It may seem obvious for J♡ Q♡, but it would not be obvious if we were dealing with thousands of items and it would also be costly to find out.

It is now a short step to describe an algorithm that implements this process in algorithm 12.8. The idea of splitting a sequence until we cannot split it any further and then merging bigger and bigger sequences is implemented by using recursion. MergeSort(A, l, h) takes an array A whose elements $A[l], \ldots, A[h]$ we want to sort. If $l \geq h$ then A contains just one element and we do not need to do anything. Otherwise, we calculate a midpoint in line 2 and call MergeSort on each of the two parts, that is, MergeSort(A, m, h)

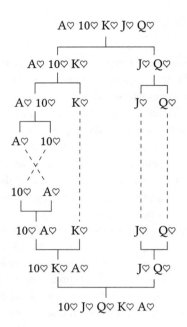

Figure 12.13
Sorting a poker hand with merges.

and MergeSort(A, $m + 1$, h). During each call the same things will happen: a check if there is a need to sort; if not, two new splits will be created and the process will be applied to them. This will be repeated until we arrive at segments with just one element. When this happens, we'll start merging them to ever larger segments until we cover the whole array A. To set everything in motion, we call MergeSort(A, 0, $|A| - 1$).

To understand what is going on, have a look at figure 12.14. This figure is an example of a *call trace*, because it traces the function calls that occur during the execution of a program. Each function that is called from another function is indented with respect to its caller; we also connect it to allow easier navigation in the figure. As you can see, the initial array [84, 64, 37, 92, 2, 98, 5, 35, 70, 52, 73, 51, 88, 47] is split to smaller and smaller pieces, until we can start merging, starting from single item arrays and progressing to larger and larger arrays until we merge two parts that constitute the original array.

Figure 12.14

Call trace of merge sort.

Algorithm 12.8: Merge sort.

MergeSort(*A*, *l*, *h*)
  Input: *A*, an array of items
    l, *h*, array indices
  Result: *A* with items $A[l], \ldots, A[h]$ sorted

1 **if** $l < h$ **then**
2 $m = l + \lfloor (h - l)/2 \rfloor$
3 MergeSort(*A*, *l*, *m*)
4 MergeSort(*A*, *m* + 1, *h*)
5 ArrayMergeInPlace(*A*, *l*, *m*, *h*)

Now you can understand why in algorithm 12.7 we included l, m, h in the inputs: it is only in the last step in the execution of merge sort that we merge two parts of the whole array, thus having $l = 0$ and $h = 0$. Before that we are merging smaller parts and need to know exactly where they start and where they end.

Merge sort is a nice application of the *divide and conquer* approach to problem solving, as it sorts a set of items by dividing it in two and sorting the two halves. Beyond aesthetics, we have to worry about performance, of course, as we are looking for useful, not just nice solutions. So what is the complexity of merge sort?

The key to analyze the complexity of the algorithm is to take into account that at each recursive step we are splitting the array in half. When we split an array in half we are in effect creating a binary tree: the root is the unsplit array, the two parts are the children. You can see the tree in figure 12.14; the tree comprises the sort nodes and grows in a left-to-right, top-to-bottom fashion. Each sort node has two children, unless it is a leaf. Figure 12.15 shows the same tree in a more familiar format: each node corresponds to the array that is to be sorted, that is, a call to MergeSort(*A*, *l*, *h*).

At each level of the tree we need to perform at most *n* element comparisons. That worst case scenario will happen when in each of the merges that take place at a level all elements of the two parts to be merged have to be compared in line 15 of algorithm 12.7. In general, as we have said, one of the two parts to be merged may be consumed during the merge before the other, in which case we simply copy the remaining items without comparing them. However,

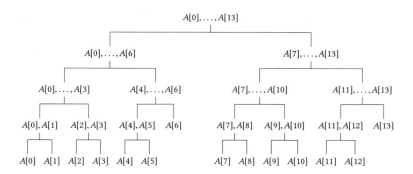

Figure 12.15
Merge sort tree.

let's deal with the worst right now, as the analysis of what may happen on average is more complicated.

We need then to find out the number of levels in the tree. At the top of the tree, we have our array A, with n elements. At each level we break each array in two, if possible. If n is a power of two, then the process cannot be repeated more than $\lg n$ times because we get arrays of size one, so we need $\lg n$ levels. If n is not a power of two, then it is between two powers of two: $2^k < n < 2^{k+1}$. The number of levels in that tree will therefore be more than k and no more than $k + 1$: that is equal to $\lceil \lg n \rceil$. In general, therefore, whether n is a power of two, our tree will have up to $\lceil \lg n \rceil$ levels. In each level, all items of A are copied twice, from the various parts of A to their scratchpads, the various C arrays of lines 1–3 of algorithm 12.7; so we have $2n$ copies. In the worst case we have n comparisons, if we need to compare all elements of every array pair in a level of the tree during lines 8–20 of algorithm 12.7. In terms of complexity we then have $O(2n\lceil \lg n \rceil + 2n) = O(n \lg n)$ copies and $O(n\lceil \lg n \rceil + n) = O(n \lg n)$ comparisons. To get from $O(n\lceil \lg n \rceil + n)$ to $O(n \lg n)$ we used the fact that $n\lceil \lg n \rceil + n \le n(\lg n + 1) + n = n \lg n + 2n$.

To add to this improvement in sorting performance, we can do better with merge sort if we take advantage of arrays, or parts of them, that are already sorted to each other. Imagine the more general case where we split an array in two parts, we sort the two parts independently of each other, and then we find out that all the elements of the first part are less than or equal to the elements of the second part. Then we do not need to merge the two parts; we just need to concatenate the second part to the first part. In practice, that is easy to do. After the calls to MergeSort in algorithm 12.8, we check whether $A[m]$ is less than or equal to $A[m + 1]$. If yes, no merge is needed.

Merge sort is a sorting algorithm that is used in practice and is implemented in standard libraries of programming languages. Its main disadvantage is the amount of space it requires: as we saw, we need to copy for each merge the array A to an auxiliary array C. Therefore, merge sort requires an amount of n extra space for sorting an array with n elements. That may be an important limitation when sorting big arrays.

12.5   Quicksort

The application of divide and conquer to sorting brings us to the single most important, for computer scientists, sorting algorithm, the one algorithm that every computer programmer knows, the one that we mean when we talk about sorting without naming an algorithm. The algorithm is called *quicksort* and was developed by C. A. R. (Tony) Hoare in 1961.

The intuition behind quicksort is simple. We take an item among the items we want to sort. We want to put this item into its final position: the position it will have in the sorted array. How do we find that position? The item will be into its final position when all elements that are smaller than itself are before that item, and all elements that are greater than itself follow the item. So we move elements around until we achieve that. If we have an array A that we want to sort, suppose we do that and are left with item $A[p]$, for some p, in its final position. Then the items $A[0], A[1], \ldots, A[p - 1]$ and $A[p + 1], A[p + 2], \ldots, A[n - 1]$, where $n = |A|$, need to be put into their final positions. We repeat the same procedure for the two parts $A[0], A[1], \ldots, A[p - 1]$ and $A[p + 1], A[p + 2], \ldots, A[n - 1]$. That will provide us with another two elements in their final positions and will give us the opportunity to continue the process in the two parts that are created for each of $A[0], A[1], \ldots, A[p - 1]$ and $A[p + 1], A[p + 2], \ldots, A[n - 1]$.

Suppose you have a number of kids and you want to put them in line, in ascending order of height. Quicksort is like picking one among them, say Jane, and telling the others: "Those who are shorter than Jane move to the front of Jane, those who are taller than Jane make a line behind Jane." Then you go to the line in front of Jane, pick another kid, and do exactly the same thing. You also go in the line behind Jane and do the same thing. You repeat the process until everybody is in the correct position in the line.

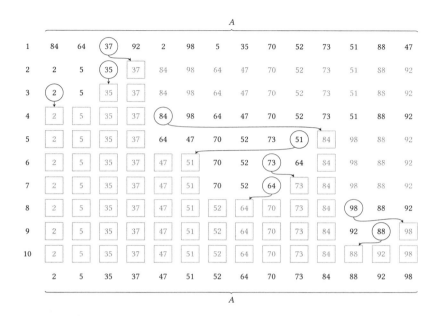

Figure 12.16
Quicksort example.

The process is shown in action in figure 12.16. We start by picking the number 37. In the second row we have moved all items less than 37 to its left and all items greater than 37 to its right. The number 37 is now in its final position, which we indicate by putting it in a box. In each row we deal with a group of items—those that are lower or greater than an item we have put into its final position. We gray out the rest of the items, and leave painted black those items that we deal with in the row; these are the items that, in the kids example above, we pick one among them and ask them to position themselves with respect to the chosen one.

So we turn our attention to items 2, 5, and 35. We pick the number 35; this is in fact already in its correct position, as it is greater than both 3 and 5. Then we have to deal with 2 and 5, which also do not need any moving. In row four we go to the rest of the items, those that are greater than 37. The active items in row four are all the items from 84 to the end, 92. We pick 84, move the items, and continue in this way from row five onward, until all items are in their sorted position.

Algorithm 12.9: Quicksort.

Quicksort(A, l, h)
  Input: A, an array of items
    l, h, array indices
  Result: A with items $A[l], \ldots, A[h]$ sorted

1 **if** $l < h$ **then**
2    $p \leftarrow$ Partition(A, l, h)
3   Quicksort(A, l, $p - 1$)
4   Quicksort(A, $p + 1$, h)

The process can be rendered as the pretty short algorithm 12.9. The algorithm is a recursive one, like merge sort, and looks in fact quite similar to it. At line 4 of the algorithm we partition the array A in two parts, from $A[0], A[1], \ldots, A[p-1]$ and $A[p+1], A[p+2], \ldots, A[n-1]$. The element that lies at position p is the partitioning element and we call it *pivot*, because in some sense the rest of the elements move around it. The elements $A[0], A[1], \ldots, A[p-1]$ are smaller than the pivot element, and the elements at $A[p+1], A[p+2], \ldots, A[n-1]$ are greater than or equal to the pivot element. Having partitioned the array, we apply Quicksort to the two partitions. The whole process makes sense as long as the array segment has at least one element, as indicated by the condition in line 1. To start sorting we call Quicksort(A, 0, $|A| - 1$), similarly to merge sort.

There is a missing part in algorithm 12.9, the definition of the Partition function that makes all the magic happen. There are several ways to partition an array to two sets, smaller and greater than an element. One way to do it goes like this. First we pick a pivot element. We want to put this element into its final, sorted position, but we don't know which is that position yet, so for the moment we just swap it with the element at the end of our items to get it out of the way.

We want to find the final position of the pivot element. That is the position that will partition the items after we have gone through all of them; the boundary separating the two sets, those that are less than the pivot element, and those that are not. Initially we have not partitioned anything, so we may set that boundary at zero. We traverse the elements to be partitioned. Whenever we find an element that is less than the pivot element, we know immediately two things: that this element must go before the pivot element's final

---

Algorithm 12.10: Partitioning.

Partition(A, l, h) $\rightarrow b$
    Input: A, an array of items
            l, h, array indices
    Result: A is partitioned so that $A[0], \ldots, A[p-1] < A[p]$ and
            $A[p+1], \ldots, A[n-1] \geq A[p]$, for $n = |A|$
    Output: b, the index of the final position of the pivot element

1    $p \leftarrow$ PickElement(A)
2   Swap($A[p], A[h]$)
3    $b \leftarrow l$
4   **for** $i \leftarrow l$ **to** h **do**
5   **if** Compare($A[i], A[h]$) < 0 **then**
6   Swap($A[i], A[b]$)
7            $b \leftarrow b + 1$
8   Swap($A[h], A[b]$)
9   **return** b

---

position, and the final position of the pivot element will be one greater than what we had supposed so far. When we finish our traversal, we move back the pivot element to its final position, such as it has been established by the traversal. Algorithm 12.10 describes the procedure in detail.

In a way similar to merge sort, algorithm 12.10 takes as parameters an array A and two indices l, h, and partitions the part of the array between and including the two indices. If $l = 0$ and $h = |A| - 1$, then it will partition the whole array; otherwise it will partition the items $A[l], \ldots, A[h]$. We want this capability for exactly the same reason that we wanted it in merge sort: during quicksort's recursive calls, we need to partition parts of A, not necessarily the whole of A. Quicksort sorts A in place, so we indicate in the algorithm description that it has both a result and an output.

In line 1 of the algorithm, we pick the pivot element. We swap the pivot element with the element at the end of A in line 2 and set the position separating the partitioned elements at the start of the area to be partitioned. We use the variable b for that position, as it is the boundary between those values that are smaller than the pivot element and those values that are not. In the loop of lines 4–7 we traverse the area to be partitioned. Every time we find an element with a value less than the pivot element, we swap it with the element

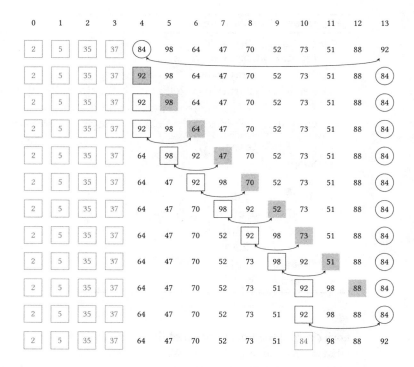

Figure 12.17
Partitioning example.

at the current position b and advance the boundary position b by one element. After the loop we put the pivot element that we had placed at the end of the items to its correct, final position, which is position b, and we return its index.

To make this clearer, you can have a look at figure 12.17, which is a blown-out version of what happens between rows four and five of figure 12.16. We have $l = 4$ and $h = 13$. We pick element 84 and swap it with the item at $A[13] = 92$. Initially $f = l = 4$; we indicate the position b, the provisional final position, with a rectangle. We use a borderless gray rectangle for the current value of i in lines 5–8 of algorithm 12.10. At each step of the partitioning algorithm we increase i, thus we move the gray borderless rectangle one position to the right. Whenever we find that $A[b] < 84$, we swap the values of $A[i]$ and $A[b]$ and increase the value of b. Note that the final value of i is $h - 1$ because $A[h]$ contains the pivot element. This agrees with the values i can take in line 5

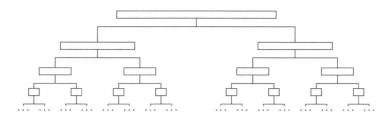

Figure 12.18
Optimum quicksort tree.

of the algorithm. When we are done with the loop, we swap $A[h]$, the pivot element, with $A[b]$, to put it into its correct final position.

There is another missing part to complete the quicksort picture, and that is the function PickElement. If you look at figure 12.16, in rows three and eight we picked the first (in row three there were only two elements to select from) element, in rows 2, 5, 7, 9 we picked the last element (in row 9 there were also two elements to select from), and in the other rows we picked some other element between. In essence, we picked an element *in random* each time. Sometimes it happened to be the first, or the last, but other times it turned out to be something else. You may wonder why we pick elements at random instead of using some other straightforward rule like picking the first element ($A[l]$) or the last element ($A[h]$) or the middle element. There is a reason for picking elements in random, and it has to do with the performance characteristics of quicksort.

Quicksort can be visualized as a tree, like merge sort. When the array is partitioned, we get two recursive applications of quicksort. Suppose that we always pick the median element, that is, the element that partitions the array in two arrays with an equal number of elements. Then we get a tree like the merge sort tree, as you can see in figure 12.18. The tree is balanced because each time we split the array in half we get two equal partitions (give or take an item, if the number of elements to be partitioned is an even number).

At the first level of the tree the partitioning requires doing n nodes in the array A because all nodes have to be compared with the pivot. In the second level of the tree the partitioning requires $n-1$ comparisons because we partition two arrays with $n-1$ elements in total; remember that we took out the pivot element in the first level. Because the tree is a binary tree like the one in merge sort, we have $O(\lg n)$ levels in the tree; in each level we have at

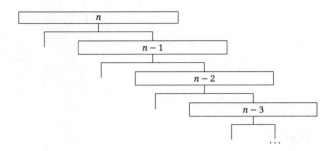

Figure 12.19
Worst case quicksort tree.

most n comparisons and also no more than n swaps, so the complexity of the algorithm is $O(n \lg n)$.

Now suppose that each time we pick as a pivot element the smallest available item. One way for this to happen is if A is already sorted, and we pick as pivot element the elements of A from start to finish. If we do that, the partitioning will be completely unbalanced. Each time we select a pivot element we'll get two partitions with the following characteristics: one will be a degenerate partition, with no elements at all, and the other will have all the remaining elements. For example, if we want to partition the items [1, 2, 3, 4, 5] and we pick as pivot element the number 1, we'll get two partitions: an empty one, [], and [2, 3, 4, 5]. If we continue by picking as pivot element the number 2 we'll get again [] and [3, 4, 5].

The situation is illustrated in figure 12.19. We start by partitioning n elements, then $n - 1, n - 2, \ldots, 1$ elements. Thus, the tree will have n levels this time. In each of the levels except the last, in which we have an array with a single element, the pivot element is compared to all remaining elements of the level, so we have $n + (n - 1) + \cdots + 1 = n(n - 1)/2$ comparison operations. Therefore, if the array is already sorted in ascending order, and we pick as the pivot element the first, smallest item each time, quicksort will have $O(n^2)$ complexity, instead of $O(n \lg n)$.

In sum, in the best case quicksort has $O(n \lg n)$ complexity, in the worst case it has $O(n^2)$ complexity. The best case requires that we somehow always pick the best pivot element, the one that will partition the array in the most balanced way. This is something we cannot do in practice because the cost of searching for such an element would add to the complexity of the algorithm, making it impractical.

Picking the pivot element in random guards against the worst case scenario. Even better, it can be proven that the quicksort tree that results from choosing a pivot randomly is not much worse than the optimum quicksort tree. Although it may seem counterintuitive, picking elements at random ensures that the *expected* complexity of quicksort remains $O(n \lg n)$.

Notice the emphasis on the word "expected" in the previous paragraph. Quicksort with random selection of the pivot element introduces an element of chance in the behavior of the algorithm. Because we pick elements randomly, we cannot be sure that we may not end up with the worst case scenario. We may end up so, in which case quicksort will perform abysmally. However, the chances of arriving at such a dire behavior are vanishingly small. Therefore, we expect, although we cannot formally guarantee, that quicksort will perform well.

How vanishingly small are the chances that we'll get the worst possible behavior? If we pick pivot elements randomly, the probability that we'll pick the smallest element the first time is $1/n$, if we suppose that all elements have different values. The probability that we'll pick the smallest element the second time is $1/(n-1)$. We continue reasoning in this way until we have an array with two elements, when the probability is $1/2$. The probability that we pick up the worst possible element every time is then:

$$\frac{1}{n} \times \frac{1}{n-1} \times \cdots \times \frac{1}{2} = \frac{1}{1 \times 2 \times \cdots \times n} = \frac{1}{n!}$$

The value $1/n!$ is small indeed; for just ten elements we get $1/10! = 1/3628800$, less than one chance in 3.5 million.

Quicksort is an example of a *randomized algorithm*, an algorithm whose behavior depends on probabilities. Quicksort is a good randomized algorithm because on average it behaves well, and the probability that it does not behave well is too small to be a practical concern.

There is an underlying requirement in quicksort, which in fact extends to all randomized algorithms, and this is that we must be able to pick numbers in random; in quicksort, these numbers correspond to pivot indices. Although this is not trivial, any programming language worth its salt will have good functions available in programming libraries that play that role. In chapter 16 we will have much more to say about randomized algorithms and we will also spend some time into random number generation.

If quicksort has on average the same complexity as merge sort and in addition we run a risk, however tiny, that it may behave worse, you may wonder why we bother with it at all, or why its name is not an exercise in hubris. The answer is that quicksort does deserve its name and is probably the most used sorting algorithm. In contrast to merge sort, it does not require a lot of additional space. Also, the way the algorithm is structured makes for fast implementation in computers. The loop in lines 4–7 of algorithm 12.10 involves incrementing a variable and comparing an indexed value with some other value. These two are fast operations and can be executed in great speed.

12.6   Spoilt for Choice

We have seen five sorting methods, and there are many more. Even among the five we have seen, is there an overall winner, a method that one should always choose?

There is no such superior method. Different methods have their own advantages and disadvantages. Consider merge sort and quicksort. Merge sort goes through the elements to be sorted one after the other. Quicksort needs to be able to access the elements in completely arbitrary order. As long as we are dealing with standard arrays, that makes no difference, because a core feature of arrays is that all elements can be accessed in the same, constant time. But if we are dealing with data in some other arrangement where going from one element to the next is faster than accessing any random element, then merge sort will still perform as expected, whereas quicksort will suffer. Quicksort is therefore not suitable for sorting lists of items where you can access an item only by following a link from an item next to it, as is the case with lists.

Heapsort and merge sort have a guaranteed upper limit of $O(n \lg n)$, whereas quicksort has an expected performance of $O(n \lg n)$ and a performance of $O(n^2)$ in rare cases. In many cases the difference is moot. But there may be critical cases where we do need a guarantee that sorting will take no more than $O(n \lg n)$, making quicksort unsuitable.

Merge sort and heapsort have the same performance guarantees, but their internal workings are different. Merge sort is an algorithm that can be parallelized; that is, parts of it can run concurrently and independently of other parts, on different computers, processors, or processor cores. For example, if we have 16 processing elements at our disposal, we can divide and conquer our data four times, so that we have 16 segments to sort and then merge. We can distribute each one of these segments to a different processing element, for a sixteen-fold improvement in speed for their sorting.

Merge sort is also suitable for sorting data residing in *external storage*. We have described algorithms that operate in data in the computer's main memory. The problem of sorting data stored in secondary storage is different, as the cost of moving along the data and reading is different when we work with external storage than when we work with internal memory. Merge sort is suitable for external sorting, whereas heapsort is not.

Having reached a computational complexity of $O(n \lg n)$, it is natural to ask whether there is a place for algorithms like selection sort and insertion sort that achieve only a $O(n^2)$ performance. The answer is that there is a place. We have been counting only comparisons and exchanges in our performance analyses, as these two are the major costs when sorting large amounts of elements. However, that is not the whole picture. All code takes some time to execute and results in some computational cost. Recursion, for instance, has its costs. In each recursive call the computer has to record the complete state of the function that it is currently executing, it has to set the scene for the recursive call to take place, and it has to restore the state of the function that made the recursive call when we returned from it. As a result of all these hidden costs, it may be faster to run a simple algorithm like selection sort or insertion sort when our dataset is small, and the advantage of $O(n \lg n)$ to $O(n^2)$ does not have the opportunity to show. One way to exploit this is to have quicksort or merge sort revert to one of the simpler methods when we get down to sorting a small number of elements, say 20.

Another consideration when selecting a sort method is the amount of space that we have available. We saw that merge sort requires additional space equal to the space required to store our elements, $O(n)$. Quicksort also requires additional space, although this is not immediately obvious. It has again to do with its recursive nature. On average the quicksort tree has a depth of $O(\lg n)$; therefore, we need that much extra space to keep track of recursion, the storing of state between calls as we go one level deeper. All the other methods, selection sort, insertion sort, and heapsort, have minimal demands on extra space: just space for one element to do each exchange.

Apart from speed and space we may also be interested in how our sorting algorithm handles ties, that is, records that have the same key values. To return to sorting cards again, look at the cards in figure 12.20. We want to sort them by their rank. If we use heapsort we get the situation in figure 12.20a. If

(a) Heapsort: unstable sort.

(b) Insertion sort: stable sort.

Figure 12.20
Stable and unstable sorting.

we use insertion sort we get the situation in figure 12.20b. In heapsort the relative order of 5♣ and 5♡ was reversed in the sorted array, whereas in insertion sort it was preserved. We say that insertion sort is a *stable sorting* method and heapsort is an *unstable sorting* method. The actual definition is this: a sorting algorithm is stable if it preserves the relative order of records that have the same keys. So, if we have two records R_i and R_j with keys K_i and K_j, respectively, so that $\texttt{Compare}(K_i, K_j) = 0$ and, moreover, R_i is before R_j in the input to our algorithm, the algorithm is stable if R_i comes before R_j in the output of the algorithm. From the algorithms we examined, insertion sort and merge sort are stable, whereas the rest of them are unstable.

All this discussion about sorting has barely scratched the surface of sorting algorithms; this is a subject that could easily fill a whole book (and it has). There are many more sorting algorithms than the five we have presented here. For most cases, however, these five suffice. In fact, for most cases knowledge of quicksort suffices. But there are always cases that go beyond the usual and cases where a different algorithm, or a different variant of an algorithm, can bring huge potential benefits in terms of speed or space. The choice and application of an algorithm in a given setting is a creative endeavor, not a cookbook execution.

Notes

Herman Hollerith invented the tabulating machine that bears its name, paving the way for modern computers [3]. Selection sort and insertion sort were already around by 1956, when they were included in a bibliographical survey of sorting [72]. Robert W. Floyd presented an initial version of heapsort in 1962, calling it treesort [66]. J. W. J. Williams gave an improved version, with the name heapsort, in June 1964 [218], which was followed by another version by Floyd, called treesort 3, in December 1964 [68]. Merge sorting was proposed by John von Neumann in 1945 [114, p. 158]. Quicksort was introduced by C. A. R. Hoare in 1961 [93, 94, 95].

Exercises

1. Implement merge sort, using algorithm 12.8, so that it outputs its call graph during execution. To make it readable, the call graph should be indented: recursive calls should be indented a number of spaces to the right, compared to the calling function. Hence, the call graph should be like the one in figure 12.14, without the connecting lines.

2. Implement merge sort, using algorithm 12.8, so that it outputs the call graph as in figure 12.14, including the connecting lines. The connecting lines can be composed from simple characters like "|", "_", and "+".

3. The in-place array merge, algorithm 12.7 uses an array C of length $h - l + 1$. Because C may be smaller than A, we need to be careful with the various indices in C by using the variables cm and ch and subscripting with $k - l$ in line 2. Implement the algorithm assuming that C is as large as A so that both can share the same range of indices.

4. For short arrays insertion sort or selection sort can be faster than merge sort. Measure your implementations of insertion sort, selection sort, and merge sort, and find what the threshold is where merge sort runs faster than the other two.

5. Implement merge sort, taking into account the potential savings from sorted arrays that do not need merging. Check whether $A[m]$ is less than or equal to $A[m + 1]$ and merge only if $A[m] > A[m + 1]$.

6. If we change line 15 of algorithm 12.7 so that we use a strict comparison ($<$), is merge sort still a stable sorting algorithm?

7. Instead of selecting a pivot element in random each time we carry out a partitioning in quicksort, we can shuffle randomly the elements of the array A before

we start. Then the elements of *A* will be in random order, and we can pick as a pivot element the first element of each array to be partitioned. Use this strategy to implement quicksort.

8. Another way to select a pivot element is instead of picking it in random, to select three elements, such as the first, the last, and the one in the middle of the array to be partitioned, and then use as the pivot element the median of the tree elements, that is, the element with the middle value. It turns out that this strategy also works well in practice, with the probability of slow behavior being low. Use this strategy to implement quicksort.

9. Like merge sort, it usually pays off to combine quicksort with some other, simpler algorithm like insertion sort for shorter arrays. Implement quicksort combining it with insertion sort, so that when the array to be partitioned becomes smaller than a certain threshold, it switches to using insertion sort. Carry out experiments to find out what this threshold would be.

13 The Cloakroom, the Pigeon, and the Bucket

When you hand in your coat or bag to a cloakroom attendant you get a ticket in return. When afterward you want to retrieve your belongings in order to leave the premises, you hand over your ticket and the coat or bag is handed over to you in return.

If you think a bit about the problem this process solves, it is a problem of searching and locating an item. Your item is what you hand over to the cloak attendant; it is located via the ticket and then returned to you. The way this works is that the cloakroom has numbered racks, on which coats are hung, and numbered compartments on which bags are placed. Your ticket corresponds to a position on a clothes rack or a compartment. The attendant needs only to make sure that your item is put into the right place and is removed with the correct ticket.

When people think of searching they usually think of going through some items until they find the one they want; the process becomes easier when the items are sorted, so that we can move around them in a more organized way when we search. The cloakroom shows that there is actually another way to search: to translate an item to a location where it will be stored and to retrieve it directly from that address. In the cloakroom, the address is printed on the ticket. The attendant does not really look for your item: the attendant reads the address of the item, from the ticket, and goes directly to the address to fetch it for you.

It is easy to generalize that technique of *locating without searching*: instead of searching for an item, derive an address where it will be stored. Associate the item with the address, and then go directly to the address each time you want to find the item.

Now bring that to the computer realm, where our items are records that contain attributes. We want to be able to go directly from the record to an address where we store it; that address will be a number corresponding to a location in storage memory. The crux of the problem is exactly how to associate the address with the item. We need a fast and reliable method, and we cannot rely on any form of attendants. Since when we are looking for a record we are looking for it in terms of one or more attributes, which form a key for the record, we need a method for deriving an address from a record's key. As the address is a number, we need a method that takes us from keys to numbers. In other words, we need a function, say $f(K)$, that takes the key K of a record R and returns a value $a = f(K)$. The value a is the address where the record will be stored, and we go on and store it there. Every time we want to retrieve the record using its key, we make again the same function call $f(K)$, which will return the same address value a, from which we will fetch the required record. The function must be fast so that it can calculate the address quickly, at least as fast as we would need if we were to search through the records to find the one we want. If it is not that fast, it simply is not worth it. If we do have such a function, though, we have solved our locating problem in a novel way: instead of us searching for an item, the item will tell us where to find it—the function will do the telling.

13.1   Mapping Keys to Values

Suppose we have n distinct records and we know all of them in advance. Then the problem becomes one of finding a function f such that for every one of the keys of the n records f produces a different value from 0 to $n - 1$. Having that, we can store each record R in a table T, in fact an array, of size n, so that if $f(K) = a$, where K is the key of R, then $T[a] = R$. You can see such an arrangement in figure 13.1, where the items are on the left, the table on the right, and the arrows show the effect of each function call $f(K)$, that is the address of the associated table cell.

Coming up with such a function f for a set of records is not easy. We can handcraft f, but that is tedious and complicated. Algorithm 13.1 shows a function that maps each of 31 of the most common English words to a number from -10 to 29 (so we can add ten to get all positive table indices). Warning: you are not expected to understand algorithm 13.1. Just bear with it for a while.

The algorithm uses a function Code that takes a character and assigns a numerical value to it. The character is taken from the input string s, which we assume is at least four characters long, from $s[0]$ to $s[3]$. If the word has

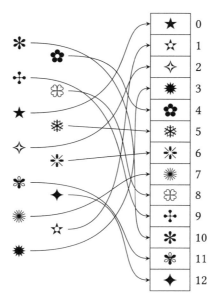

Figure 13.1

Associating a set of elements with table positions.

less than four characters, then we assume it is padded at the end with spaces. The Code will first assign the value zero for a space, one for the character "A" two, for the character "B", and so on. It will then add one if the assigned value is greater than nine and another two to the resulting value if it is greater than 19. The codes assigned to each of the first three characters of a word are mangled together and a unique number is produced for each word.

You are justified in thinking that all this looks like hocus-pocus, but it does work, as you can see with its output on the input set of the common English words in table 13.1. It is a *perfect mapping*, in that all words are mapped to different values. It is also fast, as it only requires a definite number of trivial operations. However, it is not practical for any other set of words. It may not work if we change a single word, as it may produce the same value for two different words, thus giving the same address for two different items. You were asked to bear with the algorithm not because it is useful, but to see with your own eyes that a good mapping function can indeed be difficult to find.

Even though algorithm 13.1 does assign a unique address to each word, it leaves holes in the assignment. We have 31 words and the values of the

---

Algorithm 13.1: A perfect mapping of 31 of most common words in English to numbers.

PerfectMapping(s) $\rightarrow r$
    Input: s, a string among a predefined list of 31 of the most common
           words in English
    Output: r, an address in the range $-10, 1, \ldots, 29$

1    $r \leftarrow -\text{Code}(s[0])$
2    $s \leftarrow \text{Code}(s[1])$
3    $r \leftarrow r - 8 + s$
4   **if** $r \leq 0$ **then**
5        $r \leftarrow r + 16 + s$
6    $s \leftarrow \text{Code}(s[2])$
7   **if** $s = 0$ **then**
8   **return** r
9    $r \leftarrow r - 28 + s$
10   **if** $r > 0$ **then**
11   **return** r
12   $r \leftarrow r + 11 + s$
13   $t \leftarrow \text{Code}(s[3])$
14   **if** $t = 0$ **then**
15   **return** r
16   $r \leftarrow r - (s - 5)$
17   **if** $r < 0$ **then**
18   **return** r
19   $r \leftarrow r + 10$
20   **return** r

---

function are $-10, -9, \ldots, 30$ so there are nine function values that do not correspond to a word. That does not make the function incorrect, but we may wish to reduce waste.

One idea is to use the first character of each key, the last character of each key, and the number of characters in the key. We can assign a numerical code to the first and the last character and derive a value as follows: $h = \text{Code}(b) + \text{Code}(e) + |K|$, where K is the key, $|K|$ is the length of the key, b is the character at the beginning of the key, and e is the character at the end of the key. The resulting value would be the index of the table. The problem,

Table 13.1

Mapping of 31 most common English words to the numbers -10 to 30.

A	7	FOR	23	IN	29	THE	-6
AND	-3	FROM	19	IS	5	THIS	-2
ARE	3	HAD	-7	IT	6	TO	17
AS	13	HAVE	25	NOT	20	WAS	11
AT	14	HE	10	OF	4	WHICH	-5
BE	16	HER	1	ON	22	WITH	21
BUT	9	HIS	12	OR	30	YOU	8
BY	18	I	-1	THAT	-10		

of course, is to find the proper numerical codes for such a scheme to work. The Code function that we used before is not suitable because it does not produce unique values. For example, the word "ARE" is mapped to the value 9 (by $1 + 5 + 3$), as is the word "BE" (by $2 + 5 + 2$).

If we search for a suitable encoding we find that it does indeed exist, and we incorporate it in algorithm 13.2; it is the array C in the algorithm. Each position in the array corresponds to a numerical code that we assign to a character. Position 0 of the array contains the code for "A", position 1 of the array contains the code for "B", and so on for the rest of the characters. The function Ordinal(c) returns the ordinal position of a character c in the alphabet, starting from zero. The array C contains several entries equal to -1; these are dummy entries for characters that do not appear as first or last in our data set. For example, none of our words contains "C" as its first or last letter.

Algorithm 13.2 maps 31 words to 31 different addresses, from 1 to 32, as you can see in table 13.2. This is a minimal perfect mapping, as it maps all words to distinct values, and it maps n words to n distinct values, the minimum possible number.

Is this an improvement over the previous algorithm? Yes. We have a correct mapping and we do not waste space. It is also a much simpler algorithm. Is it a general, practical solution to our problem? No—it is a solution only if we know all our keys in advance and we can derive a suitable encoding for the letters. This is not always possible. If our dataset contained the word "ERA", the algorithm would not work because "ERA" would have exactly the same mapped value as "ARE". That could be fixed by tweaking a bit algorithm 13.2, but the problem remains: it is not a sure-fire way that would map keys to

Algorithm 13.2: A minimal perfect mapping.

```
MinimalPerfectMapping(s) → r
```
    Input: s, a string among a predefined list of 31 of the most common
        words in English
    Output: r, an address in the range $1, \ldots, 32$
    Data: C, an array of 26 integers

1    $C \leftarrow [$
2   3,   23,   -1,   17,   7,   11,   -1,   5,   0,
3   -1, -1, -1,   16,   17,   9,   -1,   -1,   13,
4   4,   0,   23,   -1,   8,   -1,   4,   -1
5    $]$
6    $l \leftarrow |s|$
7    $b \leftarrow \text{Ordinal}(s[0])$
8    $e \leftarrow \text{Ordinal}(s[l-1])$
9    $r \leftarrow l + C[b] + C[e]$
10   **return** r

Table 13.2

A minimal perfect mapping of 31 of the most common English words to the numbers one to 31.

A	7	FOR	27	IN	19	THE	10
AND	23	FROM	31	IS	6	THIS	8
ARE	13	HAD	25	IT	2	TO	11
AS	9	HAVE	16	NOT	20	WAS	15
AT	5	HE	14	OF	22	WHICH	18
BE	32	HER	21	ON	28	WITH	17
BUT	26	HIS	12	OR	24	YOU	30
BY	29	I	1	THAT	4		

addresses reliably over an unknown set of keys. Moreover, we skipped the interesting part of how we found the array C in the first place. We had to use a specialized algorithm just for that. So things are more complex than they appear.

13.2   Hashing

The solution we want is to have a general purpose function that takes keys and produces values in a prescribed range and works even without previous knowledge of the items and their keys. The function must guarantee that, no matter what the key, it will return a value in the range that we want. The function must also avoid as much as possible mapping different keys to the same values. We used the phrase "as much as possible" with good reason: if the number of possible keys is greater than the range of the mapped values, then it is impossible not to duplicate mappings. For example, if we have a table of size n and $2n$ possible keys, then at least n keys will be mapped on the same values with other keys.

Time for some terminology. The technique we are talking about is called *hashing*. It comes from the meaning of the word "to hash" as cutting and chopping meat into small pieces, mixing them together, and making them a mess (no relation to psychoactive agents). The idea is that in a similar way we take a key, cut it, scramble it, and mangle it so as to get an address out of it that we can use for searching. We want the addresses to be distinct, if it is possible, so we are in a sense scattering the keys on an address space; that is why sometimes the technique is also called *scatter storage*. The function we use is a *hash* or *hashing function*, or *hash function*. The array, or table, on which we map the keys is called a *hash table*. The entries of the table are called *buckets* or *slots*. If the function manages to map all keys to distinct values, it is called a *perfect hash function*. If it manages to map all keys to distinct values without wasting any space, so that the range of the generated addresses is equal to the number of the keys, then it is called a *minimal perfect hash function*. When this is not possible and the function maps two different keys to the same address, we say that we have a *collision*. As we said, if the address space is smaller than the number of possible keys, then it is impossible to avoid collisions. The point is rather how to avoid collisions as much as possible, or how to handle them, if they occur.

This situation is a manifestation of an important principle in mathematics, the *pigeonhole principle*, which states that if you have n items, m containers, with $n > m$, and you want to fit the items into containers, then at least one container will contain more than a single item. Although obvious if you think of it, see figure 13.2, the pigeonhole principle has some counter-intuitive applications.

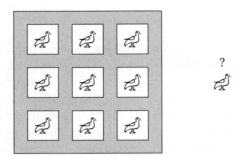

Figure 13.2
The pigeonhole principle.

One of them is that you can prove that in any big city there will be at least two people with exactly the same number of hairs on their heads. The average number of hairs on a human head is about 150,000. The actual number of hairs on a person may of course vary, but we can be sure that there can be no person with, say, 1,000,000 hairs on the head. Therefore, in any city with more than 1,000,000 inhabitants there will be at least two people with exactly the same number of hairs on their head.

Another example is the so-called *birthday paradox*, which asks you to name what is the minimum amount of people you need to get into a room so it is probable that two of them have the same birthday. Call this probability $P(B)$. It is easier to calculate $P(B)$ by approaching the opposite problem, that is, what is the probability that in a group of persons in a room there will be no common birthday? By the basic laws of probability, if we call that probability $P(\overline{B})$, we have $P(\overline{B}) = 1 - P(B)$. Now for this to happen all birthdays need to fall on different dates. If we take the persons in turn, the birthday of the first person can be on any day of the year and the probability of this happening is 365/365 (we discount leap years). The birthday of the second person can be on any day apart from the day of the first person's birthday. There are 364 such days, so the probability is 364/365 and the probability of the two first persons having different birthdays is $365/365 \times 364/365$. We continue with the same line of thinking, and for n persons we get the probability of all of them having different birthdays being $365/365 \times 364/365 \times \cdots \times (365 - n + 1)/365$. If we do the calculations we find that for $n = 23$, we have $P(\overline{B}) = 365/365 \times 364/365 \times \cdots \times 343/365 \approx 0.49$. That means that $P(B) \approx 0.51$, so if you get 23 people in a room it is more likely than not that two of them have their birthday on the same day. Of course if $n > 23$ the probability is even better; you may try bets at a cocktail party, and chances are you will win. If the result seems surprising, notice that we do not ask for two people to share a specific birthday or to find somebody with your birthday, but for any two people to have the same birthday.

13.3   Hashing Functions

Returning to hashing functions, the quest is to find hash functions that minimize collisions. For example, suppose that our keys are composed of 25 characters, consisting of a street name and number. The number of theoretically possible keys is $25^{37} = 1.6 \times 10^{39}$: each character can be one of 26 letters, or a space, or one of ten digits, 37 cases in all, and we have 25 characters in total. The number of possible keys in practice is of course much less, because not all strings are valid street addresses; and in a given application the number of addresses that we will encounter will probably be less than the number of all valid street addresses in the world. Let's say that we expect to have about 100,000 keys, or street addresses, which we do not know in advance. Then we are looking for a hash function that will map from a range of size 1.6×10^{39} to a set of 100,000 distinct values. By the pigeonhole principle it is impossible to guarantee not to have collisions. But we can try to find a function that maps keys to as many different values as possible. If the function does a good job, then it will not create many collisions for the 100,000 keys that we may encounter.

If our keys are numeric, instead of strings, then a family of functions that has proved to be good is the simple remainder, or modulo, of the division of the key by the size of our address table:

$$h(K) = K \bmod m$$

where m is the size and K is the key. The result will be by definition between 0 and $m - 1$ and so it will fit in the table. The calculation leads to the trivial algorithm 13.3. Perhaps the only thing that needs explaining is that the algorithm works for all integer keys, not just for non-negative ones, because the modulo operation works for both positive and negative numbers.

For example, suppose that we have to handle records that contain some country information and each record's key is the country's international call code. Table 13.3 contains the first 17 countries in the world in terms of their

---

Algorithm 13.3: An integer hash function.

IntegerHash(k, m) $\rightarrow h$
    Input: k, an integer number
              m, the size of the hash table
    Output: h, the hash value of k

1   $h \leftarrow k \bmod m$
2   **return** h

Table 13.3

First 17 countries in terms of population with international call codes (2015).

China	86	Japan	81
India	91	Mexico	52
United States	1	Philippines	63
Indonesia	62	Vietnam	84
Brazil	55	Ethiopia	251
Pakistan	92	Egypt	20
Nigeria	234	Germany	49
Bangladesh	880	Iran	98
Russia	7		

population, along with their international call code. If we start adding countries in a hash table of size 23 using their call codes as keys, then the situation after adding the first ten countries will be as in figure 13.3. If we have this hash table, then we can find every country, provided we have its call code, by calculating $h(K) = K \bmod 23$.

When we said above that the remainder functions have proved to be good, we meant that these are functions that do well in terms of collisions; that is, collisions do not happen often. This, however, depends on the judicious choice of the table size. If the keys are decimal numbers, then a table size that is a power of ten, 10^x for some x, is a poor choice. The reason is that the remainder of the division of a positive integer by 10^x is simply the last x digits of the number. For example, 12345 mod 100 = 45, 2345 mod 100 = 45, and so on. In general, as every positive integer with n digits $D_n D_{n-1} \ldots D_1 D_0$ has value $D_n \times 10^n + D_{n-1} \times 10^{n-1} + \cdots + D_1 \times 10^1 + D_0 \times 10^0$, for every power of ten, 10^x, we have:

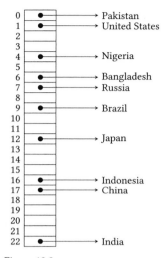

Figure 13.3

Hash table of size 23 containing the first ten countries in terms of population, keyed by call code.

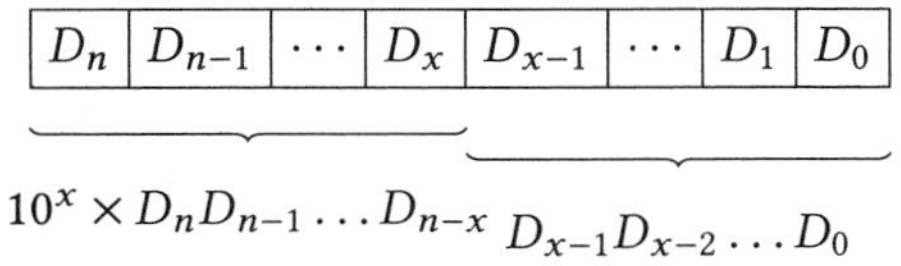

$$\boxed{D_n}\;\boxed{D_{n-1}}\;\boxed{\cdots}\;\boxed{D_x}\;\boxed{D_{x-1}}\;\boxed{\cdots}\;\boxed{D_1}\;\boxed{D_0}$$

$$10^x \times D_n D_{n-1} \ldots D_{n-x} \quad D_{x-1} D_{x-2} \ldots D_0$$

Figure 13.4

Break-up of a positive integer modulo a power 10^x.

$$\frac{D_n D_{n-1} \ldots D_1 D_0}{10^x} = 10^x \times D_n D_{n-1} \ldots D_x + x_{x-1} D_{x-2} \ldots D_1 D_0$$

If $x \le n$, then the first part of the sum is the quotient and the right part the remainder. If $x > n$, then the first part, the quotient, does not exist at all; therefore, it is always:

$$D_n D_{n-1} \ldots D_1 D_0 \bmod 10^x = D_{x-1} D_{x-2} \ldots D_1 D_0$$

This follows straight from the fact that the value of a digit d at position x of a positive integer is simply $d \times 10^x$; you may check figure 13.4 to see how this affects the modulo operation: all numbers ending with the same x digits will have the same hash value.

If our number is a negative integer, then the same problem appears and only the last x digits matter in the modulo operation. If we use the definition of modulo we find that $-12345 \bmod 100 = 55$, $-2345 \bmod 100 = 55$, and so on. It is not just a matter of chopping the leading digits of the number, but we are still in trouble.

Following the same reasoning, another bad choice, if we are dealing with numbers in the binary system, is a table size that is a power of two. In general, we do not want to use a table size that is a power of the base of the numbering system that our keys use. In all these cases, only a subset of the digits of our keys will be taken into account—the lower x digits, if the table size is b^x, where b is the base of the numbering system. What we need is a way to have a balanced distribution of keys on the hash table, so that the probability of a collision is minimized. Ideally we would like our hash function to distribute all keys to the different table entries with equal probability, that is, the hash values should be *uniformly distributed*. If only the lower x digits are taken into account when hashing, then we will immediately get collisions for all numbers that end with the same x digits, no matter how different the preceding digits are. A similar problem exists if our choice for the table size is an even number. All even keys will map to even hash values and all odd keys will map to odd hash values. Ideally we would like all keys to map with equally probability to any hash value to avoid biases, so even numbers are out of consideration for modulo divisors.

Taking all the above into account, the best choice for a table size is a prime number. In practice if your table can store up to 1000 keys, you will not go for a table of size 1000, but a table of size 997, which is a prime.

Up to this point, we assumed that the keys are integers. If the keys are strings, then we can treat them as numbers in a numeric system with a suitable base, for example, 26 if we only have letters in the alphabet. The value of the string is then calculated as we would calculate any value in any positional number system. If s is a string of n characters, then its value is $v = \mathrm{Ordinal}(s[0])b^{n-1} + \mathrm{Ordinal}(s[1])b^{n-2} + \cdots + \mathrm{Ordinal}(s[n-1])b^0$ and the hash value is $h = v \bmod m$. This can be directly written as algorithm 13.4. If we apply the algorithm to the string "HELLO" for $b = 26$ and $m = 31$ we get:

$$v_0 = \mathrm{Ordinal}(\text{``H''}) \cdot 26^4 = 7 \cdot 456,976 = 3{,}198{,}832$$

$$v_1 = 3{,}198{,}832 + \mathrm{Ordinal}(\text{``E''}) \cdot 26^3 = 3{,}198{,}832 + 4 \cdot 26^3 = 3{,}269{,}136$$

$$v_2 = 3{,}269{,}136 + \mathrm{Ordinal}(\text{``L''}) \cdot 26^2 = 3{,}269{,}136 + 11 \cdot 26^2 = 3{,}276{,}572$$

Algorithm 13.4: A string hash function.

StringHash(s, b, m) $\rightarrow h$
    Input: s, a string
            b, the base of the number system
            m, the size of the hash table
    Output: h, the hash value of s

1   $v \leftarrow 0$
2   $n \leftarrow |s|$
3   **for** $i \leftarrow 0$ **to** n **do**
4       $v \leftarrow v + \text{Ordinal}(s[i]) \cdot b^{n-1-i}$
5   $h \leftarrow v \bmod m$
6   **return** h

$$v_3 = 3{,}276{,}572 + \text{Ordinal}(\text{"L"}) \cdot 26^1 = 3{,}276{,}572 + 11 \cdot 26 = 3{,}276{,}858$$
$$v_4 = 3{,}276{,}858 + \text{Ordinal}(\text{"O"}) = +3{,}276{,}858 + 14 = 3{,}276{,}872$$
$$h = 3{,}276{,}872 \bmod 31 = 17$$

where v_i is the value of v in the ith iteration of the algorithm.

This procedure is equivalent to treating the string with n characters as a polynomial of degree $n - 1$:

$$p(x) = a_{n-1}x^{n-1} + a_{n-2}x^{n-2} + \cdots + a_0$$

where each coefficient a_i is the ordinal value of the ith character of the string, counting from the left. The polynomial is evaluated for $x = b$, where b is the base of our invented system, the number of possible characters in general. At the end we apply a modulo operation. In our particular example with the string "HELLO" the polynomial is $p(x) = 7x^4 + 4x^3 + 11x^2 + 11x + 14$, and we evaluate it for $x = 26$.

That is a naive way to evaluate a polynomial. For a polynomial of degree n, $p(x) = a_nx^n + a_{n-1}x^{n-1} + \cdots + a_0$, we start computing all the powers from the left to the right, which is wasteful. For the moment, to simplify the discussion, we assume that all coefficients are non-zero; the argument we make holds for the general case where we may have zero coefficients as well. If we calculate x^n we have already calculated x^{n-1}, but we do not make use of that anywhere. For the term a_nx^n the algorithm needs $n - 1$ multiplications (for calculating the power) plus one multiplication of the power with the coefficient a_n; in all, n multiplications. Similarly, the term $a_{n-1}x^{n-1}$ needs $n - 1$ multiplications. In total the algorithm needs $n + (n - 1) + \cdots + 1 = n(n - 1)/2$ multiplications and also n additions to sum the terms.

A better way to evaluate a polynomial is to go from the left to the right, re-using the powers we calculate for subsequent factors. So, if we have calculated x^2, we do not need to start the calculation of x^3 from scratch because $x^3 = x \cdot x^2$. If we do that, then we need one multiplication for a_1x, two multiplications for a_2x^2 (one to get x^2 from x and one to get a_2x^2), again two multiplications for a_3x^3 (one to get x^3 from x^2 and one to get a_3x^3), and in general two multiplications for every term up to and including a_nx^n. In total that makes $2n - 1$ multiplications, and we need n additions to sum the terms. That's a good improvement over the previous scheme.

We can do even better if we use an approach called *Horner's rule*. Mathematically, the rule shows how to re-arrange a polynomial as follows:

$$a_0 + a_1x + a_2x^2 + \cdots + a_nx^n = (\ldots(a_nx + a_{n-1})x + \cdots))x + a_0$$

We evaluate the expression by starting with the innermost part, where we take a_n, multiply it by x, and add the previous coefficient a_{n-1}. We multiply the result by x and add the previous coefficient a_{n-2}. We repeat the process until at the end we are left with a partial result that we multiply by x and add a_0. In effect we start the evaluation by the innermost nested factor, $x(a_{n-1} + a_nx)$, and then go outward to $x(a_{n-2} + x(a_{n-1} + a_nx))$, substituting the inner value that we have found, then go outward again, until we go through the whole expression. This is easily expressed as algorithm 13.5. An illustration of Horner's rule is in figure 13.5, where we indicate the results with r_n, which is trivially $a_n, r_{n-1}, \ldots r_0 = r$. The right side of the figure shows the application of Horner's rule in the polynomial corresponding to "HELLO", $p(x) = 7x^4 + 4x^3 + 11x^2 + 11x + 14$ for $x = 26$.

By checking algorithm 13.5 we see that line 3 is executed n times. Polynomial evaluation now takes just n additions and n multiplications, so that's the way to go.

Now we can notice something else. We evaluate a polynomial, which may result in a big value; at least x^n for a polynomial of degree n. At the end of the hash operation, however, we will get a result that fits into the hash table. So from something as big as x^n we will get down to something less than the size of the table, m. Indeed, in our example, we go up to 3,276,872 only to go down to $h = 3{,}276{,}872 \bmod 31 = 17$.

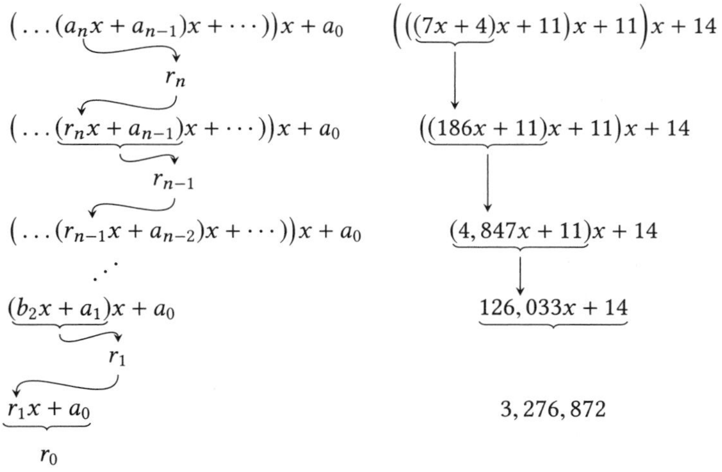

$$\big(\ldots(a_n x + a_{n-1})x + \cdots)\big)x + a_0 \qquad \Big(\big((7x + 4)x + 11\big)x + 11\Big)x + 14$$

$$r_n \qquad\qquad\qquad \downarrow$$

$$\big(\ldots(r_n x + a_{n-1})x + \cdots)\big)x + a_0 \qquad \big((186x + 11)x + 11\big)x + 14$$

$$r_{n-1} \qquad\qquad\qquad \downarrow$$

$$\big(\ldots(r_{n-1}x + a_{n-2})x + \cdots)\big)x + a_0 \qquad (4{,}847x + 11)x + 14$$

$$\ddots \qquad\qquad\qquad \downarrow$$

$$(b_2 x + a_1)x + a_0 \qquad\qquad 126{,}033x + 14$$

$$r_1$$

$$r_1 x + a_0 \qquad\qquad\qquad 3{,}276{,}872$$

$$r_0$$

Figure 13.5
Horner's rule.

A feature of the modulo operation is that we can apply it to the constituents of a bigger expression according to these rules:

$$(a + b) \bmod m = \big((a \bmod m) + (b \bmod m)\big) \bmod m$$

$$(ab) \bmod m = \big((a \bmod m) \cdot (b \bmod m)\big) \bmod m$$

By combining the properties of the modulo operation with Horner's rule we derive algorithm 13.6; instead of raising directly to successive powers, the exponentiation happens by the repeated multiplication of the previous hash value with the base of the number system in line 4 and taking the remainder of the operation at each iteration. Each step of the iteration is a direct application of Horner's, where we substitute b for x and Ordinal(c), where c are successive characters of the string, for the polynomial coefficients.

If we apply algorithm 13.6 to the string "HELLO" we will find the same value as before, as expected, but with much less hassle in calculating the numbers:

$$h_0 = \text{Ordinal}(\text{``H''}) \bmod 31 = 7 \bmod 31 = 7$$

$$h_1 = \big(26 \cdot 7 + \text{Ordinal}(\text{``E''})\big) \bmod 31 = (182 + 4) \bmod 31 = 0$$

$$h_2 = \big(26 \cdot 0 + \text{Ordinal}(\text{``L''})\big) \bmod 31 = 11 \bmod 31 = 11$$

Algorithm 13.5: Horner's rule.

HornerRule(A, x) $\rightarrow r$
  Input: A, an array containing the coefficients of a polynomial of
      degree n
      x, the point at which to evaluate the polynomial

  Output: r, the value of the polynomial at x

1   $r \leftarrow 0$
2   **foreach** c **in** A **do**
3       $r \leftarrow r \cdot x + c$
4   **return** r

Algorithm 13.6: An optimized string hash function.

OptimizedStringHash(s, b, m) $\rightarrow h$
  Input: s, a string
      b, the base of the number system
      m, the size of the hash table
  Output: h, the hash value of s

1   $h \leftarrow 0$
2   **foreach** c **in** s **do**
3       $h \leftarrow \big(b \cdot h + \mathrm{Ordinal}(c)\big) \bmod m$
4   **return** h

$$h_3 = \big(26 \cdot 11 + \mathrm{Ordinal}(\text{``L''})\big) \bmod 31 = (286 + 11) \bmod 31$$
$$h_4 = \big(26 \cdot 18 + \mathrm{Ordinal}(\text{``O''})\big) \bmod 31 = 482 \bmod 31 = 17$$

where h_i is the value of h in the ith iteration of the algorithm. Implementations of algorithm 13.6 with suitable b and m are in use by programming languages that provide hash functions for strings.

Having established hash functions for strings (algorithm 13.6) or integers (algorithm 13.3), the next piece of the puzzle is how to handle real numbers, usually called *floating point numbers*. One way is to convert a floating point to a string and hash the string as we know with algorithm 13.6. However, converting numbers to strings can be slow. Another idea would be to turn floating point values to integers by taking out the decimal point. Under this

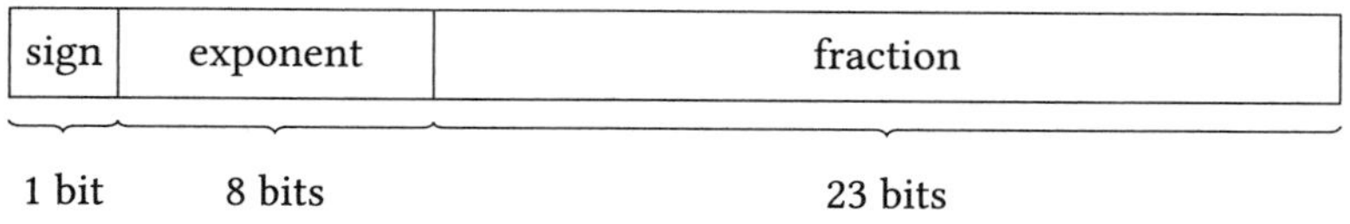

sign	exponent	fraction

1 bit   8 bits   23 bits

Figure 13.6
Floating point representation.

scheme, 261.63 would become 26163, which is an integer, which we would then hash using algorithm 13.3. However, we cannot do exactly that, because "taking out the decimal point" is something we can do if the floating number is indeed represented in a computing using an integer part, a decimal point, and a part to the right of the decimal point. This is not how floating numbers are usually represented in computers, though.

13.4   Floating Point Representation and Hashing

Computers use something akin to *scientific notation* for representing real numbers, that is, for *floating point representation*. With this notation numbers are represented as a product of a signed number with absolute value between 1 and 10 and a power of 10:

$$m \times 10^e$$

The number m is variously called *fraction part, characteristic, mantissa,* or *significand.* The number e is simply the *exponent.* So we have:

$$0.00025 = 2.5 \times 10^{-5}$$

and

$$-6{,}510{,}000 = -6.51 \times 10^6$$

Floating point numbers in computers are similar to that. We use a predefined number of bits for their representation. Usually two choices are possible: 32 bits and 64 bits. Let's deal with the 32 bits; 64-bit numbers are similar. If we use 32 bits in our computer to represent floating point numbers, we arrange them as in figure 13.6.

To render humanly comprehensible the value of a number represented in this way, we must take it apart and calculate:

$$(-1)^s \times 1.f \times 2^{e-127}$$

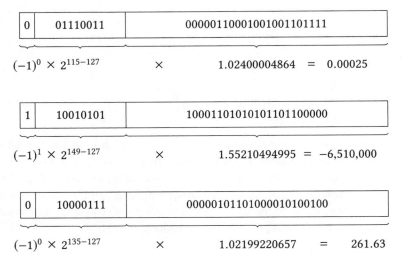

Figure 13.7

Floating point representation examples.

where s is the sign, f is the fraction, and n is the exponent. When the sign is 0, $(-1)^0 = 1$ and the number is positive. When the sign is 1, $(-1)^1 = -1$ and the number is negative. The part $1.f$ is a *binary* fractional number. A binary fractional number is not that different from a decimal fractional number. A decimal number like $0.D_1 D_2 \ldots D_n$ has value $D_1 \times 10^{-1} + D_2 \times 10^{-2} + \cdots + D_n \times 10^{-n}$. A binary number like $0.B_1 B_2 \ldots B_n$ has value $B_1 \times 2^{-1} + B_2 \times 2^{-2} + \cdots + B_n \times 2^{-n}$. In general, a fractional number $0.X_1 X_2 \ldots X_n$ in a positional number system with base b has value $X_1 \times b^{-1} + X_2 \times b^{-2} + \cdots + X_n \times b^{-n}$. If a number has both an integer and a fractional part, its value is simply the sum of the two parts. So the number $B_0.B_1 B_2 \ldots B_n$ has value $B_0 + B_1 \times 2^{-1} + B_2 \times 2^{-2} + \cdots + B_n \times 2^{-n}$. In this way, the number 1.01 in binary is equal to $1 + 0 \times 2^{-1} + 1 \times 2^{-2} = 1.25$ in decimal. Figure 13.7 shows how our examples are represented in a computer as floating point numbers.

There are four cases to consider regarding the interpretation of bits in a floating number represented as in figure 13.6. The first case is when we have both $f = 0$ and $e = 0$; then the number is 0. In particular, there are two kinds of 0. If $s = 1$ we have -0 and if $s = 1$ we have $+0$. The second case is when we have $e = 0$ but $f \neq 0$; then the number is interpreted slightly differently from

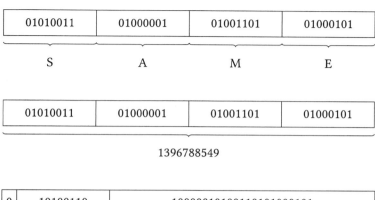

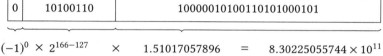

Figure 13.8
Interpretation of same bit pattern: ASCII string, integer number, real number.

the formula we gave above as:

$$(-1)^s \times 0.f \times 2^{e-127}$$

The difference is that we have a leading 0 instead of 1 left to the fraction. We say then that the number is not normalized. The third case is when we have $e = 255$ and $f = 0$; then the number denotes infinity. If $s = 1$ we have $-\infty$ if $s = 0$ we have $+\infty$. Finally, if $e = 255$ and $f \neq 0$, then we interpret the value as being *not a number* or NaN. This typically means an unknown value, or an invalid result in a calculation.

This wraps up our digression to floating point arithmetic. It might seem like computer arcana. Perhaps they are. The truth is, the value of knowing them is appreciated when stuck debugging a program that produces nonsensical numerical results. Also note that although we do have a representation for infinity, *this is only relevant for calculations with floating point numbers.* There is no equivalent representation of infinity for integer numbers.

From this point it is straightforward to return to hashing. The number 261.63 is represented as 01000011100000101101000010100100 in the computer. We treat this sequence of bits as an integer number. For a moment we forget that we have stored a floating point, and we behave as if we had stored an integer number with the same bit pattern. We have:

$$(01000011100000101101000010100100)_2 = (1132646564)_{10}$$

We simply take 1132646564 as our key to hash—we use the $(X)_b$ notation to show that the number X is in number system b. In short, for any floating point number, we can interpret it as an integer and use algorithm 13.3, as usual. That's efficient, as we do not really need to do any conversion. We just treat the same pattern of bits differently.

This leads to an important point about computers in general. Computers know only bits: zeroes and ones. They have no idea what they stand for. A pattern of bits in a computer's memory may stand for anything. It is up to particular programs to make sense of what they mean and treat them appropriately. In figure 13.8 you can see how the same bit pattern means three different things in a computer: it may be interpreted as a string, an integer, or a floating point number. Treating a bit pattern differently from what it is intended to mean is a bad idea. There are exceptions, like the one we adopt here, but keep in mind that the rule says otherwise.

13.5   Collisions

Now that we have established a reliable family of hash functions, for both numerical keys and strings, are we done? Let's return to table 13.3 and suppose that we add the next country in terms of population. That happens to be Mexico, with call code 52. This creates a conflict with Bangladesh: 52 mod 23 = 880 mod 23 = 6, so the key of Mexico ends up in the same position of the table with the key of Mexico, as you can see in figure 13.9.

Because of the pigeonhole principle, we will always have collisions. A good hash function will do its best to minimize them, but it is mathematically impossible to avoid them altogether. So for a hashing scheme to work, we must have a way to work around collisions when they do occur.

The most popular method to handle collisions is to arrange for the buckets of a hash table not to contain simple records, but to point to lists of records. Each bucket of the table will point to a list that will contain all the records whose keys hash at the same value; that is, it will contain all the records whose keys conflict together—that explains the name "bucket" because in a sense it contains a set of records. If there are no conflicts for an entry, then the list will

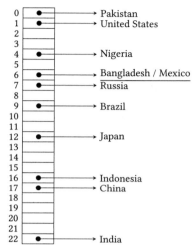

Figure 13.9

Hash table of size 23 containing the first 11 countries in terms of population, keyed by call code.

contain a list with a single item. If there are no keys that hash to a bucket, then the bucket will be an empty list, pointing to NULL. We often use the term *chain* for a list of records that hash to the same value. As we use one chain for each hash value, we call this scheme *separate chaining*. In figure 13.10 you can see how this resolves the problem with the collision of Bangladesh and Mexico in figure 13.10. We use the symbol ∅ to denote a pointer to NULL. As we want this operation to be as fast as possible, we generally use a simple, single linked, unsorted list. Items are added to the head of the list, as indeed happened with Mexico and Bangladesh.

In this way we can add more countries to our table. Some of them will go to single item chains, whereas some of them will collide with other countries in the hash table so they will end up in the chain that contains all countries whose key code hashes to the same value. If we have in total 17 countries, like in figure 13.11, we get single item chains, chains with two items, and even a chain with three items, as Iran, Mexico, and Bangladesh have area codes that hash to the same position in the hash table.

The whole purpose of a hash table is to be able to retrieve items from it quickly. The first step to retrieve an item is to calculate the hash value of its key. We then go and look at the hash table at the position indicated by the

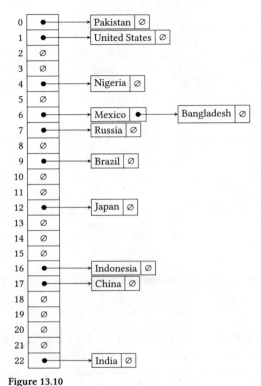

Figure 13.10
Hash table of size 23 containing the first 11 countries in terms of population, keyed by call code, with separate chaining.

hash value. If it points to NULL, then we know that the item does not exist in the hash table. If it points to a list, then we start going through the list until we find it, or we reach the end of the list without finding it. So, in figure 13.11, if we are given the key 880, we will calculate its hash value, which is 6, and then we will start traversing the list pointed by position 6 of the hash table. We will compare the key of each item in the list with 880. If we find it, we know this is Bangladesh. This will happen after checking three items, as Bangladesh is at the end of the list. Now suppose we are searching for the country with call code 213, which is Algeria. The number 213 also hashes to 6. We will traverse the list, but we will not find any item in the list with a key equal to 213, so we can safely determine that Algeria is not in our table.

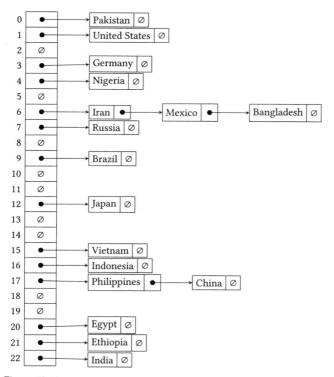

Figure 13.11

Hash table of size 23 containing the first 17 countries in terms of population, keyed by call code, with separate chaining.

Algorithm 13.7 handles insertion in a hash table with chained lists. For a record x we need a function $\mathsf{Key}(x)$, which gets the key of x. The function $\mathsf{Hash}(k)$ calculates the hash value of key k and can be any of the hash functions that we have seen, depending on the type of the key. Because the hash table contains lists of items, if our hash table is called T, then $T[h]$ is the list containing the items with keys whose hash value is h.

Searching an item in a hash table starts the same way as insertion; see algorithm 13.8. Then when we find the bucket that should hold the list with the item we are looking for, we just search the list in the bucket. $\mathsf{SearchInList}(L, i)$ searches for item i in list L, so we actually need to call $\mathsf{SearchInList}(T[h], x)$. Recall that the function $\mathsf{SearchInList}$ returns the item we are looking for or NULL if the item is not in the list. If we want to remove items from a

---

Algorithm 13.7: Insertion in hash table with chained lists.

InsertInHash(T, x)
    Input: T, a hash table
            x, a record to insert in the hash table
    Result: x is inserted into T

1 $h \leftarrow$ Hash(Key(x))
2 InsertInList($T[h]$, NULL, x)

Algorithm 13.8: Search in hash table with chained lists.

SearchInHash(T, x) $\rightarrow$ TRUE or FALSE
    Input: T, a hash table
            x, a record to lookup in the hash table
    Output: TRUE if found, FALSE otherwise

1 $h \leftarrow$ Hash(Key(x))
2 **if** SearchInList($T[h]$, x) = NULL **then**
3   **return** FALSE
4 **else**
5   **return** TRUE

---

hash table, we use again a variation of the same theme, as in algorithm 13.9, using function RemoveFromList(L, d) that removes the first node containing d from the list and returns it, if d is present in the list, otherwise returns NULL.

From algorithm 13.8 it follows that the cost of looking for an item with hashing with separate chaining varies, depending on the item. First, we have to take into account the cost of the hash function. If we are hashing numeric keys, this is the cost of algorithm 13.3, which is the time taken by a division operation. We take it as constant, $O(1)$. If we are hashing strings, this is is the cost of algorithm 13.6, which is $\Theta(n)$, where n is the length of the string. As the algorithm is fast, and it only depends on the key, not on the number of items we hash, we also treat that as constant. To that we have to add the cost of the operations required after we have found the hash value. This may be $O(1)$, if the bucket points to NULL, or $O(|L|)$, where $|L|$ is the length of the list L, because searching in a list takes linear time as we go from one item to the next. The question then is, how long can a list be?

Algorithm 13.9: Removal from hash table with chained lists.

RemoveFromHash(T, x) → x or NULL
    Input: T, a hash table
            x, a record to remove from the hash table
    Output: x, the record x if it was removed, or NULL if x was not in the
                 hash table

1   $h \leftarrow$ Hash(Key(x))
2   **return** RemoveFromList($T[h], x$)

The answer depends on the hash function. If the hash function is a good one, so that it distributes all keys evenly in the hash table, with no bias whatsoever, then we expect the length of each list to be about n/m, where n is the number of keys and m is the size of the hash table. The number n/m is called the *load factor* of the table. For an unsuccessful search we need the time to calculate the key and $\Theta(n/m)$ to get to the end of the list. For a successful search we have to go through the items in the list until we meet the item we are looking for. Because items are added in the beginning of the list, we have to go through the items in the list that were added to the list after the item we are looking for. It can be proved that the time for the search in the list is $\Theta(1 + (n-1)/2m)$.

We see that in both successful and unsuccessful searches, the time required to go through the list depends on n/m. If the number of keys is proportional to the size of the table, that is, $n = cm$, then the time to search a list becomes constant. Indeed, for an unsuccessful search we have $\Theta(n/m) = \Theta(cm/m) = \Theta(c) = O(1)$. An successful search cannot take longer than a successful one, so again it takes $O(1)$ time. In both cases we achieve constant time.

Constant average performance is a remarkable feat, and as a result hash tables are popular storage mechanisms. There are two major caveats to take into account, though. First, there is no ordering in hash tables. The records are inserted in the table in random places, if the hash function is a good one. So if we want to search for items in some order (say, numerical, or alphabetical), where we find an item and then we want to find the item following it in that ordering, hash tables are not suitable. Second, the performance of the hash table depends on the load factor. We saw that the time to search when $n = cm$ is bound by c; we would like to ensure then that c does not get very large. For example, if we know we will insert n items, we can create a hash table of

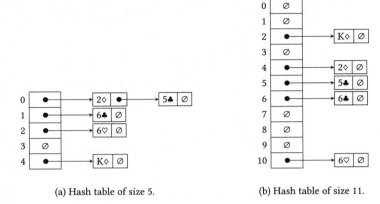

(a) Hash table of size 5.   (b) Hash table of size 11.

Figure 13.12
Hash table resizing.

size $2n$ so that on average the search will take no more than two comparisons. But what happens if we do not know the number of items in advance, or if our estimate is wrong? If this happens we *resize* the hash table. We create a new, bigger hash table, we take all items from the overloaded hash table, we insert them into the new bigger one, we discard the old table, and we use the new hash table from that point onward. A resize operation is computationally expensive, so it pays to have a good estimate of our needs in order to avoid it. Otherwise, most hash table implementations monitor their load factor. When this reaches a threshold, such as 0.5, they resize it. In this way lookup in a hash table will remain constant, on average, but insertion will be slow when inserting an item entails resizing the hash table.

An example of resizing is in figure 13.12. Initially we have a hash table of size 5 and we insert records whose keys are playing cards. Each card has a numerical value: the ace of clubs is 0, up to the king of clubs with value 12; then the ace of diamonds is 13, the ace of hearts is 25, and the ace of spades is 38; the highest value goes to the king of spades with 51. In figure 13.12a, the table has size 5 and the load factor is 1. We then decide to increase the size of the table. In order to have a prime number for the modulo operation, we go beyond 2×5 to 11. We re-insert the cards as in figure 13.12b; any new cards will be inserted in the enlarged table.

It is important to understand that the performance of hash tables is probabilistic. With a good hash function, the probability that search will take more than n/m is very small, but it exists. We cannot guarantee that every chain will be short but that on average the probability that it will grow more than the average size is small. Also, when we resort to resizing, performance will suffer while resizing is going on.

Hash tables vary and have found many different uses in a great deal of applications. Their probabilistic behavior gives us an opportunity to trade off time versus speed, allowing us to fine-tune applications that use hash tables. If space is not a problem and speed is, we just create a hash table as large as we can. If space is at a premium, then we compromise on speed by stuffing more keys into a smaller table.

As hash tables do not order their contents, a common use is for implementing data structures where we are only interested in finding and storing something, not in its order. One such data structure is the *set*. Sets contain items, and items are required to be unique. Hash tables accommodate these requirements directly: if we define a hash function for the items, we just insert the items to the hash table, provided they are not already there. If we want to check whether an item exists in a set, then we just check whether it exists in the hash table, using the hash function on the item. Sets are not ordered: the items are just inserted into the hash table, and as we have seen there is no notion of ordering of the items in the way they are put in place. The lists stemming from each bucket are ordered, but that does not correspond to any sorting rule, say alphabetical, or numerical, for the items themselves. This does not matter because sets in mathematics are unordered anyway.

Another common data structure that is well accommodated with hash tables is the *dictionary*, also called a *map* or an *associative array*. A dictionary handles key-value pairs, like an ordinary dictionary that contains entries (keys) and definitions (values). We use a key to retrieve the associated value, as we do in a real dictionary where from a word we get its definition. Unlike a real dictionary, these dictionaries are not ordered, as the hash tables underlying them do not provide ordering. Real dictionaries are ordered to facilitate search; hash tables do their magic so that we do not have to search at all. A dictionary is like a set where the elements of the set are key-value pairs; these we can represent internally in the dictionary with a two element array. If we want to insert a new key-value pair, we hash the key and insert the key-value pair in the hash table, as in algorithm 13.10. Note that we must first check whether the key-value pair is already in the dictionary. The function SearchInListByKey($T[h]$, k) searches through the list in $T[h]$ for the item that is the key-value pair with key k and returns it when it finds it, or

---

Algorithm 13.10: Insertion in a dictionary (map).

InsertInMap(T, k, v)
    Input: T, a hash table
        k, the key of the key-value pair
        v, the value of the key-value pair
    Result: value v is inserted into the dictionary associated with the
        key k

1   $h \leftarrow$ Hash(k)
2   $p \leftarrow$ SearchInListByKey($T[h]$, k)
3   **if** $p = $ NULL **then**
4       $p \leftarrow$ CreateArray(2)
5       $p[0] \leftarrow k$
6       $p[1] \leftarrow v$
7   InsertInList($T[h]$, NULL, p)
8   **else**
9       $p[1] = v$

---

it returns NULL if it does not. That is slightly different than SearchInList, which searches for a particular item, checking for equality with the item. SearchInListByKey searches for a particular item checking for equality with the *key* of the item. That is quite a common pattern: search functions in data structures often take a parameter that specifies how to check equality, say using a particular attribute of an item, or a combination of attributes, instead of the whole item.

If the item is not there, then we insert it in line 7 using the function call InsertInList($T[h]$, NULL, p). If it is, we redefine the dictionary entry for k by assigning the second element of the existing key-value pair to the new value.

If we want to retrieve the value associated with a key in the hash table, we hash the key, we fetch the key-value pair stored in the hash table, and if we find it we return the value; see algorithm 13.11. Finally, if we want to remove a key-value pair from a dictionary, we hash the key and remove the key-value pair corresponding to the key from the hash table; see algorithm 13.12. We use a function RemoveFromListByKey(L, k) that removes the key-value pair with key k from the list L and returns it, if it exists, or returns NULL if it does not exist. RemoveFromListByKey is similar to RemoveFromList in the same way

---

Algorithm 13.11: Lookup in a dictionary (map).

Lookup(T, k) → v or NULL
    Input: T, a hash table
           k, a key
    Output: v, the corresponding value, if it exists, or NULL otherwise

1   $h \leftarrow$ Hash(k)
2   $p \leftarrow$ SearchInHash($T[h], k$)
3   **if** $p =$ NULL **then**
4   **return** NULL;
5   **else**
6   **return** $p[1]$

---

that SearchInListByKey is similar to SearchInList: it finds what to remove by searching the list for an item checking equality with the given key.

This triplet of algorithms is not much different than plain handling of entries in hash tables that we saw above.

Algorithm 13.12: Removal from dictionary (map).

RemoveFromMap(T, k) → $[k, v]$
    Input: T, a hash table
           k, a key to remove the corresponding key-value pair from the
           dictionary
    Output: $[k, v]$, the key-value pair corresponding to k if it was
              removed, or NULL if no corresponding key-value pair was
              found in the dictionary

1   $h \leftarrow$ Hash(k)
2   **return** RemoveFromListByKey($T[h], k$)

13.6   Digital Fingerprints

The idea of hashing is a fundamental component of applications that deal with identifying a piece of data. If you have a record of a person, consisting of a number of attributes, then it's easy to identify a record: you just check whether you already have a record with the same keys. Now imagine that your "record" does not fit nicely into the mould of attributes and keys. Your record may be an image, or a sound, say a song. You want to find out whether you have encountered that song before. There are no predefined attributes attached to a song. The song's title, performer, and composer are outside the song. When you are handed data containing a recording of a song, you only have a recording of the sound frequencies that make up a song. Your record, if you want to think of it that way, is a set of frequencies. How do you search for it?

What you want to do is to derive something unique from the sound recording, so that you can use that unique feature as a key for identifying it. Let's use a different example for a moment, and suppose that you need to identify a human. It is not easy to identify an unknown person and match that person to a set of known persons of interest. You have to use something unique for that person and try to match it against something unique for each of the persons in the known persons set. A method we have been using for a couple of hundred years is to take fingerprints as pieces of identification. We have the fingerprints of the known persons and we also get the fingerprint of the person we want to identify. If we can match the fingerprint of the unknown person to a person we know, then the person ceases to be unknown: we have identified the person.

In the digital realm we have *digital fingerprints*. These are some features of digital data that we can use to identify data reliably. In practice, say you have a sound clip from a song and you want to find out which song this is. You have a big database of songs, whose digital fingerprints you have already calculated. You calculate the digital fingerprint of the sound clip, and you try to find a match with a fingerprint in the songs database. If you do, you've found a song. Hashes come into play because you may have millions and millions of songs and therefore millions and millions of fingerprints. You must be able to find a match (or determine that no match exists) very fast. Also, there is no notion of ordering in the song fingerprints. So a big hash table is ideal for that purpose. The keys are our fingerprints and the records are the details of each song, like title, artist, and so on.

To establish a digital fingerprint for sound we have to recall that a sound is a vibration that propagates through a medium, usually air. Each sound has one or more frequencies associated with it. A pure note has a single frequency, for example, the note A has a frequency 440 Herz (Hz) in an even tempered scale and the note C has a frequency of 261.63Hz. A sound clip has many frequencies, changing over time, as different instruments and voices combine

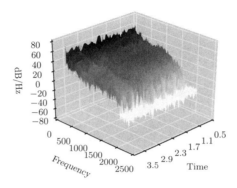

Figure 13.13
3D representation of energies, frequencies, and time.

together. Moreover, some frequencies sound louder than others, such as when one instrument is played more loudly than the rest. The difference in sound intensity are differences in the energy of the corresponding frequencies. Different frequencies have different energies at different points in time in a song, as some of them get louder, some of them get softer, or some of them may even die out.

We can represent graphically a song with a 3D plot of energies, frequencies, and time. A 3D representation of energies, frequencies, and time for a segment of 3 seconds of a song is in figure 13.13. Note that the (0, 0, 0) point is at the far side of the graph, and we start half a second into the song (because there is too much silence at its beginning). The figure tells us that this song segment has predominantly low frequencies, as they have the most energy: at each point in time, the low frequencies have the highest z-values. In the z-axis we measure frequency energy as decibels (dB) by Herz. The negative sign comes into play because a decibel is logarithmic. It represents the ratio of two values: $10 \log(v/b)$, where b is the base value. In our case we have $b = 1$, so for $v < 1$ we have negative values.

Instead of using a 3D representation like the one in figure 13.13 we usually restrict ourselves to two dimensions, using just the color to denote the energy value at each time and frequency point. We call this representation a *spectrogram*. Figure 13.14a is the spectrogram corresponding to figure 13.13.

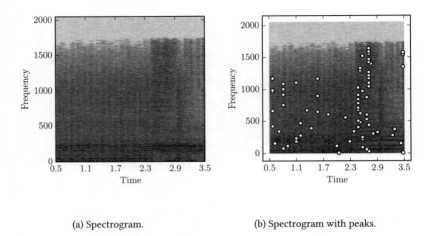

(a) Spectrogram.   (b) Spectrogram with peaks.

Figure 13.14
Spectrogram and frequency energy peaks.

You probably agree that this representation is much easier to grasp than the previous one, yet no information has been lost. Less is more arises pretty often in visualizing data.

In the spectrogram you can see that the energy does not change smoothly over time and frequencies. There are places where a spot with high energy (dark) is bordered by spots with low energy (bright). The equivalent in figure 13.13 is when a value is a peak, relative to its neighboring values. We can detect such peaks mathematically. If we plot them on top of the spectrogram we get figure 13.14b. Now, it turns out that the pattern of frequency energy peaks in a song can act as its digital fingerprint. Hence, we can take the peaks of a sound segment and try to see if they match the peaks of a song we already know. If our sound segment is shorter than a song, we'll try to match the peaks in a segment of the song, equal in duration. When we find a match, there is a good chance that we have indeed found the song.

In practice, having just frequencies as our fingerprint is not the best we can do. A song is better characterized by pairs of peaks and the time difference between them. If we have a frequency peak f_1 at time t_1 and another frequency peak f_2 at time t_2, instead of using f_1 and f_2 as keys into the hash table, we create a new key as $k = f_1 : f_2 : t_2 - t_1$, as in figure 13.15a. The key

k can be the string representation of the concatenation of its parts, such as "1620.32:1828.78:350", where the time difference is in milliseconds.

The number of possible pairs (f_x, f_y) in a song can be large, as it entails pairing all frequency peaks between them. Mathematically, this is equivalent to all the possible ways of choosing k items out of n items, with $k = 2$ and n the number of frequency peaks in the song, and there is even a notation for it:

$$\frac{n!}{k!(n-k)!} = \binom{n}{k}$$

This is the number of possible *combinations*, that is, selections without ordering, of k elements out of n. The notation $\binom{n}{k}$ is read "n choose k."

If formula for combinations seems cryptic, consider how we find the number of *permutation*, that is, ordered selections of k items out of a set of n items. There are n ways to choose the first item, then for each one of them there are $n - 1$ ways to choose the second item, and so on until the kth item, which is the last one left and so there is only one way to choose it. In total we have the product $n \times (n - 1) \times \cdots \times (n - k + 1)$ ways to choose in order k items out of n. But:

$$n \times (n - 1) \times \cdots (n - k + 1) = \frac{n!}{(n-k)!}$$

Because permutations are ordered, we need to divide this figure by the number of possible orderings of k items. There are k ways to choose the first item; for each one of them there are $k - 1$ ways to choose the second item, and so on as before until the last item. So there are $k \times (k - 1) \times \cdots \times 1 = k!$ possible orderings of k items. Because the number of combinations is the number of permutations divided by the number of possible orderings, we arrive at the figure for $\binom{n}{k}$.

Returning to our frequency pairings, the value $\binom{n}{2}$ can lead to a large number of keys in our hash table. If we have 100 frequency peaks in a song, it is $\binom{100}{2} = 4950$, so we need that number of keys for that song only. To avoid an explosion in the size of the hash table, we compromise and use only a subset of the possible pairs for each frequency peak; for instance, we may decide to use only up to ten pairs. The actual value, called *fan-out factor*, can be adjusted to ensure better detection with less storage and increased speed. A bigger fan-out factor requires more storage and improves detection accuracy, while requiring more time for detection. Figure 13.15b shows the pairs taken into account for calculating hashes of a single peak, when we specify a fan-out of

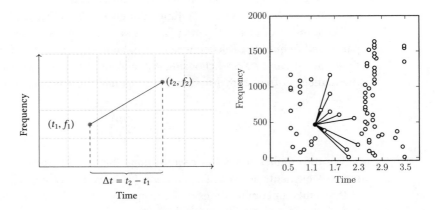

(a) Frequencies hash key is $f_1 : f_2 : \Delta t$.   (b) Hashing frequencies with fan-out ten.

Figure 13.15
Hashing frequency peaks.

ten and we require the first ten peaks following the selected one in the time axis.

To summarize, to populate the hash table we derive the spectrogram of each known song and use as keys the frequency pairings and their time difference based on a convenient fan-out factor. The records associated with these keys are the details of possible matches, such as the song title and artist. When we want to identify a song, we derive in the same way its spectrogram and its frequency pairings and search the hash table for these keys. We pick the song with the most matches as the one closest to the one we are looking for.

13.7   Bloom Filters

Hash tables are remarkably efficient for storing and retrieving data. Sometimes, if we relax our requirements from them we can achieve even greater efficiency while saving space as well. In particular, suppose we are not interested in storing and retrieving data, but in just checking whether some data exist in a set, without bothering to actual retrieve them. Moreover, suppose that we can accept being told, rarely, that the data are in the set even when they are not, although we cannot accept being told that the data are not the set when they are. We are willing to accept some *false positives*, a statement that something is true when in fact it is not, but we are not willing to accept any *false negatives*, a statement that something is false when in fact it is true.

Such situations arise in many contexts. If we have a big database, there is a cost associated with the retrieval of data from it. If we can find out instantaneously whether some data are in the database, we are spared the trouble of going to look for them in the database in vain if they are not there. A false positive is acceptable because it means that we will incur an unnecessary cost for trying to retrieve something that does not exist, but this should not be a problem if false positives are rare.

Cache mechanisms work in a similar manner. A *cache* is a temporary hold of data that is frequently accessed. We may have data stored in a variety of storage mechanisms, but some subset of the data is more frequently accessed than the rest. We put that subset in a fast storage medium, for example, main memory. When we want to fetch some data we first check whether they are present in the cache. If they are, we return them from our fast storage medium. If they are not, we have to go and fetch them from where the bulk of the data reside. A false positive means that we will believe that the data are in the cache. That is not a problem because we will quickly find out that we are mistaken and will turn our attention to the bulk storage. As long as this happens rarely this again should not be a problem.

Various kinds of filters follow the same principle. In a filter we want to tag the bad apples and let the good items through. When filtering spam e-mail, we want to tag as spam all e-mail coming from addresses that are known spammers. We definitely do not want to have false negatives, a mail from a known spammer passing through. We are willing to accept a low level of false positives, messages that end up in our junk folder marked as spam when they are not. The same logic applies to URL shorteners. A company providing a URL shortening service must do its best to guarantee that the shortened URLs that it handles do not lead to malicious sites; therefore, when a URL is up for shortening, it has to check whether it does belong to the set of misbehaving sites. The company should not tolerate false negatives, known malicious URLs that are missed. It may tolerate a small percentage of good URLs tagged as bad, as long as the percentage is low. In digital forensics we have at our disposal an inventory of malware files. We can take apart these files into blocks and insert them in our filter. Then when we want to scan some storage medium for mischievous activity, we can get the blocks of the storage medium and check whether any of them are present in our filter.

Algorithm 13.13: Insert in Bloom filter.

InsertInBloomFilter(T, x)
    Input: T, a bit array of size m
            x, a record to insert to the set represented by the Bloom filter
    Result: the record is inserted in the Bloom filter by setting the bits
            $h_0(x), h_1(x), \ldots, h_{k-1}(x)$ to 1

1   **for** $i \leftarrow 0$ **to** k **do**
2       $h \leftarrow h_i(x)$
3         $T[h] \leftarrow 1$

An efficient and popular way to implement a set membership mechanism when some false positives are not a problem is to use *Bloom filters*, named after their inventor, Burton Bloom. A Bloom filter is a large array T of bits, of size m. Initially all bits are set to zero, the filter being empty. Each time we want to add an item to the set, we hash the item with a number of k independent hash functions; by independent we mean that the hash values they produce for the same key are completely independent among functions. Each of these hash functions should have a range from 0 to $m - 1$. For each hash value we get, we set the corresponding bit of the bit array to 1. When we want to check whether an item is in the filter, we hash it with the k functions and check whether all the k hash values are set to one in the bit array. If they are, we assume that the item has been entered into the filter; there is a probability that it is actually not in the filter, because all the corresponding bits have been set by other elements already in the filter. The probability is acceptable as long as it is kept low. If not all k hash values are set, then we definitely know that the item is not in the filter.

In more concrete terms, we have at our disposal k independent hash functions $h_0, h_1, \ldots, h_{k-1}$, each one having a range from 0 to $m - 1$. If we want to insert an item x in the filter, we calculate $h_0(x), h_1(x), \ldots, h_{k-1}(x)$ and set $T[h] = 1$ for all $h = h_i(x)$, where $i = 0, 1, \ldots, k - 1$; see algorithm 13.13. If we want to check whether an item x exists in a Bloom filter, again we calculate $h_0(x), h_1(x), \ldots, h_{k-1}(x)$. If $T[h] = 1$ for all $h = h_i(x)$, where $i = 0, 1, \ldots, k - 1$ then we say that the item is present in the filter. If not, we say that it is not; see algorithm 13.14.

When we start using a Bloom filter all its entries are set to 0. Then as we enter members in the set, some of the entries are set to 1. In figure 13.16 we

---

Algorithm 13.14: Check membership with Bloom filter.

IsInBloomFilter(T, x) $\rightarrow$ TRUE or FALSE
    Input: T, a bit array of size m
             x, a record to check if it is a member of the set represented by
             the Bloom filter
    Output: TRUE if x is in the Bloom filter, FALSE otherwise

1   **for** $i \leftarrow 0$ **to** k **do**
2       $h \leftarrow h_i(x)$
3   **if** $T[h] = 0$ **then**
4   **return** FALSE
5   **return** TRUE

---

start with an empty filter with a table of 16 bits, in which we add "In", "this", "paper", "trade-offs". Each of the first three items hashes to two empty table entries. Then "trade-offs" hashes to one entry that has already been set to 1 and one empty entry. Such a partial conflict is not counted as a real conflict in a Bloom filter, so if we were checking for membership of "trade-offs" in the filter before inserting it, we would get a FALSE value. This is why we use more than one hash function: we expect that it will be more difficult for all hash values of an item to fall into already set entries of the filter. You may question how far this strategy could go, however. If we use many hash functions, then the Bloom filter will start filling up fast and we will have conflicts as most of the entries will have been set. That is a valid question. We'll see that we can configure our filter with an optimum number of hash functions.

If we continue adding items in the filter we will get a conflict, a situation where an item is reported as already being in the set, although it is not. It is a statement that something is true when in reality it is not, that is, a false positive. In particular, we'll get a false positive when algorithm 13.14 returns TRUE for a record x, although in reality the record x is not in the filter. In figure 13.17 we do just that by adding items in the Bloom filter. After inserting "among" we discover that the filter treats "certain" as if it were already there.

That may seem catastrophic, but it is not. If our application tolerates false positives, and we have already seen examples of such applications, we can live with this behavior. The real issue is what we get in return.

At this point in our example we have a false positive, but we have successfully inserted five items in the set. We have a $1/6 \approx 17\%$ false positive rate

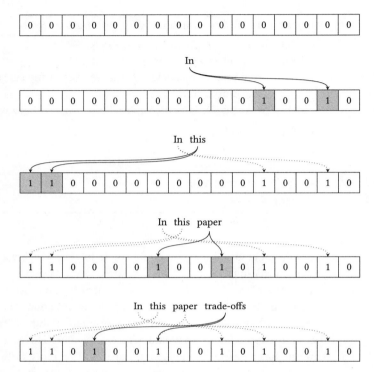

Figure 13.16
Bloom filter insertion of "In", "this", "paper", "trade-offs" in a 16 bit table.

while using a 16 bit table. Now here is a crucial part: *we do not really store the members of our set anywhere.* We just set entries in our hash table to one. A Bloom filter allows us to represent a set, without having to store the items of the set. If we had used a common hash table to represent the set words, then we would need space to store the table plus space to store the actual strings corresponding to the words. The words in our example take up 41 bytes, equal to 328 bits, assuming that each letter takes up one byte. We gain space in the order of $328/16 \approx 20$, as long as we can accept false positives.

We have used a rudimentary Bloom filter of 16 bits for a handful of words, employing two hash functions. In reality we would use a bigger filter to handle a bigger amount of items, not necessarily with two hash functions. The number m of bits of the filter (its size), the number n of items we wish to

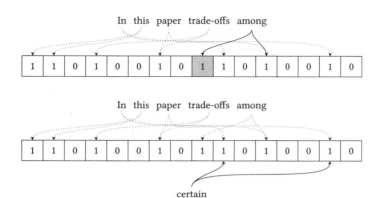

Figure 13.17
Inserting "among", false positive for "trade-offs".

handle, and the number k of hash functions are all parameters that we can balance to get the behavior we want.

If we have just one hash function, then the probability that a particular bit in the table will be set when we hash an item is $(1/m)$, so the probability that this particular bit will not be set is $(1 - 1/m)$. If we use k independent hash functions, then the probability that the particular bit will not be set is $(1 - 1/m)^k$. We can write that as $(1 - 1/m)^{m(\frac{k}{m})}$. When m is large enough we get from calculus that $(1 - 1/m)^m = 1/e = e^{-1}$. Using this fact, the probability that a particular bit will not be set is $e^{-k/m}$. If our Bloom filter contains n items, then the probability that the bit will not be set is $e^{-kn/m}$. Turning this over, the probability that the bit will be set is $(1 - e^{-kn/m})$. The probability that we'll get a false positive is the probability that, after we have inserted n items, we check for an item that is not in the filter and all k hash values of that item are in positions that are set. That is equal to the probability that k particular bits are set: $p = (1 - e^{-kn/m})^k$.

From the last expression we can calculate the optimal values for the parameters of a Bloom filter. If we have a given m (filter size) and n (number of items), using again some calculus we can derive the best value for k as $k = (m/n) \ln 2$. For example, if we want to handle 1 billion elements with a Bloom filter of 10 billion bits, equal to 1.25 Gbytes, we need to use $k = (10^{10}/10^9)/ln2 \approx 7$ different, independent hash functions. With these parameters, because $n/m = 10^9/10^{10} = 1/10$, the probability of a false positive is $\left(1 - e^{-7/10}\right)^7 \approx 0.008$,

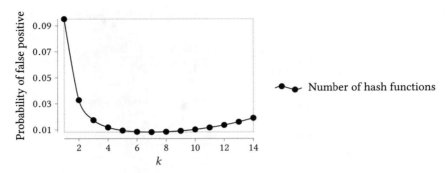

Figure 13.18
Probability of false positive in Bloom filter as a function of hash functions, k, when $n/m = 10$.

or 8‰; note that this is *per mille*, not percent. We can plot the function $\left(1 - e^{-k/10}\right)^k$ for different values of k, as in figure 13.18. The plot shows that with even five hash functions we can achieve a false positive rate of less than 1%.

If we take $k = (m/n)\ln 2$ and substitute it into $p = (1 - e^{-kn/m})^k$, then simplify the result, we get the size m of a Bloom filter that has a false positive rate of p and uses k hash functions: $m = -n\ln p/(\ln 2)^2$. For example, if we want to handle one billion items with a false positive rate of 1%, we get $m \approx 9{,}585{,}058{,}378$, about 10 billion bits, or 1.25 Gbytes, as in our example. If the average size of an item is ten bytes, then with 1.25 Gbytes we can handle 10 Gbytes of data with the computational cost of a few hash functions!

Classic Bloom filters, as we have described them, are remarkable in the savings they can produce, but apart from false positives, they have another liability that may limit the extent of their use. You cannot delete an item from a Bloom filter. If you have two items and a bit is set by both items, then if we unset the bits that correspond to one of the items we accidentally unset one of the bits that correspond to the other item as well. In figure 13.19 both "paper" and "trade-offs" hash to the same position in the Bloom filter, $T[6]$. If we want to remove one of them from the filter, then we will unset $T[6]$, which should be set because it is needed by the other item.

The solution is not to use an array of bits as the hash table, but an array of counters, for example, integers, initialized to zero. Each time we insert an element we increment by one the counters corresponding to the hash positions.

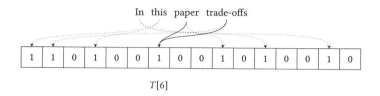

$T[6]$

Figure 13.19
The problem of deletions in Bloom filters.

Algorithm 13.15: Insert into counting Bloom filter.

InsertInCntBloomFilter(T, x)
    Input: T, an integer array of size m
              x, a record to insert to the set represented by the counting
              Bloom filter
    Result: the record is inserted in the counting Bloom filter by
              increasing by 1 the counters at $h_0(x), h_1(x), \ldots, h_{k-1}(x)$

1   **for** $i \leftarrow 0$ **to** k **do**
2       $h \leftarrow h_i(x)$
3       $T[h] \leftarrow T[h] + 1$

To remove an element we decrement the same counters. Checking for membership is the same as before, checking for zero in all the hash values of an item. We call these filters *counting Bloom filters*. Algorithm 13.15 shows how to add items and algorithm 13.16 shows how to remove items. Membership check in counting Bloom filters is the same as with normal Bloom filters.

If we use a counting Bloom filter in our example, the situation will evolve as in figure 13.20. We insert items by adding to the counter that corresponds to each hash position. When the time comes to remove an item, we simply reduce the counters that correspond to the hash position of the item we want to remove, as in the last part of the figure. Introducing counters solves our problem, but it comes with a price. In simple Bloom filters each position in the table takes the space of a single bit. In counting Bloom filters each position in the table takes the space of a counter; that could be a byte or even more. So our economies of space are less than with simple Bloom filters.

There is one last thing that we have somehow swept under the carpet. We have assumed the existence of a set of independent hash functions that for

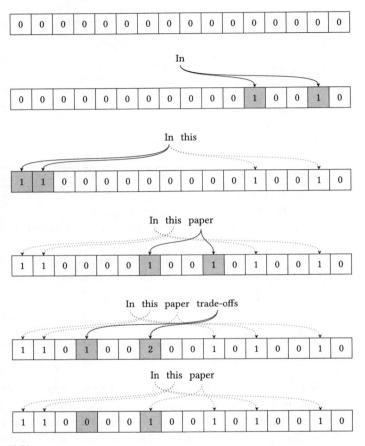

Figure 13.20
Insertions and deletion in counting Bloom filter.

Algorithm 13.16: Remove from a counting Bloom filter.

RemoveFromCntBloomFilter(T, x)
    Input: T, an integer array of size m

           x, a record to remove from the set represented by the counting Bloom filter

    Result: the record is removed from the counting Bloom filter by decreasing by 1 the counters at $h_0(x), h_1(x), \ldots, h_{k-1}(x)$

1   **for** $i \leftarrow 0$ **to** k **do**
2       $h \leftarrow h_i(x)$
3   **if** $T[h] \neq 0$ **then**
4           $T[h] \leftarrow T[h] - 1$

Algorithm 13.17: FNV-1a based 32 bits hash.

FNV-1a(s, i) $\rightarrow h$
    Input: s, a string

         i, an integer

    Output: the 32 bits hash value of s

1   $h \leftarrow$ 0x811C9DC5
2   $p \leftarrow$ 0x01000193
3   $h \leftarrow h \oplus i$
4   **foreach** c in s **do**
5       $h \leftarrow h \oplus$ Ordinal(c)
6       $h \leftarrow (h \times p)$ & 0xFFFFFFFF
7   **return** h

---

the same input produce a set of different hash values. We have not shown any such hash functions. Our hash algorithms take a specific and produce a specific output. Fortunately, there exist hash algorithms that can vary their output depending on a parameter we pass to them, and the variation in the output is such that they behave as different, independent hash functions. These are the ones we can use in Bloom filters. Algorithm 13.17 is an example of such an algorithm, based on the Fowler/Noll/Vo or FNV hash algorithm, named after Glenn Fowler, Landon Curt Noll, and Phong Vo who invented it.

The algorithm takes a string s and another parameter i and returns a 32 bits hash value. For different values of i it produces different hash values for the

Table 13.4

The bitwise AND operation.

		x	
		0	1
y	0	0	0
	1	0	1

same string s, so we can use it as a basis for a Bloom filter. To accomplish that, the hash value is initialized with a seemingly magic number in line 1. It is XORed with an integer i that we pass as parameter. Then, in line 5, it takes the value of each character of the input string and XORs it with the current hash value. This value of each character is given by the function that Ordinal(c) returns the code used for a character. This may be a Unicode code or an ASCII code, depending on the representation. In line 6 the algorithm multiples the result with another magic number p, set in line 2, and takes the last 32 bits of the result because we want a 32 bits hash value. To take the last 32 bits we perform the *bitwise* AND operation, with symbol & (an ampersand), between the product and the number 0xFFFFFFFF, which is equal to 32 bits set to 1. The bitwise AND operation takes two sequences of bits and outputs one in each position where both sequences have one, or zero otherwise; see table 13.4. In arithmetic, taking the last 32 bits is equivalent to taking the remainder of the division with 2^{32}, but with the bitwise AND operation we avoid the division altogether; we just switch off any bit beyond the 32 bits instead of calculating $(h \times p) \bmod 2^{32}$.

Incidentally, this a useful and common trick. When we want to switch off specific bits, we use a binary pattern, in our case 0xFFFFFFFF, that contains only the bits we want to remain switched on, if they are already switched on. Such a binary pattern is called a *bit mask* or simply a *mask*. In figure 13.21 you can see the application of a bit mask of four bits to a number with eight bits to switch off all bits apart from the last four. A bit mask is not necessarily composed of all ones, although that is a common situation.

While we are at that, the counterpart of the bitwise AND is the *bitwise* OR; see table 13.5. We can use a bit mask with the bitwise OR operator when we want to switch bits on, instead of off, as in figure 13.22. The symbol for the bitwise OR is usually a vertical bar (|). We had no use for bitwise OR in our algorithm, but it's good to know it because you may come across it. This

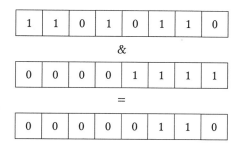

Figure 13.21

Applying bit mask 00001111 = 0xF to 11010110 with bitwise AND.

Table 13.5

The bitwise OR operation.

		x	
		0	1
y	0	0	1
	1	1	1

is particularly important because there is room for confusion in certain programming languages. In these languages, a && b means that the expression is true if both a and b are true, whereas a || b means that the expression is true if either a or b is true. These correspond to **and** and **or** in our algorithms. At the same time, a & b means to calculate the bitwise AND of a and b, whereas a | b means to calculate the bitwise OR of a and b. One pair of operators talks about truth, the other manipulates numbers in binary form. Mixing them unknowingly is not recommended.

Talking about the particularities of programming language, another feature of many languages allows us to simplify line 6 of algorithm 13.17 as just $h \leftarrow h \times p$. If the programming language stores numbers in 32 bits, then whenever $h \times p$ exceeds the greatest 32 bits number only 32 bits will actually be stored in h, because of overflow. So there is no need for any bit mask or modulo operation.

It seems like we have come full circle. We started with algorithms that looked like hocus-pocus and we have arrived at an algorithm with impenetrable numbers embedded into them. The numbers in lines 1 and 2 have proven to be good at making the output of the hash function look random. In essence, we need to take a set of bits as input (our string) and jumble it so we

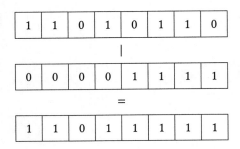

Figure 13.22
Applying bit mask 00001111 = 0xF to 11010110 with bitwise OR.

get a different set that is seemingly unrelated to the input. That is not easy to do. It requires trying several randomization strategies, and we must check carefully that the behavior we get meets our requirements: in our case that different values for i give us different hash functions that behave as if they were truly independent.

Notes

The pigeonhole principle is attributed to the mathematician Peter Gustav Lejeune Dirichlet in 1834, although he called it *Schubfachprinzip*, or "drawer principle." According to a history of hashing [118, p. xv], the idea was first mentioned by Hans Peter Luhn in an internal IBM document in January 2013. Arnold I. Dumey, the co-inventor of the postal sorting machine and a cryptanalyst for the U.S. Army's Signals Intelligence Service (SIS) and later the Natural Security Agency (NSA), presented the idea some years later, in 1956, in what was the first paper on hashing [54], although he did not use the word. The word itself was used for the idea by Robert Morris, a cryptographer and computer scientist in 1968 [146]. Morris worked at Bell Labs, where he made important contributions to the Unix operating system, and then at NSA from 1986 until his retirement. A simple example of a family of perfect hash functions has been proposed by Cichelli [37]. The encoding of the individual characters in algorithm 13.2 was found with GPERF [173].

William George Horner presented the method that took his name in 1819 [97]. However, the method had also been discovered by others before. Newton used the method some 150 years before Horner, and it was also used in 13th-century China by Ch'in Chiu Shao [113, p. 486]. A similar process was effected by Paolo Ruffini in 1804, but Horner and Ruffini seem not to have known of the earlier developments. Horner's presentation is remarkably complicated, compared with today's expositions in mathematical texts; in the original publication it was noted that "The elementary character of the subject was the professed objection; his recondite mode of treating it was the professed passport for its admission" [190, p. 232]. Algorithm 13.6 is similar to the hash function used by the Java programming language [22, pp. 45–50].

The song identification process we describe is a simplified version of the one presented by the Shazam service [212, 89]. The figures were drawn with code derived from the dejavu project (https://github.com/worldveil/dejavu). Burton Bloom presented the filters that bear his name in 1970 [23], giving hyphenation as an example use for them. Bloom's paper starts with the sentence, "In this paper trade-offs among certain computational factors in hash coding are analyzed," the beginning of which we used in our examples. Simson Garfinkel has written a short introduction on digital forensics [76]; for an application of Bloom filters to digital forensics, see [222]. The FNV hash algorithm is described in [70]. There are other hash algorithms that are commonly used in Bloom filters with arguably better results, such as MurmurHash, Jenkins, and FarmHash. You can easily find implementations of them in different languages with a web search. For a tutorial introduction and a derivation of the mathematical formulas underpinning Bloom filters, see [24]. Mitzenmacher and Upfal include Bloom filters in their textbook on randomized algorithms [144, section 5.5.3]. Broder and Mitzenmacher have written a comprehensive review of network applications of Bloom filters [30].

Exercises

1. Describe a way that you can use a hash table to find the unique elements of an unsorted array or list, and implement a program to do that. Then, do the opposite: find a way and write a program to find the elements that appear multiple times in an unsorted array or list.

2. You are given an unsorted array containing integers and another integer s. How can you find all pairs of numbers (a, b) where a and b are contained in the array, so that $a + b = s$, in time $O(n)$? Write a program which does that using a hash table.

3. How could you find the most common word in a text using a hash table?

4.   How can you implement the union, intersection, and difference of two sets using hash tables?

5.   An *anagram* is a piece of text obtained by rearranging the letters of another piece of text. For example, "alert" is an anagram for "alter". Suppose you have a dictionary containing all English words. It is possible to find all words that are anagrams of another word by using a hash table, as follows. Go through each word in the dictionary. Sort the characters of the word; for "alter" you would get "aelrt". You then use that string as a key in a hash table, whose values are all words in the dictionary composed of the same letters. Write an anagram finder that works on these lines.

14 Bits and Trees

The I Ching (易 經), or the Classic of Changes, also known as the Book of Changes, is an ancient Chinese divination text. It was probably assembled some time between the 10th and the 4th centuries BCE. The process of divination in I Ching involves picking some random numbers that correspond to a specific symbol, a *hexagram*. Each hexagram is a stack of six horizontal lines; each line may be broken or not. As there are two possibilities for each line, we have $2 \times 2 \times 2 \times 2 \times 2 \times 2 = 64$ possible hexagrams. The hexagrams are traditionally arranged in a specific order, shown in figure 14.1. The order has some interesting properties. The hexagrams form pairs; 28 of these pairs contain hexagrams that are vertical mirror images of each other (like the third and the fourth hexagram); the other eight pairs contain hexagrams that are inversions of each other, so that a solid line in one becomes a broken line in the other (like the first and second hexagrams).

The idea behind I Ching is that each hexagram has a specific meaning. Originally a number was derived by some procedure using yarrow plant stalks. The hexagram corresponding to the number would then be used to divine divine intent.

The underlying concept behind all kinds of divination is that the godly will for the future can be channelled through some medium and revealed as some sign that the initiated are able to understand. Sometimes these signs and their interpretation can be quite liberal, for example, involving reading patterns in tea leaves or coffee grounds. There is even a name for that, *tasseomancy*, meaning cup divination, from the French "tasse" meaning cup and the greek "manteia" meaning divination. The I Ching is an example of *cleromancy*; "cleros" is Greek for lot, therefore it means divination by lots.

As would be expected for an ancient classic text, there is a huge amount of commentary on I Ching. The derivation of what a chosen hexagram means in a specific case involves quite a bit of creative ambiguity, as would again be

Figure 14.1
The I Ching hexagrams.

expected because otherwise it is not possible to make 64 different outcomes fit every situation where people ask for this form of guidance.

If we set aside the possibility that the divine will is somehow manifested through I Ching hexagrams, then we can evaluate its potential by trying to find out how much each hexagram really tells us. Surely a single hexagram may be interpreted in many different ways, but all the different interpretations start from the same pattern of broken and solid lines. How much does each pattern really say? In other words, what does the divine really say to the oracle? This might seem a strange question to ask, but there is good scientific way to answer it.

14.1   Divination as a Communications Problem

We can analyze divination symbolically as in figure 14.2, which shows a general diagrammatic description of a communication system. In the general case we have an *information source* that transmits a *message*. The message can be anything: text, audio, video, and so on. In order to be transmitted it must be converted into a *signal*, which travels through a *communications channel*. When traveling inside the communication channel, *noise* may, unfortunately, pollute the signal. At the end of its journey the signal is picked up by the *receiver* who should be able to convert it back to the original message and forward it to its *destination*.

If we have two people talking to each other, Alice and Bob, a message is a thought in the brain of one of the interlocutors, say Alice. The thought is converted into a spoken sentence, which is an audio signal transmitted as sound waves through the air, which is the communications channel. The sound waves are converted to electrical signals by the ear of Bob; the ear is the receiver. The electrical signals reach Bob's brain, the destination of the

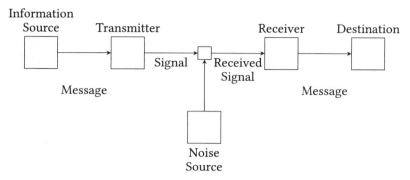

Figure 14.2
A communication system.

message. If Alice and Bob speak in a noisy environment, noise will be added to the audio waves, possibly making discussion difficult.

In modern communications the signal is typically an electromagnetic wave that travels through a wire or the air or light pulses that travel through an optical fibre. Messages are all sorts of stuff that we send around after converting them to suitable signals.

In divination, the deity sends a message converted as a suitable signal. In I Ching the signal is the number derived from the yarrow stalks. The oracle receives the signal and can turn it back to the original message. It is possible that reception may not be noise-free, in which case the interpretation of the message will be erroneous. This explains failures in determining the divine will.

A fundamental characteristic of a communications system is that it transfers *information* from the source to the destination. But what is information? In its everyday meaning, information is related to meaning and the semantics of a message. This notion of information does not concern us here. We are only interested in a technical definition of information. For that we can start by observing that we give some information when we say to somebody something that they don't already know. Information is transferred when we learn something new. Similarly, a message contains information to the extent that it is not predictable. If the contents of a message are predictable, then we can save ourselves the trouble of sending it—the recipient could easily predict the message contents anyway. The receiver does not need to wait to receive a message if it is known in advance what the message will be. So for there to be some information, there must be uncertainty in the content of the message; we must convey to the recipient something not completely pre-determined.

A simple message that fits this description is one telling us the outcome between two equally likely alternatives. This can be a choice between a "yes" and "no," a "zero" and a "one," "black" and "white," when we do not have a reason to expect that one of the outcomes is more probable than the other. The message settles the question, therefore it carries some information. The amount of information in a choice between two equally probable alternatives, or equivalently a binary choice, is called a *bit*, short for *binary digit*, because a binary digit can take one of two values, zero and one, which can represent one out of two possible outcomes. The bit is the unit of information.

The simplest yes or no message has an information content of one bit. From that point, messages can convey more information if their content represents more possibilities. If a message contains the answers to two equally likely yes or no questions, it carries two bits of information. By the same token, if the message contains the answers to n equally likely yes or no questions, it carries n bits of information.

If we have n different bits, where each one corresponds to a possibility independent of all other possibilities, we may have $2 \times 2 \times \cdots \times 2 = 2^n$ different messages. So, one way to understand the information content of a message with n bits is to view it as the amount of information that allows us to distinguish between 2^n different alternatives resulting from n equally likely different outcomes.

Each I Ching hexagram contains the answer to six binary possibilities. These correspond to 64 different outcomes. It follows that as a system of divination it boils down to the communication of a message consisting of exactly six bits. That is how much the divine tells us. It is quite impressive that answers to important questions can be conveyed in such short messages.

I Ching has something going for it: each hexagram does correspond to a six bits message. Historically deities have shown to be more taciturn. The famous Pythia, the oracle of the god Apollo at the sanctuary of Delphi in ancient Greece, was admired for her powers. When Croesus, king of Lydia, consulted Delphi about whether he should cross a river boundary and attack the Persians, he received as a reply that, "If you cross the river, a great empire will be destroyed." Believing that the Persian empire would be the one to be destroyed, he attacked to meet the destruction of his own empire. To the question "Which empire will be destroyed?" the message given by Pythia contains no information at all—a message with zero bits of information.

14.2   Information and Entropy

When we face equally likely binary choices, the amount of information is equal to the number of choices; as each choice corresponds to one bit, the amount of information is equal to a number of bits equal to the number of different choices. As we saw, for 2^n different alternatives, we need n different bits. Therefore, the amount of information in a message among 2^n equally likely messages is $n = \lg(2^n)$ bits; simply put, it is the logarithm base two of the number of possible outcomes.

This covers the information content of messages carrying equally likely outcomes, but we must cater to the situation when outcomes are not equally likely. To do this it is convenient to change the basis of our discussion from outcomes to their probabilities; and instead of talking about outcomes, we'll be talking about events, as is the custom with probabilities. The amount of information of a message m stating that an event with probability p has occurred is then defined to be $h(m) = -\lg p$. We must negate the logarithm to get a positive result because $p \leq 1$; alternatively we can use $h(m) = \lg(1/p)$, but it is easier not to have to deal with fractions. When the probability of an event is $p = 1/2$, which is the same as having two equally likely outcomes, we get $h(m) = -\lg(1/2) = 1$ bit, the same as we had before. But now we are able to generalize information beyond equally likely events. For example, suppose we know, because of historical and current meteorological data, that the probability of rain tomorrow is 80%. How much information does the statement m "It will rain tomorrow" convey? Because we have $p = 8/10$, the amount of information contained in the message is $h(m) = -\lg(8/10) \approx 0.32$ bits. If we are told the contrary statement m', "It will not rain tomorrow," we gain information equal to $h(m') = -\lg(2/10) = 2.32$ bits. We gain less information when we are told something that we were pretty sure about anyway. We gain more information when we are told something surprising: although we think it unlikely that it will rain, we are assured it will. If the probability that it will rain tomorrow is 50%, then it is really a toss what will happen. If we know that it could go either way with equal probabilities, a statement asserting that it will rain tomorrow conveys the same information with a statement asserting that it will not rain tomorrow, equal to 1 bit. The least surprising situations are when we know something will not happen, $p = 0$, or that something will definitely happen, $p = 1$. In both cases we get zero bits of information. Indeed, if $p = 1$ we have $-\lg 1 = 0$. If $p = 0$ the logarithm is not defined, but when we know with certainty that something will not happen it is the same as saying with certainty that the opposite will happen, so we can talk about the complementary probability $1 - p$ that has again zero bits of information.

Let's leave the weather aside and move to English texts. Texts are composed of characters. The appearance or not of a specific character in a particular position in a text is an event; we can therefore investigate the amount of information carried by each individual letter. Keep in mind that we are always talking about the technical definition of information, as a measure of bits, and not the everyday meaning of the term, where the information of a text means something completely different. If we have the frequencies of occurrence of the letters, we can pass from frequencies to probabilities and calculate the information carried by them by taking the base two logarithm of the probabilities. Table 14.1 shows letters, frequencies, their probabilities, and the associated information. The most common English letter, "E", has one third of the information content of the least common English letter, "Z". That's because there are many more Es than Zs in English texts, so an appearance of Z is more surprising than an appearance of E.

Having calculated the information for *each* individual letter, we may wonder, what is the *average* information of an English letter? Because we know the probability of occurrence and the information of each letter, to find the average value, we work as we always do to find averages. We multiply each value with the probability it appears, and we sum all the products. Equivalently, we multiply each value with the number of times it appears divided by the total number of occurrences of all values—that's the proportion of times the value appears, the probability of the value—and sum the products. It is common, especially in more technical texts, to speak of the *expected value* instead of the average.

To calculate the average information of an English letter we need only multiply each probability by the number of bits of information and sum all products. If $p(A), p(B), \ldots, p(Z)$ are the probabilities, that is equal to:

$$p(A)h(A) + p(B)h(B) + \cdots + p(Z)h(Z)$$

The sum gives us 4.16 bits as the average information content of an English letter. In fact, this value is too high because it assumes that letters are independent of each other. Letters in a text are not independent and can be predicted based on the letters that precede them; a more accurate value is around 1.3 bits per letter.

Table 14.1

English letter information.

Letter	Frequency	Probability	Information
E	12.49	0.1249	3.0012
T	9.28	0.0928	3.4297
A	8.04	0.0804	3.6367
O	7.64	0.0764	3.7103
I	7.57	0.0757	3.7236
N	7.23	0.0723	3.7899
S	6.51	0.0651	3.9412
R	6.28	0.0628	3.9931
H	5.05	0.0505	4.3076
L	4.07	0.0407	4.6188
D	3.82	0.0382	4.7103
C	3.34	0.0334	4.904
U	2.73	0.0273	5.195
M	2.51	0.0251	5.3162
F	2.40	0.0240	5.3808
P	2.14	0.0214	5.5462
G	1.87	0.0187	5.7408
W	1.68	0.0168	5.8954
Y	1.66	0.0166	5.9127
B	1.48	0.0148	6.0783
V	1.05	0.0105	6.5735
K	0.54	0.0054	7.5328
X	0.23	0.0023	8.7642
J	0.16	0.0016	9.2877
Q	0.12	0.0012	9.7027
Z	0.09	0.0009	10.1178

The calculation we just carried out is the definition of the average information content of an outcome x_i out of a set of possible outcomes $X = \{x_1, x_2, \ldots, x_n\}$, each one with probability $p(x_i)$. A setup of outcomes x_i out of a set of outcomes X with probabilities $p(x_i)$ is called an *ensemble*. In our example with English text x_i is a letter, X are all letters, and $p(x_i)$ is the probability of the particular letter x_i. In general mathematical terms the definition of the *average information content* for an ensemble with n different outcomes is:

$$H(X) = p(x_1)h(x_1) + p(x_2)h(x_2) + \cdots + p(x_n)h(x_n)$$
$$= -p(x_1)\lg p(x_1) - p(x_2)\lg p(x_2) - \cdots - p(x_n)\lg p(x_n)$$

$$= -\Big[p(x_1)\lg p(x_1) + p(x_2)\lg p(x_2) + \cdots + p(x_n)\lg p(x_n)\Big]$$

The value $H(X)$ is called the *entropy* of the set of outcomes X. The formula above says, in three different ways, that the entropy of a set of outcomes is the average information content of an outcome, or the expected information content of an outcome.

These definitions of information and entropy are due to Claude Elwood Shannon, who presented them in 1948. It is common to refer to the technical definition of information as *Shannon information* or *Shannon information content*; sometimes we also use the word *surprisal*, as it indicates how surprised we should be by seeing the contents of a message. The founding of information in mathematical terms allowed the development of a whole new discipline, Information Theory, which underpins modern communications, data compression, but also extends to subjects such as linguistics and cosmology.

Although related, information content and entropy are not the same. Entropy is defined by way of the information content. The information content is the amount of bits associated with an event. Entropy refers to ensembles and is the average information content of *all events in an ensemble*.

To see the difference, we can talk about the information content of a heads or tails outcome when flipping a coin. If the coin is fair, then the probability of heads p is equal to the probability of tails q, and we have $h(p) = h(q) = -\lg(1/2) = 1$ bit. If the coin is not fair and p is more likely than tails, say $p = 2/3$ and $q = 1/3$, then we have $h(p) = -\lg(2/3) = 0.58$ bits and $h(q) = -\lg(1/3) = 1.58$ bits. A head is less surprising than a tail, therefore a message saying that we got heads carries less information than a message saying that we got tails.

When we talk about the coin, it does not make sense to talk about its information content. We can only talk about the average information content of its outcomes, that is, the average information content of the two outcomes head or tails. That is the coin's entropy. If the coin X is fair, then we have $H(X) = -p\lg p - q\lg q = -(1/2)\lg(1/2) - (1/2)\lg(1/2) = 1$ bit. If the coin is loaded with $p = 2/3$ and $q = 1/3$, then we have $H(X) = -p\lg p - q\lg q = -(2/3)\lg(2/3) - (1/3)\lg(1/3) \approx 0.92$ bits. The loaded coin is more predictable than the fair coin and has therefore lower entropy. We can plot a graph showing how entropy changes as p and q change; you can see the result in figure 14.3. The entropy is indeed maximized when $p = q = 0.5$, at which point it becomes exactly 1 bit.

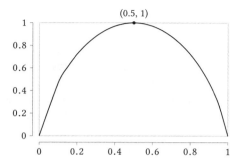

Figure 14.3
Entropy of an ensemble of two events with probabilities p and $q = 1 - p$. The probability p is on the x axis and the entropy of the ensemble is on the y axis.

Why entropy? Why is the average information content of an ensemble called that? The notion of entropy was first introduced in physics by the Austrian physicist Ludwig Boltzmann, in 1872, and the American scientist J. Willard Gibbs, in 1878. Both definitions are related to the amount of disorder of a system. Intuitively, the less ordered a system is, the higher its entropy is.

To understand entropy in physics, we can start by observing that a system has both external and internal states. The *external state* is how it looks from the outside. The *internal state* is what happens inside. For example, suppose we have a transparent jar full of two kinds of molecules, black and white (they could be molecules of black and white ink). The internal state of the jar consists of the position of each molecule. The external state of the jar consists of the color of its contents. There are many more internal states where the color we see is gray than internal states where we see a clear separation of colors, with half the jar white and half the jar black. That's because the second external state requires that all molecules of the same color have grouped together, where the first external state makes no such requirements. There are therefore more ways to distribute the molecules throughout the jar randomly than ways that require to separate them according to their color. The uniform color external state has more internal states than the black and white one; its entropy is therefore higher.

The internal states of the system arise from the state of its constituent parts and are called *microstates*. The external state of the system is a variable describing some aspect of it and is called *macrostate*. With these definitions, the entropy S of a system in a particular macrostate was defined by Boltzmann as:

$$S = k_B \ln \Omega$$

where Ω is the number of microstates, all with equal probabilities, that are consistent with the specific macrostate and k_B is a physical constant, called Boltzmann's constant. The formula counts occurrences and takes the natural logarithm, so it is somewhat similar to Shannon's entropy. The similarity between physical entropy and information entropy becomes more apparent when we consider Gibb's formula for S:

$$S = -k_B \Big[p(x_1) \ln p(x_1) + p(x_2) \ln p(x_2) + \cdots + p(x_n) \ln p(x_n) \Big]$$

where $x_1, x_2, \ldots, x_n$ are the different microstates of the system and $p(x_i)$ is the probability of each microstate. Gibb's formula is a generalization of Boltzmann's, as it does not require equal probabilities. Apart from k_B and the use of natural logarithms instead of base two logarithms, this is the same as the definition given by Shannon.

Glancing closely at the syntactic similarity between entropy in physics and entropy as information, it is tempting to think that there may be some deeper reason behind this. Indeed, there has been a lot of discussion on what it might mean. One way to approach the issue is to think of Gibb's entropy S as the amount of information required to define precisely a particular microstate of the system, such as the position and momentum of each black or white molecule in the jar.

14.3   Classification

We humans have a remarkable, innate ability to assign entities into groups. We apply this ability to all sort of entities, animate or inanimate; it is called *classification*. It is essential to our survival, as we do not need to learn explicitly that a specific striped, big cat is potentially harmful to our well-being; we know that anything that looks like a tiger is probably a tiger, and we should exercise caution, even if we have never met that particular tiger before. Similarly, if we see for the first time a large animal looking like a carnivore, we probably classify it immediately as potentially dangerous, without waiting to find out.

Classification is not only essential to our survival, but for many tasks in advanced societies as well. Banks need to classify loan applicants according to whether they are good prospects for repaying their debt. Retailers want to classify potential customers as good or bad targets for promotional campaigns. Social media companies and pollsters seek for ways to classify posts as for or against specific propositions and attitudes.

There are several ways to classify things. An obvious one, and the one we will deal here, is to use a set of *attributes*, which are features pertaining to each instance that we want to classify. Attributes can be anything that is relevant to the classification task: for example, for classifying loan applicants we may use age, income, sex, educational attainment, and job status; at the same time, features such as height, although relevant for other classifications, may not be relevant for discerning good loan applicants. For classifying mushrooms as poisonous or edible we may use features such as their cap shape, gill size, stalk shape, odor, and habitat, whereas features such as their frequency or scarcity may not be relevant.

Attributes may be *numerical*, or *categorical*. Numerical attributes take numbers as their values, for example, income. A categorical attribute can take one out of a set of categories as its value. Educational attainment, for instance, may take as values "elementary school," "high school," "university," "postgraduate," "doctorate." Numerical attributes, such as height, take numbers as their values. We may also have *boolean attributes* that take as values "true" and "false." If it is convenient these may be seen as categorical attributes with two values, or as numerical values with zero standing for false and one standing for true. The class of an entity is usually determined by the value of one of its attributes, called *class attribute*, or *label*. A loan applicant may be "eligible" or "ineligible".

Given a set of attributes that we believe are useful for classifying a set of instances, the classification problem becomes this: how can we classify the instances using the attributes at hand? Sometimes the answer may seem obvious, like a jobless loan applicant with zero income and low educational qualifications. But it is rarely so clear-cut. Historically, good classification required expertise, and indeed it has been carried out by experts making their decisions using rules and hunches they had developed over time. For many cases this is no longer feasible. Today we need to classify a large number of instances, for many different purposes: just imagine the questions big retailers or social media companies have to answer daily and the volume of instances they have to classify.

What we need, therefore, is for the machines, the computers, to learn how to classify. This brings us to the realm of *Machine Learning*, which aims to develop ways by which computers can learn to do things, like classification, which we typically associate with human intellectual faculty. Machine Learning approaches fall into three categories.

In *supervised learning*, learners, that is, computers, learn how to perform a task by being presented with a dataset, called the *training set*, along with the correct answers to the task. The job of supervised learning is to use the training set and the given answers in order to infer a function that will then be used on real data. An example of supervised learning is classification. We provide a training set with entities, their attributes, and their classes, and we want the learner to derive a way to classify other entities that it has not seen yet.

In *unsupervised learning*, the learner tries to find some hidden structure in a dataset without being given any correct answers to infer the structure. Unsupervised learning approaches may only rely on the features of the data, without any explicit knowledge of any outcomes. We can use unsupervised learning to do *clustering*, that is, given a set of entities with some attributes, find a number of clusters that best partitions the entities. Each cluster is a group of entities so that the members of a group are more closely related to each other than with with members of other groups.

Finally, in *reinforcement learning* learners are presented with a training set and are called to provide answers for a task; they are given feedback, but this feedback is not in terms of right or wrong indicators, but in terms of some rewards or penalties that the learner accumulates. Robots are typical applications of reinforcement learning. They interact with their environment and based on the feedback they get they control their movements.

14.4   Decision Trees

Here we will focus on a supervised learning method for classification. We start with a training set that contains some data with known classes. We want to train the computer to be able to *predict* the class of unknown data. The method uses the divide and conquer principle. It takes an initial training set along with attributes that describe the training instances. It then partitions the dataset, based on attribute values, to smaller and smaller subsets until it arrives at subsets that map to specific classes. At the end of the training, the learner has digested the training set and has derived a way to classify using the selected attributes. Then the learner applies the knowledge it has gained to real, production data. The partitioning of the initial set to subsets can be

Table 14.2

A simple training set for weather data.

No.	Attributes			Class
	Outlook	Humidity	Windy	
1	sunny	high	false	N
2	overcast	high	false	P
3	rain	high	false	P
4	sunny	normal	false	P
5	rain	high	true	N
6	rain	normal	true	N

easily represented with a tree; such a tree is called a *decision tree*, a tree in which internal nodes represent a test on an attribute, links between parent and children nodes correspond to outcomes of the test in the parent node, and leaves correspond to classes. A decision tree is a model for predicting the class of unknown data; such models are called, not surprisingly, *prediction models*.

An example training set is in table 14.2. The training set contains weather data for six different Saturday mornings. In this tree we decide whether to undertake some activity on Saturday mornings in general, guided by what the training set tells us. We classify Saturday mornings to "P" (Play) or "N" (No play). We distinguish three attributes for the day: outlook, humidity, windy. The outlook attribute can take three values: sunny, overcast, or rain. Humidity can be high or normal. Windy can be true or false. A simple decision tree created from that training set is in figure 14.4.

To classify an object using a decision tree, we simply go down the tree according to the values of the attributes of the object. For example, say we have an instance with outlook sunny, humidity normal, and windy. The instance is not in the training set. We start at the root, as in figure 14.5a. We check the outlook attribute. It is sunny, so we go down the left branch and arrive at the humidity node, where we check the humidity attribute, in figure 14.5b. It is normal, so we go down the right branch, arriving at a leaf node P, so P is the class we assign to the instance, in figure 14.5c. We did not need to check the windy attribute.

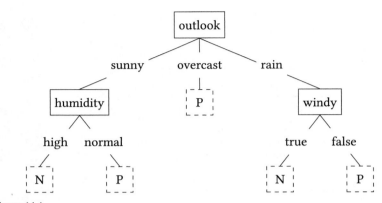

Figure 14.4
A simple decision tree.

A decision tree is equivalent to a set of rules; each path from the root to a leaf node is a set of rules that must be obeyed for an instance to be classified as in the leaf node. The example decision tree gives us six such rules:

if outlook is sunny and humidity is high then N
if outlook is sunny and humidity is normal then P
if outlook is overcast then P
if outlook is rain and windy then N
if outlook is rain and not windy then P

It is usually easier to visualize what is happening with a decision tree than with a set of rules. Also, the derived set of rules shows no indication about how we arrived at them, while the decision tree displays the attributes and the order in which we test them during tree construction.

We can trace the construction of the decision tree in figure 14.6. To create the decision tree using the training set we start at the root. Each internal node, including the root, corresponds to a test of an attribute. We use the outlook attribute at the root, which we can read as "check the outlook attribute for the observations in set {1, 2, 3, 4, 5, 6}," in figure 14.6a. The subset {1, 4} contains observations with sunny outlook. We create a branch in the tree for this subset and proceed to test the value of another attribute. We pick the humidity attribute to check in figure 14.6b. There is one instance with sunny outlook and high humidity, so we create a branch for high, containing the subset { 1 }, in figure 14.6c. Now we have arrived at a subset whose members (just one)

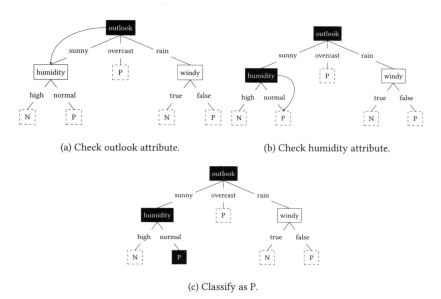

(a) Check outlook attribute.   (b) Check humidity attribute.

(c) Classify as P.

Figure 14.5
Classification using the decision tree of an instance with outlook sunny, humidity normal, and windy.

all belong to a single class, N; we have arrived at a leaf node, and it does not make sense to go further. There is also one instance with sunny outlook and normal humidity, so we create a branch for normal containing the subset { 4 } in figure 14.6d. This is again a leaf node with the class P.

Going back to the test at the root node, the second possibility for the outlook attribute is to be overcast. There is a single instance with an overcast outlook, so we create a leaf node with class P in figure 14.6e. The third possibility for the outlook attribute is to expect rain, corresponding to the subset {3, 5, 6}. We pick the windy attribute to check on that subset in figure 14.6f. If windy is true the members of the subset {5, 6} all have class N, so we create a leaf node with N in figure 14.6g, while the subset { 3 } has windy equal to false and we put it into a leaf node with class P.

14.5   Attribute Selection

There is one part of the tree construction process that we have taken as given, but we must deal with it now if we want to be able to arrive at a real decision

(a) Test outlook.

(b) Outlook sunny, test humidity.

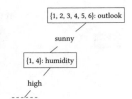

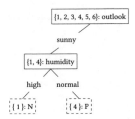

(c) Outlook sunny, humidity high.

(d) Outlook sunny, humidity normal.

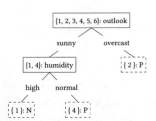

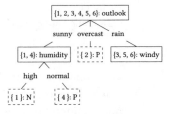

(e) Outlook overcast.

(f) Outlook rain, test windy.

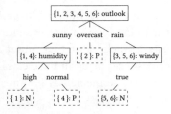

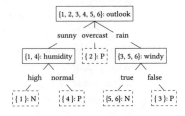

(g) Outlook rain, windy true.

(h) Outlook rain, windy false.

Figure 14.6
Decision tree construction steps.

Table 14.3

Training set for weather data.

No.	Attributes				Class
	Outlook	Temperature	Humidity	Windy	
1	sunny	hot	high	false	N
2	sunny	hot	high	true	N
3	overcast	hot	high	false	P
4	rain	mild	high	false	P
5	rain	cool	normal	false	P
6	rain	cool	normal	true	N
7	overcast	cool	normal	true	P
8	sunny	mild	high	false	N
9	sunny	cool	normal	false	P
10	rain	mild	normal	false	P
11	sunny	mild	normal	true	P
12	overcast	mild	high	true	P
13	overcast	hot	normal	false	P
14	rain	mild	high	true	N

tree construction algorithm. That is the choice of the attribute to test at each node. In figure 14.6 we selected first the outlook attribute, then the humidity attribute, then the windy attribute. But we could have done otherwise; we could have chosen different attributes, in which case we would have arrived at a different decision tree.

To examine *attribute selection*, we'll use the somewhat more complex training set in table 14.3. In the new training set we have added an attribute, temperature, which may be hot, mild, or cool. Although more complex than table 14.2, this is still definitely a toy problem. In real classification problems, training sets can have tens or even hundreds of attributes and they may comprise many thousands or many millions of instances.

Because each node in a decision tree corresponds to a decision we take with respect to an attribute, to construct a decision tree starting from the root we have to decide which attribute to use in order to make our decision to start partitioning the training set instances. There are four different attributes, so we have four possibilities to use in the root node decision. Which one is the best?

(a) Windy for root decision attribute.

(b) Humidity for root decision attribute.

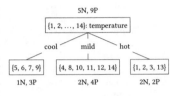
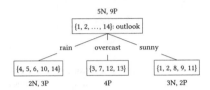

(c) Temperature for root decision attribute.

(d) Outlook for root decision attribute.

Figure 14.7
Alternative root decision attributes.

In figure 14.7 you can see the first level of the decision trees that result by choosing each of the four different attributes as the attribute to test in the root node. Again, which one is the best choice?

In trying to answer the question, our objective is to classify the training set so that we arrive at nodes of one particular class. If all instances in a node are of a single particular class, each node is completely homogeneous in terms of that class. If the instances in a node are a mixed bunch of classes, then the node is heterogeneous. The more mixed the bunch is, the more heterogeneous the node is. And this is where entropy comes in.

If a node is homogeneous, then the class attribute of each instance is predictable because it is the same with that of any other instances in the node. If the node is heterogeneous, then this no longer holds; yet, the more instances that have the same class, the more predictable the class of each instance becomes.

In figure 14.7 we see the first level of the decision tree for the four different choices for the root attribute. Along with each child node we indicate the number of instances having N and P classes. In the entire training set we have five instances of class N and nine instances of class P. In figure 14.7b the node down the normal branch has six instances with class P and a single instance with class N. If we were to stop the decision tree here and base our decision for the class of an instance, then reason would dictate to choose class P, as the odds of P over N in that node are six to one based on the observed frequencies.

The more unpredictable a situation, the higher its entropy is, because we need more bits to describe it. If, therefore, we think of entropy, the more homogeneous a node is, the lower its entropy will be; the more heterogeneous a node is, the higher its entropy will be. The entropy is defined in terms of probabilities of events; in decision trees, an event is an occurrence of an instance with a particular class attribute. The probability of an event is the frequency of an instance with a particular class attribute in a node. This ties directly with the definition of entropy as we have seen it:

$$H(X) = -p(x_1)\lg p(x_1) - p(x_2)\lg p(x_2) - \cdots - p(x_n)\lg p(x_n)$$

In this formula now X is a node containing a set of instances; each instance has a value for its class attribute; there are n such possible values; and each x_i is the event of observing the ith value of the class attribute in the node. In our weather data example, we have only two x_i, one for P and one for N. The entropy for each node in the decision tree becomes:

$$H(X) = -p(x_1)\lg p(x_1) - p(x_2)\lg p(x_2)$$

for $x_1 = $ P and $x_2 = $ N.

If we use entropy to indicate the homogeneity or heterogeneity of a node, we get the values shown in figure 14.7, where we indicate the value of H for each node; we'll see what G is in the figure in a moment.

True to what we should expect, when the probability of each class is 50%, as happens for instance in the left child of figure 14.8a, we get $H = 1$. With the same token, when the probability of a class is 100%, as happens in the middle child of figure 14.8d, we get $H = 0$. For intermediate values of heterogeneity, we get intermediate values of H. If we were to plot the values of H we would end up with figure 14.3, as in this particular example there are only two values for the class attribute, so the situation corresponds to the entropy of an ensemble of two events with probabilities p and $1 - p$.

We arrive to the crux of how we pick the decision attribute. In each one of the trees in figure 14.8, we start with an entropy at the root and two or more entropies at the level below. We want to partition the training set so that each of the offspring nodes is as homogeneous as possible. To measure the homogeneity of a single node we use its entropy. If we have m offspring

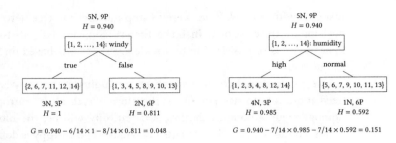

(a) Windy for root decision attribute.   (b) Humidity for root decision attribute.

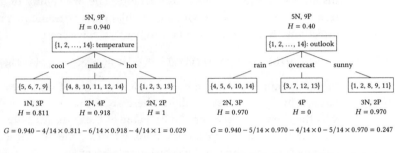

(c) Temperature for root decision attribute.   (d) Outlook for root decision attribute.

Figure 14.8
Alternative entropy and information gain values.

nodes $n_1, n_2, \ldots, n_m$, then to gauge the homogeneity of all offspring nodes we use the measure:

$$\frac{|n_1|}{n} \times H(n_1) + \frac{|n_2|}{n} \times H(n_2) + \cdots + \frac{|n_m|}{n} \times H(n_m)$$

where $|n_i|$ is the number of instances of the training set that go to node n_i. Each multiplier ratio in the above formula is a frequency ratio, a proportion, or, equivalently, a probability; each multiplicand is the value of the entropy of each node. That is the average value of the entropy of the offspring, or the expected value of the entropy of the offspring with regards to the class attribute:

$$p_1 H(n_1) + p_2 H(n_2) + \cdots + p_m H(n_m)$$

where $p_i = |n_i|/n$ is the probability that an instance belongs in node n_i.

Having calculated the entropy of the parent node and the expected entropy of the offspring nodes, we can subtract the second from the first. This will give us a value that will represent how much the entropy has *decreased* from the parent to the children. The difference between the parent entropy and the expected entropy of the children is called the *information gain*. It is the reduction in entropy that results by partitioning the examples according to the chosen test attribute. If $H(X)$ is the entropy of the parent node and a is the test attribute, then the information gain is:

$$G(X, a) = H(X) - \left[p_{1|a}H(n_{1|a}) + p_{2|a}H(n_{2|a}) + \cdots + p_{m|a}H(n_{m|a}) \right]$$

$$= H(X) - p_{1|a}H(n_{1|a}) - p_{2|a}H(n_{2|a}) - \cdots - p_{m|a}H(n_{m|a})$$

The formula seems somewhat complex, but the calculations are actually exactly the same as above. By $n_{i|a}$ we denote the ith offspring node that results after choosing a as a test variable in its parent. Similarly, by $p_{1|a}$ we denote the probability $p_i = |n_{i|a}|/n$ that an instance belongs in the offspring node $n_{i|a}$ after choosing a as a test variable in its parent. The reason we went into the trouble of introducing a in the formula is to make explicit that the tree grows by choosing the attribute a at the node we are splitting.

In more abstract terms, we could write:

$$G(X, a) = H(X) - H(X|a)$$

That is, the information gain is the difference in entropy from a node X in a decision tree to the nodes that result after using a as a test attribute. The notation $H(X|a)$ follows the convention of expressing *conditional probabilities*: $p(x|y)$ is the probability that we have x knowing that y is true.

Returning to our example, the value of the information gain we achieve with each choice of test attribute is the G that we saw at the bottom line of each subfigure in figure 14.8.

You may observe that the entropy, or information content, is reduced when we go down one level of the tree, so that the term information gain seems counter-intuitive. To see why the term is apt we have to go back tox the idea of information as a measure of how many bits we need to transfer a message. The message we want to transfer here is the average information content of an instance in a node. If we want to represent a node in a message, then we need $H(X)$ bits. If we want to represent its offspring nodes in a message, then we actually need fewer bits. The amount of bits we save is our gain, thus information gain. The gain comes from the fact that in the offspring we know something more than in the root: the value of the test attribute in each node. For example, in figure 14.8d we start with 14 instances that can contain all three values of the outcome attribute. In the offspring we know, for each node, that all instances have an outlook that is rainy, overcast, or sunny, but no node can have a mix. This knowledge allows us to dispense with some amount of information content of the offspring.

The information gain is the key to choosing the test attribute at each node in the decision tree. We calculate the information gain for each possible choice of attribute at the node, and we select the attribute with the biggest information gain. Hence, in figure 14.8 we see that the biggest information gain comes from the outlook attribute; that is the attribute we select to partition the training set at the root.

Let us pause for a minute and take stock of what we have achieved up to this point. We started by measuring information and then measuring disorder, in the form of entropy. We then saw that we can represent classification rules in tree form as classification trees. Classification trees grow by splitting our training set to finer and finer partitions, choosing in each step a suitable test attribute. The choice of the attribute is governed by how much information gain we get. We can now use this mechanism as the basis for developing a fully fledged algorithm for constructing decision trees.

14.6   The ID3 Algorithm

Entropy and information gain are the basic ingredients of the ID3 (Iterative Dichotomizer 3) decision tree construction algorithm, invented by the Australian computer scientist Ross Quinlan in the late 1970s. The ID3 algorithm starts at the root node of the decision tree; the root node contains all the training set instances. To select a test attribute to partition the training set elements, it calculates the information gain for each possible attribute and selects the attribute that produces the largest value of that measure. It partitions the training set accordingly, creating offspring nodes. Then it runs recursively for each of the newly created nodes, selecting the best partitioning attribute based on the information gain to partition the subset of the training set at the current node, and so on.

That is about all. The general idea behind ID3 is simply to pick a test attribute, partition, and repeat for each of the offspring. This being a recursive procedure, it cannot go on forever. Indeed, there are three ways in which the recursion will stop at a given node; when this happens, we create a leaf node with a corresponding class.

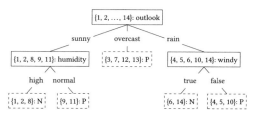

Figure 14.9
Leaf nodes contain instances of one class.

First, we may arrive at a node where the training set subset has the same value for the target class attribute (in our example, all P class or all N class). Then it certainly does not make any sense to continue, as we have arrived at a node that classifies precisely the instances coming down the path from the root. When this happens, we turn the node to a leaf node with the corresponding class. This is what happens in figure 14.9; all the leaf nodes contain instances of exclusively one class. For example, if we partition the set {1, 2, 8, 9, 11} using the humidity attribute, the two values high and normal result in one node with all instances of class N and another node with class P; we turn both instances to leaves. The same thing happens to the other branches of the tree.

The second way to stop is to arrive at a node where there are no more attributes to test but the remaining examples do not belong to the same class. As there are no more attributes, we cannot partition the remaining examples any further. We have to stop; we create a leaf node to which we assign as class the class of the majority of the remaining instances. If there is no majority because it is 50-50, then we can choose any tie-breaking rule. To see this in action, suppose that our training set consists of the instances in table 14.3 plus an additional instance, numbered 15, with sunny outlook, mild temperature, high humidity, not windy, and class P. The ID3 algorithm would create the tree in figure 14.10. When we arrive at the node containing the subset {8, 15}, we use the last available attribute, windy. Both elements of {8, 15} are windy, but instance 8 has class N while instance 15 has class P. But we have no attribute left at all to split these two. So we put them in a leaf node, whose class would ideally be the class of the majority of the instances, but we have no majority here, so we use the class P, it being the class of the last instance we examined (15).

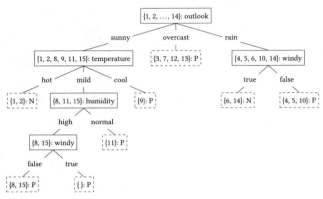

Figure 14.10
Leaf nodes with instances of more than one class.

The third way to stop is to arrive at a branch for which there are no elements to partition. When this happens we create a leaf node with the class of the majority of the instances in the parent node; again, if there is no majority, we are at liberty to choose a tie-breaking rule. With the same expanded training set example this happens in the normal branch going down the node containing the subset {8, 15} in figure 14.10. Neither instance 8 nor instance 15 are windy, so we have to create an empty leaf node, to which we attach class P. We use the same tie-breaker as before because we must find the (non-existing) majority between the class attributes of {8, 15}.

The process we described is not an algorithm yet. To get to an algorithm, we can describe it in a more structured way. The process is recursive, depth-first, and it goes like this:

- Create a tree with a single root node. If all examples are of the same class, assign the class to the root node and return the tree (first way to end recursion). Otherwise, if there are no more attributes to test, assign to the root node the most common class of the remaining examples and return the tree (second way to end recursion). Otherwise:

  - Let a be the attribute that produces the maximum information gain. This will be the test attribute for the root node. For each possible value v_i of a:

       ◦ Add a branch to the root node for v_i. Find the examples that have value v_i for a. Let this set of examples be *examples_v_i*.

         · If *examples_v_i* is empty, add below the new branch a new leaf node with the most common class in the examples of the parent node (third way to end recursion, as we do not proceed any deeper in the tree).

         · Otherwise, add below the new branch a new tree constructed recursively for *examples_v_i* and the attributes without attribute a.

• After handling all the attribute values v_i in this node, return the tree as it has grown in subsequent recursive calls.

This looks more like an algorithm, but it is not there yet. We would like to specify the process in pseudocode using the control constructs and the data structures we already know. When we do that, we arrive at algorithm 14.1. The parameters we pass to the algorithm are *examples*, the training set instances (for example, the weather data), *target_attribute*, the classifier attribute (the class attribute in the weather data), *attributes*, the rest of the attributes of the training set instances, and *attribute_values*, the values they can take.

The *examples* are represented as a list, each member of which is a single training set instance. A single training instance is a record that contains attributes describing the instance and a target attribute, which is the attribute that ascribes to each instance its class. Each training instance record is represented by an associative array, or map, that maps attribute names to attribute values. For example, the first instance of table 14.3 is a map with the following key-value pairs: (outlook, sunny), (temperature, hot), (humidity, high), (windy, false), (class, N). The *target_attribute* is simply the name of the classification attribute (class in our example), and *attributes* is a set containing the names of the other attributes of the instances; in our example, these are outlook, temperature, humidity, and windy. The *attribute_values* is a map that maps each attribute from *attributes* to a list of allowable values it can take; for example, it maps outlook to [sunny, overcast, rain].

Each node in a tree is represented by a map, which is created empty with the CreateMap function. To handle maps in the algorithm, we use one function for inserting key-value pairs and one function for retrieval. The function InsertInMap(m, k, v) inserts into the map m the value v with key k; the function Lookup(m, k) retrieves from the map m the value with key k.

Algorithm 14.1: ID3.

ID3(*examples, target_attribute, attributes, attribute_values*) → *dt*
    Input: *examples*, a list containing the training set instances
           target_attribute, the classifier attribute
           attributes, a set containing the other attributes of the
           training set
           attribute_values a map containing the allowable values for
           each one of the *attributes*
    Output: *dt*, a decision tree

1   $r \leftarrow$ CreateMap()
2   InsertInMap(*dt*, "instances", *examples*)
3   **if** CheckAllSame(*examples, target_attribute*) **then**
4       $ex \leftarrow$ GetNextListNode(*examples*, NULL)
5       $cv \leftarrow$ Lookup(*ex, target_attribute*)
6   InsertInMap(*dt, target_attribute, cv*)
7   **return** *dt*
8   **if** IsSetEmpty(*attributes*) **then**
9       $mc \leftarrow$ FindMostCommon(*examples, target_attribute*)
10   InsertInMap(*dt, target_attribute, mc*)
11   **return** *dt*
12 $a \leftarrow$ BestClassifier(*examples, attributes, target_attribute*)
13 InsertInMap(*dt*, "test_attribute", *a*)
14 **foreach** v **in** Lookup(*attribute_values, a*) **do**
15   *examples_subset* $\leftarrow$ FilterExamples(*examples, a, v*)
16   **if** IsSetEmpty(*examples_subset*) **then**
17         $mc \leftarrow$ FindMostCommon(*examples, target_attribute*)
18         $c \leftarrow$ CreateMap()
19   InsertInMap(*c, target_attribute, mc*)
20   InsertInMap(*c*, "branch", *v*)
21   AddChild(*dt, c*)
22   **else**
23   *offspring_attributes* $\leftarrow$ RemoveFromSet(*attributes, a*)
24         $c \leftarrow$ ID3(*examples_subset, target_attribute,*
25   *offspring_attributes, attribute_values*)
26   InsertInMap(*c*, "branch", *v*)
27   AddChild(*dt, c*)
28 **return** *dt*

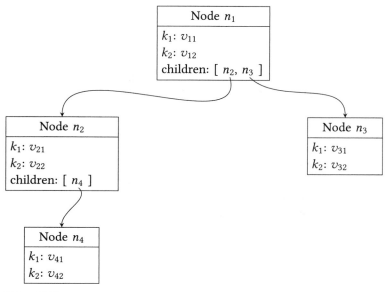

Figure 14.11
A tree represented with maps.

At this point it is worth pausing a bit to make sure you realize that the data structure we will be using for representing the tree is the map. Every node is a map: the payload of the node is represented via key-value pairs. Another key of the map has as its value a list of its children nodes. Each of the children nodes represents its payload and children in the same way. Figure 14.11 shows an example of a tree represented with maps. Each k_i and v_{ij} stands for a payload key-value pair, whereas the "children" key contains the list of children, if any.

The algorithm starts by creating a new node *dt* that contains the *examples*, in line 1. The new tree node *dt* is initially empty; this will represent the current training set instances, so we insert into it the *examples* with the key the string "instances" (line 2). To simplify things we assume that here and in other places in the algorithm where we use specific strings as keys (lines 13, 20, 26), none of them happens to be the name of any other attribute.

In lines 3–7 we check whether all instances of *examples* have the same value at their *target_attribute*. If this happens, this is the first way in which recursion should stop. To get the common value, we get the first instance, the head of the *examples* list, and we look up its value for the *target_attribute* in line 5. Then, in line 6, we insert the common value into *dt* using *target_attribute* as key. The presence of *target_attribute* is what makes it a leaf node. We return *dt*.

In lines 8–11 we tackle the situation where we have run out of attributes to test. We find the most common value of *target_attribute* in line 9 and store it in variable *mc* (most common). To do that we use function FindMostCommon. In line 10, we insert *mc* into *dt* using *target_attribute* as its key; then, we return *dt*.

Most of the work takes place when we do not end the recursion. To proceed we need to find the attribute that best partitions the training set instances. This is the attribute that gives us the largest information gain. To find it we use the function BestClassifier. We store the attribute name into variable *a*, in line 12, and we record the fact into the node *dt* by inserting the key "test_attribute" with value *a* in line 13.

The loop in lines 14–27 is repeated every time for each possible value of the attribute *a* that we established is the best one to use for partitioning. For each possible value *v*, we use the function FilterExamples, in line 15, to get those instances that have the value *v* for the attribute *a*; we put these instances in *examples_subset*.

If there are no such instances at all, which we check in line 16, then we continue in line 17 by finding the most common value of *target_attribute*, *mc*, which we'll put into a leaf node. To do that, we create a new empty node *c* in line 18. We then insert *mc* into *c* using *target_attribute* as its key in line 19. We indicate the value of the test attribute that gets us to this new node by inserting the key "branch" with value *v* to the new node in line 19. In essence, the "branch" key holds the information for the branch labels in the figures of the decision trees we have been seeing. Having done that, we make *c* a child of *dt* in line 21 using the function AddChild.

If there are instances in *examples* that have the value *v* for the attribute *a*, we can proceed by trying to find another test attribute to partition these instances further in lines 22–27. Any subsequent partition cannot use attribute *a*, so in line 23 we set *offspring_attributes* to the attributes that remain when we remove *a* from *offspring_attributes*. Then we are ready to make a recursive call in lines 24–25 using the *examples_subset* as our instances. When the recursive call returns it will give us a tree (which may be a single node) that we will add as child to the node *dt*; we do this in lines 26–27 with the same steps as in lines 20–21.

After we have dealt with all possible values of the attribute *a*, the node *dt* will be a node of the decision tree whose offspring we have also processed through the algorithm. We can therefore return *dt*.

The last page or so may have been a long walkthrough for a simple procedure that consists of choosing a test attribute, partitioning a set, and doing the same again for each of the partitions. It is true that sometimes in computer science the difference between an intuitive understanding and a rigorous description, as in an algorithm, can be wide. We cannot avoid that. The best way to grasp ID3, if it still eludes you, is to follow it step by step in figures 14.9 and 14.10 keeping in mind that the algorithm constructs the decision trees in a depth-first, left to right manner.

14.7   The Underlying Machinery

To complete the exposition we must describe the workings of the various functions in algorithm 14.1. The `CreateMap` function initializes a map. This is a matter of allocating an array that will be used in conjunction with a hashing function. Insertion and lookup in the map via the `InsertInMap` and `Lookup` functions work as normal maps built on top of hash tables. To add a child to a node in the tree we use the `AddChild` function. Each node is a map, so we can use a predetermined attribute like "children" that will have as value the list of children of the node, as we discussed above and saw in figure 14.11. Then the function `AddChild` is a function that looks up that attribute. If it finds nothing, then it creates a list with the child as its single element and inserts the list as the value of the children attribute. If it finds a list, it inserts the child into it.

`CheckAllSame` is a simple matter of getting the value of *target_attribute* for the first instance in *examples* and then going through the rest of the *examples* and checking whether the value of *target_attribute* is the same with that of the first instance. If at any instance we find that this is not so, `CheckAllSame` returns FALSE; otherwise it returns TRUE. This is what is done in algorithm 14.2. In line 1 we get the first node in the *examples* list and in line 2 we get the example instance out of the node; the function `GetData` returns the data payload in a list node. Then, in line 3, we get the value *v* for *target_attribute* in the first example. In the loop in lines 4–7 we go through the rest of the examples. Notice the technique we use to iterate through the list nodes. Each time we get the node following *n* and we assign it to *n*: then we check whether this is NULL, which means that we have reached the end of the list. Inside the loop, for each node *n* we extract the example

---

Algorithm 14.2: Check that all training set instances have the same value for a given attribute.

CheckAllSame(*examples, target_attribute*) → TRUE or FALSE
    Input: *examples*, a list of training set instances, represented by maps
          target_attribute, the attribute to check
    Output: a boolean value that is TRUE if all instances in *examples* have
          the same value for *target_attribute*, FALSE otherwise
1 $n \leftarrow$ GetNextListNode(*examples*, NULL)
2 *example* $\leftarrow$ GetData(n)
3 $v \leftarrow$ Lookup(*example, target_attribute*)
4 **while** ($n \leftarrow$ GetNextListNode(*examples, n*)) $\neq$ NULL **do**
5   *example* $\leftarrow$ GetData(n)
6   **if** Lookup(*example, target_attribute*) $\neq v$ **then**
7   **return** FALSE
8 **return** TRUE

---

instance it contains, in line 5. We then check whether it has the same value for *target_attribute*, in line 6. If not, we return FALSE in line 7. If all nodes have the same value, we return TRUE at the end of the algorithm, in line 8.

The function FindMostCommon is easy to define, as you can see in algorithm 14.3. The algorithm takes as input a list of training instances and an attribute, *target_attribute*. Each instance has a value associated with *target_attribute*, and we want to find the most common of these values. We use a map, *counts*, to count the occurrences of each value of *target_attribute*. We initialize it in line 1; in line 2 we set *mc*, the most common value we are looking for, to NULL; and in line 3 we set *max*, the current maximum number of occurrences of a value of *target_attribute*, to 0.

The loop in lines 4–14 goes through each example in the list of examples. It gets the value of *target_attribute* in the current example, in line 5, and stores it in v. Then it looks up v in *counts* and stores the result in *count*. If this is the first time we have seen the value v, *count* will be NULL, so we change it to one, in lines 7–8. If we have seen the value v before we increase *count* by one in line 10. We insert the updated *count* into *counts* in line 11. We then compare the current count with the maximum value so far in line 12. If we have a new maximum we update the maximum in line 13 and the corresponding most

---

Algorithm 14.3: Find the most common value of a given attribute in a list of training set instances, represented by maps.

FindMostCommon(*examples, target_attribute*) → *mc*
    Input: *examples*, a list of training set instances, represented by maps
            target_attribute, the attribute whose values we want to
            examine
    Output: *mc*, the most common value of *target_attribute* among the
            contents of *examples*

1   *counts* ← CreateMap()
2   *mc* ← NULL
3   *max* ← 0
4   **foreach** *example* **in** *examples* **do**
5   v ← Lookup(*example, target_attribute*)
6   *count* ← Lookup(*counts, v*)
7   **if** *count* = NULL **then**
8   *count* ← 1
9   **else**
10   *count* ← *count* + 1
11   InsertInMap(*counts, v, count*)
12   **if** *count* ≥ *max* **then**
13   *max* ← *count*
14   *mc* ← v
15 **return** *mc*

---

common value in line 14. Finally we return the most common value we have found after exhausting the loop, in line 15.

To filter the instances that have the same value for a particular attribute, as in function FilterExamples, we need to go through the instances we want to filter, test for each instance whether it meets the condition we want, and add those that do to the list of filtered instances. This is what algorithm 14.4 does. It takes as input a list of examples, an attribute *a*, and a value *v*; we want to filter the list of examples and return only those with value *v* for the attribute *a*. We create an empty list, *filtered*, in line 1. In the loop in lines 2–4 we go through each example and check whether it meets the specified condition. If it does, we add it to the list *filtered*, which we return at the end.

Algorithm 14.4: Filter training set examples.

FilterExamples(*examples, a, v*) → *filtered*
  Input: *examples*, a list of training set instances, represented by maps
         a, an attribute to lookup in *examples*
         v, the value of *a* that will be used for filtering
  Output: *filtered*, a list containing the instances in *examples* that have
         value *v* for the attribute *a*
1 *filtered* ← CreateList()
2 **foreach** *example* **in** *examples* **do**
3   **if** Lookup(*example, a*) = *v* **then**
4   InsertInList(*filtered*, NULL, *m*)
5 **return** *filtered*

At this point, to complete the description of algorithm 14.1 we need to define the BestClassifier function. As we explained, this picks in a node the attribute that produces the largest information gain, among all other attributes. We will build BestClassifier step by step.

To start, because information gain requires the calculation of the entropy at a node, we must define an algorithm for calculating the entropy. Algorithm 14.5 implements the entropy formula we have seen:

$$H(X) = -p(x_1)\lg p(x_1) - p(x_2)\lg p(x_2) - \cdots - p(x_n)\lg p(x_n)$$

The entropy formula requires us to find the proportion of each different value of the attribute we use to calculate the entropy. This means counting the number of occurrences of each different value and dividing by the total number of instances. Algorithm 14.5 takes as input a list of examples and the attribute, *target_attribute*, that will be the basis for the entropy calculation.

To count the number of occurrences of each different value of the key we will use a map *counts*, which we initialize to empty in line 1. We will keep track of the different values we encounter in the list *values*, which we also initialize as empty in line 2. In the loop of lines 3–11 we carry out the tally. For each one of the different examples we get the value of the *target_attribute* and store the value in a variable *v* in line 4. In line 5 we look up *v* in the *counts* map and store the result in *count*. If it is not there, line 6, that's the first time we encounter this particular value, so we set *count* to one, in line 7. In line 8 we add *v* to the *values* list. If we have encountered *v* before, then we increase

---

Algorithm 14.5: Calculate the entropy of a list of training instances, with respect to a given attribute.

CalcEntropy(*examples, target_attribute*) → *h*

      Input: *examples*, a list of training set instances, represented by maps
             target_attribute, the attribute whose values will be used to
             calculate the entropy

      Output: *h*, the entropy of *examples* with respect to the different
              values of *target_attribute*

1   *counts* ← CreateMap()
2   *values* ← CreateList()
3   **foreach** *example* in *examples* **do**
4   *v* ← Lookup(*example, target_attribute*)
5   *count* ← Lookup(*counts, v*)
6   **if** *count* = NULL **then**
7   *count* ← 1
8   InsertInList(*values*, NULL, *v*)
9   **else**
10   *count* ← *count* + 1
11   InsertInMap(*counts, v, count*)
12   *h* ← 0
13   **foreach** *v* in *values* **do**
14   *p* ← Lookup(*counts, v*)/|*examples*|
15   *h* ← *h* − *p* · lg(*p*)
16   **return** *h*

---

count by one, in lines 9–10. Having updated *count* we insert it into *counts* in line 11.

When we get out of the loop we can calculate the $p_i \lg(p_i)$ terms of the entropy formula. We initialize the entropy value, *h*, to zero in line 12. We go through each of the possible values we have encountered in the second loop in lines 13–15; we look up the count for each value *v* and divide it by the total number of examples; this is the value p_i every time through the loop. We subtract it from *h* and update *h* in line 15. When all this is done we return the entropy value.

You may have noticed that algorithm 14.5 is similar to algorithm 14.3; indeed, in both cases it boils down to going through a list of items and counting those items that meet some condition. A variation on the same idea solves the problem of how to calculate the information gain for each different test attribute at a node. We saw that the information gain is given by the formula:

$$G(X, a) = H(X) - p_{1|a}H(n_{1|a}) - p_{2|a}H(n_{2|a}) - \cdots - p_{m|a}H(n_{m|a})$$

This can be turned to algorithm 14.6, which in turn is similar to algorithm 14.5. The main difference between the two algorithms is that, where algorithm 14.5 counts the instances that satisfy a condition, algorithm 14.6 groups together the instances that satisfy the condition.

CalcInfoGain starts by creating a map, *groups*, in line 1, where each key-value pair is a *test_attribute* and a list containing the instances with the same value for the *test_attribute*. We will keep track again of the different values we encounter in the list *values*, which we initialize as empty in line 2. We populate *groups* in the loop of lines 3–10, which we iterate for each instance in *examples*. We look up the value of the *test_attribute* of the instance in line 4 and store it in v; then we look up the group of that value in line 5. If there is no such group (line 6), then we insert into *groups* a new key-value pair with v as key and a list with a single element, the current instance, in line 7; we also add v to *values* in line 8. If there is a group (line 9), then we add the instance to that group in line 10.

Out of the loop we calculate the entropy of the node and we store it in g, in line 11. Then, in lines 12–16, for each of the different values of the *test_attribute* we calculate the ratio of the instances of the corresponding group to the total number of instances, the entropy of the group with regard to the *target_attribute*, and we subtract their product from the entropy of the node.

With the information gain algorithm at our disposal the BestClassifier function in algorithm 14.1 is simply an iteration to pick the maximum of the possible information gains we can get by choosing different test attributes in a node, as you can see in algorithm 14.7.

We have called the function BestClassifier because each time it picks the best attribute to partition the instances into groups (classes). We have laid the reasoning for that in terms of the entropy and the information gain. But what does that mean in practice? One could argue that using these two measures is one way to partition the instances, but there may be others, equally or even more effective. That might be so; using the information gain as the basis

---

Algorithm 14.6: Calculate the information gain of a list training instances with respect to a test attribute and a target attribute.

CalcInfoGain(*examples, test_attribute, target_attribute*) → *g*
    Input: *examples*, a list of maps
              test_attribute, the test attribute
              target_attribute, the target attribute
    Output: *g*, the information gain of *examples* with respect to
               test_attribute and *target_attribute*

1   *groups* ← CreateMap()
2   *values* ← CreateList()
3   **foreach** *example* **in** *examples* **do**
4   v ← Lookup(*example, test_attribute*)
5   *group* ← Lookup(*groups, v*)
6   **if** *group* = NULL **then**
7   InsertInMap(*groups, v,* [*example*])
8   InsertInList(*values,* NULL, *v*)
9   **else**
10   InsertInList(*group,* NULL, *example*)
11   *g* ← CalcEntropy(*examples, target_attribute*)
12   **foreach** *v* **in** *values* **do**
13   *group* ← Lookup(*groups, v*)
14   p ← |*group*|/|*examples*|
15   h ← CalcEntropy(*group, target_attribute*)
16      $g \leftarrow g - p \cdot h$
17   **return** *g*

---

for our judgment rests on the premise that the decision trees that result are somehow better than alternative decision trees. In what way better, we'll see next.

14.8 Occam's Razor

Let's assume that we use an alternative implementation for BestClassifier. In this alternative implementation, instead of calculating the largest information gain to pick the test attribute at each node, we just choose the attribute

---

Algorithm 14.7: Find the best classifier attribute by finding the maximum information gain.

BestClassifier(*examples, attributes, target_attribute*) → *bc*
    Input: *examples*, a list of training instances, represented by maps
            attributes, a list of attributes to check for the maximum
            information gain
            target_attribute, the class attribute of the instances
    Output: *bc*, the attribute, among *attributes*, that gives the greatest
            information gain with respect to the *target_attribute*

1   *maximum* ← 0
2   *bc* ← NULL
3   **foreach** *attribute* **in** *attributes* **do**
4   *g* ← CalcInfoGain(*examples, attribute, target_attribute*)
5   **if** $g \geq maximum$ **then**
6   *maximum* ← *g*
7   *bc* ← *attribute*
8   **return** *bc*

---

in a predefined order: temperature, humidity, windy, outlook. The resulting decision tree is in figure 14.12.

The tree in figure 14.12 is created using the same training set as the tree in figure 14.9, yet it is blatantly different. It is much larger and deeper than the tree we get with using the information gain. Because a decision tree stands for a set of rules to classify instances, a typical rule in the tree of figure 14.9 is shorter than a typical rule in the tree of figure 14.12. This is a fundamental feature of ID3: by using the measures of entropy and information gain the algorithm picks test attributes that prefer shorter of larger trees. To put it in another way, it picks the test attribute so as to arrive at shorter, rather than longer, decision rules.

Is there a reason we should prefer shorter than longer decision rules? There exists an important problem-solving rule, or principle, called Occam's (or Ockham's) razor, which states that if several competing hypotheses predict equally well, we should pick the one with fewer assumptions. The name of the rule comes from William of Ockham (also spelled Occam), a medieval English Franciscan friar and theologian. According to the rule we should shave away

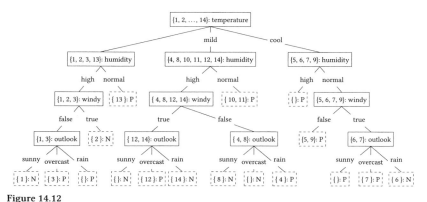

Figure 14.12

Decision tree that results from picking the test attribute in order: temperature, humidity, windy, outlook.

assumptions we do not need, thus the term "razor." An alternative formulation of Occam's razor is that, all other things being equal, we should prefer simpler explanations to more complex ones. Another version, which has been attributed to Ockham himself, although it does not survive in any of his writings, is that entities must not be multiplied without necessity.

Occam's razor is a general guide with wide application in science. We usually prefer a simpler scientific explanation over a complex one that explains the same things, and a theory that explains a natural phenomenon with fewer assumptions is preferred over a competing theory that is more complex. The same principle is at work behind the economy of ideas: an explanation is economical if it explains a lot without assuming a lot.

Somehow simplicity meshes well with our ideas on elegance, so a decision tree method that adopts a method favoring simpler trees seems to be a good way to go. It works well in practice, so that ID3 is the basis of a number of other more advanced classification algorithms that are in use classifying complex real-world data.

14.9   Cost, Problems, Improvements

Under some assumptions it is easy to analyze the computational cost of ID3. The construction of the decision tree depends on the number of levels of the tree. Suppose we have n instances in the training set and each one of them has m different attributes. We can assume that the decision tree has $O(\log n)$

levels. In binary trees the number of levels is $O(\lg n)$; here we cannot assume that the attributes are binary, so we use the more general base ten logarithm. But this does not really matter, because in terms of the big-Oh notation it is the same because $\lg n = \log n / \log 2$ and $O(\lg n) = O((1/\log 2) \log n) = O(\log n)$.

The worst case scenario is that all levels are full, so that at each level we work with all n instances. So, to construct all levels by checking one attribute at each level it costs us $O(n \log n)$. However, we check more than one attribute at each level: at the root level we check all m attributes and at level i we check $m - i + 1$ attributes (level one is the root). To keep things simple, let's assume that we check m attributes at all levels; we are looking for an upper limit, so we may do with one that is not as tight as possible. Then the total computational cost for constructing the decision tree is $O(mn \log n)$, which is efficient.

Efficient it may be, but ID3 as we have described is not generic enough, as it requires that all attributes are categorical, that is, they can take only a small number of predefined values. This does not cover numerical values. Temperature, for instance, could be given in degrees Celsius. These are real numbers; even if we round them to the closest integer, we could not use temperature as a test attribute because we would need as many branches as the possible temperature values, which would not result in a good decision tree. A way to solve the problem is, simply, to turn the decision to a binary one. We pick the median value, that is, the value that splits the instances in half, with half the instances below that value and half the instances above that value. The test becomes $x \geq median$, which produces a two-way split.

A related problem is *highly branching attributes*, which are attributes with a large number of possible values. Numerical attributes fall into this category, but it also encompasses attributes that are not numerical, like dates or attributes that uniquely identify an instance. When this happens we end up again with a node that has too many branches. For example, suppose that we include in the potential test attributes of table 14.3 the serial number of the observation in the first column. We start at the root node trying to find the attribute that gives us the maximum information gain. We check how the serial number fares. There will be 14 children to the root node, one for each different value of the serial number. The entropy of each child is exactly $1 \lg 1 = 0$ because each child has a single class attribute. Therefore, the information gain of the serial number will be $G(root, serial\_number) = H(root) - 0 - 0 - \cdots - 0 = H(root)$. That is the maximum possible information gain, so we would have to pick the serial number as the test attribute. That

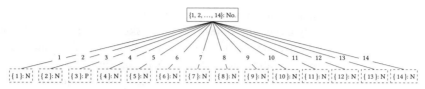

Figure 14.13
Highly branching attribute.

would get us to the tree in figure 14.13. That tree perfectly classifies the training set with a single, and very simple, rule, checking the value of the serial number of the instance. That tree can classify nothing else, however, because no other instance will have any of the serial numbers in the training set. It is therefore completely useless. True, nobody sane would use a serial number or any other form of ID as a test attribute, but it is not unreasonable to pick a date, or some other attribute that, even though it does not identify an instance, has a lot of different values spread among instances.

The problem stems from the fact that highly branching attributes lead to high information gain. To solve the problem we must guard against that. Instead of using information gain as our measure for picking the test attribute we can use a modification of information gain called *gain ratio*. We start by introducing a new term, called *split information*, defined for a node X and a candidate test attribute a that takes c different values as:

$$SI(X, a) = -p(y_{1|a})\lg p(y_{1|a}) - p(y_{2|a})\lg p(y_{2|a}) - \cdots - p(y_{c|a})\lg p(y_{c|a})$$

where each $y_{i|a}$ is the proportion of instances in our set that has a particular value for a. Split information is, again, entropy. But while to this point we were concerned with entropy with respect to the target attribute, now we are concerned with entropy with respect to the candidate test attribute. The gain ratio is then:

$$GR(X, A) = \frac{G(X, a)}{SI(X, a)}$$

The gain ratio penalizes high branching attributes. Every attribute that completely partitions the training set to subsets with one instance each will have, if there are n instances, $SI(X, a) = -(1/n)\lg(1/n) - (1/n)\lg(1/n) - \cdots - (1/n)\lg(1/n) = -\lg(1/n) = \lg n$. By contrast, an attribute that partitions the training set to two equal subsets will have $SI(X, a) = -(1/2)\lg(1/2) - (1/2)\lg(1/2) = \lg 2 = 1$.

The gain ratio does not completely solve the problem because if one of the p_is is very large it becomes very large, skewing the results. To avoid that we can first calculate the information gain and apply the gain ratio as a second step, for those attributes with above average information gain.

Another problem that arises in applications is that real-world data often lack values for some attributes. These are called *missing values*. Taking temperature again as an example, it may turn out that we do not have temperature measurements for all our data. We can waive away the problem by positing that a missing value is still a value, even though it looks special. We may assign a specific value standing for not available (for example, "NA"), and pretend that this is, for instance, another temperature measurement. This is straightforward and will do, but not always; in such cases we must employ other, most sophisticated workarounds.

Finally, an important issue that arises in all classification approaches, and indeed a serious concern in Machine Learning in general, is *overfitting*. In Machine Learning we start with a training set that we use to teach the computer to perform a certain task. In classification, we start with a training set that contains some data with known classes and we arrive at a prediction model, in the form of a decision tree, that we use to predict the class of other data. Overfitting occurs when our prediction model, our tree, is too precise to be any good. The tree in figure 14.13 is an extreme example of overfitting; in fact it is so extreme that it is not a problem because we can easily spot that it's wrong. But overfitting may not be so obvious, so we may get a decision tree that looks sensible but in practice fails at its classification task.

Overfitting is an insidious problem, and there are not easy solutions for it. The best we can do is to recognize that it can occur and guard against it. We can, for example, use *holdout data*, a part of our training set that we do not use during training, but use afterward for testing how well the decision tree performs on it. This is no panacea; overfitting can still occur, and it is often an empirical call whether it does. If it is any consolation, overfitting is the bane of even seasoned professionals in Machine Learning.

Notes

Claude Elwood Shannon launched Information theory in a paper where he set out to introduce a "mathematical theory of communication" [181]; this seminal work is also available in book form, accompanied by a helpful introduction [183]. That was not his first achievement. Before that, at the age of 21, when he was a student studying for his master's degree at the Massachusetts Institute of Technology, he showed that boolean algebra can be used as a basis for electrical circuits. Shannon also worked on an estimate for the entropy of English letters, giving values between 1.3 bits and 1.5 bits for pieces of text 16 letters long [182]. More recently, Thomas Cover and Roger King arrived at an estimate of 1.3 bits per letter [43]. To really appreciate the depth and wealth of Information Theory, you should look into some of the books treating the subject. James Stone has written a tutorial introduction [193]; the book by MacKay [131] is a somewhat more advanced text that segues to other topics like probabilities, inference, and neural networks. Thomas Cover (who arrived at the 1.3 bits per letter estimate) and Joy Thomas have written a comprehensive introduction [44]. For a rigorous mathematical treatment, see the book by Robert Gray [83]. For a non-technical overview of the role of information in modern societies and their economies, see César Hidalgo's book [91].

The ID3 algorithm is a relative of an older approach, called Concept Learning System (CLS), developed in the 1950s [100]. Ross Quinlan, after publishing ID3 [158, 159, 160], went on to improve it in several ways. A popular extension of ID3 that has found widespread use is C4.5 [161]. The weather data example we have used comes from the original ID3 publications. CART (Classification and Regression Trees) is another popular algorithm that has many similarities with ID3 [28].

The field of Machine Learning is vast. Tom Mitchell's book is a classic introduction [142]. Popular books on the subject include the textbook by Hastie, Tibshirani, and Friedman [90] and the primer by James, Witten, Hastie, and Tibshirani [102]; Bishop's book on pattern recognition and Machine Learning [20]; and the introduction by Alpaydın [2]. Murphy's book approaches the subject through a Bayesian probabilistic perspective that has proved very fruitful [148]. An introductory text for Data Mining, a subfield of Machine Learning, is the book by Witten, Frank, and Hall [219]. You can also check the top ten algorithms in Data Mining, as identified in a topic conference in 2006 [220].

There are no extant writings of William of Ockham (about 1287–1347) that contain the eponymous rule, and in fact similar rules predate Ockham by a long time. For example, Aristotle (384–322 BCE) gives a similar rule in his Posterior Analytics (Book I, 25), stating that among competing hypotheses, the best is the one with the fewest requirements, presumptions, and assumptions. More recently, Frank Wilczek, winner of the Nobel Prize in Physics, cast the rule as: "We say that an explanation, or more generally a theory, is *economical* if it assumes little and explains a lot...It seems reasonable, intuitively, to prefer economical explanations over their opposites—explanations that invoke many assumptions to explain a limited range of facts or observations" [216].

A cautionary tale for prediction models comes from Google. Google Flu Trends is a service that predicts flue prevalence from flu-related searches on the Internet [78]. It was launched in 2008, and its estimates over the years matched those of the US Centers for Disease Control and Prevention (CDC); but then, in 2013 the predictions went awry [49]. The culprits seem to be overfitting and "big data hubris," the implicit assumption that big volumes of data can substitute, rather than supplement, traditional data collection and data analysis [122].

As algorithms, particularly those that leverage big data, have gained ground on more and more aspects of human activity, their adoption brings forward ethical questions. Algorithms can be used to spot potential lawbreakers, screen job applicants, calculate insurance premiums. When they are used for such purposes it is important to understand how they work and why they give the results they do [152]. Algorithms can lighten our workload, not our responsibility.

Exercises

1. The Latin phrase "Ibis redibis and per bella peribis" has two meanings, depending on where you place a comma. The variant "Ibis, redibis, nunquam per bella peribis" means "You will go, you will return, never in war will you perish." The alternative "Ibis, redibis nunquam, per bella peribis" means "You will go, you will never return, in war you will perish." The phrase is attributed to the oracles of Dodona, in ancient Greece (but they spoke Greek, not Latin, so it's probably apocryphal). What is the entropy of the phrase?

2. Figure 14.3 shows the entropy of a coin, for various probabilities of heads and tails. Can you make a plot of the entropy of a die, where one event is "It will land one" and the other event is "It will land two, three, four, five, six"? At which

probability of the first event is the entropy maximized? What is the maximum value of the entropy?

3. Implement the ID3 algorithm but using as a classifier a simpler method by which you pick each attribute in turn, like we did in figure 14.12.

4. Implement the ID3 algorithm incorporating the gain ratio correction.

5. The *Gini impurity measure* is another rule that can be used for partitioning the examples in a classification tree node. If $p(x_i)$ is the probability that an instance belongs in class x_i, then $p(1 - x_i)$ is the probability that the instance does not belong in class x_i. If we pick an instance at random, then the probability that it will belong in class x_i is $p(x_i)$. If we assign the instance in a class at random, then the probability that we will classify it incorrectly is $1 - p(x_i)$. Therefore, the probability that we'll pick at random an instance from class x_i and will classify it incorrectly if we just classify it at random is $p(x_i)(1 - p(x_i))$. The Gini impurity is the sum of these probabilities over all n items:

$$p(x_1)(1 - p(x_1)) + p(x_2)(1 - p(x_2)) + \cdots + p(x_n)(1 - p(x_n))$$

Gini impurity is zero when all examples in a node fall into the same category. Now, instead of using the information gain to partition our examples, we can use the reduction in Gini impurity to guide our decision. Modify the ID3 algorithm so that it uses the Gini impurity measure.

15 Stringing Along

When scanning through a lengthy piece of text in your browser, you probably hit the search in page facility (or some equivalent by any other name). You type in part of the text that you are interested in, and your browser highlights on the page the parts where the part appears. The same functionality is present in all kind of documents, like PDF, for example. It is a staple of word processors and editors; correcting a term in a document is a simple matter of doing a find and replace, where the program will find all occurrences of a problematic part and replace it with its corrected version.

All these are instances of the same underlying operation: *string matching*, also called *string search*. All text in computers is internally represented as strings, which are typically arrays of characters encoded in a particular way as numbers. As arrays, the positions in an array representing a string start from zero. A paragraph, page, or book can all be represented as strings of varying length. Searching for something in a string is essentially trying to find where a particular string occurs inside another string: think of looking for a particular word inside a paragraph. If both strings have the same length, then we are actually trying to find out whether the two strings have the same content. This is also string matching, of a degenerate sort, and as such it is a simpler problem than the more general problem of looking for a match of a small part of a big string, because we only need to see whether the strings are the same when compared on a character by character basis.

String matching has a much wider application than looking for something inside text. The same principles apply to any situation where we try to find something inside something else, where both the search item and the search area are sequences of symbols from the same alphabet. The alphabet may be the alphabet of a human language or something else entirely.

In biology, the *genetic code* is the set of rules by which DNA and RNA encode proteins. The DNA is composed by sequences of bases. There are four

Table 15.1

The DNA genetic code.

(1)	(2) T		C		A		G		(3)
T	TTT	Phenylalanine	TCT	Serine	TAT	Tyrosine	TGT	Cysteine	T
	TTC		TCC		TAC		TGC		C
	TTA		TCA		TAA	Stop	TGA	Stop	A
	TTG		TCG		TAG	Stop	TGG	Tryptophan	G
C	CTT	Leucine	CCT	Proline	CAT	Histidine	CGT	Arginine	T
	CTC		CCC		CAC		CGT		C
	CTA		CCA		CAA	Glutamine	CGA		A
	CTG		CCG		CAG		CGG		G
A	ATT	Isoleucine	ACT	Threonine	AAT	Asparagine	AGT	Serine	T
	ATC		ACC		AAC		AGC		C
	ATA		ACA		AAA	Lysine	AGA	Arginine	A
	ATG	Methionine / Start	AGC		AAG		AGG		G
G	GTT	Valine	GCT	Alanine	GAT	Aspartic acid	GGT	Glycine	T
	GTC		GCC		GAC		GGC		C
	GTA		GCA		GAA	Glutamic acid	GGA		A
	GTG		GCG		GAG		GGG		G

bases in the DNA: adenine (A), guanine (G), cytosine (C), and thymine (T). A triplet of bases, called a *codon*, encodes one particular amino acid. A sequence of codons encodes a particular protein; such a codon sequence is a *gene*. DNA resides in the chromosomes; the proteins corresponding to genes are constructed in other parts of the cell. The code for each particular protein is carried by RNA, in particular messenger RNA (mRNA), which uses again four bases: A, G, C, and uracil (U) instead of thymine.

The unraveling of the genetic code has been a triumph of molecular biology. There are only 20 amino acids that compose all proteins, and these 20 amino acids are encoded in DNA and RNA by codon sequences. There are also special codons that define the start and end of each protein encoding, much like white space demarcates a word from another word in the text. The genetic code is, therefore, a set of rules written with an alphabet of four characters. You can see all DNA codons in table 15.1. The circled numbers on top of the table refer to the first, second, and third letters of each codon. The intersection of the first column and the column corresponding to the second letter is the column with all different possibilities for the third letter; by picking a letter from the column headed by the circled three, we get a specific amino acid.

String matching comes into play in molecular biology when we want to find a particular DNA or RNA sequence. Thus, we are looking into a strand of DNA or RNA for a particular sequence of codons. These sequences can be long, containing tens of thousands of bases; the full human genome, which is the complete set of amino acid sequences, is estimated to contain about 3.2 billion bases. String matching at this scale is a serious proposition.

Electronic surveillance is another area where big amounts of data are subject to string matching. Typically some entity is interested in finding some pattern, a message, in a mass of data that are being intercepted. The message may be a code word, a phrase, or an incriminatory transaction. The intercepting agency goes through the data trying to find pattern matches. Unfortunately, intercepting agencies tend to cast a wide net, collecting all sorts of data, most of them completely innocuous; so to be able to do their job they must have recourse to fast string matching mechanisms.

Computer forensics, the gathering of evidence in computers and storage media, uses string matching to identify pieces of information, typically resulting from some particular user behavior. For example, authorities may be looking for evidence that the user has visited sites with specific URLs, or that particular cryptographic keys have been used.

Another application is *intrusion detection*, in which we try to establish whether a computer system has been infiltrated by some harmful software (malware). If we know some byte sequences that can identify the malware, then intrusion detection can use string matching techniques to find the malware lurking inside computer memory or storage. Better still, we can use string matching for *intrusion prevention* by monitoring the network traffic, that is, the traffic of bytes traveling across a system's boundaries. Again, if we know what byte sequences to look for, we can catch malware before it invades our system. We need fast string matching algorithms, so that the matching will not slow down traffic.

Detection of offending text is also essential in *spam detection*; spam is composed of boilerplate text, so a mail filter can use string matching to help the classification of emails as junk. Repeating text occurrences are key in catching instances of plagiarism; cheaters can be caught by checking for the same chunks in essays, assignments, or programs. That said, plagiarists may take care to alter the stuff they copy. Happily, there exist algorithms that take this into account, so it is much more difficult to outwit them.

Text extraction from websites, also called *web scraping* or *screen scraping*, works with string matching. There is a wealth of information over the web rendered in HTML web pages. Such text is semi-structured, in that it is demarcated by particular HTML tags, such as `<li>` and `</li>` for list items. That allows us to extract from a page text that meets a particular condition, such as text between particular tags.

Different string matching applications have different requirements. For example, we may be interested in *exact matching*, where we want to find precisely a string, or *approximate matching*, where we want to find variants of it. We may be dealing with a large alphabet, or with a short one (think of DNA with only four characters). We may be willing to sacrifice speed for easy to understand and implement algorithms, or we may be looking for fast solutions. Here we start with the simplest approach, which will do when speed is not a top priority, before presenting more complex but more efficient algorithms.

String matching concerns finding one string in another string. To make clear what we are trying to match in what, we will call *pattern* the string we are trying to find and *text* the string in which we are trying to find the pattern. This helps the prose, but is not completely precise. The text can be any kind of string, not just humanly readable text. But if we keep that in mind, there is no harm in using this nomenclature. It is common in the field anyway.

15.1   Brute Force String Matching

The most straightforward way to do string matching is the naive brute force approach of starting at the beginning and checking for a match letter by letter. It is a *brute force method* because we do not apply any form of cleverness; you can see it in algorithm 15.1.

We have two strings as input: the pattern we are looking for, p, and the text in which we search for the pattern, t. We will store the results, which will be the indices of t where we find p, in a queue q, so that it is straightforward to access them afterward in the order they are found. If there are no matches, q will be empty. In line 1 we create the output queue, then in lines 2 and 3 we store the length of the pattern, in variable m, and the text, in line n. We enter a loop, in lines 4–9, starting from the beginning of t up to $n - m$ positions in it; the current index in t is given by i. Obviously there cannot be a match after that, because the pattern would fall off the searched text. Each iteration of the loop proceeds one position in t. In each new position, we prepare and enter another loop, in lines 5–7. This inner loop starts at the beginning of p and uses j as an index in it; it checks with $j < m$ that we have not exhausted p. For each character in p, given by $p[j]$, we then check whether it is the same with the jth character of p starting from its current, ith, position. If this happens, we advance j by one. Thus, j shows the number of characters we have matched in t for each different position that we try to find p in it. Note that the checks in

---

Algorithm 15.1: Brute force string search.

```
BruteForceStringSearch(p, t) → q
        Input: p, a pattern
               t, a text
        Output: q, a queue containing the indices of t where p is found; if p
               is not found the queue is empty
 1     q ← CreateQueue()
 2     m ← |p|
 3     n ← |t|
 4     for i ← 0 to n − m do
 5         j ← 0
 6         while j < m and p[j] = t[i + j] do
 7             j ← j + 1
 8         if j = m then
 9             Enqueue(q, i)
10     return q
```

---

line 6 must be in that order; we assume that short-circuit evaluation is at work here, so that we never check beyond the end of p. There are two ways to exit the inner loop, corresponding to the two checks in line 6. If we have $j = m$, then we have exited the loop without any character mismatch, and therefore we have found the pattern we are looking for. Then we add to the queue q the index i of the position in t where we found the match. If we have exited the loop because we found a mismatch, that means p is not present starting at the ith position of t; therefore, we need to try the next position in t, going round a new iteration of the outer loop. At the end we return q.

Figure 15.1 shows what is going on when we are searching for "BARD" in "BADBARBARD". You can think of the whole algorithm as sliding a transparent slide with "BARD" written on it on top of "BADBARBARD". Each value of i corresponds to a different position of the slide; we move the slide one position rightward every time we detect a mismatch between "BARD" and the letters underneath. In the figure we indicate as white-on-black the characters where we establish the mismatch. The characters of "BARD" following the mismatch are grayed out because we do not need to check them; this corresponds to the second check of line 6 of the algorithm. The first two columns in the figure show the values of i and j at the end of each inner loop iteration.

i	j	B	A	D	B	A	R	B	A	R	D
0	2	B	A	R	D						
1	0		B	A	R	D					
2	0			B	A	R	D				
3	3				B	A	R	D			
4	0					B	A	R	D		
5	0						B	A	R	D	
6	4							B	A	R	D

Figure 15.1
Brute force string matching.

i	j	0	0	0	0	0	0	0	0	0	1
0	3	0	0	0	1						
1	3		0	0	0	1					
2	3			0	0	0	1				
3	3				0	0	0	1			
4	3					0	0	0	1		
5	3						0	0	0	1	
6	4							0	0	0	1

Figure 15.2
Worst case brute force string matching.

You can verify that the value of j shows the number of characters matched for each value of i.

The slide metaphor gives as a way to approach the complexity of brute force string search. The outer loop will be executed $n - m$ times. The worst case for the inner loop is to check all characters of p and find a mismatch in the last character each and every time. For example, this will happen when p and t contain only two characters, say 0 and 1, and p matches at the end of t, while the first $m - 1$ characters of p match in all the previous positions; see figure 15.2. Clearly something like that is unlikely to happen in human texts, but they can occur when we are looking for patterns in digital data in general.

In such pathological cases, we will need m iterations of the inner loop for each iteration of the outer loop. As we have $n - m$ iterations of the outer loop, the resulting product is $m(n - m)$; thus, in the worst case the performance of brute force string matching is to the order of $O(m(n - m))$. We often simplify this to $O(mn)$ because n is usually much longer than m, so that $n - m \approx n$.

15.2   The Knuth-Morris-Pratt Algorithm

If you go back to figure 15.1, you may notice that we actually wasting some of our time with comparisons that are doomed to fail. For example, consider how we start:

```
B   A   D   B   A   R   B   A   R   D
B   A   R   D
    B   A   R   D
    B   A   R   D
    B   A   R   D
```

Our first attempt fails when we try to match R against D. Then we try to mach B against A, we fail, and then B against D, and we fail again. But we already know that the second and third character of our text are A and D, respectively. How? Because initially we went as far as the third character of our pattern. So we know that the first three characters of the text are BAD. The first three characters of our pattern are BAR. There is no way we can slide BAR over BAD and get any kind of match; we can go directly one character beyond, which is equivalent to shifting the pattern three places to the right, and start comparing with the rest of the text:

```
B   A   D   B   A   R   B   A   R   D
B   A   R   D
            B   A   R   D
```

But then the same thing happens when we attempt to match at this point.

```
B   A   D   B   A   R   B   A   R   D
            B   A   R   D
                B   A   R   D
                B   A   R   D
                B   A   R   D
```

We know that at the current position the text reads BARB because we have just read it. There is no way that we can slide BARD over BARB one or two places and get a complete match; so we can slide BARB three places to the right and start directly from there:

```
B A D B A R B A R D
    B A R D
        B A R D
```

Let's see another example where the pattern is ABABC and the text in which we search is BABABAABABC.

```
B A B A B A B C A B C
A B A B C
```

We immediately get a mismatch, so we shift the pattern one position to the right and we try again:

```
B A B A B A B C A B C
  A B A B C
```

This time we manage to match four characters from the pattern and meet a mismatch at the fifth character. The part of the text that we have tried to match is ABABA and the pattern is ABABC. We might be tempted to slide the pattern four positions, as we have matched four characters from it:

```
B A B A B A B C A B C
        A B A B C
```

That would be a mistake because by doing it we would miss the match we get by shifting the pattern by two positions:

```
B A B A B A B C A B C
    A B A B C
```

So it seems that we can try matching in a more intelligent way than the naive approach, by shifting the pattern an appropriate amount to the right. We must be careful, though: too much shifting and we will miss a match. What is the general principle at work here?

The method we have been using follows the Knuth-Morris-Pratt algorithm (named by its inventors) and works like this. We proceed character by character in the text. Let's say that at position i of the text we have matched j characters of the pattern. We increase i by one, to $i + 1$. We then check whether the $(j + 1)$th of the pattern matches the $(i + 1)$th character of the text. If yes, we continue increasing i and j. If not, we try to find out: knowing that we have matched j characters in position i but that we cannot match $j + 1$ characters in position $i + 1$, how many characters can we really match in position $i + 1$? We update j accordingly and continue.

	i		*i*
$i = 0$	B A B A B A B C A B C	$i = 1$	B A B A B A B C A B C
$j = 0$	A B A B C	$j = 0$	A B A B C
	j		*j*

	i		*i*
$i = 2$	B A B A B A B C A B C	$i = 3$	B A B A B A B C A B C
$j = 1$	A B A B C	$j = 2$	A B A B C
	j		*j*

	i		*i*
$i = 4$	B A B A B A B C A B C	$i = 5$	B A B A B A B C A B C
$j = 3$	A B A B C	$j = 4$	A B A B C
	j		*j*

	i		*i*
$i = 5$	B A B A B A B C A B C	$i = 6$	B A B A B A B C A B C
$j = 2$	A B A B C	$j = 3$	A B A B C
	j		*j*

	i
$i = 7$	B A B [A B A B C] A B C
$j = 4$	A B A B C
	j

Figure 15.3
A trace of the Knuth-Morris-Pratt algorithm.

In figure 15.3 you can see the Knuth-Morris-Pratt (KMP) algorithm in action in our example. Instead of showing the pattern sliding over the text we show the two pointers i and j that show how many characters we have matched in the text and the pattern, respectively.

We start with both $i = 0$ and $j = 0$. There is a mismatch, but we have not matched any characters in the pattern, so we just increase i and try again. This time we get a match and advance both i and j. We get matches and continue advancing both i and j until we have $i = 5$ and $j = 4$. Then we have a mismatch and have matched a number of characters in the pattern. We want to know where we should start matching the pattern; that is, to what value we should reset j. It turns out, we'll see shortly how, that the correct value for j is 2. So we let $j = 2$ and start again, advancing both i and j as long as we get a match. In the end we have matched all of j, so the position of the match is equal to $i - j + 1$ (we add one because strings are zero-based).

If you prefer to visualize the workings of the algorithm as shifts instead of changes in i and j, the two positions shift we showed before happens when we increase i and we have to reset j to a lower value. This corresponds to shifting the pattern to the right by $s = j_c - j$ positions, where j_c is the current value of j. You can verify that this shift happens when $i = 5, j = 2$. So this:

$$
\begin{array}{llll}
 & & i & \\
i = 5 & \text{B A B A B A B C A B C} & & i = 5 \\
j = 4 & \text{A B A B C} & & j = 2 \\
 & \hspace{1.5em} j & &
\end{array}
\qquad
\begin{array}{l}
\hspace{2em} i \\
\text{B A B A B A B C A B C} \\
\text{A B A B C} \\
\hspace{3em} j
\end{array}
$$

is the same with this:

$$
\begin{array}{l}
\text{B A B A B } \boxed{\text{A}} \text{ B C A B C} \\
\text{A B A B } \boxed{\text{C}}
\end{array}
\quad\longrightarrow\quad
\begin{array}{l}
\text{B A B A B } \boxed{\text{A}} \text{ B C A B C} \\
\hspace{2em}\text{A B } \boxed{\text{A}} \text{ B C}
\end{array}
$$

The Knuth-Morris-Pratt algorithm tries to match the pattern with the text character by character. With this shifting, when it encounters a mismatch, it tries to save as much of the already matched part of the pattern as possible, instead of discarding everything and starting from the beginning of the pattern.

To complete the algorithm we need to know exactly how we determine which part of the pattern to reuse when we encounter a mismatch. To see this, let's take a brief detour in terminology. A part of a string is called a *substring*. A part of the string at the start of a string is a *prefix*; a part of the string at the end of a string is its *suffix*. A string can have many prefixes: all A, AB, ABA, ... are prefixes of the string ABAXYZABA. The corner cases are the empty string, which is considered to be a prefix of every string, and the whole string, which is considered to be its own prefix. A *proper prefix* is a prefix that is not the whole string. Similarly, a string can have many suffixes: all A, BA, ABA, ... are suffixes of ABAXYZABA. Again we consider the empty string and the string itself to be valid suffixes. A *proper suffix* is a suffix that is not the whole string. In the literature you may also find definitions that require proper prefixes and suffixes not to be empty strings. We will be dealing with non-empty prefixes and suffixes.

A *border* is a proper prefix of a string that is also a proper suffix of the same string; so ABA is a border of the string ABAXYZABA. The *maximum border* of a string is the border with the maximum length: all A, AB, and ABA are borders of the ABAYXABA string. The maximum border is ABA. We define the length of the maximum border of the string to be zero if the string has no border at all. Usually a string with a border looks something like this:

We indicate the prefix and the suffix of the border with a dotted pattern. Note that the prefix and the suffix of a border may overlap, like in the string ABABABA where the border is ABABA, but this need not concern us here, and does not have any impact on the discussion.

With this terminology at hand we can tackle the answer to the question of which part of the pattern we can reuse in a mismatch. Suppose we encounter a mismatch like the following:

On the top we have the text and on the bottom the pattern. We indicate with a hatch pattern the part of the text that we have not yet read; the grey parts are the parts that have found that they match and the black parts are the mismatched characters. In a situation like this, let's also suppose that we will get a match up to and including the mismatched character by shifting the pattern to the right a certain number of places:

This time we indicate the parts that match with a dotted pattern. Now imagine that we shift back the pattern to its original position. It will look like:

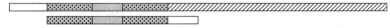

Because we know that the grey parts match *and* the dotted parts match, the only way we can obtain the above is if the dotted part repeats at the end of the pattern; otherwise there would be a mismatch before the originally mismatched character. So we get:

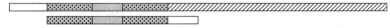

Then it turns out that the prefix of the pattern that we have matched must have a border! That gives the solution to our problem: when we encounter a mismatch, we may be able to reuse a part of the pattern we have matched, if this part is a border. It is not necessary that we will get a match with a border, but we should try; moreover, we should try to get a match with the *maximum* border and then with smaller borders, in decreasing order, lest we miss a potential match. That is because a *longer* border results in a *shorter* shift; taken in reverse, *longer shifts* correspond to *shorter* borders. Compare this:

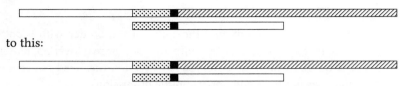

to this:

The second example has a longer border and therefore is shifted less to the right than the first example. This is just a consequence of the expression $s = j_c - j$ that gives the number of shifts. The larger j is, the smaller the shift to the right. So, as we remarked, starting with the maximum border and proceeding with decreasing borders ensures that we are not going to skip over a match. Say we are looking for the pattern AABAAA in the text AABAABAA. We get a mismatch after five characters:

```
A A B A A B A A
A A B A A A
```

The matched prefix of the pattern is AABAA, which has a maximum border with length two, AA, and another border, A, with length one. We must use the border with length two, AA, resulting in a shift of three positions and a match:

```
A A B A A B A A A A
    A A B A A A
```

If we skip that border and try with the border with length one, A, resulting in a shift of four positions, then we will miss the above match:

```
A A B A A B A A A A
      A A B A A A
```

Because we will be using borders of different prefixes of p as we search for a match, we must precompute them so that whenever we want, if we have a prefix of p of length j, we can directly find the maximum border of that prefix of p. If we precompute the borders, it is handy to put them in an array b so that $b[j]$ will contain the length of the maximum border of the prefix of p that has length j.

Figure 15.4a shows the border array for the pattern ABCABCACAB. The array is at the bottom of the figure; on the top of the figure you can see the length of each successive prefix of the array. For a prefix of length zero we define its length to be zero. If you take the prefix with length five, that is, ABCAB, you can see that it has a border AB of length two. Similarly, if you take the prefix with length seven, that is, ABCABCA, you can see that it has a border ABCA of length four.

j	0	1	2	3	4	5	6	7	8	9	10
		A	B	C	A	B	C	A	C	A	B
$b[j]$	0	0	0	0	1	2	3	4	0	1	2

j	0	1	2	3	4	5	6
		A	A	B	A	A	A
$b[j]$	0	0	1	0	1	2	2

(a) Border array for pattern ABCABCACAB.   (b) Border array for pattern AABAAA.

Figure 15.4
Border arrays.

Note that the border array contains the maximum border for each prefix. So, in figure 15.4b you can see that the prefix of length five, that is, AABAA, has two borders: AA and A. The maximum border is AA with length two, which is what is in the corresponding cell of the border array.

If we have a function FindBorders(p) that creates the array b for pattern p, then we have algorithm 15.2 that renders the discussion so far in algorithmic form.

The algorithm is a straight application of the ideas we have been describing, and the best way to understand it is to read it by going through an example, such as the one in figure 15.3 or the one in figure 15.5; note that we stop the traces at the time of the first match. In lines 1–4 we lay down the groundwork. We create the return queue, we calculate the length of the pattern and the text, and we calculate the borders array. Then in line 5 we initialize j, which will count how many characters we have matched in the pattern. Another variable, i, will count how many characters we have read from the text. Lines 6–13 is a loop that proceeds through each character from the text. For every new character we read, if we have already read and matched part of the pattern and we find a mismatch with the current character of the text, we need to reset j to the length of the maximum border of the matched prefix of the pattern. This is the task of lines 7 and 8. Note that this is a loop, because we may find a mismatch at the border, so that we have to try a shorter border, and so on. In effect, lines 7–8 check successive increasing shifts, until we find a match. This is what happens in figure 15.5, when we have $i = 5$ and $j = 5$ and then while keeping i unchanged we set $j = 2$ and then $j = 1$. This occurs because for $j = 5$ the matched part of the pattern is AACAA, which has a border of length two. This leads us to set $j = 2$, but we still get a mismatch; therefore we try the border of the prefix of length two, AA, which is just A, of length one. Therefore, we set $j = 1$.

Algorithm 15.2: Knuth-Morris-Pratt.

```
KnuthMorrisPratt(p, t) → q
    Input: p, a pattern
           t, a text
    Output: q, a queue containing the indices of t where p is found; if p
            is not found the queue is empty
 1   q ← CreateQueue()
 2   m ← |p|
 3   n ← |t|
 4   b ← FindBorders(p)
 5   j ← 0
 6   for i ← 0 to n do
 7       while j > 0 and p[j] ≠ t[i] do
 8           j ← b[j]
 9       if p[i] = t[i] then
10           j ← j + 1
11       if j = m then
12           Enqueue(q, i − j + 1)
13           j ← b[j]
14   return q
```

When we find a matching character, we simply have to increase the value of j, as we do in lines 9–10. If we manage to match all characters of the pattern, which we check in line 11, then we have a complete match; we add the position of the match to a queue q, in line 12. Then before we go on to read the next character of the text, we must reset j to the longest border, in line 13, which corresponds to the shorter shift we can do without missing another potential match.

To complete the description of the Knuth-Morris-Pratt algorithm, we need to define the function FindBorders. We work as follows. If we have already found that for a prefix of length i we have a border of length j, as in figure 15.6a, we can easily check whether the prefix of length $i + 1$, which ends at position i, has a border of length $j + 1$, which ends at position j. The only way this can happen is if the character in position j of the pattern, the $(j + 1)$th character of the pattern, is the same with the character in position i of the pattern, the $(i + 1)$th character of the pattern; see figure 15.6b. If this does not

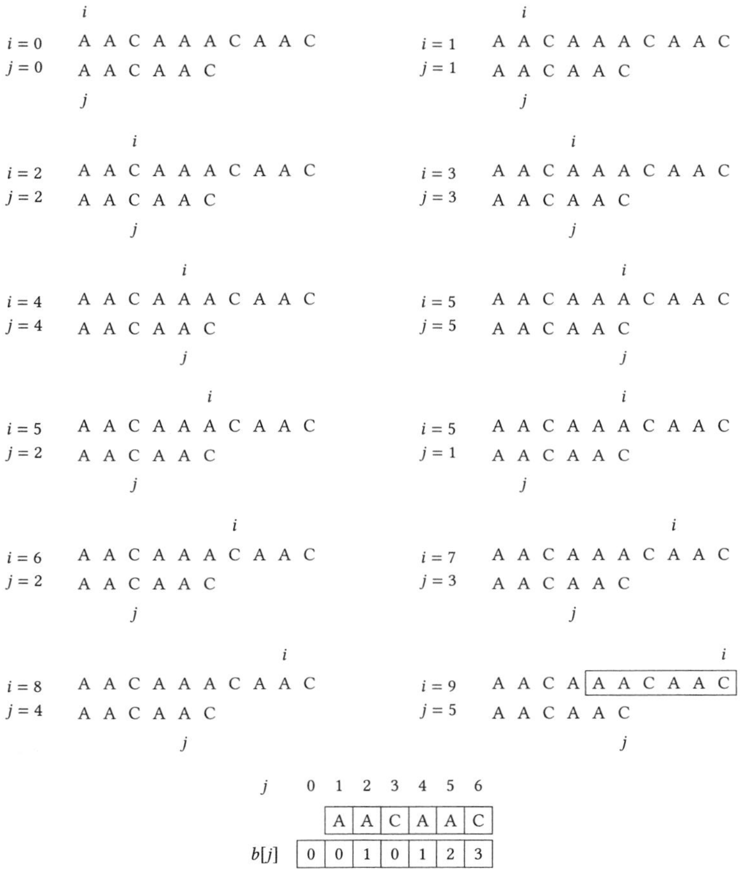

```
              i                                    i
i = 0   A A C A A A C A A C        i = 1    A A C A A A C A A C
j = 0   A A C A A C                j = 1    A A C A A C
        j                                   j

                i                                    i
i = 2   A A C A A A C A A C        i = 3    A A C A A A C A A C
j = 2   A A C A A C                j = 3    A A C A A C
            j                                    j

                  i                                      i
i = 4   A A C A A A C A A C        i = 5    A A C A A A C A A C
j = 4   A A C A A C                j = 5    A A C A A C
              j                                    j

                  i                                      i
i = 5   A A C A A A C A A C        i = 5    A A C A A A C A A C
j = 2   A A C A A C                j = 1    A A C A A C
            j                                    j

                    i                                        i
i = 6   A A C A A A C A A C        i = 7    A A C A A A C A A C
j = 2   A A C A A C                j = 3    A A C A A C
            j                                    j

                      i                                          i
i = 8   A A C A A A C A A C        i = 9    A A C A A A C A A C
j = 4   A A C A A C                j = 5    A A C A A C
              j                                    j
```

```
        j    0  1  2  3  4  5  6
                A  A  C  A  A  C
       b[j]  0  0  1  0  1  2  3
```

Figure 15.5
Another trace the Knuth-Morris-Pratt algorithm; the borders array is at the bottom.

happen, then the best we can do is check the immediately shorter border, of length say $j' < j$, and see whether that border's last character matches the $(i + 1)$th character of the pattern; see figure 15.6c. If, again, this does not happen, then we try the immediately shorter border, and so on. If at any time we find out that there is no such border, then clearly the border for the prefix of length $i + 1$ is zero.

This leads to a method for finding borders. We work with increasing prefixes of the string whose borders we are trying to find. For a prefix of length

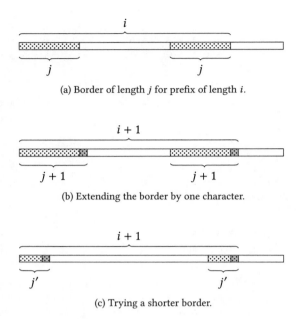

(a) Border of length j for prefix of length i.

(b) Extending the border by one character.

(c) Trying a shorter border.

Figure 15.6
Finding borders of a string.

zero and length one, the length of the border is zero. Then if we have a prefix of length i, we work as above: we check whether we can extend the existing border by one character; if not, we try shorter borders, until there are no borders. That is the task of algorithm 15.3. The algorihtm takes as input a string p and returns an array b so that $b[i]$ is the length of the border of the prefix of p with length i.

Algorithm 15.3 starts by doing some housekeeping: counting the length of the string, in line 1, creating the output array, in line 2, setting the length of the current border, j, to zero in line 3, and setting the length of the borders of the prefix of p of length zero and one in lines 4–5; these are zero, as we have said. Then we enter a loop, in lines 6–11, for each character of p starting from its *second* character onward. We start from the second character because we already know that the prefix of p of length one has a border of length zero.

In lines 7–8 we try to find a shorter border that could match, if the current border does not. In lines 9–10 we extend the border, whichever border we found (it could be a zero border), by one, if it is possible. Then in line 11

Algorithm 15.3: Find the borders of a string.

FindBorders(p) $\rightarrow b$
    Input: p, a string
    Output: b, an array of length $|p| + 1$ containing the lengths of the
                 borders of p; $b[i]$ contains the length of the border of the
                 prefix of p of length i

 1   $m \leftarrow |p|$
 2   $b \leftarrow$ CreateArray$(m + 1)$
 3   $j \leftarrow 0$
 4   $b[0] \leftarrow j$
 5   $b[1] \leftarrow j$
 6   **for** $i \leftarrow 1$ **to** m **do**
 7   **while** $j > 0$ **and** $p[j] \neq p[i]$ **do**
 8          $j \leftarrow b[j]$
 9   **if** $p[j] = p[i]$ **then**
10          $j \leftarrow j + 1$
11       $b[i + 1] \leftarrow j$
12   **return** b

---

we store the length of the border in the appropriate position in the array b. Because the first two elements of b have already been set, we must set the element at position $i + 1$. Finally we return the borders array. A trace of the algorithm finding the borders of the string ACABABAB is in figure 15.7. Each row of the figure shows the values of i, j, and the contents of b at the beginning and end of each iteration of the outer loop.

The remarkable thing about algorithm 15.3 is that it is pretty much the same with algorithm 15.2. Indeed, in algorithm 15.2 we are matching a pattern p with a text t; in algorithm 15.3 we are matching a pattern p with itself. We use essentially the same process, first to find the borders of our pattern, then, having found the borders, to carry out the matching per se. The Knuth-Morris-Pratt algorithm may not be the simplest one to grasp, but once you do, you can appreciate its elegance.

Knuth-Morris-Pratt is not only elegant, it is fast. Because algorithms 15.2 and 15.3 are essentially the same, we only need to analyze one of the two. The outer loop of algorithm 15.2 runs n times. In each of these iterations we have some iterations of the inner loop of lines 7–8. This is repeated as long as

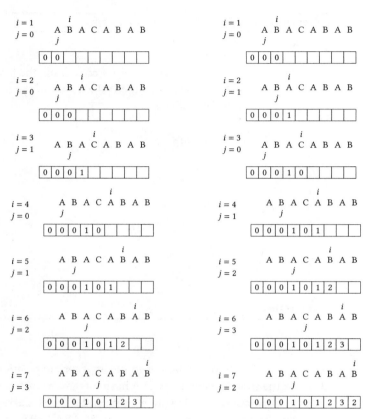

Figure 15.7
Trace of finding the borders of ABACABAB.

$j > 0$, and at each iteration j is decreased. Moreover, j can only be increased once, in line 10, during an iteration of the outer loop. Therefore in all the iterations of the inner loop, j cannot be decreased more than n times, which means that the inner loop cannot be repeated more than n times in total. It follows that the computational complexity the algorithm, without taking into account FindBorders, is $O(2n) = O(n)$. With a similar analysis, the computational complexity of FindBorders is $O(m)$. So the total time taken by the Knuth-Morris-Pratt algorithm, including the preprocessing step of finding the pattern's borders, is $O(m + n)$. To this we must add a small price in space: we

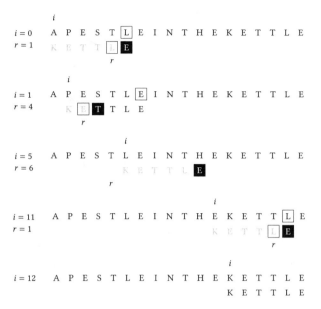

Figure 15.8
The Boyer-Moore-Horspool algorithm.

need to store the b array with the borders. Its length, though, at $m + 1$, is not normally a problem.

15.3   The Boyer-Moore-Horspool Algorithm

Up until now we have been scanning the text from the left to the right. If we change tack and think about scanning the text from the right to the left, then we can work with another, simple, algorithm, which works well in practice. The algorithm is called Boyer-Moore-Horspool, again after its inventors.

In figure 15.8 we are searching for the pattern KETTLE in the text string APESTLEINTHEKETTLE using the Boyer-Moore-Horspool algorithm. We place KETTLE at the beginning of the text. Then instead of starting to check the characters for matches from the left to the right, we start from the right to the left.

We come immediately upon a mismatch; the last character of KETTLE, E, against the last character of the prefix APESTL of the text, the latter L. Therefore, we can start sliding the pattern to the right. Because the rightmost character we have read is the character L, our next effort for matching should be by moving the KETTLE so that the L in the pattern matches the L in APESTL. In other words, when we start reading the text at position $i = 0$, we find a mismatch that we try to amend by moving the pattern to the right by $r = 1$ positions.

We try again, going from the right to the left. This time we come upon a mismatch on the character T of the pattern. The last character that we have read from the text is the character E; therefore, the best we can do is slide the pattern rightward so that the next occurrence of E in the mattern matches the character E, the last character of the prefix APESTLE of the text. That corresponds to a slide rightward by $r = 4$ positions.

The resulting position results in an immediate mismatch. Moreover, the last character of the text that we have read, the character H, does not exist in the pattern at all. So, we can move the pattern all the way to the right of the character H, which corresponds to a slide rightward by $r = 6$ positions.

When we do that, we are at position $i = 11$ and a mismatch of L and E, like the one when we started our search. Again we move one position to the right, to $i = 12$, where we finally find a complete match of the pattern with the text.

As you can see in figure 15.8, the approach allows us to skip a lot of characters from the text; but for it to work, we need a way to know how many characters to slide the pattern rightward each time. As it turns out, the rule is straightfoward.

If there is a mismatch and the mismatched character is nowhere in the pattern, then we slide the pattern m positions to the right, where m is the length of the pattern because we must go past the character that we have no chance of matching; see figure 15.9a.

If there is a mismatch and the mismatched character in the text exists in the pattern at position $r \geq 1$ counting from the *right* of the pattern, then we slide the pattern r positions to the right. There may be multiple occurrences of the character in the pattern. For the scheme to work, r is the index of the *rightmost* occurrence of the mismatched character in the pattern, counting from the right; see figure 15.9b.

To make the algorithm work we need a way to find the index of the rightmost occurrence of each character in the pattern. A way to do that is to create a special table. The table will be an array as long as the alphabet of the text

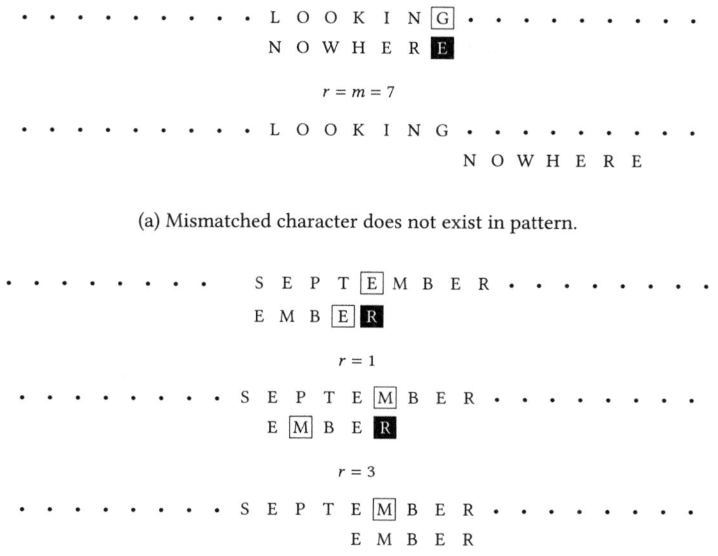

· · · · · · · · · · L O O K I N [G] · · · · · · · · · ·
N O W H E R [E]

$r = m = 7$

· · · · · · · · · L O O K I N G · · · · · · · · · ·
N O W H E R E

(a) Mismatched character does not exist in pattern.

· · · · · · · · · S E P T [E] M B E R · · · · · · · · ·
E M B [E] [R]

$r = 1$

· · · · · · · · · S E P T E [M] B E R · · · · · · · · ·
E [M] B E [R]

$r = 3$

· · · · · · · · · S E P T E [M] B E R · · · · · · · · ·
E M B E R

(b) Mismatched character appears in pattern.

Figure 15.9
Mismatched character rule.

and the string. For example, if we are using the ASCII alphabet, the table will contain 128 elements. Following what we have been saying above, if we call this table rt, the contents of $rt[i]$ will be the index of the rightmost position $r \geq 1$ of the ith ASCII character in the pattern, counting from the end of the pattern, if the character is present in the pattern, or the length m of the pattern otherwise.

For the pattern KETTLE, the table rt will have all entries equal to six, except for the entries 69 (ASCII code for E), 75 (ASCII code for K), 76 (ASCII code for L), and 84 (ASCII code for T). The values for the letters in the pattern and their corresponding indices, in decimal and hexadecimal format, are on the left of figure 15.10. On the right of the figure we show the same information for the pattern EMBER; the logic is the same with the one for KETTLE. Note that the value corresponding to the letter R is equal to 5. That is because if we find a mismatch with it, then we need to slide the pattern all over its length to try again for a match with the text. That is consistent with the definition of the

Letter	K	E	T	T	L	E		E	M	B	E	R
ASCII (decimal)	75	69	84	84	76	69		69	77	66	69	82
ASCII (hexadecimal)	4B	45	54	54	4C	45		45	4D	42	45	52
Occurence from right	5	4	2	2	1	4		1	3	2	1	5

Figure 15.10
Rightmost occurrences of letters in patterns.

	0	1	2	3	4	5	6	7	8	9	A	B	C	D	E	F
0	6	6	6	6	6	6	6	6	6	6	6	6	6	6	6	6
1	6	6	6	6	6	6	6	6	6	6	6	6	6	6	6	6
2	6	6	6	6	6	6	6	6	6	6	6	6	6	6	6	6
3	6	6	6	6	6	6	6	6	6	6	6	6	6	6	6	6
4	6	6	6	6	6	**4**	6	6	6	6	6	**5**	**1**	6	6	6
5	6	6	6	6	**2**	6	6	6	6	6	6	6	6	6	6	6
6	6	6	6	6	6	6	6	6	6	6	6	6	6	6	6	6
7	6	6	6	6	6	6	6	6	6	6	6	6	6	6	6	6

(a) Rightmost occurrences table for KETTLE.

	0	1	2	3	4	5	6	7	8	9	A	B	C	D	E	F
0	5	5	5	5	5	5	5	5	5	5	5	5	5	5	5	5
1	5	5	5	5	5	5	5	5	5	5	5	5	5	5	5	5
2	5	5	5	5	5	5	5	5	5	5	5	5	5	5	5	5
3	5	5	5	5	5	5	5	5	5	5	5	5	5	5	5	5
4	5	5	**2**	5	5	**1**	5	5	5	5	5	5	5	**3**	5	5
5	5	5	5	5	5	5	5	5	5	5	5	5	5	5	5	5
6	5	5	5	5	5	5	5	5	5	5	5	5	5	5	5	5
7	5	5	5	5	5	5	5	5	5	5	5	5	5	5	5	5

(b) Rightmost occurrences table for EMBER.

Figure 15.11
Rightmost occurrences tables.

mismatch character rule, which requires that $r \geq 1$. If a character only occurs at the end of the pattern, its position from the right is zero and $r \geq 1$ does not hold, so we treat it as the other entries in the table that do not appear in the pattern. That ensures that a mismatch there will lead to a slide over the whole length of the pattern.

In figure 15.11a we show the rightmost occurrences table for KETTLE, always assuming that the alphabet consists of the 128 characters in the ASCII encoding. The figure arranges the array rt in a tabular format and highlights

---

Algorithm 15.4: Create rightmost occurrences table.

CreateRtOccurrencesTable(p, t, s) $\rightarrow q$
    Input: p, a pattern
            s, the size of the alphabet
    Output: rt an array of size s; for the ith letter of the alphabet, $rt[i]$
             will be the index of the rightmost position $r \geq 1$ where the
             character appears in p, counting from the end of the pattern,
             or the length of the pattern p otherwise

1   $rt \leftarrow$ CreateArray(s)
2   $m \leftarrow |p|$
3   **for** $i \leftarrow 0$ **to** s **do**
4       $rt[i] \leftarrow m$
5   **for** $i \leftarrow 0$ **to** $m - 1$ **do**
6       $rt[\text{Ord}(p[i])] \leftarrow m - i - 1$
7   **return** rt

---

the positions of the characters that exist in KETTLE. The first row and the first column contain hexadecimal values so that characters are easy to find, working with figure 15.10. You can check, for instance, that the entry 0x4C in the table, corresponding to the character L, has value 1. In reality, rt is a simple one-dimensional array with indices going from 0 to 127, but this would be unwieldy to display in a figure.

In both parts of figure 15.11, most of the entries in the tables are equal to the length of the pattern. That is why the Boyer-Moore-Horspool algorithm can be efficient: most of the characters in the alphabet will not be present in the table of rightmost occurrences; this will enable us to skip over the whole pattern whenever we come upon any of these characters. However, if the pattern contains a lot of the characters of the alphabet, then the algorithm may not be efficient, but this happens rarely.

We need a way to create the rightmost occurrences table. That is the task of algorithm 15.4. Although we have been talking about ASCII in our examples, the algorithm is more general and can handle any alphabet, provided we pass the size of the alphabet as argument. The function Ord(c) returns the position of the character c in the alphabet, counting from zero. The algorithm starts by creating the array rt (line 1) and then calculates the length, m, of the pattern, p, in line 2. In lines 3–4 it sets all the contents of the array rt to m. Then in

Figure 15.12
Finding the rightmost occurrences in EMBER.

lines 5–6 we go over each character i in the pattern, except from the last, and we calculate how far from the right it is; we set the contents of rt to the result. Finally, we return the array rt.

There are two things to note. First, we do not go over the last character because, as we have said, a mismatch there, if the character does not exist anywhere else in the pattern, requires shifting the whole pattern anyway, so the correct value for it is m. Second, during the execution of the algorithm the contents of $rt[i]$ may change, if we find the same character later on. Figure 15.12 shows how algorithm 15.4 changes the values of the table rt for EMBER in the execution of the loop of lines 5–6. The table is shown vertically; columns correspond to the state of the table before the loop of lines 5–6 and then for each value of i in the loop iterations. The leftmost column shows the letters that are mapped to the table positions; to save space we only show the relevant letters, with vertical dots used for the rest of the letters. Before the loop starts, all values of the table have been set to 5. In the first iteration, the value for E changes to 4; then the value for M changes to 3; after that, the value for B changes to 2; and finally, the value for E changes again to 1.

Having developed the algorithm for the rightmost occurrences, we are ready to tackle algorithm 15.5, the Boyer-Moore-Horspool algorithm itself. It takes as input the search pattern, p, the text, t, in which we will search for the pattern, and the size, s, of the alphabet. It returns a queue, q, containing the indices of t where p is found.

Algorithm 15.5: Boyer-Moore-Horspool.

BoyerMooreHorspool$(p, t, s) \rightarrow q$
  Input: p, a pattern
     t, a text
     s, the size of the alphabet
  Output: q, a queue containing the indices of t where p is found; if p
     is not found the queue is empty

 1 $q \leftarrow$ CreateQueue()
 2 $m \leftarrow |p|$
 3 $n \leftarrow |t|$
 4 $rt \leftarrow$ CreateRtOccurrencesTable(p, s)
 5 $i \leftarrow 0$
 6 **while** $i \leq n - m$ **do**
 7 $j \leftarrow m - 1$
 8 **while** $j \geq 0$ **and** $t[i + j] = p[j]$ **do**
 9   $j \leftarrow j - 1$
 10 **if** $j < 0$ **then**
 11   Enqueue(q, i)
 12 $c \leftarrow t[i + m - 1]$
 13 $i \leftarrow i + rt[\mathrm{Ord}(c)]$
 14 **return** q

The first four lines are housekeeping: creating the return queue (line 1), getting the length of the pattern (line 2), getting the length of the text (line 3), and getting the rightmost occurrences table (line 4), by calling algorithm 15.4.

The real work is in the loop of lines 6–13, and it carries out the process in figure 15.8. Having set i to 0 in line 5, the loop will execute as long as it is possible to match p with t; that requires $i \leq n - m$, otherwise p will fall out the right of t. The variable j starts from the end of p, in line 7, and works leftwards towards the start, in the loop of lines 8–9, as long as there are still characters in the pattern to check and $p[j]$ matches the corresponding character in t, $t[i + j]$. When we exit the loop, if we have exhausted the characters of the pattern, then we will have $j < 0$ and have found a match that we enter into the queue in lines 10–11. Match or no match, we need to slide the pattern to the right. The amount of characters to shift the pattern is determined by the contents of the table rt for the character of the text that falls under the last

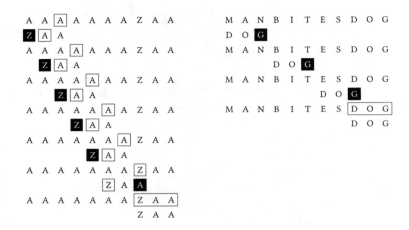

(a) A worst case scenario.   (b) A best case scenario.

Figure 15.13
Boyer-Moore-Horspool worst and best cases.

character of the pattern. We find that last character and save it in c in line 12. Then we retrieve the shift from rt simply by getting the corresponding entry, and we update i accordingly in line 13. Finally, we return our results, if any, in line 14.

The Boyer-Moore-Horspool algorithm is simple to implement. Its performance is usually very good, for most p and t, although in degenerate cases it can get as slow as brute force matching. Figure 15.13a shows a worst case example: we have $n - m$ iterations of the outer loop *and* $m - 1$ iterations in the inner loop for each of them except the last, in which we have m inner iterations to determine a match. Overall, that results in a running time of $O(nm)$, equal to that of brute force matching. Figure 15.13b shows a best case scenario, where the pattern skips repeatedly m characters until it finds a match at the end; this results in a running time of $O(n/m)$. This may look too good to be true, but it turns out that most real searches are like figure 15.13b: the search string contains only a few of the characters of the alphabet, so we can on average expect an $O(n/m)$ running time. The time to create table rt is $O(m)$, so it does not change the overall picture because usually n is significantly longer than m. The actual drawback that may exist with Boyer-Moore-Horspool is the size of the rightmost occurrences table. An ASCII-encoded alphabet requires a table size of 128, which is of no concern to applications, but if our alphabet runs into thousands of characters, space may be an issue.

Notes

The history of string matching is an interesting interplay of theory and practice. Stephen Cook showed in 1971 that there should exist an algorithm for string matching running at $O(m + n)$ [40]. Earlier than that, trying to solve a practical problem while implementing a text editor, James H. Morris had devised an algorithm with a complexity of $O(n + m)$, although that was not clear at the time. Working independently, Donald Knuth set out to develop an algorithm following Cook's theoretical construct. Knuth showed his work to Vaughan R. Pratt, who suggested improvements; Pratt in turn showed the result to Morris, who recognized that it was essentially the same with his own algorithm. The three of them published the algorithm together in 1977 [116]. An alternative version of the algorithm was proposed in 1997 by Reingold, Urban, and Gries [164].

The Boyer-Moore-Horspool algorithm was proposed by R. Nigel Horspool in 1980 [98]; we followed the presentation of Lecroq [123]. Its complexity was analyzed by Baeza-Yates and Régnier [7]. It is actually a simplification of a more complex algorithm, the Boyer-Moore algorithm, invented by Robert S. Boyer and J Strother Moore in 1977 [26]. The original Boyer-Moore algorithm has a worst case complexity of $O(n + m)$ when the pattern is not found in the text and $O(nm)$ where the pattern is found in the text. A version of the algorithm had also been discovered independently around the same time by R. W. Gosper, a founder of the hacker (not cracker) community. Zvi Galil showed in 1979 how the algorithm can be modified to achieve a complexity of $O(n + m)$ even when the pattern is found in the text [73].

The material we presented scarcely does justice to the wealth of work in string matching. For more you can consult the books by Gusfield [85] and Crochemore, Hancart, and Lecroq [45].

Exercises

1. All the algorithms we have described in the chapter return all the matches they can find. With minor modifications they will return just the first match; write the first-match-only algorithms.

2. The Boyer-Moore-Horspool algorithm uses a table to hold the rightmost occurrences so that lookup time for each character is as small as possible. However, this results in a waste of space if the pattern is a small subset of the alphabet. Try using a different data structure, like a hash table or a set, instead. Although lookup time should still be constant, it will take longer than a simple table. Compare the performance of running implementations of the original Boyer-Moore-Horspool algorithm and the space-saving one.

3. A reason we are using queues to return the results in our string matching algorithms is that if they are implemented so that they support concurrent access to them, users of the algorithms can start getting results immediately, instead of having to wait for all the text to be processed. Check the libraries and the capabilities of your programming language and implement the algorithms so that they allow concurrent, synchronized access to the results.

16 Leave to Chance

Chance is fickle and in many cases we abhor it; far better to walk with stable and predictable steps than to take risks with uncertain outcomes. Computers are deterministic machines. We do not expect them to behave erratically. Indeed, when we start getting different answers to the same question, we start suspecting that there may be a bug lurking somewhere.

Similarly, we are not likely to make important decisions based on chance. We normally weigh the knowns and the unknowns and make a decision with due consideration, trying to eliminate bias; it is really a compliment to be able to say that we have left nothing to chance.

And yet, chance can solve many important problems. Apart from the remote probability that it can solve your material needs by winning at the casino, we can employ an element of chance in our computational procedures to solve many important problems for which no other practical, or no easier, or no appropriate, method exists.

The important property of luck and chances is that they are unpredictable. A fair coin has a 50-50 chance of coming heads or tails; if we know that it is not loaded in any way, we do know that the outcome of its flips will not be biased, and we know there is no reason to predict that it will come out one way or another.

Unpredictability lies behind *randomness*. Randomness is the lack of any regularity in a series of events or data. Something is *random* when there are no patterns on it, no matter how we perceive it. White noise, the noise of static on the radio (not accessible on digital radio, though), is random. The series of numbers coming out of a fair die are random. Brownian motion is the motion of particles suspended in a fluid. The particles collide with the atoms or molecules of the fluid (gas or liquid). The collisions cause the particles to change their course. The collisions and the course are random. A trace of particle in Brownian motion is a picture of a random path.

A lack of regularity can be a great asset. Think of an opinion poll. Because in most cases it is impossible to survey all the population, pollsters have to use a manageable subset, a *sample* of the population. The holy grail of polling is to have a *representative sample*, that is, a sample that has the same characteristics as the population at large, so that it is not biased in any way. A *population* is not necessarily a set of human beings; it can be any set of entities that we wish to study. The term population has stuck, however, and is used with this expanded meaning in mathematics, statistics, and computer science.

As an example of sampling bias, *survivorship bias* results when we sample only those subjects that are still around during the time of sampling, whereas the survey concerns some event that extends backwards. Consider a survey of firms taken after a financial crisis. Because this will necessarily exclude all firms that did not survive the crisis, the sample will be biased.

A *random sample*, that is, a sample taken from the population at random, removes bias. As there is no preference or regularity in what to include in the sample, there is no reason to suppose that the sample is not representative of the population at large.

To obtain a random sample we have to use a process that incorporates randomness—otherwise the sample will be predictable. That process, expressed algorithmically, will be a *randomized algorithm*, an algorithm that uses randomness in its operation.

There is an important conceptual leap here. Normally we expect algorithms to be fully deterministic, so that for the same input they always produce the same output. If we accept that the output of an algorithm may depend on its input *and* a degree of randomness, a whole new set of possibilities opens.

There are problems that we do not have any practical algorithm to solve; what is more, there are problems for which we know there is no practical algorithm to solve. By practical we mean within the computational, storage, and time resources that are acceptable for our task. There are also problems for which we do have practical algorithms to solve, but for which there are randomized algorithms that are much simpler than any non-randomized algorithm we currently know.

Of course there is a price for our dependence on randomness. The algorithm will not be entirely predictable. Unpredictability may manifest in various ways: sometimes the algorithm may fail to produce a correct result or it may take a long time to execute. The key to a successful randomized algorithm is to quantify "sometimes." We need to know how rarely an algorithm may fail to produce the right answer or what its expected and worst performance is. Also, the degree of correctness may be something that is arranged on demand. An algorithm may give an answer that is correct within a certain interval of values, and the longer we allow it to run, the narrower the interval, and therefore the accuracy of the answer will be.

The value of randomized algorithms is one of the most important outcomes of research in Computer Science in the last decades. We could write volumes upon volumes on them, but that is not our task here. We will limit ourselves to only a small sample of randomized algorithms, spanning different application areas; you will get a glimpse of what taking some chances can do for you.

16.1   Random Numbers

Before we embark on anything related to randomized algorithms, we must deal with a fundamental problem: how to get the randomness we need in the first place. Typically, this means getting a random number, or a sequence of random numbers, that we feed into the algorithm. But where do we find random numbers? Where do we find a *random number generator*, as we call it, an implementation in a computer that gives us the random numbers we need?

One of the most famous quotations in computer science hails back to 1951 and was made by one of the leading pioneers in the field, John von Neumann, who remarked:

Any one who considers arithmetical methods of producing random digits is, of course, in a state of sin.

Even if we do not find random number generators in any circle of Dante's inferno, the case remains that if you try to produce random numbers algorithmically, you are doomed to fail. There is no way that a deterministic machine, executing a deterministic algorithm, will produce something completely random. That is simply a contradiction in terms. If someone gives you an algorithm that produces random numbers and that algorithm starts spewing out results, it is easy for you to predict what the next number will be. Just notice the current state of the algorithm and execute the next steps yourself. You will be able to predict the next number with 100% accuracy. So down goes randomness.

The real random number generators use as a source of their randomness some physical process that, as far as we know, is completely random.

Such random number generators are called True Random Number Generators (TRNGs). There are several TRNGs. You can use a Geiger counter on a nuclear decay radiation source. You can detect photons targeting a semi-transparent mirror. Due to quantum effects, photons will go through or reflect from the mirror with equal probabilities, so the outcome is random. You can pick up atmospheric radio noise, that is, noise caused by atmospheric processes such as lightning discharges. There are hardware random number generators that can be embedded in computers, and that work with real random sources; however, they are not available everywhere and they may not be able to produce random numbers at the rate that we need them.

If, for any reason, we do not have a TRNG at our disposal, or if it does not suffice for our needs, we have to settle for a Pseudorandom Number Generator (PRNG). A PRNG is that sinful plot: a deterministic algorithm that will produce numbers that look random, even if they are not; they are just pseudorandom. That said, it is not easy to define what "look random" means. A common requirement is that we want the PRNG to produce numbers that follow a *uniform distribution*. A uniform distribution of a finite set of numbers is one in which each number is equally likely. So a uniform distribution of the set of numbers 1 to 10 would contain the number 1 one tenth of the time, the number 2 one tenth of the time, and so on all numbers up to and including the number 10.

Keeping in mind that the numbers that are produced by a PRNG are pseudorandom numbers, we will simply call the output of such algorithms random numbers without saying specifically that they are pseudorandom.

A uniform distribution is desirable but not enough. Continuing with the previous example, the sequence of numbers:

$$1, 2, \ldots, 10, 1, 2, \ldots, 10, 1, 2, \ldots, 10, \ldots$$

that is, a repeating sequence of the numbers 1 to 10 in order, is a uniform distribution, but it does not look random at all. A PRNG will produce a uniform distribution that does look random. To ensure that this happens, there are statistical tests that check a sequence of numbers for randomness. These statistical tests, given a sequence of numbers, indicate whether they deviate significantly from what a truly random sequence of numbers would be.

A simple PRNG that has been used for a long time is given in algorithm 16.1. The algorithm is an implementation of the following computational method, called the *linear congruential method*:

Algorithm 16.1: Linear Congruential Random Number Generator.

LinearCongruential$(x) \rightarrow r$
   Input: x, a number $0 \leq x < m$
   Data: m the modulus, $m > 0$
         a the multiplier, $0 < a < m$
         c the increment, $0 < c < m$
   Output: r, a number $0 \leq r < m$

1    $r \leftarrow (a \times x + c) \bmod m$
2   **return** r

$$X_{n+1} = (aX_n + c) \bmod m, \quad n \geq 0$$

The method produces a new random number X_{n+1} given a previous one, X_n. It multiples X_n by a special multiplier a, adds a special increment c to the product, and then takes the remainder of the division with, again, a specially chosen modulus m. To jump-start the method, we need to feed it with an initial value, X_0, which is called the *seed*.

The algorithm works in exactly the same lines. The algorithm takes a value, X_n, called x in the algorithm, and produces a new value, X_{n+1}, called r in the algorithm. Initially we call it with an initial value, s, the seed; then we call it feeding it with input the output from the previous call. That means that we have a series of calls:

$x \leftarrow$ LinearCongruential(s)
$x \leftarrow$ LinearCongruential(x)
$x \leftarrow$ LinearCongruential(x)

and so on. In each call we get a new value, x, that we will use as our random number and as our input in the next call to LinearCongruential.

In implementations of the linear congruential method, as with other PRNGs, we do not pass x to each call. Instead, these calls are wrapped into higher level calls. There is usually a separate call to set the seed, and then new random values are produced by calling a function that takes no parameters—because x is maintained in some hidden variable. Initially you make a call like Seed(s), and then for every random value you make a call like Random(). Yet what actually happens is what we just described.

It is obvious that the sequence of numbers produced by algorithm 16.1 will depend on the initial seed value. The same seed will always give the same sequence of numbers. This is actually a good thing in PRNGs, because when we write programs using them and we want to check the correctness of the program, we usually want to give away randomness and be able to get completely predictable results.

We mentioned that the values a, m, and c are special. They must be selected with care. A PRNG will never produce more values than m. When it steps on a value that it has already produced, it will start producing the same values it produced before. In effect, the method has a *period* of repeating numbers. We must choose a, m, and c so that the period is as big as possible, ideally m, and the numbers in the period follow a uniform distribution. Poor choices result in short periods, and therefore immediately predictable numbers after the first period come along very soon. For example, if we set $s = 0$, $m = 10$, $a = 3$, and $c = 3$, we will get:

$$3, 2, 9, 0, 3, 2, 9, 0, \ldots$$

To get a full period, equal to m, for any seed value, a, m, and c must meet three requirements. First, m and c must be relatively prime, that is, one must not divide the other. Second, $a - 1$ must be divisible by all the prime factors of m. Third, $a - 1$ must be divisible by 4 if m is divisible by 4. We need not go into the mathematics of why this is so; moreover, we need not go around searching for numbers meeting these requirements. Usually we settle for some parameters that are recommended for use by researchers in the field. For example, one parameter set is $s = 2^{32}$, $a = 32310901$, c an odd number, and m a power of two.

The linear congruential method produces numbers between 0 and $m - 1$, inclusive, that is, the range denoted by $[0, m - 1]$. If we want numbers in some other range, for example, $[0, k]$, we can multiply the result by $k/(m - 1)$. We can also add an offset x to get a range of the form $[x, k + x]$. The special case of numbers between 0 and 1, denoted by $[0, 1]$ is obviously obtained by dividing with $m - 1$. We often need the range between 0 and 1 without including 1, denoted by $[0, 1)$, which we get by dividing with m.

Over the last few years, quite some research has been carried out on whether the numbers generated by the linear congruential method are fit for purpose (i.e., whether they appear to be random enough). In the same vein, other methods have been proposed as being better because they pass more tests of randomness. A promising alternative, which has the additional

---

Algorithm 16.2: xorshift64*.

XORShift64Star(x) $\rightarrow r$
    Input: x, a 64-bit integer different than 0
    Output: r, a 64-bit number
1   $x \leftarrow x \oplus (x \gg 12)$
2   $x \leftarrow x \oplus (x \ll 25)$
3   $x \leftarrow x \oplus (x \gg 27)$
4   $r \leftarrow x \times 2685821657736338717$
5   **return** r

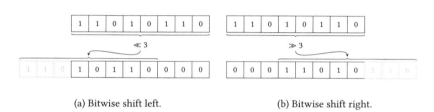

(a) Bitwise shift left.   (b) Bitwise shift right.

Figure 16.1
Bitwise shift operators.

advantage of being very fast, is the xorshift64* (read XOR shift 64 star) generator, which you can see in algorithm 16.2. The xorshift64* generator produces numbers of 64 bits.

The algorithm is straightforward, if you know the $\ll$ and $\gg$ operands. The symbol $\ll$ is the bitwise *shift left operator*; $x \ll a$ means to move the bits of the number x left by a positions. For example, $1110 \ll 2 = 1000$; see also figure 16.1a for an example of shifting a whole byte three bits to the left. In a symmetrical way, the symbol $\gg$ is the bitwise *shift right operator*; $x \gg a$ means to move the bits of the number x right by a positions. For example, $1101 \gg 2 = 0011$; see figure 16.1b.

The xorshift64* algorithm is used in the same way as the linear congruential method. It takes a value and produces a new value that we take as our random number and we use it as input in the next call to the algorithm. The first time we feed it with a seed, which must not be zero.

The output is constructed by manipulating the bits of x, shifting them right, and xoring the shifted bits with x itself in line 1. We repeat a similar operation shifting to the left and xoring in line 2, then shifting to the right and xoring

---

Algorithm 16.3: xorshift1024*.

XORShift1024Star(S) $\rightarrow r$
    Input: S, an array of 16 unsigned 64-bit integers
    Data: p, a number initially set to 0
    Output: r, a 64-bit random number

1   $s_0 \leftarrow S[p]$
2   $p \leftarrow (p+1)\ \&\ 15$
3   $s_1 \leftarrow S[p]$
4   $s_1 \leftarrow s_1 \oplus (s_1 \ll 31)$
5   $s_1 \leftarrow s1 \oplus (s_1 \gg 11)$
6   $s_0 \leftarrow s_0 \oplus (s_0 \gg 30)$
7   $S[p] \leftarrow s_0 \oplus s1$
8   $r \leftarrow S[p] \times 1181783497276652981$
9   **return** r

---

in line 3. After we are done with that, we multiply x by a seemingly *magic number* and return it. A magic number in an algorithm is a number without apparent meaning; in our case, the number is special because it ensures that the output does look random.

The xorshift64* algorithm is fast and produces decent random values; moreover, it has a period of $2^{64} - 1$. If you want something even better, then you can up the ante and go for xorshift64*'s big sibling, xorshift1024*, which you can see in algorithm 16.3. The xorshift1024* generator produces again 64-bit numbers, even though its name would seem to suggest otherwise. But a whole lot more of them.

Compared to xorshift64*, xorshift1024* has a much larger period of $2^{1024} - 1$ and produces random numbers that pass even more tests of statistical randomness. The algorithm uses an array S of 16 unsigned 64 bit integers, which it takes as input. The first time the algorithm is called this array is the seed, and it is recommended that it contains 16 numbers produced from xorshift64*. In every subsequent call the contents of S change in the algorithm, and the S with the new values must be used as input in the next call of xorshift1024*. The array S provides part of the algorithm's name, as $16 \times 64 = 1024$.

The algorithm also uses a counter p that goes around the integers in the array S; p must be initialized to zero before the first call, and is updated in the algorithm in each subsequent call. The algorithm returns a random 64 bit integer by manipulating parts of the array S. In particular, in each call it works with two elements of S. The one is pointed by p and is stored in s_0 in line 1. Then p takes its next value, in line 2, and we get the second element of S for this call of XORShift1024*and store it in s_1, in line 3. Line 2 is an efficient way to have p act as a counter from 0 to 15, then back to 0, and so on. That is what the bitwise AND with 15 does. If you are in doubt, recall that 15 is 1111 in binary, so the bitwise AND with 15 results in keeping the lowest four bits as they are and setting all the others to zero; for example, 1101 & 1111 = 1101. If $p + 1 < 16$, the AND does nothing to the sum because $p + 1$ has only the last four bits set, which are left untouched. If $p + 1 = 16$, the AND turns $p + 1$ to zero because 16 & 15 = 10000 & 1111 = 0.

The rest of the algorithm is all about manipulating the bits of S in fancy ways. With these operators, in line 4 we shift s_1 left by 31 bits and we XOR the result with s_1 itself. In lines 5–6 we do a similar manipulation with s_1 using shift right and then another manipulation with s_0 using shift left. We XOR the resulting s_0 and s_1, store it back to $S[p]$, and return the product of $S[p]$ with another magic number.

The xorshift1024* algorithm is a piece of intricate precision machinery, with carefully chosen constants used as operands in a series of choreographed operations. It is the result of serious work and effort. It produces randomness, yet nothing in it is there by luck. This brings us to the second quotation on randomness and computers, by Donald Knuth, one of the foremost authorities in computer science:

random numbers should not be generated with a method chosen at random

A grid of 10,000 random bits is shown in figure 16.2a; zero bits are in black and white bits are in white. You probably fail to discern any patterns in the figure, which is just as well; were you able to see patterns, the numbers would be blatantly non-random (or you would be a victim of *pareidolia*, the phenomenon where you see patterns where they do not exist). Even without patterns, though, randomness may provide interesting aesthetic results, as you can see in figure 16.2b, which contains 400 random numbers depicted as black or white squares, scaled and rotated according to their value.

The random number generators we have seen to this point are fine for most applications, but they are *not suitable* for producing random numbers that are to be used for cryptograhic purposes. There are many aspects of cryptography that require random numbers, like one-time pads, cryptographic key generation, and *nonces*, arbitrary numbers that are to be used only once in specific

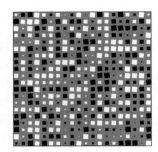

(a) 10,000 random bits.   (b) A randomly generated image.

Figure 16.2
Images of randomness.

protocols. When we need random numbers for cryptography, it is not enough to have numbers that pass some statistical tests for randomness. The numbers must also be resistant to specific attacks. In particular, there must be no polynomial time algorithm that can start predicting the coming numbers; also, there must be no way that, given the state of the algorithm, one can work backward and deduce the previously generated numbers.

In cryptography we use special random generators, called, predictably, Cryptographically Secure Pseudorandom Number Generators (CSPRNGs). Their design is much more complex than the methods we have seen so far, and their validation is through continuous examination and tests by the cryptographic community. A CSPRNG is usable as long as all attacks against it have failed.

To get an idea of how a CSPRNG works, we will give an overview of a popular algorithm called Fortuna, after the Roman goddess for fortune. Fortuna works diagrammatically as in figure 16.3.

To ensure that the numbers it produces are not predictable, Fortuna uses an *entropy accumulator*. Its job is to collect unpredictable data. Unpredictable data can be loosely understood as entropy, hence its name. The entropy must come from sources outside the algorithm. Such sources are user events, like keypresses and mouse moves; network events, such as the arrival or despatch of data; and disk events, like disk writes. Information on these events, as

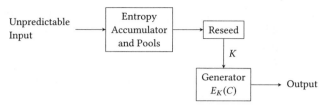

Figure 16.3
The Fortuna Cryptographically Secure Pseudo Random Number Generator.

they happen, is harvested and saved in *entropy pools*. These pools function as sources of real randomness for the rest of the algorithm.

The generator module is responsible for producing the random numbers we want. It works by using an internal counter C and a key K. It takes the key and encrypts the value of the counter with a block cipher using K as the key to the block cipher. The result, $E_K(C)$, is the output. The key is equivalent to the seed we have used in the other methods. To ensure that the outputs are not predictable, we want the key to change from time to time. This is the purpose of Reseed. Reseeding takes input from the random data that have been accumulated to the entropy pools and produces a new key at certain intervals. The result is that the generator module changes state both because the counter C changes after encrypting a new block and because it acquires a new key K between short intervals; so even if somebody were to guess the value of the counter, there would still be the value of K to be guessed, and this value depends on really random data.

There are many fine details in Fortuna to make it as robust and attack-resistant as possible. A CSPRNG is a different kind of beast than a plain old PRNG, and we've barely scratched the surface. But always keep in mind, if you do need random numbers for cryptography, you need to go the extra mile and use Fortuna or some other strong CSPRNG.

16.2   Random Sampling

We started our discussion with random sampling, so it makes sense to explore how we can actually sample a population randomly. If we have a population of size n and we want to sample m members of the population at random, a straightforward idea is to go through each member of the population and select it in our sample with a probability m/n. Unfortunately, this idea is wrong. It will select m members from the population only *on average*, not every time, and we want a random sample of size m *every time*.

To solve the problem, imagine that we have already gone through t items and selected k items for our sample. Our population has, again, n members, and we want a random sample of size m. Because we have gone through t items, we still have $n - t$ items that we have not examined at all, and we have yet to add $m - k$ items in our sample. In how many ways can the process unfold from that point onward? That is equal to the number of different ways we can choose the missing items for our sample from the remaining items in the population; more precisely, the number of different ways, call it w_1, we can choose $m - k$ items from $n - t$ items. This is the number of possible combinations, that is, selections without ordering, of $m - k$ elements out of $n - t$, so we have $w_1 = \binom{n-t}{m-k}$. If you are not familiar with this notation, refer to section 13.6. Thinking in exactly the same lines, if we have gone through $t + 1$ items and selected $k + 1$ items for the sample, the number of ways the process can unfold from that point onward, call it w_2, is $w_2 = \binom{n-t-1}{m-k-1}$. Taking everything together, the probability that we will go from t and k to $(t + 1)$ and $(k + 1)$ is w_2/w_1:

$$\binom{n-t-1}{m-k-1} \bigg/ \binom{n-t}{m-k} = \frac{m-k}{n-t}$$

The right part of the equation follows immediately by taking the left and substituting $\binom{a}{b} = \frac{(a)!}{(b)!(a-b)!}$.

We now know that the $(k + 1)$th item should be selected with probability $(m - k)/(n - t)$ if t out of k items are already selected. This enables us to arrive at *selection sampling*, algorithm 16.4, which implements a sampling process that meets our requirements.

Algorithm 16.4 takes as input an array P containing the items of the population and the size of the random sample, m. We put the items of the random sample in an array S of size m, which we create in line 1. The variable k represents the number of already selected items during the execution of the algorithm; initially it is zero, in line 2. Similarly, the variable t represents the number of items we have gone through; we set it to zero in line 3. We store the size of the population in line 4.

We repeat the loop of lines 5–10 until we have selected enough items. In each iteration of the loop we generate a uniformly distributed random number, u, between 0 and 1, not including 1, in line 6. We use a function Random(0, 1) that does that, returning a number in the range $[0, 1)$. Based on what we

---

Algorithm 16.4: Selection sampling.

SelectionSampling(P, m) → S
   Input: P, an array containing the items of the population
            m the number of items to select
   Output: S, an array with m randomly selected items from P

1   $S \leftarrow$ CreateArray(m)
2   $k \leftarrow 0$
3   $t \leftarrow 0$
4   $n \leftarrow |P|$
5   **while** $k < m$ **do**
6        $u \leftarrow$ Random(0, 1)
7   **if** $u \times (n - t) < (m - k)$ **then**
8             $S[k] \leftarrow P[t]$
9             $k \leftarrow k + 1$
10       $t \leftarrow t + 1$
11 **return** S

---

have said above, we want to include the current item we are examining, $P[t]$, with probability $(m - k)/(n - t)$; this will happen if $u < (m - k)/(n - t)$. The actual test we use is $u \times (n - t) < (m - k)$ because it is usually easier to do multiplications than divisions. If the condition in line 7 holds, then we insert $P[t]$ in s (line 8) and increase the number of items we have selected (line 9). Whichever way the condition goes, we increase the number of items we have seen by one in line 10; we round up the algorithm by returning S.

To prove that the algorithm works we need to show that it does return m randomly selected items, no more, no less, with the right probability. Concerning the probability, it is exactly the one we wanted. If we have selected k items after going through t items, then the probability that we will select the $(k + 1)$th item is, as we saw, $(m - k)/(n - t)$. It can be shown that the overall probability that any item will be selected is then exactly m/n. By "overall probability" we mean the probability that an item will be selected regardless of whether we have selected the previous k out of t. For the reader who wonders about the mathematics, the pass from $(m - k)/(n - t)$ to m/n hinges on the difference between *conditional* and *unconditional probabilities*. The conditional probability for an event is the probability that it will happen provided that another event has happened; that is the $(m - k)/(n - t)$ figure in our case. The unconditional probability is the probability that something will happen, period. That is the m/n figure for us; it is the item being selected no matter what has happened before.

Now about the number of items selected. Suppose we arrive at a situation where we have $n - t$ items left to examine and also $n - t$ items to select, so that $m - k = n - t$. Then $u \times (n - t) < m - k$ becomes $u < 1$ and we will definitely select the next item. Recall that Random(0, 1) returns numbers in the range $[0, 1)$ so the inequality will hold. The same situation will then arise for $k + 1$ and $t + 1$, then for $k + 2$ and $t + 3$, and so on until the last item of the array P. In other words, the probability check in line 6 will work so that all the remaining $n - t$ elements in P will be selected. Therefore, there is no way the algorithm can terminate having selected less than m elements. If, on the contrary, we have already selected m items before the end of P, the loop will exit and will not select any more. In fact, that is saving time, but not strictly required. If the loop did continue to run, we would have $u \times (n - t) < m - k$ becoming $u \times (n - t) < 0$, which is impossible; so the algorithm would not select any other item until it reached the end of P. Therefore, we will definitely select at most m elements. Because we can select at least m elements and at most m elements, the only possibility that is feasible is to select exactly m elements. So the algorithm does behave as it should.

The loop in the algorithm will execute at most n times, if the last element in P finds its way to the random sample. Quite often, though, it will execute fewer times. The probability for each item to be selected is m/n; therefore, the probability for the last item to be selected is also m/n, and the probability that the algorithm will stop before reaching the last item is $1 - (m/n)$. It can be shown that the average number of elements that we consider before the algorithm stops is $(n + 1)m/(m + 1)$.

Selection sampling demands that we know the size of the population n. We may not always have this information, however. The population may consist of records in a file, and we may not know how many records there are in the file. We could read all the file and count them and then run selection sampling, but this requires going over the file twice, the first time only for counting. In another scenario, the population may be streamed to us without us knowing when the streaming will stop, at which point we should be ready to come up with a random sample over the items that will have been streamed to us without going back to read them all over again. It would be much better if we had at our disposal an algorithm that can handle these cases as well.

Such an algorithm exists and is called *reservoir sampling*. The idea is that if we want a sample of m randomly selected items, then we fill up a reservoir of m items as soon as we find them; that is, we put the first m items directly in the reservoir. After that, we want to get each new item and change the contents of the reservoir so that each item in the reservoir has an m/t probability of actually being there, where t is the number of items we have encountered. When we read the whole population, each item in the reservoir will be there with probability m/n, if n is the size of the population. Reservoir sampling is an *online algorithm*, as it does not have to wait for all its input to be fed to it.

To see how we can achieve that, suppose we do have m items in the reservoir where each one of them was selected with probability m/t. In the beginning, when we add all the first m items, the probability is $m/t = m/m = 1$ so the condition trivially holds. Knowing that the condition holds for some t, we want to show that it holds for $t + 1$.

When we get the $(t + 1)$th item, we add it into the reservoir with probability $m/(t + 1)$, replacing one of the items already in the reservoir. We choose the item to take out of the reservoir randomly, so each item in the reservoir has probability $1/m$ of being taken out.

Because we choose the probability appropriately, the item entering the reservoir does so with the required probability $m/(t + 1)$. We must investigate what the probabilities are for the items that remain in the reservoir. The probability that a particular item in the reservoir is replaced is the probability that the new item enters the reservoir and the particular item at hand is picked to leave it: $m/(t + 1) \times (1/m) = 1/(t + 1)$. Conversely, the probability that an item remains in the reservoir is $1 - 1/(t + 1) = t/(t + 1)$. Because the item was already in the reservoir with probability m/t, the probability that an item was already in the reservoir and remained there is $(m/t) \times t/(t + 1) = m/(t + 1)$. Therefore, both the newly and previously inserted items are in the reservoir with the correct probability after reading and handling the $(t + 1)$th item.

In summary, if we are at item $t \leq m$, then we just put it into the reservoir. If we are at item $t > m$, then we add it into the reservoir with probability m/t and take out randomly an item already in the reservoir. This is algorithm 16.5 that implements reservoir sampling.

The algorithm reads the items of the population from a *scr*, which can be anything that has a function GetItem that returns a new item from *scr* or NULL, if there are no more items. It also takes as parameter the size of the sample; it returns an array of m randomly selected items from *scr*.

Algorithm 16.5: Reservoir sampling.

ReservoirSampling(*scr, m*) → *S*

    Input: *scr*, a source of items of the population

            m the number of items to select

    Output: *S*, an array with *m* randomly selected items from *scr*

1    $S \leftarrow$ CreateArray(m)

2   **for** $i \leftarrow 0$ **to** m **do**

3        $S[i] \leftarrow$ GetItem(scr)

4    $t \leftarrow m$

5   **while** $(a \leftarrow$ GetItem(scr)) $\neq$ NULL **do**

6        $t \leftarrow t + 1$

7        $u \leftarrow$ RandomInt($1, t$)

8   **if** $u \leq m$ **then**

9            $S[u - 1] \leftarrow a$

10   **return** S

Algorithm 16.5 starts by creating s, which will be the reservoir, in line 1 and putting the first m items of scr directly into s, in lines 2–3. Then, in line 4, it sets t to the number of items we have read. The loop in lines 5–9 is executed as long as there are more items available. The return value of GetItem(scr) is saved in variable a; if a is NULL, then the loop will exit; otherwise we execute lines 6–9.

The first thing we do inside the loop is increase the value of t to $t + 1$ in line 5. Then in line 7, and this is the key to the whole algorithm, we call RandomInt($1, t$) that returns a random integer u from 1 to t inclusive, that is, in the range $[1, t]$. The condition $u \leq m$ (line 8) is the same with $u/t \leq m/t$; so we replace an item in the reservoir if the condition holds. To pick up at random an item that has been entered previously in the reservoir we reuse u: it is, after all, a random number between 1 and m, so we just need to put a in position $u - 1$ of the zero-based array s (line 9). When we have exhausted the scr and exited the loop, we return s in line 10.

An example of reservoir sampling in action is in figure 16.4. We sample four items out of sixteen. The reservoir is on the left. At the top of the figure we fill the reservoir with the first four items. Then, depending on the value of u in each iteration, we put the current item, shown in thick border, in the reservoir. Note that it is possible that during the execution of the algorithm the same

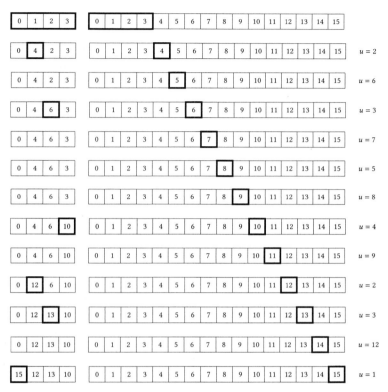

Figure 16.4
Reservoir sampling of four items out of sixteen.

position in the reservoir takes on more than one new value; that happens with positions one and two of our example. In this particular example, the reservoir keeps changing until the end; that, of course, is not necessary as it depends on the random value of u.

16.3   Power Games

Does a vote count? How much? These are important questions in all kinds of elections, and the answers may not be obvious. Of course, if a voter casts a vote, then the voter expects that the vote has some significance, otherwise the voter would not bother to vote, or would not accept, with good justification, a political system that gives the power to vote without power.

In general elections, where we follow the principle of One Person One Vote (OPOV), it is not easy to answer that question. Among million of votes cast, the probability that an individual vote will make any difference is very small. Elections are usually decided by more than a one-vote difference. This leads to a paradox: if the probability that your vote makes a difference is small, then, unless voting is mandatory and can be enforced, it is not rational to vote. Voting takes time, so a vote that makes no difference means that the voter squanders time without any outcome. Still, people vote in large numbers. This has come to be called *the paradox of voting*, and quite a bit of research has been carried out to resolve it.

How much a vote counts is important in other settings as well, not just in general elections. There are settings where we can analyze the power each voter yields in a meaningful way to derive interesting and sometimes even counter-intuitive results.

As a real-life example, in 1958, the precursor of today's European Union was set up as the European Economic Community (ECC). The founding members were six countries: France (FR), the Federal Republic of Germany (DE; Germany was divided back then), Italy (IT), Belgium (BE), The Netherlands (NL), and Luxembourg (LU). One of the governing bodies of the ECC was the Counting of Ministers. Ministers of the member countries would convene and vote on matters of ECC policy.

An immediate problem that had to be resolved is how exactly the countries would vote. A system like One Country One Vote makes each country equal to the others. That, however, fails to take into account the great differences in resources and populations among the different countries. Is it fair that small Luxembourg should have equal say as a much larger country like France? It was therefore decided that in the Council of Ministers, each country would have a vote with a specific weight: France, Germany, and Italy got four units each. Belgium and The Netherlands got two units each. Luxembourg got one unit. In order for a vote to pass, it should gather at least 12 units.

It is immediately obvious that the big countries had more weight than the medium-sized countries, and all countries had more weight than Luxembourg. That looks acceptable. We would expect that Luxembourg by itself would not command a majority and that the bigger countries could drive a majority with greater ease than the smaller countries. Unfortunately, the system had a fundamental flaw.

Table 16.1
Voting in the first Council of Ministers in the European Economic Community.

FR (4)	DE (4)	IT (4)	NL (2)	BE (2)	LU (1)	Sum
✓	✓	✓				12
✓	✓		✓	✓		12
✓		✓	✓	✓		12
	✓	✓	✓	✓		12

In table 16.1 we have listed all possibilities for achieving 12 votes. We can arrive at that threshold if all three big countries vote together, or if two of the big countries and two of the middle countries vote together. Of course, if more countries join them, so much the merrier, but it is not necessary. The problem is that Luxembourg is not needed at all. In any vote, a majority is achieved no matter what Luxembourg does. So Luxembourg may have been awarded a vote, but that vote does not translate to any real power. It could have been awarded no votes at all, and there would be no difference in practice.

This is an extreme problem, in that a voter is effectively disenfranchised. In other situations there may be subtler problems: even though a voter is not disenfranchised, how much power does a voter have in relation to other voters? Returning to the ECC example, how much more powerful is Germany than Belgium? The units tell us that somehow Germany is twice as powerful, but is that true?

To tackle this kind of question, we must adopt a systematic approach. We say that we have a set of voters, $V = \{v_1, v_2, \ldots, v_n\}$, and a set of weights, $W = \{w_1, w_2, \ldots, w_m\}$. Voter v_i votes with weight w_i. We say that in order for a decision to be taken, it needs to meet a *quota Q*. In the example of the ECC, we have $Q = 12$. The setup of V, W, and Q is called a *voting game*.

Each subset of voters is called a *coalition*. A coalition that reaches the quota is called a *winning coalition*. A coalition that fails to reach the quota is called a *losing coalition*. If we add more voters in a winning coalition, then we get another winning coalition. In the ECC example, a winning coalition is {DE, FR, IT}; another one is {DE, FR, IT, BE}. Thus, a winning coalition can grow larger without making any real difference. What is of more consequence is what happens if we make a winning coalition smaller. If we start with the winning coalition {DE, FR, IT, BE} and take out BE, then we get the winning coalition $\{DE, FR, IT\}$. But if we take the winning coalition $\{DE, FR, IT\}$ and remove any country from it, then the resulting coalition is not a winning one. A *minimal winning coalition* is a winning coalition, such as the removal of any of its members results in obtaining losing coalition. A voter is *critical* in a winning coalition, also called a *swinger* or a *pivot*, if its removal from the coalition makes the coalition a losing coalition. In a minimal winning coalition, all its members are critical, but a member may be critical in a winning coalition that is not minimal: consider removing DE from $\{DE, FR, IT, BE\}$.

A critical voter is a voter that is able to affect the outcome of an election. The voter is critical because at least one winning coalition will be turned to a losing one if the voter leaves it, so the whole election result can depend on the behavior of that particular voter. A voter that is not critical in any coalition is a voter that is not able to affect the outcome of an election at all. Such a voter is called a *dummy*. Luxembourg is a dummy voter in the ECC example. Even if Luxembourg is part of a winning coalition, its departure from the coalition will not turn it into a losing one; no matter what Luxembourg does, the election outcome will not be affected.

We are now in a position to define a measure of voting power, called the *Banzhaf index*, after John F. Banzhaf III who proposed it and made it known. We start with defining the *Banzhaf score* of voter v_i, which is the number of coalitions in which voter v_i is critical. We denote the Banzhaf score of voter v_i by $\eta(v_i)$. The Banzhaf score by itself does not provide much information. That is because it gives no indication of the importance of the number of coalitions in which voter v_i is critical in the large scheme of things. A voter may be critical in a sizable amount of coalitions, but there may be many more coalitions in which the voter is not critical. To put the Banzhaf score into perspective, we use the Banzhaf index of voting power, which is the number of coalitions in which v_i is critical, divided by the total number of critical coalitions for all voters. It is the ratio of critical coalitions ascribed to a particular voter v_i. If we think of the total voting influence as a pie, then then Banzhaf index is the part of the pie, the ratio of the influence, that goes to each voter. We denote the Banzhaf index by $\beta(v_i)$, so we have:

$$\beta(v_i) = \frac{\eta(v_i)}{\eta(v_1) + \eta(v_2) + \cdots + \eta(v_n)}$$

As an example, take four voters $V = \{A, B, C, D\}$ with corresponding weights $W = \{4, 2, 1, 3\}$ and quota $Q = 6$. The critical coalitions are (we underline the critical voters) $\{\underline{A}, \underline{B}\}$, $\{\underline{A}, \underline{D}\}$, $\{\underline{A}, \underline{B}, C\}$, $\{\underline{A}, B, D\}$, $\{\underline{A}, C, \underline{D}\}$, $\{\underline{B}, \underline{C}, \underline{D}\}$.

	x	y	z
$\varnothing$	0	0	0
$\{z\}$	0	0	1
$\{y\}$	0	1	0
$\{y,z\}$	0	1	1
$\{x\}$	1	0	0
$\{x,z\}$	1	0	1
$\{x,y\}$	1	1	0
$\{x,y,z\}$	1	1	1

Figure 16.5
Correspondence between subsets of a set and binary numbers.

Note that $\{A, B, C, D\}$ is winning, but not critical. Counting the critical coalitions for each voter we get $\eta(v_A) = 5$, $\eta(v_B) = 3$, $\eta(v_C) = 1$, and $\eta(v_D) = 3$. With these we then get the Banzhaf indices $\beta(v_A) = 5/12$, $\beta(v_B) = 3/12$, $\beta(v_C) = 1/12$, $\beta(v_D) = 3/12$. The results may come as a surprise to you. Although all voters have different weights, voters B and D have the same proportion of the total voting influence ascribed to them. Voter D has a greater voting weight than voter D, yet that does not translate into more voting power. Voter D may bask in a delusion of voting grandeur, while voter B may lurk in glee, having more power than what comes across at first sight.

We calculated the Banzhaf index by hand; to do that we had to find the critical coalitions and the swingers in each one of them. It is easy to do that with pencil and paper, when the number of voters and possible coalitions is small, but it does not scale to bigger voting games.

The Banzhaf index is a *relative measure*. It is like measuring the proportion of the total income of a group that accrues to each particular member; instead of income, think of voting power. We are also interested in an *absolute measure* of voting power, similar to the size of a person's income, not related to the distribution in the group.

To derive such a measure, we start by observing that a coalition is a subset of V, the set of voters, so the total number of all possible coalitions is the number of all possible subsets of V. The number of all possible subsets of a set S with n elements is 2^n. To see that, imagine a binary number with n digits. Digit i of our number corresponds to element i of set S. Any subset of S can therefore be represented as the n digit number with the corresponding bits set to 1; check out figure 16.5 for an example involving a set $S = \{x, y, z\}$. Hence, the number of all possible subsets of S is the number of different binary numbers with m digits, which is 2^n. The set containing all the subsets of a set S is called the *power set* of S, and its symbol is 2^S. So, the number of all possible subsets of S is the number of elements in its power set, 2^S, and that is, as we just saw, 2^n.

If each coalition is equally likely, then the probability for one particular coalition to occur is $1/2^n$. If we take voter v_i out of V, then we have a set of $n - 1$ voters, so the total number of coalitions of the set $V - v_i$ is 2^{n-1}. The *swing probability* for voter v_i, that is, the probability that the voter is a swinger, is the probability that one of the coalitions of $V - v_i$ becomes critical with the addition of v_i. The probability is equal to the number of critical coalitions with v_i divided by the number of all coalitions without v_i. That is the Banzhaf score $\eta(v_i)$ divided by 2^{n-1}, and it defines the *Banzhaf measure of voting power*, or simply *Banzhaf measure*, symbolized by $\beta'(v_i)$:

$$\beta'(v_i) = \frac{\eta(v_i)}{2^{n-1}}$$

That is the absolute measure we were looking for. It gives us the probability that if we don't know how v_i will vote, when the votes are counted, if voter v_i were to switch its preference, then the outcome of the vote would change as well. Alternatively, it is the probability that, if we know how v_i will vote, the outcome of the voting would change if v_i were to change opinion.

Let's return to our simple, small voting game. We have four voters, $V = \{A, B, C, D\}$, their associated weights, $W = \{4, 2, 1, 3\}$, and a quota, $Q = 6$. We want to find the Banzhaf measure of voter A. We have $2^3 = 8$ coalitions without A. Of them, five become critical with the addition of A; the situation is laid down in table 16.2. The Banzhaf measure of A in this voting game is 5/8. If we carry out the same procedure for the other three voters, we find their Banzhaf measures as $B = 3/8$, $C = 1/8$, $D = 3/8$.

Note that the numbers we found are not normalized (i.e., they do not add up to one). That is because the Banzhaf measure is not a relative measure, which

Table 16.2

Calculating the voting power of A in a simple voting game with votes $A = 4$, $B = 2$, $C = 1$, $D = 3$ and quota $Q = 6$.

Coalitions without A	Coalitions with A	Votes	Winning	Critical
$\varnothing$	$\{A\}$	4		
$\{B\}$	$\{A, B\}$	6	✓	✓
$\{C\}$	$\{A, C\}$	5		
$\{D\}$	$\{A, D\}$	7	✓	✓
$\{B, C\}$	$\{A, B, C\}$	7	✓	✓
$\{B, D\}$	$\{A, B, D\}$	9	✓	✓
$\{C, D\}$	$\{A, C, D\}$	8	✓	✓
$\{B, C, D\}$	$\{A, B, C, D\}$	10	✓	

would show how the overall voting influence is divided among the voters. It is an absolute measure, as was our goal, showing how much influence each voter has. Therefore, we can use the Banzhaf measure and compare voters' influence across different elections, which does not make much sense to do with the Banzhaf index. If we want to, we can get from the Banzhaf measure to the Banzhaf index by rescaling $\beta'(v_i)$ so that the sum of all $\beta(v_i)$ sums up to one. We have:

$$\beta(v_i) = \beta'(v_i) \times \frac{2^{n-1}}{\eta(v_1) + \eta(v_2) + \cdots + \eta(v_n)}$$

We can therefore treat the Banzhaf measure as the primary concept and the Banzhaf index as a derivative concept.

This enumeration procedure we used in our example to calculate $\beta'(v_i) = \eta(v_i)/2^{n-1}$ is fine, as long as the number of voters is small. Calculating the value of $\beta'(v_i)$ for a large number of voters is a challenge. The denominator of $\beta'(v_i)$, 2^{n-1}, is a big quantity, but that is not so much of a problem because we can calculate it directly. As a power of two, it is just the binary number of n digits with one as its first digit and all other digits zero. The problem is the numerator, $\eta(v_i)$. There is no known way to calculate $\eta(v_i)$ efficiently. We can think of more intelligent approaches than simple enumeration (e.g., once we know that a coalition reaches the quota, there is no reason to consider supersets of that coalition), but they do not change the overall complexity of the task, which is not amenable to a polynomial time algorithm. We need a different approach for working with a substantial number of voters.

The different approach leverages chance. Instead of enumerating all possible coalitions and checking whether they are critical, we can just pick up coalitions at random and do the same check. If the coalitions we pick are really random, after some time we will have checked a random sample of all the possible coalitions. In sampling terms, our population comprises all possible coalitions with a particular voter and we are sampling from that population. If our sample is large enough, then the ratio of critical coalitions over all possible coalitions should be about the same with the ratio of the critical coalitions in our sample over all the coalitions in our sample.

That is an instance of a *Monte Carlo method*, a computational method that uses random sampling to arrive at its results. The name comes from the famous casino. Monte Carlo methods have a distinguished pedigree; they were devised by the people behind the first digital computers. They have a great variety of applications, from the physical sciences and engineering, to finance and business.

Before seeing how a Monte Carlo method can be harnessed to calculate the Banzhaf measure, it is instructive to see a simpler application. A straightforward Monte Carlo method, similar in concept to the one we will be using for calculating the Banzhaf measure, can be used to calculate the value of π. If we have a square whose sides are two units of length each, its area will be four square units. If we inscribe a circle in the square, its diameter will be two units and its radius one unit. The area of the circle will therefore be π. If we scatter some small objects, say, grains of rice, on the square, some of them will land inside the circle and some of them outside. If we scatter enough objects, the ratio of those landing inside by the total number of objects thrown will then be $\pi/4$. In figure 16.6 we show the evolution of the process after scattering 100, 200, 500, and 1000 random points. You can see the value of π estimated and the *standard error* (s_e) for each approximation. Note that there is no improvement in the value of the estimate when we move from 200 to 500 points, but there is an improvement in its accuracy, as the standard error decreases. When we get to 1000 random points, we get to $\pi \approx 3.14$ with a standard error of 0.005.

You may wonder how we got the error values. Because our procedure is randomized, we cannot expect to hit on the exact correct value: that would be highly unlikely. There will always be an amount of error in our result. We get a measure of the amount of error from statistics. Each point can be inside or outside the circle. We define a variable X that is equal to zero if the

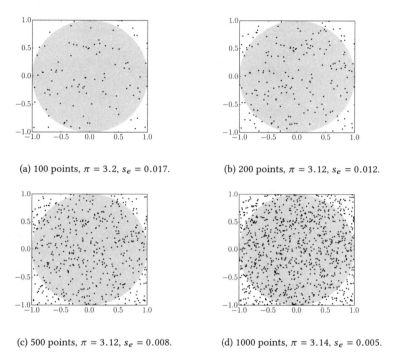

(a) 100 points, $\pi = 3.2$, $s_e = 0.017$.   (b) 200 points, $\pi = 3.12$, $s_e = 0.012$.

(c) 500 points, $\pi = 3.12$, $s_e = 0.008$.   (d) 1000 points, $\pi = 3.14$, $s_e = 0.005$.

Figure 16.6
Monte Carlo calculation of π.

point is inside the circle and equal to one if the point is outside the circle. The *expected value* of X is $E[X] = \pi/4 \times 1 + (1 - \pi/4) \times 0 = \pi/4$. The *variance* of X is $\sigma^2 = E[X^2] - (E[X])^2$. We have $E[X^2] = (\pi/4) \times 1^2 + [1 - (\pi/4)] \times 0^2 = \pi/4$. So $\sigma^2 = \pi/4 - (\pi/4)^2 = (\pi/4)(1 - \pi/4)$. The standard error is then $s_e = \sigma/\sqrt{n}$, where n is the number of points and σ, the square root of the variance, is the *standard deviation*. This formula gives the standard errors in figure 16.6. According to statistics, with a standard error s_e we expect with probability 95% that the true value of π will be within a margin of $\pm 1.96 s_e$ of the calculated value.

Although this method for π is a nice example to introduce Monte Carlo methods in general, it is not a particularly good method for calculating π. There are much more efficient methods, but we've let pedagogy trump efficiency here.

Algorithm 16.6: Random subset generation.

RandomSubset(S) → RS
    Input: S, a set
    Output: RS, a random subset of S

```
1   RS ← CreateList()
2   foreach m in S do
3       r ← Random(0, 1)
4       if r < 0.5 then
5           InsertInList(RS, NULL, m)
6   return RS
```

Returning to voting, we will be generating coalitions in random and checking whether they are critical. The ratio of those that are critical to all those that we generate will give us an approximation of the Banzhaf measure. A random coalition is a random subset, so the first thing we need to do is find a way to generate random subsets.

That is the task of algorithm 16.6. The input to the algorithm is a set S, and it returns a random subset RS of elements of S. In the beginning, in line 1, RS is initialized to the empty list. Then, in the loop in lines 2–5, we iterate over the elements of S. For each element we essentially flip a coin to decide whether we will include it in the random subset. We do that by taking a random number in the range $[0, 1)$, in line 3, and comparing it with 0.5 (line 4). If it is less than 0.5, then we include it in RS in line 5. We return RS, as it has been filled, in line 6.

Algorithm 16.6 is a general random subset generation algorithm, not limited to generating coalitions. We can use it in any task we have to take a random sample, of random size, from a set. In the specific application of calculating the Banzhaf measure using a Monte Carlo method, it allows us to arrive at a simple algorithm for the calculation, algorithm 16.7.

The algorithm takes as input the voter v, whose Banzhaf measure we want to calculate, a list ov containing the other voters, the quota q required to pass, an associative array w containing the weight for each voter, and the number t of tries we will try to find a critical coalition.

We keep count of the number of tries in the variable k, which we initialize to zero in line 0. We keep count of the critical coalitions we have found in the variable nc, which we also initialize to zero in line 1. The loop in lines 3–10 is

---

Algorithm 16.7: Monte Carlo Banzhaf measure.

BanzhafMeasure(v, ov, q, w, t) $\rightarrow b$

    Input: v, a voter

                ov, a list containing the other voters

                q, the quota required

                w an associative array containing the weight of each voter

                t, the number of tries

    Output: b, the Banzhaf measure for voter v

1   $k \leftarrow 0$

2   $nc \leftarrow 0$

3   **while** $k < t$ **do**

4       $coalition \leftarrow \mathsf{RandomSubset}(ov)$

5       $votes \leftarrow 0$

6   **foreach** m **in** $coalition$ **do**

7            $votes \leftarrow votes + \mathsf{Lookup}(w, m)$

8   **if** $votes < q$ **and** $votes + \mathsf{Lookup}(w, v) \geq q$ **then**

9            $nc \leftarrow nc + 1$

10      $k \leftarrow k + 1$

11 $b \leftarrow nc / k$

12 **return** b

---

repeated t number of times. For each iteration of the loop, we get a random coalition, using algorithm 16.6. We need to find the number of votes in each random coalition; initially this is zero, set in line 5. Then for every member of the coalition (loop in lines 6–9), we add the member's votes to the running total, in line 7. If the running total is less than the quota but it reaches the quota with the votes of voter v (line 8), then we have a critical coalition, so we increase that count (line 9). We increase the loop counter at the end of the loop (line 10). At the end of the algorithm we return the ratio of critical coalitions over all coalitions (line 11) and then return it.

As with the Monte Carlo calculation of π, we need to know how many iterations to carry out to achieve a target accuracy. The mathematics are a bit more involved; it turns out that if we want our result to be within $\pm\epsilon$ with probability δ, the required number of samples is:

Table 16.3

U.S. electoral college, number of electors, and Banzhaf measure.

CA	55	0.475	MD	10	0.076	UT	5	0.038
TX	34	0.266	MN	10	0.076	WV	5	0.038
NY	31	0.241	WI	10	0.076	HI	4	0.030
FL	27	0.209	AL	9	0.069	ID	4	0.030
IL	21	0.161	CO	9	0.068	ME	4	0.030
PA	21	0.161	LA	9	0.068	NH	4	0.030
OH	20	0.153	KY	8	0.061	RI	4	0.030
MI	17	0.130	SC	8	0.060	AK	3	0.023
GA	15	0.114	CT	7	0.053	DC	3	0.023
NC	15	0.114	IA	7	0.053	DE	3	0.023
NJ	15	0.114	OK	7	0.053	MT	3	0.023
VA	13	0.099	OR	7	0.053	ND	3	0.023
MA	12	0.091	KS	6	0.046	SD	3	0.023
IN	11	0.084	MS	6	0.046	VT	3	0.023
MO	11	0.084	AR	6	0.045	WY	3	0.023
TN	11	0.084	NE	5	0.038			
WA	11	0.083	NM	5	0.038			
AZ	10	0.076	NV	5	0.038			

$$k \geq \frac{\ln \frac{2}{1-\delta}}{2\epsilon^2}$$

We can use algorithm 16.7 to calculate the Banzhaf measure of a real-life example, that of electing the U.S. president. The U.S. president is not elected directly by the people, but by the U.S. electoral college. The electoral college consists of a number of electors for each state and the District of Columbia. After the election, the party that wins the elections to each state and the District of Columbia appoints all the electors there (almost: Maine and Nebraska can split their electors, but we will ignore that possibility). Then the electors vote for the president, who is elected with a majority vote. The total number of electors is 538, so the president is elected with a quota of 270 electors.

The number of electors per state changes depending on the latest census. In 2015, California had 55 electors, whereas Vermont had 3 electors. Using these data we get the Banzhaf measure for the states and the District of Columbia in table 16.3. The table is sorted in descending order of Banzhaf measure.

California holds the biggest clout, but even tiny Vermont is no dummy. California's Banzhaf measure is about 20.65 times that of Vermont. The electoral college of California is about 18.33 times that of Vermont. So California gets a bit more power than one would expect just from observing the electoral ratios. The interested reader could check other pairs to detect any discrepancies. In terms of the accuracy of the results, the Monte Carlo approach was run with $\epsilon = 0.001$ and $\delta = 0.95$. That required 1,844,440 samples for each Banzhaf measure. Not a small number, but a trifle compared to the number of possible subsets of a set of 51 members.

16.4   Searching for Primes

In many applications of cryptography, it is essential to find large prime numbers. In these applications, large prime numbers are typically prime numbers of m bits, where m is a large power of two (1024, 2048, 4096, ...). The security of several cryptographic algorithms, like RSA and the Diffie-Hellmann key exchange, depends on that, as do several cryptographic protocols that are embedded in the programs and devices that we use in our everyday life.

Finding large prime numbers is a challenge. We know that there are infinitely many prime numbers. We also know approximately how many prime numbers there are less than or equal to a number n. According to the Prime Number Theorem, if n is large, the number of primes less than or equal to n is approximately $n/\ln n$. The problem is how to find one of them.

One approach is to find all prime numbers with m bits, which are all prime numbers less than or equal to $n = 2^m$, and pick one of them. There are several methods for finding all primes less than or equal to n. The best known one is the Sieve of Eratosthenes, an ancient algorithm, named after Eratosthenes of Cyrene, c. 276–c. 195/194 BCE, a learned ancient Greek mathematician. The algorithm finds primes by ticking off the numbers that are not prime. Those that remain are primes—hence, the name sieve. We start with the number 2, which is prime. We mark all numbers less than or equal to n that are multiples of 2; these are of course composite numbers. We then go from the last prime number we found, 2, to the first number that has not been marked as a composite. That is the number 3, and it is a prime. Again we mark all numbers less than or equal to n that are multiples of 3. We then go again from the last prime we found, 3, to the first number that has not been marked as a composite. That is the number 5, and it is a prime. We continue like this until we exhaust all the numbers to n. The general idea is that every number p that we find that is not marked is prime because we have marked all the multiples of all numbers less than p; therefore, p is not a multiple of any number, and therefore is a prime. In the end, all unmarked numbers are prime.

Figure 16.7
The Sieve of Eratosthenes for $n = 31$.

You can see the operation of the sieve for $n = 31$ in figure 16.7. We check the multiples of 2 and 3; then the number 4 has already been marked as a composite, as have all its multiples, so we proceed with the number 5. After that we realize that there are no more composites left. That is not an accident. For any n, all composites that are greater than or equal to $\sqrt{n}$ are marked when we check the multiples of the numbers $p \le \sqrt{n}$. Indeed, any composite c such that $\sqrt{n} \le c \le n$ can be written as the product of two factors $c = f_1 \times f_2$, where at least one of $f_1 \le \sqrt{n}$ or $f_2 \le \sqrt{n}$ holds (we have equality when $c = n$); but then it will have already been marked as composite, being a multiple of f_1 and f_2.

We can also note something else. When we start ticking off the multiples of a number p, we can start directly at the pth multiple, p^2. That is because all of $p \times 2, p \times 3, \ldots, p \times (p-1)$ have been checked when we were checking the numbers $2, 3, \ldots, p-1$.

The Sieve of Eratosthenes is algorithm 16.8. It takes as input a natural number $n > 1$ and returns an array *isprime* such that if $p \le n$ is a prime, *isprime*$[p]$ is TRUE, otherwise it is FALSE. In the beginning, in lines 1–5, we create and initialize the array *isprime* so that all its elements apart from the first two are TRUE, that is, we mark them tentatively as prime; the numbers 0 and 1 are not considered prime. Note that the array is of size $n + 1$ in order to represent all numbers from 0 to n, inclusive. Then we set p equal to 2, in line 6, as 2 is a prime. The loop in lines 7–13 marks the composite numbers. In line 7 we use the condition $p^2 \le n$ instead of $p \le \sqrt{n}$ because usually the calculation of the square root is more time consuming that the calculation of squares. If p has not been marked as a composite (line 8), then in lines 9–12 we mark as composites the numbers $p \times p, p \times (p+1), \ldots, p \times \lfloor n/p \rfloor$. We set j equal to p in line 9, then we go through a loop as long as j is not greater than $\lfloor n/p \rfloor$

Algorithm 16.8: The Sieve of Eratosthenes.

```
SieveEratosthenes(n) → isprime
```
   Input: n, a natural number greater than 1
   Output: *isprime*, a boolean array of size $n + 1$ such that if $p \leq n$ is a
       prime, *isprime*[p] is TRUE, otherwise it is FALSE

1   *isprime* ← CreateArray($n + 1$)
2   *isprime*[0] ← FALSE
3   *isprime*[1] ← FALSE
4   **for** i ← 2 **to** $n + 1$ **do**
5   *isprime*[i] ← TRUE
6   $p \leftarrow 2$
7   **while** $p^2 \leq n$ **do**
8   **if** *isprime*[p] = TRUE **then**
9           $j \leftarrow p$
10   **while** $j \leq \lfloor n/p \rfloor$ **do**
11   *isprime*[$j \times p$] ← FALSE
12              $j \leftarrow j + 1$
13      $p \leftarrow p + 1$
14 **return** *isprime*

(line 10). In the loop we form the multiple $j \times p$ and mark the corresponding entry in *isprime*, in line 11, then we go to the next j, in line 12. If p has
already been marked as composite, it is the multiple of a number $p' < p$ we
have examined previously, therefore all its multiples are multiples of p' and
we do not need to go through the lines 9–12. We increase p in line 13 so that
we can start another outer loop. When all loops are done, we return *isprime*
in line 14.

The outer loop of the algorithm is executed $\sqrt{n}$ times. Inside the loop we
strike off all the multiples of 2, which are $\lfloor n/2 \rfloor$; then all the multiples of 3,
which are $\lfloor n/3 \rfloor$; then all the multiples of 5, which are $\lfloor n/5 \rfloor$; and so on for all
primes until the largest prime k with $k \leq \sqrt{n}$. Therefore, we strike off at most
$n/2 + n/3 + n/5 + \cdots + n/k$ primes, which is equal to $n(1/2 + 1/3 + 1/5 \cdots + 1/k)$. The sum $(1/2 + 1/3 + 1/5 \cdots + 1/k)$ is the sum of the reciprocal of primes
not greater than $\sqrt{n}$. In general, it can be proven that the sum of the reciprocal
of primes not greater than a number m is $O(\log \log m)$. Therefore, the total

time we spend striking off primes is $O(n \log \log \sqrt{n}) = O(n \log \log n)$, which is the complexity of the algorithm.

There are more efficient algorithms for finding all primes less than, or equal to a number. They run in times of $O(n)$ and even $O(n/(\log \log n))$. That's efficient, you are temped to think, so they could be the way to go for finding primes.

Unfortunately, things are not so simple. The figure $O(n)$ or $O(n/(\log \log n))$ counts complexity in terms of the size of the number, but this hides the size behind n. As we said, it is $n = 2^m$, for some large m, so the actual complexity that $O(n)$ requires is $O(2^m)$ steps: that is exponential in terms of the bits of the input number, not linear as we might have thought initially. For a number of 4096 bits we get $O(2^{4096})$, an impractical quantity. The $O(n/(\log \log n))$ figure just divides that number somewhat, without changing the overall picture.

Because finding all primes is not expedient, and because we know there are about $n/\ln n$ primes lying out there, we can try our luck and see what happens if we pick one number less than or equal to n and check it for primality. If we pick all n numbers we expect to find $n/\ln n$ primes; if we pick one number, then the probability that we'll hit a prime is $1/\ln n$. Conversely, probability theory tells us that in order to find a prime we would expect to try $\ln n$ numbers. Say we are looking for a prime number of 4096 bits. We need to try $\ln(2^{4096})$ numbers to expect to find a prime. We have $\ln(2^{4096}) = 4096 \ln 2 \approx 2840$, which is a pretty reasonable number. However, we do have to check, for each one of them, whether the number is indeed a prime.

The simplest way to check whether a number is prime is simply to see whether it is divided by any other number apart from one. For a number n it suffices to check whether it is divided by any number up to $\lfloor \sqrt{n} \rfloor$. The reason that $\sqrt{n}$ suffices is the same as with the Sieve of Eratosthenes: a number greater than $\lceil \sqrt{n} \rceil$ can produce n only if it is multiplied by a number no greater than $\lfloor \sqrt{n} \rfloor$, which we have already checked. We can also half that number because we can skip all even numbers greater than 2: if n is divisible by any even number greater than 2, then it is also divisible by 2 anyway. If we assume that division takes one step, then this algorithm would take up to $O\left((1/2)\sqrt{n}\right) = O(\sqrt{n})$ steps, which does not look bad. Once more, though, this is deceptive. The size of our input is the size of the number n. Again, in binary this is 2^m, which means that the algorithm will need $O\left(\sqrt{2^m}\right) = O\left((2^m)^{1/2}\right) = O(2^{m/2})$. Even if we need to pick at random a small number of numbers, we need a large amount of time to check whether the randomly picked number is prime.

Fortunately, there is an efficient way to check if a number is prime. The method we will describe will always tell us that a prime is indeed a prime—therefore, there are no false negatives, saying that a prime is composite. It will also tell us that a composite is a composite *most of the time*. There will be a probability that it will fail to flag a composite as such and will report, erroneously, that it is prime—a false positive. However, we will see that we can ensure that this probability is low enough that it does not matter for all practical purposes. This is a *probabilistic primality test*, where the chances really work in our favor.

The test relies on some facts from number theory. If the random number we want to test for primality is p, then p must be odd; otherwise, if it is even we immediately discard it as composite. Therefore, $p - 1$ must be even. If we divide any even number repeatedly by 2, then we will either arrive at 1 or some other odd number. For example, if we divide 12 repeatedly by 2, we get 6, then 3. So $12 = 2^2 \times 3$. If we divide 16 repeatedly by 2, then we get 8, 4, 2, 1. So $16 = 2^4 \times 1$. In general we have $p - 1 = 2^r q$, where $r \geq 1$ and q is an odd number.

Now let's take another random number x so that $1 < x < p$ and calculate $y = x^q \bmod p$. If $y = 1$, that is, $x^q \bmod p = 1$, we have $(x^q)^t \bmod p = 1$, for any $t \geq 0$. Indeed, this follows from the fact that for any integers a and b we have $[(a \bmod p)(b \bmod p)] \bmod p = (a \cdot b) \bmod p$. By taking $a = b$ and applying repeatedly we have $(a \bmod p)^t \bmod t = a^t \bmod p$, so if $a \bmod p = 1$ we have $a^t \bmod p = 1$. Then by substituting 2^r for t in $(x^q)^t$, we get $(x^q)^{2^r} \bmod p = 1$, $x^{2^r q} \bmod p = 1$, or $x^{p-1} \bmod p = 1$. According to Fermat's Little Theorem, if p is a prime, then this relationship must necessarily hold. Conversely, if the relationship holds, then p is *probably* prime, but it may not be. We have encounted Fermat's Little Theorem before, in the RSA cryptosystem, section 5.2.

Let's sum up what we have done until now. We have picked a random number p that we want to test for primality. We write it as $p = 1 + 2^r q$. Then we take a random number x such that $1 < x < p$ and calculate $y = x^q \bmod p$. If $y = 1$, then we can say that p is probably prime. We will call this situation "Exhibit A", for reasons that will become clear in a short while.

If $y = x^q \bmod p \neq 1$, then we can start a squaring process, producing the values:

$$(x^q)^2 \bmod p = x^{2q} \bmod p$$

$$(x^{2q})^2 \bmod p = x^{4q} \bmod p$$

$$\cdots$$

$$(x^{2^{r-1}q})^2 \bmod p = x^{2^r q} \bmod p = x^{p-1} \bmod p$$

If p is prime, then again, thanks to Fermat's Little Theorem, this sequence of values will end with 1. In fact, we may get 1 well before we reach the rth squaring—all subsequent squarings will continue producing 1, as we saw above. Moreover, the value we get before the first 1 must necessarily be $p - 1$.

An aside on why this is so (if you trust that it is, you can skip to the next paragraph). It comes from number theory. For any number y, if we have $y^2 \bmod p = 1$, where p is a prime, it means that $y^2 = kp + 1$, for some integer k, or $y^2 - 1 = kp$, or $(y - 1)(y + 1) = kp$. For this to happen, if $k \neq 0$ the number p should have $(y - 1)/k$ or $(y + 1)/k$ as a factor, which it cannot, because p is a prime. Therefore we must have $k = 0$; then it must be $y - 1 = 0$ or $y + 1 = 0$, which means we can only have $y = 1$ or $y = -1$. So, in the squaring sequence, before the first time we get $y = 1$ we must have $y = -1$. We must cast this in terms of modulo arithmetic, where $0 < y < p$. Recall that the mathematical definition of the modulo, $a \bmod b$, is the number $c \geq 0$, the remainder, such that $a = qb + c$, where q is the floor of the division of a/b, $\lfloor a/b \rfloor$. We encountered this definition in section 4.2, where we introduced the modulo operator. Therefore, we get $c = a - b\lfloor a/b \rfloor$. The remainder of the division of -1 by p is then $-1 \bmod p = -1 - p\lfloor -1/p \rfloor = -1 - p(-1) = p - 1$. So, indeed, immediately before we get $y = 1$ we must get $y = p - 1$.

Time to recap again. If we start squaring repeatedly $y = x^q \bmod p$ and p is a prime, we will at some point arrive at $y = p - 1$; then the next squaring (which we do not need to do) will give $y = 1$. Conversely, if we arrive at $y = p - 1$ without knowing anything about p, it is *probable* that p is a prime, although it may not be. We will call this situation, with $y = p - 1$, "Exhibit B".

If we arrive at $y = 1$ *without* having got $y = -1$ in the previous squaring, then we know definitely that p is *not* a prime, because all the arguments in the previous paragraphs show that if it were a prime, we would have got $y = -1$ immediately before. We will call this situation, with $y = 1$ without having got $y = p - 1$ before, "Exhibit C".

Finally, if we arrive at $y = x^{2^r q} \bmod p = x^{p-1} \bmod p$ and $y \neq 1$, then also by Fermat's Little Theorem we can be sure that the number is *not* a prime. This will be our "Exhibit D".

Algorithm 16.9: A witness for composite numbers.

WitnessComposite(p) $\rightarrow$ TRUE or FALSE

   Input: p, an odd integer

   Output: a boolean value that is TRUE if the number is definitely
            composite, FALSE otherwise

1    $(r, q) \leftarrow$ FactorTwo($p - 1$)

2    $x \leftarrow$ RandomInt($2, p - 1$)

3    $y \leftarrow x^q \bmod p$

4   **if** $y = 1$ **then**

5   **return** FALSE

6   **for** $j \leftarrow 0$ **to** r **do**

7   **if** $y = p - 1$ **then**

8   **return** FALSE

9        $y \leftarrow y^2 \bmod p$

10   **if** $y = 1$ **then**

11   **return** TRUE

12   **return** TRUE

We have therefore found reliable, definitive, indicators that a number p is a composite number: Exhibit C and Exhibit D; at the same time, we have probabilistic indicators that the number p is prime: Exhibit A and Exhibit B. We call a function that attests to a particular attribute of interest a *witness*: we can therefore use the results of our discussion to build a witness for p being composite; the witness is algorithm 16.9.

The witness algorithm is remarkably short for all the arguments we've put forward for it. It is essentially a simple method with quite a bit of foundation below.

We start by calling, in line 1, FactorTwo($p - 1$), which returns r and q such that $p - 1 = 2^r q$; we'll come back to FactorTwo shortly. Then, in line 2, RandomInt($2, p - 1$) produces an integer in the range from 2 up to and including $p - 1$. In line 3 we calculate $x^q \bmod p$ and store it in y. From Exhibit A, we know that if $y = 1$ (line 4), the number p is probably prime, so we return FALSE in line 5. If it is not so, we start to square repeatedly, at most r times, in the loop of lines 6–11. If $y = p - 1$ in any iteration of the loop (line 7), then the next squaring will produce $y = 1$, and from Exhibit B we deduce that the number is probably prime and return FALSE in line 8. After squaring y, modulo p, in line 9

Algorithm 16.10: Miller-Rabin primality test.

MillerRabinPrimalityTest(p, t) $\rightarrow$ TRUE or FALSE
  Input: p, an odd integer
        t, the number of times the witness primality function will be
        applied
  Output: TRUE if the number is prime with probability $(1/4)^t$, FALSE if
        the number is definitely composite

1   **for** $i \leftarrow 0$ **to** t **do**
2   **if** WitnessComposite(p) **then**
3   **return** FALSE
4   **return** TRUE

---

we check to see whether we got $y = 1$. If this happens, it does without having gone through $y = p - 1$, and therefore we definitely know from Exhibit C that the number is composite and we return TRUE. If we exit the loop then we have Exhibit D and we return TRUE, that p is definitely composite, in line 12.

In order for the witness algorithm to be practical, we must know that the probability that it will err is acceptably low. It turns out that the probability that the algorithm will be wrong is at most $1/4$ of the time. That is the key to its use in practice. If we use it just once, then we have a $1/4$ probability that it will report a composite number as a prime. If we use it twice, then the probability will be $(1/4)^2$ that it will be wrong both times. By calling it more times, we can lower the probability to any absurdly low level we want. For example, if we call it 50 times, the probability that it will falsely report a prime will be $(1/4)^{50}$, which should be enough for all practical purposes.

The repeated application of the witness algorithm is called the Miller-Rabin primality test, after Gary L. Miller and Michael O. Rabin, on whose ideas it is built. Given WitnessComposite(p), the Miller-Rabin algorithm is straightforward; see algorithm 16.10.

In terms of complexity, the Miller-Rabin test is efficient. Going back to algorithm 16.9, the modular exponentiation in line 3 takes place only once and can be performed efficiently in $O((\lg p)^3)$, as $q < p$. Indeed, we saw how to perform fast modular exponentiation in section 4.5, where we also met these complexity figures. The loop of lines 6–11 is executed $O(r)$ times, where $r < \lg p$, so we have $O(\lg p)$ iterations. In each iteration we perform a modular squaring. Taking into account that all $y < p$, the modular squaring needs $O((\lg p)^2)$ time;

Algorithm 16.11: Factor n as $2^r q$, with q odd.

FactorTwo$(n) \rightarrow (r, q)$
    Input: n, an even integer
    Output: (r, q), such that $n = 2^r q$

1   $q \leftarrow n$
2   $r \leftarrow 0$
3   **while** $q \bmod 2 = 0$ **do**
4      $r \leftarrow r + 1$
5      $q \leftarrow q/2$
6   **return** (r, q)

---

taken over all iterations, we get $O((\lg p)^3)$. We can assume that the time taken up by RandomInt is less than that.

The only piece still missing is the function FactorTwo, which provides the factor of $p - 1$ that is multiplied by the biggest possible power of 2. We can write this function as a series of repeated divisions; see algorithm 16.11. This algorithm works by setting q to its input, n, in line 1; at the end of the algorithm q will be an odd number that is the remainder of n by a power of 2. The power of 2 that we are looking for is r, which we set initially to zero in line 2. In the loop of lines 3–5, we check whether q is even (line 3); if yes, we know it is divisible by 2, so we increase r (line 4) and do the division (line 5). If q is odd, then we are done and we return (r, q).

The repeated division entails that the number of steps of the whole process is the base two logarithm of its input, which is the number $p - 1$ that we use in WitnessComposite, so the complexity of FactorTwo is $O(\lg p)$. That does not affect the overall complexity of WitnessComposite, which therefore requires $O((\lg p)^3)$ steps. That is very good. For t iterations of WitnessComposite we get $O(t \cdot (\lg p)^3)$, so we have a practical method for finding large primes with size reaching p. We keep guessing for a prime; each guess takes $O(t \cdot (\lg p)^3)$ steps to check, and we expect to guess about $\ln p$ times.

By the way, 50 iterations are probably overkill. It may be more likely than $(1/4)^{50}$ that your computer will produce an error for any unrelated reason: hardware malfunctioning, some kind of electromagnetic interference, even cosmic rays penetrating the atmosphere and reaching its circuit boards.

Notes

The effort to create random numbers in computers is about as old as computers. The Ferranti Mark I computer, built in 1951, included a hardware-based random number generator, adopting a suggestion by Alan Turing. Derrick Herny Lehmer proposed a linear congruential generator in 1949 [127]. John von Neumann's quote on randomness and sin appeared in an early collection of papers on the Monte Carlo method [211]. The advice against random use of random methods comes from the introductory material on random numbers in Knuth [113, section 3.1].

Tables of good values for m, a, c are given by Pierre L' Ecuyer [124]. L' Ecuyer and Richard Simard have written a comprehensive library for testing random number generators [125]. The xorshift64* and xorshift1024* generators were invented by Sebastiano Vigna [209] based on the xorshift generators introduced by George Marsaglia [133]. Figure 16.2b, was produced based on a recipe for creating Hinton maps included in the matplotlib examples gallery; the initial idea is attributed to David Warde-Farley.

The Fortuna CSRNG was invented by cryptographers Niels Ferguson and Bruce Schneier [62, chapter 10]; it is also described in an updated version of the original book [63, chapter 9]. It was proposed as the successor of the popular Yarrow generator [106]. Testing the security of a CSRNG is a continuous effort; so a security analysis of Fortuna found that there is room for improvement [53].

Selection sampling, along with other methods, was described by C. T. Fan, Mervin E. Muller, and Ivan Rezucha in 1962 [59]; it was also independently described in the same year by T. G. Jones as a method to get a "random sample of precisely n records from a tape film containing N records"; the description took no more than 24 single-column lines [103]. Yves Tillé's book gives a comprehensive treatment of different sampling algorithms [202]. Selection sampling is also known as algorithm S and reservoir sampling as algorithm R and are discussed in Knuth [113, section 3.4.2]. Knuth attributes reservoir sampling to Alan G. Waterman; it has also been presented by McLeod and Bellhouse [136] and Jeffrey Scott Vitter [210]. Tillé notes that it is a special case of a method proposed by Chao [35]. You can find a Perl one-liner for selecting a random line from a file in the *Perl Cookbook* [36, p. 314] (so this is a solution to exercise 1 below). The weighted sampling method presented in exercise 2 is by Efraimidis and Spirakis [55].

The first publication on measuring voting power was by Lionel Penrose in 1946 [156]; Penrose essentially described the Banzhaf measure, but his paper went completely unnoticed. The field really got going in 1954 with a paper by Lloyd S. Shapley and Martin Shubik [184], who introduced a different measure, the Shapley-Shubik index of voting paper. John F. Banzhaf published his paper in 1955 [9]. The number of iterations required to get a target accuracy of the Banzhaf measure is derived in [6]. A survey of algorithms for calculating power indices in weighted voting can be found in [134]. A detailed description of voting power is in the book by Felsenthal and Machover [61]; see also the book by Taylor and Pacelli [200]. More recently, Banzhaf analysis has been criticized as not corresponding to real-world voting because different probabilistic assumptions apply there [77].

For an analysis of the complexity of prime number sieves, see the report by Sorenson [191]. Gary L. Miller first proposed a primality test in 1975 [140]; that test is deterministic, not probabilistic, but relies on an unproven mathematical hypothesis. Micheal O. Rabin modified it a few years later to produce a probabilistic algorithm that does not depend on unproven mathematics [162]. Knuth noted that cosmic radiations are more likely to create a problem than wrong guesses from Miller-Rabin [113, section 4.5.4].

Exercises

1. How would you select one line in random from a file, without reading it all in memory? That means that you do not know how many lines there are. You can use reservoir sampling, where the reservoir is of size one. That means that when you read the first line, you pick it with probability equal to 1. When you read the second line, if it exists, you pick it with probability equal to 1/2, so line 1 and line 2 have equal probability of being selected. When you read the third line, again if it exists, you pick it with probability equal to 1/3. That means that lines 1 and 2 have 2/3 probability of being selected, which they share equally, because we saw that each one of them had 1/2 probability of being selected previously; so each of the three lines has 1/3 probability of being selected. We continue in this way until the end of the file. Implement reservoir sampling to pick a random line from a file. Note that this version of reservoir sampling can be much smaller than the general one.

2. There are applications where we need to sample according to some predefined weights: that is, the probability that an item is sampled must be proportional to its weight. This is called *weighted sampling*. We can do that with a variation of reservoir sampling. We start by inserting the first m items in the reservoir, but we associate with each item i a key equal to u^{1/w_i}, where w_i is its weight and

u is a random number selected uniformly in the range from 0 to 1 (included). Then for each item k that follows, we get again a random number u in the range $[0, 1]$ and calculate its key u^{1/w_k}; if this is greater than the smallest key in the reservoir, we insert the new item in the reservoir, replacing the one with the smallest key. Implement this scheme using a minimum priority queue to find each time the item that has the smallest key in the reservoir.

3.   In the Sieve of Eratosthenes, we mentioned that we used the condition $p^2 \le n$ instead of $p \le \sqrt{n}$, because it is usually faster. Check the situation for yourself: implement both of them and measure how much time each one of them takes.

4.   There are many elections that use vote weights; calculate the Banzhaf measure for an election of your choice. Vary the number of samples between program executions and check the accuracy and the time required. A good idea is to make a plot of the sample size and accuracy against the execution time of the program.

Bibliography

[1] Ravindra K. Ahuja, Kurt Mehlhorn, James Orlin, and Robert E. Tarjan. Faster algorithms for the shortest path problem. *Journal of the ACM*, 37(2):213–223, April 1990.

[2] Ethem Alpaydın. *Introduction to Machine Learning*. The MIT Press, Cambridge, MA, 3rd edition, 2014.

[3] Geoffrey D. Austrian. *Herman Hollerith: Forgotten Giant of Information Processing*. Columbia University Press, New York, NY, 1982.

[4] Bachrach, El-Yaniv, and M. Reinstädtler. On the competitive theory and practice of online list accessing algorithms. *Algorithmica*, 32(2):201–245, 2002.

[5] Ran Bachrach and Ran El-Yaniv. Online list accessing algorithms and their applications: Recent empirical evidence. In *Proceedings of the Eighth Annual ACM-SIAM Symposium on Discrete Algorithms*, SODA '97, pages 53–62, Philadelphia, PA, USA, 1997. Society for Industrial and Applied Mathematics.

[6] Yoram Bachrach, Evangelos Markakis, Ezra Resnick, Ariel D. Procaccia, Jeffrey S. Rosenschein, and Amin Saberi. Approximating power indices: Theoretical and empirical analysis. *Autonomous Agents and Multi-Agent Systems*, 20(2):105–122, March 2010.

[7] Ricardo A. Baeza-Yates and Mireille Régnier. Average running time of the Boyer-Moore-Horspool algorithm. *Theoretical Computer Science*, 92(1):19–31, January 1992.

[8] Michael J. Bannister and David Eppstein. Randomized speedup of the Bellman-Ford algorithm. In *Proceedings of the Meeting on Analytic Algorithmics and Combinatorics*, ANALCO '12, pages 41–47, Philadelphia, PA, USA, 2012. Society for Industrial and Applied Mathematics.

[9] John F. Banzhaf, III. Weighted voting doesn't work: A mathematical analysis. *Rutgers Law Review*, 19:317–343, 1965.

[10] Albert-László Barabási. *Linked: The New Science Of Networks*. Basic Books, 2002.

[11] Albert-László Barabási and Eric Bonabeau. Scale-free networks. *Scientific American*, 288(5):50–59, May 2003.

[12] J. Neil Bearden. A new secretary problem with rank-based selection and cardinal payoffs. *Journal of Mathematical Psychology*, 50:58–59, 2006.

[13] Richard Bellman. On a routing problem. *Quarterly of Applied Mathematics*, 16(1):87–90, 1958.

[14] Frank Benford. The law of anomalous numbers. *Proceedings of the American Philosophical Society*, 78(4):551–572, 1938.

[15] Arthur Benjamin, Gary Chartrand, and Ping Zhang. *The Fascinating World of Graph Theory*. Princeton University Press, Princeton, NJ, USA, 2015.

[16] Jon Bentley. *Programming Pearls*. Addison-Wesley, 2nd edition, 2000.

[17] Jon L. Bentley and Catherine C. McGeoch. Amortized analyses of self-organizing sequential search heuristics. *Communications of the ACM*, 28(4):404–411, April 1985.

[18] Michael W. Berry and Murray Browne. *Understanding Text Engines: Mathematical Modeling and Text Retrieval*. Society for Industrial and Applied Mathematics, Philadelphia, PA, 2nd edition, 2005.

[19] N. Biggs, E. K. Lloyd, and R. J. Wilson. *Graph Theory, 1736–1936*. Clarendon Press, Oxford, UK, 1986.

[20] Christopher M. Bishop. *Pattern Recognition and Machine Learning*. Springer, New York, NY, 2006.

[21] Joshua Bloch. Extra, extra—read all about it: Nearly all Binary Searches and Mergesorts are broken. `http://googleresearch.blogspot.it/2006/06/extra-extra-read-all-about-it-nearly.html`, June 2 2006.

[22] Joshua Bloch. *Effective Java (2nd Edition) (The Java Series)*. Prentice Hall PTR, Upper Saddle River, NJ, USA, 2nd edition, 2008.

[23] Burton H. Bloom. Space/time trade-offs in hash coding with allowable errors. *Communications of the ACM*, 13(7):422–426, July 1970.

[24] James Blustein and Amal El-Maazawi. Bloom filters—a tutorial, analysis, and survey. Technical report, Dalhousie University, Faculty of Computer Science, 2002.

[25] J. A. Bondy and U. S. R. Murty. *Graph Theory*. Springer, New York, NY, 2008.

[26] Robert S. Boyer and J Strother Moore. A fast string searching algorithm. *Communications of the ACM*, 20(10):762–772, October 1977.

[27] Steven J. Brams. *Mathematics and Democracy: Designing Better Votign and Fair-Division Processes*. Princeton University Press, Princeton, NJ, 2008.

[28] Leo Breiman, Jerome H. Friedman, Richard A. Olshen, and Charles J. Stone. *Classification and Regression Trees*. Wadsworth International Group, Belmont, CA, 1984.

[29] Sergey Brin and Lawrence Page. The anatomy of a large-scale hypertextual web search engine. *Computer Networks and ISDN Systems*, 30(1–7):107–117, April 1998.

[30] Andrei Broder and Michael Mitzenmacher. Network applications of bloom filters: A survey. *Internet Mathematics*, 1(4):485–509, 2003.

[31] Kurt Bryan and Tanya Leise. The $25,000,000,000 eigenvector: The linear algebra behind google. *SIAM Review*, 48(3):569–581, 2006.

[32] Russell Burns. *Communications: An International History of the Formative Years*. The Institution of Electrical Engineers, Stevenage, UK, 2004.

[33] Stefan Büttcher, Charles L. A. Clarke, and Gordon Cormack. *Information Retrieval: Implementing and Evaluating Search Engines*. The MIT Press, Cambridge, MA, 2010.

[34] R. Callon. Use of OSI IS-IS for routing in TCP/IP and dual environments. RFC 1195, December 1990.

[35] M. T. Chao. A general purpose unequal probability sampling plan. *Biometrika*, 69(3):653–656, 1982.

[36] Tom Christiansen and Nathan Torkington. *Perl Cookbook*. O'Reilly, Sebastopol, CA, 2nd edition, 2003.

[37] Richard J. Cichelli. Minimal perfect hash functions made simple. *Communications of the ACM*, 23(1):17–19, January 1980.

[38] Douglas E. Comer. *Internetworking with TCP/IP, Volume 1: Principles, Protocols, and Architecture*. Pearson, 6th edition, 2013.

[39] Marquis de Condorcet. *Essai sur l'application de l'analyse à la probabilité des décisions rendues à la pluralité des voix*. Imprimerie Royale, Paris, 1785.

[40] Stephen A. Cook. Linear time simulation of deterministic two-way pushdown automata. In *IFIP Congress 1*, pages 75–80, 1971.

[41] Thomas H. Cormen. *Algorithms Unlocked*. The MIT Press, Cambridge, MA, 2013.

[42] Thomas H. Cormen, Charles E. Leiserson, Ronald L. Rivest, and Cliffort Stein. *Introduction to Algorithms*. The MIT Press, Cambridge, MA, 3rd edition, 2009.

[43] T. M. Cover and R. King. A convergent gambling estimate of the entropy of English. *IEEE Transactions on Information Theory*, 24(4):413–421, September 2006.

[44] Thomas M. Cover and Joy A. Thomas. *Elements of Information Theory*. Wiley-Interscience, Hoboken, NJ, 2nd edition, 2006.

[45] Maxime Crochemore, Christophe Hancart, and Thierry Lecroq. *Algorithms on Strings*. Cambridge University Press, Cambridge, UK, 2014.

[46] Joan Daemen and Vincent Rijmen. *The Design of Rijndael: AES—The Advanced Encryption Standard*. Springer-Verlag New York, Inc., Secaucus, NJ, USA, 2002.

[47] Sanjoy Dasgupta, Christos H. Papadimitriou, and Umesh Vazirani. *Algorithms*. McGraw-Hill, Inc., New York, NY, 2008.

[48] Easley David and Kleinberg Jon. *Networks, Crowds, and Markets: Reasoning About a Highly Connected World*. Cambridge University Press, New York, NY, USA, 2010.

[49] Butler Declan. When Google got flu wrong. *Nature*, 494(7436):155–156, 2013.

[50] W. Diffie and M. E. Hellman. New directions in cryptography. *IEEE Transactions on Information Theory*, 22(6):644–654, November 1976.

[51] E. W. Dijkstra. A note on two problems in connexion with graphs. *Numerische Mathematik*, 1(1):269–271, December 1959.

[52] Roger Dingledine, Nick Mathewson, and Paul Syverson. Tor: The second-generation Onion Router. In *Proceedings of the 13th USENIX Security Symposium*, Berkeley, CA, USA, 2004. USENIX Association.

[53] Yevgeniy Dodis, Adi Shamir, Noah Stephens-Davidowitz, and Daniel Wichs. How to eat your entropy and have it too—optimal recovery strategies for compromised rngs. Cryptology ePrint Archive, Report 2014/167, 2014. http://eprint.iacr.org/.

[54] Arnold I. Dumey. Indexing for rapid random-access memory. *Computers and Automation*, 5(12):6–9, 1956.

[55] Pavlos S. Efraimidis and Paul G. Spirakis. Weighted random sampling with a reservoir. *Information Processing Letters*, 97(5):181–185, 2006.

[56] Leonhardo Eulerho. Solutio problematis ad geometrian situs pertinentis. *Commetarii Academiae Scientiarum Imperialis Petropolitanae*, 8:128–140, 1736.

[57] Shimon Even. *Graph Algorithms*. Cambridge University Press, Cambridge, UK, 2nd edition, 2012.

[58] Kevin R. Fall and W. Richard Stevens. *TCP/IP Illustrated, Volume 1: The Protocols*. Addison-Wesley, Upper Saddle River, NJ, 2nd edition, 2012.

[59] C. T. Fan, Mervin E. Muller, and Ivan Rezucha. Development of sampling plans by using sequential (item by item) selection techniques and digital computers. *Journal of the American Statistical Association*, 57(298):387–402, 1962.

[60] Ariel Felner. Position paper: Dijkstra's algorithm versus Uniform Cost Search or a case against Dijkstra's algorithm. In *Proceedings of the 4th Annual Symposium on Combinatorial Search (SoCS)*, pages 47–51, 2011.

[61] Dan S. Felsenthal and Moshé Machover. *The Measurement of Voting Power: Theory and Practice, Problems and Paradoxes*. Edward Elgar, Cheltenham, UK, 1998.

[62] Niels Ferguson and Bruce Schneier. *Practical Cryptography*. Wiley Publishing, Indianapolis, IN, 2003.

[63] Niels Ferguson, Bruce Schneier, and Tadayoshi Kohno. *Cryptography Engineering: Design Principles and Practical Applications*. Wiley Publishing, Indianapolis, IN, 2010.

[64] Thomas S. Ferguson. Who solved the secretary problem? *Statistical Science*, 4(3):282–289, 08 1989.

[65] R. M. Fewster. A simple explanation of Benford's law. *The American Statistician*, 63(1):26–32, 2009.

[66] Robert W. Floyd. Algorithm 113: Treesort. *Communications of the ACM*, 5(8):434, August 1962.

[67] Robert W. Floyd. Algorithm 97: Shortest path. *Communications of the ACM*, 5(6):345, June 1962.

[68] Robert W. Floyd. Algorithm 245: Treesort 3. *Communications of the ACM*, 7(12):701, December 1964.

[69] L. R. Ford. Network flow theory, 1956. Paper P-923.

[70] Glenn Fowler, Landon Curt Noll, Kiem-Phong Vo, and Donald Eastlake. The FNV non-cryptographic hash algorithm. Internet-Draft draft-eastlake-fnv-09.txt, IETF Secretariat, April 2015.

[71] Michael L. Fredman and Robert Endre Tarjan. Fibonacci heaps and their uses in improved network optimization algorithms. *Journal of the ACM*, 34(3):596–615, July 1987.

[72] Edward H. Friend. Sorting on electronic computer systems. *Journal of the ACM*, 3(3):134–168, July 1956.

[73] Zvi Galil. On improving the worst case running time of the boyer-moore string matching algorithm. *Commun. ACM*, 22(9):505–508, September 1979.

[74] Antonio Valverde Garcia and Jean-Pierre Seifert. On the implementation of the Advanced Encryption Standard on a public-key crypto-coprocessor. In *Proceedings of the 5th Conference on Smart Card Research and Advanced Application Conference—Volume 5*, CARDIS'02, Berkeley, CA, USA, 2002. USENIX Association.

[75] Martin Gardner. Mathematical games. *Scientific American*, 237(2):120–124, August 1977.

[76] Simson L. Garfinkel. Digital forensics. *American Scientist*, 101(5):370–377, September–October 2013.

[77] Andrew Gelman, Jonathan N. Katz, and Francis Tuerlinckx. The mathematics and statistics of voting power. *Statistical Science*, 17(4):420–435, 11 2002.

[78] Jeremy Ginsberg, Matthew H. Mohebbi, Rajan S. Patel, Lynnette Brammer, Mark S. Smolinski, and Larry Brilliant. Detecting influenza epidemics using search engine query data. *Nature*, 457(7232):1012–1014, 2009.

[79] Oded Goldreich. *Foundations of Cryptography: Basic Tools*. Cambridge University Press, Cambridge, UK, 2004.

[80] Oded Goldreich. *Foundations of Cryptography: II Basic Applications*. Cambridge University Press, Cambridge, UK, 2009.

[81] David Goldschlag, Michael Reed, and Paul Syverson. Onion routing. *Communications of the ACM*, 42(2):39–41, February 1999.

[82] Michael T. Goodrich, Roberto Tamassia, and Michael H. Goldwasser. *Data Structures & Algorithms in Python*. John Wiley & Sons, Hoboken, NJ, 2013.

[83] Robert M. Gray. *Entropy and Information Theory*. Springer, New York, NY, 2nd edition, 2011.

[84] John Guare. *Six Degrees of Separation: A Play*. Random House, New York, NY, 1990.

[85] Dan Gusfield. *Algorithms on Strings, Trees and Sequences: Computer Science and Computational Biology*. Cambridge University Press, Cambridge, UK, 1997.

[86] David Harel and Yishai Feldman. *Algorithmics: The Spirit of Computing*. Pearson Education, Essex, UK, 3rd edition, 2004.

[87] P. E. Hart, N. J. Nilsson, and B. Raphael. A formal basis for the heuristic determination of minimum cost paths. *IEEE Transactions on Systems, Science, and Cybernetics*, 4(2):100–107, July 1968.

[88] Peter E. Hart, Nils J. Nilsson, and Bertram Raphael. Correction to "A formal basis for the heuristic determination of minimum cost paths". *SIGART Bulletin*, 37:28–29, December 1972.

[89] Fiona Harvey. Name that tune. *Scientific American*, 288(6):84–86, June 2003.

[90] Trevor Hastie, Robert Tibshirani, and Jerome Friedman. *The Elements of Statistical Learning: Data Mining, Inference, and Prediction.* Springer, New York, NY, 2nd edition, 2009.

[91] César Hidalgo. *Why Information Grows: The Evolution of Order, from Atoms to Economies.* Basic Books, New York, NY, 2015.

[92] Theodore P. Hill. A statistical derivation of the Significant-Digit law. *Statistical Science,* 10(4):354–363, 1995.

[93] C. A. R. Hoare. Algorithm 63: Partition. *Communications of the ACM,* 4(7):321, July 1961.

[94] C. A. R. Hoare. Algorithm 64: Quicksort. *Communications of the ACM,* 4(7):321, July 1961.

[95] C. A. R. Hoare. Algorithm 65: Find. *Communications of the ACM,* 4(7):321–322, July 1961.

[96] John Hopcroft and Robert Tarjan. Algorithm 447: Efficient algorithms for graph manipulation. *Communications of the ACM,* 16(6):372–378, June 1973.

[97] W. G. Horner. A new method of solving numerical equations of all orders, by continuous approximation. *Philosophical Transactions of the Royal Society of London,* 109:308–335, 1819.

[98] R. Nigel Horspool. Practical fast searching in strings. *Software: Practice and Experience,* 10(6):501–506, 1980.

[99] D. A. Huffman. A method for the construction of minimum-redundancy codes. *Proceedings of the IRE,* 40(9):1098–1101, September 1952.

[100] Earl B. Hunt, Janet Marin, and Philip J. Stone. *Experiments in Induction.* Academic Press, New York, NY, 1966.

[101] P. Z. Ingerman. Algorithm 141: Path matrix. *Communications of the ACM,* 5(11):556, November 1962.

[102] Gareth James, Daniela Witten, Trevor Hastie, and Robert Tibshirani. *An Introduction to Statistical Learning: With Applications in R.* Springer, New York, NY, 2013.

[103] T. G. Jones. A note on sampling a tape-file. *Communications of the ACM,* 5(6):343, June 1962.

[104] David Kahn. *The Codebreakers: The Comprehensive History of Secret Communication from Ancient Times to the Internet.* Scribner, New York, NY, revised edition, 1996.

[105] Jonathan Katz and Yehuda Lindell. *Introduction to Modern Cryptography.* CRC Press, Taylor & Francis Group, Boca Raton, FL, 2nd edition, 2015.

[106] John Kelsey, Bruce Schneier, and Niels Ferguson. Yarrow-160: Notes on the design and analysis of the Yarrow cryptographic pseudorandom number generator. In Howard Heys and Carlisle Adams, editors, *Selected Areas in Cryptography,* volume 1758 of *Lecture Notes in Computer Science,* pages 13–33. Springer, Berlin, 2000.

[107] Jon Kleinberg and Éva Tardos. *Algorithm Design.* Addison-Wesley Longman Publishing Co., Inc., Boston, MA, 2005.

[108] Jon M. Kleinberg. Authoritative sources in a hyperlinked environment. In *Proceedings of the Ninth Annual ACM-SIAM Symposium on Discrete Algorithms,* SODA '98, pages 668–677, Philadelphia, PA, USA, 1998. Society for Industrial and Applied Mathematics.

[109] Jon M. Kleinberg. Authoritative sources in a hyperlinked environment. *Journal of the ACM,* 46(5):604–632, September 1999.

[110] Donald E. Knuth. Ancient babylonian algorithms. *Communications of the ACM,* 15(7):671–677, July 1972.

[111] Donald E. Knuth. *The TEXbook.* Addison-Wesley Professional, Reading, MA, 1986.

[112] Donald E. Knuth. *The Art of Computer Programming, Volume 1: Fundamental Algorithms.* Addison-Wesley, Reading, MA, 3rd edition, 1997.

[113] Donald E. Knuth. *The Art of Computer Programming, Volume 2: Seminumerical Algorithms.* Addison-Wesley, Reading, MA, 3rd edition, 1998.

[114] Donald E. Knuth. *The Art of Computer Programming, Volume 3: Sorting and Searching.* Addison-Wesley, Reading, MA, 2nd edition, 1998.

[115] Donald E. Knuth. *The Art of Computer Programming, Volume 4A: Combinatorial Algorithms, Part 1.* Addison-Wesley, Upper Saddle River, NJ, 2011.

[116] Donald E. Knuth, James H. Morris, Jr., and Vaughan R. Pratt. Fast pattern matching in strings. *SIAM Journal on Computing*, 6(2):323–349, 1977.

[117] Donald E. Knuth and Michael F. Plass. Breaking paragraphs into lines. *Software: Practice and Experience*, 11:1119–1194, 1981.

[118] Alan G. Konheim. *Hashing in Computer Science: Fifty Years of Slicing and Dicing.* John Wiley & Sons, Inc., Hoboken, NJ, 2010.

[119] James F. Kurose and Keith W. Ross. *Computer Networking: A Top-Down Approach.* Pearson, Boston, MA, 6th edition, 2013.

[120] Leslie Lamport. *LaTeX: A Document Preparation System.* Addison-Wesley Professional, Reading, MA, 2nd edition, 1994.

[121] Amy N. Langville and Carl D. Meyer. *Google's PageRank and Beyond: The Science of Search Engine Rankings.* Princeton University Press, Princeton, NJ, 2006.

[122] David Lazer, Ryan Kennedy, Gary King, and Alessandro Vespignani. The parable of Google flu: Traps in big data analysis. *Science*, 343(6176):1203–1205, 2014.

[123] Thierry Lecroq. Experimental results on string matching algorithms. *Software: Practice and Experience*, 25(7):727–765, 1995.

[124] Pierre L'Ecuyer. Tables of linear congruential generators of different sizes and good lattice structure. *Mathematics of Computation*, 68(225):249–260, January 1999.

[125] Pierre L'Ecuyer and Richard Simard. TestU01: A C library for empirical testing of random number generators. *ACM Transactions on Mathematical Software*, 33(4), August 2007.

[126] C. Y. Lee. An algorithm for path connections and its applications. *IRE Transactions on Electronic Computers*, EC-10(3):346–365, September 1961.

[127] D. H. Lehmer. Mathematical methods in large-scale computing units. In *Proceedings of the Second Symposium on Large-Scale Digital Calculating Machinery*, pages 141–146, Cambridge, MA, 1949. Harvard University Press.

[128] Debra A. Lelewer and Daniel S. Hirschberg. Data compression. *ACM Computing Surveys*, 19(3):261–296, September 1987.

[129] Anany Levitin. *Introduction to the Design & Analysis of Algorithms.* Pearson, Boston, MA, 3rd edition, 2012.

[130] John MacCormick. *Nine Algorithms That Changed the Future: The Ingenious Ideas that Drive Today's Computers.* Princeton University Press, Princeton, NJ, 2012.

[131] David J. C. MacKay. *Information Theory, Inference, and Learning Algorithms.* Cambridge University Press, Cambridge, UK, 2003.

[132] Charles E. Mackenzie. *Coded Character Sets, History and Development.* Addison-Wesley, Reading, MA, 1980.

[133] George Marsaglia. Xorshift rngs. *Journal of Statistical Software*, 8(14):1–6, 2003.

[134] Tomomi Matsui and Yasuko Matsui. A survey of algorithms for calculating power indices of weighted majority games. *Journal of the Operations Research Society of Japan*, 43:71–86, 2000.

[135] John McCabe. On serial files with relocatable records. *Operations Research*, 13(4):609–618, 1965.

[136] A. I. McLeod and D. R. Bellhouse. A convenient algorithm for drawing a simple random sample. *Applied Statistics*, 32(2):182–184, 1983.

[137] Alfred J. Menezes, Scott A. Vanstone, and Paul C. Van Oorschot. *Handbook of Applied Cryptography*. CRC Press, Inc., Boca Raton, FL, USA, 1996.

[138] Ralph C. Merkle. A certified digital signature. In *Proceedings on Advances in Cryptology*, CRYPTO '89, pages 218–238, New York, NY, USA, 1989. Springer-Verlag New York, Inc.

[139] Stanley Milgram. The small world problem. *Psychology Today*, 1(1):60–67, 1967.

[140] Gary L. Miller. Riemann's hypothesis and tests for primality. In *Proceedings of Seventh Annual ACM Symposium on Theory of Computing*, STOC '75, pages 234–239, New York, NY, USA, 1975. ACM.

[141] Thomas J. Misa and Philip L. Frana. An interview with Edsger W. Dijkstra. *Communications of the ACM*, 53(8):41–47, August 2010.

[142] Thomas M. Mitchell. *Machine Learning*. McGraw-Hill, Inc., New York, NY, 1997.

[143] Michael Mitzenmacher. A brief history of generative models for power law and lognormal distributions. *Internet Mathematics*, 1(2):226–251, 2004.

[144] Michael Mitzenmacher and Eli Upfal. *Probability and Computing: Randomized Algorithms and Probabilistic Analysis*. Cambridge University Press, Cambridge, UK, 2005.

[145] E. F. Moore. The shortest path through a maze. In *Proceedings of an International Symposium on the Theory of Switching, 2–5 April 1957*, pages 285–292. Harvard University Press, 1959.

[146] Robert Morris. Scatter storage techniques. *Communications of the ACM*, 11(1):38–44, 1968.

[147] J. Moy. OSPF version 2. RFC 2328, April 1998.

[148] Kevin P. Murphy. *Machine Learning: A Probabilistic Perspective*. The MIT Press, Cambridge, MA, 2012.

[149] Simon Newcomb. Note on the frequency of use of the different digits in natural numbers. *American Journal of Mathematics*, 4(1):39–40, 1881.

[150] Mark Newman. *Networks: An Introduction*. Oxford University Press, Inc., New York, NY, USA, 2010.

[151] Michael A. Nielsen and Isaac L. Chuang. *Quantum Computation and Quantum Information*. Cambridge University Press, Cambridge, UK, 2000.

[152] Cathy O'Neil. *Weapons of Math Destruction: How Big Data Increases Inequality and Threatens Democracy*. Crown, New York, NY, 2016.

[153] Christof Paar and Jan Pelzl. *Understanding Cryptography: A Textbook for Students and Practitioners*. Springer-Verlag, Berlin, 2009.

[154] Vilfredo Pareto. *Cours d' Économie Politique*. Rouge, Lausanne, 1897.

[155] Richard E. Pattis. Textbook errors in binary searching. *SIGCSE Bulletin*, 20(1):190–194, February 1988.

[156] L. S. Penrose. The elementary statistics of majority voting. *Journal of the Royal Statistical Society*, 109(1):53–57, 1946.

[157] Radia Perlman. *Interconnections: Bridges, Routers, Switches, and Internetworking Protocols*. Addison-Wesley, 2nd edition, 1999.

[158] J. R. Quinlan. Discovering rules by induction from large collections of examples. In D. Michie, editor, *Expert systems in the micro electronic age*. Edinburgh University Press, Edinburgh, UK, 1979.

[159] J. R. Quinlan. Semi-autonomous acquisition of pattern-based knowledge. In J. E. Hayes, D. Michie, and Y.-H. Pao, editors, *Machine Intelligence*, volume 10. Ellis Horwood, Chichester, UK, 1982.

[160] J. R. Quinlan. Induction of decision trees. *Machine Learning*, 1(1):81–106, 1986.

[161] J. Ross Quinlan. *C4.5: Programs for Machine Learning*. Morgan Kaufmann Publishers Inc., San Francisco, CA, 1993.

[162] Michael O. Rabin. Probabilistic algorithm for testing primality. *Journal of Number Theory*, 12(1):128–138, 1980.

[163] Rajeev Raman. Recent results on the single-source shortest paths problem. *SIGACT News*, 28(2):81–87, June 1997.

[164] Edward M. Reingold, Kenneth J. Urban, and David Gries. K-M-P string matching revisited. *Information Processing Letters*, 64(5):217–223, December 1997.

[165] R. L. Rivest, A. Shamir, and L. Adleman. A method for obtaining digital signatures and public-key cryptosystems. *Communications of the ACM*, 21(2):120–126, February 1978.

[166] Ronald Rivest. On self-organizing sequential search heuristics. *Communications of the ACM*, 19(2):63–67, February 1976.

[167] Phillip Rogaway and Thomas Shrimpton. Cryptographic hash-function basics: Definitions, implications, and separations for preimage resistance, second-preimage resistance, and collision resistance. In Bimal Roy and Willi Meier, editors, *Fast Software Encryption*, volume 3017 of *Lecture Notes in Computer Science*, pages 371–388. Springer Berlin Heidelberg, 2004.

[168] Bernard Roy. Transitivé et connexité. *Comptes rendus des séances de l' Académie des Sciences*, 249(6):216–218, 1959.

[169] Donald G. Saari. *Disposing Dictators, Demystifying Voting Paradoxes*. Cambridge University Press, Cambridge, UK, 2008.

[170] David Salomon. *A Concise Introduction to Data Compression*. Springer, London, UK, 2008.

[171] David Salomon and Giovanni Motta. *Handbook of Data Compression*. Springer, London, UK, 5th edition, 2010.

[172] Khalid Sayood. *Introduction to Data Compression*. Morgan Kaufmann, Waltham, MA, 4th edition, 2012.

[173] Douglas C. Schmidt. GPERF: A perfect hash function generator. In Robert C. Martin, editor, *More C++ Gems*, pages 461–491. Cambridge University Press, New York, NY, USA, 2000.

[174] Bruce Schneier. *Applied Cryptography: Protocols, Algorithms, and Source Code in C*. John Wiley & Sons, Inc., New York, NY, USA, 2nd edition, 1995.

[175] Markus Schulze. A new monotonic, clone-independent, reversal symmetric, and Condorcet-consistent single-winner election method. *Social Choice and Welfare*, 36(2):267–303, 2011.

[176] Robert Sedgewick. *Algorithms in C—Parts 1–4: Fundamentals, Data Structures, Sorting, Searching*. Addison-Wesley, Boston, MA, 3rd edition, 1998.

[177] Robert Sedgewick. *Algorithms in C++—Parts 1–4: Fundamentals, Data Structures, Sorting, Searching*. Addison-Wesley, Boston, MA, 3rd edition, 1998.

[178] Robert Sedgewick. *Algorithms in C—Part 5: Graph Algorithms*. Addison-Wesley, Boston, MA, 3rd edition, 2002.

[179] Robert Sedgewick. *Algorithms in C—Part 5: Graph Algorithms*. Addison-Wesley, Boston, MA, 3rd edition, 2002.

[180] Robert Sedgewick and Kevin Wayne. *Algorithms*. Addison-Wesley, Upper Saddle River, NJ, 4th edition, 2011.

[181] C. E. Shannon. A mathematical theory of communication. *The Bell System Technical Journal*, 27(3):379–423, July 1948.

[182] C. E. Shannon. Prediction and entropy of printed english. *The Bell System Technical Journal*, 30(1):50–64, January 1950.

[183] Claude E. Shannon and Warren Weaver. *The Mathematical Theory of Communication*. University of Illinois Press, Urbana, IL, 1949.

[184] L. S. Shapley and Martin Shubik. A method for evaluating the distribution of power in a committee system. *American Political Science Review*, 48:787–792, September 1954.

[185] Peter W. Shor. Polynomial-time algorithms for prime factorization and discrete logarithms on a quantum computer. *SIAM Journal on Computing*, 26(5):1484–1509, October 1997.

[186] Joseph H. Silverman. *A Friendly Introduction to Number Theory*. Pearson, 4th edition, 2012.

[187] Simon Singh. *The Code Book: The Secret History of Codes and Code-breaking*. Fourth Estate, London, UK, 2002.

[188] Steven S. Skiena. *The Algorithm Design Manual*. Springer-Verlag, London, UK, 2nd edition, 2008.

[189] Daniel D. Sleator and Robert E. Tarjan. Amortized efficiency of list update and paging rules. *Communications of the ACM*, 28(2):202–208, February 1985.

[190] David Eugene Smith, editor. *A Source Book in Mathematics*. McGraw-Hill Book Co., New York, NY, 1929. Reprinted by Dover Publications in 1959.

[191] Jonathan Sorenson. An introduction to prime number sieves. Computer Sciences Technical Report 909, Department of Computer Science, University of Wisconsin-Madison, January 1990.

[192] Gary Stix. Profile: David Huffman. *Scientific American*, 265(3):54–58, September 1991.

[193] James V Stone. *Information Theory: A Tutorial Introduction*. Sebtel Press, Sheffield, UK, 2015.

[194] Michael P. H. Stumpf and Mason A. Porter. Critical truths about power laws. *Science*, 335(6069):665–666, 2012.

[195] George G. Szpiro. *Numbers Rule: The Vexing Mathematics of Democracy, from Plato to the Present*. Princeton University Press, Princeton, NJ, 2010.

[196] Andrew S. Tanenbaum and David J. Wetherall. *Computer Networks*. Prentice Hall, Boston, MA, 5th edition, 2011.

[197] Robert Tarjan. Depth-first searcn and linear graph algorithms. *SIAM Journal on Computing*, 1(2):146–160, 1972.

[198] Robert Endre Tarjan. Edge-disjoint spanning trees and depth-first search. *Acta Informatica*, 6(2):171–185, 1976.

[199] Robert Endre Tarjan. *Data Structures and Network Algorithms*. Society for Industrial and Applied Mathematics, Philadelphia, PA, 1983.

[200] Alan D. Taylor and Allison M. Pacelli. *Mathematics and Politics: Strategy, Voting, Power and Proof*. Springer, 2nd edition, 2008.

[201] Mikkel Thorup. On RAM priority queues. *SIAM Journal on Computing*, 30(1):86–109, April 2000.

[202] Yves Tillé. *Sampling Algorithms*. Springer, New York, NY, 2006.

[203] Thanassis Tiropanis, Wendy Hall, Jon Crowcroft, Noshir Contractor, and Leandros Tassiulas. Network science, web science, and internet science. *Communications of the ACM*, 58(8):76–82, July 2015.

[204] Jeffrey Travers and Stanley Milgram. An experimental study of the small world problem. *Sociometry*, 32(4):425–443, 1969.

[205] Alan Turing. Proposed electronic calculator. Technical report, National Physical Laboratory (NPL), UK, 1946. http://www.alanturing.net/ace/index.html.

[206] United States National Institute of Standards and Technology (NIST). Announcing the ADVANCED ENCRYPTION STANDARD (AES), November 26 2001. Federal Information Processing Standards Publication 197.

[207] United States National Institute of Standards and Technology (NIST). Secure hash standard (SHS), August 2015. Federal Information Processing Standards Publication 180-4.

[208] United States National Institute of Standards and Technology (NIST). SHA-3 standard: Permutation-based hash and extendable-output functions, August 2015. Federal Information Processing Standards Publication 202.

[209] Sebastiano Vigna. An experimental exploration of Marsaglia's xorshift generators, scrambled. *CoRR*, abs/1402.6246, 2014.

[210] Jeffrey S. Vitter. Random sampling with a reservoir. *ACM Transactions on Mathematical Software*, 11(1):37–57, March 1985.

[211] John von Neumann. Various techniques used in connection with random digit. In A.S. Householder, G. E. Forsythe, and H. H. Germond, editors, *Monte Carlo Method*, volume 12 of *National Bureau of Standards Applied Mathematics Series*, pages 36–38. U.S. Government Printing Office, Washington, D.C., 1951.

[212] Avery Li-Chun Wang. An industrial-strength audio search algorithm. In *Proceedings of the 4th International Conference on Music Information Retrieval (ISMIR 2003)*, Baltimore, MD, October 26–30 2003.

[213] Stephen Warshall. A theorem on boolean matrices. *Journal of the ACM*, 9(1):11–12, January 1962.

[214] Duncan J. Watts. *Six Degrees: The Science of a Connected Age*. W. W. Norton & Company, New York, NY, 2004.

[215] T. A. Welch. A technique for high-performance data compression. *Computer*, 17(6):8–19, June 1984.

[216] Frank Wilczek. *A Beautiful Question: Finding Nature's Deep Design*. Penguin Press, New York, NY, 2015.

[217] Maurice V. Wilkes. *Memoirs of a Computer Pioneer*. The MIT Press, Cambridge, MA, 1985.

[218] J. W. J. Williams. Algorithm 232: Heapsort. *Communications of the ACM*, 7(6):347–348, June 1964.

[219] Ian H. Witten, Eibe Frank, and Mark A. Hall. *Data Mining: Practical Machine Learning Tools and Techniques*. Morgan Kaufmann Publishers Inc., San Francisco, CA, 3rd edition, 2011.

[220] Xindong Wu, Vipin Kumar, J. Ross Quinlan, Joydeep Ghosh, Qiang Yang, Hiroshi Motoda, Geoffrey J. McLachlan, Angus Ng, Bing Liu, Philip S. Yu, Zhi-Hua Zhou, Michael Steinbach, David J. Hand, and Dan Steinberg. Top 10 algorithms in data mining. *Knowledge and Information Systems*, 14(1):1–37, January 2008.

[221] J. Y. Yen. An algorithm for finding shortest routes from all source nodes to a given destination in general networks. *Quarterly of Applied Mathematics*, 27:526–530, 1970.

[222] Joel Young, Kristina Foster, Simson Garfinkel, and Kevin Fairbanks. Distinct sector hashes for target file detection. *Computer*, 45(12):28–35, December 2012.

[223] G. Udny Yule. A mathematical theory of evolution, based on the conclusions of Dr. J. C. Willis, F.R.S. *Philosophical Transactions of the Royal Society of London: Series B*, 213:21–87, April 1925.

[224] Philip Zimmermann. Why I wrote PGP. Part of the Original 1991 PGP User's Guide (updated), 1999. Available at https://www.philzimmermann.com/EN/essays/WhyIWrotePGP.html.

[225] Philip Zimmermann. Phil Zimmermann on the importance of online privacy. The Guardian Tech Weekly Podcast, 2013. Available at http://www.theguardian.com/technology/audio/2013/may/23/podcast-tech-weekly-phil-zimmerman.

[226] George Kingsley Zipf. *The Psycho-Biology of Language: An Introduction to Dynamic Philology*. Houghton Mifflin, Boston, MA, 1935.

[227] George Kingsley Zipf. *Human Behavior and the Principle of Least Effort: An Introduction to Human Ecology*. Addison-Wesley, Reading, MA, 1949.

[228] J. Ziv and A. Lempel. A universal algorithm for sequential data compression. *Information Theory, IEEE Transactions on*, 23(3):337–343, May 1977.

[229] J. Ziv and A. Lempel. Compression of individual sequences via variable-rate coding. *Information Theory, IEEE Transactions on*, 24(5):530–536, September 1978.

Index